21st-Century Statecraft

21st-Century Statecraft

Reconciling Power, Justice and Meta-Geopolitical Interests

Nayef R.F. Al-Rodhan

The Lutterworth Press

THE LUTTERWORTH PRESS

P.O. Box 60
Cambridge
CB1 2NT
United Kingdom

www.lutterworth.com
publishing@lutterworth.com

Hardback ISBN: 978 0 7188 9574 7
Paperback ISBN: 978 0 7188 9575 4
PDF ISBN: 978 0 7188 4835 4
ePUB ISBN: 978 0 7188 4836 1

British Library Cataloguing in Publication Data
A record is available from the British Library

First published as *Neo-Statecraft and Meta-Geopolitics* by LIT Verlag, 2009

This edition published by The Lutterworth Press, 2022

Text copyright © Nayef R.F. Al-Rodhan, 2022

Contents

List of Figures & Tables

Acknowledgements

The author would like to thank the following people for their important assistance with the production of this book: Adrian Brink, Samuel Fitzgerald, Dorothy Luckhurst, Christine Garnier-Simon, Ioana Puscas, Ines Gassal-Bosch, Virginia Raffaeli and Louison Mazeaud.

I am also immensely grateful for the support of my colleagues at St Antony's College, Oxford University (UK), at the Geneva Centre for Security Policy (Switzerland) and at the Institute of Philosophy, School of Advanced Study, University of London (UK).

1

Statecraft in the Twenty-First Century

In Search of a New Paradigm

What does it take to be an effective statesman or stateswoman? Throughout history, from early Mesopotamia to the ancient Greek polis, from the Han empire in eastern Eurasia to the Arab-Islamic empires, to the time of European states and colonial rule, through two world wars and a cold war into contemporary democracy and autocracy, state leaders have always had to make complex decisions to secure their authority over geographic areas and manage their populations. In the maelstrom of change, some challenges to statecraft reverberate and resurface across centuries and continents, such as conflicts over resources and territory, and some historical legacies continue to be enshrined in present geopolitical constellations. At the same time, and as humanity pushes new frontiers, both in space and science, unprecedented opportunities emerge and, with them, unknown perils. Today's blend of conventional and new challenges requires a fresh approach to the art of statecraft. Traditional geopolitical helmsmanship no longer suffices to steer ships of state through the turbulent waters of the third millennium. The main purpose of this book is thus to offer a new understanding of statecraft, one that is capable of navigating the risks, and of leveraging the opportunities, of an increasingly digitised and globally interconnected twenty-first century.

Although we all have an intuitive understanding of the term, statecraft remains a contested notion. Traditional approaches tend to define it as the art of conducting state affairs and achieving policy objectives effectively.

Whilst some include domestic policy in their conception of statecraft, however, others focus exclusively on interstate strategic actions.[1] Effective statecraft is understood in this book to include all internal and external actions that create an environment in which the state can flourish and secure the well-being of its inhabitants in the long run.

As the world has become more complex, so has statecraft. Today, more and more people negotiate between multiple cultural allegiances, compelling state leaders to create a common identity out of populations increasingly diverse in religion, cultural affinities, and world views. As we move further into the twenty-first century, new frontiers are about to open in science, bringing about opportunities and risks that are difficult to anticipate yet need to be prepared for. The rapid processes of globalisation and digitisation have multiplied transnational challenges, of which cyber threats and pandemics are just two examples. These threats make it imperative for states to work together on questions for which there are often no time-tested answers. Despite a heightened need for cooperation, an increasing number of states and actors are competing for influence and dominance through a variety of means, ranging from economic policy to political subversion.[2]

How should state leaders confront the ever-shifting array of contemporary challenges? In this book, I argue that, for a state to thrive in the twenty-first century, it has to leverage the interdependence of the world through what I call *reconciliation statecraft*. In other words, effective statecraft today is a delicate balancing act between the well-being of individuals, the interests of the nation, economic development, the sustainability of the environment, regional and international obligations, cultural interests (such as linguistic or religious traditions) and different moral outlooks.[3] As tensions between these diverse interests constitute a major source of international conflict, their reconciliation promotes global and national prosperity and peace and should therefore be the ultimate goal of twenty-first century statecraft. To achieve this goal, the traditional tools of statecraft need to be complemented by new ones. This book introduces five innovative tools and additional concepts that equip state leaders to navigate the international circumstances of the third millennium.

1.1 Structure of the Book

This book begins by discussing traditional concepts of statecraft and geopolitics in chapters two and three, illustrating their limitations in light of contemporary challenges. The following chapters introduce five innovative concepts that serve as the main tools of reconciliation statecraft. These include, first of all, a new geopolitical analysis method I have termed *meta-geopolitics*. To pursue an effective foreign policy, state leaders need to study the geography of the broader area in which their state is located and the balance of power among surrounding states. They need to know how geographic, economic and demographic factors impact international relations (IR). The study of these factors is encapsulated in the discipline of geopolitics. That discipline's traditional focus on territory and resources, however, is no longer sufficient to capture the complex dramas unfolding on today's world stage. As I explain in chapter four, *meta-geopolitics* provides a more nuanced and comprehensive map that helps practitioners of statecraft orient themselves in the maze of international relations. *Meta-geopolitics* moves beyond classic geopolitical assumptions to include a wider range of variables that reflect the complexity of contemporary power dynamics. More specifically, it deals with seven 'state capacities': social and health issues, domestic politics, economics, environment, science and human potential, military and security issues, and international diplomacy. Assessing the geopolitical strengths and weaknesses of states by taking into account these seven factors provides a more accurate picture of worldwide dynamics in the twenty-first century. It also helps to identify the breadth of often interrelated security threats that states face but which remain largely hidden in more classic geopolitical analyses.

The second major tool of reconciliation statecraft is a new form of governance that prioritises human dignity. Applying neuroscientific findings to political analysis, chapter five argues that *dignity-based governance* allows a state to promote domestic stability, prosperity and peace by unlocking the best in human nature and, thus, in its constituents' behaviour. The extent to which domestic factors versus the international environment influence states' choices has been part of a long debate. What is certain, however, is that domestic structures and foreign policy affect one another.[4] Dignity-based governance allows a state to fully leverage its resources – human, natural and otherwise – thus realising its geopolitical potential.

As chapter five illustrates, dignity-based governance must be accompanied by a *symbiotic realist* approach to international relations, which is the third tool of reconciliation statecraft. *Symbiotic realism* is premised on the idea that, since we live in an interconnected and interdependent world, international politics can no longer rely on zero-sum gains (i.e., gains at the cost of others) but rather must strive for non-conflictual competition and absolute gains that are to the benefit of all.

Despite global interdependence and porous borders, state leaders often over-focus on narrowly defined national interests, with disastrous consequences, especially in the field of security.[5] In the twenty-first century, promoting international security is a key ingredient in, and often is identical with, enhancing a state's national security. The concept of *sustainable* national security that I propose in chapter five recognises that no state today can achieve security through gains at the expense of other states, nor can it be realised at the cost of the environment or individual well-being. In fact, national security is highly connected with human, transnational, environment and transcultural security. This requires international collaboration and what I call *transcultural synergy*, which implies mutually beneficial exchanges between members of different nations and cultures.[6]

Finally, a reconceptualisation of power is required for statecraft to reconcile diverse interests and create common ground in an age of increasing polarisation. Chapter six outlines the theoretical foundations for how both soft- and hard-power tools should be employed before introducing the new concept of *just power*, which argues that the promotion of justice should be the aim of twenty-first century statecraft. This is imperative – not for altruistic reasons, but because it is the only sustainable way states can promote progress and stability in a globalised world. Put differently, it is in the national interest of each state to promote the well-being of humans all over the world, regardless of their nationality.

Table 1.1 summarises the five concepts I believe are conducive to an improved statecraft paradigm suited for the twenty-first century.

Having outlined the main tools of reconciliation statecraft, chapter seven illustrates how they enable state leaders to solve the dilemmas raised by different interests represented by individuals, states and groups of individuals, as well as more general global interests such as environmental protection. Whilst these interests are not mutually exclusive, they may at times conflict with one another. A failure to reconcile them poses severe risks to the peace, security and prosperity of each country and of the entire planet. As chapter seven highlights, reconciliation statecraft is an approach focused on long-term sustainability and global progress rather than short-term gain.

Chapter eight presents case studies that apply the framework of *meta-geopolitics* to evaluate the geopolitical realities and dilemmas of twenty-six states and one union of states, the EU. Chapter nine builds on these case studies to identify the future trajectories and key geostrategic imperatives they must abide by if they are to flourish as states under

Table 1.1 Tools of Reconciliation Statecraft

Comprehend the world through a new geopolitical analysis method: 'META-GEOPOLITICS'

Adopt a new form of governance ('DIGNITY-BASED GOVERNANCE') that reconciles human dignity needs with the emotional amoral egoism that is innate in all human beings.

Pursue multi-sum games and win-win situations (i.e., 'SYMBIOTIC REALISM') in its conduct of international relations.

Promote 'SUSTAINABLE NATIONAL SECURITY' by adopting a multi-sum approach to security that includes human, environmental, national, transnational, and transcultural security and focuses on transcultural synergies.

Integrate hard, soft, smart and 'JUST POWER' tools that foster equality and respect of different cultures and human dignity.

all seven state capacities. Chapter ten draws conclusions from the case studies and identifies the world's most volatile geopolitical area: a north-south corridor that runs from the Arctic to the Antarctic and includes the greater Middle East and East Africa. I call this the *tripwire pivotal corridor* (TPC). Without stability in the TPC, I argue, there can be no stability at the international level. This chapter also identifies the problems affecting some of the most unstable states in the TPC, problems that have turned into transnational threats. It also discusses the geopolitical significance of the corridor in terms of both strategic natural resources and crucial maritime passageways. Finally, it identifies a number of pivotal states that have the necessary resources to promote regional stability within the corridor and warns against major powers' interference for narrow national interest and gains.

The book closes, in chapter eleven, with a more general glimpse into the future, drawing on the meta-geopolitical lens to analyse a series of global trends that are likely to affect geopolitics in the coming years. Climate change, the melting of the Arctic ice cap, space debris and militarisation and a multiplicity of technological and scientific innovations and developments, both military and civilian, are only a few issues that are likely to have a strong impact on power relationships among states in the decades ahead. I refer to these issues as *civilisational frontier risks* because they have the potential to fundamentally alter our lives and, if handled badly, could even lead to the collapse of human civilisation or the extinction of the human species. This book endeavours to bring these risks to the attention of statecraft practitioners, and to provide tools that could help leaders to make great strides in meeting the challenges of tomorrow.

This book is geared towards a broad audience, including scholars, policy makers and the interested public. It is my hope that the new concepts introduced in this book will be useful and can be developed and applied further by practitioners and political scientists alike.

2

Traditional Approaches to Statecraft

Statecraft can be defined broadly as the art of conducting state affairs, which implies that it is as old as the first state-like entities.[1] To a large extent, historical experiences (along with their interpretations and the lessons drawn from them) have shaped the different ways thinkers have defined statecraft.

In the fifth century BCE, for example, Greek historian Thucydides used the writing of the *History of the Peloponnesian War* to deduce principles of policy behaviour. In doing so, he clearly sought to provide guidance to future leaders who might find themselves in situations similar to those experienced by the leaders he described in his historical work. 'It will be enough for me', Thucydides wrote, 'if these words of mine are judged useful by those who want to understand clearly the events which happened in the past and which (human nature being what it is) will, at some time or other and in much the same ways, be repeated in the future.'[2] Note that, for Thucydides, theorising about statecraft was inseparable from thinking about history, a history determined by human nature.

Niccolò Machiavelli similarly studied great leaders of the past, and also carefully observed the actions of contemporary leaders of various Italian principalities, in order to develop a set of guidelines for policy makers, which he described in *The Prince*.[3] Machiavelli also highlighted the interconnections between politics and human nature. In *The Discourses*, he stressed the immutability of the human passion which drives the course of history:

> Whoever considers the past and the present will readily observe that all cities and all peoples are and ever have been

> animated by the same desires and the same passions; so that
> it is easy, by diligent study of the past, to foresee what is likely
> to happen in the future.[4]

In other words, the study of history teaches us that there are some constants in statecraft regardless of the historical period. Among these is human nature. Other constants include cooperation and rivalries among state entities, and the dilemmas surrounding the question of whether to use armed force.[5] This last issue is the gravest and most consequential decision any statesman or woman can face.

More recent approaches to statecraft are reflected in a definition given by former US Middle East envoy and chief peace negotiator Dennis Ross. He defines statecraft as: 'the use of the assets or the resources and tools (economic, military, intelligence, media) that a state has to pursue its interests and to affect the behaviour of others, whether friendly or hostile'.[6] Ross further explains that statecraft 'involves making sound assessments and understanding where and on what issues the state is being challenged and can counter a threat or create a potential opportunity or take advantage of one'.[7] A similar view of statecraft is also reflected in Margaret Thatcher's 2003 book *Statecraft: Strategies for a Changing World*,[8] in which she argues that, although all contemporary problems require global solutions, states should cease to rely on international institutions to address them. On the contrary, according to Thatcher, states should return to the exercise of state power in pursuit of national interest.[9] The balance between this national interest and morality is, according to Henry Kissinger, central to foreign policy.[10] In his famous book *Diplomacy*,[11] Kissinger argues that the traditionally different views of human nature, one as more good, and the other as driven by self-preservation, are what have determined the different approaches to foreign policy traditionally adopted by the United States, on one side, and European countries, on the other.

Despite varying definitions of statecraft, most agree that leaders of all political entities have to make the right decisions and take the actions necessary to preserve the territorial integrity and the political independence of their countries. They need to gauge potential dangers and threats that might jeopardise their citizens. They have to establish cooperative relationships with neighbouring states and enter into appropriate alliances. They are responsible for securing favourable trade agreements so that their countries' economies may prosper. In short, statecraft is the art of using appropriate policy tools to achieve policy objectives effectively. This chapter reviews how the tools of statecraft have been traditionally conceived before illustrating the need for a complementary suite of innovative tools to navigate the twenty-first century.

2.1 Hard, Soft and Smart Power

The tools of statecraft have traditionally been described in two ways: hard and soft.[12] One way or another, statecraft always involves the use of a state's power to achieve policy objectives, either through the 'hard' tools of coercion (such as military force), or the 'soft' tools of persuasion (such as diplomacy). Only in 2007 was a new paradigm added, 'smart power'.[13] Power, broadly defined, is the ability to get what one wants. By extension, power is also, as one author has put it, 'the ability to influence the behaviour of others to get the outcomes one wants'.[14] There are, of course, different ways to get others to do what one wants, ranging from reward to punishment.

In international politics, power has traditionally been defined quite narrowly as military and economic might.[15] Today, these traditional sources of state power are referred to as *hard power*. The stronger (and the more technologically advanced) a state's military, the better a state can influence other states' behaviour by threatening the use of military force. Moreover, the larger a state's economy, the more influence it can exert on others by promising economic incentives for desirable behaviour or by threatening economic sanctions to punish undesirable behaviour.

Hard power is not the only way one state can influence another. Attraction and co-option are other powerful ways to get others to do what one wants. To describe these non-coercive types of power, Joseph S. Nye Jr coined the term *soft power*, defining it as 'attractive power'.[16] It is the ability to get others on one's side without using force or economic bribes. Soft power uses 'an attraction to shared values and the justness and duty of contributing to the achievements of those values' as a means to get others on board.[17] It will be much easier for a state to win the cooperation of other states that are attracted to the state's culture and that share its political ideology and foreign-policy objectives.

Economic power can be either a hard-power tool or a soft-power tool. It can be used coercively by threatening sanctions (hard power). At the same time, however, a country's wealth can serve as a point of attraction for other states that might have the same economic goals or are keen to have access to the country's domestic market. The promise of investment or aid may also convince other states to cooperate closely with a wealthy country.

During the Cold War, both the United States and the Soviet Union used a combination of hard- and soft-power tools to carve out their spheres of influence around the world. The ideological appeal of communism might have prompted some leaders in the developing world and Eastern Europe to join the communist camp, but covert military operations or outright interventions (such as the invasion of Hungary in 1956) helped to keep the Soviet spheres of domination together. In post-war Western Europe, the United States secured its sphere of influence not just through military alliances and a nuclear umbrella, but also by offering attractive economic incentives through the Marshall Plan. Force and persuasion – hard and soft power – are both important tools of statecraft.

Economic sanctions and incentives are hard power tools that have become more frequent and more prominent since the end of the Cold War. One example of the successful use of incentives to promote security and stability occurred after the dissolution of the Soviet Union. When Ukraine and Kazakhstan became independent, both countries had large, Soviet-era nuclear-weapons stockpiles on their territories. Russia and the West successfully offered a series of incentives to the two countries to give up their nuclear-weapons capabilities. These incentives included economic assistance, improved diplomatic relations and security guarantees.[18] The incentive provider always acts from a position of strength, which implies that, if the target country does not accept the offered incentive to alter its behaviour, the incentive-providing state can resort to more unpleasant, coercive measures.[19] Such inducements are best used in cases where there is no immediate crisis.

Among the frequently used incentives offered by economically and politically powerful states are improved economic and political relations. Indeed, access to the international system of trade and the maintenance of regular diplomatic relations with the world's major powers can be a powerful incentive for states to abide by acceptable standards. A particularly powerful incentive, especially, but not only, for developing countries, is access to advanced technology, which is so important for economic prosperity today. As some states are particularly interested in improving their military capabilities, offering access to purely civilian technology might be the best way to offer incentives without the negative side effect of helping the recipient country to increase its military potential.[20]

Incentives can help to change internal political dynamics within a state in the way desired by the incentive provider. The promise of access to international markets and advanced technology, for instance, can be used to support peaceful integration into the international community and the acceptance of cooperative security arrangements. As one expert has observed, political constituencies (such as business elites and the middle class) that have the most to gain from international free trade are usually less inclined to support assertive nationalism or the acquisition of weapons of mass destruction by their country.[21] Hence, outside incentives may motivate such groups to lobby their government even harder to abandon behaviour that goes against the cause of international peace and security.

Incentives can be provided not just in response to a desired action but also in anticipation of positive reciprocity. A case in point is President George H.W. Bush's unilateral withdrawal of nuclear artillery and short-range missiles from Europe in 1991. Bush's initiative was matched by Soviet President Mikhail Gorbachev's dismantling of tactical nuclear weapons from Soviet land forces and naval vessels.[22] Initiating incentives is a good way of demonstrating goodwill and building trust while inviting the other state to promote further cooperation by reciprocating.

The use of sanctions as a tool of statecraft has been the subject of much controversy and debate in recent years. Do sanctions work? Do they target the 'right' people? One of the most common misperceptions regarding sanctions is the notion that economic hardship will automatically turn a population against the government targeted by the sanctions and thus force the government to step down or change its behaviour.[23] Indeed, economic sanctions may sometimes achieve the opposite. If a target regime is able to portray the outside world as hostile and threatening to the population, it may be able to increase popular support for the 'victimised' regime and promote nationalist feelings. This may especially be the case in countries with authoritarian regimes where the flow of information is restricted and citizens have little access to outside media sources.

In some cases, sanctions may also inadvertently enrich governing elites that are able to generate revenue from the black-market trade in commodities rationed by the ruling regime.[24] This was the case in Haiti, for example, where military and business elites close to the ruling regime enriched themselves through the black market and thus were able to strengthen the very regime the sanctions sought to weaken.[25]

In other cases, however, sanctions succeed at weakening the target regime and speed up internal political change. Such was the case in South Africa, where well-organised domestic opposition groups were able to win large segments of the population over to their side. These opposition groups were able to convince the public that the regime, through its unjust policies, was to blame for the international sanctions that were causing the country's economic hardship.[26] In fact, the opposition African National Congress (ANC) even encouraged the international community to stiffen its sanctions to strengthen the ANC's civil-resistance campaign against the incumbent regime.[27]

Hence, in cases where a country already has a strong opposition movement, sanctions may be more successful at achieving the intended outcome.

Still, general economic sanctions continue to evoke moral concerns, considering that the population at large, and especially the poorest part of it, often bears the brunt of the hardship caused by the sanctions while the elites continue to live comfortably. Especially in dictatorships, where the population has little influence on the government and did not vote it into power, there is the question of whether punishing an entire population for the actions of a small elite can be morally justified.

Sanctions may target a country's elites if they are aimed at the financial sector. Measures might include 'the freezing of foreign assets, the cancellation of debt rescheduling, the withholding of credits and loans, and restrictions on travel, commerce and communications'.[28] These types of financial sanctions usually hurt the economic and political elites the most, while they do not cause the kind of humanitarian hardship associated with broader trade sanctions. In fact, one study has found that the success rate of financial sanctions (41 per cent) is considerably higher than that of general trade sanctions (25 per cent).[29]

As this analysis of the dual, hard and soft nature of economic power illustrates, the idea in international relations of a dichotomy between hard and soft power remained largely unchanged for decades. In 2007, however, Nye and Richard L. Armitage coined the term *smart power*. As I discuss in greater depth in chapter six, following the US invasion of Iraq, Nye and Armitage found that, when it comes to choosing between hard and soft power tools, the 'smart' thing to do is to find the appropriate balance between them to meet the circumstances and the type of goal pursued. Only by integrating hard and soft power tools and thus implementing smart power can global challenges be addressed effectively.[30]

In fact, although a lot of scholarly attention has focused on incentives and sanctions as instruments of statecraft, existing literature identifies a wide range of hard- and soft-power tools at the disposal of statesmen and women, which can all be utilised in a complementary manner and, therefore, as 'smart power' tools. Table 2.1 provides an overview of these tools.

Table 2.1 Traditional Tools of Statecraft

TOOL	DESCRIPTION
Negotiation (direct or through diplomacy)	Formal discussions to solve an issue of conflict. Agreement possible only if 'both sides' objectives, though different, are compatible'. Direct negotiations take place between the holders of political power in states, while *diplomacy* is undertaken by appointed representatives of the state who themselves do not hold political power. *Track II diplomacy* refers to informal negotiations undertaken by unofficial representatives of states – often a good way of broaching potentially explosive bilateral issues in an unofficial, non-confrontational atmosphere.
Mediation	Act as intermediary or neutral facilitator in negotiations between two or more state parties (may be undertaken by the holder of political power or by an appointed representative).
Propaganda	Spread information and ideas among the population of another state in the hope of inspiring a reaction or attitude favourable to the foreign policy of the state.
Intelligence-gathering/ espionage	Gathering of information by a state's diplomats or secret agents inside another state that is helpful to the foreign policy of the state.

(*continued*)

Table 2.1 (continued)

Incentives	Offer of some form of reward in exchange for a desired action or to provide a motive for a state to take a particular course of action. Best used when conflict situation has not yet evolved into a state of crisis. Incentives serve as conciliatory gesture and help ease tensions. Good way of creating 'long-term foundations for peace and cooperation'. Most effective if used from a position of strength (which includes the implied capacity to use negative inducements as well). Can also be used without explicit conditionality to help a state stabilise and develop its economy, and to foster good relations.
Sanctions	Inflict economic harm on target state by withholding import goods and services or access to technology to pressure the state to change its behaviour. Usually takes time to bear fruit (on average almost three years). 'Most effective when economic costs are high for the target but low for the initiator, when initiator is much larger than the target, and when the target and initiator have extensive trade relations.'
Coercion (deterrence, compulsion and war)	Involves the threat or actual use of military force. Can be effective to stop or deter overt aggression and deadly conflict. Deterrence can be implicit (the sheer military power of a state can deter other states from taking a particular initiative against the state) or explicit through troop mobilisation and the stationing of troops along borders. War refers to an actual military attack on another state's territory or military installations.

2.2 Diplomacy

A wealth of literature discusses diplomacy in analysing statecraft. Although diplomacy is a crucial part of statecraft, it does not encompass everything that statesmen and women do. Statecraft is concerned with the big picture regarding a state's general foreign-policy direction, as well as with the particularities of specific momentary challenges confronting a state. It involves strategic decisions that will determine the future direction and geopolitical agenda of the state in question. Statecraft is exercised by actual holders of political power, while diplomats merely act as representatives of governments, or as intermediaries between two governments.[31] It is not the job of a diplomat to contribute to the formulation of foreign policy. A diplomat simply executes or represents a foreign policy that has already been decided on by the holders of political power.[32] Whilst being an important means to the ends of statecraft, diplomacy must therefore not be equated with the latter.

In his 1822 *Manuel diplomatique* (subsequently republished as *Le Guide diplomatique*, from which edition I quote), Charles de Martens defined diplomacy as 'the science or art of negotiation'.[33] This definition, however, is at the same time both too broad and too narrow. It is too broad in the sense that the holders of political power can also negotiate directly, and diplomacy only encompasses activities undertaken by state representatives and intermediaries. The definition is also too narrow, as diplomacy encompasses other activities besides negotiation, such as the gathering of information inside another country and conveying that information to one's government.[34] Diplomats also serve as important points of contact between two governments.

In *The Pure Concept of Diplomacy*, José Calvet de Magalhães offers the following comprehensive definition of diplomacy: 'Diplomacy is an instrument of foreign policy for the establishment and development of peaceful contacts between the governments of different states through the use of intermediaries mutually recognized by the respective parties.'[35]

Some argue that the tools of diplomacy need to be adjusted to meet the changing demands of our global information age so that diplomats can serve their states more effectively. As former British diplomat Shaun Riordan has observed, the diplomatic function of conveying information from his home country to his host country is becoming almost superfluous in an age of email and instant messaging (which makes it so the information might as well be sent directly by a government department to the foreign office of the other state).[36] The importance of the representational function of diplomats may also be further diminished due to increased international mobility.

What is increasingly needed instead are experts in different fields of policy concerning a variety of transnational threats. Instead of training diplomats as generalists, writes Riordan, 'the new diplomatic agenda requires experts – in environment, finance, economics, human rights, health issues, organised crime, security issues, terrorism, technology.'[37]

Public diplomacy is becoming an increasingly important aspect of diplomacy in the twenty-first century. An important feature of the new century is the increased melting away of the distinction between foreign and domestic policy, made necessary by globalisation and the increase in issues which have both domestic and international repercussions, ranging from terrorism and violent extremism to economics and even pandemics.[38] States today have an interest in winning the support of foreign publics when trying to achieve their policy objectives. This may range from getting foreign public support for a war or an international treaty all the way to encouraging a foreign public to seek peaceful democratic change at home. Most governments today need domestic political approval for their foreign-policy actions and they need the approval of the foreign public with whose government they are trying to seal a deal.[39]

States also increasingly have to make the negotiation, treaty-drafting and policy-formulation processes transparent if they want to earn the trust and support of their own and foreign publics. In doing so, they need to involve and consult the broad range of stakeholders that shape foreign affairs today, including non-governmental organisations (NGOs) along with, Riordan adds, 'less formal groupings, businesses, supra-national, national and sub-national governments'.[40] Only in this way can their trust and support be won. As will be seen in the case studies later on, collective entities such as the European Union (EU) really struggle from this perceived lack of legitimacy, since, even more so than in individual states, citizens feel removed from the decision-making processes which define multi-state entities.[41] The example of the EU also demonstrates how important the support of not only the domestic but also the foreign public is, since states must gain the support of citizens in other member states if they are to receive the necessary budget approval from their respective governments in the EU Council.[42]

States care (and have to care) about their image abroad. For instance, national companies trying to sell products and do business abroad partly depend on the image and reputation of their country of origin. Furthermore, states need to acquire a sufficient amount of international credibility and trustworthiness if they want to act as a mediator in international disputes or to secure support for an international initiative they feel strongly about.

In today's information age, it is not just governments and their agencies abroad that shape the image of their country. International companies, cultural icons, internet news sites and blogs, for example, also contribute to shaping a country's image. Hence, governments need not only to reach the broader civil society of foreign countries, they also need to make use of different civil-society agents to spread their message and their values. Riordan suggests that 'the public diplomacy agenda must involve all aspects of Western civil society from governments to educators, schools, NGOs, business, informal groupings of citizens to individual citizens'.[43] For this reason, during the COVID-19 pandemic, many governments, including that of the US, chose to enlist celebrities from all fields to spread messages encouraging people to get vaccinated, wear masks and comply with social distancing measures.

Under the leadership of Condoleezza Rice, the US State Department put forward a concept known as transformational diplomacy. At its core, this implies that diplomacy needs to go beyond its traditional functions of representation and negotiation. Instead, diplomats need to be able to engage with civil society in the country in which they are stationed and work with host governments and civil society organisations to build resilient democratic states. A former special adviser to Rice explains:

> You need a diplomatic corps that's not just watching, observing and reporting, but a diplomatic corps that is helping with local partners to actually make change happen on the ground. What does that mean? That means things like advising them on how to build a better court system, on how to build a stronger border security system, on how to train their police.[44]

The concept thus suggests that diplomats should actively contribute to nation-building and democratisation processes in states undergoing a democratic transition or suffering from instability and lawlessness. Effective embassies should thus be concerned not only with influencing foreign governments, but also with engaging foreign citizens directly.

The concept has its drawbacks, however, as it ignores potential resistance to foreign interference or even fears of neo-colonialism or of political subversion that might arise if Western governments become involved in domestic politics to such an extent.[45] If a state has a positive image abroad and is able to convince the public in foreign countries of its genuine willingness to help them build better institutions and better lives, it can be a highly effective addition to traditional diplomacy. It can be a way for developed democracies to promote national and international security by helping to stabilise states and thereby preventing many of the security threats associated with state failure, including the proliferation of transnational crime, the uncontrolled spread of diseases and so forth. It is a way for developed democracies to promote long-term development. Helping developing countries to make their institutions strong, efficient and transparent will make those countries more attractive for domestic and international investors, which will set the stage for long-term economic development.[46]

2.3 Subversion

Subversion is another important means through which states pursue their interests and achieve their objectives. In international relations, subversion can be defined, as Jill Kastner and William C. Wohlforth do, as 'the practice of trying to gain an advantage by directly influencing a foreign country's domestic politics against its wishes. By manipulating events inside another country's borders, a subverter hopes to change the policy of an existing regime – or change the regime itself.'[47] There are different ways to interfere in the internal affairs of other governments, ranging from the age-old tactics of propaganda to supporting resistance movements seeking to overthrow governments.[48]

Throughout history, subversion has served as an important tool of foreign policy. In the writings of Thucydides, one finds ample examples of how ancient Athens practised subversion, for example, by promising financial aid to other city-states.[49] Similarly, during the late 1950s, the Eisenhower administration resorted to subversion when provoking a major rebellion and civil war in Indonesia with the aim of replacing its political leadership.[50] In the future, great-power conflict is likely to play out primarily through subversion, be it through fake news or the waging of proxy warfare (i.e., the empowering of non-state actors with the intention of undermining the state authority of an adversary). Iran, for instance, has adopted a foreign policy aimed at destabilising neighbouring governments through the use of terrorist groups, which is the reason behind Iran's support of the Houthis in Yemen or Hezbollah in Lebanon.[51] Violent extremist and terrorist groups themselves, such as Hezbollah, continue to use the techniques of infiltration, dissimilation, and population control which were perfected during the Cold War, combining them with contemporary strategies such as internet-based propaganda.[52] In 1947, for example, Major General Sir Stewart Menzies, head of the British Secret Service, developed an elaborate and far-ranging plan of anti-Soviet subversion that included deception, while also 'throwing ridicule' on Soviet officials and creating a 'general nuisance' in Soviet-controlled territory.[53] Similar tactics were also employed by Russia against Western countries and also by multiple states in Latin America, triggering instability and the collapse of regimes such as the one in Guatemala.[54]

Subversion appears a more attractive instrument of statecraft than conventional force for a number of reasons. To name a few, conventional force is more costly, is legally proscribed and is irreconcilable with economic interdependence, whilst the secrecy attending subversion allows the attacker to avoid detection to some degree.[55]

Today, subversion is often used with the aim of undermining state authority and promoting ungoverned space. In other words, division, rather than conquest, is the aim of modern forms of subversion.[56] Ungoverned space, however, poses severe threats to human, national and international security.[57] Subversion has a long history (as demonstrated by the numerous cases of subversion which took place in both Europe and Latin America during the Cold War[58]) but the virtual realm offers new opportunities for foreign powers to manipulate political events and public opinion in another country by spreading fake news. Indeed, cyber operations are becoming an increasingly popular instrument of subversion.

Even more so in cyberspace compared to the physical word, subversive operations are less costly and easier to mount. Yet, and for all the strategic advantages it offers, subversion via cyber operations faces numerous operational constraints. As Lennart Maschmeyer argues, intensity, speed and control are negatively correlated with regard to cyber operations. This means that, for example, increasing control (i.e. decreasing the risk of unexpected effects) takes time because it requires high familiarity with the adversary's system to find vulnerabilities that can be exploited without detection. This negative correlation is illustrated by various incidents, including the hack on Ukraine's power grid and the Petya malware attack. The former required months of preparation and temporarily caused intense disruption yet the attackers swiftly lost control over the incident (due to the switch to manual control to restore power). Consequently, the economic and long-term psychological impact was minimal. Similarly, the Petya malware attack, which caused billions of dollars in damage, entailed unanticipated consequences and strategic costs (i.e. sanctions). In sum, cyber operations that promise a greater scale of effect also carry a higher risk of loss of control.[59]

Notwithstanding its constraints, and for all the reasons mentioned above, future great-power conflict is likely to play out mainly via subversion, be it through fake news or the waging of proxy warfare (i.e. the empowering of non-state actors with the intention of undermining the state authority of an adversary). Cyber operations are, and will continue to be, a favourite strategy in subversive tactics because of their overall strategic promise: 'low costs, low risks, yet high payoffs', prompting all parties affected to go on the offensive, and yet not quite leading to (cyber) war.[60]

2.4 *Challenges to Traditional Statecraft*

Traditional approaches tend to define statecraft in terms of the aforementioned tools, or focus on its relationship with diplomacy, as discussed above. Several contemporary factors are calling for a revised understanding of statecraft, however.

For one, there is a multiplicity of actors in today's international arena. Unlike the nineteenth century, when there were a handful of great powers, today there are almost two hundred sovereign states. The principle of sovereign equality accords every state equal rights and responsibilities, regardless of its size – at least in principle. States also need to deal with an array of non-state actors, including NGOs (lobbying for issues such as environmental protection or human rights), transnational corporations, private security firms, international terrorist networks and so forth.[61]

States are also constrained in their actions by the alliances and intergovernmental organisations they have joined. Military alliances such as the North Atlantic Treaty Organization (NATO) and political unions such as the EU spring to mind. Various international bodies oblige states to honour their treaty obligations. For example, signatories of the Geneva Conventions have to observe certain limitations on their conduct of war, while members of the World Trade Organization (WTO) voluntarily submit to the organisation's dispute-settlement procedures.

Greater access to the mass media and the internet increasingly pushes state leaders to respond to public opinion and political pressure from within their own countries, particularly as more and more states today have democratic forms of government.[62] States also have to be increasingly concerned about how their own actions are viewed by people in other states and worry about their international image – an integral component of their power.

Furthermore, challenges to traditional understandings of statecraft are posed by a number of high-impact challenges that loom ahead. These challenges, which I call civilisational frontier risks, are discussed in more detail in the final chapter of this book. If left unaddressed, these risks could lead to the collapse of human civilisation or even human extinction. Here I briefly outlines the ten major civilisational frontier risks, which I shall discuss in more detail in the final chapter of his book.

Civilisational frontier risks include, first, those that have started to emerge from outer space. Despite our growing dependence on space, and for all the threats posed by space debris and weaponisation, outer space remains largely under-regulated.[63] We still lack an efficient liability regime and adequate solutions to the practical problems of identifying and removing space debris. In fact, we have advanced little with regard to regulating outer space since the adoption of the 1967 Outer Space Treaty.[64] The lack of regulation of outer space presents serious geopolitical challenges both in the present and in the future, since we rely heavily on space for our daily activities, from the internet, to flights and navigation.[65]

Another set of civilisational frontier risks is posed by emerging technologies, including artificial intelligence (AI), quantum computing and neuromorphic computing. In brief, AI encompasses computer systems that are capable of performing tasks that normally require human intelligence,[66] while quantum computing harnesses the potential of quantum mechanics to solve highly complex problems[67] and neuromorphic technology seeks to mimic the neural network architecture of the brain.[68] All three technologies have the potential to fundamentally change our daily lives and even human nature. In the coming decades, they will bring about enormous societal and economic challenges, ranging from loss of jobs through automation to new forms of warfare to increased inequalities, within and between states. If a state achieves superiority in one of these fields, all others will face grave security vulnerabilities, as I shall explain later in the book. The geopolitical impact of emerging technologies thus merits close attention.

Pandemics – albeit not a new phenomenon – are likely to occur with heightened frequency in the twenty-first century, requiring state leaders to prepare for them. The fight against COVID-19 has made us acutely aware of the adverse long-term consequences of pandemics for human well-being and for national and international politics. Pandemics not only have drastic negative effects on public health (including mental health) but also pose a challenge to the socio-economic foundations of our lives, increasing inequality and poverty.[69] In today's globalised world, national epidemics may evolve into planetary pandemics much faster than ever before, in addition to being far more difficult to contain. In 2017, two years before the COVID-19 pandemic, the US federal agency, the Centers for Disease Control and Prevention, published a special issue titled, 'Why It Matters: The Pandemic Threat'. This document emphasises that 'when a pathogen can travel from a remote village to major cities on all continents in thirty-six hours, the threat to our national security is greater than ever'.[70] Experts warn that more pandemics are coming as climate change releases long-dormant viruses and bacteria which have been preserved in permafrost for centuries.[71] Whilst we are progressing rapidly in the areas of sanitation and medical research, modern mobility and increased urbanisation (including urban slums) allow infections to spread much more easily across the globe.[72] The COVID-19 pandemic laid bare the gaps in our knowledge and capabilities to confront the rapid spread of dangerous diseases.[73]

Other civilisational frontier risks are associated with the increasing range of applications of synthetic biology, CRISPR and mRNA, as well as by the growing human-machine symbiosis fostered by brain-computer interfaces (BCIs). For all the benefits they offer, these technological innovations also expose humanity and the environment to hazards that state leaders must seek to mitigate. The aim of synthetic biology is not only to modify existing organisms but also to create novel ones with characteristics not found in nature.[74] Releasing synthetic organisms into the environment may have unanticipated negative effects on both the environment and human health, however.[75] The gene-editing technology CRISPR, and technology based on mRNA, can have similarly dangerous off-target effects.[76] These technologies can also be abused by state or non-state actors to, for example, engineer pathogens and biological weapons.[77]

BCIs are likewise fraught with risks as they continue to blur the line between medical treatment and human enhancement.[78] Among other possible effects, they have the potential to severely curtail our free will and raise difficult ethical questions that state leaders must attempt to answer with the help of neuro-ethicists. Neuro-ethics is a subfield of bioethics that aims to ensure that technologies capable of influencing the human mind are developed in an ethical manner.[79] In fact, neuro-ethics can help policy makers develop appropriate regulation that maximises the benefits and minimises the harms associated with technological innovations.

Climate change is another large-scale harm that state leaders cannot afford to ignore. Climate change entails rising sea levels, ocean acidification, severe storms and droughts, and damage to vulnerable ecosystems.[80] The combined effect of climate change, biodiversity loss and pandemics, which are both causes and consequences of one another, may threaten the future of humanity.[81] Unfortunately, extinction rates are accelerating[82] and, within the next few generations, may lead to a 'sudden' biosphere collapse,[83] which could lead to wars, mass migrations, social instability and mass deaths.[84]

Further challenges to statecraft are posed by the growing significance of the virtual realm. These include future financial crises resulting from cyber attacks caused by rogue states or non-state actors. Cyber attacks could result in the collapse of critical infrastructure, or a dangerous disruption of nuclear or biological facilities.[85] Digital technologies and the emergence of social media platforms have also accelerated the spread of fake news. Anyone anywhere today can become a creator and messenger of all sorts of falsehoods. Fake news has the capacity to destabilise political and civic institutions, and to create circumstances in which emotions such as anger or fear are more influential in shaping public opinion than objective facts.[86]

Statecraft also needs to adapt to advances in weapons technology (especially weapons of mass destruction, or WMD, and bioweapons). There are opposing views as to whether or not such weaponry will increase the likelihood of states resorting to the use of force.[87] It is certain, however, that whichever country succeeds in developing new types of WMD and bioweapons or defence systems first will have the upper hand in the geopolitical arena. If biological weapons were to be used on a mass scale, the effects would potentially endanger the existence of our species. State leaders must therefore collaborate to prevent the release of such weapons into the world.

Scientific advances in numerous fields, including genome editing, synthetic biology and superintelligence, are opening new frontiers for human enhancement that could augment our biological and cognitive abilities far beyond the current limitations of our organism.[88] Our attempts to improve our bodies and minds could ultimately change human nature so dramatically that the trans-human stage might be reached by our species in the twenty-first century.[89] Trans-humanism, however, does not necessarily imply progress. It is fraught with challenges, including the risk of increasing inequalities between the enhanced and non-enhanced.[90]

Intrusive tech-enabled surveillance poses another significant civilisational frontier risk. Big data, machine learning and predictive analytics enable massive intrusion into people's lives. Failure to regulate surveillance technology can give rise to grave violations of civil liberties.[91] This, in turn, can threaten the social contract between citizens and the state, and lead to the perception that government is no longer legitimate.[92]

The main risks posed by emerging technologies stem from the present lack of regulation[93] or self-regulation.[94] In fact, regulation is unlikely to keep up with the speed of the scientific developments themselves.[95] As a result, transformative technologies could be harnessed by the powerful and wealthy for egoistic and violent purposes.

Yet, for all their inherent risks, transformative technologies might have the capacity to solve today's most urgent problems,[96] and to drive development and progress across multiple sectors. AI, for example, can introduce rational techniques into decision making processes. Transformative technologies like AI and quantum computing[97] can contribute to improving national and international security by allowing us, for example, to develop stronger encryption systems and gather information.[98] In sum, emerging technologies are a double-edged sword that state leaders need to handle wisely.

In light of these civilisational frontier risks, a new approach to statecraft is needed, one that enables it to adapt to an ever-evolving and transnational amalgam of challenges. In fact, and as political scientists Paul Gorden Lauren, Gordon Craig and Alexander George explain, 'adaptation to accelerated change has become the major problem of modern statecraft'.[99] In the chapters that follow, I introduce five innovative tools that can help state leaders successfully navigate the rapidly changing and increasingly complex geopolitical landscape of the twenty-first century.

The first tool for successful statecraft in the twenty-first century that I propose is the new geopolitical analysis method I call *meta-geopolitics*. To navigate today's rapidly changing and increasingly interdependent world, skilled statecraft needs to be based on an accurate and solid understanding of international dynamics and the power relationships among states. A good map of the macro-picture of international relations is needed to make decisions at the micro-level of day-to-day statecraft. Only by knowing where his or her state stands in relation to other states and within the global environment can a state leader effectively decide where he or she wants to go and what the state is capable of doing, given its global position and relative capabilities. The analysis of international dynamics has traditionally been called geopolitics[100] but existing approaches to geopolitics are widely insufficient to describe the complexity of today's world. *Meta-geopolitics* yields a more reliable macro-picture of international dynamics by taking into account the increasingly complex determinants of state power and international politics. Before moving on to an in-depth analysis of *meta-geopolitics* in chapter four, however, I first provide in the next chapter a brief overview of more traditional approaches to geopolitics.

3

Rethinking Geopolitics

Statesmen and women cannot devise prudent policies if they do not have a sound understanding of where their country stands in relation to the rest of the world. Certainly, such leaders need a map – a map that tells them about their state's geographic location, its maritime access routes and the size of its territory compared to other regional powers. However, this basic information is not sufficient for good statecraft. To devise effective policies, they need to consider questions regarding the state's relative position *vis-à-vis* the rest of the world, including how populous the state is compared to its neighbours, how strong its military capabilities are, whether the state's military will be able to fend off an emerging regional power that is threatening to alter the global balance of power and whether there are alternative passageways through which essential commodities can be supplied to the state in case of a closure of the regular trade routes the state uses.

Such questions can be answered through geopolitics. Geopolitics has been traditionally defined as the study of how geographic factors (such as boundaries, natural resources etc.) impact politics, particularly political relationships among states. It looks at the power dynamics among states seeking to control territory and to acquire reliable access to strategically important locations and resources.[1] Looking at international relations from a geopolitical point of view leads to strategic prescriptions that have a strong focus on geographical realities. This chapter reviews both traditional and contemporary conceptualisations of geopolitics. In doing so, it highlights the need for a new and more comprehensive approach to geopolitical analysis.

3.1 Traditional Concepts of Geopolitics

Formerly, geography – the static physical features of our planet – was the major ingredient of geopolitics, and some of the early theorists had strong backgrounds in geography and the natural sciences. Increasingly, however, the field has been overtaken by social scientists focusing on human action and socio-economic systems to determine international power relationships.[2] Nevertheless, scholars such as Saul Cohen and Stephen Walt have been reintegrating the study of geography into their geopolitical analyses. As the description of their approach in Table 3.1 suggests, both place major emphasis on the geographic location of states to determine power relationships.

Historically, the study of geopolitics has had its ups and downs. Following its inception at the end of the nineteenth century, geopolitics developed into a respectable 'science' in the early twentieth century, as a series of competing geopolitical hypotheses and theories circulated among academics, military strategists and politicians. After the defeat of the Axis powers in 1945, geopolitics came into disrepute. The concept became strongly associated with Germany and Japan's expansionist policies (the attempt to colonise territories for access to more resources and strategic world dominance). The study of geopolitics appeared less relevant for a while during the Cold War, during which the Northern Hemisphere remained rather static, carefully divided between the US and Soviet spheres of dominance and influence. The nuclear stalemate between the world's only two superpowers prevented open territorial competition in the Northern Hemisphere, although competition over resources and strategic locations occurred in the Southern Hemisphere through proxy wars. The end of the Cold War and the resulting regional fragmentation and new multipolar power dynamics led to a revival of geopolitical thinking in politics and in academia.[3] The following table provides a concise overview of some of the key concepts of geopolitics listed in chronological order.

3.2 Contemporary Critiques of the Geopolitical Approach

One frequent criticism of classical concepts of geopolitics is that the emphasis on geography can lead to an overly deterministic view of world politics. It is as if to say that the natural environment in which

Table 3.1 Concepts of Geopolitics[4]

AUTHOR	CONCEPT	SHORT DESCRIPTION
Aristotle (384-322 BCE)	**Natural environment impacts individuals and societies**	- Natural environment helps determine an individual's choice of occupation, which in turn impacts the type of political arrangement people choose - Heterogeneous territory leads to heterogeneity among inhabitants, which makes it difficult to build a united and peaceful state - Isolated geographic location of a state fosters longevity and stability, as the state is protected from military attacks and revolutionary ideas coming from abroad
Jean Bodin (1530-1596)	**Climatic theories**	- Natural environment shapes human character and influences regime types of political communities
Alfred Thayer Mahan (1840-1914)	**Importance of sea power in world politics**	- Most important ingredient of a state's international power is a strong navy, control of long coastlines and significant ports - Expected rivalry over world dominance to take place between Russian land power and British sea power in Asia, and argued that Britain and the United States together could surround Eurasia from key bases and keep Russian power in check

(continued)

Table 3.1 (continued)

AUTHOR	CONCEPT	SHORT DESCRIPTION
Rudolph Kjellen (1864-1922)	**Geopolitics**	- Coined the term 'geopolitics' in 1899, defined as the "science of the state", which, in practice, he believed to be mostly the science of war, as he saw political process to be spatially determined
Friedrich Ratzel (1844-1904)	**Organic theory**	- Like organisms, states compete with each other to increase their living space (*Lebensraum*) in order to thrive
Sir Halford Mackinder (1861-1947)	**Heartland theory**	- Rivalries between states will shift from the sea to the interior of continents - Most important area to be contested will be control over the northern and interior parts of Eurasia ('Pivot Area' of world politics), including important river networks to the seas and lakes - Germany, Russia and China are well-positioned to gain control of the Pivot Area and dominate maritime powers
General Karl Haushofer (1869-1946)	**Theory of pan regions**	- World consists of three blocs of power: (1) Anglo-America, United States as core (with periphery of Latin America); (2) Europe, Germany as core (with periphery of Africa and India); and (3) Japan (with periphery of Southeast Asia) - Advocated that Germany, as Europe's leading power, would expand its sphere of domination eastwards (ideas taken up by Nazi Germany)
Nicholas Spykman (1893-1943)	**Environmental determinism; 'Rimland' theory**	- Northern Hemisphere more important than Southern Hemisphere - Importance of 'Rimland', including Western Europe, Middle East, South Asia, South-east Asia and Far East

(*continued*)

Table 3.1 (continued)

Alexander de Seversky (1894-1974)	**Importance of air power (air supremacy equals global control)**	- Whoever controls the skies controls the world - United States and Soviet Union have air dominance over their respective spheres, but have to compete for air dominance over 'Area of Decision' (including Anglo- America, Eurasian heartland, maritime Europe, North Africa, Middle East)
Hans Morgenthau (1904-1980)	**Power politics/ realism**	- A state's power (made up of its economic might, armed forces, demographics, etc.) is more important than its geographic location - Power by its very nature will expand until stopped by countervailing power
George F. Kennan (1904-2005)	**Containment/ industrial base/ peripheral defence**	- Focus defence on the world's major centres of industrial power - Block expansion of aggressive power
Samuel Huntington (1927-2008)	**Clash of civilisations**	- The world's 'hot spots' where wars and hostilities are most likely to occur are located along the fault lines between the world's different civilisations - The wars of the future are most likely to occur among civilisations rather than among states
Saul Cohen (present)	**Geostrategic regions**	- Two main regions: Maritime (dependent on trade) with the United States, Europe and Japan as first-order states or regions; and the Eurasian Continental Realm (interior-directed) with China and the Soviet Union as first-order states

(*continued*)

Table 3.1 (continued)

Immanuel Wallerstein (present)	World systems theory	- Geographical division of labour within world economy consisting of three subsystems: (1) core states (advanced economic powers with strong state structures exploiting the periphery); (2) periphery (weak states with little autonomy, often former colonies); semi-peripheral areas (serve as buffers between core and periphery) - System is rigid, almost impossible for countries on the periphery to ever reach the economic level of the core
Thomas P.M. Barnett (present)	Pentagon's New Map	- World divided into 'Functioning Core' and 'Non-Integrating Gap' - Need for 'Global Transaction Strategy' to connect Gap to the Core through civil-military engagement and integration
Stephen Walt (present)	Balance of threat/loss-of-strength gradient/ offshore balancing	- Geographic proximity strongly affects threat perception between two states - States balance against their most proximate threat, so geographically isolated states are less likely to be opposed by antagonistic Alliances
Joseph Nye (present)	Three-dimensional space	- International relations today has three dimensions: (1) military realm, unipolar (defined by US military dominance); (2) multipolar economic dimension; (3) 'floating' non-state actors

(*continued*)

Table 3.1 (continued)

Francis Fukuyama (present)	**'End of history'**	- Values of free-market capitalism and liberal democracy will triumph over all other political and economic systems, and they will become a source for international security and stability wherever these values are adopted
Nayef Al-Rodhan (present)	***Meta-geopolitics***	- Threats to international peace and security can emanate from seven different areas of state power that are interrelated and mutually reinforcing (social and health issues, domestic politics, economics, environment, science and human potential, military and security issues, international diplomacy) - These seven dimensions of state power need to be taken into account in addition to traditional and critical geopolitics

a state happens to be located invariably determines its relative power in the region and its international influence. This claim, however, does not withstand empirical scrutiny. To name just one of many examples, geography has not condemned a country like Switzerland, which has few natural resources, little fertile farmland and is land-locked, to remain an economically backward and poor country isolated from the outside world. Geopolitics, in its narrow, deterministic sense, thus fails to incorporate important human factors in political and economic processes. It also does not account for historical contingencies. Certain political systems may either support or discourage technological development and thus help to determine a state's ability to compete with the outside world or make new territorial conquests. Religious taboos may equally influence the way a nation relates to, and makes use of, its natural environment and geographic location. Sometimes pure luck will lead to a discovery that enables a nation to overcome geographic or geopolitical obstacles and become a powerful state.

The process of globalisation has been radically transforming geostrategy. Arguing from various perspectives, numerous scholars have challenged traditional notions that look at the world as dominated by threats emanating primarily from the rivalries of states with fixed boundaries.[5] Such notions are a poor foundation for devising a relevant security strategy as external threats to states are now transnational and no longer emanate from states alone.

The liberal international school is the most forceful critic of geography-based explanations of international relations today. The school commonly bases its opposition to geopolitical approaches on two observations. First, globalisation has blurred the distinction between domestic and international politics to the point that distinguishing between the two has become meaningless. Second, today's information-based economy has changed economic power relationships and the ability of states to offer political incentives.[6]

As a result of these two premises, the liberal international school has put forward five main arguments for why geopolitics is an outmoded way of explaining international relations. First, the size of a country's territory is no longer necessarily a measure of its economic and political strength.[7] A country's human potential and technological sophistication allows it to overcome geographic adversity and have a geopolitical relevance that is not reflected by its size and geographic location on a world map. Furthermore, large states with an unstable political system that are plagued by domestic political turmoil are often unable to take advantage of their privileged strategic location or their important strategic resources.

Second, economic capital can often be a more significant measure of a country's power and influence in international affairs than the size of its military.[8] International economics, this argument goes, is slowly replacing geopolitics as the most relevant gauge of actual power relationships in the world.

Third, international politics is no longer a zero-sum game. The accumulation of economic wealth by one state can lead to economic growth in the entire region and can thereby benefit other states as well.[9] In fact, it has been found that the globalisation of production fosters regional economic integration, which in turn can lead to increased regional security cooperation.[10]

Fourth, the conquest of territory through war, especially in the developed world, is no longer of any advantage to states embedded in an international free-market economy. As Stephen G. Brooks argues in his book *Producing Security*, economic success strongly depends on multinational corporations, whose research, development and production of goods are geographically dispersed over a number of countries. Multinational corporations also strongly rely on international subcontracting, outsourcing and alliances between companies to remain competitive in the global marketplace.[11] Hence, the conquest of territory – and with it industrial bases – is no longer a lucrative way for states in the developed world to increase their economic might due to the broad dispersal of the value chain of modern production. A state engaged in military conquest will suffer economic setbacks, as their actions might provoke an international embargo and will certainly discourage foreign direct investment. A state with a knowledge-based economy that is conquered and controlled by another power is also unlikely to generate the same degree of technological innovation as it did when the state was free and independent.[12]

Fifth, liberal internationalists argue against the geographical or physical determinism of the geopolitical approach. They argue that ideas are more important than geography, as ideas can change the global system and the conflict behaviour of states, while the geographic setting remains the same. An early proponent of the idea that political systems influence conflict behaviour was the German philosopher Immanuel Kant. In his essay, 'Perpetual Peace: A Philosophical Proposal', Kant argued that there would be no wars if people, who naturally feel a common human bond with the rest of humanity, were left to govern themselves and formed a pacific federation of free states instead of being the subjects of power-hungry monarchs.[13] Similarly, Woodrow Wilson famously argued that democracies do not go to war with each other. The conflict behaviour of states is thus not just determined by geography but, more importantly, by political systems and ideational factors. The latter has become a popular subject of investigation for political scientists. In particular, the school of critical geopolitics illuminates the transformative power of perceptions and ideas in international relations. The following section will look at this school of thought in more detail.

3.3 Critical Geopolitics

Critics of traditional concepts of geopolitics, whether they emphasise geography or social scientific aspects to explain the dynamics of international politics, argue that representations and perceptions of states and different population groups also shape international dynamics. A new school of thought called *critical geopolitics* has formed around the notion that geographic representations of the world are highly subjective. The school is based on the postmodern deconstructivist notion that no text or term possesses an intrinsic and fixed meaning, and that all concepts used to interpret the world are just discourses imposed by a dominant ideology, class, gender or race.[14] Proponents of critical geopolitics would thus stress the importance of recognising that leaders of the world's most powerful and influential states shape the way we see international politics. Countries that are on friendly terms with the United States, for instance, are likely to adopt US perceptions of which states are posing a threat to international security. It is no coincidence, for example, that the US president's narrative of the world is more influential than that of a poor state in the global South.[15] In other words, the most powerful states in the world tend to be able to impose their views of international political relationships on the rest of the world.

Gearóid Ó Tuathail was the first systematic proponent of this new school of thought and referred to geopolitics as an unstable and historically contingent concept.[16] As he explains in one article, geopolitics is a 'historically ambiguous and unstable concept'.[17] Geographical space and the world map are represented differently in different historical periods. For Tuathail, a geographic survey cannot be separated from a strategic agenda. In other words, drawing maps is, by its very nature, an act of interpreting and representing physical reality.[18]

Critical geopolitics thus deals with perceptions and interpretations of global processes. The school argues that geography is not an objective science. Our location, as well as our gender and social status, help shape the way we interpret geographical space. Critical geopolitics further argues that factors such as race, class and gender help shape the way individuals are affected by, and cope with, geopolitical processes, be they wars or changes in the global economy.[19] Feminist scholars, such as Donna Haraway, have argued that women and children experience geopolitical processes, such as wars or geo-economic processes, in a different way from men. For instance, women in the South are usually less mobile than men and thus can take less advantage of migration opportunities related to globalisation.[20] For individuals on the ground, geopolitical and geo-economic processes are much more personalised. Looking at these diverse personal trajectories thus gives a much more complex and contradictory picture of international processes than the macro-view of geographical space and power relationships offered by traditional geopolitical analysis.[21]

Critical geopolitics distinguishes between three different levels of perceptions and descriptions of global processes: formal, practical and popular. Formal refers to the theoretical and systematic way academics explain geopolitics. Depending on the theory or school of thought adopted by the scholar, a slightly different interpretation of geopolitical relationships will result. If one believes, for instance, that economic factors are what mostly determine geopolitical relationships, one would emphasise economic power centres like the United States and the EU. If demographic factors are emphasised, however, countries like China and India would figure more prominently when representing geopolitical dynamics.[22] To give another example, during the Cold War, US scientists significantly contributed to the portrayal of the world as being divided between the free world under the leadership of the United States and an evil empire dominated by the communist Soviet Union, a portrayal that shaped the geopolitical worldview of an entire generation.[23]

Practical geopolitics describes the way policy makers and political leaders represent international political dynamics. An extension of this level is politicians' use of maps and geopolitical interpretations as propaganda tools. The use of maps in political propaganda can often give a false impression of objectivity to the target audience. As L.K.D. Kristof explained in 1960, 'A poster with a true or pseudo-geopolitical map is ... attractive and seems to tell merely a self-evident truth. Men have already learned to distrust words and figures, but they have not yet learned to distrust maps.'[24]

Popular geopolitics involves the way the media and popular culture represent geopolitical processes and thus shapes how ordinary citizens perceive global politics.[25] During the Cold War, for example, Western cartoons, movies and the mass media reinforced the notion of a world divided into two camps and the portrayal of the Soviet Union and Eastern Europe as a dark and backward area from which all kinds of threats might emerge. In recent history, the Muslim world is portrayed in Western cartoons, movies and mass media as an antagonistic and backward area from which terrorist threats might emerge, thus perpetuating Western typecasting of the Islamic world as a monolithic religious and political entity. This has dangerous implications for intercultural relations, which may even give rise to justifications of foreign interference, including military invasion in Muslim countries.[26] As Robert A. Saunders rightly remarks, 'in the contemporary realm of international relations, images have been weaponized in an unending war of ideas'.[27] His book *Popular Geopolitics: Plotting an Evolving Interdiscipline* offers a good example of how popular culture, new media and public diplomacy may impact nation branding and shape national image and statecraft.

Of course, all three types of discourses are interrelated. Politicians borrow some of their concepts from academics, academics can be influenced by popular culture, and the media can help to shape the perceptions of policy makers. We all use abstract and simplified images that help us to make sense of the world, and these images are influenced by cultural factors. Critical geopolitics therefore maintains that geopolitics is a cultural construct and that international dynamics are not quantifiable scientific processes that can be objectively described.

3.4 Strategic Geography

The political scientists Geoffrey Kemp and Robert E. Harkavy coined the term *strategic geography*. In contrast to *geopolitics*, this term more specifically describes 'the tactical elements of geography that contribute to grand strategy'.[28] According to the authors, strategic geography is the study of how access to, or control over, land, water and air space impacts a state's national security and economic prosperity. The concept incorporates all areas of modern geography. On the one hand, there is *physical geography*, which describes the topographical make-up of continents. It also includes the natural resources that exist in different geographic areas. The physical geographic make-up of the world changes slowly – natural resources may become depleted due to human activity; rivers may change course or be diverted as a result of dam projects.

On the other hand, strategic geography includes *human* geography, which describes factors that impact geographic space as a result of human activities, including political, economic and military activities. The *political* geography of a country or region describes the decision-making apparatus that governs the people within a defined geographic space. Wars of conquest or internal political revolutions can dramatically change the political geography of a region, as can the break-up of an empire or the partition of a single political entity into two or more separate states. Mass migration can alter the politics of an entire region. New alliances or shifts in alliances can also change the landscape of international politics rather dramatically. One example would be the rift that developed within the Sino-Soviet communist bloc and the subsequent rapprochement between the United States and China under US President Richard Nixon in the 1970s.[29]

Economic geography refers to a country's industrial and rural infrastructure and trade patterns.[30] Changing market conditions, the discovery of valuable natural resources on a state's territory, a radically new technological innovation or the blockage of an important trade route (or choke point) can have a decisive impact on countries and regions and may affect internal politics, international political alignments or even provoke a war. One current issue in this context, which will be discussed in more detail later, is the international politics surrounding the construction of oil pipelines from the land-locked Caspian basin to ports on open waters. While Russia, of course, wants the pipelines to run through its territory, the United States and the EU are lobbying Central Asian states to build pipelines through Turkey. The route chosen will have an important impact on the economies and economic security of Europe, as well as on the countries that the pipelines cross.[31]

Military geography, another important subcategory of human geography, describes the military capabilities of a state and the way these assets are deployed. New developments in weapons technology can change the military geography of countries and regions. The development of new aircraft and missile technologies, for instance, has decreased the importance of geographical obstacles such as distance or high mountain chains. A change in political regime might similarly alter a state's military posture from a defensive to a more offensive one. Taking into account both physical and human geography and its many subcategories, strategic geography provides a more nuanced way of studying how access to, or control over, physical space influences power relationships among states.

Since the coining of the term 'strategic geography' by Kemp and Harkavy, a lot of work has been done on military, economic and human geography.[32] Together, these works highlight the need for state leaders to take into account the military, economic and human realities of their geographic environment. Still, and as I illustrate further below, there are even more factors that state leaders must incorporate in their geostrategic deliberations.

3.5 The Continued Relevance of Geopolitics

There are strong arguments to support the notion that classical geopolitics is outdated and of little use to students of international relations today. Globalisation has multiplied interrelationships between states and has made national boundaries porous. Today, geographic boundaries between states, such as rivers or mountain chains, tell us little about a particular state's relative power, safety or level of international integration. Furthermore, the development of long-range missiles, strategic bombers and air-borne fuel tankers has made distance and geographical obstacles less of a problem for war planners. De-territorialised threats emanating from cyberspace further call into question the use of a 'territorial' paradigm.[33]

I would argue, however, that states will continue to be constrained by the geographic limitations of their territories, even if less so than in the recent past. Discounting geography entirely and focusing exclusively on social factors leaves a skewed picture of international relations. Despite the human ability to overcome a range of environmental and geographic obstacles, the natural environment and a state's location in terms of control of important coastlines or access to waterways nevertheless remains important.[34] Although it is true that today's economy is, to a large extent, based on knowledge, the resources and industry that enable the production of software in the first place remain the basis for economic wealth and power. A technologically advanced country still cannot thrive without reliable access to oil and an industrial infrastructure, whether at home or abroad. These important industries and resources remain spatially distributed. The fact that they are distributed unevenly around the world makes geopolitics a highly relevant component of strategy in the twenty-first century.[35] Geopolitical analysis therefore remains important for statecraft yet must be adjusted to capture the changed realities of the twenty-first century. New features that contribute to state power today must be added to any map featuring geographical details and resource distribution among and within states.

The argument that the process of globalisation erodes state borders to a level of irrelevance and thus renders geography a superfluous concept in the national strategic thinking of states lacks evidence. Certainly, threats to states today are often transnational and asymmetrical. Most developed states fear terrorist or guerrilla attacks more than conventional military attacks by neighbouring states. However, the example of the US war against terrorism that followed the terrorist attacks of 11 September 2001 demonstrates the continuing importance of state actors in international relations. Clearly, the attack was perpetrated by a small group of non-state actors.[36] Furthermore, ideologically minded non-state actors can succeed in taking over formerly state-controlled territories and consequently become a spatial threat – or at least spatially relevant – in geopolitical terms. The example of Islamic State shows how quickly a non-spatial threat can turn into a spatial one.

The liberal economic argument that the interconnectedness of global commerce and states' strong mutual economic dependence raises the economic cost of war to an unacceptable level does not rest on solid empirical foundations. History has shown that people fight wars for reasons other than economic enrichment. As one author puts it: 'People are still attached to their culture, their language, and a place called home. And they will sing for home, cry for home, fight for home, and die for home. Which is why globalisation does not, and will not, end geopolitics.'[37]

The argument has been made that globalisation promotes increased intercultural understanding and friendships by intensifying interactions between people from different cultures. This purportedly decreases the potential for demonising foreign cultures and reduces the risk of conflicts between states. Nevertheless, historical experience has also shown us that wars often take place between states that share a strong cultural bond. The First World War is a case in point. The war was fought between major European powers that all shared strong cultural affinities, similar cultural tastes and religious beliefs, and they all had engaged in intense cultural borrowing over the centuries. Despite the intense mixing of cultures brought about through the process of globalisation, special interstate politics cannot be left out of the picture. State units, individual states' strategic needs and power dynamics between states need to be included in any accurate analysis of international relations.[38]

Moreover, geopolitics does not need to be geographically deterministic. In fact, many contemporary geopoliticians acknowledge that it is not geography *per se*, but rather the interaction between the natural environment and human entrepreneurship that determines the geostrategic power of a particular state. Modern geopoliticians understand that the strategic location of a country may help shape its political values and systems, but also that it does not determine them. Geopolitics does not claim to be a natural science and has no aspiration to be one. As Kristof noted: 'The modern geo-politician does not look at the world map in order to find out what nature *compels* us to do but what nature *advises* us to do, given our preferences.'[39]

Today, technological sophistication, knowledge and the ability to spread influential information contribute enormously to a country's power. Even so, a spatial analysis of the world continues to serve as the foundation for grand strategy in the information society of the twenty-first century. Besides mountains and strategically significant natural resources, a geopolitical analysis of today's world may also include the spatial concentration of software and human resources.[40] Just as a spatial analysis of how natural resources are concentrated across the world's different continents has provided clues to classical geopoliticians about global power relationships, so does a spatial analysis of how software resources are globally distributed demonstrate where today's power centres lie. As long as elements of state power are distributed unequally across the globe (whether they be natural resources, national armies, industry or software), geopolitics remains relevant.

We nonetheless require a new geopolitical analysis tool to do justice to today's increasingly complex and nuanced interaction between geography, international politics and international relations. The following chapter thus proposes *meta-geopolitics* as a new geopolitical framework that more accurately represents the spatial distribution of hard-, soft-, smart- and just-power resources and international power dynamics in a globalised world.

4

Meta-Geopolitics **and the Seven Dimensions of State Power**

Geopolitical analysis is an important pillar of effective statecraft because it enables statesmen and women to understand the current world system and attain their political objectives. The complexity of today's world, however, requires us to take an all-encompassing approach to the analysis of international relationships. The concept of *meta-geopolitics* offers an innovative and holistic approach that differs from traditional concepts of geopolitics, as it proposes a multidimensional view of power. More precisely, it considers seven major areas of state power, or 'capacities', to demonstrate the highly complex strategic relationships between states. These include (1) social and health issues, (2) domestic politics, (3) economics, (4) the environment, (5) science and human potential, (6) military and security issues and (7) international diplomacy. In fact, threats to international peace and security can emanate from these seven different areas of state power and are often interrelated and mutually reinforcing.

These seven capacities can be used to evaluate not only states, but also international relations and international power relationships. In today's interconnected and technologically sophisticated world, geography alone no longer tells us much about the strengths of particular regions in relation to others. Instead, all seven dimensions of state power identified in this study need to be taken into account to understand power relationships in the twenty-first century.

The meta-geopolitical approach not only enables us to evaluate all of the soft- and hard-power tools used across the seven areas described above. It also allows us to make predictions about the ability of a state

Figure 4.1 The Concept of Meta-Geopolitics

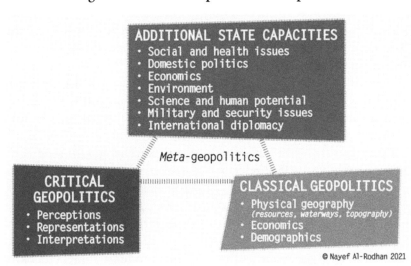

to continue to project its power in the future. It takes into account such variables as projected population growth, demographic make-up, public health and human and scientific potential. These factors help us gauge whether a country will retain, increase or lose its current geopolitical status.

More traditional geostrategic concepts usually identify and revolve around one type of threat or focus on one great power or geographic region that needs to be contained. These concepts usually lead to the conclusion that a country's limited resources should be marshalled to deal with this one identified type of pre-eminent threat. Looking at some of the geopolitical concepts listed in the previous chapter will illustrate the one-dimensionality of more classic geopolitical concepts.

For Hans Morgenthau, for example, military and economic capabilities are the most important features of a state in the global game of geopolitics. His concept of geopolitics suggested that the most important measure states can take to ensure their future national survival is to strengthen their militaries. A state basing its geostrategic decisions on Morgenthau's worldview would have neglected to train its military to engage in stabilising missions in a failed state. Morgenthau's worldview would have also led national-security officials to ignore the need to protect citizens sufficiently from possible terrorist attacks or pandemics.

Similarly, Alexander de Seversky's concept would have urged great powers to invest heavily in building up excellent air-power capabilities, while Alfred Thayer Mahan's concept would have led them to enlarge their naval fleets. Doing so would have taken a state's limited resources away from preparing for other security threats. A geostrategy based too heavily on military defence may leave some states heavily armed but with a failing internal security structure, an unhealthy population or a society suffering under the tyranny of transnational criminal networks.

Other geostrategists focus on the significance of certain geographic areas. Sir Halford Mackinder, for instance, based his theory on the geopolitical importance of the 'Eurasian Heartland'.[1] His worldview would have led geostrategists to conclude that control of the northern and interior parts of Eurasia should be their country's primary geostrategic goal. Yet, focusing only on one particular geographic area lets states ignore the emergence of other possible great military powers. Looking at the world through the spectrum of *meta-geopolitics* allows states to detect potential shifts in the global balance of power early. It draws their attention to states that may experience rapid population growth along with impressive economic growth and technological progress. This could lead geostrategists to rethink their country's strategic orientation and include rising world powers in their security- and foreign-policy calculations.

Samuel Huntington's theory of a 'clash of civilisations' predicted that future wars would occur primarily between different civilisations, such as the 'Islamic civilisation' and the 'West', rather than between states. His theory would have prompted national security officials to focus on promoting harmony and understanding between different civilisational entities. Doing so would have led states to ignore the fact that most violence in the world still occurs between groups that belong to the same civilisational entities and often even to the same state. Huntington's reasoning could have prevented states from marshalling sufficient resources to tackle security threats associated with state failure, which is always accompanied by civil violence (which can be a cause or a consequence of state failure).

These classic theories of geopolitics all single out one state capacity – be it military capability or geographic location – as the most important one in global geopolitics. Today's countries, however, face a broad variety of decentralised and often interrelated threats. To illustrate the twenty-first-century security environment, G. John Ikenberry compares the global environment to an urban setting:

> If the world of the twenty-first century were a town, the security threats faced by its leading citizens would not be organized crime or a violent assault by a radical mob on city hall. It would be a breakdown of law enforcement and social services in the face of constantly changing and ultimately uncertain vagaries of criminality, nature, and circumstances.[2]

Ikenberry concludes that: 'these more diffuse, shifting, and uncertain threats require a different sort of grand strategy than one aimed at countering a specific enemy, such as a rival great power or a radical terrorist group'.[3] Using the concept of *meta-geopolitics* likewise forces a security analyst to look at all areas in which potential instabilities and threats to global security could arise.

Ikenberry rightly points out the huge uncertainties regarding future threats. It is not possible to know right now what the main threat to the national security of a particular state will be ten or fifteen years down the line.[4] Even if we could single out two or three major threats, Ikenberry posits that such threats will likely 'be complex and interlinked with lots of other international moving parts'.[5] For instance, a state that experiences a lot of civil violence and whose government enjoys little legitimacy may become a failing state. It is unlikely that a failing state will be able to stop the spread of organised crime or a contagious disease. The transnational threats emanating from such a state could then be as diverse as a pandemic, money laundering, drug trafficking and terrorism.

In sum, any geostrategy that is based on *meta-geopolitics* will account for the diffuse and shifting nature of today's security threats. Focusing a country's geostrategy on one single security challenge will leave a country dangerously unsafe, as doing so will make it ignore other threats that might come up or 'miss the dangerous connections between these threats', says Ikenberry.[6]

I now turn to a more detailed description of the seven capacities of state power and explain their relevance for assessing power relationships between states in the twenty-first century.

4.1 Social and Health Issues

The first capacity assesses the state of society in each country, including demographic factors, ethnic make-up, degree of social peace and cohesion, and health issues affecting the population.

4.1.1 Demographic Factors

Extreme population growth – whether too high or too low – can have a negative impact on the relative strength of a country. First, let us look at the possible destabilising effects of too-rapid population growth. Most population growth will likely occur in poor places where basic resources, especially water and arable land, are scarce, where governments lack sufficient resources to provide education and adequate health care to a growing population and where the local economy is unable to absorb a rapidly growing labour force.[7] In rural areas, increased tensions may arise over access to resources. In urban areas, rapid population growth can lead to social and political instability if the economy is unable to create new jobs fast enough to absorb the growing working-age population.[8]

It has also been found that the possibility of ethnic conflict is enhanced if urban areas have a high proportion of fifteen- to 25-year-olds.[9] For countries affected by rapid population growth, this may mean growing social unrest. For strategists looking at these demographic developments from the outside, this may mean potential emigration flows from these countries to other states, including their own.

While some countries struggle with a population that is growing too rapidly, such as Nigeria, for instance, others, such as Japan and China, worry about ageing and population decline. The trends of increasing longevity and falling fertility are affecting many countries, but they are particularly pronounced in the developed world. In much of the developed world, which is currently the engine for technological innovation and the global economy, the shrinking and ageing of national populations poses a formidable challenge to states' economic and military strength.[10]

Europe, Japan and China are all affected by an increasingly ageing population. In addition, in Europe the population is expected to shrink in the long term.[11] Citing a 2001 United Nations (UN) projection, Richard Jackson points out that, by 2050, 'there will be 28 per cent fewer working-age Germans than there are today, 36 per cent fewer working-age Japanese, and 42 per cent fewer working-age Italians'.[12]

For the European Union, a shrinking and ageing population is expected to have negative consequences for its overall geopolitical posture. EU countries will have to dedicate a growing portion of their gross domestic product (GDP) to pensions and health care for the elderly. Spiralling health care costs are also worrisome, as the number of people aged 85 and over – the most expensive age group in terms of health care costs – is projected to triple by 2050.[13]

Countries in Europe and Japan, where taxes are already high, may opt to raise taxes even more to finance generous public retirement systems. Alternatively, they may start to borrow excessive amounts of money to pay for their pension schemes, which could potentially lead to debt crises in some of these countries.

European governments in countries with generous pension schemes and public health-care systems may find it politically almost impossible to make painful cuts to social services. Massive cuts in the pension system may hit the most vulnerable among the population the hardest, however. Besides the human costs, such a development may also weaken the state itself, as trust in government is fading among populations throughout Europe.[14]

Ultimately, population decline can result in a stagnating economy and lower living standards. With a shrinking labour force, there is less investment in capital expansion and fewer opportunities for technological innovation. An ageing labour force also 'possibly lack[s] the creative and entrepreneurial drive associated with youth', Neil Howe and Richard Jackson have suggested.[15] Stagnating economies do not bode well for social peace and future macroeconomic developments within countries: 'cartels, beggar-thy-neighbour protectionism and anti-immigrant populism' are some of the possible defensive mechanisms that states may use to try to cope with economic stagnation.[16]

To pay for rising retirement benefits, countries are likely to make cuts in the defence sector. They may turn increasingly inwards, with little money and human resources to spare to engage in an activist foreign policy. Together, all these developments will lead to a diminished global position for those affected by population decline.

Russia, in particular, will face formidable strategic challenges as a result of population decline. If the current trends of low birth rates, high death rates and emigration continue, the Russian population may drop significantly by 2050. As a consequence, Russia may no longer have enough people to settle and cultivate – and thus control – its large territory, especially in the east and in Siberia. Meanwhile, a growing number of Chinese immigrants are settling in Russia's east and Siberia, which could intensify tensions between these two historic rivals.[17] On the other hand, a large and growing population does not automatically make a country strong and prosperous either. Rapid population growth can also weaken a state that has insufficient resources to accommodate its growing population.[18]

Demographic growth has often been perceived as an important prerequisite for a state to thrive in the long term. Howe and Jackson argue, for example, that 'virtually every rising power in history has also been a demographically expanding power'.[19] Yet, the population imbalance between the developed and developing world has so far had no effect on the global balance of power. The developed world continues to dominate the world militarily, economically and technologically, while the countries that make up the vast majority of the world's population remain weak. Furthermore, modern advances in weapons technology have allowed countries to fight wars with less manpower. Similarly, technological progress allows countries to substitute automation for a declining workforce and remain economically strong. Nevertheless, ageing and population decline are becoming important factors in assessing the predicted strength of a country in the coming decades. The state capacity of demography is thus important for assessing a country's geopolitical posture.

4.1.2 Social Issues

The degree of social cohesion and peace within a country has an impact on its ability to sustain a prosperous economy and a stable government. Social cohesion can be defined as the absence of large social and economic divisions within a society. Members of a socially cohesive society share the same basic values and have a sense of living towards a common future. By contrast, ethnic divisions and hostilities can erode a country's social fabric. So can a wide gap between the rich and the poor, which is an indicator of widespread inequality – perhaps also inequality of opportunity – among a population. If the poor see no prospects for the betterment of their living standards, they may demand radical social and economic change and divide or destabilise a country's political landscape. A government that loses legitimacy among a large portion of the population may not be able to ask for many sacrifices from its people, whether for economic austerity programmes or for military operations, or even compliance with social distancing measures during the COVID-19 pandemic.[20] Hence, social factors are an important measure of a country's resilience in times of adversity.

Socially cohesive societies are much more resilient in the face of hardship and adversity. A case in point is the 1997 financial crisis in Southeast Asia. South Korea, displaying a high degree of social cohesion, was able to weather the economic turmoil without suffering social or political upheavals. In a display of solidarity, ordinary citizens even sold some of their personal treasures in an effort to improve the financial situation in their country.[21] Meanwhile, in the Southeast Asian countries that lacked a similar sense of social solidarity, financial crisis translated into increased social violence and political turmoil.[22]

States whose citizens have a high degree of social cohesion usually maintain more stable governments. In countries without major social divisions and where citizens share a strong sense of solidarity, governments tend to be more prone to care for the public good and refrain from policies that discriminate against particular social groups.[23] Indeed, opportunistic politicians are less able to exploit ethnic or socio-economic divisions in socially cohesive societies.[24]

4.1.3 Health Issues

The health of the population is another factor affecting the demographic capacity of a state. Good measures of the general condition of a population's health are maternal and infant mortality rates, as well as life expectancy at birth. The prominence of, for example, HIV/AIDS, malaria or tuberculosis within a country can tell us something about the state's ability to contain the spread of infectious diseases and the effectiveness of its health-care system. It can also tell us something about the general health of the population.

The widespread prevalence of an infectious disease within a country can have serious consequences for that country's economy and its ability to defend itself militarily. According to one study, Africa's GDP would be 'nearly one-third higher if malaria alone had been eliminated several decades ago'.[25] This estimate includes both indirect costs, such as loss of productivity and commerce, and direct economic costs, including medical expenses.[26] In Russia, HIV/AIDS is a major burden.[27] HIV/AIDS and other infectious diseases can cause labour shortages and impede economic development. In sub-Saharan Africa, almost nine out of ten children and adolescents were living with HIV in 2019, according to UNICEF.[28] HIV/AIDS deprives children of parents, potential teachers and social leaders and leads to the untimely death of important human capital in the public and private sectors.[29] In Africa, infection rates are high among soldiers, so the disease may weaken a country's ability to defend itself.[30]

The quality and accessibility of health care in a country usually improves with economic growth. Health is also a core ingredient of the human capital without which economic growth cannot be achieved in the first place. A 2005 Chatham House report found that, in both developing and developed countries, improved public health positively affects economic productivity and growth.[31] The report states: 'In fact, it is not an exaggeration to say that no society has seen sustained economic progress when it has neglected investment in its people's education and health.'[32] Making sure public health conditions are good is a crucial investment in the economic growth, productivity and global competitiveness of any state. Problems in this particular state capacity will therefore have an effect on any forecasts of the country's long-term economic growth and thus its geo-economic standing in the world.

4.2 Domestic Politics

The domestic political situation in a country impacts its policy and ability to act in foreign affairs. Countries that face internal political turmoil can become introverted. They often lack the decisive power to pursue a strong and consistent foreign policy. Authoritarian governments that enjoy only flimsy popular support may be limited in their ability to pursue certain policy options. Sometimes, authoritarian governments try to deflect domestic problems by painting the outside world as hostile and by giving the impression that their country is constantly under siege. This can produce a rally-around-the-flag effect and make it easier for governments to make their people accept their legitimacy and the need to make personal sacrifices.[33] This can also make a state adopt an aggressive posture in foreign policy.[34]

Governments that are unable to impose law and order throughout their territory contribute to regional instability. The ability of such governments to prevent transnational criminal networks, including drugs and arms traders, from operating in their country is limited.[35] Moreover, weak governments may find it difficult to contain the spread of contagious diseases or enforce environmental-protection measures, particularly when it comes to pollution and toxic waste, which can cause havoc across borders.[36] Massive flows of refugees or migrants could further compromise the security of neighbouring states, as is the case, for instance, in Lebanon, which is adding a massive influx of migrants and refugees to an already fragile domestic context.[37]

The peace researcher Quincy Wright, who in the 1950s collected a vast amount of information about the causes of war, pointed to a variety of domestic political factors that play a role in a state's conflict behaviour.[38] He distinguished between the government, the state, the people and the nation. To assess a state's propensity for engaging in conflict, one first, he wrote, would need to understand the decision-making process in a particular government and identify those individuals with the largest amount of influence over national policy making. Second, at the state level, one would need to know the constitutional and legal checks on the executive branch, and whether the legislature had the power to veto an executive decision. Third, it is important to evaluate public opinion towards the government, the conflict situation and the opponent. Is public opinion in favour of a peaceful resolution of the conflict, or is the public putting a lot of pressure on the national government to act forcefully against the enemy? Fourth, one would need to analyse the traditions, culture and ideology of the nation concerned. How does the nation see itself, how has it historically related to the enemy and what kind of grudges does it hold against that enemy? Furthermore, the strength and resolve of a nation's national military would need to be evaluated, as well as a nation's resilience and willingness to make sacrifices.[39]

As Sara Kuepfer and I elaborated in a previous work, several factors contribute to the internal stability of a state.[40] One prerequisite is a stable political system. Currently, liberal democratic systems tend to be the most stable in the long term. As we wrote in 2007: 'They enjoy broad-based domestic support, are able to bring dissenting voices into the political process, and ensure political and institutional continuity through autonomous political institutions and a professional civil service'.[41] A good domestic political system will contribute to a country's stamina, which in this context can be defined as 'the ability of any human organization to sustain a collective effort'.[42] As Niall Ferguson explains, the importance of a country's ability to maintain the morale of its people is 'one of the oldest lessons of military history'.[43] Democracies derive their morale from a shared sense of the legitimacy of their government and the notion that their government's decisions reflect the will of the majority of citizens.[44] Their merits notwithstanding, however, today's leading democracies face a number of severe challenges – such as rising levels of inequality and polarisation – that can only be remedied through a stronger focus on fulfilling the requirements of human dignity, as I explain in chapter five.

Political upheavals may await so-called nominal democracies, where judicial and legislative checks and balances are weak or missing. In nominal democracies, power can become monopolised by a powerful political faction that represents and promotes the interests of only one particular social, ethnic or religious group within the country. This will heighten social divisions and set the country up for political upheavals in the short and medium term.[45]

A state's ability to ensure public order is a prerequisite for durable political institutions, as is recognised in the concept of the rule of law. The longer a state's political system has been in place without disruption, the more durable, and hence stable, a state usually is. A 2003 study conducted by the US organisation Fund for Peace identified four state institutions that are crucial to maintaining the stability of states: (1) a 'competent and professional domestic police force and corrections system'; (2) a professional civil service; (3) an independent judicial system based on the rule of law; and (4) a 'professional and disciplined military accountable to a legitimate civilian authority'.[46] The study concluded that the four identified institutions need to have sufficient autonomy so that they cannot be monopolised by any particular political faction or ethnic group within the state.[47] Government arbitrariness can be prevented to a large degree if policies are implemented by neutral state bureaucracies. In states where the civil service is made up of professionals instead of political appointees, governmental transitions following popular elections will happen more smoothly, as the government bureaucracy can ensure a measure of continuity.[48]

The international community is affected by the disintegration of any state's political system and thus needs to take an interest in the domestic political conditions of all states. A state is considered 'failed' if the central government is no longer able to control its entire territory, promote law and order and provide basic public services to its population.[49] States described as 'weak' or 'failing' only partly fulfil basic state functions and are at risk of collapsing, with detrimental consequences not only for their own citizens, but also regional and global stability.

In sum, a good domestic political system will enable a state to draw on its human resources, to demand sacrifices from its people for the good of the country, thereby strengthening its ability to project power abroad. Chapter five will focus in more detail on the main characteristics of good domestic governance.

4.3 Economics

Economic power has become of immense geopolitical importance – perhaps even more so than traditional military capabilities. For this reason, some argue that economic competition is to some extent replacing military competition between the great powers today.[50] At the same time, states tend to be less and less in control of economic developments even within their own borders. Globalisation, the abolition of trade barriers and the increasing power of multinational and transnational corporations are limiting the ability of national governments to regulate or greatly influence macroeconomic processes if they want to remain integrated in the global economy.[51] Nevertheless, assessing a state's economic strength, weaknesses and future potential is vital to understanding a country's geopolitical position. Its economic dependence on particular outside resources, for example oil and gas, economic aid or a single trading partner tells us more about a state's economic and strategic vulnerabilities.

Some states, such as Russia and Saudi Arabia, which alone possess a significant percentage of the world's fossil fuel energy sources, are blessed with an abundance of natural resources and/or fertile farmland. This allows these states to have independent access to important primary resources without having to buy them on the international market. Yet, an important factor is the distribution of these resources among the state's population. In some states, as is the case in Brazil,[52] for instance, resources are concentrated in the hands of small elites, which can lead to large economic inequalities and social tensions.[53] In other states, such as Russia[54] or Iran,[55] governments own the resources, which can lead to a rentier system[56] as explained further below. In general, the more people who have access to a country's resources, the more stable and peaceful a society will be.[57]

States can provide an environment conducive to economic growth and development. This starts with a functioning infrastructure, including good transportation, communications, financial-services networks, reliable utilities distribution and sufficient energy supply. As the Organization for Security and Co-operation in Europe (OSCE) has observed, '[g]ood infrastructure attracts investment by connecting firms to their customers and suppliers, in effect enlarging the size of the market'.[58] Especially in developing and transitional economies, a state's ability to attract foreign direct investment and promote the development of small and medium-sized enterprises is crucial for economic growth and development.[59] Furthermore, a state can facilitate economic growth and investment by maintaining stable political institutions and a transparent legal system.[60]

Last but not least, it needs to be kept in mind that, without cheap and sufficient energy, no country can attain economic growth.[61] This again demonstrates the interconnectedness of the seven state capacities when it comes to geopolitical power relationships.

A weak military, unstable domestic conditions or the lack of economic and technological development can keep wealthy states from fulfilling their geopolitical potential and make them relatively weak international actors, as has been the case for many states in Latin America[62] or the Middle East.[63] Another argument can be made that real geo-economic power lies neither with resource-rich states nor with commodity producers, but with those controlling financial power, such as the International Monetary Fund (IMF), the World Bank (WB) and the largest contributors to those institutions.[64]

4.4 Environment

All countries in the world struggle with problems of environmental degradation and pollution, and some more than others. The health of entire populations is affected by air and water pollution or soil erosion.[65] In rising global powers undergoing rapid economic development, such as China, it is predicted that environmental destruction and pollution will considerably slow economic growth in the near future.[66] This will have an impact on the relative power such countries can wield. In short, a state that consumes its natural resources at an unsustainable level is unlikely to maintain its current level of power indefinitely and, in the medium term, will struggle with an increase in pollution-related illnesses among its population, as well as with a slowing economy.[67]

As the following examples will show, water scarcity is a serious issue for many countries. Mismanagement of water resources, population growth, a high degree of pollution and the more frequent occurrence of droughts in some parts of the world are all contributing to the problem.[68] From a geopolitical perspective, severe water scarcity can weaken state power in several ways. First, the lack of access to safe drinking water and sanitation causes the spread of many water-borne infectious diseases, such as diarrhoea, typhoid fever or cholera,[69] and thus has an impact on public health. Lack of water also slows economic growth in agriculture and industry. Second, water scarcity can lead to domestic unrest, as governments struggle to provide sufficient food and water supplies to their citizens.[70] Third, water scarcity can lead to regional conflicts among different states. For example, Turkey's or Israel's ability to disrupt the water supply of neighbouring countries may increase its geopolitical leverage but may also make it more vulnerable to conflicts with its downstream neighbours.[71] Indeed, water is a vital strategic resource, as it provides the foundation for a country's economic prosperity, human and environmental health and, ultimately, peace and stability within and between countries.[72]

Global warming will have significant strategic implications. Flooding or the rise in sea level as a result of melting ice sheets may render parts of a state's territory uninhabitable or make it disappear entirely, as will be the case within the next few decades for many low-lying coastal areas in the Pacific.[73] Otherwise fertile coastal land may become unusable for agricultural production as a result of frequent flooding.[74]

Rising sea levels are likely to cause a variety of legal disputes among maritime nations. If rocks and low-lying islands claimed as part of a country's sovereign territory become submerged, those countries will no longer be able to claim the surrounding waters as part of their exclusive economic zones. As a result, seabed resources, especially oil and gas, that used to be within the exclusive economic zones of coastal states could then be exploited by other powers. Such a situation could lead to serious international disputes.[75]

An increase in droughts and flooding as a result of global warming may lead to vast numbers of environmental refugees, which could have security implications in neighbouring states. Strong hurricanes, which are becoming more frequent with rising ocean temperatures, can also cause a variety of economic and social stresses on communities and states.[76]

As I explore at length in the final chapter, the melting of permanent ice sheets is freeing up new maritime passages. This is the case with the thawing of the permafrost on Russia's northern shores, which is opening the area to shipping. Canada's northern waters will also soon become open to shipping all year round. The northern seas would become a highly lucrative trade route between Asia and North America. Protecting this strategically and economically important line of maritime communication could pose new military challenges.[77]

The melting of the Arctic ice cap is also exposing unknown deposits of valuable natural resources such as oil, gas and minerals that have thus far been inaccessible. This is leading to disputes among five potential claimant states: Russia, the United States, Canada, Denmark and Norway,[78] as well as China.[79]

The higher frequency of natural disasters and humanitarian crises – including mass evacuations and massive refugee flows – places increased burdens on national militaries, which in most cases are the only entities with the equipment and skills necessary to deal with such large-scale emergencies.[80] Tying up national militaries in disaster-relief operations can reduce their capacity and could affect power relationships between states.[81] It can be argued that, of all factors, climate change will have the largest impact on traditional geostrategy, and its consequences are likely to affect the strategic and security situations of every country in one way or another.

4.5 Science and Human Potential

The quality of a state's human resources is an important measure of state power and of its potential to project that power abroad. A reliable and steady supply of workers is a prerequisite for consistent economic growth. Furthermore, a good education system that produces highly skilled workers is a prerequisite for maintaining economic competitiveness. The quality of a country's local labour force can be determined by its skill range and its dedication and motivation to work hard.

A country's investment in research and development (R&D) may influence its ability to remain competitive in the long term. Thriving economies in the developed world are dominated by information technology and ideas-based value production. Countries unable to keep up with new technological developments risk being left further and further behind in their overall economic development. Indeed, as one author has put it, 'Wealth is no longer dependent on the possession of land and natural resources, but on the intellectual capital and social organisation to produce high quality, high technology products. Such wealth cannot be efficiently acquired by war or conquest.'[82] In other words, the size of a country's military and of its wealth alone do not tell us everything about the power of a state in a postmodern global environment.

The state of technological development within a country is also important from a military perspective. Throughout the world, weapons systems are becoming ever more sophisticated, and retaining a cutting edge in science and technology is crucial for any country's national security. One example is aerospace technology: states that have mastered the delivery of satellites into orbit have at their disposal sophisticated missile technology that could also give their militaries a competitive edge.

However, international hostilities do not take place solely at the military level. Cyber attacks can cause as much havoc and damage as conventional military attacks. A 2007 report on the future of NATO found that 'war could be waged without a single bullet being fired, and the implications of this need to become part of strategic and operational thinking'.[83] To fend off cyber attacks, a state needs the necessary manpower and ability to develop new software to defend itself from calamitous disruptions in its network infrastructure. Information technology is the pillar of network-centric warfare (or cyber warfare). Being one step ahead in cyber technology will mean keeping the upper hand should a cyber war break out between two states. In this regard, a state's scientific and technological output and progress can become as important as the size of its military for trying to gauge a country's ability to retain its current level of power on the world stage.

4.6 Military and Security Issues

This category includes internal, transnational and external security challenges affecting different states. The first two types of security challenges, in particular, can considerably weaken a state's government and social cohesion, and also make it less attractive for foreign investment and tourism.

Internal challenges might include a secessionist movement by an ethnic-minority group or a high crime rate, as is the case, respectively, in Xinjiang[84] and South Africa.[85] Transnational security threats that could weaken a country include pandemics and a high level of transnational criminal activity, for example, human trafficking and the illicit trade in drugs and arms. Such activities undermine law and order within a state, jeopardise the growth of the formal sector and lead to human-rights violations.[86] Through the broad-based use of corruption and bribes, criminal networks could even succeed in undermining a state's autonomy.[87] There could be a further internal or transnational security threat from either home-grown insurgent or terrorist groups or from transnational or international terrorist organisations.

In terms of military security, external challenges could come from a hostile state or result from foreign claims on a part of a state's national territory. The size of a state's army, the quality of its weaponry and the percentage of its GDP spent on defence can help gauge the relative strength of a state's military power and thus its ability to fend off hard-power security challenges. As will be seen from the case studies in Chapter 8, all the world's major superpowers are large military spenders.[88]

From a geopolitical perspective, it is essential to assess a state's potential ability to develop nuclear weapons. This is the one kind of weapon whose acquisition by a state can dramatically change power relationships around the world and trigger nuclear arms races in the neighbourhoods of the states that acquire them.

Another important security concern for many states is energy security. Currently, many states are dependent on oil- and gas-producing countries for fossil fuels. Yet renewable energies are likely to replace some fossil fuels by 2050.[89] A country's dependence on other states for its energy needs has wide-reaching implications for its economic vulnerability and its political manoeuvrability.[90] Energy needs could force a country to ally itself with oil-producing states or make political concessions to countries that may go against its interests. The uneven geographic distribution of energy resources can have a strong impact on geopolitics, elevating the importance of particular regions.[91]

In other words, a country's political leverage in international affairs cannot be measured by the size of its military alone. Its relative dependence on other states for crucial energy needs is also important.

4.7 International Diplomacy

International diplomacy, the last of the seven capacities, describes a state's involvement in international organisations and the issues and challenges it faces on the diplomatic front. Membership and activity in international organisations can be an indicator of a state's standing in the international community. Diplomatic priorities vary. Some countries might aspire to gaining a permanent seat on the United Nations Security Council (UNSC) or resolving a conflict with a neighbouring state. Others allow their foreign policies to be strongly guided by economic interests. China is an example of a country whose foremost diplomatic priority is to establish good relations with resource-rich countries to secure access to vital resources, especially oil, which will enable it to maintain its rapid economic growth.[92]

A state's diplomatic leverage is not necessarily proportional to its economic and military power. Its particular strategic location or ideological appeal might also contribute to its soft-power capabilities. As the relevant case studies in chapters eight and nine show, in the case of the EU, we see a disconnect between its strong economic power and its relatively weak leverage in foreign policy.[93] It is also in danger of becoming increasingly self-absorbed in streamlining internal policy and in dealing with new member states.[94] Hence, our seventh capacity considers a state's standing in the international community with regard to its ability and desire to exercise soft-power tools.

It might be tempting to argue that a country's economic power, as measured in terms of GDP, is a good indicator of its power and influence in the world. For a country to be able to project its economic power abroad and translate it into global influence, it needs to be actively involved in international diplomacy and international institutions. As Ferguson has pointed out, although Great Britain was the major world power in the nineteenth century, the United States has had a larger GDP than Britain since the 1870s.[95] However, the United States was inward-looking at that time and was not greatly involved in world affairs. Its entry into the First World War and its participation in the post-war settlement catapulted the United States onto the world stage. Only then could it be referred to as a true global power.[96]

International diplomatic power also has an important unquantifiable, psychological aspect. International credibility goes a long way when a state is trying to achieve anything on the diplomatic level. Credibility has to be earned through diplomatic behaviour over a long period. Switzerland is an example of a nation that has substantial diplomatic power despite its small size. It has earned the role of a host of international meetings and as a neutral mediator in many conflicts due to its long-held policy of strict neutrality in international affairs, its active engagement in humanitarian causes and conflict resolution around the world, as well as its domestic political stability, sound economy and its good overall international image.[97] Together with New York, the small Swiss city of Geneva is one of the world's two largest centres of international cooperation. Geneva hosts the largest number of international conferences and meetings per year in the world.[98] Investing in multilateral institutions, and, especially, actively supporting the UN through constructive participation in the reform of its institutions and submitting to the principles of its Charter, is a way for states to improve their credibility and standing on the international diplomatic stage.[99] An additional effect of this is that the more states become actively involved in the UN system and abide by its Charter, the more international law is strengthened.[100] Every state ultimately benefits from a more predictable, secure and peaceful international system. Hence, international diplomacy is a good gauge of the contribution a state makes towards that end.

4.8 *The Seven State Capacities*

Assessing the geopolitical strengths and weaknesses of states using the seven capacities provides a nuanced picture of geopolitics in the twenty-first century. Most states have strengths and weaknesses – not only among the various capacities but also within a single capacity. A state may have a strong military but be highly dependent on other states for energy to maintain its military capabilities in case of war. Or a state may have strong human resources but be unable to create enough new jobs to employ its whole population. Another example might be a state that has a good health infrastructure but fails to provide affordable access to it for a large segment of the population, as is the case in the United States.

Tables 4.1 and 4.2 describe two models for evaluating a state's geopolitical posture and power using the seven capacities of state power. In the tables below, the left-hand column lists the capacities, while the right-hand column lists certain key issues that need to be addressed to describe and evaluate each state capacity. Table 4.2 lists the areas where growth and change are needed for each issue going forward.

For an illustration of how these tables can be applied to individual countries, chapters eight and nine feature case studies of 26 geopolitically important states and one collectivity of states, the EU, using these table models to assess the strengths and weaknesses of each state across the seven capacities.

An evaluation of state power using all seven capacities highlights how states are constrained in their behaviour by more than geographic factors. A low level of education among a particular population[101] or a poor transportation or energy infrastructure might slow a state's economic-development plans despite its wealth in natural resources or its favourable geographic location.[102] In the sphere of international diplomacy, states face constraints on their actions by other states, be they allies or foes. As states depend on each other's support and on a favourable image abroad, they often heed constraints coming from the international diplomatic sphere even if they are powerful enough in terms of resources to disregard a diplomatic censure. In a majority of cases today, states are willing to submit to international law even if their violation of a particular rule may not lead to any serious short-term consequences. States today often prefer to submit to international law than to the law of raw power, as they see a long-term advantage in upholding the rudimentary legal order that guides an otherwise anarchical world.[103]

Table 4.1 Meta-Geopolitical Analysis of Present State Realities

ISSUE AREA	GEOPOLITICAL REALITIES AND DILEMMAS
1 Social and Health Issues	• Population size and growth rate • Ethnic and/or social divisions • Prevalence of infectious diseases and common causes of death • State of health-care infrastructure and accessibility to health care (common measure is maternal and child mortality rates)
2 Domestic Politics	• Form of government, degree of democracy • Internal challenges to domestic political order
3 Economics	• GDP growth rate • Key economic sectors • Poverty • Economic infrastructure, ability to attract foreign investment
4 Environment	• Key environmental problems (man-made and natural causes)
5 Science and Human Potential	• Literacy rate and quality of education system • Strengths and skills of population • Investment in R&D as a percentage of GDP
6 Military and Security Issues	• Military and defence capabilities • External security threats and ongoing border disputes • Internal security threats
7 International Diplomacy	• Foreign-policy priorities and diplomatic initiatives • Relationships with key regional and global players

An analysis of a country's relative power in the context of *meta-geopolitics* is best done using the table format presented in this chapter. When looking, for example, at the case of China through the prism of the seven capacities and with regard to its geographic location, we notice the huge influence it can have in the future on Pacific Rim countries. It is likely to exert this influence not through military conquest, but by shaping these countries' foreign and domestic policies and dominating their economies. Indeed, with its geographic proximity to the Pacific Rim, along with its huge population, China seems to have a distinct advantage over the world's current superpower, the United States, in terms of dominating this geographic area in the future.[104]

Table 4.2 Meta-Geopolitical Analysis of Future State Trajectories

Issue Area	Geostrategic Imperatives & Future Trajectories
1 Social and Health Issues	▶ Social challenges ▶ Improvements needed in health sector
2 Domestic Politics	▶ Domestic political challenges to be overcome
3 Economics	▶ Measures to be taken to spur economic growth and development
4 Environment	▶ Environmental challenges to be addressed and overcome
5 Science and Human Potential	▶ Improvements required in education sector and scientific infrastructure
6 Military and Security Issues	▶ Improvements required to promote internal security ▶ External threats and border conflicts that need to be addressed
7 International Diplomacy	▶ Future diplomatic challenges ▶ Future foreign-policy priorities

Ferguson makes an interesting point that state power is not determined by the tools (a strong economy, natural resources, weapons) a country possesses so much as by its ability to use those tools abroad: 'Power is about monopolizing as far as possible what might be called the means of projection (of power). A list of these would have to include manpower, weaponry, and wealth but also knowledge and, since a rationally organized bureaucracy is a formidable resource, administrative efficiency.'[105]

Finally, there remains a big unpredictability factor that makes history interesting and statecraft so difficult. No one can predict the future, yet analysing international geopolitical dynamics within the seven state capacities will help make the geopolitical decisions of statesmen and women more informed, even if by no means a foregone success. As Lauren, Craig and George put it:

> Those responsible for statecraft never fully know all that they need to know. They operate in partial darkness because of the complexities of the world, the uncertainties and sometimes the irrationality of human behaviour, ignorance and the capacity for self-delusion, and the incomplete and often ambiguous nature of intelligence information and analysis. There can be unforeseen and unintended consequences, and sometimes things go wrong even in the best of plans.[106]

Geopolitics provides a compass that helps statesmen and women navigate the labyrinth of international relations. Using the tool of *meta-geopolitics* can help make this geopolitical map more detailed and more accurate. Of course, it cannot prevent unpredictable turns of events or shifts of power. Nevertheless, the application of *meta-geopolitics* can help statesmen and women gauge potential threats early and take the necessary precautionary measures. Through *meta-geopolitics*, a highly sophisticated picture of geopolitical dynamics in the early twenty-first century can be established, and the areas most vulnerable to international conflict and instability can be located geographically. *Meta-geopolitics* is thus an indispensable tool for equipping statesmen and women with a better comprehension of the world they have to navigate.

5

Statecraft and Neurophilosophy

All state leaders are confronted with the destructive potential of human nature. They therefore need to understand how to unlock the best in their citizens' behaviour and curtail the worst facets of human nature. Knowing what people instinctively strive towards and what they need to thrive are of paramount importance to devising effective public and global policies that ensure peace, security and prosperity for all. This requires an appreciation of how our brains work. State leaders can therefore greatly benefit from incorporating neurophilosophical reflection into political analysis. Neurophilosophy emerged in the late 1980s and has since fostered insightful synergies between neuroscience and other disciplines that have traditionally sought to comprehend the human mind and political behaviour.[1] My neurophilosophical approach draws on cutting-edge research in the field of political neuroscience that includes, among others, computational approaches that explore the mechanisms underlying political behaviour, neurocognitive perspectives that harness neuroimaging and psychophysiological methods, and behavioural studies that analyse how these mechanisms play out across cultures and social contexts, and, importantly, how such findings can be used to improve policy and decision making.[2] Admittedly, the workings of the brain are a phenomenon so complex that its study is fraught with difficulties. Challenges are posed by the diversity of approaches used to make sense of complex brain data, that is, to make the connection between brain activity and what it represents.[3] In addition, whilst both academics and policy makers have become increasingly interested in using insights from the behavioural sciences in order to inform policy making, their conclusions are often based on oversimplified understandings of what knowledge behavioural science actually yields.[4]

As I argue in this chapter, neurophilosophy can contribute to an improved statecraft paradigm in at least three ways. First, state leaders need to understand how our innate tendencies shape the world we live in. Only then will they be able to devise domestic policies that bring out the best in their citizens, thus allowing their countries to thrive. For a country to fully leverage its key resources, human and otherwise, it has to adopt what I call dignity-based governance, as I explain below. Second, states are a reflection of the character of human beings, so understanding human nature enables us to better comprehend state behaviour in the international arena. In this chapter, I offer a new neurophilosophical approach to international relations, *symbiotic realism*, which provides greater explanatory leverage than conventional approaches that rely on speculative accounts of human nature. Finally, an enhanced understanding of human nature can help statesmen and women achieve what I call *sustainable* national security, as the last part of this chapter illustrates.

Before I delve into a more detailed analysis of these three innovative concepts, and of how they contribute to an improved practice of statecraft, let me briefly review the most recent neurophilosophical insights into human nature.

5.1 What State Leaders Must Know about Human Nature

Arguing from a neurophilosophical vantage point, my book *Emotional Amoral Egoism: A Neurophilosophy of Human Nature and Motivations* identifies three primordial features of the basic character of human beings: emotionality, amorality and egoism. These three characteristics are universal and timeless, being genetically coded into our DNA. At the same time, they are subject to influences from our environment. Contrary to many long-revered beliefs, human beings are the products of both nature and nurture, which continuously interact with, and shape, one another.[5] What do I mean when I say human being are emotional amoral egoists?

First, I draw on the extensive research into the human brain that has revealed the centrality of emotions in human experience and their interaction with key cognitive processes, such as learning or memory formation.[6] Second, in using the term *amoral*, I do not mean to suggest that people are indifferent to, or unaware of, the concepts of right and wrong. On the contrary, I believe that most human beings are capable of forming moral judgements. There is, however, a wealth of evidence suggesting that human beings are born without an innate understanding of good and evil, and that their moral judgements shift according to circumstances, both personal and political.[7] Studies on stress, for example, reveal that, in the face of moral dilemmas, stress leads to more egocentric decisions.[8]

Finally, I use the term *egoism* to mean that we do not enter the world as the entirely blank slate envisioned by Locke. Instead, I conceive of the human mind as a *predisposed tabula rasa*.[9] I argue that we are 'predisposed' in the sense that we are endowed by nature with a powerful survival instinct, one that makes us engage in actions that maximise our chances of survival. Whilst humankind is capable of performing good and evil deeds, survival instincts are so powerful that, in most situations, people act according to what they perceive to be their general self-interest.[10]

Although we are born with a predisposition towards egoistic behaviour, our upbringing and environment help us to develop a moral compass that might allow us to move beyond the dictates of self-interest. Furthermore, and despite lacking inborn moral concepts, we possess a number of innate pro-social emotions, such as empathy and sympathy, which may lead us to more altruistic forms of behaviour. Our pro-social affinities, however, are often biased towards in-group members and do not necessarily make us better human beings. Empathy, for example, often leads us to make unjust decisions since empathy is, as Ingmar Persson and Julian Savulescu have found, 'spontaneously biased to individuals who are spatio-temporally close, as well as discriminatory in other ways, and incapable of accommodating large numbers of individuals'.[11] In fact, there is ample evidence that empathy and morality are two independent motives for behaviour.[12]

Not only do our emotions have the upper hand in driving human behaviour; the human brain is also pre-programmed to feel good, neurochemically speaking, and seeks this type of neurochemical gratification through five main drivers of human action. I have called them the *Neuro P5: power, profit, pleasure, pride* and *permanency*.[13] The latter, in particular, is closely connected to our egoism, since it refers to our desire to survive death, be it through the transmission of our genes or through our historical legacy. The malleability of our brains and our receptivity to socialising influences means that the sources of our neurochemical gratification are not predetermined but are largely shaped by our environment.[14]

How can statesmen and women benefit from these insights into human nature? Because human nature is malleable, its development is informed by a multitude of external factors. The right form of governance is key to creating a context that harnesses people's inborn tendencies for the better, and that prevents our inborn egoism and emotionality from generating conflict, aggression and crime. Whilst being overwhelmingly driven by emotions, sometimes reason, reflection and conscious moral judgements guide us to act not only in our own interest but with regard to the well-being of others. Our capacity for reason can only flourish, however, in an environment where our requirements for dignity are fulfilled.[15] What I call dignity-based governance can therefore channel our innate tendencies and talents not only in a way that maximises human capital, thus contributing to a country's innovativeness and prosperity, but also in a way that contributes to sustainable peace and stability.

5.2 Dignity-Based Governance

As I have emphasised, domestic structures and foreign policy affect one another. The extent to which domestic factors, as opposed to the international environment, shape states' choices has been part of a long debate in the field of international relations.[16] What is certain, however, is that unstable domestic conditions prevent countries from fulfilling their geopolitical potential. In other words, the domestic political situation shapes the ability of a state to project power abroad. For example, a government that suffers from a legitimacy deficit may not be able to ask its population to join a military operation abroad.[17] Likewise, a government that is unable to impose law and order in its country has a limited ability to fend off transnational security threats (such as drug trafficking or infectious diseases). This, in turn, can contribute to regional instability.[18]

Recent neuroscientific research, and the field of neurophilosophy, has started to grapple with the link between governance and the requirements for human dignity. *Dignity-based governance* can secure the consent of the governed and unlock the best in human behaviour – a statement that may appear self-evident, yet it was not studied from a neuroscientific viewpoint until recently. By 'dignity' I do not merely mean the absence of humiliation. Rather, and in light of insights from neuroscience, I use this term to denote a set of universal and permanent human needs, namely: *reason, security, human rights, accountability, transparency, justice, opportunity, innovation* and *inclusiveness* (see

Figure 5.1 A New Governance Paradigm:
Dignity-Based Governance

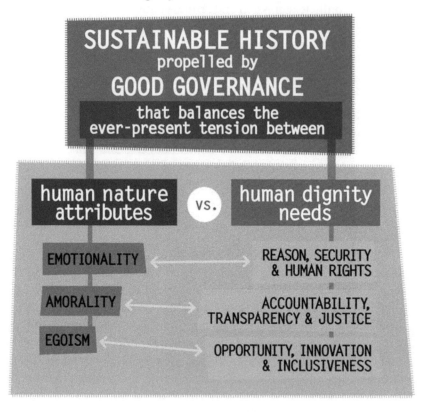

© Nayef Al-Rodhan 2020

Figure 5.1).[19] What follows will illustrate what each of these nine human needs implies, and why dignity-based governance is one of the primary tools of effective statecraft.

Our egoism continuously pushes us to seek our own welfare with no regard for others' requirements for dignity, and this is particularly true when resources are scarce, and when insecurity prevails. The emergence of pro-social behaviour is dependent on good governance that reconciles our *emotional amoral egoism* with others' requirements for dignity.[20] This requires a threefold balancing act. First, our emotionality has to be balanced with *reason, security* and *human rights*. In other words, state leaders must recognise that, in order to assuage vitriolic human emotionality, they need to promote a reason-based society through high-quality education for all and a commitment to established facts and reasoned arguments, rather than populist appeals to emotions. Furthermore, they must be committed to protecting society as a whole against violence, hunger, disease, natural disasters and disadvantages resulting from disabilities, sickness and old age. The promotion of human rights is also conducive to curtailing the negative potential of our emotionality. This includes, among other things, ensuring that individuals' rights to privacy are respected in the context of big data, or guaranteeing freedom of expression whilst prohibiting incitement to religious, racial or national hatred.[21]

Second, state leaders must recognise that morality will usually be trumped by self-interest – unless our environment has inculcated specific values in us that make us act with regard to the well-being of others. In shaping people's moral compasses, *justice, accountability* and *transparency* play a vital role. Public institutions must be accountable and transparent in order to limit the misuse and abuse of power. Justice should be ensured by impartial judicial systems focused on rehabilitation and not just punishment.[22]

Finally, dignity-based governance channels human egoism to benefit society through *opportunity, inclusiveness* and *innovation.* Opportunity means creating circumstances that are conducive to the positive physical, mental and social development of every member of society. This includes the provision of adequate housing, nutrition, education and health services, including widely available and affordable psychotherapeutic care. Moreover, dignity-based governance leverages human egoism through opportunities for professional, scientific and intellectual growth, which not only benefit the individual's ego, but also foster an innovative society. Since innovation contributes to economic growth, its promotion also fosters prosperity across all sectors. States should therefore invest in R&D in all areas. Importantly, opportunities must be fairly distributed among the population. This requires reducing income gaps as well as sustained policy efforts to eliminate all forms of discrimination and marginalisation, which fuel social divisions.[23]

By prioritising the requirements for human dignity, dignity-based governance creates an environment that channels our quest for the *Neuro P5* (i.e. *power, profit, pleasure, pride* and *permanency*) into productive enterprises. Through schooling, political discourse, the broadcasting and news media, gaming and entertainment industries, it associates 'feeling good' with behaviour that is beneficial to the individual and the country as a whole. For example, it encourages people to derive pride from charitable acts or innovations which contribute to the innovativeness of a nation and the world.[24]

In sum, dignity-based governance enables a state to fully unlock its positive potential and to encourage the best behaviour from its population. It is the prerequisite of what I call a *sustainable history*, which denotes progress and lasting improvement in the human condition.[25] For all its merits, and despite being more stable than most other systems, democracy in its current forms does not constitute any Hegelian final point in history. In fact, today's leading democracies struggle with high levels of polarisation, marginalisation and injustice. The shortcomings that can be observed in democratic countries are mainly due to policies devised with little understanding of human nature. Practitioners of statecraft can greatly benefit from enhancing their understanding of what most deeply motivates and drives people. Only if they recognise the key importance of satisfying the requirements for human dignity will they be able to lead their countries into a better future.

As I illustrate in the next section, dignity-based governance must be accompanied by a new approach to international relations in navigating today's interstate strategic environment. Dignity-based governance, coupled with *symbiotic realism*, will enable state leaders to steer their countries on a sustainable and beneficial course in the long run.

5.3 Symbiotic Realism

Statecraft is about managing interstate relations. The aforementioned tension between the requirements for human dignity and our *emotional amoral egoism* is present not only within countries but also among states. Resolving this tension brings about collective gains for all. *Symbiotic realism* stresses the critical importance of such absolute gains in today's interdependent world, where a plethora of challenges – climate change and pandemics not the least of them – belie the belief that international relations are zero-sum games where one side has to lose for the other side to win. In reality, we shall all lose if we fail to collaborate on counteracting global warming or the spread of deadly viruses. In so arguing, *symbiotic realism* is far from echoing liberalism or neoliberalism, as this chapter will illustrate.

Despite the urgent need to strengthen international cooperation, the current world order is increasingly characterised by competition between the world's major powers, especially between the United States and China and Russia.[26] This is due to our *emotional amoral egoism*, which pushes not only individuals but also states to seek their own welfare even at terrible cost to other individuals and countries. It can easily lead to a clash of national interests even in areas that require global collaboration and absolute gains, such as climate change. This section discusses why statecraft can no longer follow the traditional zero-sum logic that typically underwrites conflictual competition between states. Instead, state leaders need to adopt *symbiotic realism* in their conduct of international relations.

Symbiotic realism was developed in response to realism, the most prominent concept in the field of international relations. Realism constitutes a theoretical orientation, rather than a single theory. In general, realists see power politics as a zero-sum game in which states seek to increase their power by taking it away from others. Due to the absence of a world government with the authority to regulate state behaviour, the international state system remains anarchical, an unregulated space in which every state is ultimately left to fend for itself. Realists conceived of states as unitary rational egoists, behaving on the basis of rationally calculated decisions about outcomes that maximise self-interest. In the absence of an overarching authority capable of enforcing commitments, morality is assumed to have no place in international relations.[27]

The realist concept suffers from several shortcomings that my theory of *symbiotic realism* seeks to overcome. Above all, *symbiotic realism* posits that state leaders need to adapt to an increasingly interdependent world by escaping the zero-sum logic and promoting symbiotic (mutually enriching) interstate relationships. In arguing this, *symbiotic realism* does not echo liberalism or neoliberalism, far from it. It is true that liberalism also stresses the interdependence of states and their capacity for cooperation where it occurs within the framework of shared norms and values.[28] Likewise, neoliberalism emphasises the prospects for cooperation through the cultivation of shared norms, mutual trust and the building of institutions. In terms of economic policy, this leads to a support for free trade and international capital mobility, among other policies.[29]

Symbiotic realism departs from its liberal and neoliberal forebears in significant ways, however. *Symbiotic realism* draws on neurophilosophical insights into human nature, whilst liberal and neoliberal theorising about international relations is dependent on widely unverified and speculative assumptions about human behaviour.[30] In fact, whilst all accounts of international politics are based on certain visions of the human, most IR scholars do not sufficiently reflect on these assumptions and do not adequately substantiate them through empirical evidence.[31]

The nature of IR itself, as a 'rational enterprise capable of producing knowledge about the world of international politics' has, indeed, long been up for debate.[32] Whereas I have chosen to rely on neurophilosophy as a lens through which to approach statecraft, many IR scholars have turned to traditional philosophy of science in the search for a foundation for the discipline, and particularly towards instrumentalism, social constructivism and scientific realism.[33] Although there are obviously some differences within these ideal positions,[34] they can be broadly summed up as the following. According to instrumentalists, who adopt a positivist approach, 'reliable knowledge comes only from what can be observed via the senses'.[35] For Kenneth Waltz, therefore, theories are merely instruments for the apprehension of reality.[36] For social constructivists, on the other hand, it is impossible to know the world independently of its social context and, consequently, to know the world objectively. They adopt, in this sense, an anti-positivist stance.[37] Finally, according to scientific realists, scientific knowledge perfectly reflects reality.[38]

As of yet, no consensus has been found on what the philosophical foundation of IR is and what this ought to look like.[39] Not only is it therefore still unclear how IR as a science should be conducted[40] but, and more relevant to the challenges under discussion in this volume, this may also have contributed to IR scholars' widespread neglect of controversies within the life sciences.[41] This, in turn, has meant that most debates on world politics are characterised by 'either analytically insignificant or dangerously reifying' ideas of the human.[42] As stated in previous sections of this chapter, one cannot separate IR from the human beings it concerns. *Symbiotic realism* thus seeks to close this gap by bringing neuroscientific insights to bear on understandings of human and state behaviour, and herein lies part of its originality.

Indeed, as claimed by Nuno P. Monteiro and Kevin G. Ruby, whichever philosophy of science approach to IR one takes, there will still be a point in which the theory is based on a foundation which requires a 'leap of faith', which manifests as a form of 'logical circularity' in the case of scientific realism.[43] For this reason, they contend that it is possible that the bridge between IR and science in its most strict interpretation will never be closed.[44] However, irrespective of where one stands in relation to the philosophical foundations of IR, what the philosophy of science debate can offer us is the idea that we must be open-minded about the boundaries of IR as a science. Importantly, as stated by Monteiro and Ruby, it is possible and it may also be necessary to borrow from different approaches to knowledge when seeking answers to IR questions.[45] This is the intellectual context in which the theory of *symbiotic realism* is situated.

Drawing on recent neuroscientific findings, *symbiotic realism* does not share the liberal and neoliberal view of states as rational actors.[46] Instead, it regards emotions as central to the decision making of states, as I explore in more detail in section 5.3.1 on the *emotional amoral egoism* of states. Moreover, it complicates traditional notions of rationality by taking into account the substantive influence emotions exert on cognitive functions such as perception and problem solving (see section 5.1. above).

In addition to being based on a neurophilosophical and thus significantly different account of human nature, *symbiotic realism* reconceptualises the relationship between individual and collective gains. Liberalism and neoliberalism assume that states only care about their own individual gains, whilst they are indifferent to the gains achieved by others.[47] *Symbiotic realism*, however, argues that, in today's interdependent world, no state can afford to be indifferent to the loss of other states, even if such a loss leaves its individual gain unaffected at the first glance. In the long term, however, the misery of other states, no matter how distant, will affect us in one way or another, as I illustrate at various places throughout this book.

Finally, *symbiotic realism* rejects many of the core assumptions of neoliberalism, which some critics see as the root cause of many of today's major problems, such as inequality.[48] It will be remembered that neoliberalism began as an intellectual movement in the 1930s, before becoming politicised by Reagan and Thatcher in the 1980s and finding a more technocratic form in the 'Washington Consensus' of the 1990s. The basic presuppositions uniting the complex of neoliberal policies, ideas and institutional changes include the privatisation of public assets, the deregulation of labour markets, and the vision of individualised competition in the marketplace as the only effective mechanism for the distribution of rewards.[49] Neoliberalism has thus involved a departure from Fordist Keynesian institutions, which were marked by an extensive welfare state and state intervention.[50] *Symbiotic realism* sees none of these mechanisms as the key to progress. Scholarly research has shown from various vantage points, including the evolutionary perspective, that 'the free market is an unsuitable alternative to liberal democracy's shortcomings'.[51] Instead, it argues that dignity-based governance at the global and national level and a focus on multi-sum games are the harbingers of lasting progress and human well-being.

As some critics tend to conflate my theory of *symbiotic realism* with neoliberalism, I shall take the liberty to repeat the primary points of difference between my approach to international relations and that of neoliberal thinkers:

1) *Symbiotic realism* draws on neuroscientific research and neurophilosophical analysis in its efforts to explain state behaviour, whilst neoliberal theorising about international relations relies on widely unverified and speculative assumptions about human behaviour;
2) Neoliberalism assumes that states only care about their own individual gains, whereas *symbiotic realism* argues that no state can afford to be indifferent to the loss of others;
3) Unlike neoliberalism, *symbiotic realism* argues that states must pursue multi-sum games and dignity-based governance, at both the national and the global levels.

Symbiotic realism involves adopting a mindset that recognises the extent to which globalisation and the information revolution have resulted in instant connectivity and interdependence, which has decisively altered the international system. Soft-power capabilities have become increasingly significant components of a state's relative power, such as a state's ability to portray a favourable image of itself and its policies abroad. Now, moreover, non-state actors, such as non-governmental organisations and transnational corporations, have greater influence in international affairs. There is now a multiplicity of actors besides states in international affairs and any theory of international relations needs to reflect this diversity.[52]

Alongside states, therefore, *symbiotic realism* considers a number of other important actors that have been largely overlooked by classical realist approaches. I have identified these different actors in a previous publication: *Symbiotic Realism: A Theory of International Relations in an Instant and an Interdependent World*.[53] These actors include the individual, the state, large collective entities, international organisations, transnational corporations, the environment, natural resources, and information and communications technology.[54] Whilst international organisations reflect power relations within the global political system, they still play an important role in mediating relations between states and in providing a means to address global issues such as migration or climate change.[55] The environment and natural resources are 'reactive actors' that transform the world in response to human activity. One example is climate change, a human-caused phenomenon that is having a major impact on international politics.[56] Given the degree of human mobility and instant connectivity today, we must also acknowledge the relevance of collective identities, which are groups of people sharing a common culture, ethnicity, religion or ideological commitment. They should not be conceived in a static way but as fluid entities that are likely to display inner contradictions.[57] In addition, *symbiotic realism* recognises how gender is affected by and, at the same time, helps to shape the global system.[58] The fact that states today deal with a multiplicity of actors suggests that leaders of states will need to expand the supranational bodies that regulate the different non-state actors. Furthermore, states should try to benefit from the expertise of NGOs and international organisations in their efforts to address global challenges such as environmental degradation and global warming.

Besides introducing multiple actors, *symbiotic realism* emphasises four dynamics that define today's interstate strategic environment: *instant connectivity, interdependence, global anarchy* and the *neurobiological predilections of human nature* (see Figure 5.2).

Figure 5.2 *Symbiotic Realism*

states / transnational corporations / women / the biosphere / civilizations

© Nayef Al-Rodhan 2020

Instant connectivity refers to the widespread availability of information and communications technology, such as the internet, which allows information to be exchanged and spread around the world within seconds. This inevitably affects international relations. Governments, for example, often have to react to information spread by private news agencies or even foreign actors. One major downside of instant connectivity is the accelerating spread of fake news.

Interdependence refers to the fact that states today can no longer be studied as independent units but are mutually dependent due to increased trade, labour mobility and the widespread cooperation required to solve common problems and pursue common interests. Consequently, states can increase their power and security not by making others weaker or less secure, but by working together with other states. In short, *symbiotic realism* emphasises the feasibility of achieving absolute gains in international affairs.

International anarchy – the absence of a world government – does not have to lead to competitive relations and relative gains at the expense of others, as realists argue. Through conscious efforts, states can be encouraged to comply with humanitarian norms and strive for collective gains for all, even in the absence of enforcement mechanisms.[59] Moreover, if collaboration between states is repeated, greater trust and shared norms may be conducive to reducing insecurity in an anarchic international system. Whether or not international anarchy leads to relative rather than absolute gains depends on how statecraft channels the defining features of human nature.

The fourth element shaping international politics is *human nature*. This is a point of similarity with classical realism, which placed human nature at the centre of theorising on national and international politics, largely relying on a man–state analogy. In other words, according to realism, the character of states mirrored the eternal features of human nature. The latter subscribed, however, to a narrow and rather pessimistic view of human nature. In light of recent insights into human predilections, especially those provided by neuroscience, the tenets of realism must be revisited, and the fundamental character of states must be redefined as '*emotional amoral egoism*'.

Table 5.1 will help the reader to situate my theory of *symbiotic realism* in relation to other key approaches to international relations.

Table 5.1 A Comparison of Key Theories of International Relations[62]

	Classical Realism	Neorealism	Classical Liberalism	Neoliberalism	Constructivism	*Symbiotic Realism*
Key theoretical proposition	Assumption that states are self-interested and continuously compete for power or security in a system of international anarchy.	Focus on the unequal distribution of capabilities and the anarchical structure of the state system that compel states to act in certain ways.	Emphasis on freedom, institutionalised peace and prosperity, and progress, with cooperation, rather than force, being considered key to advancing each state's respective interests.	Belief in the capacity of self-regulating free markets to enable progress and a better world.	Conviction that ideas, collective norms, images, identities, and belief systems (especially elite beliefs) shape state behaviour and world politics.	Emphasis on the critical importance of absolute gains and the four key dynamics of today's interstate strategic environment: 1. instant connectivity; 2. inter-dependence; 3. global anarchy; and 4. the predilections of human nature and emotionality of states.
Main actors in the international system	Sovereign states	International system	States, international institutions, multinational corporations	Individuals, states, non-state actors	Individuals (especially elites), transnational networks, NGOs	Individuals, the state, large collective entities, international organisations, transnational corporations, the environment, natural resources, information and communications technology

(continued)

Table 5.1 (continued)

	Classical Realism	Neorealism	Classical Liberalism	Neoliberalism	Constructivism	*Symbiotic Realism*
Assumptions about human nature	States are believed to be egoists, behaving on the basis of rational decisions about outcomes that maximise their self-interest, with conflict being a reflection of the competitive and dominating nature of human beings.	The rationalist mode of theorising the human leads to a strong focus on rational calculations of states that seek to maximise benefits and minimise losses.	The positive view of human nature as perfectible is conjoint with faith in human reason, which is deemed capable of triumphing over fear and the desire for power.	The neoliberal worldview sustains the image of *homo economicus* using practical rationality to calculate the costs and benefits of decisions.	Human interests and identities are believed to be malleable and shaped by historically and socially constructed norms, beliefs, and values, with political interactions occurring on the basis of partially shared, if contested, interpretations of reality.	Neuroscientific account of human nature that complicates traditional notions of state rationality by underlining the *emotional amoral egoism* that drives state behaviour and each nation's strategic culture.
Main state objectives and instruments to achieve them	Self-preservation and power-maximisation are a nation's foremost priority, with power being both a means and an end; force and deceit are considered effective tools for furthering national interests.	Ensuring survival is the overriding goal which requires states to be mindful of their capabilities and continuously seek security.	International institutions, global commerce and the promotion of democracy serve as instruments to achieve a liberal world that is conducive to world peace and the happiness of individual beings.	Privatisation of public assets, the deregulation of labour markets and the vision of individualised competition in the marketplace are deemed important tools to achieve a thriving state.	Ideas, discourse, community building through interaction and shared normative frameworks are regarded as key means of improving international relations.	*Dignity-based governance* at the global and national level and a focus on multi-sum games are the harbingers of lasting progress and human well-being. *Dignity-based governance* reconciles the ever-present tension between our innate emotional, amoral and egoistic tendencies and the nine dignity needs of others.

Attitude towards cooperation vs competition	Assumption that international relations are inevitably conflictual and that conflicts are resolved by force.	Belief in the limited potential for cooperation and the prevalence of conflict.	Conviction that mutually beneficial cooperation is possible when people behave rationally.	Cooperation is believed to be fostered by the cultivation of shared norms, mutual trust and building of institutions.	Global prospects for cooperation and conflict are regarded as dependent on prevailing ideas and values.	Emphasis on the importance of mutually beneficial cooperation to satisfy human dignity needs (not just political freedoms) and to address 21st-century challenges.
Stress on relative or absolute gains?	Power politics are believed to be a zero-sum game, with states seeking to increase their power by taking it away from others out of fear that their own survival might be compromised by the relative advantages of rivals.	States are assumed to be primarily concerned with relative rather than absolute gains, with each state trying to improve its position in comparison to others.	States are believed to care only about their own individual gains and to be indifferent to the gains achieved by others.	States are assumed to be preoccupied with maximising their own individual gains and are less concerned with the gains or losses of others.	Preoccupation with relative gains is believed to dominate relations with the out-group members, whilst focus on absolute gains is likely to dominate in social exchanges with in-group members.	Interdependence and globalisation have created the heightened imperative to pursue absolute gains since the loss of other states, no matter how distant, will affect us in one way or another in the long term.

(continued)

Table 5.1 (continued)

	Classical Realism	Neorealism	Classical Liberalism	Neoliberalism	Constructivism	Symbiotic Realism
Key theorists	Thucydides (460–400BCE), Machiavelli (1469–1527), Hobbes (1588–1679), Reinhold Niebuhr (1892–1971), John H. Herz (1908–2005), George Kennan (1904–2005), Raymond Aron (1905–83), Hans Morgenthau (1904–80)	Kenneth Waltz (1924–2013), John J. Mearsheimer (born 1947)	John Locke (1632–1704), Jeremy Bentham (1748–1832), Immanuel Kant (1724–1804), John Stuart Mill (1806–73), Adam Smith (1723–90), Benjamin Constant (1767–1830)	Friedrich Hayek (1899–1992), Milton Friedman (1912–2006), James M. Buchanan (1919–2013), Margaret Thatcher (1925–2013), Ronald Reagan (1911–2004), Alan Greenspan (born 1926)	Alexander Wendt (born 1958), Martha Finnemore (born 1959), John Ruggie (1944–2021), Kathryn Sikkink (born 1955), Peter Katzenstein (born 1945)	Nayef Al-Rodhan (born 1959)

Sources: M.B. Steger and R.K. Roy, *Neoliberalism: A Very Short Introduction* (Oxford: Oxford University Press, 2021); R.H. Jackson, G. Sorensen and J. Moller, *Introduction to International Relations: Theories and Approaches*, 7th edn (Oxford: Oxford University Press, 2019); D. Jacobi and A. Freyberg-Inan (eds), *Human Beings in International Relations* (Cambridge: Cambridge University Press, 2015); M. Griffiths (ed.), *Encyclopedia of International Relations and Global Politics* (New York: Routledge, 2013); M. Zehfuss, *Constructivism in International Relations: The Politics of Reality* (Cambridge: Cambridge University Press, 2002); J. Haynes, P. Hough, S. Malik and L. Pettiford, *World Politics: International Relations and Globalisation in the 21st Century* (London: Sage, 2017).

5.3.1 Emotional Amoral Egoism of States

There is ample historical evidence that states are survival-oriented, pursuing self-interest and self-serving actions at all times.[60] Whilst realists are thus right to perceive interstate conflict as a reflection of the egoistic nature of human beings, they generally over-focus on rational calculations to the neglect of the pivotal role played by emotions. Indeed, the traditional account of rational statecraft has been invalidated by evidence that human behaviour is primarily motivated by emotions, which are inextricably linked with our cognitive functions, as I have explained elsewhere.[61] The myth of rational statecraft practitioners is also belied by a wealth of historical evidence, as discussed further below. Yet, the assumption – shared by realists, liberals and neoliberals alike – that rational decisions shape foreign policy has led to a widespread neglect of the role that emotions play in world politics. Admittedly, realists as well as liberals have held implicit ideas about a limited number of emotions – such as fear, hate and the lust for power – but these assumptions have been largely speculative, poorly theorised and overrationalised. For example, classical liberalism rationalises various emotions into different kinds of utilitarian self-interest.[63] However, recent interdisciplinary insights into human emotions require us to reconceptualise the role played by a variety of emotions in international dynamics.

In light of emerging neurophilosophical understandings of how the human mind works, *symbiotic realism* contends that, in the same way as individuals, states are emotional, amoral and egoistic. Scepticism over the notion of state emotionality is often due to the erroneous 'no body, no emotion' assumption: 'Because emotion happens in biological bodies, not in the space between them, it is hard to imagine emotion existing at anything other than the individual level of analysis.'[64] However, a narrow focus on the individual level of analysis overlooks the power of group-level emotion that is irreducible to the individual experience. In fact, people associate with states (through shared culture, history or common interests) in ways that give rise to group-level emotions and even 'a consciousness indiscernible to their inhabitants'.[65] These are the product of a complex process in which 'group members share, validate, and police each other's feelings; and these feelings structure relations within and between groups in international politics'.[66]

Viewing states as exhibiting emotional responses to qualia helps to undermine the 'oftentimes problematic dichotomy in much scholarship between individuals as monological conscious agents and other actors as either metaphorical or purely rational'.[67]

I argue that some of the most powerful emotions that determine the relations between states are tied to the *Neuro P5* (*power, pleasure, profit, pride* and *permanency*). Wars are often waged in vindication of national pride or national permanency, that is, the desire to survive and produce a collective memory that stresses the superiority of a certain nation. The quest for power likewise permeates state behaviour. When power is unconstrained by democratic controls or systems of good governance, its holders may succumb to its addictive potential and, as a result, display severe distortions in judgement, cognition and behaviour, making states act in a ruthless way to maintain and enhance their power.[68] All too often, *fear-induced pre-emptive aggression* lies at the root of state aggression.[69] Fear constitutes a powerful motivator to 'strike first' and disproportionately and entails a whole range of reactions to satisfy the need for safety.[70] In other words, foreign policy decision making is heavily influenced by emotions, and especially those tied to the *Neuro P5*.[71]

Whilst the drug-like effect of the *Neuro P5* can inflate some negative traits of states to maximal levels, emotions *per se* are not necessarily detrimental to the decision making of states.[72] Until the early 2000s, IR scholars generally believed that emotions were harmful to the quality of decision making. New findings in neuroscience have shown, however, that emotions can also serve an adaptive function by facilitating effective and quick decision making.[73] In recent years a wealth of research has looked at the ways affective experience shapes state behaviour. For example, Marcus Holmes has explored the decision of British leaders to build up the Royal Navy before the First World War to illustrate the role of pre-analytical affective intuition yielding relevant knowledge. Welch Larson has similarly stressed the role of intuitive judgement to explain why Harry Truman decided to arrange an airlift in response to the Soviet blockade of West Berlin in 1949.[74] In light of recent findings, *symbiotic realism* argues that states, like humans, are not driven exclusively by rational calculations and the pursuit of domination but by a wide range of affective needs, such as the desire for a sense of belonging and a positive identity, that have the potential to both improve and hinder foreign decision making.[75]

Whether or not the emotionality and egoism of states leads to constructive or destructive state behaviour in the international arena depends on the surrounding circumstances. States, like humans, are intrinsically neither 'good' nor 'bad' but amoral.[76] By referring to states as 'amoral' I do not negate the fact that state leaders have moral sensitivities, or that foreign policy is frequently pursued on the basis of moral judgements. Instead, by 'amoral' I mean that the moral compass of any state is shaped by influences from history, culture, the domestic and international environment, which can significantly recalibrate the intuitions that drive political leaders. Their behaviour will thus fluctuate significantly, on the basis of perceived fears, collective memory, national identity, social norms, cultural practices and many other variables.[77]

Given the emotional, amoral and egoistic tendencies of states, the theory of *symbiotic realism* recognises the importance that shared values play in mitigating conflicts and hostilities among states. It posits that collaboration and *transcultural synergy* should be the guiding principle in the search for better ways to manage relations between states.[78] I elaborate on the implications of *transcultural synergy* in the next chapter. Briefly put, it means that, through collaboration and *transcultural synergy*, states are able to achieve more than they could on their own. Hence, innovative solutions for today's many global challenges and threats can best be found if exchanges between the world's different cultures become second nature. Indeed, *symbiotic realism* holds that the formation of a global cultural superstructure based on universally shared values is needed to address the challenges associated with globalisation and technological advances.

Finally, *symbiotic realism* emphasises the need to privilege dignity in interstate relations as a way to channel the *emotional amoral egoism* of states into enterprises that favour more peaceful and prosperous outcomes for all. This means that the nine requirements for dignity described in the previous chapter need to be fulfilled at not only the national level but also the global level.

In sum, *symbiotic realism* serves as an important basis for statecraft in an increasingly interconnected world. Senior British diplomat Robert Cooper has described the EU as the best-developed example of a postmodern state system based on mutual interdependence and transparency to a point where national borders among members become increasingly irrelevant. EU member countries have come together voluntarily based on the conviction that close cooperation and the merging of domestic and foreign policy is more likely to result in mutual prosperity and security than if every state were left to fend for itself in a system based on national sovereignty and characterised by mutual suspicion. Furthermore, the EU member states have adopted the principle of peaceful resolution of conflicts and seek to prevent distrust among members through mutual transparency and surveillance.[79] The EU model, albeit in need of improvement, exemplifies the movement towards absolute gains and *symbiotic realism*. National egoism, however, often transforms the EU's quest for absolute gains into a zero-sum game. For the world to evolve towards win-win situations, nationalist egoism must be abandoned in recognition of the fact that in today's globalised world no state can sustainably flourish at the cost of others.

As the world becomes more and more interdependent, zero-sum approaches to international affairs become increasingly detrimental to a state's own national interests. By pursuing *symbiotic realism* in their conduct of international affairs, state leaders can build harmonious relations with other states that maximise collective gains for all. The need for collective gains becomes particularly evident when looking at the ways in which national security and broader international security are intertwined. The following section will discuss how an improved statecraft paradigm must rethink the nature of national security.

5.4 Sustainable *National Security*

National security policy is an integral part of modern statecraft. Every statesman and stateswoman has the responsibility to defend the territorial integrity and political independence of his or her state, as well as to ensure the well-being and safety of the people living within its territory.

Not every state, of course, is equally independent in its ability to pursue its security objectives alone. The size and relative power of each state determines its ability to do so. Small and weak states often need to form alliances or accept protection from a stronger state to maintain their territorial integrity.[80]

A state's geographic particularities – both its natural resources and geographic location – will have an impact on its national security agenda. A high mountain range may provide extra security for a state, but the same state might be particularly vulnerable to economic embargoes due to its lack of arable land. Extensive oil and gas resources may give a state a lot of economic leverage in its dealings with other states but may also make a state more attractive to potential invaders.

To a certain extent, security has objectively definable physical characteristics, such as whether a country's borders are safe from attack. There is also, however, an important subjective dimension to the notion of security that concerns people's perceptions of their personal security or that of their country.[81] Statecraft thus involves not just addressing security threats *per se*, but also reassuring citizens that the security strategy being pursued by the state will increase people's safety. At the same time, of course, statesmen and women should not let themselves be influenced by exaggerated threat perceptions among citizens. As noted before, statecraft needs to include effective public diplomacy to lessen threat perceptions among the public, both at home and abroad.

5.4.1 Threats to National Security in a Transnational World

National security concepts have expanded in recent years, especially since the end of the Cold War. Most developed countries are no longer primarily occupied with securing their territorial integrity and political independence.[82] Their state borders enjoy a high degree of international legitimacy and the UN legal framework, which includes nearly every country in the world, outlaws territorial conquest.[83] Instead, so-called non-traditional threats have begun to play an increasingly important role in national security concepts around the world. Non-traditional threats by definition do not involve state armies; rather, they include an array of transnational threats that are impossible for individual governments to eliminate. Examples include the spread of infectious diseases, environmental pollution and global warming, international organised crime and terrorism. Many of these non-traditional threats are exacerbated by the weakness or failure of a state, which can result in its inability to enforce law and order or ensure public health across its entire territory. Due to the growing interconnectedness and interdependence of states today, a threat to one country can spill over to other countries much faster and more easily than in the past.

In my book *The Three Pillars of Sustainable National Security in a Transnational World*, I identified eleven key challenges to national security in the twenty-first century:

1) *Changing global power structures, state failure and regional conflicts.* These include various factors affecting international power relationships and international stability, including the increased influence of multinational corporations, state failure, rogue states and ethnic, tribal and religious warfare.
2) *The security implications of population growth, migration and refugee flows.* All three developments can lead to shortages of local resources, social tensions and ethnic conflicts.

3) *The information revolution and national security.* New communication and information technology can be used in harmful ways against states through information warfare and cyber attacks and as a tool to organise international terrorist or criminal activities.

4) *Transcultural interactions.* The intensification of transcultural interactions due to globalisation.

5) *Growing economic cleavages and energy security.* Persistent poverty and continuously growing economic inequality among the world's population can lead to state instability, increased violence within and between states, national economic collapse and global economic instability. The uneven geographic distribution of finite energy resources, together with existing barriers to renewable energy technologies, may increasingly lead to struggles among energy-importing states over the control and influence of energy-rich territories.

6) *Transnational organised crime.* Transnational organised crime can undermine a state's economic development and internal political stability; it can also weaken a state's social fabric and promote violence.

7) *Non-state actors, terrorism and asymmetrical warfare.* Threats to state stability posed by armed intrastate groups or international terrorists using unconventional means of warfare and often harsh brutality against civilians.

8) *Proliferation.* The horizontal proliferation of WMD and conventional small arms poses security threats to individual states and the international system.

9) *The privatisation of security.* The use of private security companies by states lessens state accountability for military actions and may lower the threshold for states to engage in adventurous actions.

10) *Health, diseases and biosecurity.* The uncontrollable spread of diseases can be caused by, or result in, state instability; countries affected by epidemics may suffer economic decline, social and political tensions, and conflicts.

11) *Environmental security.* Environmental degradation and pollution, droughts, and rising sea levels as a result of global warming may make entire areas uninhabitable;

food shortages and the loss of people's livelihoods can lead to many environmental refugees and increasing social conflicts.[84]

As these diverse and interconnected challenges continue to blur traditional distinctions between internal and external threats, states must overcome zero-sum approaches to security which – as I argued above – no longer suffice to describe the multifaceted and often transnational nature of today's security issues. In previous publications, I developed a new national security concept, called *sustainable* national security, premised on the notion that a state can only advance its long-term security needs by helping others to enhance their safety and well-being. More specifically, *sustainable* national security rests on three pillars:

1) *symbiotic realism* (a prescription for conducting international relations in an interdependent world based on a neurophilosophical understanding of human nature);
2) the *multi-sum security principle* (a prescription for global security based on justice, multidimensionality and multilateralism, as well as on a deeper appreciation for different strategic cultures); and
3) *transcultural synergy* (a prescription for dealing with collective sub-national and supranational entities).[85]

Whilst I discussed the first concept, the implications of *symbiotic realism* in the previous section, I briefly examine the latter two concepts in the remainder of this chapter.

5.4.2 Global Security and the Multi-sum Approach
In an interconnected and interdependent world, security challenges are multidimensional. In my book *The Five Dimensions of Global Security: Proposal for a Multi-sum Security Principle*, I argue that any comprehensive global security concept today needs to include five dimensions: *human, environmental, national, transnational* and *transcultural*.[86] I further maintain that a state that seeks to maximise its security must apply principles of justice in all five spheres, as injustice in one sphere will lead to insecurity in other spheres (justice and just power are discussed in the next chapter).[87] Figure 5.3 illustrates the *multi-sum security principle*.

Figure 5.3 The Five Dimensions of Global Security and the *Multi-sum Security Principle*

In a globalised world, security can no longer be thought of as a zero-sum game involving states alone. Global security, instead, has five dimensions that include human, environmental, national, transnational, and transcultural security, and, therefore, global security and the security of any state or culture cannot be achieved without good governance at all levels that guarantees security through *justice* for *all* individuals, states, and cultures.

© Nayef Al-Rodhan 2020

National security. National security has become 'the catch-all justification for all sorts of actions taken by governments'[88] and yet it eludes a clear-cut definition. Historically, it was widely understood in terms of ensuring the right to govern and defending that claim against both internal and external challengers.[89] In other words, it traditionally implied the protection of a country from external physical attack or internal subversion, and it meant ensuring the rule of law within state territory. In the course of history, the idea of national security has been expanded to include aspects such as the organisational stability of a social order and the legitimacy of a regime.[90] A country's definition of national security is also significantly impacted by its historical experiences and collective memory. For example, a country that has suffered extensively under occupation is likely to adopt a security culture different from that of a country that has never experienced occupation.[91] Other factors that affect national security priorities include access to natural resources. A country that is dependent on foreign energy resources is likely to place greater weight on energy security than one that is blessed with ample oil resources, for example.[92]

As mentioned above, the twenty-first century has witnessed an increasing blurring of the internal-external dichotomy that characterised traditional thinking about security.[93] Today, it is widely acknowledged that, alongside military matters, national security encompasses other issues such as cyber, environmental protection, health or migration.[94] These issues transcend national borders and affect not only the national but also the *human, environmental, transnational* and *transcultural* dimensions of security. The multi-sum security principle seeks to reflect this fact by taking a holistic view of the interplay among the multiple dimensions of global security.

Human security. State-centric approaches to security cannot always sufficiently guarantee the security of individuals. Some states are unwilling or unable to promote the security of all their citizens. Some people may be stateless or may have fled their country of origin and thus have no state that is looking after their safety and welfare. Furthermore, intra-state conflicts, pandemics, famine and the devastating impact of natural disasters all demonstrate that security involves more protecting territorial integrity. Hence, the concept of *human security*, which takes the individual as the primary referent object of security, was developed.[95] The multi-sum security principle counts human security among its five security dimensions.

Human security is commonly defined as the 'protection of individuals from risks to their physical or psychological safety, dignity and well-being'.[96] The concept of human security was first expounded in the UN Development Programme's 1994 Human Development Report, *New Dimensions of Human Security*. This report equates security with the protection of people, rather than territory.[97] Since its publication, a vivid debate has evolved seeking to determine the core implications of human security.[98] In 2001, for example, the International Commission on Intervention and State Sovereignty (ICISS) issued a report arguing that state sovereignty must be redefined as a responsibility to prevent violent conflicts and human rights abuses, and to assist states in their efforts to do so. To protect citizens' lives, should preventive measures fail, the report deems the use of coercive measures and even military force permissible.[99] This stands in contrast to the purely civilian concept of human security outlined in the 1994 UN Development Programme report.

Similarly, in 2004, the UN High-level Panel on Security sought to reconceptualise state sovereignty as the state's duty to protect the well-being of its citizens and that of the wider international community, without, however, clarifying the question of whether military force was justified.[100] In 2006, the EU commissioned a report entitled 'A Human Security Doctrine for Europe',[101] proposing that Europe should develop an improved kind of human security capability that involves civil-military integration and legal principles to safeguard individual rights to security.[102]

Today, there are numerous UN programmes committed to fostering security through a people-centred and preventive approach that focuses on context-sensitive solutions to the threats that endanger individuals' survival, livelihood and dignity.[103] Unfortunately, the promotion of human security is often complicated by the continued prevalence of narrow conceptions of national security, especially as multilateral efforts to protect human security (such as those of the International Criminal Court or the Ottawa Convention to ban anti-personnel landmines) are dependent on the cooperation of states.[104] Moreover, and as I discussed in a previous publication, human security 'relies on states having the institutional and financial means with which to provide for people's basic health, housing, food, physical security and justice needs'.[105] Finally, and in light of the transnational nature of many threats to human well-being, international collaboration is key to achieving human security objectives.[106]

Environmental security. Another important security dimension identified in the multi-sum security principle is environmental security. Natural disasters – human-induced or not – and environmental pollution and degradation cause hundreds of thousands of deaths per year. They can lead to the loss of people's livelihood, large refugee flows, political instability, economic decline and sometimes even armed conflicts. The protection of the very basis of our existence, nature, needs to be part of any security strategy today.[107]

Already, climate change is affecting water and food security, and is likely to make numerous currently inhabited areas of the globe uninhabitable in the not-so-distant future.[108] Natural disasters are increasing in number as a result of global warming, putting at risk not only human lives but also social and economic infrastructure.[109] Political instability and economic weakness are among the factors that exacerbate the effects of climate change in a way that increases the risk of instability, violent conflict and mass migration. Political instability and poor governance prevents states from effectively adapting to physical changes in the environment brought about by climate change, while economic weakness makes countries unable to afford expensive adaptation technologies or to compensate for reductions in state finances resulting from droughts or floods.[110] This, in turn, increases the likelihood of food insecurity and mass migration. In host countries, increased migratory pressures may breed xenophobic fears, leading to a rise in support for ultra-nationalism.[111] 'Where states have not failed but are failing, climate change could strike the blow that leads them to fail.'[112]

Moreover, a wealth of evidence suggests that global warming increases health risks from waterborne diseases, such as malaria and cholera, thus posing a severe threat to human health.[113] Climate change is also creating new theatres of geopolitical competition. Melting Arctic ice will open new shipping routes and make available oil and gas deposits, which is likely to trigger disputes over shipping lanes and resources among the five Arctic powers (the US, Russia, Canada, Denmark and Norway).[114] The development objectives of the Arctic powers may also threaten the rights of the indigenous peoples of the region.[115]

In other words, climate change has wide-ranging security implications that will affect every country in one way or another. I discuss them in more detail in the final chapter of this book, which deals with the major civilisational frontier risks facing humanity.

Competing interests at the national level, business lobbies, and state policies that focus excessively on short-term interests to the neglect of the long term are some of the main barriers to achieving environmental security.[116] While all states will benefit from measures taken to prevent or reduce environmental damage, we must ensure justice in burden sharing and bearing the economic costs of environmental regulations.

Transnational security. Transnational threats are those that transcend national borders and state jurisdictions. Because they affect a number of states simultaneously, they cannot be solved at the national level alone. Transnational challenges have moved from the periphery to the centre of state leaders' attention. As mentioned above, these threats may take the form of cyber attacks, water pollution, transnational terrorist networks, the trafficking of weapons, drugs and human beings, intentional or unintentional misuse of emerging technology, or biological risks (resulting from the spread of infectious diseases, or laboratory accidents, for example).[117] Ozone depletion is another risk that will affect the entire globe simultaneously, and could lead to dangerous disruptions of ecosystems, as well as severe health problems in humans (such as increased risk of skin cancer and respiratory conditions).[118] Environmental and transnational security are inextricably linked.

It is worth noting that a growing number of transnational challenges originate with non-state actors, even individuals using unsophisticated means, which makes them asymmetric in nature, with no easily identifiable source. The internet, in particular, can create asymmetric capabilities enabling individuals to cause large-scale disturbance. Many of the frameworks used to tackle transnational threats remain state-based, which makes them largely inadequate to guide effective policy responses.[119] Instead, states need to work closely together, from establishing epidemiological surveillance systems to developing effective environmental protection capabilities, to ensuring harmonised legislation to criminalise various violations of transnational security.

Transcultural security. Any concept dealing with security today must also take into account cultural entities and their interactions with one another. I refer to this third dimension of global security as *transcultural security.* Ensuring the security of groups and cultures within states is particularly important within the context of migration and the xenophobic and exclusionary tendencies found in many societies today.[120] With intensified migration, many states are now pluri-cultural, comprising a number of overlapping collective identities. The goal of transcultural security is, first, to foster social cohesion by ensuring the peaceful coexistence of people from different cultural backgrounds. Second, it aims at promoting cross-fertilisation between different cultures (see section 5.4.4, on *transcultural synergy*).

Importantly, transcultural security does not require all cultures to merge into one dominant form. Instead, it presupposes greater tolerance and respect for diversity and understanding of different belief systems, values and cultural practices, which can mitigate some of the most pressing security concerns of our day, such as violent intrastate conflicts.[121]

As I explain in *Emotional Amoral Egoism: A Neurophilosophy of Human Nature and Motivations*, a positive identity and a sense of belonging are crucially important for human well-being.[122] Part of what sustains and defines a person's identity is his or her group membership, be it national, ethnic or religious. If this group is not recognised or is even vilified, a person's identity as a member of that community will be negatively affected. This gives rise to resentments that may easily trigger tensions, the securitisation of collective identities, defensive actions and, ultimately, conflict.[123] Unfortunately, the securitisation of collective identities for selfish political purposes and the stereotyping of certain groups – such as migrants, refugees or particular ethnic and religious communities – is quite prevalent. Negative stereotyping breeds discrimination and can lead to insecurity on the part of those who are being stereotyped.[124]

Political discourse, schools, the mass media and the entertainment and gaming industries have a critical role to play in fostering respect for diversity, and in promoting inclusive national and global identities that contribute to transcultural security.[125] Acknowledging the interdependencies between national security and the multiple dimensions of global security, as well as the role of transcultural security, requires states to rethink their strategic culture, as I explain in the next section.

5.4.3 Strategic Culture and Pragmatic National Interest

Strategic culture is usually defined, as Alan G. Stolberg does, as 'a set of shared beliefs, assumptions, and modes of behaviour, derived from common experiences and accepted narratives (both oral and written), that shape collective identity and relationships to other groups, and which determine appropriate ends and means for achieving security objectives'.[126] In other words, strategic culture shapes how states craft national security strategy, and how they perceive their regional and international roles.

The argument that culture plays an important role in shaping national security policy is as old as the writings of Thucydides and Sun Tzu.[127] The national character studies of the 1940s, used for threat assessment during the Second World War, were some of the first modern attempts to explore the ties between culture and state behaviour.[128] In the 1970s, Jack Snyder brought these ideas into the realm of modern security studies, establishing the first generation of theories of strategic cultures by reinterpreting Soviet nuclear strategy 'as a result of this socialization process, a set of general beliefs, attitudes, and behaviour patterns with regard to nuclear strategy has achieved a state of semi-permanence that places them on the level of "cultural" rather than mere policy'.[129] It was with the advent of the Constructivist school that the paradigm of strategic culture was revived, giving rise to a new generation of work exploring the pervasive influence of culture, national histories and values on security and doctrines of military strategy.[130] Without seeking to rectify culture, these works provide a culturally informed explanation of how strategic policies are constructed and why states sometimes act in a way that contradicts 'realist' interests of maximising power. For example, they help us to better understand the confrontation between China and Japan regarding the Senkaku Islands (or Diaoyu, as the islands are known in China). The islands have minimal strategic or resource value, and the resources that have been invested in disputes over them have far exceeded any material or strategic advantage either side would gain from their possession. Disputes over them must thus be understood as part of a historical narrative permeated by cultural pride and grudges.[131]

Symbiotic realism also sees strategic culture as an important explanatory variable, but it moves beyond dominant or exclusionary definitions of culture and focuses instead on the *interplay* between neurobiological processes and environmental factors. The concept of strategic culture has traditionally been heavily permeated by the emotionality (national pride and prestige) and the egoism (the pursuit of national interests) of states to the extent that it became mistaken for a concept that reifies differences. It is fundamental to note, however, that *sustainable* national security is irreconcilable with an ethnocentric strategic culture permeated by vilification of other countries, ideas of superiority, us-versus-them thinking, and insensitivity to the cultures of other states. To the contrary, it is in the pragmatic national interest of all states to pursue a strategic culture which aspires to move beyond the egoism of states to strive for multi-sum games.[132] *Symbiotic realism* incorporates recent findings from cultural neuroscience, which is an emerging research discipline that investigates 'cultural variation in psychological, neural and genomic processes as a means of articulating the bidirectional relationship of these processes and their emergent properties'.[133] These findings lead us to refute the constructivist claim that there are no antecedent essences to society, since our neurobiological processes certainly provide structure that shapes how we perceive and interpret the world.[134] At the same time, *symbiotic realism* acknowledges that this structure is malleable by experience and external influences, as the brain is a 'dynamic growing organ in which we can see the evidence for the self-constructivist principle in development'.[135] This means that strategic culture, everywhere, is permeated by our innate predispositions, that is, the emotionality (national pride and prestige) and the egoism of states (the pursuit of national interests). Furthermore, and due to humankind's innate amorality, there is not one but many value systems that underlay different national strategic cultures. Whilst our *emotional amoral egoism* influences our preferences and actions in security and defence policy, it is in turn open to influences from cultural practices. Depending on these influences it can, on the one hand, foster moral cosmopolitanism and international cooperation yet, on the other hand, lead to rabid nationalism which subscribes to zero-sum

Figure 5.4 The Ocean Model of Civilisation

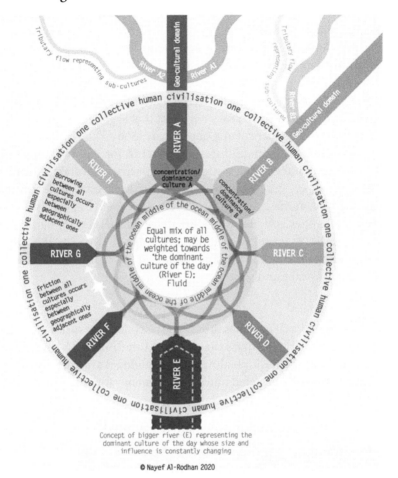

Concept of bigger river (E) representing the
dominant culture of the day whose size and
influence is constantly changing

© Nayef Al-Rodhan 2020

thinking and may give rise to aggression against other states.[136] It is in
the pragmatic national interest of all states to pursue a strategic culture
which aspires to move beyond the egoism of states to strive for collective
gains.[137]

5.4.4 Transcultural Synergy

Exchanges of knowledge and customs among different cultures have
enriched human societies since the beginning of time. Just as an
ocean is fed by many rivers, so human civilisation and progress is an
accumulation of contributions from different geo-cultural domains. This
idea is encapsulated in my 'ocean model' of civilisation (see Figure 5.4).

Cross-cultural exchanges are almost a prerequisite for cultural entities to develop and grow – without external stimuli, they would become stagnant and ossified.[138]

Globalisation is furthering and intensifying this process of cross-cultural fertilisation. These exchanges can help spur human creativity in efforts to come up with solutions to the many security issues confronting countries today. Synergy between 'a plurality of cultures', as I have previously argued, 'can have a net effect that is greater than the impact of the efforts of members of any one culture alone'.[139]

Synergies between cultures are useful for human progress and constitute a vital element for fostering international stability and peace. Through synergy, a global collective consciousness can be formed that is based on mutual respect and the conviction that cultural diversity and exchanges are necessary to drive humanity forward. Synergy presupposes transcultural understanding, in the absence of which cultural prejudices and tension are poised to become exacerbated at the expense of peace and security.

* * *

To sum up, this chapter has proposed the concept of *sustainable* national security, which recognises the intimate interlinkages between national security and the multiple dimensions of global security. Whilst global security may be divided into five elements for analytical purposes,

Figure 5.5 *Sustainable* National Security

© Nayef Al-Rodhan 2020

the five are often interconnected, requiring statesmen and women to adopt *symbiotic realism* in their conduct of international relations. In other words, practitioners of statecraft need to collaborate across borders and sectors and pursue collective gains for all in today's interdependent world. To do so, they need to tap into *transcultural synergy* by encouraging members of different cultures to work together to address pressing transnational security concerns. A challenge facing statesmen and women is therefore to identify points of overlap between value systems as a means of promoting transcultural dialogue and understanding. As I put it in the book *The Three Pillars of Sustainable National Security in a Transnational World*:

> Sustainable peace and security can only be achieved if states focus on the multi-dimensionality of today's security environment, form mutually beneficial security relationships with other states in every security dimension, and enrich their own culture and boost human creativity through fruitful exchanges and interactions with other cultures and civilizations.[140]

Figure 5.5 summarises the reasoning behind the concept of *sustainable national security* and illustrates the concept's ideational components.

Considerations of justice are also key to efforts to create a safer world. At the heart of many grievances expressed through violence and crime is a lack of justice. As I argue in the next chapter, the only way to use power to advance national interests in a sustainable fashion is in accordance with the principle of justice. By striving for a fair distribution of opportunities and justice in all areas of policy, ranging from international trade agreements and diplomatic negotiations all the way to military interventions, states will contribute to enhanced stability, economic progress and peace in the world. In doing so, they will enhance their own national security and prosperity. The next chapter will thus introduce the fifth innovative tool of statecraft proposed in this book: the concept of just power. This concept explains the underlying moral principles on which the pursuit of a *sustainable* national and international policy must be based.

6

Just Power

Statesmen and women have a wide range of tools at their disposal to implement foreign policy and promote their objectives. The question is how, and according to what principles, these tools ought to be employed.

A national security policy based solely on the employment of hard-power tools will leave other states less secure and can be counterproductive in today's interconnected and interdependent world. At the same time, there are legitimate reasons for states to use hard power. The realist school of political thought, which dominated international relations thinking in the latter half of the twentieth century, focused almost exclusively on hard power. The role and effective use of soft power to advance state interests has only gained increased prominence in recent decades. In 2007, a group of US scholars articulated a set of guidelines to help the US government to make use of the country's vast array of soft- and hard-power policy tools more effectively. Their efforts led to the new concept of *smart power*, which calls for the intelligent employment of different policy tools to advance US national interests.[1] This reflection on hard- and soft-power tools inspired numerous countries in their conduct of statecraft.[2]

It is difficult to argue with the proposition that states need to better integrate soft-power tools in international affairs, where hard power is sometimes overvalued as a means of solving conflicts and eliminating threats. This chapter takes this argument one step further, however, proposing a new set of guidelines for statesmen and women in their exercise of foreign policy. A state's foreign policy should not just be *smart*, it should also be *just*. Justice in international affairs is best pursued if states do whatever they reasonably can to advance human dignity around the world. This can be done by helping to enhance international security and economic prosperity for all human beings in the world. Using a state's power to advance justice for all is ultimately the only way to promote *sustainable* national and international security.

6.1 Realism and Overreliance on Hard Power

The realist school of international relations has traditionally considered hard power to be the only type of power that is of any consequence in relations between states. Political realism maintains that, in an anarchic world that lacks an overarching authority regulating state behaviour, a state needs to rely on its own hard-power capabilities to secure its existence. According to realists, the need for self-preservation drives state action. An early statement in support of this view can be found in the works of the ancient Greek historian Thucydides, who famously concluded in his *History of the Peloponnesian War* that 'the strong do what they have the power to do and the weak accept what they have to accept'.[3] Thucydides held that, in international affairs, the military conquest of weak states by strong states was a fact of life, and the primary duty of every statesman was thus to accumulate sufficient hard-power capabilities to prevent his state from suffering the fate of conquest.

Niccolò Machiavelli came to a similar conclusion in the sixteenth century. Writing during a time when the Italian peninsula was subject to regular invasions by French, Spanish and Holy Roman armies, and where Italian city-states changed hands and alliances often, Machiavelli concluded that a state could only rely on itself and its own (preferably citizens') army to ensure its survival.[4]

The seventeenth-century English philosopher Thomas Hobbes similarly maintained that humans, by their very nature, have a 'general inclination' towards 'a perpetual and restless desire of power after power, that ceaseth only in death'.[5] He wrote in *Leviathan* that, without an authority to regulate state interactions, states have to rely on their own capability to protect themselves from the onslaught of foreign armies.[6]

For the realist school, if states have any responsibility *vis-à-vis* the international system at all, it is to help maintain global order. Order, for the realists, is achieved by maintaining a sustainable global balance of power.[7] A good case in point for such an equilibrium would have been the nineteenth-century European system, in which two alliances made sure that no single power would be able to overpower the continent, and where the incentives for one power to start an aggressive war were minimal due to the alliance system that kept individual state ambitions in check. At the same time, the major European powers, which set up the system at the Congress of Vienna, themselves considered the balance-of-power arrangement fair and just. Besides the power-political constellations that created a power equilibrium on the continent, the European powers' shared sense that the system was legitimate reinforced the lack of revisionist ambitions following the defeat of Napoleon. As Henry Kissinger put it in one of his studies of the period: 'The balance of power reduces the opportunities for using force; a shared sense of justice reduces the desire to use force.'[8]

The realist school rightly maintains that a set of values alone cannot support an international system of states. The establishment of international order and security is a necessary prerequisite for promoting values of international justice. As Paul Ramsey explains, there is an asymmetry between the values of order and justice: 'We must attend to the preservation of an ordered polity and an orderly interstate system so that there can be the conditions for improving the justice actualised among men and between states.'[9]

In a world made up of different cultures that have different values, it is difficult to come up with a value system of international relations that all states can agree on. With the establishment, following the Second World War, of a rudimentary system of international law and the United Nations, the principle of collective security became a guiding notion in international relations. Collective security is based on states' common opposition to aggression. Denying another state's right to political independence and territorial integrity is deemed unjust *a priori*, and the UN system gives states the right to self-defence, and collective self-defence, in the face of aggression. Furthermore, the UN system serves as a guarantor of international order through its Security Council, which can authorise the use of force to resist any state action it deems a threat to international peace and security.

The principled opposition to aggression *per se* goes against the realist notion that states should only employ military power in collective self-defence if doing so furthers their own national security and power. Still, the UN system of collective security, which is backed up with hard power, is a step towards achieving a more ordered international system. It lays the foundation for states to go beyond their common opposition to aggression and agree on other commonalities and shared values that will help them build an ever more extensive system of international justice. Alternative viewpoints to realism often emphasise factors motivating state actions other than the use, or threat, of force.

Other schools of international relations have notably highlighted the role of norms, identities and structures in driving international politics. Rather than fully relying on capabilities for security and global order, less palpable elements such ideologies or structures constructed by experience, time and space matter. Social constructivism goes beyond the common understanding of 'neo-utilitarian' theories of international relations which emphasise 'interests', 'preferences' and 'forces' as binding elements for the international system.[10] Rather, actors, their consciousness and social experiences but also collective beliefs (like the opposition to aggression mentioned above) shape the behaviour of states on the international scene.[11] These aspects have often been neglected as they elude easy empirical demonstration yet determine decisions for interventions, collective security norms and create the conditions for cooperation.[12] As explained by John G. Ruggie, realism and neoliberalism cannot account for all international dynamics.[13] While the common domains of realism such as interests and preferences matter, actors and their continuously constructed identities do have a strong influence on outputs. John G. Ruggie calls for 'paradigmatic (ir)reconcilability' to fully account for international dynamics in an inclusive way.[14] This notion enables a more diverse and inclusive approach to global governance, including global security governance.

Going further, the concepts of smart and just power discussed in this chapter show more sustainable alternatives to the use of force in international relations.

6.2 The Concept of Smart Power

As put by Joseph S. Nye, 'when we restrain our definition of leadership to only top-down, king of the mountain, we miss the crucial role of soft power in effective leadership'.[15] In response to the US invasion of Iraq, a group of foreign-policy practitioners, former politicians and political scientists formed a commission, hosted by the US Center for Strategic and International Studies (CSIS), in 2007.[16] These senior experts and practitioners were united by one common concern: that the United States was relying too much on hard power in its war on terrorism. In doing so, the United States was neglecting important soft-power tools, such as public diplomacy, the building and strengthening of international institutions and alliances, and economic aid and cooperation, to project its strength and win reliable allies around the world. This failure, the group concluded, was leaving the United States weaker, as a dominant military was not enough to create a world that is peaceful, prosperous and in harmony with American values. What was needed, the experts agreed, was for the United States to employ a better balance of both soft and hard power to confront the plethora of threats to US national security.

Although threats emanating from rogue states, for example, might best be dealt with through hard power, other threats, including terrorism, infectious diseases, environmental pollution and global warming, afford the additional employment of soft-power tools, or 'the ability to get what you want though attraction rather than coercion and payment'.[17] The 'smart' thing to do, the commission maintained, is to adjust the type of power used to meet the circumstances and the type of goal pursued. The group thus coined the term 'smart power', which describes the integration of hard and soft power to tackle global challenges.[18] The goal of tackling *global* challenges is key: not only is US security ultimately dependent on global security and well-being, but tackling global challenges will also help to improve America's image in the world and strengthen its world leadership. If other states are attracted to American values and recognise the benefits that close collaboration with the United States can bring in terms of solving their problems, the United States will have a better chance of gaining the support of other states when pursuing its own security objectives.

The commission laid out five areas that a smart-power strategy should focus on:

1) *Alliances, partnerships and institutions.* The United States must reinvigorate the alliances, partnerships and institutions that serve our interests and help us to meet twenty-first-century challenges.
2) *Global development.* Elevating the role of development in US foreign policy can help the United States align its own interests with the aspirations of people around the world.
3) *Public diplomacy.* Bringing foreign populations to our side depends on building long-term, people-to-people relationships, particularly among youth.
4) *Economic integration.* Continued engagement with the global economy is necessary for growth and prosperity, but the benefits of free trade must be expanded to include those left behind at home and abroad.
5) *Technology and innovation.* Energy security and climate change require American leadership to help establish a global consensus and develop innovative solutions.[19]

The smart-power concept, as defined for the United States, is a big step forward from traditional power politics. It clearly recognises that even the world's strongest military cannot prevent deadly attacks perpetrated by non-state actors dressed in civilian clothing; it cannot halt environmental degradation and pollution causing hundreds of thousands of deaths every year; nor is it able to promote employment and prosperity. Rather, sustainable power in international affairs belongs to states that are able and willing to contribute to the good of the international community as a whole. These are states that drive the development of clean technologies, promote economic integration and strengthen international institutions that promote global security.

6.3 The Concept of Just Power

The smart-power concept rightly maintains that a sustainable foreign policy requires a 'smart' combination of both hard and soft power. This book, however, takes this idea one step further by stressing that the combination of hard- and soft-power tools needs to serve the cause of justice for the policy to be sustainable. In short, the overarching principle that should guide modern statesmen and women is global justice.

What is global justice? To what extent are statesmen and women responsible for justice in the international realm, and how does international justice differ from social justice within the framework of the nation-state?

Global justice is a theoretical stand focused on the just treatment of individuals in different areas, in terms of both recognitional and distributive justice, and the responsibilities we have to one another in the age of globalisation.[20] My own approach to global justice is, first, inspired by moral cosmopolitanism, viewing individual human beings as the primary object of concern, with national boundaries implying no constraint on the deliverance of justice.[21] It is also, second, rooted in a neurophilosophical understanding of the requirements for human dignity, which include the need for justice.

The primary obligation of a statesman or woman is therefore not restricted to promoting the physical well-being, and the physical security and economic prosperity, of the people he or she represents. Good statecraft looks beyond just ensuring these two material aspects of a successful nation. As Joseph S. Nye Jr argues, statesmen and women also have to look after the psychological well-being of their nation's inhabitants. He posits: 'A prudential statesman approaching his task with utter realism must take moral views of citizens into account in weighing his actions. ... He or she must, insofar as possible, consider all the consequences of the actions he directs, now and in the future.'[22] Whilst most of our moral beliefs are learned, we possess a natural inclination towards justice, which forms part of our requirements for dignity and informs our attribution of legitimacy.[23] 'Offering the basis for rule by consent, rather than coercion, legitimacy therefore promotes constructive relations between the state and its citizens, and is vital for regime maintenance', Nye contends. A statesman whose domestic or foreign-policy actions are perceived as legitimate by a majority of citizens will find it easier to harness popular support for the policy pursued. If the policy is viewed as just, citizens are more likely to support their government and make necessary sacrifices, for example, in case their country finds itself at war, or if their government raises taxes to fund foreign aid or peace missions abroad.

Statesman and stateswomen benefit from projecting just power not only domestically, but also internationally. A state that has a proven track record of honouring international agreements and obeying international law will be more successful at securing binding commitments from other states. Statesmen and women must pursue the long-term interest of their states, and not act rashly, out of a sense of expediency. For example, failing to honour an agreement because doing so might not serve the immediate interest of the state may have negative long-term consequences, as the state may lose the trust of the international community. Moreover, citizens want to be part of a state of which they can be proud, and the international reputation of their state will reflect on their own sense of identity and self-worth. Also, a statesman will only be able to secure the psychological well-being of citizens and maintain the state's positive international image (from which future generations will benefit) if his or her foreign policy is perceived as just.

Finally, a state that plays by the rules and pursues a just and fair foreign policy makes a contribution to building a more reliable and peaceful international order based on mutual trust and shared values. Every state will benefit from such an international order with regard to both national security and prosperity.

In other words, state power needs to be employed in accordance with basic principles of justice at all times. The reason this needs to be done is not necessarily moral in character, but rather pragmatic: because it is the only sustainable way to promote national interests and achieve national security. By promoting justice and thus the interests of the international community as a whole, a state will be able to make its influence over others sustainable and achieve its own national interest. Consequently, it will be able to count on the support and cooperation of other states when needed. As argued in a previous work, the use of military power alone will not provide lasting security if it leads to real or perceived injustices. If a state or groups within a state feel that the use of hard power by another state has left them worse off than before, opposition and disgruntlement against the perpetrator of hard power will remain, and in one form or another will come to haunt it.[24] By pursuing justice, even the world's most powerful state will be able to marginalise extremist ideologies directed against its dominance, as these ideologies will lose their mass appeal.[25] The pursuit of justice is a prerequisite for long-term security.

My definition of justice in international relations consists of five elements. First, any foreign policy needs to respect the intrinsic requirements for dignity of individual human beings. Second, a state's foreign policy has to be respectful of other peoples' cultures and religions. Instead of alienating people of different cultures and religions, universal human values shared by all cultures need to be emphasised. Third, any state committed to justice will contribute to increased global equality. This means promoting fair rules for trade and the flow of capital to foster global economic prosperity, and making sure that the voices of developing states are heard and taken seriously in international institutions.[26]

Fourth, a state's foreign policy should, whenever possible, respect international law and honour its obligations under international treaties. Doing so will greatly enhance the state's international credibility with others. International law serves an important regulating function that brings order and predictability to the otherwise anarchic international state system. As to the use of force, basic just-war principles should be adhered to unconditionally. These commonly recognised principles limit the use of force by states to legitimate self-defence, collective self-defence, the use of force sanctioned by the UN Security Council and to rescue people threatened by genocide.[27] When a state finds itself in a war, international laws of warfare govern the conduct of the war. These laws prohibit the direct targeting of civilians and require the humane treatment of prisoners of war.

Fifth, good statesmanship will empower people by listening to people's policy concerns at home and abroad. It will make sure to include and listen to all parties to international conflicts in order to gain a comprehensive understanding of the underlying grievances that have led to violence and insecurity. People who feel that their concerns and grievances are taken seriously by statesmen and women of more powerful countries are more likely to support the policies of that particular state. After all, states in today's information age depend on a favourable world public opinion of their foreign-policy actions to be fully successful.[28]

Admittedly, it is not always clear what the 'just' solution may be in every international relations issue. Political philosopher Michael Walzer, for example, correctly observes that states 'operate in a world of conflicting interest and values where they are constantly forced into compromises which are, as we say, morally compromising'.[29] Nevertheless, justice is a principle to which every statesman and stateswomen should aspire in his or her foreign policy pursuits. My definition of global justice as consisting of five elements is meant to provide state actors with a helpful tool to discern the fairest solution even among conflicting interest and values.

Just power seeks to promote the aforementioned five dimensions of global justice. In so doing, its guiding principles are *fairness, equality* and *impartiality*, which I have discussed in a previous work.[30] The principle of *fairness* mostly applies to international negotiations. It implies that all parties involved in an issue that is being negotiated be adequately represented, and that their interests and concerns be addressed and taken into consideration in any negotiated solution. The negotiation process has to be transparent and fair in order to make a balanced outcome more likely.

The principle of *equality* means that a state, in exercising power, must ensure that all other states are being treated as equals regardless of culture and economic clout. When it comes to sharing burdens, however, what should count is equality of effort, not necessarily of result. For instance, both poor and rich countries should contribute to the good of the international community according to their respective abilities. They may invest an equal proportion of their GDP – as opposed to an equal amount of money – in a particular international project. Finally, the *impartiality* principle implies that good statesmen and women take an unbiased approach to each negotiating party and do not allow personal preferences and prejudices to cloud their ability to apply rational standards of justice and equality to all parties involved.

In sum, just power employs the tools of soft and hard power according to principles of justice. Hard-power tools should be employed in a minimalist way – only in self-defence or to prevent impending genocide (as acknowledged by the global community as a whole). In observing this minimalist principle, wars fought for moralistic reasons (e.g. to shape the world according to one's subjective view of justice) should be avoided as there always exist different ideological outlooks. Soft-power tools are by their very definition non-coercive. A state may thus try to win over other states through persuasion. States will hardly be attracted to messages of hatred and discord if the world's powerful and wealthy states pursue a foreign policy guided by principles of justice. Statecraft based on the principle of just power will thereby lead to global stability and lasting peace.

6.4 Are There Just Wars?

The notion that there should be moral constraints on war is ancient and global. Here, I briefly review the most influential position on the question of whether there are just wars before discussing the implications of just power on this issue.

Every major civilisation and world religion deals with the question of whether, and under what circumstances, there are legitimate reasons to use military force, and what kind of restrictions need to be observed by armies in the heat of battle. The concept of a just cause for war was present in Roman law, for example. A war is justified, it stipulated, if it is preceded by an offence by another party. As put by Cicero: 'No war can be undertaken by a just and wise state, unless for faith or self-defence.'[31] Roman law also included a series of procedures that sought to ensure that all other means of resolving a conflict would be exhausted prior to the resort to war. In his writings, Cicero listed a limited number of just causes for war; they included: 'the recovery of lost goods, self-defence of territory or citizens, and punishment of [an] enemy's misdeeds'.[32]

The Jewish tradition lays out three instances in which going to war are justified for a Jewish state. First, there are wars God commanded the Jews to fight. Second, there are defensive wars following an attack on the Jewish people or to pre-empt an attack that is about to happen. ('Whoever sheds the blood of man, by man shall his blood be shed.' Genesis 9:6) Third, there is the category of 'optional wars', which can be fought for a justified reason after all peaceful means of resolving the situation have been exhausted.[33] The latter point is central to Jewish tradition, namely that a war should always be the last resort and can only be legitimate if a peaceful solution to a conflict has been ruled out. While a war is being fought, Jewish tradition forbids the targeting of non-combatants and calls upon Jewish armies to allow civilians to leave areas of combat before the start of combat.[34]

Although the early Christians were mainly pacifists and refused to take part in any wars, the Christian tradition evolved to accept the view that certain wars may have to be fought in the name of justice. The early Christian theologian St Augustine expressed views on warfare that became the foundation for the Christian just-war tradition. He argued that it was morally justified for the ruler of a state to use armed force in order to protect his subjects from physical harm and to restore peace. In the thirteenth century, the theologian St Thomas Aquinas further developed St Augustine's ideas on warfare and laid down three conditions for a war to be just: legitimate authority, just cause and right intention.[35] These elements were used to justify crusades occurring between 1095 and 1291 to conquer lands from Muslims.[36] The invasion of Jerusalem and the treatment inflicted on its inhabitants is today widely regarded as an example of violations of fundamental ethical principles.[37]

Islam also provides guidelines as to what situations justify war and stipulates ethical constraints on the conduct of war. In general, Islam permits the use of military force in self-defence, to come to the defence of other Islamic states that have been attacked and to go to war against a state that is oppressing its Muslim citizens.[38] As for the conduct of war, the Koran calls upon Muslims to fight wars in a disciplined way and with the minimum necessary force. Moreover, it calls for the protection of non-combatants and the humane treatment of prisoners of war.[39] According to Islamic teachings, wars should be limited, and peace should always be favoured over violence.

The term *jihad* in Arabic literally means *struggle* or *effort*. It can refer to a believer's internal struggle to resist temptations and live the life of a good Muslim. It can also refer to the broader effort of building a just Muslim society; and it can take on the meaning of a holy war in defence of Islam, sometimes even through the use of force.[40] Islamic law, however, places clear restrictions on *jihad* if the term is taken in the narrow meaning of a military struggle to defend Islam. If the faith or territory of Muslims is under attack, Islamic law allows them to take up arms, but only under a set of strict preconditions. Legitimate reasons for *jihad* are self-defence or to protect the freedom of Muslims to practise their faith or free them from oppressive rule. *Jihad* cannot be invoked to forcibly convert non-Muslims to Islam or to conquer territory for reasons of economic gain or to enhance a ruler's prestige.[41] As for the conduct of *jihad*, detailed rules are laid out. Among them are the protection of innocent people, women, children and the elderly; the obligation to tend to the wounded; the just treatment of the enemy; and the obligation to halt armed hostilities if the enemy asks for peace. A further rule forbids Muslim armies to 'poison wells', which can be read today as a broader precept against chemical and biological warfare.[42]

Hinduism encompasses a variety of religious groups in India, yet most Hindus believe that war is justified in self-defence. If the cause for going to war is justified, the Hindu scriptures set down a series of rules regarding the conduct of wars and impose moral restraints on soldiers. The Hindu scriptures do not allow soldiers to attack women, children, the elderly or the sick, to attack someone from behind, or to poison the tip of an arrow.[43]

In general, the religious traditions summarised above share a series of common principles regarding warfare. First, there is the strong notion that peace is always preferable to war, and that war should be a last resort after all other means of resolving a conflict or injustice have been exhausted. Second, war should be limited to correcting the injustice that led to conflict and should not be used to conquer new territory. Third, wars should be fought in a disciplined way and unnecessary destruction of property should be avoided. Fourth, non-combatants should never be targeted, and enemy forces, once captured or having surrendered, are to be treated humanely. The concept of just power incorporates all of these general principles regarding warfare.

In Western Europe, the Christian just-war tradition strongly influenced the development of modern international laws of warfare. Despite its Christian origins, just-war theory increasingly found proponents in the secular world. In the late fifteenth and early sixteenth centuries, Francisco de Vitoria argued that 'difference of religion' does not justify war.[44] He made this argument in response to the invasion and pillaging of Latin America by the Spanish Conquistadores, implying that spreading the faith to non-Christian lands did not constitute a just cause for going to war.

A prominent follower of Vitoria's thinking was the seventeenth-century philosopher Hugo Grotius, who further secularised Christian just-war theory. Grotius was also of the conviction that wars of expansion to impose a particular religion on other nations were unacceptable. Grotius thought that there needed to be clear, universally accepted (i.e. not emanating from a particular church or religious authority) rules regulating state relations. In the course of the peace settlement of Westphalia, which followed the Thirty Years' War (1618–48) in Europe, Grotius sought to make just-war principles part of the modern international legal canon that was to regulate state relations following the peace settlement. State sovereignty was the basic principle of the Westphalian settlement, and any use of armed force that violated the territorial integrity and political independence of a sovereign state was deemed both unjust and illegal. The universal, secular principle of state sovereignty thus trumped any particularistic religious justification to conquer another state. In turn, using armed force to defend national sovereignty would be justified, as states have a God-given right to determine their own future and build a just and prosperous society without outside interference. Grotius famously stated:

> He who wills the attainment of a given end, wills also the things that are necessary to that end. God wills that we should protect ourselves, retain our hold on the necessities of life, obtain that which is our due, punish transgressors, and at the same time defend the state. ... But these divine objectives sometimes constitute causes for undertaking and carrying on war. ... Thus it is God's Will that certain wars should be waged. ... Yet no one will deny that whatsoever God will, is just. Therefore, some wars are just.[45]

As European society became more secular and the Church lost its role as a moral authority in state relations, international law started to fill the void. After the devastation of the First World War, states understood the necessity of regulating war and putting constraints on armies during warfare, especially with regard to non-combatant protection. After all, World War I was the first war in history in which the number of civilian deaths was higher than military deaths.[46]

Following that war, a series of international treaties sought to impose on states further legal limitations on the use of force. In the Covenant of the League of Nations, signatory states pledged 'to promote international co-operation and to achieve international peace and security by the acceptance of obligations not to resort to war [and] by the prescription of open, just and honourable relations between nations'.[47] The founding document of the League's successor organisation following the Second World War, the United Nations, limited the legitimate resort to war to self-defence, collective self-defence and actions authorised by the UN Security Council deemed necessary to preserve international peace and security.[48]

Both just-war theory and international law observe the distinction between *jus ad bellum* and *jus in bello*. *Jus ad bellum* addresses the question of what constitutes a legitimate reason for going to war. *Jus in bello* deals with the legitimacy of the means with which a war is fought. First and foremost, *jus in bello* is concerned with the principle of non-combatant immunity. The distinction between the two just-war categories is significant to the extent that an unjust war can still be fought with just means, while a just war can be fought with unjust means.

A prominent reviver of modern just-war theory today is the political philosopher Michael Walzer. In his classic work *Just and Unjust Wars*, he discusses both *jus ad bellum* and *jus in bello* from a secular moral perspective.[49] In principle, writes Walzer, the use of power is justified only in the case of aggression against a sovereign state. By attacking a political community, the aggressor deprives citizens of the ability to determine their form of government and way of life. This forces people to make a choice between fighting or abandoning their human rights to life and liberty, which, according to Walzer, 'are somehow entailed by our sense of what it means to be human'.[50]

In addition to aggression, Walzer lists a few exceptional circumstances where military action might be justified. These are all circumstances in which the expected consequences of inaction would be detrimental to the safety of a state or its people. One such exception would be a pre-emptive military attack by one state against another state that is just about to launch an attack on the first.[51]

Another exception where states can legitimately use military power, writes Walzer, is to rescue people threatened by massacre. The difficult question of how just power can be employed to save human lives in other states is discussed in more detail in the next section.

In his just-war theory, Walzer applies thin, or minimalist, principles of justice, as the theory regulates relations between states that can be culturally very diverse. These thin moral values in just-war theory include the right of a legitimate political community to territorial integrity and political self-determination, the concept that unarmed civilians should not be targeted during warfare and the notion that the systematic persecution and killing of a population group is a heinous crime against humanity and warrants a rescue operation on behalf of the persecuted.

A frequently heard criticism of just-war theory, even if it is phrased in secular terms, is that the inclusion of any type of moral arguments when talking about state behaviour can lead to moral disagreements. If two states are going to war and both claim the moral high ground by stating that their reason for military action is moral and just, there is no higher authority to rule as to which state is acting more morally. Different nations with different religious outlooks may make different moral judgements in a particular situation. Hence, most secular just-war theorists today have adopted a legalist, as opposed to a moralist, paradigm to make their case.[52] By applying legal rather than moral principles to evaluate the justness of a war, secular thinkers today are better able to avoid clashes in moral outlook between different nations and cultures.

Although modern international law has borrowed from and incorporated moral principles derived from the just-war tradition, law and justice remain two different things. An action deemed legal by international law does not necessarily make the action just. My own approach, just power, views military intervention as the *ultimate ratio* to prevent horrific violations of the requirements for human dignity, as I shall discuss in the next section. The main focus of just power, however, is to identify ways of actively preventing wars. Through its emphasis on fairness, equality and impartiality, it seeks to counteract the casual factors of war, including marginalisation, oppression and fear-induced pre-emptive aggression.

6.5 *Just Power and Humanitarian Intervention*

The question of humanitarian intervention poses a moral dilemma in that it pits two ethical principles in international relations against one another. On the one hand, there is the principle of national sovereignty, which gives political communities the right to territorial integrity and political independence. Any foreign infringement upon their national territory would thus, strictly speaking, be in violation of this fundamental state entitlement. On the other hand, there is the principle of human rights, which states that every human being – by virtue of being human – has a series of basic, inalienable rights, including the right to life and freedom from oppression. The question of whether the need to protect human rights should trump the right of states to national sovereignty is a difficult one that has not been fully resolved in the existing international system of sovereign states. This was at the centre of the concept of 'responsibility to protect' which emerged in the early 2000s after conflicts in Rwanda and Yugoslavia. The principle of a 'responsibility to protect' civilians was finally adopted by the UN World Summit in 2005.[53]

The realist school of political thought has long been sceptical about foreign intervention in states to address inherently domestic issues. In his 1951 book *American Diplomacy*, George F. Kennan objected to a 'moralistic-legalistic' approach to foreign policy.[54] He and other realist thinkers believe that the world would become a much more violent place if a number of powerful states started to fight wars to change regimes and rescue people from political oppression. Instead of taking the moral high ground and pursuing a moralistic foreign policy, realists maintain countries should limit their military actions to the pursuit of their individual national-security needs and objectives. While realists are not opposed to ethics and morality *per se*, they caution against the inappropriate use of morality in international affairs, which is sometimes referred to as 'moralism'.

Realists have put forward three main arguments against the use of state power for moralistic purposes. First, there is the danger that states will adopt, often unconsciously, a stance of moral superiority over other nations and cultures, and project a black-and-white view of the world. This can lead to a fixation on the evils of one single nation and let states ignore other evils that occur elsewhere in the world or even in their own countries. In morally demonising a particular state, a country also tends to burn bridges with states it may one day have to rely on if strategic circumstances change.[55]

Second, moral outrage can become so emotional that the facts on the ground are no longer scrutinised objectively. This can lead to the hasty use of force even while the actual roots of atrocities happening inside a state are not studied to the extent needed in order to devise the best policy possible to restore long-term order and peace in the area in which massive human-rights violations are occurring.[56]

Third, realists caution that respect for human rights cannot be imposed by foreign cultures but has to be integrated into existing political systems by the political community in question. Foreign interventions in the name of human rights can be counterproductive, in the sense that human-rights principles become associated with the foreign imposition of a political system and are not seen for what they really are: principles that grant every human being the right to life and human dignity.

Just power, however, is based on the notion that, in today's interconnected world, the need to prevent or halt massive atrocities and persecutions inside a state trumps the need to respect that state's right to sovereignty. The moral justification for military intervention in a state engaged in massive human-rights violations has been eloquently expressed by Walzer: 'People who initiate massacres lose their right to participate in the normal (even in the normally violent) processes of self-determination' and 'their military defeat is morally necessary'.[57] In other words, a state that is no longer able to fulfil its basic function – ensuring the safety of its own citizens – temporarily loses its right to sovereignty until stability and peace are restored. This determination, however, is not always clear and will need broad agreement in the international community.

Another important principle in humanitarian intervention is proportionality. Intervention should not cause more human suffering than non-intervention. Moreover, there needs to be a reasonable expectation that order and peace can be restored following the use of military force. As Fernando Tesón puts it, 'Foreign armies are morally entitled to help victims of oppression in overthrowing dictators, provided that the intervention is proportionate to the evil which it is designed to suppress.'[58]

Humanitarian interventions are based on the notion that the intervention is welcomed by those whose human rights are being violated on a massive scale. Although it is not always possible to get the consent of these people prior to a planned intervention, the international community should be reasonably convinced that their intervention indeed is welcomed by the local population and is in their genuine interest.[59]

According to Stanley Hoffmann, there are two types of situations in which intervention on moral grounds is justified. One instance would be when states, due to their internal condition, pose a threat to international peace and security. These might be so-called failed states, where governments have lost control over their territories and are unable to protect their citizens from harm or prevent criminal activities on their territories. A second type of situation where, for Hoffmann, a humanitarian intervention is justified, is the threat of genocide, mass killings and mass expulsions.[60]

When it comes to the justification of the use of armed force, there seems to be a growing gap between international law and principles of universal justice and morality. It becomes ever harder to uphold the legal principle of non-intervention when there are documented cases of massive human-rights violations inside a state. Also, the existence of failed and inherently unstable states clearly poses a threat to surrounding states and beyond and cannot be ignored as an internal problem of the state that finds itself in domestic turmoil. It is almost a moral 'gut-feeling' that motivates bystanders to call for humanitarian intervention. As one author has put it, 'There is a powerful moral intuition at work in thinking of those who advocate interventions that apparently go beyond current international law and depart from the self-defense model.'[61] It is this 'moral intuition', backed up by the verification of real facts on the ground and a plan that promises a reasonable chance of success, that is involved in the exercise of just power by states.

The principle of just power does not seek to impose a foreign culture on states where humanitarian disasters are happening, nor does it advocate a benign form of imperialism. Interventions must never be carried out unilaterally by one or a small coalition of states. Given the sensitivity and consequences of such military actions, expansive multilateral agreements have to precede interventions. It is thereby important that justifications for such interventions spring from true regard for the requirements for human dignity and are not used as fronts for geopolitical goals or to pursue narrow national interests. The just power concept advocates the use of power to rescue people subject to large-scale persecution or atrocities if the rescue operation is expected to result in the successful establishment of peace and order in the region. Such rescue operations, however, must be undertaken through multilateral institutions, especially the UN Security Council. To make the intervention a lasting success, just power needs to be employed not just to stop atrocities but to provide for a stable post-intervention settlement – the topic of the next section.

6.6 Occupations and Jus Post Bellum

A just intervention undertaken to save human lives and remove a threat to international security caused by a failed state has to have an outcome that guarantees peace and security inside the state. This principle also applies to post-war situations in wars that have been fought 'justly' against an aggressor state. The use of military force either in a humanitarian operation or to repel an aggressor could lead to a temporary occupation of the state that the force is directed against. Under the just-power principle, states fighting wars need to take responsibility for a post-war settlement that is equitable and guarantees lasting peace.

Michael Walzer describes the justice of an occupation in the following way:

> What determines the overall justice of a military occupation
> is less its planning or its length than its political direction
> and the distribution of the benefits it provides. If its steady
> tendency is to empower the locals and if its benefits are widely
> distributed, the occupying power can plausibly be called just.[62]

A just occupation, therefore, should help to protect and promote
the human rights of the local population. It should help locals build a
stable order so that the state will no longer pose a threat to international
peace and security. Rather than trying to enrich itself, the occupying
power has a moral obligation to make sure that economic resources are
distributed fairly among the local population and that the economy is
developed to serve the future interests of the state. Only by ensuring
that the state is able to build a viable economy can peace and stability
be preserved.

The philosopher Brian Orend has put together a series of guidelines
for a state seeking to exercise just power after it has fought a war.[63]
According to Orend, any peace settlement should be fair and not serve as
a punishment. Instead of demanding unconditional surrender, a realistic
settlement needs to be found that takes account of the grievances of the
aggressor state.[64]

People who have violated human rights and international law need
to be punished in a targeted manner. Instead of punishing an entire
population, those political leaders and soldiers who committed serious
crimes need to be dealt with separately.[65] Finally, and most importantly,
a state needs to ensure that any peace settlement respects the human
and community rights of the aggressor state's population. These rights
are non-negotiable and need to be guaranteed in any settlement.

6.7 Just Economic Power

A commitment to human dignity and individual well-being across the
world cannot be pursued with military power alone. The use of force
will sometimes be necessary to protect people from physical harm, but
it cannot protect them from severe economic deprivation and hunger.
Hence, economic power also needs to be employed justly. Although a
complete redistribution of global wealth is unrealistic and would be
counter-productive, wealthy states have a moral responsibility to make
the global economic order more just to ensure that every human being

is able to make a decent living. As Jon Mandle argues, 'Global inequality *as such* is not objectionable as long as basic human rights are protected, including secure access to a sufficient supply of basic resources.'[66]

There are tremendous economic inequalities in the world. Nearly half of the world's population has to live with US$5.50 a day while billionaires' wealth saw a twelve per cent increase in 2018. This especially affects women who globally earn 50 per cent less than men.[67] Even so, it should be noted that some of the huge gap between countries had been alleviated by roughly 34 per cent between 1993 and 2017. The COVID-19 pandemic, however, had a further devastating impact on inequality and global divergence between richer and poorer nations. As noted by the World Bank, whatever steady progress had been achieved previously, the projections estimated by late 2021 showed that 'the gap between nations is expected to increase for the first time in a generation'.[68]

These economic inequalities are so great that it would not take much for rich countries to ensure that the basic economic rights of those currently living in extreme poverty are met. According to one calculation, if the world's richest 225 people contributed four per cent of their combined wealth to the alleviation of extreme poverty, every human being could have 'universal access to basic education', 'basic health care … [including] reproductive health care for all women, adequate food … and safe water and sanitation'.[69]

The question of the extent to which wealthy states have a moral obligation to share some of their wealth with less wealthy states can be approached from both a state-centred perspective and from a human-rights perspective. From a state-centred perspective, one could argue that governments only have an obligation to care for the well-being of their own citizens. However, as philosopher Charles Jones puts it, 'nation-state borders lack any fundamental ethical standing'.[70] A further argument against the state-centred approach to economic justice is that people in wealthy states have inherited, and not earned, their privileged position.[71] They have been born into affluence and have been given the opportunity to receive a good education and succeed in the job market. So, in many ways, the ability to have a decent human existence depends on one's place of birth and thus is pure coincidence.

The just-power perspective maintains that economic power can only be employed justly if distributive justice is approached from a human-rights angle. From such a perspective, one would argue that every human being has the right to an economic minimum: a job, adequate shelter and sufficient food. From a humanitarian point of view, it can be argued that we all have a moral responsibility to make sure that certain minimum standards are provided to forestall 'starvation or severe malnutrition and early death from easily preventable diseases', which affects all people living in severe poverty.[72] Hence, this automatically places a responsibility on the 'haves' to ensure that the poorest of the world have an economic minimum that allows them to live decently. Again, this is a moral responsibility that states have towards non-citizens in the minimalist, or thin, sense: states have to do what they can to ensure that the basic human rights of every human being in the world are protected. Just power in the economic realm does not call for a total redistribution of the global wealth. This is why a rights-based approach is useful. As Thomas Nagel explains: 'Rights are a guarantee to each of us of a certain protected status, rather than a net benefit to the aggregate.'[73]

Indeed, Walzer's concept of thick and thin moral principles is highly useful with regard to the question of global economic justice. As Walzer explains, every human society shares the notion that social goods must be distributed justly. Nevertheless, different cultural groups define the notion of just distribution differently, as they assign different values to different social goods in accordance with their individual value systems.[74] The principle of just distribution is a thin, and thus universal, moral principle. It is up to each individual state, however, to give this principle concrete meaning and to translate it into laws and public policies. As noted before, Walzer stresses that thick moral principles apply to relationships within states, while thin moral values apply to relationships between states. In a state-based international system, the state remains the primary entity for the pursuit of social justice. Echoing Walzer, philosopher John Rawls similarly argued that principles of social justice need to be set up as part of a 'social contract', in which citizens of a state express their particular concept of justice.[75]

At the same time, every state has an obligation to help build a global economic order, sustained by global institutions, that enables every state in the world to ensure that its citizens have secure access to essential resources. In other words, the global economic system has to enable every state to pursue social and economic justice at home in accordance with its own thick cultural values. At the same time, global institutions should assist states and give them incentives to build a domestic political system that is fair and representative and that ensures that the basic economic needs of all citizens are met.

When it comes to building a just economic order, wealthy states have a greater role to play than developing states simply because they have more economic resources to do so. Moreover, Mandle argues that former colonial powers have a particular responsibility to work towards a more just global economic order because of their history of imposing an unequal economic relationship on their former colonies, which they used to enrich themselves at the colonies' expense.[76]

It is important that wealthy states negotiate fair-trade agreements with developing states. This means, first, that wealthy states accept a level playing field when it comes to international trade. For example, government subsidies enable farmers in the United States and the EU to sell their products below their production costs. These subsidies put poor nations at a disadvantage because without them farmers in poor countries would be able to compete with farmers from rich countries on the international market.[77]

High tariff barriers set up by wealthy states are another issue that makes the global economic order unjust. As one Oxfam study notes, 'When developing countries export to rich-country markets, they face tariff barriers that are four times higher than those encountered by rich countries. Those barriers cost them $100bn a year – twice as much as they receive in aid.'[78] To make the global trading system more just, so that all the countries of the world can increase their wealth through trade, trade barriers and the high level of agricultural subsidies in rich states need to be phased out. The current polarisation of global wealth is unsustainable. Conditions of desperate poverty, where people have no prospect for a better future, will only breed more resentment against the rich world and the process of globalisation. Such feelings may provide fertile ground for instability and forced migration.

Just power demands that wealthy states use their economic power to further the cause of justice inside other states. A wealthy state that pursues economic relations with a state that promotes and tolerates severe injustices domestically has a moral responsibility not to assist that state in any way to continue such practices. As Nagel explains: 'Even if internal justice is the primary responsibility of each state, the complicity of other states in the active support or perpetuation of an unjust regime is a secondary offense against justice.'[79] A telling example is the arms trade through which wealthy and producer states are complicit with violations committed by receiving countries, including those against civilians.[80]

Just power further calls for the use of targeted, or 'smart', sanctions. Smart sanctions target the regime of a state that is violating international norms, as opposed to the entire population, which is already suffering under that regime. Examples of sanctions that mostly target the government and wealthy elites are asset freezes, travel bans and arms embargoes.[81] When economic power is employed coercively, states have to observe the same principles of justice as when using military power. In addition, saving innocent civilians from harm and keeping 'collateral damage' to a minimum are prerequisites for using economic sanctions justly.

6.8 Applying Justice to All Five Global Security Dimensions

As I have argued, any comprehensive security concept today needs to include five security dimensions: *human, environmental, national, transnational* and *transcultural*.[82] This *multi-sum security principle* further maintains that, to maximise security, a state needs to apply principles of justice in all five security dimensions, as injustice in one sphere will lead to insecurity in other spheres. I summarise what this means below.

In the area of *human security*, it is important that national governments and international institutions cooperate to ensure that the basic needs of all humans are met. Individual governments have to promote social justice at home by ensuring a fair distribution of scarce resources and providing every citizen with access to education and health care.[83] In post-conflict situations, the international community needs to ensure human security by building a just post-war order that allows people to live in peace and safety. Post-conflict settlements should always focus on promoting reconciliation, such as through truth-and-reconciliation commissions.[84]

Second, in the area of *environmental security*, justice may be pursued in several ways. This security dimension is a prime example of where a state's long- and short-term interests may collide. As I have suggested, a statesman's or stateswoman's responsibility lies in protecting the state's long-term interests. Hence, to do justice to future generations of citizens, as well as to humans around the world, states ought to do whatever they reasonably can to conserve the environment, reduce pollution and use non-renewable natural resources sparingly, as it is in every state's long-term interests to do so.[85] Furthermore, in terms of environmental justice, wealthy states have certain moral obligations (for the sake of the planet) towards developing nations that lack the financial means to pursue effective environmental policy and often see themselves forced to deplete their natural resources for short-term economic gain. Moreover, developing nations are often hit harder by the effects of global warming, which is primarily caused by wealthy economies. Hence, the principle of environmental justice demands that wealthy nations make a determined effort to fight global warming, invest in clean technologies and assist developing states to improve their environmental standards.

Third, a *national security policy* based on justice not only protects state borders but promotes the well-being of all citizens. Government policies that are considered just by citizens will be most effective in keeping the country stable domestically and in protecting the homeland from foreign invasion. A government that protects the human rights and civil liberties of its citizens and ensures that public goods are distributed fairly among its population will minimise the chance of being overthrown from within, and, at the same time, it will maintain enough citizen support to be able to mobilise national security forces to protect the country from security threats.[86]

Fourth, just policies by states and international institutions will help to remove many incentives for states and non-state actors to threaten the security of states. *Transnational security* can be promoted through a just international economic order and through fair and effective international cooperation in law enforcement. Furthermore, transnational security can be enhanced by providing the necessary means and know-how to help weak and failing states to become independent and stable entities.[87]

Transcultural security, defined as the absence of discrimination based on a person's heritage and the absence of hostile clashes between members of different cultures, constitutes a fifth area of comprehensive international justice. States can contribute to the goal of transcultural harmony by working against discrimination on the basis of nationality, religion or ethnicity at home and abroad. Cultural exchanges can help enhance cultural understanding between different nations.[88]

With its five dimensions of security, the multi-sum security principle serves as the comprehensive theoretical underpinning for the employment of just power and sustainable security.

6.9 Comparing the Concepts of Smart and Just Power

This chapter makes the case that states should employ power not just smartly but also justly. Tables 6.1 and 6.2 provide an overview comparing the similarities and differences between the two approaches, as well as the advantages of each concept.

Table 6.1 Comparing the Concepts of Smart Power and Just Power

	SMART POWER	JUST POWER
Author, Date	J.S. Nye, Jr., R. Armitage, 2007	Nayef R.F. Al-Rodhan, 2009
Definition	Skillful combination of hard- and soft-power tools to achieve foreign policy objectives	Use of hard- and soft-power tools according to principles of justice in order for the national interest (and even regional or global dominance) to be sustainable
Philosophical Foundations/ Principles	**Realism and idealism:** - Norms-based internationalism (including respect for international law and institutions) - National security - Human rights and democracy - Fair-trade rules - Public diplomacy - Promoting US image - Promoting US values and interests through international institutions	**Symbiotic realism, multi-sum security principle and justice** - Absolute gains - Burden-sharing - Non-conflicting progress and cooperation among states - Just-war principles - Human rights and human dignity - Global economic justice - Multilateral and multidimensional - Allows for different geo-cultural domains and rejects the imposition of a particular set of values onto others
Key Initiatives (Soft Power)	**New multilateralism:** - Reform current international institutions (UN, WB, IMF) - Strengthen and maintain alliances - Create new multilateral groups that coordinate and implement global strategies to solve specific global threats - Seek global consensus on fighting climate change - Fight communicable diseases through a global health network - Provide universal access to safe drinking water and sanitation - Increase education level worldwide - Make development and humanitarian assistance a key theme in foreign policy - Increase educational exchanges - Promote more equitable terms of trade so every state can benefit from global trade - Invest in R&D of clean technologies - Promote the global good with help of UN institutions (especially peacekeeping and peacebuilding, counter-terrorism, global health, energy and climate)	**Promotion of justice:** - Eradicate extreme poverty worldwide - Promote fair-trade rules that enable developing countries to develop their economies - Provide worldwide access to affordable basic healthcare - Strengthen international legal framework - Promote an international cooperative/ burden-sharing framework that addresses a broad variety of security threats - Assist states in governing justly as a way of preventing suffering and conflicts within and between states
Advantages of Approach	- Enhance and maintain international credibility - Promote increased international cooperation to help US and global security objectives - Address threats to international and national security through international institutions	- Enhance the state's international credibility - Serve as model for others - Address threats to international and national security through international institutions - Allow for cultural specificities as long as they meet a common standard
Disadvantages	- Possible domestic opposition to spending increases for UN fees and humanitarian assistance - Bureaucratic obstacles to unified development policy	- Perception of potential clashes between a state's pragmatic national interest (i.e., a government's responsibility to promote the interests and well-being of its citizens) and the global good, despite the fact that they are intertwined

Table 6.2 Application of Smart- and Just-Power Tools

Application of Hard-Power Tools

SMART POWER	JUST POWER
▶ Use of military power and coercive economic measures are sometimes justified and necessary ▶ Needs to be last resort and employed only if soft-power tools have failed ▶ Use of hard-power tools to be coordinated with allies and international institutions ▶ Respect international legal norms and obligations when using hard power	▶ Same as for smart power ▶ Strictly observe just-war principles (both *jus ad bellum* and *jus in bello*) ▶ Saving human lives and promoting human rights and dignity are at the forefront of any multilateral hard-power action

Application of Soft-Power Tools

SMART POWER	JUST POWER
▶ Use a variety of soft-power tools and make soft-power the preferred foreign policy tool ▶ Stress humanitarian assistance, public diplomacy, educational exchanges, multilateral diplomacy, multilateral institution-building when using hard power	▶ Same as for smart power ▶ Make justice and human dignity the guiding principles in the application of soft-power tools

Even more so than smart power, *just* power is based on the recognition that state-centric paradigms cannot effectively address the complex and interrelated threats the international community is facing. Furthermore, just power no longer considers the state to be the only entity that needs protection. Basing itself on the theory of *symbiotic realism*, the concept of just power considers additional global actors that deserve policy consideration and security guarantees. These are individuals, large collective entities and the biosphere itself, among others.[89]

Ultimately, the concept of just power suggests that justice should be the foundation of all human, group and state interactions. States should pursue justice because it is the only way they can pursue *sustainable* national security. In an interconnected world, an individual state can only enhance its national security if all other states and the individuals living within those states can be more secure. Hence, by pursuing just power, a state is simply pursuing its own national interest. If states do not act according to principles of justice, the injustices they perpetrate will harm not just other states but ultimately also their own national interest. Because today's world is so interconnected, any injustice committed against people or states will, in one way or another, come to affect all other countries.

6.10 Justice in a Transnational World

Globalisation has not only facilitated the international movement of goods and people. Intense and frequent interactions with people from different countries and cultures, as well as global media connectivity, have transformed the way people think about responsibility and justice in relation to other human beings. Knowing more about the plight of others in far-off corners of the globe morally compels citizens and politicians to address human suffering and major wrongdoing wherever they occur. Global markets are connecting humans on an economic level more than ever before. We are all consumers of goods produced in many different parts of the world. The fates of individuals around the world are thus interlinked. Regional and international organisations, such as ASEAN or the UN, give expression to the aspirations of many states to transcend national borders when it comes to issues like human rights and environmental protection.

In the absence of a world government and an international body that defines and regulates global justice, states remain on their own to work for a more just world. Still, the next best thing is a network of effective global organisations and institutions that can help states exercise just power. Such institutions facilitate the coordination of humanitarian aid and the worldwide protection of human rights, thus furthering the cause of global justice.

Just as international law is being expanded, we are seeing the rise of universal moral standards that no state today can violate without causing international outrage. Global security depends on actions that guarantee that all human beings are of equal worth and dignity. Cosmopolitanism has won over national or ethnic particularism when it comes to respect for the equal value of human beings, regardless of gender or cultural background.[90] States that use their power in the name of justice will be guided by a determination to protect human rights. It is important for states, especially powerful states, to act consistently, when it comes to defending human rights, to convince weaker states that their intentions are good and that their employment of military power serves the purpose of promoting international justice and not some cynical political objective or geopolitical goal.[91]

In sum, the principle of just power starts from the premise that the protection of human dignity is the foremost objective of any state. A state will use power only if it can reasonably be expected that human suffering can be reduced and international peace and stability can be promoted. Just power calls upon states to observe just-war principles and to fight wars only if faced with aggression or to rescue people who are being systematically persecuted or killed within another state that is unable or unwilling to stop such atrocities. When using any hard-power tools, states will observe the principle of non-combatant immunity and do everything within their power to protect innocent civilians from harm. In all cases, international legitimacy and multilateral cooperation must be sought before using force.

Furthermore, the concept of just power demands that states, especially wealthy states, take on an active role in building a more just international economic order. Such an economic order would ensure that world trade is truly free and fair and gives poor states an opportunity to grow and to develop their economies and to provide a better life for their citizens. The concept of just power maintains that states have an obligation towards humankind to do as much as they can to ensure that the basic human rights of every human being are protected. Initiatives may include refusing to support regimes that violate human rights or refraining from imposing high trade tariffs that prevent developing nations from being able to compete in the global market. Just statecraft requires statesmen and women to consider the interests of many different parties, not just those of their own state. Figure 6.1 provides an overview of the four types of power concepts discussed in this chapter.

Figure 6.1 Just Power

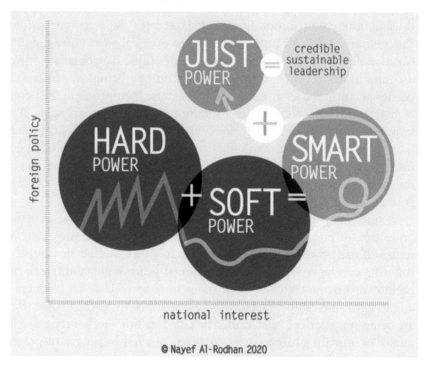

© Nayef Al-Rodhan 2020

Statecraft in the twenty-first century requires extraordinary abilities to reconcile a series of crucial interests that are relevant in the realm of international politics. Justice as a guiding principle prompts statesmen and women to strive towards harmony and the reconciliation of different interests as opposed to pursuing a state's national interest at the expense of other states and entities. In chapter seven, I elaborate on the idea of reconciliation by describing eight crucial global interests that modern statecraft cannot afford to ignore. Before summing up these eight global interests, however, the chapter first looks at what is ahead and reviews some of the challenges states are expected to face in the coming decades.

7

The Concept of Reconciliation Statecraft

In the previous chapter, I introduced five innovative concepts that provide statesmen and women with effective tools to navigate today's world. These tools will enable them to look beyond narrowly defined national interests to recognise and leverage the interdependence of states in the twenty-first century. More specifically, they enable them to address the conflicts and dilemmas raised by different interests represented by individuals, states, groups of individuals and groups of states, as well as more general global interests, such as environmental protection. Along with growing interdependence comes the challenges of balancing these diverse interests, which are not mutually exclusive yet, at times, conflict with one another. A failure to reconcile them will negatively affect global peace and security, as is illustrated below.

This chapter identifies eight different interests that are highly relevant in twenty-first-century statecraft. These interests are individual, group, national, regional, cultural, global, planetary and moral. Next, it discusses how state leaders can balance these different interests and work towards what I call *reconciliation statecraft*, thereby fostering not only the thriving of their state but also the promotion of global peace, security and prosperity for current and future generations.

7.1 Individual Interests

Individuals living in different countries of the world all have sets of interests they pursue. It is primarily the task of national governments to enable citizens to pursue those interests freely, as long as this does not compromise the ability of others to do the same. Individual interests include making a decent living and ensuring a certain quality of life. For most adult individuals, this will include employment, affordable housing, public and private safety, good schools for their children, affordable health care and social services provided by the state.

Citizens who are well-off and enjoy a certain degree of social security do not have to worry about day-to-day basic necessities and may have interests that are less material. With regard to international politics, citizens might consider it as being in their interest to belong to a state with a good international image, as that image might also enhance their self-esteem and their individual interests. They may want their state to contribute actively to international peace missions or development projects in the developing world. The owners or employees of a company that sells products abroad have an interest in their country's image, as a positive image might facilitate their marketing efforts. Individuals want their state to be safe and secure and thus rarely approve of foreign policy moves that increase the vulnerability of their country. Individuals in most states, even if their government is not representative, usually dislike external interference in their domestic politics.

Despite this, individuals who suffer from the consequences of state brutality or do not feel protected by their government might welcome foreign pressure on their state to change its political behaviour or even a foreign intervention. In short, individuals want their human rights and requirements for dignity to be protected at all times.

According to the theory of *emotional amoral egoism* that I outlined earlier, people are unlikely to observe moral norms if their basic needs are not met. If humans find themselves deprived of sufficient food, shelter, security and basic health care, they will prioritise these needs before they will care for the well-being of others. When in danger, humans will rarely put their individual survival instinct second. To act morally towards others, individuals must have a positive self-identity and a sense of belonging to a larger community in whose well-being the individual member is genuinely interested, as his or her own well-being will depend on the well-being of other members of the community. In contrast, fear, want and humiliation often lead to aggressive behaviour, power struggles and greed.[1] Hence, statesmen and women need to ensure that basic individual interests – both material and emotional – are met at both the national and global level in order to secure international stability, security and peace.

7.2 Group Interests

International borders often do not correspond to ethnic and religious settlement patterns. This has meant that many ethnic groups are part of a multi-ethnic state or that belong to several multi-ethnic states. Such ethnic groups have rights, as the UN has held. Group rights may include the right to maintain a common language and culture, as well as rights to state protection of minorities. Group rights are based on the notion that humans have a basic need to form cultural attachments, and that cultural units deserve some degree of protection from mainstream society. Group interests that are sometimes asserted *vis-à-vis* the state are, as Azam Kamguian writes, the 'rights [of a people] to govern themselves, have guaranteed political representation, or [be] exempt from generally applicable law'.[2]

Besides ethnic and religious minorities, there are other groups with common interests: women, for example. As a group, women pursue interests such as equal pay for equal work and reproductive rights, as entrenched in the 1979 UN Convention on the Elimination of All Forms of Discrimination against Women.[3] Children also share common interests, including those reflected in the 1989 UN Convention on the Rights of the Child, such as the rights to care, protection, education and health care.[4] Disabled people have also organised to advance their group interests for better accessibility to public places and more safety, as well as access to employment and educational opportunities. The 1975 UN Declaration on the Rights of Disabled Persons seeks to ensure that the human dignity of disabled people is protected and that the disabled receive the necessary support and care they need to lead as normal a life as possible.[5]

Possible conflicts between group interests and individual interests. Groups can sometimes be oppressive to the individual. For instance, if a group's cultural practices violate the human rights and freedoms of a certain member of the group, calls to protect and respect the group's cultural autonomy and calls to protect the individual human rights of group members may clash. The protection of group rights should not be extended to practices that violate women's rights to equality and self-determination. Cultural traditions that violate principles of human dignity and equality will need to be modified to ensure that the dignity of every human being is guaranteed.[6]

As long as group interests are granted only to the extent that they are an extension of individual human rights and not in opposition to them, conflicts between group and individual rights can be minimised. Still, tensions between the individual and the group can never be entirely eliminated. After all, societies only function when individuals submit to society's norms and rules. Meanwhile, individuals benefit from an ordered and functioning society, and if the society's laws and rules are fair, both individuals and smaller groups within a state will find their interests protected and promoted.

7.3 National Interests

National interests are to a large extent shaped by the values of the people and government of each individual state. These values can be influenced by the geographic location and natural resources of the state, the culture and historical experience of its inhabitants and the material needs of the population.[7] Current international circumstances and domestic political dynamics also impact the formulation of national interests.

The most important national interest of every state, however, is to preserve its territorial integrity and political independence, as well as the well-being and safety of its people. National security implies safe borders and internal security so that citizens can live free from physical harm. It can also refer to more subjective dimensions, namely the degree to which people *perceive* themselves to be secure from harm.[8] In summarising the ambiguity of the security concept, the political scientist Arnold Wolfers writes: 'Security, in an objective sense, measures the absence of threats to acquired values, in a subjective sense, the absence of fear that such values will be attacked.'[9]

A country's ability to pursue its national interests independently will depend on how powerful it is. EU member states have submitted to a supranational entity to achieve national interests that they could not achieve to the same extent on their own. Together, they have adopted a common currency and agreed to defer to the European Central Bank in order to increase national prosperity. Small and weak states often join alliances or accept protection from a stronger power to protect themselves from harm. Doing so implies giving up some of their freedom of action in exchange for increased security.[10]

Meanwhile, as I have suggested, citizens also want to belong to a country that has a good image abroad and that is a positive force in international affairs. In today's ever more interconnected world, a narrow definition of national interest without regard to the interests of other states will not be effective. Such behaviour can increasingly marginalise countries in the international community, on whose cooperation they depend in areas ranging from trade to the fight against a variety of transnational security threats. The long-term national interest of states thus increasingly coincides with the interests of the international community as a whole. Moreover, states find their core interests to preserve territorial integrity and political independence protected by the international legal framework and the UN's collective security system, as long as a state does not relinquish these privileges by systematically violating the human rights of its citizens or engaging in unilateral aggressive or destabilising behaviour.

Possible conflicts between national interests and individual and group interests. A state's national interest, as proclaimed and interpreted by its government, may conflict with individual interests if the state maintains an oppressive and dictatorial form of government that violates individual rights for the purpose of holding on to political power. Individuals may suffer from their government's increased spending on weapons and the military in the name of national security as opposed to investing in education and health care. Citizens may also see certain economic policies as being against their individual interests. Farmers, for instance, might oppose their state cutting of tariffs on agricultural imports – a policy that might be in the country's long-term national interest, but not necessarily in their interest.

Finally, the national interest can conflict with the interests of certain groups within a country. While the former stresses national cohesion and unity, the latter may ask for more group autonomy within the state. States, however, are often reluctant to grant such autonomy for fear of separatism and the dissolution of the state's territorial integrity. Hence, group interests will sometimes have to give way to national interests.

Some effective special-interest groups may heavily influence national foreign policy and can alter a state's international relations and effectiveness in a negative way. States should therefore prohibit excessive lobbying by interest groups, as this can damage a country's credibility and security. A state needs to maintain an impartial approach to global problems for the sake of its own security, as well as the security of the international community.

7.4 Regional Interests

'Regions' in international relations are sometimes difficult to delineate. They include groups of countries that share not just a common geographic space, but often also a common history, cultural affinity and strong economic relations. States enter into regional associations or organisations when they feel that they can serve their national interest of increasing national security and prosperity best through regional integration and cooperation. Many transnational threats today require regional approaches. Even when such threats are global and need global responses in the long term, regional blocs are often able to act faster and more decisively in the short term. In fact, it is much easier to reach a regional rather than global consensus on an action plan against a particular threat. Regional organisations can thus meet both the national interests of member states and a set of global interests.[11]

In addition, many transnational threats to international security start regionally, including those originating in state instability, massive migration flows, water and air pollution, and over-fishing of common bodies of water. Even the proliferation of weapons of mass destruction will most likely first threaten adjacent states before having global implications. Note, for example, the spillover effects of the Syrian civil war, which diffused conflict beyond the Middle East region through international terrorism, an economic downturn[12] and a refugee flow, which in turn have provoked a racist and populist backlash in Europe.[13] Through good regional cooperation, potential global threats can be contained and eliminated at the regional level. Barry Buzan is interested in regional security complexes, which he defines as 'a group of states whose primary security concerns link together sufficiently closely that their national securities cannot reasonably be considered apart from one another'.[14] Buzan and Ole Wæver have stressed the importance of geographical proximity for security cooperation: 'Adjacency is potent for security because many threats travel more easily over short distances than over long ones.'[15] Many transnational threats that have regional implications before they have global ones, including state instability, massive migration flows, water and air pollution, and overfishing of common bodies of water. Even the proliferation of weapons of mass destruction will most likely first threaten adjacent states.

Furthermore, because regions are made up of a limited number of states, they can often act faster and more decisively than it would take to reach a global consensus on an action plan against a particular threat. Regional organisations can thus meet both the national interests of member states and a set of global interests. Regional interests are reflected in the many regional organisations that have sprung up since the end of the Second World War. The member states of ASEAN, for instance, joined together to strengthen the Southeast Asia region economically, which benefits each individual member state. An alliance like NATO seeks to protect the common interests of Europe and North America through the pledge of collective self-defence. Some neighbouring states have joined together to form regional free trade areas within which trade among participating countries is mostly unrestricted. Three cases in point are: the North American Free Trade Agreement (NAFTA), which includes Canada, the United States and Mexico (now replaced by the United States-Mexico-Canada Agreement (USMCA)); the Andean Community (CAN), whose member states are Bolivia, Venezuela, Colombia, Ecuador and Peru; and the Regional Comprehensive Economic Partnership (RCEP), which brings together all ten members of ASEAN and Australia, China, Japan, New Zealand and South Korea.

Regional interests also exist in the environmental sphere, and neighbouring states may thus work together to create a healthier environment to the benefit of all inhabitants of the region. For instance, a group of coastal states may work on ways to prevent overfishing of maritime resources that all countries within the region depend on. Indeed, there are a growing number of regional maritime treaties aimed at the conservation of threatened species and natural areas.[16] The United Nations Environment Programme (UNEP) recognises the importance of regional approaches to environmental protection. The 1976 Barcelona Convention for the Protection of the Mediterranean Sea against Pollution, a UNEP treaty, constitutes the first of a number of 'regional seas' treaties.[17]

The EU is a community of states that has created a unified economic bloc in Europe. In addition, its neighbourhood policy expresses the EU's interest in seeing good, stable governments in states bordering the EU. The EU's security strategy states: 'Neighbours who are engaged in violent conflict, weak states where organised crime flourishes, dysfunctional societies or exploding population growth on its borders all pose problems for Europe.'[18] The EU's regional security interest is thus to have a 'ring of well governed countries' along its borders and around the Mediterranean.[19] Although few states in the areas around the EU aspire to membership of it, EU policy holds that, without being embedded in a peaceful region, it will never be able to prosper in the way it would like to. Hence, the EU's regional interest is in good governance and law and order in bordering countries so that transnational threats such as human and drug trafficking can be stopped before they reach the EU.

Regional interests can also be asserted at the sub-state level. Some countries have extremely unequally developed regions, and the inhabitants of a region that suffers from economic hardship might pursue their interests for economic development with their government. Regions with important natural resources, whether they be sub-national or span several states, may have specific regional interests pertaining to their resource and its sale on the international market.

Possible conflicts between regional interests and individual, group and national interests. Individuals and groups *within* a state may find that their interests are not sufficiently met if their state aligns its national interest with the regional interest. In the case of free trade regions, some individuals or groups may find their economic security compromised. For instance, if regional economic integration allows for the free movement of labour, some individuals and professional groups may face increased competition from better-skilled workers from neighbouring states applying for the same kinds of jobs. Farmers in one state may also suffer from competition coming from within the larger regional trading zone.

Some EU member states may sometimes find their national interest for self-determination and political independence compromised by their pledge to submit to EU legislation and adjust national legislation to correspond with EU laws. Yet, EU member states continue to believe that the occasional sacrifice of smaller national interests in one area or another is a necessary evil for the larger good of reaping the economic and security benefits of belonging to the EU. In other words, submitting to the regional interest will help to fulfil the long-term national interests of increased prosperity and security, and by working closely together with the regional organisation, individual states can achieve more in terms of economic growth and enhanced regional security than they ever could on their own.

7.5 Cultural Interests

Groups of people that share a common culture have an interest in perpetuating their cultural practices among their members in an unhampered way, including their language, religion and traditional economic base – which is often a key part of their sense of identity. Usually, cultural minorities within a state have an interest in preserving their culture without state interference, while states have an interest in protecting cultural particularities that make their societies unique.

Cultural groups face a series of challenges to their way of life, unity and security. Migration, demographic pressure and competition for limited resources can pose threats to the interests of cultural groups. As cultural groups share a common identity, they are easy targets for other groups, competing for the same resources, to single out and use as scapegoats. Migration by other groups into areas with a homogeneous cultural community can sometimes be seen as a threat to the community's way of life and trigger xenophobic reactions. At the same time, cultural minorities can be exposed to the same type of xenophobia by members of the dominant culture within a state, as is the case in many countries in the world, where the dominant group may perceive the minority as a threat to national stability and become increasingly hostile.[20]

Furthermore, many cultures today feel threatened by the cultural dominance of Western, and especially US, popular culture. Countries like France and South Korea provide public funding and protection for indigenous film producers to prevent their national movie culture from being completely marginalised by American blockbusters.[21]

Basic cultural interests have even been elevated to the level of a group right. In 1966, the International Covenant on Economic, Social and Cultural Rights was added to the Universal Declaration of Human Rights, thus acknowledging the rights of cultural groups to practise their traditional ways of life.[22]

Although it is important that such groups be free to practise their culture without facing discrimination, it should not be the basis for cultural exclusivity. It is ultimately in the interest of all cultural groups that constructive cross-fertilisation and intercultural cooperation be intensified. Promoting cultural interests should not be confused with cultural isolationism. As my theory of *transcultural synergy* suggests, no cultural entity in the world can afford to go it alone.[23] The world's problems are too large and complex for them to be resolved by one cultural group by itself. Rather, each cultural group needs the ideas and knowledge of as many cultures as possible to come up with creative solutions to the world's problems.[24] Maintaining cultural diversity is in the world's interest. At the same time, fostering cross-cultural fertilisation and cooperation is equally important. Only in this way can humanity as a whole benefit from cultural diversity and thus the broad range of ideas and approaches to life taken by the world's different cultures.

Possible conflicts between cultural interests and individual, group, national and regional interests. Cultural relativism could potentially provoke a rift between individual and cultural interests. Cultural relativism posits that human values are not universal but differ according to cultural perspectives. In contrast, the notion of human rights argues that certain rights are inviolable and cannot be trumped by any group or cultural right. Hence, there can be tensions between cultural or group interests and individual interests if a cultural practice is deemed to be in violation of individual human rights. As one author has put it: 'Traditional culture is not a substitute for human rights; it is a cultural context in which human rights must be established, integrated, promoted and protected.'[25] The same is true for cultural interests versus individual interests: the cultural context should assist individuals in pursuing their interests while limiting the excesses of self-interest.

The interests of a cultural minority within a state may conflict with the national interest of the state to promote a unified, homogeneous national culture to foster national cohesion. The idea that cultural minorities speak a different language, for example, may make states fear that the minority will fail to integrate and identify with the cultural majority and will call for political independence. Repression of minority cultures within a state may in turn violate the cultural interests or even the cultural rights of the minority group.

7.6 Global Interests

Global interests refer to the common interests of the international community of states and those of the world population as a whole. States share a common interest in preserving the state system and maintaining their independence. They therefore all want to prevent as many threats to their national security and the quality of life of their citizens as possible. As I mentioned earlier, threats to the security of states today are diffuse and come from a broad variety of sources. They are often transnational in character. Chief among them are the ten civilisational frontier risks introduced in chapter two. These threats range from climate change to the uncontrolled spread of contagious diseases. It is in the shared interest of all states to contain these global risks.

To fulfil global interests, states are required to work closely together. Multilateral instruments and institutions need to be set up to confront large-scale challenges effectively. As my theory of *symbiotic realism* posits, in a transnational world, global security cannot be achieved through zero-sum games. It can only be achieved through strategies aimed at benefiting everyone – in other words, through win-win solutions.

The UN system, aimed at strengthening the global order and improving the welfare and well-being of people around the world, is the most significant global instrument set up through multilateral efforts. Through projects on health, education, environmental protection and human rights, the UN addresses a broad variety of global problems.[26] In addition to the UN framework, states have formed multilateral regimes, treaties and organisations to tackle transnational issues, including non-proliferation, the fight against international terrorism and transnational crime, human trafficking, the spread of communicable diseases and environmental pollution. Many of these multilateral measures have been joined by so many nations that they are almost universal.[27] Their universality clearly reflects the fact that solving these problems is in the global interest of the international community.

The UN's Sustainable Development Goals reflect what the international community has deemed the most pressing global issues – such as poverty, inequality and environmental pollution – that need to be addressed in order to achieve a better future for all. The seventeen goals 'recognize that ending poverty and other deprivations must go hand-in-hand with strategies that improve health and education, reduce inequality, and spur economic growth – all while tackling climate change and working to preserve our oceans and forests'.[28] Achieving these goals will help to narrow the gap between the developed and the developing world. It will help the international community establish more environmental sustainability while poor countries are raising their standards of living, and not just increase them at a huge global cost in coming years.[29] It is in the global interest that the international community succeeds in meeting these goals.

In fact, the interest of poor nations in increasing their people's standard of living will equally benefit rich nations. First, the argument is often made that desperate poverty breeds violence and criminal activity, causing a series of transnational threats that make the world less safe.[30] Second, wealthy nations will find the opening of new consumer markets and the increased purchasing power of many people around the world equally beneficial. Indeed, as one author has put it, 'Economic principles state that everyone gains from free trade because global resources are more efficiently allocated and goods will be optimally priced.'[31]

Meanwhile, the citizens of all states share the interests of peaceful and civilised states to a large extent. They want to live in a state that rests securely within its borders and that has a low crime rate, a clean and safe environment and a prospering economy. As the collective opinion of all individual human beings, the global interest also demands respect for individual human rights, dignity and freedom everywhere in the world.

Possible conflicts between global interests and individual, group, national, regional and cultural interests. Long-term individual interests are unlikely to collide with the global interest. A businessperson may have to adhere to global trading standards, and individuals in wealthy countries may have to curtail consumption and reduce their CO_2 emissions to conserve the global environment. Ultimately, however, individuals will benefit from acting in the global interest, as they will come to benefit from fair trade rules and a cleaner environment down the line.

The global interest in maintaining global stability is only served if all states obey international laws and norms and refrain from acting unilaterally. Some states may sometimes see it as being in their national interest to use force unilaterally without consulting with allies or the UN. Clearly, 'when numerous states pursue security, clashes among them are unavoidable'.[32] Yet it is important for states to recognise that pursuing national security objectives while disregarding long-term international security goals will not make them safer. On the contrary: doing so will alienate other states on whose help the state acting unilaterally might one day depend. The late international relations scholar Inis Claude concluded that 'the intelligent pursuit of national security must blend concerns for the order of the whole and safety of the part'.[33]

If one interest shared globally is a fair economic trading system that benefits all nations of the world and that allows all nations of the world to prosper, this global interest can collide with the national interests pursued by individual states. States often pursue their narrow, short-term national interest in trying to increase economic prosperity for their own countries and populations to the highest degree possible, without consideration of how other states in the international trading system will fare. Governments in the United States and EU see it in their national interest to protect their national industries – be it agriculture or the automobile industry – by imposing import quotas and high tariffs on foreign goods in these designated categories, as well as subsidising some of their industries to make them more competitive on the global market.[34] This, however, hurts other, often poorer states that want fair competition and unfettered access to US and EU markets. Although one could argue that it is in the long-term national interest of every state to participate in a free and fair global trading system, not all states today see it as being in their current national interest to abandon their protectionist policies. Wealthy states today would need to pursue a generous conception of their long-term interest to abandon all their current trade advantages.

A further case in which the national interests of states, the human-rights interests of individuals and the global interest in peace and global prosperity can clash is in the face of humanitarian crises. Often, wealthy states with the capacity to improve the humanitarian situation in many parts of the world are unwilling to sacrifice a large amount of resources for the sake of people outside their own country. The development aid that wealthy states give is insufficient to lift the least developed countries out of poverty, or at least to provide all humans in the world with safe drinking water. Similarly, states are often only willing to intervene in crisis situations when some of their own national-security interests are at stake. By contrast, in cases where states are required to make large sacrifices to intervene in a humanitarian crisis, the national interest of states often trumps a government's humanitarian impulse.

The global interest in growing interconnectedness among states and the freer movement of people and goods may collide with groups' cultural interests. In today's globalising world, many cultural groups fear the increasing homogenisation of culture and thus feel that their cultural interests are jeopardised. Conflicts of interest thus may arise between the forces of globalisation – the increased intermixing of cultures – and the loss of cultural diversity.

Regional interests may collide with global interests in certain circumstances. If a group of states within a geographic region forms a collective defensive bloc to better protect itself against outside threats, this may enhance suspicion among other states and lead to the creation of other regional defence associations. Such a development will eventually violate the global interest of preserving a global collective security system where aggressors are deterred by the rule of law, not by self-help associations.

Some have argued that regional free trade agreements (serving regional interests) conflict with the interest of global free trade agreements, particularly the WTO system. They argue that free trade agreements encourage differential treatment among a small group of nations and promote isolation within the regional group.[35] Others, however, counter that regional free trade areas serve as good preparation, and thus as a stepping stone, for countries with more or less closed economies to open up their markets to a small number of states before eventually joining the WTO system. This way, regional trade agreements can be viewed as contributing to the global interest of having a global free trade area, as they help to prepare non-members to join. There is no conclusive answer as to whether regional agreements further or impede the expansion of the WTO trading system.[36]

7.7 Planetary Interests

The interest of the planet lies in the preservation of the biosphere and biodiversity. The planet needs to be able to maintain its ecological equilibrium, which has been severely disturbed by human settlements, toxic emissions and the depletion of natural resources. The main planetary interests include reversing global warming, preventing the further destruction of the environment through deforestation and air and water pollution, and protecting all species.

This mission becomes essential given the current levels of emissions which already produced irreversible damage. According to the Intergovernmental Panel on Climate Change (IPCC), the current trend is likely to raise temperatures above 1.5°C, breaching the Paris Agreement and creating even more extreme weather events such as floods, heatwaves and fires.[37] Amidst these forecasts, scientists are trying to raise the alarm that policy makers of this generation will be the last ones with the capacity to implement substantial actions to reverse or rather mitigate this devastating process.

Deforestation can cause major disruption to ecosystems. Forests play a key role in supplying the atmosphere with new oxygen and are thus one of the keys to maintaining the stability of the atmosphere, on which all life on Earth depends.[38] Forests also play a crucial role in maintaining the supply of fresh water. Forest soil can act as a natural water reservoir that is able to provide steady water supply to rivers.[39] By absorbing and storing large amounts of water, forests in hilly areas prevent the risk of flooding and ensure continued water supply during dry seasons.[40] Finally, forests provide a habitat for a large number of plant and animal species. The maintenance of biodiversity is a crucial planetary interest, as the extinction of one animal species can cause serious imbalances for the rest of its ecosystem. The extinction of a large number of birds, for example, can lead to the rapid growth of insect populations, which in turn can have devastating effects on plants, and thus also on animals depending on the nutrition coming from those plants. The extinction of insects at an alarming rate could, however, also severely damage ecosystems, as birds and other animals rely on insects for their own survival, and insects play a critical role in the fertilisation of plants.[41]

Through biodiversity, ecosystems maintain a wide variety of nutrients in the form of plants, insects and animals, which helps every living organism, including humans, to meet their nutritional needs. Many chemicals found to have a healing effect and contained in human medicines are found in plants, animals and micro-organisms.[42]

The environment and natural resources are therefore, as I have written elsewhere, 'reactive actors' and a 'non-conscious form of agency'. They are relevant as part of today's interactive global system in the sense that they are 'reacting to human activities in such a way as to call into question current levels of civilization and to transform aspects of the global system, for example, through climate change'.[43]

One can look at biodiversity from two different perspectives and thus use two different arguments as to why biodiversity needs to be maintained. The first looks at biodiversity as a value in itself and not in relation to its use for human beings. Those who believe in the intrinsic value of biodiversity argue for the protection of all species, regardless of their function.[44]

The second perspective takes a utilitarian approach by stating that biodiversity needs to be maintained because humankind depends on it. This argument tends to stress the economic, aesthetic and recreational value of biodiversity.[45] As a consequence, people who defend this point of view prioritise the protection of those species that are of particular value to humans. My concept of planetary interest uses the former approach. Humans are a part of the planet, as is every other species. Just as reconciliation statecraft looks at the different interests of all human entities, so it also must consider the interest of the planet on which all life depends.

Possible conflicts between planetary interests and individual, group, national, regional, cultural and global interests. There should be no actual conflicts between the interests of the planet and those of individuals and states. In the long term, human life as we know it will not be able to thrive without a healthy planet. In the short term, however, there are fierce clashes of interests. For instance, wealthy states are taking great pains to reduce their greenhouse-gas emissions and lead a less-polluting lifestyle. Developing states that have made rapid economic development a key national priority will pursue economic growth without much consideration for the natural environment. Many individuals, whether poor or wealthy, are unwilling to compromise their lifestyles to help conserve the environment. Yet they may all agree, in theory, that doing so would be desirable.

Certain cultural practices may also go against planetary interests. The hunting of endangered species, such as certain types of whales and seals, are cases in point. For the Makah Indians of northern California, for instance, the hunting of grey whales is a 2,000-year-old tradition. The Makah, for whom the whale hunt is of important cultural significance, continue to find themselves in battles with environmental groups and US legislation that prohibits the slaughter of whales in US waters without a permit.[46]

Similarly, the Inuit in northern Canada consider the annual seal hunt an important way to maintain their culture and local economy. The cruel practice of clubbing seals has been fiercely opposed by animal-rights activists around the world. Opponents of the seal hunt further argue that the population size of seals is not large enough to sustain a healthy gene pool. Meanwhile, the World Wildlife Fund (WWF) has changed its adversarial stance towards the seal hunt. In 2006 the organisation stated in a letter: 'WWF recognizes that the hunting of the harp seal (*Phocagroenlandica*) is part of the local economy, culture and traditional heritage in many coastal communities in Atlantic Canada and other parts of the world,'[47] and that this can be achieved in a sustainable manner.[48] The organisation reached this conclusion on the basis that the cultural interest of the Inuit can be made compatible with the 'WWF's mission ... to stop the degradation of the planet's natural environment and to build a future in which people live in harmony with nature'.[49] By working together with the Inuit to ensure 'sustainable resource management, species and habitat protection, as well as ecological restoration',[50] the WWF believes that planetary interests and cultural interests can be reconciled.

7.8 Moral Interests

There are a set of universal moral principles that all cultures of the world agree on. As discussed earlier, these are thin, or minimalist, moral principles. Some of them have been enshrined in international law, especially international humanitarian law. In particular, it is in the moral interest of humankind that innocent civilians everywhere be protected from being targeted during armed conflict; that everyone has a right to a basic standard of living; and that the environment be protected so that future generations can live a healthy life on the planet.

Humans are not naturally governed by morality, but by emotional self-interest. Humans are 'amoral' but have moral sensitivities. It is the role of society and the global system to encourage humans to act morally. The way to make them more moral is: (1) to package moral acts in self-interest paradigms; and (2) to set societal and global norms of conduct that are more moral through incentives, laws, education, the broadcast and newspaper media and the entertainment industry.[51]

Morality requires that humans also consider the well-being of others. It sometimes requires that humans sacrifice their own interests for the sake of being good. However, humans are highly unlikely to let their moral compasses guide their behaviour if their basic needs are not met, if they do not feel that they are part of a community or if their life is in immediate danger.[52] Hence, an important moral interest is to make sure the ground rules for moral behaviour are guaranteed. The higher the stakes, the less individuals, groups and states will behave in a moral way.

If individuals are uprooted and lack jobs and money, moral principles are likely to take second place in their struggle for survival. Groups within a state that are persecuted and denied the right to maintain their cultures may be tempted to resort to violence to fight for their group rights. A state that faces imminent military defeat is likewise prone to disregard international laws of warfare when fighting for the state's survival.

It is in the interest of universal morality that all entities, from individuals to coalitions of states, observe universal moral principles in all their actions. To enable and facilitate moral behaviour among all international actors, conditions need to be created in which no individual or state faces threats to their existence or well-being. Moral interests stress our common humanity above all else. Failure to help people who are suffering compromises our common humanity – no matter where in the world the suffering occurs.

Possible conflicts between moral interests and individual, group, national, regional, cultural, global and planetary interests. The interests of individuals, groups and nations may sometimes collide when interests of self-preservation drive their actions During the Second World War, for instance, the British Air Force, chose to carpet-bomb German cities, such as Dresden thus deliberately targeting civilians, partly in retaliation to German bombing of British cities and in order to terrorise the German population thereby pressuring Germany to surrender.[53] This was also a means to showcase the power of the British Air Force to the Soviets who were advancing on the other side, not to aid them on the Eastern front.[54] In this case, the need for self-preservation and power projection of Britain trumped the universal moral interest of upholding non-combatant immunity.

Similarly, conflicting moralities can sometimes exist among different interest entities. A statesman has a moral obligation towards his citizens to protect their country and promote their well-being. It is possible for statesmen and women to find themselves between two conflicting moralities: moral obligations towards their state's citizens and towards the rest of humankind. For instance, should a statesman be required to spend taxpayers' money for humanitarian assistance abroad when some of his or her citizens are going hungry or cannot afford medical treatment at home?

Extending the notion of human solidarity beyond our immediate kin group or nation to all humans makes the moral principle thinner and more diffuse. As one author has put it, 'Rather than being locked into forms of membership that tend to be narrow and exclusive, modern solidarity seeks the broadest inclusion possible.'[55] This can cause new moral dilemmas. For instance, a state that has the capacity to prevent starvation in one country but not in two will have to make the difficult moral choice of which of the two countries is to benefit from the country's aid. The universal principle that all people deserve one's help equally cannot always be applied in practice. Choices have to be made; priorities have to be set.

Ironically, then, when tasked with making moral decisions as to who is to benefit from one's limited capacity to help, group interests may again become relevant. Indeed, the more universal values require us to project our solidarity to all humans in the world, the more 'the ability to relate to people becomes ... abstract and fragile'.[56] Hence, 'traditional bonds of proximity', which may be based on kinship ties, common ethnicity or shared nationality, may gain renewed importance.[57] The COVID-19 pandemic triggered similar reflexes, notably in sharing vaccine doses or protective equipment, and, while many states supported others, short-term national interests prevailed over other considerations.[58] People will probably never be able to identify to the same extent with the plight of strangers, nor feel the same kind of connections with people with whom they have little in common, than they do with members of their immediate community or country. The self-interest of individuals and nation-states will also frequently prevent people from always serving the moral interest of humanity as a whole. These dilemmas, however, can be partially resolved by dividing moral values and obligations into those that are 'thick' and those that are 'thin'. People have thin moral obligations towards all other human beings, as mentioned earlier. The closer our ties, the thicker our moral obligations towards fellow human beings become. I may sell my house to pay for the cancer treatment of a relative, but not for the treatment of another member of society. I may volunteer my time to help earthquake victims in my own country but not in a neighbouring state. As one study asserts, 'Surely, when hard choices have to be made, what is owed to the national realm tends to prevail over what is owed to the international realm.'[59]

As national borders become increasingly blurred and the world becomes more interconnected, the national interest is converging more and more with that of the international community. So, while there will remain moral tensions between the notion of universal solidarity and the solidarity we feel towards our closest kin group and fellow citizens, the minimum of fulfilling the basic, or thin, moral interests of humanity as a whole can and should nevertheless be achieved. Meanwhile, global interests are unlikely to clash too much with moral interests. After all, moral values such as peace and human dignity are also in the interests of the citizens of the world as a whole and of those of the majority of states.

Finally, moral values have traditionally been applied to relationships between humans only. It is becoming increasingly understood that environmental protection is a moral duty as well, as it goes hand-in-hand with the moral duty we have towards future generations of human beings. Still, there can be conflicts. What if a rescue operation to save the lives of a group of people requires the cutting down of a forest in an area with a delicate ecosystem?

Furthermore, we all have a moral duty to make sure the global population is properly fed. Ensuring everyone's right to basic subsistence and to be free from hunger is a universal moral interest. However, overfishing is depleting fish stocks in the world's oceans, and growing crops and increasing the size of pastures for cattle requires cutting down additional forests and is destroying animal habitats. The use of fertilisers to improve crop yields is polluting groundwater and rivers. Genetically modified crops may pose an environmental hazard to nearby plants and animals. Balancing the moral obligations we hold towards fellow human beings that live in the world today with our moral obligation towards future generations, as well as the natural environment, remains a key task for statesmen and women today.

7.9 The Need to Reconcile the Eight Interests

Different theories of international relations have focused on different sets of interests as the determining factors in international dynamics. Some theorists place geography and the state system at the centre of their study of international relations, while others instead emphasise class struggles or the needs of individual human beings as the determining units in shaping global history.[60]

National and regional interests are geographically circumscribed. Both are related to geopolitics. First and foremost, national and regional interests are concerned with how to best secure their relevant geographic entity – a single country or a group of countries – and how to project their power abroad. Some authors thus suggest that the notion of national interest is related to a 'geopolitical understanding of international relations'.[61] Nevertheless, focusing exclusively on geographic features is insufficient in today's world, as Jean-Marc Coicaud and Nicolas J. Wheeler rightly conclude:

> While the geographic anchoring remains significant, it has been balanced in recent times by the changes brought about by the deterritorialization of politics at the national

and international level – a deterritorialization that includes normative factors such as identification with human-rights imperatives, the influence that it has on individual and collective interests and values and their interaction, as well as on policies at home and abroad.[62]

The importance of national interests is stressed above anything else in realism, which is international relations theory's dominant frame of reference. Realist political theory considers the national interest of states to be the only interest that impacts international relations among states, and thus considers it the driving force of international politics. For realists, states are the main actors in international relations. As the primary interest of states is to ensure their own survival and well-being, the national interest of other states and any other of the eight interests identified above are secondary.[63]

Viewing international relations primarily in terms of competing national interests leads states to conclude that the world is a hostile place and that looking after one's own interest and focusing on self-defence is the only way to ensure long-term survival. In the eyes of a realist, so-called global interests are not neutral; rather, they are defined and shaped by the most powerful states of the world to benefit their own national interest.[64]

Liberal political theory, which has challenged the realist paradigm for decades, emphasises global interests (i.e. common interests of the international community) and the interests of individuals (mainly through the notion of human rights) in addition to national interests. Liberalism has always stressed the importance of international cooperation to improve the well-being and security of all states and their inhabitants.[65] Furthermore, liberalism has moved away from the state-centred view of international relations and considers the impact of non-state actors on international dynamics. Liberal theorists would study, for instance, the role of domestic interest groups or transnational networks in shaping a country's foreign policy (and thus their indirect impact on international relations). Liberals have also acknowledged the interdependence of states and the fact that states have more interests in common than realists are ready to admit.[66]

The radical-left tradition of international relations theory has sought to break away entirely from the state-centred view of international relations. Followers of this tradition picked up on Immanuel Kant's notion that the primary units of international relations are individual human beings. Kant believed that, although individuals are part of smaller state units, their primary allegiance is to the community of humankind.[67] Marxist scholars in particular have stressed that class solidarity among humans is stronger than allegiance to nation-states.[68] Expressed in the language of interests, for Marxists, it is the group interests of social classes and not the national interests of states that transform international relations and move history forward.

Historical experience, however, has shown that neither class interests, national interests nor global interests can be singled out as the determining driving force of international relations. In fact, today's key challenges – such as climate change – simultaneously pose major threats to national, global, individual and environmental interests. In other words, all eight interests identified above are important. While they may be linked and do not naturally compete with one another, some conflicts of interest can arise from time to time. The important task of statecraft in the twenty-first century is to reconcile these interests. The concept of reconciliation statecraft maintains that peace and human progress in the twenty-first century depend on the ability of the international community of states to reconcile all eight interests. Violating only one of the eight interests will lead to insecurity and discord in other spheres of interest. For instance, violating individual human rights will generate popular dissatisfaction and create national instability, thus conflicting with the national interest of the state to have domestic peace and order. Polluting the environment will violate not just planetary interests but also the interests of states and the international community as a whole.

The five new concepts introduced in the preceding chapters are important tools to achieve the reconciliation of all eight interests. *Meta-geopolitics* provides us with an important analysis method that can reveal potential clashes of interest as well as ways to resolve them. Dignity-based governance is the main tool for reconciling diverse interests at the individual, group, cultural and national levels. *Symbiotic realism* contributes to achieving absolute gains that accommodate the various interests of different states. It is based on the idea that international relations today can no longer be a zero-sum game. Interests do not exclude one another. The theory of *symbiotic realism* states that 'synergy should be the guiding principle in the search for better ways to manage culturally pluralistic societies and relations between civilisations'.[69] The benefit of *transcultural synergy* is that states and cultural groups are able to achieve more than they could on their own.

Likewise, the *multi-sum security principle* acknowledges that, in today's interdependent world, no actor or entity can pursue long-term security without helping to further the security and well-being of everyone else. Otherwise, the pursuit of security will be unsustainable. It provides statesmen and women with a comprehensive security concept that acknowledges the interdependence of five security dimensions: human, environmental, national, transnational and transcultural.[70] The multi-sum security principle contributes to *sustainable* national security.[71] This means that the national security structure needs to be significantly broader than those that exist in different states today. Indeed, it needs to deal with a broad range of security issues, as well as with long-term threat prevention and the maintenance of ethical standards in the conduct of security policy.

The new national security doctrine developed in this book thus elaborates on how the national interest can be pursued in a sustainable way in a transnational world by including ensuring that national, environmental, global and ethical interests are included in the formation of national security policy. As I have written elsewhere, 'sustainable peace and security can only be achieved if states focus on the multi-dimensionality of today's security environment, form mutually beneficial security relationships with other states in every security dimension, and enrich their own culture and boost human creativity through fruitful exchanges and interactions with other cultures and civilizations'.[72] Finally, just power, with its emphasis on fairness, equality and impartiality, is an important tool for reconciling different interests.

Reconciliation statecraft is the best way of promoting peace and justice for all humans in a transnational world. The principle of *awareness*, which I have elaborated elsewhere, is also crucial in this context.[73] Awareness refers to knowledge of other people's culture, history and mores. With such awareness, misunderstandings, fear and exclusion will be minimised both within states and among nations.[74] Education and media programmes that aim at fostering intercultural understanding are a key ingredient for reconciling cultural and national interests.

Another key principle is *empowerment*. I have argued that, in the context of globalisation, where local communities often feel powerless *vis-à-vis* global economic forces and cultural homogenisation, it is important for local communities to reclaim control over their lives. This is particularly important in the context of development and capacity building aimed at eliminating poverty and improving health. Looking after the group interest of local communities to gain control over their lives and individual interests of securing basic human needs will also meet global interests of reducing transnational security threats resulting from human desperation, diseases and violent backlashes against symbols of globalisation.[75]

States that enter into peaceful multilateral agreements and obey international law will not only act in their own interest but will also contribute to the global interest of promoting international peace and stability. Only through multilateral cooperation can transnational threats be tackled effectively and obeying international law will generate mutual trust and predictability among states.

Interestingly, national interests can change if the adoption of new values by members of a state leads to a changing national identity.[76] A case in point is the belief in human rights, which is a founding pillar of Western democracies. The belief in human rights has become so strongly entrenched in the national identities of Western democracies that promoting the value of human rights has become part of the foreign policies of these states even if they often fail to meet their own high moral standards. If, therefore, the belief in human rights is part of a state's national identity, standing up for human rights in international politics will fulfil the national interest of the state along with individual, global and moral interests. Kathryn Sikkink describes this eloquently:

> The emergence of human rights policy is not a simple victory for ideas over interest. Instead, it demonstrates the power of ideas to reshape understandings of national interest. The recent adoption of human rights policies did not represent the neglect of national interests but rather a fundamental shift in the perception of long-term national interests. Human rights policies emerged because policy makers began to question the principled idea that the internal human rights practices of a country are not a legitimate topic of foreign policy and the causal assumption that national interests are furthered by supporting regimes that violate the human rights of their citizens.[77]

In sum, it is only through synergy and cooperation that we can find creative and effective solutions to solve the twenty-first century's complex challenges. This idea is encapsulated in the five tools of effective statecraft that I have proposed in this book. It is in the interest of all entities that the broad variety of threats and problems affecting individuals, groups and states, ranging from diseases to environmental pollution, be solved. Meanwhile, synergies among the world's cultures are happening all the time as a result of globalisation, instant communication and increased human mobility. Through fostering these synergies, reconciliation statecraft can contribute to the creation

Figure 7.1 Reconciliation Statecraft

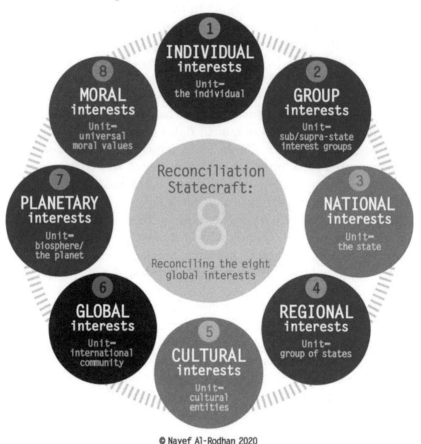

© Nayef Al-Rodhan 2020

of a global cultural superstructure based on common human values. Statecraft that not only pursues the security and well-being of the state but that is equally guided by universal human values and the long-term global interest for peace and environmental sustainability will succeed at reconciling the eight global interests. To summarise this chapter, Figure 7.1 illustrates the eight global interests.

8

Case Studies

Geopolitical Realities and Dilemmas of Twenty-seven Selected States

What follows is a series of twenty-seven case studies that are used to evaluate the geopolitical realities of states according to the seven capacities described in chapter four: (1) social and health issues; (2) domestic politics; (3) economics; (4) environment; (5) science and human potential; (6) military and security issues; and (7) international diplomacy. Many of the twenty-six states and the one community of states (the EU) chosen are major players in international relations or, at the very least, influential in the geopolitics of their region. The aim of this chapter is to identify some of the key dilemmas that characterise the twenty-first-century globalised world we live in today. The countries are ordered alphabetically and represent all areas of the globe, including North, Central and South America, northern and sub-Saharan Africa, Europe, Central Asia, East Asia and Oceania. Since some states face more challenges than others, or may be more involved in foreign affairs, the case studies will not be all equally complex or lengthy. In each case study the table describes the current status of each state and lists its strengths and weaknesses, pinpointing areas of improvement as well as state capacities in which it is leading the way and setting a positive example for others.

1. Australia
2. Brazil
3. China
4. Egypt

5. European Union
6. France
7. Germany
8. India
9. Indonesia
10. Iran
11. Israel
12. Japan
13. Kazakhstan
14. Lithuania
15. Mexico
16. Nigeria

17. Pakistan
18. Russia
19. Saudi Arabia
20. South Africa
21. South Korea
22. Sweden
23. Switzerland
24. Turkey
25. Ukraine
26. United Kingdom
27. United States

Case Study 1A: Australia

Issue Area	Geopolitical Realities and Dilemmas
1. Social and Health Issues	• Growing population • Large ethnic and racial diversity[1] • Persistence of racial discrimination towards Indigenous Australians, including Aboriginal Australians and Torres Straits Islanders[2] • Excellent public-private hybrid health-care system[3]
2. Domestic Politics	• Regarded as having one of the least asylum-seeker-friendly systems in the world, which includes forms of indefinite offshore detention[4]
3. Economics	• One of the world's strongest and most stable economies, with trade agreements particularly with ASEAN countries. However, it is vulnerable to tariffs imposed by China due to their political disagreements • Involved in multiple free trade agreements, including the RCEP[5] • Its complete border shutdown for over a year to prevent the spread of COVID-19 has dramatically reduced the influx of migrants who are a key part of the Australian workforce
4. Environment	• Large emitter of greenhouse gases and producer of fossil fuels[6] • Recurring and devastating bushfires • Increasing loss of biodiversity[7]
5. Science and Human Potential	• Lags behind other developed countries in R&D[8] • Has some of the world's leading universities[9]
6. Military and Security Issues	• Small but highly technologically equipped military with a large budget[10] • Creation of a new space force[11] • Involved in the South China Sea disputes
7. International Diplomacy	• Increasing diplomatic, economic and military tensions with China[12] • Member of Five Eyes[13]

Case Study 2A: Brazil

Issue Area	Geopolitical Realities and Dilemmas
1. Social and Health Issues	• High levels of inequality and social exclusion, particularly towards indigenous peoples[14] • Universal public health care[15] • Highly successful at containing spread of HIV/AIDS • Persistent spread of malaria and dengue, recurring waves of the Zika virus following the major outbreak in 2015–16[16]
2. Domestic Politics	• Corruption issues[17] • Progress has been made towards strengthening the rule of law
3. Economics	• Dominant agricultural and commodity-based sectors; diversified export commodities[18] • Growth in medium-sized and high-tech firms • High debt, high government spending[19] • Largest oil producer in the region[20]
4. Environment	• Sixth-largest emitter of greenhouse gas emissions and notable absentee of the Escazú Climate Agreement[21] • Rapid deforestation of the Amazon rainforest[22] • Creation of Madeira dams has had a negative impact on people and wildlife[23]
5. Science and Human Potential	• Low-quality primary education; low enrolment rates in secondary education and colleges and high numbers of dropouts • Over the past decade, progress has been made towards improving the quality of Brazilian universities and to making them more accessible[24] • Low levels of R&D investment by the public sector but high levels by the private sector[25] • Leading role in deep-water oil exploration, manufacturing of regional jet aircraft and production of sugar-cane-based ethanol[26] • Controls the full nuclear fuel cycle
6. Military and Security Issues	• High crime rate in major cities, often related to drugs gangs[27] • No disputes with neighbouring states
7. International Diplomacy	• Points of disagreement regarding nuclear programme[28] • Leading power in the Americas, role in collective security efforts[29]

Case Study 3A: China

Issue Area	Geopolitical Realities and Dilemmas
1. Social and Health Issues	• Population of nearly 1.4 billion, growing by 0.5 per cent per year[30] • Due to the one-child policy in place until January 2016 (now three children allowed) the country may face a youth demographic problem • Skewed sex ratio in favour of boys[31] • 150–200 million internal migrants per year, mostly rural-urban migration[32] • Discrimination against rural migrants in cities and growing urban-rural resentments[33] • Inadequate health care in rural areas[34] • Respiratory and heart diseases caused by air pollution, a leading cause of death[35] • Rise in mental-health problems over the past few decades • Decrease from one of the highest suicide rates to one of the lowest[36]
2. Domestic Politics	• Centralised, single-party socialist political system that aims at 'building socialism with Chinese characteristics'[37] • Localised protests by workers and farmers[38] • Some corruption[39] • Some human-rights concerns[40] • Allegations of discrimination towards ethnic-minority groups such as the Muslim Uighurs and Tibetan Buddhists[41] • Chinese government policy of economic liberalisation before political liberalisation to maintain social peace and internal stability
3. Economics	• World's second-largest economy; steady annual growth rate of more than six per cent[42] • WTO member since 2001 • Influx of rural workers into cities has boosted construction and manufacturing industries[43] • Large income gap between urban and rural residents (2.11:1 in 2011)[44]
4. Environment	• World's largest emitter of greenhouse gases • Massive air pollution largely due to coal-burning energy plants[45] • Severe water pollution[46] • Water scarcity in the north, soil erosion and desertification[47]
5. Science and Human Potential	• Strong government support for scientific and technological development, especially biotechnology and computer technology[48] • Active and impressive space programme[49]

6. Military and Security Issues	• Main national-security concern is the preservation of social order and internal stability • Very long land border to defend; boundary disputes with neighbours, including sovereignty disputes over the South China Sea[50] • Regional threats posed by North Korea; tensions with Taiwan[51] • Energy security concerns, especially US domination of the Strait of Malacca[52] • Heavy investments in arms build-up and high-tech weaponry
7. International Diplomacy	• Strong relations with natural-resource-rich states • Supports regional security mechanisms for consultation and confidence building[53]

Case Study 4A: Egypt

Issue Area	Geopolitical Realities and Dilemmas
1. Social and Health Issues	• Most populous country in Arab world, densely populated along the Nile[54] • Highly homogeneous, with a 5,000-year history as a unified state[55] • Poverty, especially in rural areas[56] • Widely accessible health-care services, good control over communicable diseases[57] • High maternal and infant mortality rates[58]
2. Domestic Politics	• Recovering steadily from the Arab Spring chaos[59] • Human rights concerns
3. Economics	• Second-largest economy in Africa[60] • Significant economic growth between the 1970s and 2011, but devaluation following the political crisis[61] • Decrease in trade deficit • Reliance on tourism, remittances, oil and revenues from Suez Canal
4. Environment	• Natural disasters, including droughts, earthquakes, flash floods • Environmental hazards, including air and water pollution, oil pollution, soil salination and desertification[62] • Putting strain on Egypt's only significant water source, the River Nile[63]
5. Science and Human Potential	• Low adult literacy rate[64] • Increasing investment in R&D[65]
6. Military and Security Issues	• Low crime rate[66] • Violent extremism and terrorism due to the Muslim Brotherhood[67] • Challenges from instability in Libya due to Turkey's introduction of violent non-state actors[68]
7. International Diplomacy	• First Arab country to make peace with Israel; remains important player in Israeli-Palestinian dispute[69] • Leading role in Arab affairs; Cairo is headquarters of the Arab League[70] • East Mediterranean tensions with Turkey[71] • Tensions with Ethiopia over the Grand Ethiopian Renaissance Dam[72]

Case Study 5A: European Union

Issue Area	Geopolitical Realities and Dilemmas
1. Social and Health Issues	• Ageing population • New social divisions due to rising hostility towards immigrants • Rising health-care costs[73]
2. Domestic Politics	• No ratified constitution[74] • Lack of overarching political authority • Democratic deficit[75] • Rise of populism in member states jeopardises integration[76]
3. Economics	• One of the major economic areas in the world • Slow economic growth • Unemployment[77]
4. Environment	• Air pollution especially through ozone and particulate matter[78] • Major emitter of greenhouse gases • Net-zero target by 2050[79]
5. Science and Human Potential	• Highly skilled labour force[80] • A world leader in science and technology, including a space programme • Relatively low investment in R&D (EU average 2.19 per cent of GDP)[81]
6. Military and Security Issues	• Agent for peace in Europe • Security strategy stresses new, non-conventional security threats • Highest priorities on security agenda are terrorism and cyber crime[82]
7. International Diplomacy	• Remarkable soft-power capabilities[83] • Weak international presence and foreign policy • Economic weight does not translate into political weight[84] • Promotes the strengthening of global institutions and international law[85] • Potential challenges of Brexit[86] • Fluctuating EU-Transatlantic relations[87] • Need and fear of Russia[88] • Confused role in balancing US-Russia tensions[89]

Case Study 6A: France

Issue Area	Geopolitical Realities and Dilemmas
1. Social and Health Issues	• Highest birth rate in the EU[90] • Excellent health care[91] • Large numbers of immigrants[92] • Challenges in the integration of immigrant communities, particularly Islamic ones[93] • Significant discrimination against immigrants • Secular extremisms a challenge to civil liberties • Need to decolonise its history, and come to terms with its brutalities, particularly in North Africa[94]
2. Domestic Politics	• Rising nationalism[95]
3. Economics	• Member of the G7 and seventh-largest economy in the world by nominal GDP[96] • Largest foreign direct investment recipient in Europe[97] • Fifth-largest trading nation in the world • Leading agricultural power in the EU[98]
4. Environment	• Heavily dependent on nuclear power[99] • Smallest emitter of carbon dioxide in the G7 • Scarce investment in renewable energy • Considered to be one of the most environmentally conscious countries in the world[100]
5. Science and Human Potential	• Elitist education system[101] • Europe's second-largest spender in R&D[102] • One of the most innovative countries in the world[103] • Biggest contributor to the European Space Agency[104] • One of the world leaders in nuclear technology[105]
6. Military and Security Issues	• Fifth biggest military spender in the world[106] • Nuclear arsenal[107] • Major arms seller[108] • One of the world leaders in cybersecurity[109] • Terrorism major security issue[110]
7. International Diplomacy	• Member of the UNSC Permanent 5 • Leading force in the EU[111] • Large aid development donor[112] • Significant influence over its former African colonies[113]

Case Study 7A: Germany

Issue Area	Geopolitical Realities and Dilemmas
1. Social and Health Issues	• Most populous country in the EU and second most populous in Europe[114] • Very low birth rate[115] • Excellent universal health care[116] • Obesity issues[117] • Large immigrant population[118]
2. Domestic Politics	• Rising populist rhetoric[119]
3. Economics	• Largest economy in Europe and fourth-largest in the world by nominal GDP (US$3.86 trillion in 2019) • World's third-largest exporter and third-largest importer of goods[120] • Strong automotive industry[121]
4. Environment	• Phasing out nuclear energy • 40 per cent of energy produced through renewable sources[122] • Focus on the Paris Agreement[123]
5. Science and Human Potential	• Good quality education overall, but facing inequalities within the system on the basis of social class and economic background[124] • One of the most innovative countries in the world[125] • Major contributor to the European Space Agency[126]
6. Military and Security Issues	• Eighth highest military expenditure in the world • Only 1.2 per cent of GDP is spent on its military, below the NATO target of two per cent[127] • Army has an exclusively defensive nature, but interpreted in a broad sense to include foreign threat • Contributes to peacekeeping missions[128]
7. International Diplomacy	• Strong leadership role within the EU[129] • Strong alliance with the US[130] • Second-biggest aid donor in the world[131] • Member of the G7 but not of the Permanent 5 in the UNSC • Gas relations with Russia leading to tensions with the US[132]

Case Study 8A: India

Issue Area	Geopolitical Realities and Dilemmas
1. Social and Health Issues	• Large population (1.13 billion); 1.6 per cent population growth per year[133] • Has taken great strides in containing many infectious diseases, but malaria and tuberculosis are still prevalent[134] • Increased frequency of diabetes, heart disease and cancers[135] • Decreasing maternal and child mortality rate[136] • Underfunded health infrastructure, especially in poor states[137] • Significant and unchanging social divisions along religious and caste lines[138] • Discrimination towards the Dalit (untouchables) and the Muslim community[139]
2. Domestic Politics	• Parliamentary democratic system – in place since 1947 – enjoys widespread popular legitimacy; not reconcilable with large and deep societal discrimination practices[140] • Hindu-nationalist Bharatiya Janata Party (BJP), led by Prime Minister Narendra Modi, has been in power since 2014[141]
3. Economics	• GDP of 2.87 trillion in 2019 with an unsteady growth rate[142] • Ongoing economic liberalisation reforms • Growing services sector spurred by IT industry[143] • Growing, highly skilled urban middle class[144] • Poverty on the decline, but six per cent of the population still living in extreme poverty[145] • Large informal sector (the informal economy in India still accounts for more than 80 per cent of non-agricultural employment)[146] • Rigid labour-market regulations and regulatory controls impede formal-sector growth • Large investment in infrastructure in an attempt to boost the economy[147]
4. Environment	• Soil erosion and deforestation • Severe air and water pollution through chemical and industrial waste[148] • Environmental regulations and institutions in place but need to become more effective[149] • Growing water shortages due to pollution and extensive overuse of groundwater[150]
5. Science and Human Potential	• Illiteracy rate of circa 25.5 per cent – but quotas for disadvantaged groups in higher education[151] • Growing, well-educated middle class • Competitive IT and high-tech sectors, including aerospace technology[152]

6. Military and Security Issues	• Second-largest military force in the world, including nuclear capability[153] • Internal security threats posed by separatist groups and extremists • Weak neighbouring states provide safe havens for human-trafficking networks • Unresolved border dispute over Jammu and Kashmir with Pakistan[154]
7. International Diplomacy	• Strategic partnership with Russia, India's major weapons supplier[155] • Strongly interested in multilateral cooperation and in affirming a leadership role within a multipolar framework • Strong economic relations but tensions with China over borders[156] • Aspires to a permanent seat on the UN Security Council

Case Study 9A: Indonesia

Issue Area	Geopolitical Realities and Dilemmas
1. Social and Health Issues	• The world's fourth-largest population, the largest Muslim population in the world[157] • Culturally and ethnically highly diverse[158] • Shortages in medical personnel, especially in less developed, rural areas[159] • Significant rate of HIV/AIDS infection; another common communicable disease is dengue fever[160]
2. Domestic Politics	• Successful, though imperfect, transition to democracy after President Suharto was deposed in 1998[161] • Human rights discrepancies[162]
3. Economics	• The only G20 member from Southeast Asia[163] • Large investment in infrastructure[164] • World's leading exporter of liquefied natural gas and considerable oil producer[165] • Positive balance of trade
4. Environment	• Seventeen thousand islands; high level of biodiversity[166] • Flooding, earthquakes and volcanic eruptions • Deforestation, air and water pollution[167]
5. Science and Human Potential	• Adult literacy rate at around 95.6 per cent[168] • Unequal quality of education across regions • Skills mismatch problem[169]
6. Military and Security Issues	• Instability in Aceh and Papua[170] • No conventional external threat to its territorial integrity
7. International Diplomacy	• Leading member of ASEAN and non-aligned movement[171] • Islamic solidarity a major value in foreign policy[172]

Case Study 10A: Iran

Issue Area	Geopolitical Realities and Dilemmas
1. Social and Health Issues	• High percentage of young people[173] • Good, low-cost public health care[174] • Serious drug-addiction problem[175] • Poor infrastructure and social security[176]
2. Domestic Politics	• Shiite theocracy led by the Supreme Leader Ali Khamenei • Hard-line conservatives won the 2021 elections[177] • Human rights and civil liberties issues, especially in non-Persian regions[178]
3. Economics	• Economy hurt by embargoes on trade and financial sanctions[179] • Fluctuating unemployment rates[180] • Stagnating agricultural sector, uncompetitive industrial sector[181] • State revenues dependent on oil • High inflation (estimated at 39.9 per cent in 2019)[182]
4. Environment	• Water shortages; desertification and deforestation[183] • Poor air quality in urban centres • Pollution of the Gulf and Caspian Sea due to oil and chemical spills[184] • Frequent deadly earthquakes[185] • One of the only countries in the region not to have ratified the Paris Agreement[186]
5. Science and Human Potential	• Well-educated, large young labour force; insufficient number of jobs to make use of the country's human potential[187] • Increased funding in R&D since 2012, when it was only 0.3 per cent of GDP, to 0.8 per cent in 2017[188]
6. Military and Security Issues	• Long, porous border[189] • Ethnic minorities and insurgent groups, resenting poverty, unemployment and government repression, are prone to launch local uprisings[190] • Weak military capabilities[191] • Considers the United States its main enemy[192] • Major founder and funder of disruptive and violent militias in the region (Iraq, Syria, Lebanon, Yemen)[193] • Declared policy of destabilising regional politics[194] • Remains a 'revolution' not a 'state'[195] • Securitisation and militarisation of religions/sectarianism[196] • Maritime insecurity in the Gulf

| 7. International Diplomacy | <ul><li>Foreign policy influenced by ideological commitment to spread its fundamentalist sectarian revolution to other Muslim states[197]</li><li>Inability to establish trust and sustainable good relations and to refrain from interfering in neighbouring countries</li><li>Pragmatic foreign policy towards East and South Asian countries (pursuit of economic and strategic objectives)[198]</li><li>No diplomatic or commercial relations with the United States since 1979 revolution and hostage crisis; conflicts with United States over Iran's nuclear programme[199]</li><li>Concerns about the military nature of the nuclear programme</li><li>Close commercial relations with Russia[200]</li><li>Recent long-term deal with China</li><li>Continued occupation of three Emirati islands[201]</li></ul> |

Case Study 11A: Israel

Issue Area	Geopolitical Realities and Dilemmas
1. Social and Health Issues	• 9.32 million inhabitants in 2021, 73.9 per cent of them Jewish[202] • Large minority of Arab-Israelis facing significant forms of exclusion and discrimination[203] • Discrimination against African, Sephardi and Mizrahi Jewish minorities[204]
2. Domestic Politics	• Fragmented political system dependent on diverse coalitions to form governments[205] • Lack of proportionality in dealing with provocation to instil fear and subjugate the Palestinian population[206] • Persistent de-humanisation of the Palestinian population
3. Economics	• Diversified, technologically advanced economy with strong high-tech sector[207] • Economic well-being dependent on the state of the peace process and of the global economy[208] • Highest defence spending per capita in the world[209]
4. Environment	• Turned a severe water crisis into a source of power and innovation[210] • Industrial pollution[211]
5. Science and Human Potential	• Free, high-standard education system[212] • Many educational opportunities at the post-secondary level, including adult-education programmes for new immigrants[213] • Highly skilled workforce, relatively young population[214] • Immigration brings many highly educated people into the country[215] • Very high investment in R&D[216]
6. Military and Security Issues	• Continuing occupation of Palestine, compromise of Palestinian human rights a cause of persistent insecurity due to lack of peace[217] • Military alliance with, and security assistance/guarantees from, the United States[218] • *De facto* nuclear weapons state[219]
7. International Diplomacy	• Persistent refusal to see the need for a viable two-state solution within the 1967 borders by maintaining a long-term, low-intensity conflict[220] • Major challenge going forward of being Jewish and democratic without a two-state solution with the Palestinians according to UN Resolutions

Case Study 12A: Japan

Issue Area	Geopolitical Realities and Dilemmas
1. Social and Health Issues	• Highly homogeneous society, widespread prejudices against non-Japanese[221] • Highly urbanised (in 2020 only 3.3 per cent of population employed in agriculture)[222] • Very high life expectancy[223] • Universal health coverage[224]
2. Domestic Politics	• Governments dominated by Liberal Democratic Party[225] • Political disengagement[226]
3. Economics	• World's third-largest economy[227] • Highly competitive in international trade[228] • High savings and investment rate[229] • Highest public debt of any developed nation[230]
4. Environment	• Frequently hit by earthquakes[231] • Air pollution in densely populated urban areas[232]
5. Science and Human Potential	• Economy reliant on science and technology sector[233] • Very well-educated workforce[234] • Advanced space technology[235]
6. Military and Security Issues	• Constitution outlaws war as a means of achieving national security[236] • United States serves as guarantor of Japan's security[237] • Territorial disputes with China, Russia and South Korea over occupied islands that Japan claims[238]
7. International Diplomacy	• Strained relations with South Korea and China due to the legacy of the Second World War[239] • Stresses economic causes of war and thus uses economic aid to stabilise regional powers[240] • Major aid donor and provider of global capital and credit • Contributes about 20 per cent of the UN budget and covets a permanent seat on the UN Security Council[241]

Case Study 13A: *Kazakhstan*

Issue Area	Geopolitical Realities and Dilemmas
1. Social and Health Issues	• Ethnically diverse, but no major ethnic tensions[242] • Major destination for migrants[243] • Free, but underfunded public health care[244] • Major challenges are tuberculosis, cancer, tobacco and alcohol abuse[245] • Growth of HIV/AIDS cases[246]
2. Domestic Politics	• Stable government[247] • Parliamentary and presidential elections have fallen short of OSCE standards[248]
3. Economics	• Largest and strongest performing economy in Central Asia[249] • Weak rate of foreign investment[250] • Large decrease in poverty and 4.5 per cent unemployment[251] • Major uranium producer[252]
4. Environment	• Long-term nuclear pollution in the north-east as result of Soviet-era nuclear testing[253] • Polluted water supply[254] • Desertification, including desiccation and heavy pollution of Aral Sea[255] • Massive urban pollution[256]
5. Science and Human Potential	• Quality of public education system has declined in the post-Soviet era, while percentage of GDP spent on education has also declined[257] • Very low R&D expenditure[258]
6. Military and Security Issues	• No major internal or external threats to national security; stable relations with all neighbouring states[259] • Low defence spending[260] • Instability in Afghanistan is perceived as a security threat[261] • Close military cooperation with Russia, which provides equipment and personnel training[262] • Water insecurity[263]
7. International Diplomacy	• Seeks to develop closer relations with major powers interested in its oil wealth (especially Russia, China, the United States and the EU)[264] • Leader in terms of Central Asian regional integration[265] • Foreign policy strongly determined by pragmatic commercial interests

Case Study 14A: Lithuania

Issue Area	Geopolitical Realities and Dilemmas
1. Social and Health Issues	• Second fastest-shrinking population in the world[266] • Increasing levels of immigration[267] • High rates of poverty and income disparity[268] • Health concerns[269]
2. Domestic Politics	• Historic first in 2020 as three parties led by women formed a government[270]
3. Economics	• Largest economy among the three Baltic states[271] • Surplus budget in 2017[272] • GDP contracted by only 1.8 per cent in 2020, the best result in the eurozone[273] • High levels of foreign investment[274]
4. Environment	• High levels of pollution[275] • Decreasing greenhouse gas emissions but increasing per capita[276] • Slow steps being taken to 'green' the economy[277]
5. Science and Human Potential	• Science and high-tech industry known for its lasers and biotechnology,[278] IT and start-up hub • Education a top priority for the Eighteenth Government (December 2020)[279] • High rates of university graduates[280] and among the most-educated population in the EU (over 90 per cent of the population has a high school or college education; 92 per cent of women – highest in the EU)[281]
6. Military and Security Issues	• Lithuanian Armed Forces contribute to international operations and missions under EU, NATO and UN coordination[282] • Military budget amounts to ~2 per cent of GDP (rising trend)[283] • Hosts several NATO regional centres[284] • Largest contributor to the NATO Energy Security Excellence Centre[285]
7. International Diplomacy	• Member of the EU and NATO • Tensions with Belarus[286] • Quit the China '17 + 1' bloc in Eastern Europe in May 2021, and urged stronger unity within the EU[287]

Case Study 15A: Mexico

Issue Area	Geopolitical Realities and Dilemmas
1. Social and Health Issues	• Reduction of widespread poverty but significant income inequality[288] • Indigenous population asking for more autonomy and suffering from discrimination[289] • Life expectancy of 75.05 years[290] • Growth in non-communicable diseases (causing 80 per cent of deaths in Mexico)[291]
2. Domestic Politics	• Political violence[292] • High levels of corruption[293]
3. Economics	• World's fifteenth-largest economy[294] • Highly dependent on US economic cycle[295] • Major oil exporter[296] • Heavy reliance on workers' remittances ($40.61 billion in 2020)[297]
4. Environment	• Deforestation, coastal pollution, urban pollution[298]
5. Science and Human Potential	• Adult literacy rate of 95.38 per cent[299] • Low levels of R&D investment and decreasing productivity growth[300] • Very strong science and technology capabilities; high public spending on education[301] • Considerable brain drain[302]
6. Military and Security Issues	• No border disputes or threats to its territorial integrity • Violent crime and frequent kidnappings[303] • Large transit country for drugs trade and producer of heroin[304] • Small armed guerrilla groups[305] • Violence related to drugs gangs and active government crackdowns[306] • Illegal migration into the United States and human trafficking[307]
7. International Diplomacy	• Strong relations with the United States and Canada (USMCA partners)[308] • US-Mexican relations: issue of illegal migration into the United States[309]

Case Study 16A: Nigeria

Issue Area	Geopolitical Realities and Dilemmas
1. Social and Health Issues	• Most populous country in Africa (200 million people in 2019) and high fertility rate[310] • Over 250 ethnic groups; 48.8 per cent Muslim, 49.3 per cent Christian[311] • Interfaith conflicts between Christians and Muslims[312] • Discrimination, child labour, human trafficking[313] • Very bad health conditions and low life expectancy (55 years)[314] • HIV/AIDS ('second-largest number of people living with HIV'); Africa's highest tuberculosis rate; polio and malaria remain challenges[315]
2. Domestic Politics	• Fledgling democracy after 47 years of military rule[316] • Government controls the country's huge oil wealth[317] • Corruption[318] • Human rights issues persist
3. Economics	• Economy highly dependent on oil and gas sectors • 40.1 per cent live below the poverty line[319] • Limited infrastructure in non-oil-related sectors[320] • An estimated 80 per cent of economically active Nigerians work in the informal sector[321]
4. Environment	• Only 70 per cent of the population have access to water supply, 44 per cent to sanitation[322] • Deforestation (141 kha of humid forest lost between 2002 and 2021) and desertification[323] • Air, water and soil pollution through waste, oil spills, automobiles and industry[324]
5. Science and Human Potential	• 62 per cent literacy rate; fewer than a third of school-age population attends secondary school[325] • Education system in crisis[326] • Underdeveloped human capital[327]
6. Military and Security Issues	• Interfaith and inter-ethnic violence • Violence, kidnappings and attacks on oil installations in the Niger Delta[328] • Major transit point for illegal drugs trafficked into Europe[329]
7. International Diplomacy	• Predominant power in West Africa; Africa-centred foreign policy but lost influence due to recent challenges[330] • Aspires to permanent seat on the UN Security Council

Case Study 17A: Pakistan

Issue Area	Geopolitical Realities and Dilemmas
1. Social and Health Issues	• Rapid urbanisation[331] • Refugees and internally displaced persons[332] • Low-level insurgencies and unrest in Baluchistan[333] • Relatively low life expectancy and high infant mortality rate[334] • Poor health conditions and severely underfunded health care[335] • High-risk country for HIV infection[336]
2. Domestic Politics	• Democratic transition in 2013[337] • Historically dominant position of military in politics and society • Corruption issues[338]
3. Economics	• Significant economic growth[339] • Process of economic liberalisation[340] • Growing services and manufacturing sectors[341] • Decreasing but still high poverty rates[342]
4. Environment	• Deadly earthquakes due to tectonic movements in the Himalayan region[343] • Regular floods due to monsoon rains • Air and water pollution; deforestation[344] • Water scarcity[345]
5. Science and Human Potential	• Very low government investment in education and poor quality of schools[346] • Low overall literacy rate of 59.1 per cent (2017), and only 46.5 per cent (2017) of women are literate[347]
6. Military and Security Issues	• Unresolved border conflict with India over disputed territories of Jammu and Kashmir[348] • *De facto* nuclear weapons state[349] • Frequent attacks by extremist groups
7. International Diplomacy	• Bilateral trade relations meant to help normalise India–Pakistan relations[350] • Maintains alliances with both the United States and China[351]

Case Study 18A: Russian Federation

Issue Area	Geopolitical Realities and Dilemmas
1. Social and Health Issues	• Population decline due to low birth rates[352] • Westward migration and depopulation in Russia's far east and the north[353] • Insufficient funding for health care[354] • Poor public-health conditions, including HIV/AIDS epidemic (1.2 per cent of population is infected)[355]
2. Domestic Politics	• Separatist movements by ethnic minorities threaten national unity • Growing nationalism[356] • Human rights issues[357] • Corruption remains an issue[358]
3. Economics	• Economic growth due to large energy sector[359] • Government restrictions on the private sector and nationalisation of energy sector[360] • Decreasing unemployment (4.4 per cent in 2020)[361]
4. Environment	• Water and air pollution • Contamination through nuclear and other hazardous waste[362]
5. Science and Human Potential	• Very high literacy rate and high numbers of graduates[363] • Low investment in R&D, especially in the private sector[364] • R&D efforts focus on aerospace technology and machinery[365] • Unexploited potential in human-capital-intensive sectors and lack of government policies to develop Russia's human capital[366] • Increasing brain drain[367]
6. Military and Security Issues	• Separatist movements among some of Russia's ethnic minorities • Perceived threat by NATO expansion to Eastern European countries and former Soviet states • Conflict with Ukraine, which started in 2014 and led to the invasion of Ukraine by Russia in February 2022[368] • Involvement in the Syrian[369] and Libyan[370] conflicts
7. International Diplomacy	• Formally withdrew from the G8 (now G7) following the sanctions imposed because of its annexation of Crimea • Diplomatic leverage has increased due to oil wealth • Maintains strong ties with former Soviet states; strong security interests in formerly Soviet states with pro-Russian minorities, such as Ukraine and Georgia • Interdependence with the EU, but tense relationship with both the EU and NATO linked to the conflict with Ukraine[371]

Case Study 19A: Saudi Arabia

Issue Area	Geopolitical Realities and Dilemmas
1. Social and Health Issues	• High birth rate and high proportion of young people[372] • Increasing involvement of women in public life[373] • Impressive improvement in public health-care provision (citizens have free, unlimited access to medical care) and drastic reduction in infectious diseases[374]
2. Domestic Politics	• Steps towards political, economic, social and theological reform under way[375]
3. Economics	• World's leading oil exporter; oil sales make up 62 per cent of government revenues;[376] stable banking sector[377] • Growing and innovative private sector[378] • Creating six new economically powerful cities[379] • Heavily dependent on foreign labour force[380] • Ambitious '2030 Vision' to diversify the economy and increase high-level tech employment[381]
4. Environment	• Major energy country (not just oil but also green energy, including hydrogen, solar, wind etc.)[382] • Water scarcity and lack of arable land[383] • Effort underway to plant ten billion trees in the country[384]
5. Science and Human Potential	• Free public education and new reforms to address the lack of correlation between education and business needs[385] • Significant investment in education, with large numbers of new universities and research centres[386] • Very large numbers of native Saudis educated as scientists, engineers and medical professionals[387]
6. Military and Security Issues	• Military alliance with the United States • Important arms importer • Significant efforts and funding towards regional stability[388] • Involvement in stabilising Yemen since 2015[389]
7. International Diplomacy	• Large donor of foreign aid[390] • Role in promoting solidarity among Muslim countries[391] • Fosters cooperative relationships with other oil-producing and significant oil-consuming countries[392] • Significant and deep relations with global powers (especially the US, Russia, China, the UK and EU states) on economic, political, security and defence issues[393] • Role in solving Palestine problem[394] • Significant and pro-active founder of several UN programmes • Member of the G20

Case Study 20A: South Africa

Issue Area	Geopolitical Realities and Dilemmas
1. Social and Health Issues	• Crippling HIV/AIDS epidemic[395] • High levels of inequality[396] • Latent racial divisions
2. Domestic Politics	• Political system seems stable, but stability threatened by vast economic inequalities, widespread poverty and unemployment and other social ills[397] • Corruption[398]
3. Economics	• Strong financial and manufacturing sectors, rich in natural resources[399] • Widespread poverty and unemployment, especially among black South Africans[400] • Electricity shortages negatively impact economic growth[401]
4. Environment	• High per capita CO_2 emissions[402] • Efforts to shift to renewable energies[403] • Water pollution as a result of the mining industry[404] • Leadership role on issues of climate change, conservation and biodiversity[405]
5. Science and Human Potential	• Brain drain and skills shortages[406] • Good higher education for the elite, but many young people among the poor black population lack adequate education[407]
6. Military and Security Issues	• High crime rate[408]
7. International Diplomacy	• Active UN member; advocate for African interests[409] • Leading role in conflict resolution, institutional reform and development issues in Africa[410]

Case Study 21A: South Korea

Issue Area	Geopolitical Realities and Dilemmas
1. Social and Health Issues	• Highly homogeneous society in ethnic and linguistic terms but growing migration[411] • Very densely populated (51.7 million people)[412] • Very low fertility rate; rapid population ageing[413] • High level of urbanisation (over 81 per cent of population)[414] • High life expectancy, but extremely high incidence of chronic diseases[415] • Highest suicide rate in the Organisation for Economic Co-operation and Development (OECD)[416]
2. Domestic Politics	• Multiparty democracy[417]
3. Economics	• World's tenth-largest economy in 2021[418] • Large exporter, slowing domestic demand[419] • China's largest trading partner[420] • Growing per capita income, large income inequalities and significant poverty rate[421] • High percentage of irregular workers[422]
4. Environment	• Air pollution, high level of CO_2 emissions[423]
5. Science and Human Potential	• Very strong education system, highly educated population[424] • Very strong high-tech sector, leading role in digital revolution[425] • Almost universal tertiary education, but also problem of over-education and skills mismatches[426]
6. Military and Security Issues	• Technically still at war with North Korea[427] • US troops providing additional security guarantees[428] • Threats from North Korea but also the growing influence of China in the region[429]
7. International Diplomacy	• Foreign policy strongly influenced by economic considerations[430]

Case Study 22A: Sweden

Issue Area	Geopolitical Realities and Dilemmas
1. Social and Health Issues	• Welfare state despite challenges[431] • High life expectancy[432] • High health-related expenditures[433]
2. Domestic Politics	• Parliamentary democracy • Constitutional monarchy • Rise of populism[434]
3. Economics	• Good forecast for 2021 GDP[435] • High employment rate[436] • 'Brain business jobs' for most citizens[437]
4. Environment	• Low air pollution[438]
5. Science and Human Potential	• Significant research and development[439] • High-skilled students[440] • Quality tertiary education
6. Military and Security Issues	• Rise of populism and tensions over immigration[441] • Cybersecurity challenges in line with increased digitisation[442] • Tensions in the Baltic sea
7. International Diplomacy	• Neutrality[443] • Funding of international organisations[444] • EU member despite some disagreements[445]

Case Study 23A: Switzerland

Issue Area	Geopolitical Realities and Dilemmas
1. Social and Health Issues	• Social stability, low crime rate[446] • High average life expectancy (84 years)[447] • High-quality health-care system and universal coverage • High health-care expenditures (11.88 per cent of GDP in 2018)[448]
2. Domestic Politics	• Very stable political system
3. Economics	• Almost completely dependent on exports (the world's twentieth-largest exporter)[449] • Powerful and significant banking commodity and financial centre[450] • Large amount of foreign investments in relation to GDP[451]
4. Environment	• Air pollution by ozone, nitrogen dioxide and fine dust particles regularly exceeds threshold values[452]
5. Science and Human Potential	• Highly skilled workforce • Well-developed and varied education and research infrastructure[453] • High level of investment in R&D, especially in private sector[454]
6. Military and Security Issues	• Faces no conventional military threats • Affected by transnational security threats that have been exacerbated by globalisation[455] • Strategy based on 'security through cooperation'[456] • Policy of neutrality precludes Switzerland from supporting any warring state or joining a military alliance[457]
7. International Diplomacy	• Close relations with the EU due to a series of bilateral agreements, but no EU membership expected in the near future[458] • Active in international peacekeeping, mediation and providing humanitarian aid[459]

Case Study 24A: Turkey

Issue Area	Geopolitical Realities and Dilemmas
1. Social and Health Issues	• Rapid population growth[460] • Underfunded public health care[461] • Discrimination against ethnic minorities[462] • Domestic violence against women[463]
2. Domestic Politics	• Asymmetric power structures[464] • Threat to secularism[465] • Kurdish minority calls for autonomy/independence/minority rights[466] • Human rights violations[467] • Persistent conflict with the Kurdistan Workers' Party (PKK)[468]
3. Economics	• Large economy[469] • Increasing importance as energy transit hub[470] • High regional income inequalities[471] • Large informal sector, which keeps productivity low[472] • Booming pharmaceuticals and biopharmaceuticals industry[473]
4. Environment	• Water and air pollution[474] • Water scarcity[475] • Vulnerability to earthquakes[476]
5. Science and Human Potential	• Low investment in R&D (0.96 per cent of GDP in 2018)[477] • Inequality in access to education[478]
6. Military and Security Issues	• Criminal networks active in the trafficking in drugs and humans through Turkey[479] • Significant regional interference in Libya,[480] Syria,[481] Egypt, Iraq and other states • Major tensions linked to East Mediterranean borders and energy routes[482]
7. International Diplomacy	• Ongoing disputes with Cyprus over the Turkish-populated northern part of the island and territorial sea boundaries[483] • Strong supporter of the Muslim Brotherhood group • EU accession negotiations halted[484] • Long-standing but turbulent alliance with the US and NATO[485]

Case Study 25A: Ukraine

Issue Area	Geopolitical Realities and Dilemmas
1. Social and Health Issues	• Life expectancy of 71.8 years[486] • Social inequalities between urban and rural areas[487] • Low spending on health care (3.2 per cent of GDP)[488]
2. Domestic Politics	• Divided between unity and federalism[489] • Influence of the EU and Russia[490] • Conflict in the Donbas[491]
3. Economics	• 4.6 per cent growth expected in 2021[492] • Significant informal economy[493] • 9.48 per cent of unemployment in 2020[494]
4. Environment	• Poor air quality due to 'aging industrial infrastructures, power generation, coal mining, food processing, vehicle emissions and forest fires'[495] • Emissions level too high despite ratification of the Paris Agreement[496]
5. Science and Human Potential	• 60,000 researchers and four hundred research institutions[497] • 0.7 per cent of GDP in R&D[498] • Research principally funded by businesses and the government[499]
6. Military and Security Issues	• Annexation of Crimea by Russia in 2014[500] • Security situation deteriorated in Eastern Ukraine and led to the formation of the separatist self-proclaimed pro-Russian Republics of Donetsk and Luhansk[501] • Invasion of Ukraine by Russia in February 2022 • Hybrid warfare including cyber attacks[502] • Instability due to being caught in the middle of the tensions between Europe and Russia[503]
7. International Diplomacy	• Cooperation with and aspiration to join the EU and NATO[504] • Tensions with Russia

Case Study 26A: United Kingdom

Issue Area	Geopolitical Realities and Dilemmas
1. Social and Health Issues	• Improvements in life expectancy and mortality have stalled[505] • High income inequality[506] • Racial inequality[507] • Long history of immigration[508]
2. Domestic Politics	• Aftermath of Brexit[509] • Anti-immigration policies implemented by the Conservative government[510]
3. Economics	• Fifth-largest economy by GDP[511] • Second-largest financial centre in the world[512] • Large aerospace and pharmaceutical industries[513]
4. Environment	• Air pollution[514] • Decreasing greenhouse gas emissions[515]
5. Science and Human Potential	• Good quality education but inequality of access[516] • Highly innovative country[517] • Comparatively low R&D spending[518]
6. Military and Security Issues	• Risk of terrorism[519] • One of the top ten military spenders in the world[520] • Nuclear power[521]
7. International Diplomacy	• Member of NATO and Permanent Member of the UNSC • Fragile relations with the EU following Brexit • Strong ally of the US • Strong economic relations with China but growing tensions[522]

Case Study 27A: United States of America

Issue Area	Geopolitical Realities and Dilemmas
1. Social and Health Issues	• Ethnic and racial diversity • Racial discrimination[523] • Widening gap between the rich and poor[524] • Excellent health care but increasingly unaffordable to many[525]
2. Domestic Politics	• Political landscape dominated by two parties, Democrats and Republicans • Persistent domestic political discourse[526]
3. Economics	• World's largest economy with strong international economic influence[527] • Significant national debt[528]
4. Environment	• The world's second-largest emitter of greenhouse gasses[529] • Air and water pollution[530] • Hurricanes on east coast; risk of major earthquakes on west coast[531] • Drought conditions in the south-east and the west[532]
5. Science and Human Potential	• High level of investment in R&D[533] • Has many of the world's leading universities and research centres[534] • Uneven quality of primary and secondary schools[535]
6. Military and Security Issues	• Increasing tensions with both Russia and China[536]
7. International Diplomacy	• Non-proliferation of nuclear weapons: concerns with North Korea, Iran[537] • International counterterrorism cooperation • Persistent and significant bias in favour of Israel in Arab-Israeli conflict and prevention of viable and contiguous Palestinian statehood[538]

This chapter has sought to identify some of the key geostrategic dilemmas and geopolitical realities which define the world we are living in today. In order to do so, it analysed twenty-six states and one community of states, the EU, and evaluated them according to the seven state capacities we previously identified in chapter four. This exercise demonstrates that all of these states perform better in relation to some state capacities than to others, that all of them face challenges ranging from population shifts, to lack of inclusivity, to political instability and economic fragility, to inflation or deflation, to threats stemming from porous borders, terrorism, cyber attacks, or WMDs, to diplomatic tensions and clashes between opposite ideologies. The fact that states across the world face geopolitical dilemmas and challenges does not mean that these are insurmountable, however. The following chapter will seek to determine not only what these states' future trajectories may look like based on their present geopolitical realities, but also to identify some solutions to the dilemmas they are currently facing in order to strengthen their performance in all seven state capacities.

9

Case Studies

Geostrategic Imperatives and Future Trajectories of Twenty-seven Selected States

The previous chapter examined twenty-six states and the EU, identifying the geopolitical realities and dilemmas they are facing today according to the seven separate states capacities identified in chapter four. Most of the countries previously examined performed better under some indicators and less well under others. There is no doubt, however, that all of them have the potential to become stronger, more stable, more equitable and better places for the overall social and economic well-being of their inhabitants. The following tables therefore seek to identify some of the key geostrategic imperatives facing the twenty-six states and the EU, and to identify their future trajectories. The order of the countries remains identical with that of chapter eight, as does the choice to develop some case studies more than others. The tables seek to pinpoint those areas of policy where each state will need to focus its resources and attention in order to strengthen its record within the seven capacities.

Case Study 1B: Australia

Issue Area	Geostrategic Imperatives and Future Trajectories
1. Social and Health Issues	• Reduce discrimination and inequality for indigenous Australians[1] • Strengthen the balance between public and private health care[2]
2. Domestic Politics	• Eliminate offshore detention for asylum seekers[3] • Increase intake of refugees
3. Economics	• Strengthen trade deals with both ASEAN countries and the EU[4] • Reduce the impact of China's tariffs[5] • Simplify immigration policies for both skilled and non-skilled workers[6]
4. Environment	• Invest in renewable energy and become an international exporter[7] • Invest in conservation and adaptation programmes
5. Science and Human Potential	• Invest more in R&D • Invest more in university and education to remain competitive[8]
6. Military and Security Issues	• Invest in new technologies
7. International Diplomacy	• Strengthen ties with ASEAN countries • Promote reconciliation with China and regional stability[9]

Case Study 2B: Brazil

Issue Area	Geostrategic Imperatives and Future Trajectories
1. Social and Health Issues	• Promote more socio-economic mobility and close the large income gap[10] • Institute land reform[11]
2. Domestic Politics	• Further efforts to tackle corruption • Promote integration in the public sphere of black and indigenous Brazilians • Eliminate racial discrimination
3. Economics	• Raise productivity levels in agriculture and manufacturing[12] • Increase electricity production • Improve transportation infrastructure[13] • Reduce government debt, trim welfare state and invest in economic infrastructure to spur economic development • Deregulation and simplification of tax system
4. Environment	• Stop further deforestation[14] • Address the negative environmental impact of Madeira dams[15] • Join the Escazú Agreement
5. Science and Human Potential	• Attract more R&D investment from multinational corporations[16] • Promote innovation in areas of strength, including pharmaceuticals, biotechnology and renewable energies • Improve quality of public primary, secondary and higher education[17]
6. Military and Security Issues	• Fight organised crime, especially the rise in drug trafficking[18] • Address threat of instability coming from the situation in Bolivia[19]
7. International Diplomacy	• Rebuild relations with Latin American countries, as well as the US and European countries[20] • Strengthen involvement with organisations such as Mercosur and increase their importance in international fora[21]

Case Study 3B: China

Issue Area	Geostrategic Imperatives and Future Trajectories
1. Social and Health Issues	• Increase investments in rural infrastructure, including health care, schools, clean water etc. • Address ageing of Chinese society[22] • Ensure equal rights for rural migrants in urban areas[23]
2. Domestic Politics	• Address the grievances that cause social unrest, especially in the countryside, and show responsiveness to people's concerns • Pursue aggressive prosecution of corruption to prevent major negative economic and political consequences • Address human rights deficiencies and perceptions and respect the cultural rights of ethnic minorities
3. Economics	• Reduce environmental damage[24] • Tackle income disparities between rural and urban workers • Liberalise farming and food-growing policies[25] • Continue liberalisation of banking sector[26]
4. Environment	• Enforce strict environmental legislation
5. Science and Human Potential	• Promote innovation and high-tech development in private industry (not just in state-controlled science programmes)[27] • Adopt a more open innovation system[28]
6. Military and Security Issues	• Resolve remaining boundary disputes • Find peaceful solution to dispute over Taiwan
7. International Diplomacy	• Work on peaceful resolution of the South China Sea dispute with ASEAN countries[29]

Case Study 4B: Egypt

Issue Area	Geostrategic Imperatives and Future Trajectories
1. Social and Health Issues	• Create jobs, reduce poverty and inequality[30] • Strengthen efforts to root out illegal child labour[31] • Increase health care funding[32]
2. Domestic Politics	• Continue to improve human rights situation[33]
3. Economics	• Continuation of economic reform programme, especially private-sector development[34] • Reduce government involvement in economy and reduce public domestic debt[35] • Curb rising inflation[36] • Increase the formal private sector[37]
4. Environment	• Improve water and air quality • Improve water-resource management
5. Science and Human Potential	• Improve education system to increase literacy rate and develop skills most needed by the economy[38] • Turn the large number of working-age people into a developmental asset by creating more jobs and improving the quality of the labour force
6. Military and Security Issues	• Continue to fight and rehabilitate violent extremists[39] • Improve border security adjacent to Gaza and Israel
7. International Diplomacy	• Continue mediating role in Arab-Israeli peace process • Strengthen Arab regional security through increased cooperation with Arab states • Find a sustainable solution to the water conflict with Ethiopia[40] • Continue efforts to stabilise Libya, Iraq and Syria[41] • Continue to push back on regional interference in Arab countries by Iran and Turkey • Resolution of East Mediterranean maritime disputes

Case Study 5B: European Union

Issue Area	Geostrategic Imperatives and Future Trajectories
1. Social and Health Issues	• Integrate foreigners into European societies by promoting multiculturalism and cosmopolitanism • Eliminate inequalities and xenophobia towards immigrants, especially in education and the workplace[42] • Adjust to challenges with regard to the ageing population
2. Domestic Politics	• Promote renewed faith in the EU project among European citizens • Open up channels for more public input in policy-making processes[43] • Ensure inclusive political statements through the broadcase and news media and entertainment industry
3. Economics	• Reinvigorate the economy and create new jobs • Prevent rise of economic nationalism and protectionism in member states[44]
4. Environment	• Promote innovation in clean technologies[45]
5. Science and Human Potential	• Improve cooperation between research institutions of individual member states • Increase R&D investment, especially by the private sector[46]
6. Military and Security Issues	• Develop an inclusive and sustainable security policy to deal with violent extremism, international organised crime, disease control, illegal migration and asylum seekers • Tackle energy security problems[47]
7. International Diplomacy	• Continue enlargement process • Develop a consistent policy towards neighbouring countries[48] • Assert rightful place as a great power in the international community[49] • Increase diplomatic efforts to accommodate the different interests of Russia, China, the US and NATO

Case Study 6B: France

Issue Area	Geostrategic Imperatives and Future Trajectories
1. Social and Health Issues	• Prioritise policies of integration for the immigrant community[50] • Reduce secular extremism • Minimise interference in cultural/religious affairs of immigrants while ensuring law and order and security
2. Domestic Politics	• Recognise religious freedoms of minorities, such as the large Islamic one • Fight nationalism • Promote egalitarian norms between cultural groups in society • Fight systemic racism in policing, economy and education[51]
3. Economics	• Invest in the 'green transition'[52] • Invest in sustainable agriculture
4. Environment	• Reduce investment in nuclear power[53] • Invest more in renewable energy • Push for the adoption of environmental policies at the EU level[54]
5. Science and Human Potential	• Reduce inequalities within the education system • Increase investment in R&D to become more competitive with superpowers such as the US and China[55] • Continue impressive achievements in high tech and space technology
6. Military and Security Issues	• Reduce nuclear weapons arsenal[56] • Coordinate with other EU member states to tackle violent extremism[57] • Increase investment in cyber security[58]
7. International Diplomacy	• Assume leadership role within the UNSC Permanent 5 as the state representing the EU[59] • Lead the EU on issues such as climate change and environmental policies • Increase development aid for its former African colonies[60] • Reduce its military intervention in Africa • Open colonial archives and reach a cathartic decolonisation of history and acknowledge past atrocities in order to achieve reconciliation[61] • Increase goodwill with Algeria through transparency about the location of buried nuclear waste[62]

Case Study 7B: Germany

Issue Area	Geostrategic Imperatives and Future Trajectories
1. Social and Health Issues	• Address ageing population and obesity[63] • Need to prioritise integration of immigrant population[64]
2. Domestic Politics	• Tackle populism and anti-immigrant rhetoric[65]
3. Economics	• Move past the long-standing policy of austerity[66]
4. Environment	• Continue investment in and development of renewable energies • Take more pro-active steps to reduce greenhouse gas emissions[67]
5. Science and Human Potential	• Invest more in education and focus on reducing inequalities within the system[68] • Increase investment in R&D • Invest in space technology to remain competitive within the international sphere
6. Military and Security Issues	• Continue international cooperation in fighting violent extremism and other transnational crimes[69] • Address cybersecurity threats[70]
7. International Diplomacy	• Assume leadership within the EU on issues such as climate change • Recognise that other countries within the EU may have different interests and seek compromise[71] • Focus on the economic and social development of countries to which Germany provides aid

Case Study 8B: India

Issue Area	Geostrategic Imperatives and Future Trajectories
1. Social and Health Issues	• Improve public health infrastructure, especially in rural areas and poor states • Contain spread of malaria and TB and other pandemics[72]
2. Domestic Politics	• Promote national unity through peaceful means • Protect secular constitutions and pluralism • Limit nationalism and alienation of Muslims and other religious groups[73] • Take action (long overdue) to address the caste system[74]
3. Economics	• Modify labour regulations to promote the development of the formal manufacturing sector[75] • Increase investment in public infrastructure[76] • Help make agricultural sector more competitive through infrastructure investment and deregulation while not harming the livelihoods of farmers[77] • Prevent social and regional wealth disparities from growing ever wider[78] • Narrow the trade deficit[79] • Develop domestic energy sources, especially hydroelectric power[80]
4. Environment	• Increase effectiveness of environmental regulations with the help of citizen participation and incentive systems • Overhaul water infrastructure and make more efficient use of existing water resources to prevent water crisis[81]
5. Science and Human Potential	• Continue public investments in scientific infrastructure • Provide free access to basic education for all • Continue the impressive achievements in the emerging technologies and space technologies sectors
6. Military and Security Issues	• Improve internal security • Offer support to weak neighbouring states in controlling their frontier areas • Find peaceful solution to border conflict with Pakistan, especially in Kashmir
7. International Diplomacy	• Balance relations with the United States, China and Russia without alienating any of them[82] • Balance short-term needs for energy supply with long-term strategic interests[83]

Case Study 9B: Indonesia

Issue Area	Geostrategic Imperatives and Future Trajectories
1. Social and Health Issues	• Follow through successful health care reforms[84] • Contain spread of HIV/AIDS and other communicable diseases[85] • Tackle child malnutrition and high maternal mortality rate[86]
2. Domestic Politics	• Entrench accountable government; ensure direct democracy through elections at the local and national level[87] • Improve human-rights situation
3. Economics	• Tackle urban and female unemployment[88] • Increase efforts to root out corruption[89]
4. Environment	• Address rising sea levels to minimise loss of territory and biodiversity[90] • Reduce forest fires to cut CO_2 emissions • Increase pledges on reduction of emissions[91] • Provide universal access to safe drinking water[92]
5. Science and Human Potential	• Adapt university training to prioritise job-market requirements[93]
6. Military and Security Issues	• Continue and expand international efforts to eliminate violent extremism[94] • Invest in cyber security[95]
7. International Diplomacy	• Strengthen role as leader of ASEAN

Case Study 10B: Iran

Issue Area	Geostrategic Imperatives and Future Trajectories
1. Social and Health Issues	• Devise programmes for employment • Tackle drug-addiction problem
2. Domestic Politics	• Promote political liberalisation and democratisation • Improve human rights situation and increase civil liberties • Eliminate ethnic discrimination
3. Economics	• Foster job growth[96] • Loosen government control and regulation of the economy and encourage job creation in the private sector[97] • Diversify the economy to reduce dependence on market prices for oil and gas
4. Environment	• Tackle water and air pollution • Improve earthquake preparedness and construct earthquake-proof buildings
5. Science and Human Potential	• Adapt education towards the job market • Make better use of the educated young labour force, including women[98] • Increase investment in R&D[99]
6. Military and Security Issues	• Address legitimate grievances of insurgent groups and minorities while avoiding their repression through violence • Reduce sectarianism and further militarisation and securitisation of religious sects • Increase efforts in stopping drug trafficking by loyal groups[100] • Stop destabilising regional countries through militarised sectarian groups[101] • Increase goodwill and peaceful cooperation with neighbours by eliminating interference in their internal affairs • Stop the supply of drones and missiles to militias in neighbouring countries to increase trust, stability and cooperation
7. International Diplomacy	• Focus on increased political, economic and cultural cooperation with neighbours to minimise tensions and increase peace and security • Reach a transparent and sustainable understanding with the international committee regarding nuclear threats, regional non-interference, security and WMD

Case Study 11B: Israel

Issue Area	Geostrategic Imperatives and Future Trajectories
1. Social and Health Issues	• Promote awareness about pervasive racism against Arab-Israelis in schools, the government and especially the police[102] • Provide equal educational and economic opportunities to Arab-Israelis and help poor communities to improve living standards through national programmes[103]
2. Domestic Politics	• Stop systemic discrimination and segregation of Palestinians and other Jewish minorities
3. Economics	• Address poverty[104]
4. Environment	• Continue to invest in technologies to address water shortages[105] • Deal with problem of depleting water levels in the Dead Sea[106]
5. Science and Human Potential	• Improve educational opportunities for Arab-Israelis • Keep up high investments in R&D, education and high-tech industry
6. Military and Security Issues	• Find a peaceful solution to Israeli-Palestinian conflict (urgent)[107]
7. International Diplomacy	• Reconcile being accepted in the region as a legitimate neighbour while recognising the rights of others, a prerequisite towards sustainable peace, prosperity and security • Stop colonising and acknowledge the rights of Palestinians in order to avoid shifting into a colonial apartheid state • Work towards the Arab peace plan of 2002 to achieve a viable Palestinian state[108] and the return of Syrian lands to normalise relations with all Arab states[109] • Protect the special religious status of Jerusalem and of East Jerusalem as the capital of a Palestinian state

Case Study 12B: Japan

Issue Area	Geostrategic Imperatives and Future Trajectories
1. Social and Health Issues	• Deal with rapidly ageing population[110] • Foster immigrant integration to better meet the growing need for immigrant labourers[111] • Improve status and rights of women[112]
2. Domestic Politics	• Foster more active public participation in democratic politics[113]
3. Economics	• Tackle high budget deficit in the context of population ageing and increasing old-age dependency ratio[114] • Stop deflation[115]
4. Environment	• Cut greenhouse gas emissions[116]
5. Science and Human Potential	• Address labour shortages (including skilled labour) due to declining birth rate • Maintain cutting-edge technological and scientific development
6. Military and Security Issues	• Enhance US-Japanese security cooperation and question of Japanese rearmament[117] • Improve relations with North Korea • De-escalate tensions with China and increase chances of peace and cooperation[118] • Energy security: increase investment in renewable energy sources[119]
7. International Diplomacy	• Strengthen trade ties with China[120] • Expand economic and security relations with ASEAN countries and India[121] • Reach a reconciliation with Korea and China on Second World War atrocities[122]

Case Study 13B: Kazakhstan

Issue Area	Geostrategic Imperatives and Future Trajectories
1. Social and Health Issues	• Maintenance of social peace[123] • Increase investment in public health care[124] • Address rising drug-addiction problem[125]
2. Domestic Politics	• Fight corruption[126] • Promote independent judiciary and improve democratic accountability[127]
3. Economics	• Promote economic diversification[128] • Develop Astana as regional financial centre[129] • Increase foreign investment[130] • Promote more equitable economic development[131] • Draw illegal migrants out of the informal sector to increase tax revenue and fuel the more efficient formal economy[132]
4. Environment	• Work on the implementation of its new Environmental Code[133] • Implement strict environmental guidelines for the large oil industry[134] • Take a pro-active role in USAID's Regional Water and Vulnerable Environment Program[135]
5. Science and Human Potential	• Invest more in the public education system and provide incentives for qualified teachers to teach at Kazakh educational institutions[136]
6. Military and Security Issues	• Safeguard radioactive material and biological weapons facilities from falling into the hands of criminal non-state actors[137] • Improve border security and combat drug trafficking[138]
7. International Diplomacy	• Respect the terms of the 2018 Convention on the Legal Status of the Caspian Sea[139] • Manage relations with Russia, US and China wisely[140]

Case Study 14B: Lithuania

Issue Area	Geostrategic Imperatives and Future Trajectories
1. Social and Health Issues	• Addressing shrinking population[141] • Boost levels of immigration • Reduce poverty rates and income disparity[142] • Address health issues[143] • Increase funding for public health care
2. Domestic Politics	• Enhance domestic political stability[144]
3. Economics	• Enable labour market integration of less skilled workers[145] • Raise local public investment[146] • Increase investment in biotech[147]
4. Environment	• Increase pricing of environmentally damaging activities[148] • Increase investment in renewable energy and sustainable practices[149]
5. Science and Human Potential	• Increase investment in R&D[150] • Increase investment in education[151]
6. Military and Security Issues	• Mitigate threats such as xenophobia, disinformation and surveillance technologies[152] • Achieve energy security[153] • Increase defence spending[154]
7. International Diplomacy	• Strengthen military, diplomatic and economic ties with both NATO and the EU • Prioritise the diplomatic resolution of tensions with Belarus[155]

Case Study 15B: Mexico

Issue Area	Geostrategic Imperatives and Future Trajectories
1. Social and Health Issues	• Reduce poverty and make income distribution more equal[156] • Address demands of indigenous population for more group rights
2. Domestic Politics	• Tackle corruption
3. Economics	• Create jobs to mitigate unemployment[157] • Meet domestic natural gas demand and diversify imports[158] • Shrink informal sector and increase formal sector[159]
4. Environment	• Promote environmental sustainability by cutting pollution and through reforestation
5. Science and Human Potential	• Raise quality of education and improve human capital[160] • Continue to fund and improve basic science research and innovation in universities[161] • Continue to encourage R&D investments in the private sector[162]
6. Military and Security Issues	• Prevent drugs cartels and organised criminal groups from gaining more power and influencing politics[163] • Reform the judicial system and ensure its independence[164]
7. International Diplomacy	• Pursue agreement on legalising Mexican migrants in the United States[165] • Strengthen relations with Central American states[166]

Case Study 16B: Nigeria

Issue Area	Geostrategic Imperatives and Future Trajectories
1. Social and Health Issues	• Promote immunisation (especially against polio and tuberculosis)[167] • Invest in, and improve quality and affordability of, primary health care[168] • Reduce child and maternal mortality through better ante- and post-natal care • Combat HIV/AIDS and other communicable diseases
2. Domestic Politics	• Ensure fair and competitive future elections • Improve human rights record[169] • Fight corruption[170]
3. Economics	• Meet UN Sustainable Development Goals by 2030[171] • Create jobs, develop agricultural sector and diversify economy[172] • Provide electricity to rural areas and build new power plants • Improve infrastructure, including roads, railroads etc.
4. Environment	• Forestall negative effects of climate change to protect agriculture and limit conflict[173] • Take measures to reduce air, water and soil pollution
5. Science and Human Potential	• Heavily invest in education and develop the country's young human potential[174]
6. Military and Security Issues	• Find peaceful and fair solution to violence in Niger Delta • Maintain strong pressure on the terrorist group Boko Haram • Implement effective measures to combat the trafficking of drugs and humans across borders
7. International Diplomacy	• Maintain leading role in promoting peace and stability in West Africa and the rest of the continent, work on re-establishing influence with partners • Pursuit of a customs union implementation among members of the Economic Community of West African States[175]

Case Study 17B: Pakistan

Issue Area	Geostrategic Imperatives and Future Trajectories
1. Social and Health Issues	• Address grievances of Baluchistan province on the political and developmental level • Increase spending on social development and health care[176] • Devise programmes to deal with population pressure[177] • Address rising food insecurity by increasing food production and imports[178] • Provide access to clean drinking water for all citizens[179]
2. Domestic Politics	• Stabilise political situation and continue democratic reforms[180] • Reduce corruption
3. Economics	• Heavily invest in infrastructure, entice support of foreign investors[181]
4. Environment	• Address severe water shortages[182] • Improve air and water quality through regulations and investments[183] • Improve seismographic research to develop early-warning capability[184]
5. Science and Human Potential	• Drastically increase investment in public school system and universities[185]
6. Military and Security Issues	• Assert important geopolitical role to make the region and the world more stable and peaceful[186]
7. International Diplomacy	• Improve relationship and build trust with Afghanistan • Focus on peace process with India to end conflict over Jammu and Kashmir[187]

Case Study 18B: Russian Federation

Issue Area	Geostrategic Imperatives and Future Trajectories
1. Social and Health Issues	• Strengthen policies to help avert demographic crisis due to population decline[188] • Promote public health by increasing funding, preventing the spreading of sexually transmitted diseases (including HIV/AIDS) and adopting public safety measures • Increase incentives for people to stay in the north and far east of the country to prevent further depopulation of these regions[189]
2. Domestic Politics	• Encourage more accountable practices • Develop a strong civil society • Guarantee civil liberties and human rights for all • Launch awareness campaigns against xenophobia and racism; aggressively prosecute racially motivated acts of violence • Fight corruption[190]
3. Economics	• Become less economically dependent on export of raw materials and develop human-capital-intensive industries[191] • Integrate all regions into the economic-growth process[192] • Reduce restrictions on the private sector and encourage responsible foreign investment[193]
4. Environment	• Provide for public participation in addressing environmental problems[194] • Invest in safe disposal technologies for hazardous and nuclear waste • Reduce water and air pollution; cut greenhouse gas emissions
5. Science and Human Potential	• Improve general living standards • Raise government funding and encourage more private-sector investments in R&D • Prevent brain drain by offering attractive employment conditions for Russian scientists[195]
6. Military and Security Issues	• Reduce tensions with NATO • Find peaceful solutions to separatist ambitions of pro-Russian communities in former Soviet states • Assume a peace-leading role in the Syrian and Libyan conflicts and in the Palestine issue
7. International Diplomacy	• Find a peaceful solution to the conflict in Ukraine[196] • Foster close economic and political ties built on mutual trust with the EU • Resolve tensions with NATO and the United States • Foster cooperation on the Arctic while maintaining Russian national interests[197]

Case Study 19B: Saudi Arabia

Issue Area	Geostrategic Imperatives and Future Trajectories
1. Social and Health Issues	• Continue efforts to increase women's development and inclusion in the economy and government • Continue economic diversification and reduce unemployment and minimise dependence on oil
2. Domestic Politics	• Continue incremental, evolutionary liberal social reforms
3. Economics	• Diversify economy to create broader economic prosperity • Continue the ambitious and impressive Saudi Vision 2030 • Continue the development of innovative new economically powerful cities like Neom[198] • Create jobs; enlarge the private sector[199] • Strengthen measures to make private-sector jobs more attractive to Saudis[200] • Encourage self-employment • Participate in solving global financial uncertainties • Combine impressive new investments in local industries and high tech, space, cyber security[201] • Continue to invest in the development of the tourism sector
4. Environment	• Address water scarcity problem • Continue to take the lead in research in the field of marine biology and protection of marine habitats • Continue investment in the planned reforestation of Saudi Arabia and the wider region through the planting of fifty billion trees
5. Science and Human Potential	• Invest in skills development, e.g. through vocational schools, to develop skills among Saudis that are sought after by the private sector • Increase R&D through government leadership and private sector • Continue to invest in higher education, increasing the number of universities and research centres like KAUST[202] • Continue incorporating more women into the labour force[203] • Invest in cloud-seeding technology • Pioneer technologies to harness abundance of solar energy • Ensure water security for agriculture and other uses with the help of nuclear technologies
6. Military and Security Issues	• Maintain stability and security on the Arabian Peninsula • Ensure food security • Continue to be the energy leader of the world through oil, gas and more innovative new energy technologies including hydrogen, solar and blue ammonia • Continue pushing for a nuclear-free Middle East

7. International Diplomacy	• Push for a just resolution to the Israeli-Palestinian conflict through a two-state solution according to the Arab peace plan of 2002 and UN resolutions[204] • Continue to support the war on violent extremism and sectarianism • Continue to push for a peaceful Yemen with a stable government free of violent extremism, foreign interference and sectarianism • Continue to push for regional security, stability and prosperity • Unify the Arab-Islamic world culturally and politically and thus act as a significant pro-active player in global affairs • Continue to advance reconciliation efforts culturally and religiously throughout the world[205] • Continue to encourage inclusive regional economic prosperity

Case Study 20B: South Africa

Issue Area	Geostrategic Imperatives and Future Trajectories
1. Social and Health Issues	<ul><li>Drastically reduce the spread of HIV/AIDS[206]</li><li>Improve racial harmony</li><li>Reduce wealth gap/inequality</li></ul>
2. Domestic Politics	<ul><li>Effectively address social ills and economic problems (especially inequality and unemployment) to prevent political instability</li><li>Fight corruption[207]</li></ul>
3. Economics	<ul><li>Reform land ownership[208]</li><li>Reduce poverty and address unemployment[209]</li><li>Increase economic power of black South Africans to reduce racial wealth gap[210]</li></ul>
4. Environment	<ul><li>Address air and water pollution</li><li>Reduce greenhouse gas emissions</li><li>Take measures to maintain marine biodiversity and fish stocks[211]</li><li>Strengthen its leadership role in Africa in addressing the climate crisis[212]</li></ul>
5. Science and Human Potential	<ul><li>Stop further brain drain[213]</li><li>Continue education reform to ensure non-discriminatory and equal access to quality education for all South African pupils</li></ul>
6. Military and Security Issues	<ul><li>Reform justice system and police force to tackle rampant crime[214]</li></ul>
7. International Diplomacy	<ul><li>Continue impartial mediating role on African continent and support of African institution-building and economic-development efforts</li></ul>

Case Study 21B: South Korea

Issue Area	Geostrategic Imperatives and Future Trajectories
1. Social and Health Issues	• Foster multiculturalism through public policy[215] • Remove obstacles that discourage Koreans from having children[216] • Stop rise of national health insurance spending[217]
2. Domestic Politics	• Enhance effective presidential leadership[218]
3. Economics	• Reduce inequality by discouraging irregular employment[219] • Encourage and facilitate higher labour participation by women[220] • Facilitate the inflow of foreign workers[221]
4. Environment	• Reduce CO_2 emissions and other air pollutants[222] • Reduce overreliance on nuclear energy[223]
5. Science and Human Potential	• Reduce education expenses[224] • Reform education system[225] • Promote innovation through enhanced linkages between business, university and government research institutes[226] • Make better use of human capital of women, older people and migrants[227]
6. Military and Security Issues	• Prioritise the achievement of peace with North Korea and its denuclearisation[228] • Reconcile tensions with China as well as the historical animosities with Japan[229]
7. International Diplomacy	• Sign free trade agreements and strengthen ties with the other regional RCEP partners[230] • Conclude peace agreement with North Korea and continue confidence-building measures

Case Study 22B: Sweden

Issue Area	Geostrategic Imperatives and Future Trajectories
1. Social and Health Issues	• Preserve the welfare state[231] • Enhance cohesion between citizens and migrants[232]
2. Domestic Politics	• Limit the rise of populism[233]
3. Economics	• Maintain access to affordable housing • Limit tax reductions at the expense of the welfare state
4. Environment	• Keep investing in sustainable solutions[234] • Further engage on the international scene[235]
5. Science and Human Potential	• Maintain strong investment in R&D • Maintain the quality of the education system[236]
6. Military and Security Issues	• Invest in cyber security solutions • Promote the ease of tensions in the Baltic Sea[237]
7. International Diplomacy	• Maintain neutrality and active funding for international organisations • Enhance cooperation with EU member states to mitigate disagreements[238]

Case Study 23B: Switzerland

Issue Area	Geostrategic Imperatives and Future Trajectories
1. Social and Health Issues	• Improve integration of foreigners and combat xenophobia[239] • Increase labour participation of older people[240] • Increase cost-effectiveness of health care system[241]
2. Domestic Politics	• Social security reform • Ensure fiscal stability
3. Economics	• Further liberalisation of domestic economy[242]
4. Environment	• Improve air quality • Stop speed of soil erosion and improve natural habitat of endangered species[243]
5. Science and Human Potential	• Continue to maintain and improve high-quality education • Keep up level of investments in R&D
6. Military and Security Issues	• Continue reorganisation of military and national security infrastructure to meet transnational threats related to globalisation
7. International Diplomacy	• Maintain neutral but active and humanitarian approach to the international system[244] • Use its status to be a host and mediator in global diplomacy[245]

Case Study 24B: Turkey

Issue Area	Geostrategic Imperatives and Future Trajectories
1. Social and Health Issues	• Decrease population growth[246] • Create sufficient jobs for the growing population • Increase funds for public health care • Curb spread of HIV/AIDS[247]
2. Domestic Politics	• Protect secularism[248] • Grant minority rights to all minorities living in Turkey • Have PKK renounce violence and enter negotiations[249]
3. Economics	• Create economic environment conducive to the establishment of formal businesses (including lower social security and pension contribution rates, more flexible employment protection laws, adjust minimum wage to local per capita GDP levels and simplify business-sector regulations)[250] • Promote creation of new jobs
4. Environment	• Enforce stricter environmental regulations • Invest in new technologies to make better use of water resources[251] • Construct earthquake-proof buildings
5. Science and Human Potential	• Find new financial resources to invest in science and R&D • Improve quality of public schools and ensure that all Turkish students acquire solid literacy and numeracy skills
6. Military and Security Issues	• Curb transnational criminal activity • Find means to address problem of Kurdish incursions from northern Iraq, short of full-blown military intervention[252]
7. International Diplomacy	• Resolve Cyprus and Eastern Mediterranean issues peacefully • Continue to cultivate all ties to Middle Eastern states • Stop supporting destabilising groups like the Muslim Brotherhood • Stop interference in Arab states and increase political, economic and cultural ties for mutual peace and prosperity[253]

Case Study 25B: Ukraine

Issue Area	Geostrategic Imperatives and Future Trajectories
1. Social and Health Issues	• Improve life expectancy • Tackle inequalities between urban and rural areas[254]
2. Domestic Politics	• Promote national unity • Regain control of the information sphere[255]
3. Economics	• Fight the informal economy[256] • Create employment opportunities
4. Environment	• Meet Paris Agreement obligations • Implement the Ukrainian Green Deal[257] • Implement an exit strategy from the coal industry[258]
5. Science and Human Potential	• Maintain high investments in the education system[259] • Increase investment in R&D • Limit the brain drain[260]
6. Military and Security Issues	• Work to reduce tensions in Eastern Ukraine and with Russia through diplomatic means
7. International Diplomacy	• Work to ease tensions and increase cooperation with Russia • Maintain strong cooperation with EU and NATO • Reaffirm its status as a neutral 'buffer zone' between Russia and the West[261]

Case Study 26B: United Kingdom

Issue Area	Geostrategic Imperatives and Future Trajectories
1. Social and Health Issues	• Invest in public health care[262] • Reduce income inequality[263] • Re-examine racial discrimination[264]
2. Domestic Politics	• Enhance unity between the different countries in the UK[265]
3. Economics	• Need to adapt in the wake of Brexit[266] • Control increasing state borrowing[267]
4. Environment	• Goal of net-zero carbon emissions by 2050[268] • Need to combat air pollution
5. Science and Human Potential	• Tackle inequality in the education system[269] • Increase investment in R&D[270] • Continue to invest in space technologies and transformative technologies[271]
6. Military and Security Issues	• Continue strong international cooperation to mitigate violent extremism • Develop additional cyber security capacities[272] • Avoid increasing nuclear arsenal to comply with international disarmament commitments[273]
7. International Diplomacy	• Strengthen ties to NATO • Mend relationship with the EU • Sign new trade deals[274] • Improve diplomatic relations with China and Russia[275]

Case Study 27B: United States of America

Issue Area	Geostrategic Imperatives and Future Trajectories
1. Social and Health Issues	• Strengthen middle class and stop growing gap between rich and poor • Make affordable health care accessible to all Americans[276]
2. Domestic Politics	• Balance public finances and reform social security system[277] • Find a good solution for immigration reform[278] • Limit the influence of lobbyists and money in politics[279] • Minimise and mend bipartisan political fractures • Address systemic racism, exclusion, poverty and inequality
3. Economics	• Enhance economic growth potential[280] • Help stabilise global financial system in cooperation with G20 • Spearhead the elimination of global poverty and inequality in cooperation with UN
4. Environment	• Implement measures to drastically reduce CO_2 emissions[281]
5. Science and Human Potential	• Promote higher standards at the federal level for primary and secondary school curricula[282] • Increase the number of university graduates[283] • Help reduce the global technology gap • Take leadership position in biotechnological advances[284]
6. Military and Security Issues	• Continuation of counterterrorism efforts at home and abroad • Help fight misinformation, disinformation and cyber threats[285]
7. International Diplomacy	• Improve America's image abroad, especially among Muslims, through concrete actions and credible impartial policies[286] • Pursue a fair peace agreement between Israelis and Palestinians through a two-state solution[287] • Reach a workable solution to North Korea's nuclear issues[288] • Find a sustainable solution to issues tied to Iran's nuclear programme, missile programme and regionally destabilising, proxy sectarian militias[289] • Advance global justice as a national security issue • Serve as honest broker in international disputes • Avoid the misuse of human rights discourse as a political tool • Promote best practices globally in education, health, economics • Promote *transcultural synergies* and harmony through cultural diplomacy (especially through education and the entertainment industry) • Ensure, through international cooperation and new binding treaties, the peaceful use of outer space[290]

This chapter has sought to identify some of the solutions to the existing geopolitical dilemmas faced by the 26 states and one multistate entity, the EU, identified in the previous chapter. Ranging from increasing funding for education, tackling social exclusion through programmes for integration, encouraging migration and addressing population shifts, this chapter has demonstrated how in the vast majority of cases there are answers to the challenges we face and practical means for becoming not only politically stronger, but also more equitable and fair places for all. What this chapter has also done, however, is to identify these states' future trajectories, and pinpoint what the future challenges under all seven state capacities may soon be. From ageing populations in some countries, to extremely high birth rates in others, to climate change, to the militarisation of space, to the role of non-state actors, or an increasingly volatile economy, the geopolitical realities confronting us today will shape not only the present but also the future.

Having identified what the present and future challenges are, and what the answer to them may be, the following chapter will focus on a geographical region which I have labelled the tripwire pivotal corridor. As I explore in more depth later in the book, these two sets of 27 case studies have demonstrated that it is within this specific geographic region that we find the highest concentration of volatility. For this reason, this area is of extreme geopolitical significance and must be prioritised if global peace and security is to be achieved.

10

The Tripwire Pivotal Corridor and its Geopolitical Significance

A meta-geopolitical analysis of worldwide dynamics reveals that there is one area in particular that will heavily influence the state of the world in the twenty-first century: a corridor that runs from north to south between the longitudes of 30 and 75 degrees east. The corridor includes countries from three continents: Africa, Europe and Asia. In the east, it incorporates China's Xinjiang province. At its western edge, it includes the Horn of Africa and the entire east coast of Africa. The corridor also includes the Arctic Circle in the north and Antarctica in the south. Due to the corridor's international geopolitical significance and its volatility, I call it the tripwire pivotal corridor (hereafter TPC). Figure 10.1 shows the TPC highlighted on a world map.

Certain key states and regions within the corridor can be characterised as *geopolitical pivots*, a term used by Zbigniew Brzezinski in his seminal book, *The Grand Chessboard*. According to Brzezinski, 'Geopolitical pivots are the states whose importance is derived not from their power and motivation but rather from their sensitive location and from the consequences of their potentially vulnerable condition for the behaviour of geostrategic players.'[1] To paraphrase Brzezinski, these pivotal states derive their geopolitical importance from their geography: their territory may serve as a critical access route, such as a land bridge, or they may have control over a maritime passageway.[2] The term 'pivot' was originally coined by Mackinder in 1904. He used the term to refer to Central Asia and

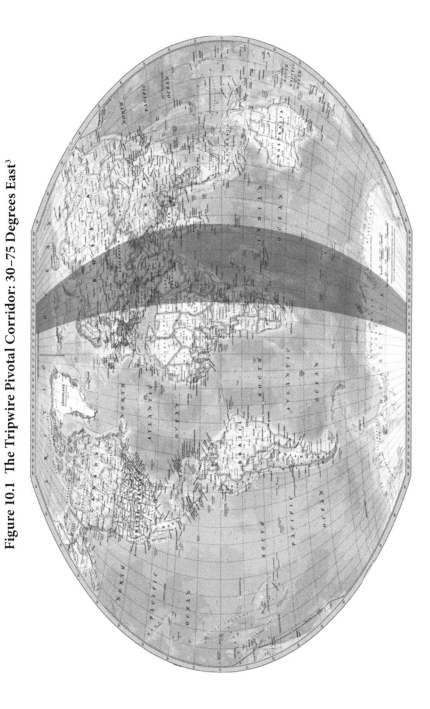

Figure 10.1 The Tripwire Pivotal Corridor: 30–75 Degrees East[3]

the Caucasus, which he saw as the key to world geopolitics. The notion of geopolitical pivots gained increased interest among geostrategists after the dissolution of the Soviet Union.[4] As I shall discuss later in this chapter, Robert Chase, Emily Hill and Paul Kennedy coined the notion of 'pivotal states' in a 1998 study.[5] Building on this theoretical framework, I proposed the concept of TPC (see next section) to single out the geopolitical and geostrategic importance of a 'corridor' of countries, which, either through natural resources or key strategic location (or both), play a central role in current global geopolitics and military affairs. The TPC, however, is also rife with vulnerabilities that may exacerbate regional and global conflict.

In this chapter I extend Brzezinski's definition of a geopolitical pivot to include the seven state capacities discussed in chapter four, all of which are important in geopolitical terms. A country's demographic trends, possession of strategic natural resources, as well as general instability factors (including ethnic or domestic political tensions that have regional reverberations), ongoing tensions and hostilities with neighbouring states and unresolved international conflicts that draw in some of the world's key geopolitical players, are equally important characteristics of key states within the TPC.

This chapter describes both the international significance and liabilities of the TPC. As to the former, the TPC contains three major choke points, which are narrow maritime passageways that many nations depend on for shipping. Furthermore, the region possesses most of the world's proven and extractable oil and gas resources on which the global economy so heavily depends. In terms of liabilities, an array of security threats that emanate from the region keeps the international community preoccupied. There are significant sources of instability, including a series of conflicts within and between states as a result of ethnic and religious tensions, water scarcity and territorial disputes. As this chapter illustrates, maintaining stability in the TPC is a crucial prerequisite for world peace.

The chapter also focuses in more detail on eight of the region's pivotal states: Iran, Israel, Saudi Arabia, Turkey, Russia, South Africa, Egypt and Pakistan. What makes these states pivotal is their size, abundance of natural resources, large population, geographic location, cultural significance and/or military capabilities. Their future stability is crucial for the stability of the entire region. As discussed below, all of these pivotal states suffer from instability factors and could turn into liabilities rather than pillars of stability in the TPC.

10.1 Geographic Location of the Corridor

Having outlined the western and eastern parameters of the TPC, the following section provides a comprehensive list of all the countries and regions included in the TPC, large and small. A short description of the area's choke points will follow in order to provide more detail about the region's geostrategic features.

10.1.1 Countries and Regions in the TPC

The following countries and regions are found within the TPC's longitudinal band:

Afghanistan
Antarctica
Arctic Circle
Armenia
Azerbaijan
Bahrain
Belarus
Burundi
China (Xinjiang province)
Djibouti
Egypt
Eritrea
Ethiopia
Georgia
India (Jammu and Kashmir)
Iran
Iraq
Israel and the Palestinian
   Territories
Jordan
Kazakhstan
Kenya
Kuwait
Kyrgyzstan
Lebanon
Madagascar

Maldives
Mozambique
Oman
Pakistan
Qatar
Russian Federation
Rwanda
Saudi Arabia
Seychelles
Somalia
South Africa
Sudan
Swaziland
Syria
Tajikistan
Tanzania
Turkey
Turkmenistan
Uganda
Ukraine
United Arab Emirates
Uzbekistan
Yemen
Zambia
Zimbabwe

10.1.2 Choke Points

Choke points are narrow international waterways that a number of states depend on for trade and military purposes. Because they are narrow, they can easily be closed off to shipping. Because of the lack of an alternative maritime route, the blockage of a choke point can have serious economic and military implications for states that depend on these maritime passageways. Indeed, maritime transport is the backbone of world trade and petroleum imports.[6] Hence, it is of vital importance for the global economy that these key sea lanes remain open.

Powerful states whose economic well-being depends on these passageways have tried to maintain influence over these key areas, mostly by cultivating friendly relations or forming alliances with states bordering the choke points. For the United States, keeping these passageways open is a crucial prerequisite for maintaining its overall global influence. Our TPC contains four major choke points:

1) The *Strait of Hormuz* is a narrow passageway that connects the Gulf of Oman and the Arabian Sea with the Persian Gulf. At its narrowest point, the strait is only about 34 kilometres wide. Oman and the United Arab Emirates are located on one side of the strait, while Iran is on the other. In 2018, 21 million barrels of oil were shipped through this strait every day to, among others, the United States, Europe and Japan. The Strait of Hormuz is considered the most vital choke point in the world.[7]

2) The *Bab el-Mandeb* connects the Red Sea with the Gulf of Aden and the Arabian Sea. Djibouti and Eritrea make up the strait's western shore and Yemen its eastern shore. Millions of barrels of oil destined for Europe, the United States and East Asia pass through the strait every day. In 2017, petroleum transported through the Bab el-Mandeb strait made up about nine per cent of total seaborne-traded petroleum in 2017.[8] The strait is vulnerable to piracy and, potentially, to attacks by extremists. Moreover, the blockage of the Suez Canal would automatically impede shipment through the Bab el-Mandeb, as the two choke points make up the southern and northern exits of the Red Sea.

3) The *Suez Canal* is on Egyptian territory and connects the Red Sea with the Mediterranean. Every day, almost two million barrels of oil are shipped through the canal, which, at its narrowest point, is only three hundred metres wide.[9] A

terrorist attack, an accident or a political crisis that brings shipping to a halt would have serious consequences for Egypt's economy, as well as for the world's. In March 2021, the Suez Canal was blocked for almost a week, which cost the global marketplace almost ten billion US dollars in lost trade.[10]

4) The *Turkish Straits* consist of a set of two narrows: the Bosphorus, which links the Black Sea and the Sea of Marmara, and the Dardanelles, which link the Sea of Marmara and the Aegean Sea. The Turkish Straits are challenging to navigate due to their convoluted structure, including narrow bends and sharp turns. An accident among the thousands of heavy oil tankers that pass through the Straits every week, or a terrorist attack, would be highly dangerous and costly. The straits play a key role in the international energy supply. They figure among the main oil export routes for Russia and a number of other Eurasian countries, including Kazakhstan and Azerbaijan.[11]

10.2 Demographic Factors of Instability

Having delineated the TPC's geographic area and its choke points, sections two, three and four of this chapter outline three themes of concern that affect most countries within the TPC: demographic concerns, cultural issues and the question of water scarcity. The present section deals with demographic trends in the TPC that have the potential to cause instability in the region: rapid population growth and increasing migratory movements.

The population of the Middle East is growing rapidly and is expected to reach almost 537 million by 2025.[12] The populations of Pakistan, Tajikistan, Turkmenistan, Uzbekistan and Kyrgyzstan are also growing rapidly.[13] These states are already having difficulties providing adequate services, including health care, for their populations. Nor have they been able to create enough jobs to absorb the millions of new job-market entrants.[14] A striking consequence of rapid population growth in these areas is the large number of young people who can be recruited into various social movements and accelerate instability.

Population pressure can also lead to migratory movements. The influx of large numbers of migrants can put pressure on resources and the economy of destination countries, which can have political implications. Migrants can also change a state's ethnic balance. Population growth in the TPC and migration will affect states outside the corridor as well. Europe, for instance, has to and will continue to deal with an increasing number of migrants in search of employment. This will have security implications when it comes to illegal migration, and it will have social implications in European states that have so far had difficulties integrating people from different faiths and ethnicities into the mainstream of society.[15]

10.3 Cultural Fault Lines

There are serious ethnic and religious divisions in many states within the TPC. These divisions threaten social peace and political stability within affected states and often have repercussions across borders. In fact, violent rivalries between different ethnic and religious factions continue to make many regions within the TPC highly unstable. In a country like Rwanda, for example, ethnic tensions led to the commission, in 1994, of a genocide.[16] In others, ethnic tensions have led to decades-long conflicts driven by deep-rooted hostility towards those perceived to be different on the basis of ethnicity or religion. In Israel and the Palestinian Territories, for example, there is conflict between Jewish Israelis on the one side, and Arab Israelis and Palestinians on the other.[17] In Turkey, low-intensity warfare has long been waged between the Turks and the Kurds.[18] These ongoing conflagrations produce a large number of refugees that often put pressure on other states' resources and also impact social dynamics in neighbouring states. This is the case, for instance, for countries such as Lebanon and Turkey which, combined, host millions of refugees escaping the conflict in Syria. Particularly in the case of Lebanon, the huge foreign presence in the country, which also represents a humanitarian crisis in itself, is threatening the country's already fragile governance system.[19] Such ethnic and religious rivalries within a single country can prompt other states to intervene on behalf of one faction. Some states risk outright fragmentation due to ethnic separatism and could become major instability factors within the entire region. A wide variety of ethnic groups inhabit Central Eurasia, and the international borders of most of the states there do not correspond to ethnic settlement patterns, which is the enduring source of friction. Section seven of this chapter will explore in more detail some of the major cultural fault lines along which conflicts occur in different countries of the region.

10.4 Water Scarcity

Fresh water is scarce in many parts of the TPC. Some states are located downstream on rivers that could easily be diverted by states upstream. This condition does not bode well for stability and security among many of these states. Here are just a few examples: Israel is highly dependent on the waters of the River Jordan, whose headwaters (the Hasbani Springs and the Yarmouk River) are also needed by Jordan and Syria. Similarly, Syria draws on water resources from the Euphrates, on which Iraq is highly dependent downstream. Both countries in turn depend on Turkey, where both the Euphrates and Tigris originate. As the population of Middle Eastern states continues to grow, water scarcity could turn into a major source of conflict in the area.[20] In fact, tensions between these countries are already escalating when it comes to water. Although Israel and Jordan struck a deal in 1994 to ensure equitable allocation of the water from the Yarmouk River, Israel has nonetheless repeatedly used water as a political weapon against Jordan by damming the water that ordinarily flows into that country.[21] In parallel, for the water security of countries dependent on the Tigris and the Euphrates, the construction of dams by Turkey is having detrimental consequences for both Syria and Iraq,[22] as is that of Iranian dams for Iraq.[23] In the latter case, in particular, if Iran continues to ignore Iraq's interests, the water scarcity caused by Iranian dams could potentially trigger not only mass migration, but also a return to war between the two countries.[24]

Egypt draws most of its water from the River Nile. However, water from the White Nile and Blue Nile also flows through Sudan, Ethiopia, Kenya, Uganda, Rwanda, Burundi, Tanzania and the Democratic Republic of Congo. As these upstream countries develop and their demand for fresh water and energy rises, several countries have plans to build hydroelectric dams along the rivers, thus reducing the amount of water that eventually flows into densely populated Egypt. The Grand Ethiopian Renaissance Dam is currently under construction and has been a source of growing tensions in the Nile River basin ever since Ethiopia began building it in 2011.[25] Despite Egypt's repeated calls for an equitable agreement on the distribution of the Nile's waters, Ethiopia has continued with the project, triggering what has, so far, been an unsuccessful diplomatic intervention by the African Union.[26] In fact, tensions between Egypt, Ethiopia and Sudan (the latter of which may suffer the impact of water depletion but will also reap the economic benefits of increased hydroelectric energy production stemming from the construction of the dam) continue to increase. If left unresolved, these tensions could lead to a serious regional geopolitical crisis which, in turn, may trigger a military conflict or the intervention of the UN Security Council.[27]

The Arabian Peninsula is extremely dry and water is thus naturally sparse. This has led some of the wealthy Gulf states to rely heavily on desalination facilities, which are expensive and require a lot of energy. A further disadvantage is that these facilities would be vulnerable assets in case of war, and thus make the states that rely on them vulnerable to even a small-scale, conventional military attack on these crucial lifelines.[28]

Water shortages are similarly expected to take on an alarming dimension in South Asia. According to the World Bank, India's extensive use of groundwater has resulted in rapidly decreasing water tables and has already led to extreme shortages in some of India's most populated regions.[29] Water pollution is another major problem for both human health and the environment, and India will need to make major efforts to build wastewater treatment plants.

Rapid population growth, economic development and urbanisation, as well as poor water management and wasteful irrigation techniques, are depleting water resources in a way that exceeds replenishment in many parts of the TPC. Droughts, which seem to be happening more frequently as a consequence of global warming, can be expected to further exacerbate water scarcity, which will translate into a decline in food production.

10.5 Antarctica's Contribution to Rising Sea Levels

Antarctica, which is also part of the TPC, may contribute to a potential global catastrophe in connection with global warming. The continental ice sheet in Antarctica holds vast amounts of water, and it has a physical tipping point beyond which ice melting can accelerate at an irreversible and catastrophic rate. According to a study published in *Nature* in 2021, if emissions are not drastically lowered, this critical threshold could be reached by 2060,[30] 'when today's elementary school kids are raising their families'.[31] The current rate of melting is already contributing to sea-level rises, a development that is expected to hit Asia particularly hard.[32]

The role of the North and South Poles as 'barometers of climate-change effects' cannot be overestimated. Global weather systems are strongly driven by the Antarctic.[33] As global warming changes that continent, global weather will change as well. Keeping Antarctica pristine and taking decisive action on planetary warming is an important prerequisite for global environmental security. The melting of ice in Antarctica should not be seen as an open invitation for further fossil fuel exploration – burning fossil fuels is what is causing the melting in the first place. Instead, the melting of Antarctic ice should be considered a warning for the international community to prevent the continued warming of the atmosphere. Antarctica thus constitutes a key spot within the TPC. The melting South Pole serves as a constant reminder and symbol for the growing threats to international security and prosperity posed by global warming.

10.6 Oil and Gas Resources

Central Eurasia (especially the Caspian basin) and the Persian Gulf together have over 70 per cent of the world's known oil and gas reserves.[34] While the region's energy supply is finite, demand for energy resources is constantly rising. Although renewable energies will play an increasingly important role in the future, we have not yet discovered a substitute for oil that is equally easily available and fit for use.[35] With rising energy demand, the region and its resources are growing in geopolitical importance for an ever greater number of countries. In addition to the actual location of the oil and gas resources, the location and direction of the pipelines that bring the resources to consumer countries and/or seaports have also become crucial and sensitive geopolitical issues.

Ironically, instability in many states within the TPC may become worse as a result of the intensified exploitation of vital strategic resources. Since some Central Asian states are weak but have lucrative natural resources, they are prone to intervention from outside. Moreover, because the population at large in most of these states is quite poor, those sections of the population that acquire control over the natural resources are often able to control or buy off the military and the police, eliminate political rivals and consequently monopolise political power.

As fossil fuels become more difficult to come by and the race for access to new fossil fuel reserves intensifies, some states are now starting to eye prospective energy reserves in the Arctic Ocean and Antarctica. Melting ice may mean that these reserves will become accessible for exploitation within the next few decades. Both the North and the South Poles could potentially become new frontiers for resource conflicts between states that lay claim to part of the resource-rich seabeds. As I already discussed, this new exploitation of carbon fuels can only exacerbate the climate change emergency.

10.6.1 *The Persian Gulf*

The Persian Gulf holds a significant proportion of the world's oil resources.[36] A blockage in the flow of oil from this region would have a severe impact on the global economy. Hence, the United States continues to consider the Persian Gulf a priority in strategic terms and maintains a considerable military presence in the region. Meanwhile, Asian countries, including India and China, are also keen to safeguard the oil supplies from the Persian Gulf region that they, too, depend on to satisfy their growing energy needs.[37] As long as the world economy remains dependent on fossil fuels, the Persian Gulf will remain of pivotal geopolitical significance.

Europe is expected to face gas shortages within the coming decade. Policymakers across Europe are trying to counteract climate change and seeking more affordable renewable energies and potential emerging technologies, such as hydrogen. They are thus reluctant to invest in the old infrastructure of the region's utilities that already face power supply problems. As a result, several European governments will be forced to import more gas from the TPC region over the coming years.[38] Asian countries, including India, are also interested in tapping into the region's energy supplies.[39]

The geopolitical importance of the Persian Gulf was made clear in 2019, when various instances of interference with and attacks against shipping vessels of other countries in the Gulf were attributed to Iran's Islamic Revolutionary Guard Corps Navy, despite Tehran's repeated denial of all involvement.[40] These malign operations led to the launch by the United States of Operation Sentinel, a coalition with Australia, Bahrain, Britain, Qatar, Saudi Arabia and the United Arab Emirates (subsequently joined by additional countries), which established a military patrolling system to promote maritime stability, ensure safe passage and de-escalate tensions in international waters throughout the Persian Gulf, the Strait of Hormuz, and other strategic chokepoints in the region in the interests of international trade and security.[41] Although there are also other security threats in the region, the main objective of Operation Sentinel was primarily to combat Iran's increasingly threatening and ambitious behaviour in the Gulf,[42] as demonstrated by the unveiling of a new – and significantly larger – Iranian warship in June 2021.[43]

10.6.2 The Caspian Basin

The Caspian Sea region is an increasingly important provider of global energy. This region includes Russia, Azerbaijan, Kazakhstan, Turkmenistan, Uzbekistan and Iran and possesses large oil and natural gas reserves from onshore fields as well as offshore deposits in the sea.[44] Development of these resources started in the 1990s, and the United States, Russia, China, Japan, India and the EU have all shown a keen interest in them.[45] The US government has maintained strong cooperation with the three independent former Soviet republics – Azerbaijan, Georgia and Turkmenistan – to develop these fuel sources and assert their independence from Russia.[46] Meanwhile, however, Russia continues to see the three former Soviet republics as part of its sphere of influence, and it resents US involvement in the region, especially given its proximity to the Black Sea and Syria.[47]

What complicates the transport of Caspian Sea resources to destination countries in Europe and Asia is that the three major oil- and gas-producing countries around the Caspian Sea – Azerbaijan, Kazakhstan and Turkmenistan – are landlocked and have no direct access to international waterways. In other words, these countries need to build pipelines that cross other states to reach seaports where the oil can be shipped to destination countries. This has important geopolitical implications.

Building pipelines through Iran may make sense from a purely geographic perspective, but it has several political and economic drawbacks. First, there is the fact that Iran is hostile to the United States. Central Asian states are reluctant to alienate the United States, not just because it is the world's only superpower, but also because US companies have heavily invested in the development of fossil fuels in the Caspian basin.[48] A further advantage of not using the Iran route and instead exporting Caspian oil through different channels – such as through the Black Sea or the Mediterranean – is that it reduces over-dependence on the Persian Gulf for oil shipment and diversifies supply lines.[49]

10.6.3 Russian Federation

Russia has the eighth-largest oil reserves in the world[50] and is one of the leading exporters of natural gas.[51] As a major energy supplier, Russia has an enviable geographical location, with its large land mass linking the European and Asian continents. Among its two main gas and oil hubs, the one in the Caspian Sea region mostly supplies states in Europe, while the other, in Siberia, delivers energy to various countries in Asia.[52]

Russia has started to make use of its energy resources to exert political pressure on other states, either implicitly or explicitly. In June 2014, Russia cut gas supplies to Ukraine in the midst of the crisis between the two countries following Russia's annexation of Crimea. While Russia claimed that it was simply trying to prompt its neighbour to pay its gas debt, Western countries widely interpreted the Kremlin's move as a method of exerting political pressure on Ukraine.[53] In 2010, a similar crisis had erupted between Belarus and Russia over gas debt.[54]

In light of threats such as these, European states are attempting to diversify the sources of their gas supplies, through the development of new projects like BP's Caspian Sea project, which enables Europe to import gas from Azerbaijan and thereby counter Russia's influence.[55] Germany and Russia's recent Nord Stream 2 pipeline moves in the opposite direction, however. The aim of this pipeline is to bring gas from Russia to Germany without having to pass through Ukraine, and thus safeguard Germany from any effect of the tensions between those two states.[56] For this precise reason, the construction of the Nord Stream 2 pipeline has been extremely controversial from the very beginning, with the US presidential administrations of both Obama and Trump issuing sanctions against all of the involved parties, including Germany.[57] In July 2021, however, the Biden administration reversed the US's previous position and expressed support for the pipeline, in a move that has been criticised as opening the doors to Russia's influence over Europe through its gas supplies.[58]

Russia is also trying to locate its new pipelines and gas-storage facilities in strategically important neighbouring countries like Hungary, Bulgaria, Greece and Turkey in order to forge closer ties with them.[59] Energy is likely to remain an important and powerful tool of diplomacy and influence in Russian geopolitics.

10.6.4 *Arctic Ocean and Antarctica*

Abundant fossil fuel resources are thought to lie underneath the seabeds of both the Arctic and Antarctica. The Arctic is expected to become ice-free in the summer by 2035,[60] which would make the exploitation of these fossil fuel reserves feasible. The resource wealth in the melting Arctic Ocean has the potential to become a serious issue of contention between coastal states that all claim rights to part of the Arctic. The five Arctic powers – Russia, the United States, Canada, Norway and Denmark – are currently in the process of making their claims on the Arctic seabed.[61] According to the UN Convention on the Law of the Sea (UNCLOS), states can claim ownership of the seabed beyond their exclusive economic zone of two hundred nautical miles if the seabed is an extension of the state's continental shelf of shallower waters.[62]

Furthermore, as I explore in more depth in chapter 10.7 and in chapter 11.1.6, the tensions between the aforementioned states over the Arctic's resources will be further compounded by the fact that the melting of the Arctic ice is opening new shipping routes, such as the Northwest Passage.[63] The combined effect of the richness in resources and the economic advantages of Arctic shipping routes (see chapter 11.1.6) will mean that the Arctic is likely to become an extremely relevant geopolitical corridor.

Antarctica is also thought to be rich in fossil fuels and minerals. Yet unlike the Arctic, Antarctica is under a well-regulated treaty regime that forbids nations from exploiting the area's natural resources and claiming new parts of its territory while the agreement is in force.[64] In the landmark treaty, drawn up in 1959, Argentina, Australia, Britain, Chile, France, New Zealand and Norway, which are close to Antarctica or have historical ties to the region, agreed to suspend their territorial claims. The United States and the Soviet Union (now Russia) also ratified the Antarctica Treaty and thus abide by the treaty's principle to keep the South Pole demilitarised. The treaty foresees a possible review of the ban on mineral and oil exploration in 2048 at the earliest.[65] Yet as countries become more desperate for fossil fuels and as the seabed becomes more easily accessible for drilling because of the melting of ice sheets, it is clear that some countries might be tempted to start drilling in Antarctica, which could lead to the dissolution of the (to date) highly successful Antarctica Treaty regime.

10.7 Zones of Instability and Conflict

10.7.1 Arab-Israeli Conflict
The Arab-Israeli conflict remains a prime source of instability in the Middle East. The prospects for a resolution of the conflict remain dim. The plight of the Palestinians remains of crucial importance for Arabs and the way they view the United States and its allies. The injustices perpetrated by Israel against the Palestinian people and the need to fight these injustices remains a central preoccupation of Middle Eastern

politics. Continued injustices and humiliation in Israel and the Palestinian Territories are often used by radical and extremist elements in the region to attract new members. The resolution of the conflict has been frozen and faces numerous obstacles, including illegal settlements, to which recent administrations have still been unable to properly react.[66]

10.7.2 Iraq

The removal of Saddam Hussein in 2003 left a power vacuum in Iraq that renders the country vulnerable to foreign influence and intervention. There are numerous indications that Iran is, at least indirectly, supporting violent sectarian militias to gain influence and promote its declared extremist sectarian politics.[67] However, because of Iraq's geopolitical significance, its future stability will be important for achieving and maintaining peace in the region. The COVID-19 pandemic, the revival of tribal divisions and the intrusion of regional powers put Iraq at further risk of division and feed distrust in institutions.[68]

10.7.3 The Persian Gulf

Since the Persian Gulf is one of the world's largest oil-producing areas, any instability in the region will have major repercussions throughout the world. Given its geopolitical significance, ongoing foreign intervention in local conflicts there is highly likely.[69]

Some states in the Persian Gulf resemble so-called rentier states. Governments in rentier states use their natural resource wealth to pay for welfare benefits and services without taxing their population. Pure rentier states run the risk of becoming highly unstable in the long term because they depend on the continued availability of the natural resource in question at sustainable prices. Rentier states therefore need to diversify their economies and develop an industrial infrastructure.[70]

Iran's position as both a regional power and rogue state in the international community keeps the region at continued risk of conflict. The recent renewal of discussions on the Joint Comprehensive Plan of Action (JCPOA) could positively influence the region's relations with other countries.[71]

10.7.4 Libya

After the fall of Mu'ammar Gaddafi's regime in 2011, former grievances reappeared to tarnish the legitimacy of the Government of National Accord (GNA), which rules from the city of Tripoli in the western part of Libya and is backed by the United Nations.[72] General Haftar from the Libyan National Army (LNA) kept control over the East until March 2021 when a government of national unity was formed.

The current efforts to unify governance in Libya are however challenged by old tensions and foreign influence. Mercenaries trained and financed by regional or global powers are still present while disagreements over security and power-sharing arrangements remain unsolved.[73] This unstable environment favoured the emergence of human trafficking networks which benefit from the severe migration crisis in the Mediterranean. Despite the fact that the European Union transferred a significant amount of money to improve crisis response, these funds ended up by being used to fund coastguards and detention centres where migrants and refugees face numerous human rights violations including torture and extortion.[74] For the country to move forward, the constant interference by Turkey, through the support of Muslim brotherhood factions, must stop.

10.7.5 Sahel

The Sahel region is defined by the United Nations as 'the vast semi-arid region of Africa separating the Sahara Desert to the north and tropical savannas to the south' and includes several countries, notably Mali, Niger and Chad.[75] This region has traditionally been inhabited by nomadic people who resisted the processes of centralisation following the establishment of borders by colonial powers.[76] In numerous cases, this resistance was echoed by violent groups which established their authority on marginalisation, fear and the lack of central governments' authority.

Mali is a perfect example of these dynamics. Indeed, in 2012, nomadic people from the north of the country started a rebellion against the central government. Violent extremist groups opportunistically used this rebellion to gain influence and seize territory. Following a request for assistance from the Malian government to the international community, France sent military forces and a UN Peacekeeping Mission was established.[77] This was the beginning of a lasting foreign presence in the whole region. Despite reinforcing states' projection in affected parts of their territory, the lack of an exit strategy further endangers the Sahel.[78] This zone has also traditionally been a center of transit and exchanges. Today, criminal networks exploit these routes and significant human rights violations including human trafficking and extortion are common.

10.7.6 Syria

Since 2011, Syria has been affected by a civil war which saw the emergence of terrorist groups such as the Islamic State (ISIS). The violence associated with the conflict has reached a terrifying level with significant human rights violations including torture, forced detention and arbitrary killings.

Foreign forces are also present, including Russia, which supports the Syrian regime against the rebels, as well as the United States as part of a wider international coalition fighting ISIS. Syrian territory has been used as a battlefield for numerous proxy wars, for instance those between Iran and Israel or between Turkey and the Kurds. Turkish and Iranian military and sectarian involvement is a very serious violation of state sovereignty and will complicate peace and reconciliation.

In addition, the Syrian conflict has created a refugee crisis with repercussions for the whole region and Europe. UNHCR reported 6.6 million refugees in neighbouring countries and 6.7 million internally displaced people.[79] The humanitarian situation, including a high level of poverty particularly affecting children and women, has worsened due to the COVID-19 pandemic.

10.7.7 Yemen

The illegitimate military coup by the Houthi sectarian group in 2014 with the support of Iran has created a massive political, economic, security and humanitarian crisis. It was condemned by the UN Security Council Resolution 2216 which reiterated its support for the Gulf state to restore the deposed legitimate government. The humanitarian crisis is mostly a result of the prevention and abuse of foreign aid by the extremist Houthi group, which to fully comply with the Stockholm Agreement and the recent Saudi proposal for peace and reconciliation.

The civil war in Yemen took a significant turn in 2015 with the Saudi-led intervention to support the government against Houthi rebels. A peace agreement brokered in December 2020 has only been partially implemented.[80] As with other conflicts in the region, the battlefield in Yemen is also the location for a proxy war, in this instance the ongoing one between Iran and Saudi Arabia. Once again, this exogeneous dimension makes the situation in Yemen volatile and dependent on the broader dynamics of global peace and security management. Settling the situation in Yemen would most likely require an overall easing of tensions in the whole region.

The conflict has triggered one of the worst humanitarian crises in the world, including the transmission of numerous diseases like cholera.[81] Insufficient access to food and water supplies is also contributing to the worsening sanitary situation. According to the World Food Programme, 16.2 million people in Yemen are food insecure and 20.1 million are in need of humanitarian assistance.[82] This crisis has been exacerbated by the Covid-19 pandemic.

10.7.8 Somalia

Somalia has been plagued by conflict since 1992 when the then president was overthrown and the country became highly divided between different military factions. Since then, violent Islamist groups, including Al-Shabaab, supported by the broader Al-Qaeda network, have tried to seize parts of the territory and worsened the security situation. This lasting civil war has created food and water insecurity.

According to the World Food Programme, 5.6 million people are food insecure and the severe floods, as well as other catastrophic climatic events such as poor rainfall and low water levels, have put food security further in danger.[83] The impact on livestock has also contributed to the rise in food prices. In addition, the spread of diseases, such as COVID-19, cholera and, more recently, desert locusts, are further worsening the precarious sanitary and food security situation.[84]

10.7.9 Central Eurasia

The states of Central Asia and their southern neighbours, Afghanistan, Iran, Pakistan and Turkey, are highly ethnically diverse and many ethnic groups are represented in several states. The borders of the seven former Soviet states of Kazakhstan, Kyrgyzstan, Tajikistan, Uzbekistan, Turkmenistan, Azerbaijan and Georgia were in most cases drawn almost arbitrarily by the Soviet Union in the 1920s and 1930s.[85] Their international borders therefore do not correspond to ethnic settlement patterns.[86] Uzbekistan is the most homogeneous among them. Large parts of the populations of Kazakhstan, Kyrgyzstan, Uzbekistan and Turkmenistan speak Turkic languages. Tajikistan, by contrast, has Persian roots.[87] Afghanistan shares common ethnic groups with Central and South Asian states: Pashtuns, the largest ethnic group in Afghanistan, also live high numbers in Pakistan; Baluchs live in Pakistan, Iran and Afghanistan; and Tajiks living in the north of Afghanistan make up over 25 per cent of the country's population.[88]

The five former Soviet Central Asian republics achieved independence in 1991 but they remain weak. Ethnically heterogeneous, they often lack national coherence and are prone to foreign influence. Russia is trying to keep them within its sphere of influence, while Iran and Turkey are competing for sway in the Muslim Central Asian states and Azerbaijan.[89]

Several territorial conflicts continue to plague the region. In November 2020, an armed conflict broke out between Armenia and Azerbaijan over Nagorno-Karabakh, a part of Azerbaijan that is predominantly settled by ethnic Armenians. Such conflicts have important regional implications because of Azerbaijan's pivotal geopolitical position with access to the resources of the Caspian basin. Brzezinski suggests that, if the country were to become stronger and more stable, and if it started to forge closer ties with ethnically related Turkey, Azerbaijan could serve as a counterweight to Russia in the region.[90] While Russia does not want Azerbaijan to forge closer ties with Turkey and the West, another powerful regional player, Iran, remains equally wary of a strong and assertive Azerbaijan. There are twice as many Azeris living in north-western Iran as there are in Azerbaijan, and Iran thus fears the rise of separatist aspirations among this minority group.[91]

These unresolved tensions remain a significant instability factor at the geostrategically significant fault lines of Central Asia and the greater Middle East. They also contribute to the lack of cooperation within the region; improving cooperation is an important prerequisite for economic development and improved security there.

Finally, the region is afflicted by transnational security challenges that also affect Europe and North America. Among these problems – which are often the consequence of poor governance and widespread corruption – are human trafficking, illegal immigration and transnational criminal activity, including illegal trade in narcotics and weapons. Russia, China, Kazakhstan, Kyrgyzstan, Tajikistan and Uzbekistan set up the Shanghai Cooperation Organisation (SCO) to increase peaceful international action to solve many of the problems afflicting the region. The SCO has taken some promising initiatives in this direction. Moreover, both NATO and the EU have important strategic incentives to resolve the stalled regional conflicts and promote stability in this area.[92]

10.7.10 Afghanistan

Located at a strategically significant point between Iran and Pakistan, Afghanistan remains one of the poorest and most unstable countries in the world.[93] Despite the toppling of their first regime by US troops in 2001, the Taliban remained a powerful and destructive force in the country and regained full control at the moment of US withdrawal in 2021.[94]

This poorly planned US exit from Afghanistan and the US deal with the Taliban group will complicate the political dynamics and regional and international security implications for many years to come. It allowed the Taliban to rapidly regain territorial control over the whole of Afghanistan; they entered Kabul on 15 August 2021. Individuals who have cooperated with the US and NATO forces are already at risk of reprisal, and thousands of people are attempting to flee the country and to seek asylum in other countries. A civil war could erupt and put in danger the already precarious national unity of the country. It remains to be seen whether responsible behaviour and assistance by the international community could prevent such a scenario.

The Afghan drugs industry also contributes to lawlessness. Since Afghanistan is a major producer of opium, the entire region is affected by drugs networks that smuggle the drugs to consumer markets outside of Afghanistan.[95] Organised crime, especially drug trafficking, is a destabilising factor in the whole of Central Eurasia.[96]

Millions of Afghan refugees also constitute a destabilising factor in neighbouring Iran[97] and Pakistan.[98] There are also (as of early 2021) four million internally displaced persons in Afghanistan,[99] comprising especially women and children, who compete with local impoverished Afghans over scarce resources, including land, shelter, clean drinking water, education, access to jobs and health facilities.[100] Desperate poverty and lawlessness increase the appeal of radical and extremist ideologies. It is in the interest of neighbouring states and the wider Central Eurasian region that Afghanistan becomes stable and moderate state.[101]

10.7.11 Kashmir

When former British India was partitioned between Pakistan and India at independence, the two states adopted different political ideologies. While India defined itself as a secular state with a socialist outlook, Pakistan identified as an Islamic state.[102]

Relations between India and Pakistan remain tense as a result of their unresolved dispute over the Kashmir region. When India and Pakistan split into two separate states – majority-Hindu and majority-Muslim, respectively – the majority-Muslim territories of Jammu and Kashmir were administered by a Hindu maharaja.[103]

India and Pakistan have repeatedly gone to war over the Kashmir region,[104] and the fact that both countries now have nuclear weapons has only raised the stakes of the simmering conflict and thus makes its resolution a necessity.[105] Tensions continue to regularly occur across the line of control and a curfew has been imposed by Indian authorities since 2016. More recently, India withdrew Jammu and Kashmir state's special status which had given it a form of autonomy, thus endangering minority rights.[106] This move, regular tensions and the lack of the prospect of peace continue to put this region at risk of major instability.

10.7.12 Xinjiang Province

The TPC includes the autonomous Chinese province of Xinjiang, which is settled by Uyghurs, a Turkic Muslim people whose language closely resembles Uzbek. The Uyghurs have intensified their attempt to separate from China since the Turkic republics of Central Asia gained independence from the Soviet Union.[107] The existence of natural resources in Xinjiang – the oil-rich Tarim basin lies within the Uighur Autonomous Province – increases the interests at stake for China.[108] For this reason, the past few years have seen an intensification of Chinese operations in Xinjiang, as well as an attempt at re-instilling 'Chinese characteristics' into the Uyghur population through intensive surveillance, re-education camps and other severe forms of repression.[109]

China is accused of committing crimes against humanity in this region including torture, forced labour and sexual abuse. Various reports and testimonies on social media, from NGOs, and from UN bodies, emerged in recent times to shed light on the problem and scale of such violations.[110] In 2019, the situation in Xinjiang gained further attention with the publication of a letter signed by numerous UN member states, notably European countries, calling for UN experts to gain access to the region.[111] China retaliated with the support of other member states, including Muslim countries, the representatives of which were invited to visit Xinjiang. Their permanent representatives to the United Nations wrote a letter praising the Chinese authorities' efforts at human rights protection.[112] This diplomatic battle took place within the context of social media campaigns and also via boycotts and investigations into potential complicity in human rights abuses by private firms operating in China. The situation only worsened the already tense situation between China and Western countries.

10.7.13 Horn of Africa

The Horn of Africa region – encompassing Yemen, Sudan, Ethiopia, Eritrea, Djibouti and Somalia – remains collectively important for the stability of the TPC. These states, torn by conflict and suffering from weak state institutions and law-enforcement capabilities, are in danger of further failure and instability.[113] In recent decades, civil conflict and bloodshed in the region have created hundreds of thousands of refugees.[114]

In addition to the large numbers of refugees and internally displaced persons, as a result of state fragility and conflict situations, negative security externalities have prevailed in the contemporary Horn of Africa, including, *inter alia*, transnational organised crime, violent extremism and terrorism, illegal cross-border trade and a flourishing trade in light weapons. According to the 2018 Global Peace Index and the State Fragility Index, the Horn is the most negatively affected region in the world.[115] Indeed, only in the Horn of Africa, out of the entire African continent, did secessionist movements succeed in breaking away from previously incorporated entities (as was the case with Eritrea and South Sudan), with significant security implications for the region.[116]

More recently, Ethiopia announced the second filling of a dam which could affect the flow of the River Nile. Both Egypt and Sudan publicly opposed the project. While it constitutes a source of national pride for Ethiopians, the dam could generate water scarcity for other countries and communities, particularly for farmers.[117] The African Union and other international actors have responded to this crisis, which is likely to continue requiring mediation. Given increasing climate hazards and the water scarcity in the region, such tensions could evolve into a serious crisis and should not remain unresolved.

10.7.14 Great Lakes Region

African states within the tripwire pivotal corridor all suffer from various levels of instability. Some of them still suffer from the after-effects of genocide and civil war, as is the case, respectively, for Rwanda and the Democratic Republic of the Congo.[118] They are all seriously affected by HIV/AIDS and other communicable diseases, including Ebola.[119] Hunger resulting from droughts and high food prices adds to the misery of many Africans.[120] Furthermore, high rates of crime, aided by the available abundance of small arms, remain a factor of instability.[121]

10.7.15 Arctic Ocean

The ice covering the North Pole is melting, which renders the Arctic Ocean increasingly accessible for shipping and resource exploration. I have already mentioned the potential for state rivalries regarding access to Arctic Ocean resources. This section deals with an additional geopolitical issue emerging from the increased accessibility of the Arctic Ocean because of melting ice: the fact that the area may soon become an important maritime passage route for the international shipping industry. The so-called Northwest Passage over North America became ice-free for the first time in human memory in the summer of 2007.[122] The ice covering vast stretches of the Arctic is now becoming thin enough for the waters to be navigable year-round, with the aid of modern icebreakers.[123] Some passageways may even become fully navigable without the aid of icebreakers.[124] In short, the Arctic Ocean may soon turn into a busy corridor for international shipping between Europe and Asia.[125]

As Arctic passages shorten the distance between Europe and Southeast Asia and between the west coast of the United States and Europe by several thousand nautical miles, the shipping industry will be able to save billions of US dollars a year.[126] The opening of these new shipping routes may relieve some of the pressure on current choke points, including the Panama and Suez Canals and the Strait of Malacca, but it may also create new choke points at the narrowest parts of the Northwest Passage, particularly around the Canadian islands and the Bering Strait, which separates Alaska (a US state) from Russia.[127] In the next chapter, I delve further into the likelihood that the five countries with Arctic Ocean shorelines (the United States, Russia, Canada, Denmark and Norway) will need to come up with a regime to police the shipping lanes and ensure safe and orderly passage.[128] Another challenge will be to keep the area non-militarised.[129]

Indeed, with Arctic ice melting fast, the North Pole could soon become a new area of conflict between major powers. As I explore in chapter 11.1.6, all five countries that border the Arctic Ocean claim territory beyond their maritime borders fixed by the UN Convention on the Law of the Sea. Some of their respective territorial claims overlap. For instance, Canada's claim to the Northwest Passage is opposed by many nations, including the United States, which considers the passage to be part of international waters.[130] Although it is possible that these territorial disputes can be resolved peacefully with the help of international legal instruments, it is important that they be resolved before the area becomes militarised. The Arctic region is thus an important focal point in the TPC that statesmen and women need to pay attention to in the coming decades and that will have increasingly serious implications for future geopolitical stability.

10.8 'Pivotal States' within the TPC

The regional powers I look at in this section are of major geostrategic importance. They serve, or have the potential to serve, as anchors in their respective neighbourhoods. On the other hand, they all have instability problems of their own. Some of these factors are domestic, including political instability, ethnic conflicts, rapid population growth, poverty and disease. Others are related more to foreign policy, such as territorial disputes or conflicts with other states over illegal weapons programmes. It will be important for other countries to help these states become fortresses of stability and solid economic growth, to enable them to have a positive stabilising influence on their more fragile and poorer neighbours.

Turkey, Egypt, Pakistan and South Africa belong to the list of 'pivotal states' that Robert Chase, Emily Hill and Paul Kennedy singled out in their 1998 study *The Pivotal States: A New Framework for US Policy in the Developing World*.[131] The authors argued that these states are all populous, developing countries with a relatively good infrastructure and sound economic growth potential whose stability and well-being is important for achieving peace and prosperity in their regions. Chase and his co-authors argued that by concentrating development aid on these states and helping them to become peaceful, democratic and prosperous, the United States and other wealthy countries would help not only the direct recipients of the aid, but also the developing countries adjacent to them, which would benefit from peaceful political ties and increased economic cooperation with regional leaders.[132] Otherwise, the authors warned, allowing these pivotal states to plunge into chaos and instability would have dangerous regional implications. In other words, they would become costly failed states, leading to large migration flows and economic turmoil in their wider neighbourhoods.

In the context of the TPC, at least four additional states – Iran, Israel, Saudi Arabia and Russia – need to be added. These are large powers – in the case of Russia, one of the world's two largest nuclear powers (with the United States) – whose future development, foreign policy and internal stability have significant regional reverberations. The following sections will focus mostly on the potential weaknesses and threats that could emanate from these pivotal states. Knowing about their areas of instability could help statesmen and women devise appropriate policies towards them as part of their efforts to promote stability in the TPC.

10.8.1 Iran

Its geopolitical position, energy resources and the size of its population make Iran a pivotal regional power. It can be singled out as an important geopolitical pivot whose stability is crucial for the overall stability of the TPC. Even as an old state, Iran's stability is less than guaranteed, as its ethnic diversity could easily translate into separatist pressures and domestic political turmoil.[133] Azeris, Kurds, Baluchs, Turkmens and Arabs form substantial minorities within the country.[134] Still, a strong sense of Persian cultural identity and nationalism persists in the country.

Iran has a nuclear programme that some countries and experts believe is meant not merely to develop nuclear technology for civilian purposes, as the regime purports, but also to enrich uranium at the weapons-grade level, which could be used to build a nuclear bomb. A nuclear-armed Iran could have two grave consequences. First, it would increase Iran's ambition to be a dominant state in the region, with negative consequences for peace and freedom.[135] Second, Iran's acquisition of nuclear weapons would prompt other regional powers to acquire nuclear weapons to balance Iran, which would put a definite end to the global nuclear non-proliferation regime.

Iran's foreign policy is strongly influenced by its ideological commitment to spread its revolutionary and violent extremist sectarian ideas to other Muslim states. As briefly mentioned above, as well as in the case study tables on Iran, this state has long favoured the use of proxy regional violent extremist militias as a means of destabilising neighbouring governments, with the aim of exerting its influence over the region while fragmenting these states. In particular, Iran provides military and financial support to groups such as Hezbollah in Lebanon,[136] the Houthis in Yemen,[137] Hamas in Israel and the Palestinian Territories,[138] as well as militias in Iraq.[139] It has also played a role in the Syrian conflict.[140]

Iran has had no overt diplomatic or commercial relations with the United States since the 1979 revolution and hostage crisis. The United States is demanding that Iran halt its nuclear-enrichment programme. President Joe Biden entered office promising to restore the Iran nuclear deal, which Trump had abandoned in 2018. Since the US quit the deal, Iran has accelerated its nuclear programme, which has strengthened Iran's position at the negotiating table. In other words, and with Russian support, Iran might resist US pressure to include in the agreement clauses requiring, for example, that Iran end its military involvement in Syria, Lebanon, Iraq or Yemen.[141]

By pretending to lend support to anti-Israel forces, Iran is – according to some commentators – diverting the world's attention from its nuclear programme while trying to increase its popularity in the region. As Anthony Cordesman explains, 'Israel's reprisals build Arab and Muslim anger against the US as Israel's allies, and make its charges that Iran is "terrorist" seem in Arab and Muslim eyes as if Iran supports "freedom fighters".'[142]

Iran's geopolitical importance in the region and the threat it presents for the stability of the Middle East and the Gulf is further compounded by its increasingly threatening behaviour in the Persian Gulf and the Red Sea. As I mentioned earlier, Iran's navy has been repeatedly accused of attacking foreign vessels, both military and civilian.[143] The possibility that Iran may gain military and economic control of the Persian Gulf, the Strait of Hormuz, and other strategic chokepoints in the region represents a serious threat for international trade and security.[144] Similar maritime threats are presented by Iran's activities in the Red Sea, where it is alleged that Iran positions military ships masked as shipping vessels to spy on neighbouring enemy states, such as Israel.[145]

While Iran considers the United States and Israel its main enemies, it has started to pursue strategic relations with a variety of key states, presumably to break its relative international isolation and to increase its international standing and diplomatic clout. Importantly, Iran is building ties with China, a relationship Iran considers to be of great strategic importance.[146] In early 2021, Iran and China signed the Strategic Cooperation Agreement reflecting a desire to intensify cooperation and trade relations over the next 25 years.[147] The growing economic and energy partnership with China makes Iran less vulnerable to economic sanctions. Stronger ties with China and Russia, both permanent members of the UN Security Council, may also benefit Iran with regard to the renegotiation of the nuclear deal.[148]

Iran could greatly benefit from the foreign investment and increased economic trade opportunities that would open up for the country if it were able to reassure the world about its peaceful nuclear intentions. Normalisation of its foreign relations will be crucial for Iran to improve domestic stability by developing its economy, creating millions of new jobs and providing a decent standard of living for its burgeoning population. This would allow Iran to become a pillar of peace and prosperity in the TPC.

10.8.2 Israel

Another state within the TPC which plays a key role in regional and global stability is Israel. Despite widespread poverty,[149] Israel has a robust economy, which has grown steadily since joining the OECD in 2010.[150] Its economic well-being is, nevertheless, dependent on the state of the peace process and not only on the state of the global economy. Indeed, by preventing the achievement of peace and demonstrating absolute disregard for the human rights of people living there, the ongoing occupation of Palestine since the 1967 war[151] and the treatment of Arab-Israelis and Palestinians in Israel are great sources of domestic insecurity, as well as international condemnation. Since Israel perceives Palestine and Palestinians as a threat to a unified Jewish state, and often groups them together with Hamas, the Iranian-backed violent extremist group fighting for Palestinian autonomy, Israeli forces often employ disproportionate means when they feel provoked, with the aim of instilling fear and completely subjugating the Palestinian population.[152]

Examples of this disproportionate behaviour include responding with airstrikes to smaller artisanal rocket attacks and employing the Israeli army against youths for throwing rocks.[153] The police often also use force against civilians for reasons that may be considered arbitrary.[154] The disproportionate use of force against the Palestinian population, which sometimes results in civilian deaths, is one of the many violations of the human rights of the large minority of Arab-Israelis and Palestinians who live in Israel or in the occupied territories. Indeed, they are subject to significant forms of exclusion and discrimination, ranging from arbitrary detention, to land confiscation, forcible transfer, lack of access to education, welfare etc.[155] Similarly, African, Sephardi and Mizrahi Jewish minorities also face systemic discrimination.[156] The fact that the political system in Israel has been dominated by unstable coalitions of right-wing conservative parties[157] who have traditionally taken strong anti-Arab and anti-Muslim stances has enabled the development of an anti-Palestinian climate in which racism, discrimination and insecurity belong to everyday life.

As mentioned above, one of the tools which Israel uses to exercise its influence over neighbouring countries is by monopolising the available water. Although the entire region has long faced a water crisis, Israel has made use of innovative technology to desalinate its waters, but has also deliberately prevented the waters from the River Yarmouk, for instance, from following their natural course and flowing into Jordan.[158]

Importantly, Israel has always been able to count on the military and political assistance of the United States. Not only has this given Israel access to some of the most sophisticated military technology, including anti-missile shield systems, but it has also provided Israel with political support in international fora such as the UNSC. This has protected Israel from the adoption of many resolutions condemning both Israel's treatment of Arabs and Palestinians, but also its aggressive behaviour towards neighbouring states and its ongoing territorial expansion.[159] Since 1967, when it first occupied Gaza and the West Bank, Israel has continued to permit hundreds of thousands of settlers to make land claims and establish Israeli settlements in Palestinian territory, displacing the local population.[160] Not only has this behaviour been condemned as illegal and a human rights violation by other states, but it is under investigation both by UN human rights experts[161] and by the International Criminal Court, on the basis that it may amount to a 'war crime'.[162] As Israel continues to refuse to return Palestinian/Syrian lands gained by military aggression in 1967, only two of its five borders are recognised by the international community.[163] Only if Israel recognises the importance of a two-state solution which allows for the existence of a Palestinian state and the return to the 1967 borders, including the Golan Heights, can long-term peace and stability be found in the region, in accordance with the Arab Peace Plan of 2002 and UN resolutions. This process would enable the gradual normalisation of relations with all Arab states and consequently play a fundamental role in the achievement of a peaceful and secure Middle East.[164]

10.8.3 Saudi Arabia

Saudi Arabia is the other pivotal state located in the Persian Gulf, in addition to Iran. Due to the fact that Islam's two holiest sites, Mecca and Medina, are located in the country, Saudi Arabia maintains a spiritual-leadership position in the entire Islamic world. Every year, millions of Muslims from all over the world visit these holy sites, which, according to the Muslim faith, every Muslim is supposed to visit once in their lifetime. In addition, the Saudi city of Jeddah is host to the headquarters of the Secretariat of the Organisation of Islamic Cooperation, an international association with 57 member states that describes itself as the 'collective voice of the Muslim world'.[165]

As the world's leading oil exporter, Saudi Arabia is a key player in global geo-economics. It can 'significantly affect market conditions and therefore the price of oil'.[166] It maintains strong relations with many oil-consuming states around the world. It also enjoys the benefits of a strong alliance with the United States and other major powers in the world (China, Russia, EU states).

Saudi Arabia has taken on a leadership role in Middle Eastern politics. It is a founding member of the Arab League and the Gulf Cooperation Council. It also uses some of its oil wealth to promote development in the Arab world. Furthermore, Saudi Arabia's role in support of an Arab-Israeli peace deal will remain crucial considering the kingdom's leverage over other Arab states. Previous Saudi-led attempts at resolving the Arab-Israel conflict include the 2002 Arab Peace Initiative.[167]

Saudi Arabia is determined to keep its pre-eminent position on the peninsula *vis-à-vis* Iran. It feels challenged by Iran's nuclear ambitions and Iran's sponsorship of violent sectarian Shia militias in Iraq, Palestine (via Hamas), Lebanon (via Hezbollah), and Yemen (via the Houthis) and it is seeking to counterbalance Iran's influence in the Muslim world.

Domestically, significant steps towards the social and economic renewal of Saudi Arabia have been taken by the Crown Prince Mohammed bin Salman in 2019, through a national programme known as Vision 2030 aimed at diversifying the Saudi economy.[168] Saudi Arabia has created six new economically powerful cities in various parts of the country, including the US$500-billion futuristic city of 'Neom'.[169] Aimed at attracting young people, these cities are home to innovative technological industries like information technology, plastics, alternative energies and petrochemicals. The country has also increased its number of high-tech universities, including the King Abdullah University for Science and Technology (KAUST).[170] All of these steps are likely to enhance Saudi Arabia's geopolitical significance.

Among the domestic challenges facing Saudi Arabia are water scarcity and a lack of arable land,[171] high birth rates and a high proportion of young people,[172] low yet increasing involvement of women in public life,[173] and dependence on a foreign labour force.[174]

Whilst Saudi Arabia is therefore a major player on the global scene, its future will be strengthened by achieving its 2030 Vision.[175] Its enhanced geopolitical power will serve as a pillar in the geostrategic balance of the TPC region, facilitating peace and prosperity regionally and internationally.

10.8.4 Turkey

Turkey has never – geographically or historically – belonged exclusively to either the East or the West. The country's unique geographic location, bridging two continents, has had a strong influence on its history. As Europe's gateway to Asia and the Middle East, it is surrounded by four seas: the Black Sea, the Aegean Sea, the Mediterranean Sea and the Sea of Marmara. As a result, it has easy access to some of the world's most important regions, including major continental trade routes and waterways such as the Mediterranean basin and the strategically significant Dardanelles and Bosphorus straits.[176]

Turkey's proximity to some of the world's largest energy exporters, including Russia and the Central Asian states, reinforces the country's strategic value. As mentioned above, the Bosphorus strait is a key supply route for energy. Turkey's role in the global energy trade has been further increased by its position at the distributing end of the Baku-Tbilisi-Ceyhan (BTC) pipeline, which transports oil from the vast reserves of the Caspian Sea region to the Mediterranean, bypassing Russia.[177] In addition, Turkey is an important exit port for oil from northern Iraq.[178]

Turkey's stability, so important for regional peace, faces both domestic and international threats. The Kurdish issue has been a major national security concern with international ramifications. Since the establishment of the Turkish Republic in 1932, the Kurdish minority has been 'torn between integration, assimilation, or rejection by the Turkish republic'.[179] In the south-east of the country, the Kurdish population has organised itself into several groups demanding self-rule or independence. The best-known among them is the Marxist-inspired Kurdistan Workers' Party (PKK), which has been active since 1984. The PKK, which wants to create an independent Kurdish state in Turkey's south-east, has been responsible for numerous terrorist attacks over the past several decades, and the violence perpetrated by PKK militants has triggered the intervention of Turkish military and police units in PKK strongholds.[180] During violent struggles with Kurdish militants in the 1980s and 1990s, 375,000 Kurds were forcibly expelled from their villages by Turkish security forces and their return has been slow.[181] In 2015, military confrontations between the Turkish central state and Kurdish nationalist groups broke out again. The conflict has international dimensions. For example, when the PKK regrouped in post-Saddam northern Iraq, Erdogan intervened militarily in northern Iraq to destroy PKK bases. The past decade has thus seen repeated clashes on the border between Turkey and Iraq, with Turkish forces conducting military operations in Iraqi territory.[182] Turkey's repeated interventions in Northern Iraq have destabilising consequences on the local population.[183] More recently, the conflict has been fed by the Syrian war, in which the parties have had a combat presence.

In recent years, Turkey has intervened militarily not only in Iraq and Syria but also in Libya, the Eastern Mediterranean and the Caucasus, in addition to supporting non-state players such as the Muslim Brotherhood, with destabilising consequences for the entire TPC.[184] In addition, major divisions exist between the secularists and traditionalists, which remain a serious instability factor within the country.[185] Moreover, Erdogan's government faces allegations that it is becoming increasingly authoritarian. Critics argue that the referendum in 2017 approved the adoption of a presidential system which has given Erdogan complete control of the executive, including the power to issue decrees and appoint his own cabinet. Although the judiciary is formally independent from the executive and the legislature, the constitutional changes that came into effect, with the referendums in 2007, 2010 and 2017, enlarged the powers of the president and the ruling party to appoint or dismiss judges and prosecutors.[186]

Turkey officially became a candidate for EU membership in 1999. EU member states remain divided, however, about the 'if' and 'when' of Turkey's accession. The ongoing disputes with Cyprus over the Turkish-populated northern part of the island and territorial sea boundaries, Turkey's relative poverty compared to other European states, its human rights record and the fact that it is a Muslim nation all remain major sticking points.[187]

The disputes over the status of Cyprus, territorial sea claims and the issue of refugees and illegal migrants trying to enter the EU have all contributed to especially fraught relations with fellow NATO member Greece, which also wants to bolster its position in the Eastern Mediterranean.[188] The tensions between the two NATO states escalated in 2020 when Turkey extended its controversial gas explorations in the Mediterranean. The situation became so hostile that many feared the countries might even fight a war.[189]

Indeed, although Turkey is a long-standing member of NATO, the past few years have seen relations between Turkey and fellow NATO countries become increasingly unstable.[190] Reasons for the deterioration of the relationship include not only the aforementioned behaviour in the Mediterranean, as well as Turkey's involvement in the Syrian and Libyan conflicts,[191] but especially its growing relationship with Russia. The factor, above all others, that has put Turkey's relations with the

United States, in particular, to the test is the 2017 signing of a deal with Russia for the acquisition of Russian S-400 surface-to-air missiles, which can be used against the American F-35 fighter jets used by many NATO states.[192] The US imposed sanctions on Turkey after the country received the first four S-400 missiles in 2019.[193] Despite that punitive measure, Turkey refused to back out of the Russian deal, arguing that the missiles are a necessary defensive and not offensive system.[194] The contentious issue remains, as of yet, unresolved.

The 2019 recognition by the US Congress of the Armenian genocide also represented an important step in US-Turkish foreign relations. By recognising the Ottoman Empire's systematic killing of 1.5 million Armenians between 1915 and 1923, the United States chose openly to go against the Turkish government's official position of denying the genocide,[195] in a move which could, potentially, one day lead Turkey to do the same. That denial is also one of the causes of many EU member states' refusal of EU accession to Turkey.[196]

10.8.5 Russian Federation

Russia aspires to regain the superpower status of the former Soviet Union and has used its revenues from energy and arms exports to renew its military capacity. It has also used its leverage as a major oil-exporting country to former Soviet republics and Eastern European states to exert political pressure. Other nations' dependence on Russian oil has enhanced its geopolitical leverage.[197] Moreover, Russia has sought to consolidate its influence and further its strategic interests by exploiting the opportunities offered in the cyber realm as well as, most recently, through vaccine diplomacy in the context of the COVID-19 pandemic.[198]

Beneath the surface, however, Russia suffers from several major weaknesses. One is demographic, as estimates show the Russian population continuing to shrink. As a consequence, Russia may soon face serious labour shortages, leading to economic decline, a financial crisis and the depopulation of vast areas, especially in the far east, north and north-east.[199] This could, in turn, lead to a 'silent occupation' of Russia's resource-rich far east by people coming from Central Asia and China, which could eventually lead to loss of control over those territories. Moreover, separatist movements, xenophobia against immigrants from Central Asia and China, and Russian nationalism all pose threats to social peace and national cohesion in Russia.[200]

Another important security issue that worries the international community are the vast weapons stockpiles that Russia inherited from its Soviet predecessor. Poorly guarded nuclear stockpiles in Russia provoke fears that nuclear material, which could be used to manufacture a radiological weapon or 'dirty bomb', could be traded on the black market.[201]

As a major supplier of nuclear technology to Iran, Russia has been involved in the controversy surrounding suspicions of Iran's intention to develop nuclear weapons. Although Russia does not want to give up its strong trading relationship with Iran (involving sales of weapons and commercial aircraft to Iran in addition to civilian nuclear technology), Russia has no intention of helping Iran to acquire the capability to develop nuclear weapons. In fact, Russia is extremely concerned about the possibility of a nuclear-armed Iran.[202]

Relations between the United States and Russia have been under enormous strain since Russia's annexation of Crimea in 2014.[203] Recent years have witnessed further escalations of tension – including cyber attacks and allegations of interference in the 2016 and 2020 US presidential elections.[204] In June 2021, US President Joe Biden and Russian President Vladimir Putin met in Geneva for a historic summit. While this was an important diplomatic step, the summit was not viewed as able to heal the major points of contention between Moscow and Washington. Likewise, relations between Russia and the EU continue to nosedive. European states have openly criticised the Kremlin's approach to domestic politics and institutions, as well as Russia's military operations in the Crimea and its energy policy towards former Soviet states.[205] As is explored in more depth in the Appendix, the tensions between Russia on one side, and Ukraine, NATO and the EU on the other, escalated to the point that Russia invaded Ukraine on 24 February 2022.[206]

Asian governments have been much less critical of Russia than their European counterparts. At the same time, Russia has not ignored the huge economic and strategic potential that Asia has to offer. Eurasianism has become an increasingly popular strategic doctrine among Russia's governing elite. The main ideologue of contemporary Eurasianism in Russia is Aleksandr Dugin, a prominent right-wing figure in Russian politics who advises high-ranking officials in the Russian defence and security policy establishment.[207] Eurasianists argue that Eurasia is a distinct subcontinent that rightfully belongs to Russia's sphere of influence. This Russia-dominated Eurasian space would thereby be anti-Western in orientation and pose a counterweight to the United States and the EU. Eurasianists believe that Russia's long-term existence depends on maintaining a large sphere of influence stretching from the Levant to the Asia-Pacific, to which they believe Russia is historically entitled.[208]

Russian Eurasianists argue that, to strengthen its geostrategic position, Russia would need to enter alliances with like-minded powers. According to Dugin's 1997 book *The Basics of Geopolitics*, 'The new

Eurasian empire will be constructed on the fundamental principle of the common enemy: the rejection of Atlanticism, strategic control of the USA, and the refusal to allow liberal values to dominate us. This common civilisational impulse will be the basis of a political and strategic union.'[209] Despite the popularity of Eurasianism in Russia, its foreign policy remains multidirectional and, although Russia may try to pursue some of the goals propagated by the Eurasianists, the country will remain dependent on a good relationship with the EU.

In sum, the Russian Federation remains a geopolitical force to be reckoned with. It is a proud country with a significant cultural heritage and military might. The West needs to treat it with respect and avoid any threatening behaviour towards it, whether real or perceived.

10.8.6 South Africa

South Africa is the second-largest economy in sub-Saharan Africa and the only African state that is part of the G20.[210] It has strong financial and manufacturing sectors as well as a good transportation infrastructure.[211] With its abundance of natural resources, the country can act as a motor for economic development in the region. Its geostrategic significance is further enhanced by its 3,000-kilometre coastline around the southern tip of the African continent. The passage around the Cape of Good Hope serves as the gateway between the South Atlantic and the South Indian oceans. Although it has lost some of its strategic relevance since the widening of the Suez Canal in the 1970s,[212] it remains of immense importance for the international commercial shipping industry.[213] South Africa thus bears key responsibilities in maintaining the shipping passage free and safe for commercial shipping. South Africa's ability to combat piracy, smuggling and illegal drug and arms trafficking in its waters is important for the security of the African continent and the smooth functioning of global trade. Although the route round the Cape is longer and more expensive, shipping companies are often willing to take these increases into account to avoid high insurance premiums on their cargo and safety risks to their crew by choosing the faster but more dangerous route through the Gulf of Aden.[214]

South Africa has significant regional influence. Its foreign policy has undergone a remarkable shift since the advent of democracy: whilst, under Mandela, it sought to turn the nation into a major international player, it thereafter concentrated on consolidating its regional leadership and on acting as an advocate for the interests of the African continent within the international community.[215] It has taken on an active role as a mediator in various conflicts on the continent, assisting in the resolution of conflicts in the Democratic Republic of Congo, Sudan, Burundi, Rwanda and the Ivory Coast. Former South African President Thabo Mbeki spent about one-fifth of his time in office on foreign missions across Africa. The country took a leading role in setting up the African Union in 2001.[216]

Despite its wealth of natural resources, South Africa continues to face severe inequalities and widespread unemployment, with almost half of the South African population living in poverty.[217] The country also struggles with inefficient government bureaucracy, restrictive labour regulations, a shortage of skilled workers, political instability, corruption and environmental problems such as high per capita CO_2 emissions[218] and water pollution through the mining industry.[219] How South Africa addresses these issues will determine whether it can serve as a force for economic prosperity and democracy and as the TPC's southern anchor of stability on a continent plagued by poverty and bad governance.

10.8.7 Egypt

With over one hundred million people and a rapidly growing population, Egypt is the most populous country in the Arab world.[220] It is one of the largest and most diversified economies of the Middle East, based on agriculture, media, petroleum imports, natural gas and tourism, and the second-largest economy in Africa.[221] At various times, the country has had a strong cultural and ideological influence on the entire Arab world. One of the world's most significant choke points, the Suez Canal, passes through Egyptian territory. The world economy depends on this crucial passageway to remain open. Egypt was also the first Arab state to make peace with Israel. It thus remains an important player in solving the Arab-Israeli conflict. For all these reasons, Egypt's stability is pivotal from a geopolitical point of view.

Yet there are serious destabilising factors in the country. Egypt has withstood the highly disruptive so-called 'Arab Spring', which was instigated by outside actors to empower the Muslim Brotherhood and take over the state.[222] The effort has, at least so far, failed and Egypt has regained its pivotal role in the region and continues to be a force of good, especially in the Arab-Israeli conflict, Libya, Syria and East Mediterranean.[223]

Egypt's success in establishing a good-governance paradigm, in developing its economy and in creating millions of new formal jobs could have positive repercussions throughout the region. Progress in the political and economic sphere in Egypt has lessened social and political discontent and thus reduced the country's risk of descending into chaos and of becoming vulnerable to the appeal of extremist ideologies. The TPC cannot become fully stabilised without a stable and progressive Egypt.

10.8.8 Pakistan

Pakistan is a populous state with nuclear-weapons capability.[224] It has an unresolved territorial dispute with nuclear-armed India over Jammu and Kashmir. Various extremist organisations have formed on Pakistani territory, which not only help to destabilise the country internally, but potentially also make the country dangerous as an exporter of radical ideologies. Pakistan will have to continue improving security features to safeguard its nuclear materiel in the interest of international security.

In addition to the threat of extremism, the country faces a wide array of demanding challenges ahead in stabilising its domestic situation. These include, among others, corruption, a high number of refugees and internally displaced persons,[225] a low overall literacy rate,[226] air and water pollution, water scarcity[227] and poor health conditions[228] resulting in relatively low life expectancy.[229]

Furthermore, Pakistan's progress remains hindered by its military conflict with India. Until this conflict is resolved, Pakistan is unlikely to reduce its enormous military budget. Doing so would free up millions of dollars to be spent on domestic infrastructure development, education and health care for the Pakistani people. Peace with India might also reduce extremism and have a moderating effect on domestic politics. Finally, a stable and moderate Pakistan will be crucial in stabilising Afghanistan, which shares a long border with Pakistan.

Overall, and especially due to the country's large population and nuclear-weapons capability, Pakistan remains of high strategic importance. Its stability and peaceful pursuit of foreign policy are crucial for peace and stability in the TPC. A prosperous, moderate and stable Pakistan will be indispensable for rendering the TPC, and with it the world, more peaceful and secure.

10.9 Great-Power Involvement in the TPC Territory

Given the TPC's geostrategic significance, the world's major powers have used diplomacy, strong economic cooperation and the signing of defence and military agreements with TPC states to secure access to the region's important resources and maritime access routes. No powerful nation can afford to neglect this corridor if it wants to maintain an influential geostrategic position in the world. However, attempts by outside powers to exert a strong influence over particular states and regions in the TPC can become a further destabilising factor in an already volatile part of the world, especially when they become entangled in local conflicts as they support opposing parties.[230] A case in point is Syria.

Many parts of the TPC have historically been a prime theatre for external powers to compete for access and resources,[231] and the twenty-first century is likely to witness increasing levels and a widening geographic range of great power competition in the region. As I have mentioned, with the melting of the Arctic ice, the North Pole could soon become a new area of conflict between major powers. Likewise, China, Russia and the United States are either expanding their footprint or scaling back their presence in many other parts of the TPC, such as the Middle East and Africa.

China has a particularly strong interest in securing reliable oil and gas supplies in the region for its growing energy needs. In fact, in 2019, it relied on the Middle East alone for about 40 per cent of its imported crude oil.[232] Furthermore, and to secure access to resources, China has invested heavily in infrastructure projects in Africa. For all the economic opportunities it has brought to the continent, China has been repeatedly accused of aggressively pursuing its interests to the detriment of local populations or at the expense of the environment.[233]

Like China, Russia has sought to cultivate its influence in the TPC and especially in the Middle East and North Africa, where it is continuously trying to expand its political and military relationships, viewing the region as an arena to contest US hegemony. The war in Syria has been viewed by the Kremlin as an opportunity to consolidate its influence in, as some have described it, 'a region that has always been of geostrategic relevance for external power projection'.[234] Russia has often acted as the arms supplier of second resort, selling to countries such as Algeria and Egypt.[235]

For decades, US strategy in the TPC has been focused on fostering societies that reject communism. More recently, however, the US has been faced with a much broader variety of challenges stemming from the TPC, including the menace of violent extremism as well as the need to secure commerce and oil flowing from the region.[236] US intervention strategies in the TPC have often displayed an inability to seek genuine cooperation with local communities and cultural understanding or long-term stability.[237]

Clearly, the United States, China, Russia and European powers (especially the United Kingdom, France and Germany) have important economic and military resources that, if employed properly, could help TPC states grow into more stable and prosperous countries. If, however, these major powers use their resources recklessly to exert political influence or stoke certain historical, cultural or sectarian conflicts between key states to gain exclusive access to some of their resources, the TPC will become less stable in the longer term and this will be counter-productive to their own long-term security and prosperity. Hence, what the international community needs is not great power rivalry but better cooperation to achieve its common aim of making the TPC more stable and secure, which will benefit everyone.

10.10 Promoting Stability in the TPC

As indicated above, there needs to be strong cooperation between developed states and those of the TPC in order to ensure lasting stability in the corridor. Because of the broad variety of threats that emanate from the TPC, there will have to be cooperation in areas as diverse as economic development, disease control, institution-building and democratisation, the fight against organised crime, nuclear non-proliferation, the management of international migration and the regulation of emerging technologies. Strong partnerships will have to be maintained between states and with international institutions in order to tackle specific problems and security threats.

One important way to promote stability is by encouraging states to work together towards the common goal of creating economic prosperity that will benefit every state in the region.[238] In order to promote entrepreneurship and economic efficiency, and to better integrate their national economies into the global market, the governments of the states concerned will need to loosen their grip on their economies and their people. They will also need to attract foreign investment.

As I have noted, competition among the world's major military powers – the United States, China and Russia and the three major European states – plays a crucial role in fuelling local conflicts within the TPC. These powers maintain a military presence in various countries. China, in particular, has started to shift its military strategies to accommodate its respective need to secure access to vital resources. Should competition between these six powers in the region escalate, the TPC will spiral into instability. The world's great powers thus have an important role and responsibility to prevent the escalation of local conflicts in resource-rich areas. An escalating rivalry – and naval arms race – between China and the United States would also entail trillions of dollars of new military expenditure for both countries – money that would be better spent on developing alternative energy sources and tackling climate change.

States can also take effective measures in the case of an imminent failure or collapse of a TPC state. Rapid intervention to stop the escalation of a conflict that could precipitate state collapse can be highly effective.[239] Helping a country to build better law enforcement institutions will encourage political reform. It will also attract more foreign investment and economic activity, which in turn can create new jobs and reduce social unrest related to poverty and unemployment.

In addition, promoting dignity-based governance structures (see chapter five) will lessen many of the region's most acute problems, such as sectarian violence, extremism and ethnic conflicts, all of which are, to a large extent, caused by political and socio-economic inequality which has been legitimised along the fault lines of culture or religion.[240] Dignity-based governance prevents ethnic tensions and violent extremism through inclusive policies and the promotion of equal opportunities and a non-exclusive form of national identity.[241] Moreover, through schooling, the broadcasting and print media, political discourse and the entertainment industry, dignity-based governance can link pro-social behaviour to the sense of 'feeling good'. In neuro-behavioural terms, humans will repeat those actions that make them 'feel good' in one way or another (which does not necessarily derive from a pro-social or positive behaviour but is rather learned and conditioned in response to one's environment, both personal and political). Governance models that place dignity at the centre thus go a long way to channel the individual's quest for the *Neuro P5* into enterprises that are beneficial to society.[242] Importantly, dignity-based governance must be implemented through a context-sensitive approach that is attentive to local cultures and histories.[243]

To resolve regional conflicts within the TPC, perhaps the most important of which is the Arab-Israeli conflict and Iran's destabilising sectarian proxies, states need to adopt *symbiotic realism* in their conduct of interstate relations. In other words, they need to prioritise absolute gains-seeking and non-conflictual competition that allows all sides to benefit.[244]

Finally, measures to increase harmony between different faiths and cultures will be important for fostering greater understanding and lessening tensions and violence among members of different religious groups within the TPC. These measures must counteract perceptions of irreconcilable cultural differences, perceptions which are often instrumentalised for political purposes (both regionally and globally) yet are profoundly erroneous.[245] Robust historical research reveals that there is only one human civilisation and that it has prospered and evolved as a result of interactions between members of different religious and cultural backgrounds. For example, Europe has thrived on borrowings from the Arab-Islamic world just as the Arab-Islamic world built on the work of others, such as the ancient Greeks, Hindus and Chinese, while rising to its golden age.[246] It is crucial to recover this aspect of history in order to prevent cultural or religious differences from being essentialised and securitised for competing political agendas. States need to recognise the ability of soft-power tools, including cultural diplomacy and educational exchanges, to promote a better understanding between different religious and cultural groups within the TPC.

Ultimately, states within the TPC will have to become stable and prosperous on their own. Developed countries outside the TPC can only offer their expertise and assistance, but TPC countries are much more likely to allow developed states to help them if they are convinced that they have good intentions. Confidence-building measures at the grassroots level will therefore be a key prerequisite for making foreign aid in the TPC effective.

While states within the TPC are responsible for their futures, it is nevertheless true, as demonstrated by ample historical and contemporary evidence, that major global powers continue to destabilise the region through narrow and short-sighted interests (cultural, economic or military). Europe has been especially guilty in this regard over the past two centuries, in addition to the United States and Russia during the latter part of the twentieth and the twenty-first century.

Building peace and stability in the TPC from the grassroots upwards is a powerful way of supplementing and reinforcing the measures that can be taken by governments and international organisations to build a cooperative framework and stabilise the region.

At the same time, we still live in a state-centric world. Global powers will need to adjust their policies to serve not just their own national-security needs (narrowly defined) but at the same time also contribute to improved security in troubled areas, especially the TPC. Doing so will be in these states' broader national interest: if problems in the TPC are not being mitigated at their source, or being deliberately accentuated, they will come to haunt states around the world. Energy security and the prevention of a host of transnational threats are high on every modern state's national security agenda. Hence, every state has an interest in stability and growing prosperity in the TPC.

Global powers also need to avoid polluting the important issue of human rights through its misuse as a pressure tool for narrow foreign policy goals. Human rights are too valuable and consequential to be instrumentalised for political ends. The same holds true for climate change politics by some states, which are misused as tools for limiting economic progress and the rise of other countries for geostrategic reasons. In other words, human rights and climate change politics need to be authentic and free from narrow or strategic goals to be believable and successful.

11

The Future State of the World and the Way Forward

In the twenty-first century, the factors determining state power continue to shift as the world undergoes enormous transformations, including technological innovations, the changing economic importance of particular resources, resource scarcities and changing geographic landscapes as a result of climate change. *Meta-geopolitics* is a helpful analytical tool targeted towards comprehending not only current but also future global developments. It has helped us to identify a number of major trends that will, to one degree or another, affect international dynamics in the coming decades. This chapter provides a broad overview of these key trends.

11.1 Civilisational Frontier Risks and their Meta-Geopolitical Implications

According to the World Economic Forum, frontier risks are 'those which could emerge as novel technologies surface, new territories are breached or societal forces shift. They are characterized by unknown likelihood, unknown impacts – or both'.[1] In what follows, I discuss ten major frontier risks that, if left unaddressed, could hinder the progress of human civilisation or even threaten the future of the human species.[2] I refer to them as civilisational frontier risks (see Table 11.1). It is in the national interest of all states to mitigate them. In chapter two, I briefly

Table 11.1 Civilisational Frontier Risks

1	Outer Space Security & Sustainability
2	Artificial Intelligence / Quantum Computing / Neuromorphic Computing
3	Pandemics
4	Synthetic Biology / CRISPR / mRNA
5	Brain-Computer Interface / Neuroethics / Free will
6	Climate / Biodiversity
7	Cyber Security / Social Media / Disinformation / Polarisation
8	WMD / Bioweapons
9	Superintelligence / Trans-humanism / Post-humanism
10	Intrusive Surveillance / Civil Liberties / Social Contract 2.0

explained how these civilisational frontier risks challenge traditional approaches to statecraft. This chapter will go one step further and consider their future implications, for which state leaders must prepare.

11.1.1 Outer Space Security and Sustainability

As I have discussed in previous publications, such as *Meta-Geopolitics of Outer Space*,[3] outer space is having and will continue to have far-reaching implications for all of us on the ground. It is a key domain of geopolitical competition.

Outer space is becoming increasingly congested and contested as both public and private actors seek to exploit the opportunities offered by outer space infrastructure and technology.[4] In recent years, space debris has increased sharply, as has space militarisation.[5] Thousands of satellites are being launched into space by both states and companies who seek profit or power, leading to increasing amounts of debris floating around, many of which have the potential to rupture spacecraft, with devastating consequences.[6] Moreover, the militarisation of space is becoming more and more acute.[7]

Currently, national militaries are using space technologies to support surveillance and communication technologies.[8] The communication and early-warning functions that satellites provide to militaries are particularly important for nuclear deterrence.[9] Reconnaissance satellites can perform functions including, as Michael Sheehan has reported, 'signals monitoring, photo reconnaissance, infra-red reconnaissance, electronic reconnaissance, ocean reconnaissance and ballistic missile attack early warning'.[10] Moreover, they 'gather visual and photographic data, eavesdrop on signals intelligence and collect radar defence information'.[11] Satellites have become invaluable for technologically sophisticated militaries.

Due to their military importance, many countries, including the United States, Russia, China and India, have been developing technologies to interfere with satellite communication or to shoot down enemy satellites with ground-based ballistic missiles. The United States is also experimenting with the development of 'space-based, kinetic-energy missile interceptors',[12] a type of ASAT (anti-satellite weapon) located directly in space rather than on Earth. To be sure, satellites, orbiting defenceless in space, are highly vulnerable to attack. Because the economy and military are both highly dependent on satellite systems, many countries see a need to develop military capabilities to protect their space assets.[13]

There are growing fears that the development of 'defensive' space-based weapons capabilities, particularly by states such as the US and China, will further complicate military relations, extending the existing competition on Earth into the space domain. If some states develop the capacity to shoot down satellites, other states that depend on satellite technology for military and civilian purposes will become highly vulnerable. Nuclear weapons states fear, moreover, that, if the United States developed a space-based, nuclear-missile interceptor system, this would considerably weaken their own nuclear deterrence capabilities, as it would no longer have to fear a retaliatory strike against its territory. Should the United States deploy such a system, Russia and China would likely increase the number of long-range, nuclear-armed missiles they maintain, starting a new arms race that could also prompt India and Pakistan, among others, to follow suit.[14]

The past few years, in particular, have seen an increasing militarisation of outer space,[15] with all the great powers in the world investing substantial sums in their space programmes and the development of new military technologies and also in the creation of so-called 'space forces'.[16] France, the United Kingdom, Canada and Japan have followed the example of the United States, Russia and China and set up 'space forces' that are separate from the rest of their air forces and militaries, with the two primary aims of defending their space assets and of deterrence.[17] Lack of regulation and high competition arguably threaten outer space security more than ever before.

In 1967, the United States and the Soviet Union signed the Outer Space Treaty, which 'bans the stationing of weapons of mass destruction (WMD) in outer space, prohibits activities on celestial bodies, and details legally binding rules governing the peaceful exploration and use of space'. China and more than one hundred other states have since signed that treaty.[18] This agreement has loopholes, however, as it does not address technologies, such as ballistic missiles, that threaten military and civilian assets in space from the ground. It also does not address newer technology developed by the United States, such as space-based, kinetic-energy missile interceptors.[19] In the face of increasing dependence on satellite systems and of the immense technological advances in space technology and the militarisation of outer space, a new treaty to prohibit or at the very least regulate arms competition in space is necessary.[20] Should the international community fail to agree on such a treaty, the complete militarisation of space is almost inevitable. This will radically alter geopolitics as we know it, since whoever achieves domination in space will also dominate the Earth.[21] In addition to transparency, cooperation and addressing gaps in space law will be critical for a sustainable space environment. More importantly, as I have written elsewhere, 'if space becomes unsafe, it will not be selectively unsafe, but rather unsafe for all'.[22]

In sum, geopolitical competition and the absence of binding rules or laws are challenging the goal of the peaceful use of outer space that was announced in the 1967 Outer Space Treaty.[23] Yet our future depends on a sustainable use of outer space, since we rely heavily on it for our daily activities, from the internet and mobile telephony to air travel, meteorology, climate research and navigation. In times of war and peace, states are highly dependent on space-based assets, including systems for diplomatic, military and security capacities.[24]

11.1.2 Artificial Intelligence, Quantum Computing,
Neuromorphic Computing

The risks associated with emerging disruptive technologies are numerous and will become even more acute in the coming decades. Recent years have seen enormous advances in numerous fields, including artificial intelligence, machine learning, quantum computing, and neuromorphic computing. These emerging technologies will profoundly affect all of the seven state capacities I identified in chapter four. If used wisely, they can help states to flourish. Otherwise they pose severe risks to society, some of which I briefly outline below.

AI commonly refers to computer systems that are capable of performing tasks that normally require human intelligence.[25] It has the potential to fundamentally alter our daily lives and what it means to be human. It could lead to various forms of human enhancement, which raises major concerns about justice, fairness, meritocracy and authenticity (see section 11.1.10 on trans-humanism). Furthermore, in combination with neurobiological and neurotechnological interventions, AI may interfere with our free will, autonomy and decision-making processes (see section 11.1.5 on BCIs).[26] The societal and economic challenges posed by AI will clearly be huge. They will range from the loss of jobs through automation to mis-profiling (due to bias contained in data sets) that will lead to increased vulnerability for certain social groups.[27] Likewise, the future of warfare will be largely determined by AI, with errors in AI systems posing dramatic threats to civilians and critical infrastructures.[28] The environment, too, will be affected by AI in a variety of ways. AI systems rely heavily on rare-earth elements (REEs), which, as Sophia Kalantzakos has reported, have become 'a focal point of geopolitical competition between China, the EU and the US'.[29] At the same time, REEs contribute to environmental pollution as the chemicals discharged to process these minerals damage soils, water, and ecosystems.[30] In short, there is no state capacity that will remain unaffected by AI in the decades ahead.

Likewise, quantum computing will play a major role in shaping our future. Quantum computing harnesses the potential of quantum mechanics – the behaviour of the universe's smallest particles – to solve a wide array of highly complex problems, promising to revolutionise many fields, from outer space to pharmaceuticals.[31] Unlike conventional computing devices, quantum computers rely on quantum bits instead of binary code and are – to date – unhackable. When perfected, quantum computers may supersede the fastest and most powerful supercomputers.[32] This would bring about not only enormous opportunities but also high risks. On the one hand, quantum computing could, for example, help to develop new catalysts for carbon capture.[33] On the other hand, it will most likely cause great economic disruption by eliminating the need for a human workforce in production sectors.[34] Whilst the full impact of quantum computing on economies, governments, national security and individual well-being is difficult to predict with any exactness, some known potential applications raise concerns, especially over national security. Quantum computers could eventually be able to crack the highest levels of encryption used by governments, endangering not only sensitive information but also critical infrastructures and the control of weapons systems.[35] In other words, if one state achieves quantum computing superiority, all other states will face severe security vulnerabilities. The race towards quantum supremacy therefore continues relentlessly, with countries investing billions in quantum development.[36]

Similarly, neuromorphic computing is an emerging technology that could exacerbate inequalities between countries. The goal of neuromorphic technology is to copy, to the extent possible, the brain's neural network architecture.[37] By imitating this architecture, neuromorphic computing enables the creation of smart chips that use very little energy whilst nonetheless computing rapidly.[38] Neuromorphic computing could eventually lead to the creation of computers capable of remembering, learning and reasoning, even surpassing the performance of the human brain.[39] This would have vast implications for a broad range of fields. Neuromorphic chips could be, for example, built into robots and drones sent into combat zones, where they would act and take decisions independently and thus replace human soldiers.[40] Such drones would also make spying more effective. Furthermore, neuromorphic computing has the potential to significantly improve a number of current technologies involved in national surveillance and facial recognition, financial forecasting, the monitoring of agriculture and so on. Such improvements, however, would render humans redundant in a multitude of jobs. In addition, they would further increase the divide between poor and wealthy countries, allowing the latter to benefit from, for example, improved surveillance technologies or machine-driven warfare. In medicine, brain-like computers could improve therapeutic procedures, but could also be used to augment human cognitive capabilities beyond their current limits. This would further contribute to a blurring of the distinctions between humans and machines, requiring us to rethink the very notion of our humanness. Equipped with human reasoning capabilities, these computers could even exacerbate some of our worst attributes, such as aggression.[41]

11.1.3 Pandemics

Another civilisational frontier risk that will dominate geopolitics in the coming years, is that of pandemics, posing challenges across all seven state capacities that the meta-geopolitical approach considers key to determining any state's future trajectory.[42] As I mentioned in chapter two, experts warn of future pandemics like COVID-19 or even more deadly pathogens, which could give rise to pandemics potentially more virulent than the coronavirus we are fighting now.[43] Melting permafrost will give rise to bacteria and viruses that may involve an even deadlier pathogen. Such a pathogen could be essentially incurable (such as Ebola[44]), nearly always fatal (like rabies[45]), extremely infectious (such as the common cold[46] or COVID-19[47]) and have a long incubation period (HIV[48]), which could lead to an extreme death toll.

The impact of future pandemics on the global geopolitical plane will be wide-ranging. Indeed, not only have infectious diseases historically been one of the greatest causes of mortality, but, as COVID-19 has demonstrated, they have the potential to severely destabilise socio-economic conditions, increasing inequality and poverty and triggering fears that exacerbate nationalism and populism.[49] Although we have made large strides in terms of sanitation and medical research, globalisation and urbanisation enable the extremely rapid spread of disease.[50]

Only through close cooperation and solidarity between states and international organisations can this type of global threat be addressed. The coronavirus pandemic has, however, demonstrated how far we are from achieving this and how, on the contrary, the spread of a disease can be used by national governments to incite hatred towards another people, as was the case when Donald Trump in the United States attacked China,[51] or by a group of states to undermine the credibility of another.[52] Despite ample evidence to the contrary, some have even suggested that the COVID-19 pandemic was triggered deliberately.[53] Although this is not the case now, it may be the case in the future, and goes to show how geopolitically relevant pandemics will become in the decades ahead. In addition to increased international cooperation, building resilience against pandemics and other types of biological hazards will require large financial investment in research and development for therapeutics, vaccine technologies and bioinformatics, as well as the development of protocols for international cooperation between governments and the corporate sector on future pandemics and biohazards.[54]

11.1.4 Synthetic Biology, CRISPR, mRNA

A quite recent interdisciplinary field, synthetic biology attempts not only to modify existing organisms but also to create novel ones with characteristics not found in nature.[55] It holds out the promise, as M.J. Poznansky reports, to 'make manufacturing greener energy production more sustainable, agriculture more robust, and medicine more powerful and precise'.[56] For example, researchers are currently working on developing genetically modified white blood cells that could search out and destroy cancer cells. They are also trying to develop a new bacterium that will absorb the carbon dioxide released into the atmosphere,[57] as well as generate an 'off' switch for plants so they could respond to environmental signals, such as dryness.[58]

Whilst state leaders must embrace the opportunities offered by synthetic biology, equally they must focus on minimising its associated risks. Releasing synthetic organisms into the environment is not without risk and may have unforeseen effects not only on the environment but also on the evolution of human nature, especially as synthetic biology is already blurring the line between treatment and human enhancement.[59] In fact, one emerging area, the application of synthetically produced cells and organs to transplantation, could eventually help to design organs surpassing human organs, in both function and survival.[60]

New frontiers have recently been reached through the possibility of synthesising human DNA. CRISPR, or Clustered Regularly Interspaced Short Palindromic Repeats, for example, is a revolutionary gene-editing technology allowing scientists to actually modify the building blocks of life.[61] Its discovery earned Emmanuelle Charpentier and Jennifer A. Doudna the 2020 Nobel Prize in chemistry. Through the tools provided by CRISPR/Cas9, genetic modifications that used to take years are now attainable within days and at much lower cost.[62] Over the past decade, the CRISPR/Cas9 gene-editing tool has had a revolutionary impact on the life sciences and on medical research, contributing to new cancer therapies and holding the potential to cure various neuro-degenerative diseases, inherited diseases and cancer.[63]

Synthetic biology has also accelerated vaccine development.[64] Both the Moderna and Pfizer-BioNTech's mRNA COVID-19 vaccines were designed and implemented using synthetic biology techniques.[65] Technology based on mRNA equips state leaders with a powerful tool to fight the current and future pandemics.

For all the benefits they offer, synthetic biology, CRISPR and mRNA are fraught with risks that state leaders need to mitigate. These include, above all, unwanted off-target effects that could have unforeseeable and highly negative outcomes for public health and the environment.[66] Moreover, these technologies could be used by state or non-state actors to, for example, engineer pathogens and biological weapons.[67] To protect their citizens, state leaders must ensure that there are appropriate international laws and regulations in place to control the development and application of these emerging technologies.

11.1.5 Brain-Computer Interface, Neuro-ethics, Free Will

The coming decades will witness an ever-increasing human-machine symbiosis fostered by brain-computer interfaces (BCIs). At present, BCIs fall into two main categories: those that 'read' the brain by decoding brain signals; and those that stimulate the function of specific brain areas by 'writing' instructions for them.[68] BCIs offer the opportunity to advance our knowledge of the human brain. At the same time, they are a much-needed therapeutic tool to restore motor control and cognitive and emotional function to people with disabilities.[69] BCIs can restore movement or communication to patients who have suffered strokes, paralysis or live with Parkinson's disease, for example.[70] In the case of brain disorders such as epilepsy or depression, they can monitor brain activity and stop an impending crisis or epileptic activity through the intake of drugs.[71] They may also help manage pain and detect and treat neurological diseases such as Alzheimer's.[72]

For all the benefits they offer, BCIs instil concerns in neuro-ethicists, especially over their impact on individuals' free will. Neuro-ethics is a subfield of bioethics that seeks to ensure that technologies capable of influencing and controlling the human mind are developed in an ethical manner in order to minimise risks associated with them.[73] These risks include a loss of the ability to make decisions for oneself and to act with free will. In fact, a number of patients who received deep brain stimulation developed impulse-control problems or a confused sense of agency.[74] Some of them have felt driven to engage in behaviour they would normally not undertake – such as compulsive gambling.[75] Furthermore, confusion over the question of whether a decision was taken by the patient or the algorithm creates a dangerous 'accountability gap'.[76] Another issue of concern is the question of how exactly BCIs can discern a person's intentions.[77] There is also reason to believe that BCIs will enable 'brainjacking',[78] that is, the exercise of unauthorised or malicious control over brain implants by cyber attackers who could, against the will of the patient or even without his or her knowledge, induce certain emotions, actions or even personality changes.[79] They could even kill people, for instance by hijacking an insulin pump.[80]

My goal here is not to provide an exhaustive review of all the harms BCIs can potentially cause. Instead, by mentioning some of them I hope to alert state leaders to the growing importance of neuro-ethics in finding answers to the ethical questions raised by emerging technologies such as BCIs. In fact, neuro-ethicists can help policy makers develop appropriate regulations for the technology sector.

11.1.6 Climate and Biodiversity

Besides the fact that countries' dependence on energy is currently having a strong influence on geopolitics, the world is also dealing with the consequences of the use of fossil fuels, which will have decisive geopolitical implications in the coming decades. The most dangerous long-term consequence is climate change, a creeping menace that will leave no area of the world unaffected, despite the possibility that climate change may be cyclical and is only partially, but unequivocally, man-made.[81] Climate change is expected to exacerbate water and food shortages and lead to devastating natural disasters, epidemics and massive refugee flows.[82]

Some of these events are interrelated and mutually perpetuating. Poorer countries will likely suffer the most, since not only can they not afford expensive adaptation technologies,[83] but many of them are also located in the areas which will be the first to go underwater or become arid.[84] Water shortages can lead to food shortages, which can result in massive migration, which can lead to further food shortages in places where a large number of migrants choose to settle and so forth.[85] The complex impact of these events on social and economic stability may also trigger conflict on a large scale.[86] The combined effect of climate change, biodiversity loss, and pandemics could even lead to our extinction.[87] Without going into detail, here it is worth summarising some of the major events related to climate change that could affect geopolitics in the coming decades.

Numerous countries, including India, will have to deal with large numbers of so-called environmental refugees as a result of massive flooding caused by rising sea levels. Millions of people living in Bangladesh, on small islands in the Bay of Bengal and in many coastal areas of India will be forced to find a new livelihood on India's mainland.[88] China is another country whose emerging economic clout on the world stage will be tempered by events related to climate change. It will be plagued in particular by desertification, which could jeopardise the livelihoods of up to four hundred million people.[89] Internal migration and social unrest resulting from such developments could also undermine the country's internal stability.[90]

Nigeria and parts of East Africa may face severe droughts, desertification and a rise in sea level.[91] In East Africa, which is part of the tripwire pivotal corridor, many countries are already weak and lack the resilience to deal with these additional stresses. The spectre of state failure will loom large for some East African countries in the near future. In the Middle East, water shortages are expected to be exacerbated at a time when the region is experiencing rapid population growth.[92]

Increasing migration from Africa and the Middle East into Europe could lead to xenophobic tensions.[93] In addition, divisions among EU member states over immigration issues could possibly lead to new border restrictions, which would impede the EU's goal of political integration.[94] In turn, an inward-looking and internally divided EU will be unable to assert itself geopolitically in a manner commensurate to its considerable economic power.

Indeed, climate change, more than anything else, will further exacerbate the gap between the rich and poor in the world. Floods, droughts and starvation will mostly affect the developing world more acutely, whilst it also has fewer means to deal with environmental changes.[95]

Climate change, and the natural disasters it brings about, is expected to be the underlying theme and exacerbating factor of strategic threats that already exist: economic recession, wars, ethnic strife and terrorism may all happen as a result of the human suffering caused by environmental disasters. As the economist Jeffrey Sachs has written, 'We sit atop ticking ecological time bombs.' 'Our era', he adds, 'will be dominated by the geopolitics of sustainability.'[96]

Global warming, conjoint with growing populations and the search for alternative sources of energy, will affect states' food and water security. Demand for sufficient water and affordable food in many parts of the world is starting to have geostrategic consequences. I address some of them in the paragraphs that follow.

Food scarcities. Food security is an issue that has taken on global proportions and is expected to affect international security and geopolitics in the coming decades. The World Food Programme's 2021 *Global Report on Food Crises* has highlighted the increasing severity and widening geographic range of acute food insecurity: 'At least 155 million people in fifty-five countries/territories were in crisis or worse ... in 2020, an increase of around twenty million people from 2019.'[97] The drivers of food crises are numerous yet often mutually reinforcing. These include pre-existing and COVID-19-related economic problems, enduring conflict and extreme weather in many parts of the world. Droughts have in recent years contributed to poor harvests in many food-exporting regions.[98] Extreme weather will be increasingly aggravated by global climate change, another development that will not be easy to reverse in the coming decades.[99]

Another reason for limited supply is that rural infrastructure in the developing world is severely underfunded, and farms there lag behind farms in the developed world in terms of production capacity and technology. The agricultural sector in the developing world is further disadvantaged by the global trading system, which allows developed countries to subsidise their agricultural industries and impose tariffs.[100]

The lack of affordable food supplies can lead – and already has led – to social unrest in developing countries, which in some instances has resulted in state instability. Food insecurity was, in fact, one of the causes of the 2011 Arab Spring.[101]

Water shortages and desalination. Besides food supply, water shortages are a growing concern for many regions around the world, including the Gulf states. It is estimated that 785 million people already lack access to clean water[102] and that by 2025 two thirds of the world's population may face water shortages.[103] One potential solution to this growing problem is to find feasible ways to remove salt from seawater, but desalination is an energy-intensive process. Fossil fuels can hardly be used for desalination, as crude oil is a finite, non-renewable resource that causes severe environmental pollution. Some countries, such as India and the Gulf states, are thus developing technologies which use solar and nuclear energy for large-scale desalination.[104]

Increasing the number of countries using nuclear technology to generate energy in order to cut carbon emissions and avoid the high price of fossil fuels certainly has a downside, however. A key challenge for policy makers in the coming decades will be to find a way for states to use carbon-free nuclear technology without enriching uranium themselves. Instead, these countries could purchase nuclear fuel through an international fuel bank.[105] Such a measure could help prevent the uncontrolled spread of nuclear-enrichment programmes.

The melting of the Arctic ice cap. Global warming may cause the Arctic ice cap to melt, a process that will have tremendous geopolitical consequences. As global temperatures rise, less of the Arctic ice that melts in the summer is refreezing in the winter. The thickness of the Arctic ice is being reduced every year, and the size of the ice cap as a whole is shrinking. Over the past 30 years, Artic sea ice has declined by 95 per cent.[106]

This reduction in the size of the Arctic ice cap is not just a consequence of global warming. It is also contributing to global warming. While a white ice cap reflects sunlight, the dark waters of the Arctic Ocean absorb solar energy. As the size of the Arctic Ocean increases as a result of the melting ice cap, it absorbs more heat and thus helps to speed up the warming of the atmosphere. This melting cycle is known as the ice-albedo feedback loop.[107]

The thick ice, which previously has prevented even the strongest ice breakers from passing through, is thinning to a point that it will soon be navigable in winter.[108] According to current trends, by 2050 ships may be able to go directly over the North Pole.[109]

The melting of the ice cap is also facilitating the exploration of natural resources which were previously hidden underneath the thick ice and were thus inaccessible. Increasing deposits of fossil fuels in particular are expected to be found beneath the melting Arctic ice, and offshore drilling of the Arctic's oil and gas deposits has become more commercially viable. Although new hydrocarbon sources will continue to be found in the Arctic, the largest known deposits in the region are off the coast of Russia, which is already involved in ongoing drilling operations.[110]

With the development of new shipping routes such as the Northern Sea Route and the Northwest Passage, states' behaviour in the Arctic is changing. The shorter maritime routes, their respective ports and natural resources are renewing global and regional interest in what was once considered an impassable area. The new shipping lanes could provide states not only with shorter transit times and strategic resource extraction, they could also be used for military activity as well as regional shipping, fishing and tourism.[111] At least at present, however, with its unpredictable seas, severe climate conditions, high costs and lack of developed infrastructure in the northern territories, there are still many obstacles for socio-economic and maritime development in the Arctic region.[112] Despite a tradition of international cooperation in the region, the Arctic is increasingly seen as an area for geopolitical competition.[113] The Arctic region is of great economic and strategic importance. As mentioned in the previous chapter, new rivalries are developing as the countries adjacent to the Arctic Ocean start laying claims to new territory. The five Arctic powers – Russia, the United States, Canada, Norway and Denmark – are starting to face off over the control of shipping lanes and resources in this newly accessible region.

Russia was the first among the five to stake a claim on Arctic territory, in 2001. Moscow claimed almost two million square kilometres of the Arctic Ocean and sought to legitimise its claim through the United Nations. When the UN rejected this request, Russia acted unilaterally and planted a flag on the seabed at the North Pole in August 2007.[114] Russia's action led Canada to start building new Arctic naval patrol vessels.[115] Meanwhile, Denmark has also made a claim to the Arctic and the North Pole via Greenland[116] and Norway has made its claims on the region as well.[117] Even China has started to increasingly engage in the Arctic. Although to this date China has claimed the benevolent intentions of fostering peace and development and improving Arctic governance, China's intentions in the region are not entirely clear. It is certain, however, that it does not want to be side-lined.[118]

The Arctic covers 30 million square kilometres, which is a sixth of the Earth's landmass.[119] There are no clear international rules as to how this region should be governed, nor is there any political framework to mediate future disputes that may arise between countries regarding the exploration of Arctic resources or the governing of shipping lanes.[120] The Arctic Council, set up to address environmental issues, lacks a mandate to deal with any security-related problems in the region.[121] Admittedly, there is the UN Convention on the Law of the Sea, which governs maritime rights. It lays down rules for how countries can claim maritime resources beyond their exclusive economic zone and provides procedures for resolving boundary disputes. Although UNCLOS might be the right instrument to address new issues arising as a result of thawing in the Arctic, the United States, one of the five Arctic powers, has not ratified the treaty and is thus not bound by it.[122] Moreover, UNCLOS does not provide clear answers as to how this geologically complex, uncharted continental shelf can be divided up among the five Arctic powers.[123]

The maritime borders between some of the five powers also remain ambiguous. In addition, the legal status of the Northwest Passage remains unclear.[124] The melting Arctic ice cap currently sits in a legal vacuum, with competing claims from major powers making the area increasingly contentious. The Arctic's enormous resource wealth and its potential to provide major international shipping lanes are beginning to make this vast maritime space a geopolitical focal point. In the near future, the implications could be immense.

11.1.7 Cyber Security, Social Media, Disinformation, Polarisation

In the coming decades, statecraft will have to confront and mitigate an ever-increasing number of risks emanating from cyberspace. Digitisation is changing and will continue to change the nature of state policy making.[125] One possible, though rather radical, scenario might be that political interactions will be fundamentally transformed as new forces, such as markets, transnational groupings and movements, and new information and communication technologies come to dominate the global village, so that state entities no longer dominate international relations.[126] As a result, according to Richard Falk, 'states will not be any longer consistently seen as the defining units of world order, and geographical boundaries and territorial sovereignty will be only one of several global indicators of how authority is located and exercised in the shaping of human behaviour'.[127]

Another scenario could be that the cyber world will become merely an instrument of international relations. In this scenario, state units would remain the dominant players in international relations within an international order based on sovereign states.[128] Still, information technology will have an impact on geopolitical hierarchies, making it so that states that control cyberspace will be able to increase their power.

In any case, the cyberworld will continue to pose immense challenges to state entities. It has greatly empowered small, non-governmental insurgent groups, allowing them to inflict harm on states, both in domestic settings and transnationally. Non-state actors can use cyberspace to recruit members, as well as to plan and execute their asymmetrical battle tactics. Various groups can also empower themselves by using disinformation and purposely misleading the conventional armies they are fighting. In non-combat settings, radical groups with various political agendas have also used the tools afforded by the digital world to spread misinformation, weaken trust in the government and public policies, with profoundly destabilising effects for domestic politics and security. The skilful use of digital technologies can allow militarily weaker groups to take the upper hand against slower-to-mobilise, hierarchically organised conventional armies.[129]

Moreover, new digital technologies and social media platforms enable anyone, anywhere to create and circulate all sorts of falsehoods including, most recently, 'deep fakes' (i.e. highly realistic manipulation of video footage). One need only look at the large number of allegations not supported by evidence which followed the 2020 elections in the United States,[130] or the false information concerning COVID-19 vaccines, to witness the power of fake news to destabilise political and civil institutions and to manipulate emotions such as anger or fear.[131] Social media also provides ample opportunities for subversive meddling as part of great-power politics.[132]

Developed states' increasing reliance on digital technologies for both civilian and military purposes makes them more vulnerable to attacks. For example, what states today refer to as 'critical infrastructure' increasingly depends on the exchange of information via the internet. Critical infrastructure includes elements such as 'electrical grids, power stations, water systems, logistical services and transportation control systems', as Kastener and Wohlforth report.[133] According to the 2020 Global Risks Report from the World Economic Forum, recent years have seen a rise in cyber attacks targeting such elements of critical infrastructure as energy, transportation and health care, to name but a few. Because individual hackers who manage to interrupt or shut down such critical communication systems can create chaos and cause enormous havoc to a state, society, and economy,[134] the report classified cyber attacks on critical infrastructure as the fifth most dangerous risk in 2020.[135]

With cyber attacks clearly presenting an increasingly dangerous threat to our security, one of the areas which is likely to be impacted the most is that of outer space technologies. Satellites, in particular, are highly vulnerable to cyber security breaches, due to the high number of data exchanges between Earth-based and space-based assets.[136] The security of outer space infrastructure depends on the security of these exchanges, since false information could be used to trigger collisions between different satellites, or to compromise navigation systems on Earth, or even to take control of private data for the purpose of surveillance.[137] Moreover, such threats come from both states and non-state actors, which is problematic in itself, making it more difficult to identify the source of an attack.[138] Threats which can impact the interaction between space and cyber security fall into five main categories: kinetic physical, non-kinetic physical, electronic, cyber and Earth-based. All of these potential threats will require international cooperation if they are to be addressed effectively.[139]

Cooperation in this sector is, however, looking unlikely. As stated above, not only are countries such as the United States, China and Russia expanding their military capabilities in outer space, but they are even developing competing global navigation satellite systems (GNSS), such as the Russian GLONASS, the Chinese Beidou, or the EU's Galileo Satellite Project, which rival the US Global Positioning System (GPS) and can be used for both civilian and military objectives.[140] Although competition in the space domain is necessary for the progress of humankind, the increasingly complex capabilities of space technologies are leaning more and more towards military and defence strategies. Whilst the EU has highlighted an increasing need for all systems to remain fully compatible and interoperable, it is highly unclear what form this cooperation and computability between different GNSS can take.[141] It is clear, nevertheless, that since GNSS messages, signal structures, carrier frequencies, codes and modulations directly affect interoperability, cooperation at the international level should take place from an early stage of development of such systems. On the multilateral level, the International Committee on Global Navigation Satellite Systems (ICG) should continue to encourage compatibility and interoperability among global and regional systems. In addition, and since there is little international law specifically regulating GNSS, the soft law framework which now applies to the internet could be useful to address the gaps until a more cohesive framework is put in place.[142]In sum, digitisation changes geopolitical dynamics in various ways. Whilst it increases the power of already strong militaries that manage to employ digital technologies effectively, it also enables foreign powers to exert unprecedented influence over domestic politics in other countries, for instance by severely damaging critical infrastructure. Cyberspace also empowers asymmetric actors, including insurgent groups, to organise themselves and inflict significant harm on states. It thus can strengthen the relative power of small, well-organised, non-state actors and give them a geopolitical significance they did not previously possess, including an increasing one in outer space.[143] Finally, digital technologies and the emergence of social media platforms have recently accelerated the spread of fake news, which has the capacity to polarise societies, thus destabilising them, and to create circumstances in which emotions such as anger or fear are more influential in shaping public opinion than objective facts.[144]

11.1.8 Bioweapons and WMD

Advances in weapons technology (and especially WMD and bioweapons) are highly relevant to geopolitics, impacting the maintenance of the existing status quo. There are opposing views as to how modern weaponry could affect a state's option to use war as a policy tool. One view argues that the existence of precision-guided weapons will increase the likelihood of states resorting to the use of force. New precision weapons allow armies to destroy their targets with a minimal loss of innocent lives. As a consequence, some experts fear that states may be more prone to resort to the use of force as wars become less costly in lives, especially for the attacking military. At the same time, it could be argued that the proliferation of liberal democracies around the world will make it less likely that states will resort to war. Governments in liberal democracies will find it hard to get funding and public approval for a war unless the war can be ended quickly and successfully, and unless the reason for going to war is widely accepted by the citizens of the state.[145]

Another view maintains that the advent of weapons of mass destruction makes war less controllable. As a consequence, some argue, wars will become futile and thus no longer an option that states can realistically pursue. The risk that a war can take on its own logic and spiral out of control or at least trigger consequences beyond the calculations of the warring parties has always existed. The advent of weapons able to destroy life on Earth as we know it could be expected to restrain states from going to war. Writers such as Jonathan Schell have argued that the advent of nuclear weapons should rule out war as a policy tool entirely. Taken to their ultimate conclusion, wars between nuclear powers would entail the destruction of all warring parties, including those using nuclear weapons; hence, there can be no 'winner'.[146]

There is, however, little doubt that, despite international commitments such as the Treaty on the Non-Proliferation of Nuclear Weapons and the Treaty on the Prohibition of Nuclear Weapons, there is still a long way to go when it comes to WMDs. As the case studies highlighted, rather than decreasing their nuclear capabilities, nuclear powers such as the United Kingdom and France are expanding their arsenals.[147] Although they both claim to be doing so for deterrence purposes,[148] this approach is doing little to encourage states such as North Korea or Iran to give up on their nuclear ambitions, rendering international disarmament efforts of little use. The nuclear deal with Iran and the one with North Korea, for instance, shows how influential WMDs remain to geopolitical discourse. Whichever country succeeds at developing new types of nuclear weapons or defence systems first will have the upper hand in the geopolitical realm, since no other state will be able to oppose it.[149]

Likewise, whichever country wins the hypersonic arms race will gain an immense strategic advantage. To qualify as 'hypersonic', a missile must travel at least five times the speed of sound, and be capable of evading counter-fire and striking with unprecedented precision.[150] In other words, such a missile would be able to neutralise existing missile defences and avoid triggering early-warning systems or detection by radar. A number of countries – including the United States, Russia, Japan, India, South Korea, Taiwan and China – are known currently to be developing supersonic and hypersonic systems for civilian or military purposes, but none of them to date is ready for deployment.[151] A ban on hypersonic missiles would provide a desirable arms control mechanism but is unrealistic to achieve, especially since some countries have already tested prototypes of the technology.[152]

Other types of WMDs, such as biological or chemical weapons are also becoming increasingly relevant to states' military and security strategies. If biological weapons were to be used on a mass scale, the effects would be unimaginable and, most likely, have the potential to escape the control of their creator. In light of the already devastating impact of a pandemic such as COVID-19, everything possible must be done to avoid the deliberate or accidental release into the world of a biological weapon or a man-made dangerous disease.[153] States should develop stronger cooperation systems to monitor each other's actions and increase regulation and safety requirements applicable to biological and medical research.

11.1.9 Superintelligence, Trans-humanism and Post-humanism

Scientific advances in numerous fields – including genome editing, synthetic biology and superintelligence – are opening up new frontiers for human enhancement.[154] Human enhancement, as I have described it previously, refers to 'the use of innovative technologies to augment a human's biological and cognitive abilities beyond the replacement of dysfunctional cellular groups and organs'.[155] Ultimately, our attempts to improve our bodies and minds might usher in a trans-human age. I used the term *trans-humanism* to refer to a stage at which a human being starts to bypass the constraints of its organism.[156] It is a transitory stage that might at some point lead to a post-human mode of existence that can no longer qualify as human. In the twenty-first century, however, post-humanism is still in the realm of science fiction and trans-humanism is the more likely next step in our evolution.[157]

Recently, we have made impressive strides towards a trans-human future. Already, we have access to a number of pharmacological and non-pharmacological methods to alter mental processes. For example, Adderall is used to increase focus and learning skills, whilst negative mental states can be mitigated through the artificial increase in levels of neurotransmitters such as dopamine and serotonin.[158] Similarly, merging our bodies with technology is a present-day reality (through pacemakers, artificial joints etc.).[159] Technologies for neurostimulation and physical enhancement are expected to grow in power rapidly, allowing us to greatly exceed our current capabilities in the near future.[160] Likewise, genetic engineering opens up new possibilities for human enhancement, and it may one day even allow us to extend the lifespan of human beings.[161] It is already possible to edit genes that will be passed on to the next generations, even if in most jurisdictions germline gene therapy is currently either prohibited or severely restricted for research purposes.[162] As synthetic biology progresses in several fields, biological neuro-technological superintelligence may eventually become feasible. It holds out the promise to bestow us with cognitive abilities that far surpass that of the smartest human mind.[163]

All these developments might change human nature in ways so dramatic that the trans-human stage might be reached by our species in the twenty-first century. It is fundamental to note that the trans-human condition does not necessarily imply a better future but will come with a host of challenges. As enhancement technologies will likely remain expensive – only affordable to those with great financial means – growing socio-economic divides between human and trans-human beings or nations seem almost inevitable.[164] Some nations, for example, could be able to turn their citizens into superintelligent and physically augmented beings, which would translate into increased productivity, innovativeness and economic growth. Furthermore, a trans-human or even superintelligent elite would have greater opportunities to engage in various activities that the political theorist Philip Pettit calls 'domination'.[165] In other words, the enhanced elite could continuously increase its power at the cost of the non-enhanced – fully eroding global justice. Furthermore, a trans-human or even post-human future may be one where the experience of happiness, or of being loved, can be easily neurochemically simulated without the attendant reality. This raises concerns about the authenticity of our existence.

These are just some of the challenges posed by enhancement technologies but they suffice to illustrate the need for a code of ethics and clear rules to guide the development of enhancement technologies in order to ensure global justice and equal opportunities for all as we approach the threshold of a trans-human era.

11.1.10 Intrusive Surveillance, Civil Liberties and Social Contract 2.0

Intrusive tech-enabled surveillance poses another significant civilisational frontier risk, with far-reaching implications for civil liberties and the social contract that defines the relationship between citizens and the state. In the age of big data, governments can collect large amounts of information about their citizens not only in much higher amounts, but also much faster than ever before. On the one hand, big data, machine learning and predictive analytics have the capacity to solve many problems and greatly benefit a range of sectors including health and crime prevention. For example, big data analytics are an important instrument in fighting contagious diseases.[166] On the other hand, big data, conjoint with AI, enables a massive intrusion into people's lives.[167] Failure to regulate surveillance technology will entail grave violations of civil liberties.

Not only is the right to privacy at risk of being compromised, but biases in predictive analytics reinforce existing discriminatory practices, such as those towards ethnic, racial or religious minorities.[168] Imbued with the bias of their creators, predictive analytics tools may identify potential troublemakers prior to actual behaviour, thus disqualifying certain individuals from, for example, employment opportunities on the basis of mere assumptions and stereotypes.[169]

Furthermore, intrusive surveillance interferes with the right to freedom of expression. Even in democracies, it increases the risk of self-censorship. In fact, following allegations of mass surveillance programmes carried out by the United States National Security Agency, a 2013 study revealed that a sizable number of US writers had resorted to some form of self-censorship.[170] In addition, algorithmic decision making has been criticised for its lack of transparency, with individuals being insufficiently aware of how their data is being used. This weakens government accountability, which is essential for the social contract.[171]

The idea of the social contract has preoccupied many great thinkers, from Epicurus to Thomas Hobbes, to Jean-Jacques Rousseau, Immanuel Kant and John Rawls. At its core, it is about an implicit agreement among members of society, and this agreement on fundamental social rules, laws and institutions shows that 'those arrangements have some normative property (they are legitimate, just, obligating, etc.)', according to the *Stanford Encyclopedia of Philosophy*.[172] Intrusive surveillance, together with a growing sense of injustice, lack of transparency and accountability threatens the social contract. It can lead to the perception that the government is no longer legitimate.

To regulate the surveillance capabilities offered by new technologies, I have previously suggested moving towards a 'social contract 2.0', which would contain the heightened imperative to protect civil rights and human dignity.[173] More specifically, we must develop regulatory frameworks that guarantee data protection, transparency and accountability, in addition to creating systems that prevent predictive models from perpetuating stereotypes and inequalities.[174]

11.2 The Coming Demographic Revolution

As I have argued, a number of civilisational frontier risks are looming, ranging from climate change to the uncontrolled spread of contagious diseases to cyber security to scientific advances in fields such as AI and synthetic biology. Alongside these risks, we are facing several additional challenges that will affect future relationships among the great powers. These include massive demographic changes. The first half of this century will witness a large-scale demographic transformation: the increased ageing of the global population. Global ageing, some believe, constitutes 'a fundamental shift with no parallel in the history of humanity'.[175] It is a trend that is irreversible in the short term. Although almost all countries of the world will be affected by a slowdown in population growth and an older age structure, those states that already have a relatively old population will be affected the most, while states with high fertility rates today will experience the least ageing.[176]

Almost all of the 'old' countries will be in the developed world, which is by nature leading technological innovation and the global economy. This demographic shift will have a huge impact on society, the economy and the domestic and foreign policies of individual states. In many developed countries, the workforce is expected to shrink, which may lead to economic stagnation or even decline. Economic slowdown can lead to a decline in innovation and entrepreneurship. Meanwhile, on the societal and domestic political levels, an older electorate could lead to the election of more conservative and risk-averse policy makers.[177] The exception among developed countries is the United States, which is the only developed country whose population size and economy is not expected to decline relative to the population sizes and economies of all other states within the next 50 years.[178]

With an ageing population, stagnating economies and lack of innovation, many developed countries may lose their attractiveness as a model that younger societies aspire to. So far, developed countries, with their liberal democracies, respect for human rights and competitive economic system, have retained a high degree of soft power on the world stage. Developed democracies may increasingly come across as ossified, privileged elites that are holding onto outdated institutions. Instead, 'illiberal regimes' might become a more attractive model, particularly in developing countries.[179] It is difficult to imagine that states with a declining and ageing population will be able to maintain their cultural appeal and strategic influence on the world stage.

The world will look much more non-Western by mid-century, which will bring both opportunities and challenges. Between now and 2050, it is expected that half of the world's population growth will be concentrated in just nine countries: India, Nigeria, the Democratic Republic of the Congo, Pakistan, Ethiopia, Tanzania, the United States, Uganda and Indonesia (ordered by their expected contribution to total growth).[180] From an ethnic perspective, 'the Western strand of world population will shrink to 13 per cent (and falling)'.[181] This will certainly have geopolitical consequences, although not necessarily negative ones.

Among the major powers, Russia and China will be most affected by ageing. Russia is facing such a population decline that it is becoming a security issue for the country.[182] Massive oil and gas revenues are currently keeping the country afloat. If its population continues to decline and its fossil-fuel reserves become depleted, however, it will not be able to rely on a more labour- and innovation-intensive economic base. As for China, the long-term impact of its one-child policy (which started in the 1970s and was only abolished in January 2016, and further amended in 2021, when the country shifted to a three-children policy) will lead to a high proportion of old-age dependency comparable to that of developed countries. The main reason for the policy shift to allowing couples to have three children was that, even after the previous one-child policy was scrapped, China still did not register the upsurge in births it expected. In contrast to developed countries, however, the Chinese government has fewer resources per capita to care for its elderly population.[183]

Countries like India, Iran and Pakistan, as well as some states in North Africa, the Middle East and East Asia, are experiencing such rapid and dramatic demographic and economic changes that they can become strategic liabilities or strengths. The combination of rapid modernisation and population growth (or in some instances growing old-age dependency) can endanger social cohesion and instability.

11.3 The Role of Women in Geopolitical Change

The economic and political empowerment of women in traditional societies around the world can decisively impact a country's future political direction, economic development and thus its geopolitical stature. In the realm of economics, the maths is easy: the more women take up paid jobs outside the home, the larger a country's workforce and thus productive potential. For instance, Southeast Asia's rapid economic growth based on the export manufacturing sector has been attributed to the large number of female manufacturing workers in the countries of the region.[184] The increased participation of women in the labour market will be crucial to offset the financial burden on states dealing with the growth of their elderly populations.

In addition, developing countries with a high female literacy rate usually perform better in terms of GDP growth than countries with a low female literacy rate. Furthermore, women who are educated tend to have fewer children. As their families have fewer children to care for, the children tend to be healthier, better nourished and better educated, which is advantageous for developing countries from both a human-resources and a societal perspective.[185]

As more women become involved in politics, governmental priorities in some countries might change. Case studies have shown that women tend to place more emphasis on issues such as health care, economic development and environmental protection. To finance these political priorities, women are often willing to cut military spending instead.[186] If these initial observations become a trend as more and more women enter politics, the empowerment of women could indeed change a country's military posture, with regional and global consequences.

11.4 The End of Unipolarity and the Beginning of Tripolarity (United States, China, Russia)

Another trend poised to shape the future of international relations is the shift towards multi-polarity, which could be a positive development for global security, assuming cooperative relationships are prioritised. In the period between the end of the Second World War and the early twenty-first century, international politics was dominated by two superpowers, the United States and the Soviet Union, large states whose economic and military capabilities, as well as ideological appeal, were omnipotent and could not be rivalled by any lesser power. Following the dissolution of the Soviet Union, the United States remained the only superpower in the world, and many started to describe the post-Cold War interlude as 'unipolar'. Now, with the ascendancy of China, and to a lesser degree Russia, the world is no longer looking so unipolar. As the Australian political scientist Coral Bell argues, the phenomenon of 'superpowerdom' is coming to an end. Instead, she writes, 'we are now back with the more familiar categories of several great powers and many more major, middle and minor powers'.[187] All these larger and smaller powers are keen to preserve their independence in international affairs, and they have the meta-geopolitical capacity to resist stronger powers and even inflict considerable military or economic harm if they choose to do so. Power is thus becoming increasingly dispersed.

An important yet disputed question is how a state qualifies as a 'pole'. According to the classic definition provided by Waltz, a state's material capabilities and its ability to translate them into influence bestow on it the status of a pole, with the power possessed by a state being measured relative to the power of the others.[188] However, in the era of globalisation, Nye argues, the international arena is better understood as a three-dimensional chess game in which power is distributed along military, economic and transnational diplomatic lines.[189] Arguing from a meta-geopolitical perspective, I extend Nye's idea to include not only three but seven state capacities, as explained in chapter four.

11.4.1 Key Players in the International Arena

Whilst a dispersion of power is observable, the US-China-Russia triangle is likely to dominate the strategic landscape throughout the twenty-first century. In fact, international peace and security in the twenty-first century may depend, to a large extent, on how relations between these three powers evolve.[190]

The rise of China in the past few decades has dramatically changed international relations. As China has become a key global political and economic actor and leader in advanced technologies, it has also assumed a more assertive posture towards the West, 'amplifying a change in international dynamics', Bruce Jones argues, 'from patterns of multilateral cooperation towards a pattern of competition'.[191] Xi Jinping is eager to challenge the status quo and reshape the international order on terms favourable to China. 'If Xi succeeds', Jones adds, 'China will position itself as an architect of an emerging era of multipolarity.'[192]

The 2017 US National Security Strategy identified China and Russia as the major rivals of the United States.[193] Russia has increasingly strengthened its relations with China, as relations between the United States and Russia have been nosediving since Russia's annexation of Crimea in 2014,[194] followed by allegations of Russian interference in the 2016 US presidential elections.[195] The rapprochement between China and Russia was favoured, among others, by the disintegration of the Soviet Union, which significantly reduced the threat from Russia in China's eyes and thus their great-power rivalry.[196] In many respects, Moscow and Beijing have common interests and their economies are complementary. In addition, US policies have at multiple times inadvertently, and to the detriment of US interests, strengthened ties between China and Russia.[197] Still, the relationship between Moscow and Beijing continues to be characterised by historic mistrust and partly conflicting national priorities.[198] Overall, relationships between the three major powers are not set in stone.

As will be elaborated upon in the Appendix, until the Russian invasion of Ukraine in February 2022, a war between twenty-first-century great powers, however, seemed highly unrealistic considering that they are all economically interconnected, and most of them have strong militaries equipped with nuclear weapons.[199] It was believed that they were likely to continue to function in a type of balance-of-power relationship, not unlike Europe's great powers during the decade of relative peace after the defeat of Napoleon in 1814.[200] During this period, none of Europe's great powers was powerful enough to conquer the others. As a result, there was a military balance among the great powers, which also cooperated to maintain peace on the continent by joining together in the 'Concert of Europe'.[201] Although it is unclear what teh long-term outcome of the Russian invasion will be for relations between Russia, NATO and the EU, and by extension also with China, there is little doubt that the consequences of this escalation will be severe anda far-reaching. Indeed, the balance of power as the world has known it for the last few decades could shift significantly as a result of the 2022 crisis.

Contrary to what we are seeing now, the great powers of the twenty-first century have a good reason to work closely together: they face common threats. Climate change, pandemics, cyber threats, WMD proliferation, inequalities and scarcities in food, water and energy will affect everyone directly or indirectly, and will occupy the national security agendas of major powers. Smaller states, often disproportionately affected by some of these challenges, will need to address these same threats under multilateral and collaborative frameworks too.

In the geopolitical chess game of the future, as I discussed in chapter ten, the tripwire pivotal corridor region will play an important role. The TPC also covers wide parts of the Islamic world, which is likely to have significant influence on global politics, with an expected 2.8 billion people by 2050.[202] Besides the Islamic world's abundant natural resources, the region can increase its international standing if individual countries adopt better domestic governance paradigms, promote economic diversification and invest heavily in education, science and technology.[203] Healing the wounds between the Islamic world and the West will be a formidable but critical task in the coming decades, but it is crucial that reconciliation be achieved on the basis of mutual respect and common interests. Relations between the Arab-Islamic world and the West will need to be cultivated to increase cooperation and reverse the rift that currently exists and has been in the making for centuries. Part of the reason for the divide with the West is the perceived religious and cultural animosity of the West towards Arab-Islamic culture and Islam, in particular, given the history of competition over the past millennium, which included the Crusades, colonialism and the deliberate dismissal and exclusion of the effect that the intellectual heritage and excellence of the golden age of Islam had on the rise of the West.[204] It is also critical that the sacred notion of human rights must not be used as a convenient tool of narrow national interests by major states, thus polluting and discrediting a valuable global goal.[205]

11.4.2 The Rise of the 'Second World'

The transition away from a unipolar world has been accompanied by an increased assertiveness and international influence of middle-income countries. Political scientist Parag Khanna refers to them as 'second-world' states, which he defines as 'those countries in eastern Europe and central Asia, Latin America, the Middle East and Southeast Asia which are both rich and poor, developed and underdeveloped, postmodern and pre-modern, cosmopolitan and tribal – all at the same time'.[206] Khanna takes note of these states' increased assertiveness, self-confidence, willingness to go their independent ways and refusal to follow the dictates of stronger powers. He describes them as 'upstart power[s] with a mind of [their] own'.[207]

Second-world countries in traditional US spheres of influence are increasingly weaning themselves off of their sole dependence on the United States. This can be observed in Latin America, an area that the United States has traditionally sought to keep free from foreign interference, the policy laid out in the Monroe Doctrine. Today, Latin American countries, and particularly those of South America, have formed strong economic relationships with China.[208]

Increasingly significant today are the growing ties between second-world powers. Numerous economic ties, ranging from oil-production alliances to foreign investment and foreign aid, are being formed among second-world powers without the involvement or help of the United States. Long-term US allies such as Japan, South Korea and Australia are becoming increasingly integrated into Asian regional organisations such as ASEAN and the East Asian Summit.[209] As Khanna observes,

'Trade within this greater Asian zone has surpassed trade across the Pacific',[210] as demonstrated by the signing in late 2020 of RCEP, the largest free trade deal in the world, by the ten members of ASEAN and Australia, China, Japan, New Zealand and South Korea. The RCEP creates a free trade zone covering about 30 per cent of the world's GDP, trade and population.[211]

In sum, the rise of an independent-minded second world makes it increasingly difficult for the United States and the EU to set the global agenda on issues like trade or environmental standards. Looking at contemporary geopolitics through the lens of an increasingly empowered second world reinforces the notion that the world will become less and less Western in outlook by mid-century. The United States cannot prevent the rise of middle-income states yearning to improve their economic prosperity and asserting their political independence on the international stage. However, what the United States can influence is how the rise of these new powers will affect the international order that it has been dominating during its 'unipolar moment'. As Fareed Zakaria cautions, if the United States wants to prevent the unravelling of the post-Second World War world order, it needs to give up some of its power and include rising powers as equal partners when decisions are made that affect the globe.[212] Only in this way can the whole world benefit from increasingly diverse international leadership.

11.5 *The International Impact of Non-State Actors*

Power is becoming increasingly diffuse, not only because of the relative increase in the power of a growing number of states, but also because of ever more powerful non-state actors that are able to exert influence or pose threats even to the most powerful states. In fact, the process of globalisation has helped to empower non-state actors such as corporations, private financial institutions and NGOs, as well as military and paramilitary groups.[213] On the one hand, globalisation has progressively weakened the control of state governments with regard to cross-border movements of goods, people and ideas. On the other hand, the intensification of cross-border movements has empowered non-state actors.[214] Globalisation allows multinational corporations to move their people and investments quickly across borders. This process has also allowed some non-state actors to become wealthier than states, and to exert their influence across borders and in every continent, as is the case, for instance, with a multinational corporation such as Google. Some corporations even have so many employees spread across the world that they resemble small states.[215]

Transnational non-governmental organisations – legal or illegal – can make effective use of the internet to recruit members and of the international banking system to transfer funds and international travel to get their members where they need to be.[216] The internet and global media make it easier for non-state actors to spread their messages. This has been the case, in particular, for terrorist and extremist messaging and violent attacks over the past decade (as demonstrated, for example, by the live streaming on Facebook of the mosque shooting in Christchurch, New Zealand, in 2019[217]). The internet and the advent of social media have also enabled non-state actors to access immense quantities of data and private information, which could be used for illegitimate purposes, as demonstrated by the Cambridge Analytica scandal.[218]

Whilst the nature of some of the non-state actors that are becoming powerful in the twenty-first century is new to our global age, there is nothing new about the observation that multinational corporations (MNCs) are gaining in power on an international level. In prior centuries, such corporations originated in the most economically and militarily advanced states of the relevant period. Examples are the British East India Company in the nineteenth century or US and Western European MNCs in the twentieth century.[219] Today, however, corporations originating from large middle-income states are becoming increasingly powerful. Significant amounts of the world's oil and gas reserves are owned by multinational corporations that are in turn owned or partly controlled by governments of emerging-market countries, such as the Chinese government-owned PetroChina, for example.[220] Traditional NGOs continue to influence states and international organisations through lobbying efforts, but they also provide states with important expertise on social, environmental and humanitarian concerns, along with a host of other important issues.[221] As I have noted, globalisation continues to help internationally active NGOs to increase their influence and effectiveness due to the ease of travel and new channels of mass communication it fosters.[222]

The non-state actors described above, however, do not have the same amount of influence in every state. According to the US National Intelligence Council, non-state actors are able to exert much more influence (mostly due to a high degree of freedom of movement) in developed countries and in weak, developing nations than they can in modernising ones. In developed countries, NGOs have the most freedom from state control and interference, as well as easy access to information and communications technology and globalised financial institutions. They also form an important part of civil society in developed states and have a variety of channels to influence policy making or provide expertise to governments.[223]

In weak states, however, NGOs tend to have significant influence due to the frailty of central state power. In these states, NGOs and even multinational corporations can take on a positive role in organising development projects, setting up health clinics or providing services that governments are unable to provide.[224] In contrast, so-called modernising states tend to give non-state actors little room to exert influence.[225] Countries such as China and Russia are highly protective of their sovereignty and dislike foreign interference. These states are also highly bureaucratic, with the central government keeping a tight grip on the management of the national economy.[226] As long as globalisation marches forward, the role of non-state actors in international affairs is a global trend that is likely to grow in the coming decades.

* * *

In sum, this chapter has illustrated some of the most important future trends that state leaders need to prepare for. An important part of meta-geopolitical thinking is the study of new developments in various areas – ranging from health and social issues to emerging technologies – that might affect the power of states and power relationships among them. Drawing on the meta-geopolitical approach, I have identified the major risks that might affect the state of the world in the coming decades. Predictions, of course, are never certain and some of the developments outlined may prove to have less of an impact on international dynamics than others. Still, state leaders are well advised to take the potential geopolitical game-changers, described above, seriously and to prepare to create opportunities from future trends whilst mitigating their associated risks. In so doing, they can greatly benefit from applying the five tools of reconciliation statecraft that I have introduced.

The following section offers some concluding thoughts on reconciliation statecraft and its role in confronting current and future challenges and in fostering a world in which no one has to suffer for the benefit of another.

11.6 Conclusion and the Way Forward

This book has taken a fresh and multidisciplinary approach to an old concept: statecraft. It has sought to provide both the practitioners and academics with a set of innovative tools to address the bewildering amalgam of challenges facing statecraft in the twenty-first century. In today's interconnected world, insecurity, political turmoil and economic misery in one part of the world can have severe implications in the most unexpected places. Statecraft requires the ability to navigate the growing interdependence of the world whilst exploiting emerging frontiers, in both space and science. It has to counteract risks arising from emerging technologies, while reaping the benefits yielded by these innovations. Transnational threats – such as climate change, cyber attacks or pandemics – require statecraft to look beyond narrowly defined national interests. While the history of humanity has been one of mutual cultural borrowings and exchanges, globalisation renders static conceptions of cultural spaces ever more obsolete as more and more people move between multiple cultural identities. Generating a bond of commonly held values amidst a diverse population is a delicate balancing act. So is balancing economic interests with the environment, or group values with individual well-being. In fact, today's statesmen and women are continuously torn between different interests represented by individuals, states, groups of individuals and groups of states, as well as more general global interests such as environmental protection. In the reconciliation of these diverse interests lies the key to effective statecraft in the twenty-first century, statecraft that is capable of ensuring the well-being of the current and future generations.

11.6.1 Five Innovative Statecraft Tools

This book has proposed five innovative tools to navigate the different pressures of the twenty-first century and reconcile what might appear to be conflicting interests. Chief among them is a new meta-geopolitical method of analysis to make sense of world affairs and accompany policy planning. *Meta-geopolitics* moves beyond the traditional focus on territory and resources. Instead, it considers a number of unevenly distributed resources, or state capacities, to understand highly complex strategic relationships between states. These seven state capacities that *meta-geopolitics* deems important for any global strategic analysis are social and health issues; domestic politics; economics; environment; science and human potential; military and security issues; and international diplomacy. Threats to international peace and security can emanate from any of the seven areas of state power and are often interrelated and mutually reinforcing.

Equally interrelated are domestic structures and foreign policy. For a state to thrive both domestically and on the international stage, it must unlock the best in its inhabitants' behaviour through what I have called dignity-based governance. This neurophilosophical governance paradigm draws on recent insights into the human brain and is the second major tool of reconciliation statecraft. It is premised on the notion that governance can positively harness our innate instincts and tendencies for the greater good of society if it reconciles the requirements for human dignity with our innate emotional, amoral and egoistic tendencies. More specifically, dignity-based governance is about, as I put it previously, '(1) assuaging vitriolic human "emotionality" by providing security, safeguarding human rights and fostering a society based on reason; (2) countering human "amorality" with justice, accountability and transparency; and (3) channelling human "egoism" to benefit society through opportunity, inclusiveness and innovation'.[227] Although our requirements for human dignity must be fulfilled if we are to live a good life in harmony with one another, especially in circumstances of scarce resources and insecurity, our egoism pushes us to seek our own welfare with little or no regard for others' requirements for dignity. This, in turn, gives rise to fear, conflict and violence which erode our society from within and manifest themselves well beyond national borders through global challenges such as violent extremism, xenophobia or organised crime. Dignity-based governance creates, among other outcomes, the conditions for human nature to overcome fundamental impulses linked to survival (which can include pre-emptive violence). Dignity-based governance thus has a pragmatic pro-social value and helps instil in us greater concern for the welfare of others, both close and distant. This is of crucial importance in an interconnected world where progress, security and prosperity must be sought in cooperation and not at others' expense.

The recognition that the world no longer operates under a zero-sum logic is also at the heart of *symbiotic realism*, the third tool of reconciliation statecraft. This innovative approach to international relations posits that international politics must be a multi-sum game focused on cooperative state behaviour, non-conflictual competition and absolute gains. Importantly, it underlines the highly pragmatic value of such a policy approach: in an interdependent world, states must act in a framework of shared global interests and gains.

Moving beyond the zero-sum logic, and recognising the multi-dimensionality of global security, also requires us to reconceptualise national security anew. In view of the multiplicity of transnational threats confronting states today, ranging from the spread of contagious diseases to organised crime and global warming, a sustainable approach to national security is an important tool of reconciliation statecraft through which to address all spheres of security, including its human, environmental, national, transnational and transcultural dimensions.

Today, states are part of an interconnected web, and state entities need to work with each other symbiotically. No culture or country in the world alone has all the ideas and talents necessary to come up with creative solutions to today's complex challenges. Forming synergies among cultures will be the best way to generate new ideas that lead to ground-breaking solutions. At the same time, *transcultural synergies* will contribute to enhanced transcultural understanding, a lack of which can often be a cause for fear, alienation, discrimination and conflicts.

Transcultural understanding still requires a large amount of work. Globalisation has led to an intensified diffusion and exchange of knowledge about different areas of the world and cultures. The average human being today is better informed and more widely travelled than ever before. Yet this has not necessarily translated into a better understanding of different cultures at a deeper level. This is mainly due to arguments, such as Huntington's clash of civilisations thesis, that establish a hierarchy between cultures encouraging prejudice, alienation and dehumanisation and securitisation of 'the other'.[228] As a result, tensions arise between different cultural groups, be it in multi-ethnic countries or in states where citizens live side-by-side with large numbers of immigrants.

Awareness of humanity's shared historical heritage and our common neuro-anatomy and neurochemistry is essential as a means of undercutting narratives that fuel conflictual relationships between members of different cultural backgrounds. *Transcultural synergies* need to be fostered in accordance with mutual respect for other cultures' intellectual heritage and approaches to problem-solving. Yet these synergies cannot only be formed among diplomats; they also need to be formed among academics, scientists, interest groups and ordinary people from different cultural backgrounds. Reconciliation statecraft thus requires the help of the population at large when trying to forge fruitful synergies. In other words, it needs to harness the power of grassroots efforts in this area.

In pursuing *sustainable* national security, another challenge for future state leaders is to create more effective global institutions that can promote and coordinate international action to address global threats. It is important for such international bodies to be able to see the interconnectedness of problems and make effective recommendations to individual states as to how they can cooperate with other states to address problems in a way that helps to advance everyone's security and well-being. Having effective mechanisms for international cooperation in place is more important than ever. Today, no power, regardless of how mighty its armed forces or economy, can afford to go it alone.

It is in the self-interest of all states to fight poverty, prevent state failure and address transnational security threats as a way of contributing to international stability. Wealthy and resourceful states retain a moral obligation to preserve human life and dignity all over the world. They need to help guarantee a minimum standard of living to people everywhere. This idea is at the core of the fifth innovative tool of statecraft discussed in this book: just power, which posits that state power should be employed with a strong consideration for justice and that it should promote international peace and stability within the framework of global norms and international law. Just power calls upon states to observe just-war principles and fight wars only if faced with aggression or to end a humanitarian crisis. In the area of economic policy, just power requires wealthy states to help to build a fair global economic order from which developing states can benefit equally.

Environmental protection is just one of many areas where the use of hard and soft power alone will not suffice. What is required, instead, is a just power that stresses fair burden-sharing. The negative effects of global warming – especially floods and droughts – are hurting the developing world more than they are affecting the developed countries of the Northern Hemisphere – and this despite the fact that the developed world carries the primary responsibility for the greenhouse gases emitted into the atmosphere throughout the twentieth century. Burden-sharing will mean that the developed world will have to cut back on consumption and do everything it can to halt the process of global warming. The notion of just power recognises that the whole human species is in the same lifeboat: planet Earth. When it comes to the well-being and survival of humanity, state borders become meaningless.

11.6.2 What Meta-Geopolitics Reveals about the State of the World

Chapters eight and nine explored 27 case studies through a meta-geopolitical analysis, highlighting the necessity to keep the seven interrelated dimensions of state power in mind when trying to understand any country or region of the world. From these case studies it emerges that there is one particular area of instability, which I have termed the tripwire pivotal corridor. This corridor deserves careful analysis in view of its enormous geopolitical relevance. The TPC contains the world's largest repositories of oil and gas resources. The TPC also includes three of the world's most important choke points, which, if blocked, would cause major havoc throughout the global economy. Moreover, many countries within the corridor suffer from a variety of instability factors, including rapid population growth, poor governance, cultural fault lines, violent extremism and territorial disputes. Focusing international resources on stabilising the TPC will go a long way towards building a stable and sustainable world order. These instability factors are accentuated by the persistent destabilising interference of major powers, which enhances severe fatalistic mistrust, instability and insecurity.

A good starting point for stabilising this volatile area is to strengthen those countries that I have singled out as the TPC's pivotal states: Iran, Saudi Arabia, Turkey, Russia, South Africa, Egypt, Pakistan and Israel. Factors such as their size and location, abundance of natural resources, large populations, cultural significance and/or military capabilities make these states important pillars for regional and global security. Turning them into forces of stability and economic growth will benefit their often weak and poor neighbouring states. These pivotal states need to become part of the solution and not part of the TPC's problems.

11.6.3 A Forecast for the Twenty-First Century

Finally, this book has drawn on the meta-geopolitical lens to identify several civilisational frontier risks. As humans venture into new territory, in space and science, an array of new threats emerges. While their future nature is difficult to predict with any exactness, their impact will certainly be wide-ranging and often destabilising. Together, they will profoundly reshape the trajectory of human civilisation in the twenty-first century. From space exploration to AI and trans-humanism to synthetic biology and cyber security, this book has explored ten nascent civilisational frontier risks that could entail particularly strong repercussions throughout the globe and beyond. If handled badly, they could bring about extreme harm to nature, human and otherwise; they could even lead to the extinction of our species. Yet, if managed wisely, they can turn into immense opportunities. In fact, and despite their disruptive potential, transformative technologies such as quantum computing or genetic engineering have the potential to solve today's most urgent problems. In sum, this book has endeavoured to bring the most urgent civilisational frontier risks to the attention of statecraft practitioners to better prepare them for the exigencies of tomorrow's world. These risks are a priority for state leaders to tackle as they will determine the state of the world in the coming decades.

11.6.4 *The Key to Human Prosperity and Flourishing*

To conclude, for a state to thrive, its leadership must master a difficult balancing act, between the well-being of its citizens and the prospects for human prosperity elsewhere in the world, between the interests of the nation and international obligations, between economic growth and environmental sustainability, between different cultural traditions and moral outlooks, between our egoistic needs and the moral imperative to ensure a dignified life for all, everywhere. In the reconciliation of these diverse interests lies the key to a better future. It must be accompanied by the authentic wish to find common ground and a sincere moral obligation to others, close and distant, which is antithetical to the instrumentalisation of human rights interventions or climate change discourse which serves narrow national interests, and which we witness all too often.

In fact, extending our sense of moral obligation to distant others is in our own self-interest, since lasting security and prosperity for a single state increasingly depends on the security and prosperity of the rest of the world. A nation that seeks rapid economic growth and thereby violates international environmental standards or the fair-trade interests of the international community may face a conflict of interest on the surface, but not when adopting a more long-term vision for the country's future. Ultimately, respecting others through non-interference and earning the goodwill and economic cooperation of other states will serve the state's national interest better. In an interdependent world, violation of a vital interest at one level – whether it is the global or the individual level – will ultimately compromise interests at other levels as well. This book has proposed five innovative concepts that equip state leaders with the tools needed to practise reconciliation statecraft. In doing so, it has incorporated cutting-edge findings from neuroscience and neurophilosophical insights into political analysis, thus opening up a completely novel perspective on the art of statecraft. Indeed, recognising how our innate tendencies motivate and shape state behaviour is key to understanding state behaviour in the international arena. Yet, it has not received the scholarly attention it deserves. By filling this gap, I hope to have contributed to an improved statecraft paradigm that enables its practitioners to work together on mutually beneficial solutions to twenty-first-century challenges whilst securing a better future, for both their own states and for the whole of humanity.

Appendix: Understanding the Conflict between Russia and Ukraine

21st-Century Statecraft: Reconciling Power, Justice and Meta-Geopolitical Interests was written, for the most part, before 2022. However, in 2022 the conflict between Russia and Ukraine reached a breaking point, culminating in Russia's invasion of Ukraine from multiple fronts on 24 February. It is therefore important to make some additional remarks.

As mentioned in the case studies on Russia and Ukraine in chapters 8 and 9 of the book, tensions between these two countries have been constant since Russia's annexation of the Crimean peninsula in March 2014.[1] In order to understand why Russia invaded Ukraine in February 2022,[2] and what the long-term consequences of such actions might be, it is necessary to reflect on what might have changed in Russia's attitude towards Ukraine and the West and vice versa.

A.1 The Causes of the Conflict

As stated above, there is little agreement as to the causes of the conflict between Russia and Ukraine. Some place all the blame on Russia and, more specifically, on President Vladimir Putin and his possible desire to re-establish the former Soviet Union.[3] Although there are some arguments for saying that Putin does dream of a Russia that returns to its former glory and re-establishes its former sphere of influence, this alone cannot fully explain the escalation of the conflict between Russia and Ukraine in the past few months.[4]

What we must focus on, therefore, are the arguments made by Russia regarding its reasons for the invasion, and the evolution of its foreign policy over the last thirty years. Although Russia has made some arguments regarding the need to stop a 'genocide of the Russian-speakers' in Eastern Ukraine and the importance of 'de-Nazifying' the country,[5] statements made by the Russian leadership over the past few months may point towards Russian's larger motivations for the invasion of Ukraine.[6]

Before exploring Russia's possible motivations in more depth, it is important to reaffirm that no argument can be used to justify an invasion such as that which has taken place, and there is little doubt that Russia's invasion of Ukraine violates Article 2(4) of the Charter of the United Nations, which prohibits the use-of-force to violate another state's territorial integrity.[7] It also violates the 1994 Budapest Memorandum, in which the Unites States, the United Kingdom, and Russia committed to 'respect the independence and sovereignty and the existing borders of Ukraine' and 'to refrain from the threat or use of force' against the country.[8] Similarly, no argument can be used to justify anything that violates international humanitarian law and norms under the Geneva Conventions and Additional Protocols.[9]

What is important to note in this context is that arguments similar to those made by Russia for its invasion of Ukraine have been used by Western states to justify military interventions in countries such as Iraq and Libya. Indeed, in the case of Iraq, the US and its Allies invaded the country, which was no threat to their national security, on the basis of false allegations regarding the possession by Iraq of weapons of mass destruction,[10] and similarly in violation of the UN Charter.[11] On the other hand, NATO justified its actions in Libya under the principle of Responsibility to Protect (R2P), which was another case of false premises leading to the ultimate weakening of the important concept of R2P.[12] In both these cases, the consequences of the military interventions by foreign states in the domestic affairs of others led to long term regional instability, humanitarian crises and endless political and economic chaos that persists to this day. The predictable failure to establish a strong government in Iraq, and the unwise dismantling of all security and military sectors, led to a power vacuum that directly enabled the brutal sectarian intervention by the Iranian Revolutionary Guard[13] and the corresponding emergence of multiple violent terrorist groups such as ISIS,[14] with extreme and horrific violence leading to ongoing human rights violations and loss of life. The instability and insecurity that dominated Iraq and Libya for decades after the interventions does not bode well for the future of Ukraine.

That said, and setting aside the arguments made by both scholars and the Russian authorities I mentioned above, the real reasons lying behind the escalation of conflict between these two countries may instead be found in Russia's increasingly tense relationship with NATO and, more broadly, the West.[15] Indeed, as stated by Mearsheimer, Russia has been vocal about its displeasure over the expansion of NATO for the past three decades.[16] Already in the 1990s, Russia claimed that the former Soviet leader, Mikhail Gorbachev, was repeatedly promised that NATO would not expand East in exchange for Germany's reunification and its NATO membership, and that NATO had breached this promise.[17] In fact, since the reunification of Germany, fourteen different countries have joined the NATO alliance, with many of them being former Soviet states.[18] Russian foreign policy documents and speeches made by the highest authorities in Russia have repeatedly called out this expansion as a breach of this alleged agreement made in 1990.[19] Since this oral promise never made it into a written document, unlike the agreement regarding the reunification of Germany, NATO has claimed that it never made Russia a binding promise, and has repeatedly disregarded Russia's expressions of concern.[20] However, even if this was the case, it is in the interest of regional and international peace and security to be sensitive to and accommodate the national security concerns of others. The West's arguably short-sighted decision to ignore Russian security concerns led George Kennan, the intellectual father of America's 'containment' foreign policy during the Cold War,[21] to decry the choice to expand NATO as a 'tragic mistake' in as long ago as 1998.[22] In a famous interview given to the *New York Times* following the US Senate's vote to approve the expansion of NATO, Kennan stated that this was 'the beginning of a new Cold War', since it would trigger adverse reactions in terms of Russian foreign policy.[23] According to Kennan, the most important thing was that, until the expansion, 'no one was threatening anybody else'.[24] It was the expansion that shifted this balance and led some to predict that nuclear threats were far from being a thing of the past when it came to the relationship between NATO and Russia.[25]

The tensions between Russia and NATO regarding the latter's rapid expansion, and that of the EU, escalated in April 2008 following the NATO Bucharest Summit Declaration, which stated that 'NATO welcomes Ukraine's and Georgia's Euro-Atlantic aspirations for membership in NATO. We agreed today that these countries will become members of NATO.'[26] Russia responded to this statement saying that Georgia and Ukraine's membership was a 'direct threat to Russia' and that this would have immense consequences for pan-European security.[27] As argued by Mearsheimer, this Declaration was one of the causes of the 2008 conflict between Russia and Georgia.[28]

Similarly, Russia is unhappy with the expansion of the EU, which now includes states that were previously members of the Warsaw Pact, such as Poland and the Czech Republic.[29] The fact that prior to the outbreak of war in Ukraine in 2014 Viktor Yanucovych's government had been in a process of signing an economic deal with the EU, which Russia then blocked, was clearly one of the causes of the 2014 anti-government uprising (referred to as the 'Euromaidan') as well as the war between pro-Europeans and pro-Russians in Ukraine that soon followed.[30] This long standing split between Western Ukraine, which tends to be more pro-European, and the East, which is more pro-Russian, is an important factor in the outbreak of hostilities in 2014,[31] and continues to play a role today through the existence and attempted expansion of the self-proclaimed Independent Republics of Donetsk and Luhansk in the Ukrainian Donbass region.[32]

Moreover, irrespective of whether Russia's long-term aim is also to establish a pro-Russian government in Ukraine, there is little doubt that Russia sees the West's push for the pro-Western governments that formed in Ukraine following the 2004-2005 Orange Revolution as highly threatening to its security interests and geopolitical standing.[33]

There are certainly many elements that contributed to the outbreak of civil and international conflict in Ukraine in 2014, to its escalation and to the Russian invasion in February 2022. However, in the light of the considerations made above, it is clear that Russia has come to see NATO, the EU, and their Western allies as an increasingly important security threat.[34] Furthermore, as highlighted by Mearsheimer, Russia views Ukraine as a region of core strategic interest due to its natural resources and advanced nuclear capacities, but also as a large buffer between its own territory and the West.[35] Following the beginning of the war between Russia and Ukraine in 2014, Mearsheimer famously blamed the Ukrainian crisis on the West.[36] He argues that by failing to take Russia's security concerns seriously, the West triggered Russia's violent response.[37] While this is most likely not the exclusive cause of the war, it is certainly one of the most, if not the most, important one. Indeed, Russia is unlikely to backtrack on its invasion until it has achieved some of its principal objectives, namely, the neutrality of Ukraine and the promise that it will not join NATO or the EU.[38] Only this will be able to assuage its fear and lead to its withdrawal from Ukraine.[39]

Indeed, as I have stated repeatedly throughout this book when illustrating my theory of *symbiotic realism* and the *multi-sum security principle*, in our instantly connected and deeply interdependent world, no state can be *sustainably* secure if every other state is not – or does not feel – secure.[40]

A.2 The West's Reaction

Having established that the main source of the conflict between Russia and Ukraine lies in Russia's belief that NATO and the West pose an important security threat, it is important to provide an overview of how the West has responded to the crisis.

Initially, the NATO and EU member states and their Western allies mostly reacted to Russia's invasion of Ukraine in the same way as they responded to the Russian annexation of Crimea in 2014, namely, through the use of sanctions[41] and the provision of weapons.[42] Economic sanctions were imposed immediately by the US, the UK, the EU and many other (mostly Western) countries against Russia, with the aim of crippling the country's economy. Members of the Russian government and military were targeted first, followed by Russian banks, companies, and even rich Russian businesspeople close to the government, the so-called oligarchs, many of whom have business in the West.[43] Such sanctions have been progressively extended to include Belarus, on the basis of its military and strategic support of Russia.[44] Who is being targeted by Western sanctions, on the basis of what evidence, and according to which legal processes, are issues that are drawing increasing amounts of attention, particularly following the adoption of these sanctions by Switzerland, a country that is known for its neutrality.[45] These sanctions were taken to a much higher level, at least symbolically, when members decided to ban selected Russian banks from the international financial messaging system known as Swift, which enables international transfers.[46]

Importantly, other kinds of measures have been adopted across the world. Both the US and European countries have banned all Russian aircraft from entering their airspace, including civilian ones, effectively cutting Russia off from the West.[47] Similarly, other measures have been adopted with the alleged aim of curtailing Russian propaganda, ranging from the shutting down of Russian cable networks RT and Sputnik in Europe and the US,[48] to an attempt by the Italian public University of Milano Bicocca to suspend a university literature course on Dostoevskij, which led to a public outcry.[49] Moreover, many private companies such as IKEA, Apple and Jaguar have suspended their operations in Russia as an attempt to protest agains the war through a 'boycott'.[50]

One of the biggest challenges for the West, and particularly for European states, in responding to the Russian invasion stems from their dependence on Russian oil and gas.[51] The possibility of Russia cutting off European supplies has increased prices of both oil and gas to new highs,[52] demontrating the relevance of economic and energy security concerns during conflicts, as has the suspension by Germany of the Russian Nord Stream 2 gas project.[53]

Although Western states such as France have made mediation attempts, the lack of willingness to concede on any of Russia's demands has so far led to no result except the increasing polarisation of the world into two factions, states that are more US-leaning, and those that are more Russian-leaning.[54] This split can be easily seen through what has recently happened in both the UN Security Council and the UN General Assembly regarding the attempted adoption of Resolutions condemning the Russian invasion of Ukraine, which were unsuccessful in the case of the former, but successful in the latter. In the first Security Council vote on the matter, Russia exercised its veto, while China abstained from voting, thereby reaffirming its neutrality and its refusal to go explicitly either for or against Russia, with whom it has increasing economic and energy ties.[55] In the UN General Assembly, on the other hand, many states who are traditionally 'non-Aligned' abstained, and both India and Pakistan voted against the Resolution, joining forces in a rather exceptional manner.[56]

A.3 The Consequences of the Conflict for the World

The announcement by Putin on 27 February 2022 that Russia would put its nuclear force on high alert triggered a feeling of terror in people all over the world who, for the first time in decades, felt that a nuclear war might not be such an unlikely event.[57] Despite this potential threat, and reports of alleged violations of international humanitarian law in Ukraine,[58] no other state seems to intend militarily intervention against Russia.[59] The reason for this lies in the fact that a military response or direct intervention in the conflict, which goes beyond sanctions and the provision of weapons, subversion (cyber- or otherwise) and financial aid, could trigger a large-scale war, potentially even a nuclear one.[60]

At present we cannot know what the long-term consequences of the war will be. Ukraine and the Ukrainian people will certainly suffer immensely, as demonstrated by the millions of asylum seekers who have already fled the country[61] and the complete destruction of large cities and key infrastructure.[62] What will happen to its government and the unity of the country is something that cannot be guessed as of the writing of this appendix.

Russia, on the other hand, will most likely suffer a significant financial crisis linked to the sanctions and the potential collapse of the Ruble.[63] Its abundance of oil, gas, metals, and its economic and energy deals with China will, however, protect it from the full extent of the desired impact of Western sanctions.[64] What role Russia will have in global geopolitics after the end of the Ukrainian war remains to be seen, as will the strength of its growing relationship with China.

Indeed, there are very few certainties regarding the short and long-term outcome of this war. What we do know, however, is that the stability of the international system and the principles that kept the system in place have shown their weakness. The United Nations has proven to be close to useless in a conflict in which one of the parties is a member of the Security Council, as has the OSCE.[65] Similarly, the principles regulating the use of force have proven meaningless in the face of one of the world's Great Powers.[66] In other words, the Russian invasion of Ukraine seriously challenges the international security framework, as the US invasion of Iraq arguably did even more so twenty years earlier.[67]

This is even clearer when we consider the extent and diversity of the measures adopted against Russia. While some of them, such as sanctions against state officials, can be considered 'standard practice', others listed above, and the lack of due process regarding their adoption, cannot. While an international response to Russia's actions is understandable, the lack of clarity as to what such a common response is, and the extreme and irrational nature of some of the measures adopted have only opened the floodgates for unforeseen consequences and extreme reactions to security threats in the future. Previously there was a set of 'standard reactions' from the international community for situations such as this one.[68] From now on, especially with the prior precedent of the Iraq invasion in 2003, every state in the world could claim to have the right to do whatever it wants, irrespective of whether this is due to direct threats or more ambiguous reasons/excuses. This is a terrifying prospect for the future of global security and stability of global order.

Nevertheless, what the conflict has shown us so far is that common security threats require persistent, transparent, accountable, symbiotic diplomacy and reconciliation.[69] Such common responses can only be found when states are willing to compromise, and thus find mutually-workable solutions while reconciling their different and competing national interests, in accordance with my proposed principle of *reconciliation statecraft*.[70]

The only way forward in this conflict is for Russia, Ukraine, NATO and the West to all come to see that zero-sum paradigms don't work and are counter-productive to *sustainable* national interests and *collective* peace and security.[71]

Notes

1. Statecraft in the Twenty-First Century: In Search of a New Paradigm

1. B.J. Cohen, Currency Statecraft: Monetary Rivalry and Geopolitical Ambition (Chicago: Chicago University Press, 2019), p. 34.
2. M. Kroenig, *The Return of Great Power Rivalry: Democracy versus Autocracy from the Ancient World to the US and China* (Oxford: Oxford University Press, 2020), p. 1.
3. N.R.F. Al-Rodhan, 'Reconciliation Statecraft: Eight Competing Principal Interests', ETH Zürich Center for Security Studies, 7 February 2018.
4. J.D. Fearon, 'Domestic Politics, Foreign Policy, and Theories of International Relations', *Annual Review of Political Science* 1 (1998), pp. 289–90.
5. N.R.F. Al-Rodhan, *The Five Dimensions of Global Security: Proposal for a Multi-sum Security Principle* (Berlin: LIT, 2007).
6. N.R.F. Al-Rodhan, *The Three Pillars of Sustainable National Security in a Transnational World* (Berlin: LIT, 2008).

2. Traditional Approaches to Statecraft

1. R. Garner, P. Ferdinand and S. Lawson, *Introduction to Politics* (Oxford: Oxford University Press, 2020), p. 465.
2. Thucydides, *History of the Peloponnesian War*, trans. Rex Warner (Harmondsworth: Penguin, 1972), p. 48.
3. P.G. Lauren, G.A. Craig and A.L. George, *Force and Statecraft: Diplomatic Challenges of Our Time*, 4th edn (New York and Oxford: Oxford University Press, 2007), p. 138.
4. N. Machiavelli, *The Discourses*, quoted in Lauren, Craig and George, *Force and Statecraft*, p. 138.
5. Lauren, Craig and George, *Force and Statecraft*, p. 270.

6. D. Ross, *Statecraft: And How to Restore America's Standing in the World* (New York: Farrar, Straus and Giroux, 2007), p. x.

7. Ibid.

8. M. Thatcher, *Statecraft: Strategies for a Changing World* (New York: Harper Perennial, 2003).

9. G.J. Ikenberry, 'Review: *Statecraft: Strategies for a Changing World*, by Margaret Thatcher', *Foreign Affairs*, September/October 2002.

10. J.P. Scoblic, 'Review: *Diplomacy*, by Henry Kissinger', *Brown Journal of World Affairs* 1, no. 2 (1994), pp. 399–404.

11. H. Kissinger, *Diplomacy* (New York: Simon & Schuster, 1994).

12. See J.S. Nye Jr, 'Hard, Soft and Smart Power', in A.F. Cooper, J. Heine and R. Thakur (eds), *The Oxford Handbook of Modern Diplomacy* (Oxford: Oxford University Press, 2013).

13. Ibid.

14. J.S. Nye Jr, *Soft Power: The Means to Success in World Politics* (New York: Public Affairs, 2004), p. 2.

15. M.F. Rasheed, 'The Concept of Power in International Relations', *Pakistan Horizon* 48, no. 1 (1995), p. 95; S. Moon, 'Power in Global Governance: An Expanded Typology from Global Health', *Globalization and Health* 15, 74 (2019), pp. 3–4.

16. Nye, *Soft Power*, p. 6.

17. Ibid., p. 7.

18. J. Kucera, 'Why Did Kazakhstan Give Up Its Nukes?', eurasianet, 15 May 2013.

19. R. Leng, 'Influence Techniques among Nations', in P.E. Tetlock, J.L. Husbands, R. Jervis, P.C. Stern and C. Tilly (eds), *Behaviour, Society, and International Conflict: Volume III* (Oxford: Oxford University Press, 1993), p. 126–89.

20. D. Cortright, 'Positive Inducements in International Statecraft', *Fraser Forum*, 2 May 2000 (based on a paper of the same title commissioned by the Fraser Institute).

21. E. Solingen, 'The New Multilateralism and Nonproliferation: Bringing in Domestic Politics', *Global Governance* 1, no. 2 (1995), pp. 214–18.

22. See D. Cortright and G.A. Lopez, 'Carrots, Sticks and Cooperation: Economic Tools of Statecraft', in B.R. Rubin (ed.), *Cases and Strategies for Preventive Action* (Century Foundation Press, 1998) pp. 113–34.

23. D. Baldwin, *Economic Statecraft* (Princeton, NJ: Princeton University Press, 1985), p. 63.

24. Cortright and Lopez, 'Carrots, Sticks and Cooperation'.

25. Ibid.

26. Ibid.

27. Peterson Institute for International Economics, 'Case Studies in Sanctions and Terrorism', 2007, https://www.piie.com/commentary /speeches-papers/case-78-8-and-92-12.

28. Cortright and Lopez, 'Carrots, Sticks and Cooperation'.

29. Ibid.
30. R.L. Armitage and J.S. Nye Jr, 'Stop Getting Mad, America. Get Smart', *Washington Post*, 9 December 2007.
31. J. Calvet de Magalhães, *The Pure Concept of Diplomacy*, trans. B. Futscher Pereira (New York: Greenwood Press, 1988), p. 51.
32. Ibid., p. 60.
33. C. de Martens, *Le guide diplomatique* (Leipzig: F.A. Brockhaus, 1866), quoted in Magalhães, *The Pure Concept of Diplomacy*, p. 50.
34. Ibid., p. 51.
35. Ibid., p. 59.
36. S. Riordan, *The New Diplomacy* (Cambridge: Polity Press, 2003), p. 110.
37. Ibid., pp. 118–19.
38. S.M. Patrick, 'John Kerry and the Blurring of the Foreign and the Domestic', Council on Foreign Relations, 22 February 2013.
39. Riordan, *The New Diplomacy*, p. 123.
40. Ibid., p. 124.
41. See T. Jensen, 'The Democratic Deficit of the European Union', *Living Reviews in Democracy*, March 2009.
42. 'Council Gives Green Light to First Recovery Disbursements', Council of the European Union, Press Release, 13 July 2021.
43. Riordan, *The New Diplomacy*, p. 126.
44. P. Zelikow, cited in J. Vaisse, *Transformational Diplomacy*, Chaillot Paper no. 103 (Paris: EUISS, 2007), p. 21.
45. Vaisse, *Transformational Diplomacy*, p. 71.
46. A. Rathmell and A. Mellors, 'Building Effective Institutions', *SDGs: The People's Agenda*, 1 March 2016; L.-M. Glass and J. Newig, 'Governance for Achieving the Sustainable Development Goals: How Important Are Participation, Policy Coherence, Reflexivity, Adaptation and Democratic Institutions?,' *Early System Governance* 2 (2019), p. 4.
47. J. Kastner and W.C. Wohlforth, 'A Measure Short of War: The Return of Great-Power Subversion', *Foreign Affairs*, July/August 2021.
48. A. Codevilla, *Informing Statecraft: Intelligence for a New Century* (New York: Free Press, 2002), p. 356.
49. G. Kruger, *Strategic Subversion: From Terrorists to Superpowers, How State and Non-State Actors Undermine One Another* (Bloomington, IN: Authorhouse, 2021), p. 139.
50. A.R. Kahin and G.M. Kahin, *Subversion as Foreign Policy: The Secret Eisenhower and Dulles Debacle in Indonesia* (New York: New Press, 1995), p. 3.
51. G.M. Feierstein, 'Iran's Role in Yemen and Prospects for Peace', Middle East Institute, 6 December 2018; J. Feltman, 'Hezbollah: Iran's Most Successful Export', Brookings Institution, 17 January 2019.
52. W. Rosenau, 'Subversion Old and New', *War on the Rocks*, 24 April 2014.
53. Ibid.
54. Ibid.

55. Kahin and Kahin, *Subversion as Foreign Policy*, p. 3.
56. Ibid.
57. M.M. Lee, *Crippling Leviathan: How Foreign Subversion Weakens the State* (Ithaca, NY: Cornell University Press, 2020), p. 5.
58. W. Rosenau, *Subversion and Insurgency*, RAND Counterinsurgency Study, Paper 2 (Santa Monica, CA: RAND Corporation, 2007), pp. 3, 13.
59. L. Maschmeyer, 'The Subversive Trilemma: Why Cyber Operations Fall Short of Expectations', *International Security* 46, no. 2 (Fall 2021).
60. Ibid.
61. Lauren, Craig and George, *Force and Statecraft*, p. 271.
62. Ibid., p. 273.
63. N.R.F. Al-Rodhan, 'What Will Space Look Like in 2021?', *Space Review*, 11 January 2021.
64. UN Office for Outer Space Affairs, Treaty on Principles Governing the Activities of States in the Exploration and Use of Outer Space, including the Moon and Other Celestial Bodies, Resolution 2222 (XXI), adopted 27 January 1967, entered into force 10 October 1967.
65. N.R.F. Al-Rodhan, '3 Disruptive Frontier Risks that Could Strike by 2040', World Economic Forum, 18 December 2020.
66. *Oxford Dictionary of Phrase and Fable*, 'Artificial Intelligence', https://www.oxfordreference.com/view/10.1093/oi/authority.201108030954 26960 (accessed 26 July 2021).
67. N.R.F. Al-Rodhan, 'Major Transformative Technologies and the Five Dimensions of Global Security', *Oxford Political Review*, 23 June 2020,.
68. N.R.F. Al-Rodhan, 'Neuromorphic Computers: What Will They Change', *Global Policy*, 18 February 2016.
69. N.R.F. Al-Rodhan, 'Meta-Geopolitics of Pandemics: The Case of COVID-19', *Global Policy*, 8 May 2020.
70. Centers for Disease Control and Prevention, 'Why It Matters: The Pandemic Threat', *Updates from the Field*, no. 26 (Winter 2017), updated 2020 and 2021.
71. Ibid.
72. L.W. Riley *et al.*, 'Slum Health: Diseases of Neglected Populations', *BMC International Health and Human Rights* 7, no. 1 (2007), p. 2.
73. Al-Rodhan, 'Meta-Geopolitics of Pandemics'.
74. N.R.F. Al-Rodhan, 'A Neurophilosophy of Two Technological Game-Changers: Synthetic Biology and Superintelligence', *Blog of the American Philosophical Association*, 29 June 2020.
75. Ibid.
76. J. Li *et al.*, 'Advances in Synthetic Biology and Biosafety Governance', *Frontiers in Bioengineering and Biotechnology* 9 (2021), p. 2.
77. J.K. Wickiser *et al.*, 'Engineered Pathogens and Unnatural Biological Weapons: The Future Threat of Synthetic Biology', *Combating Terrorism Center Sentinel* 13, no. 8 (2020), p. 3.

78. N.R.F. Al-Rodhan, 'A Neurophilosophy of Governance of Artificial Intelligence and Brain-Computer Interface', *Blog of the American Philosophical Association*, 1 June 2020; L. Drew, 'The Ethics of Brain-Computer Interfaces', *Nature* 571 (2019), pp. S19–S21.

79. Drew, 'The Ethics of Brain-Computer Interfaces'.

80. See Intergovernmental Panel on Climate Change, *Climate Change 2014: Synthesis Report: Contribution of Working Groups I, II and III to the Fifth Assessment Report of the Intergovernmental Panel on Climate Change*, ed. R.K. Pachauri and L.A. Meyer (Geneva: IPCC, 2015).

81. J.A. Patz *et al.*, 'Global Climate Change and Emerging Infectious Diseases', *JAMA: Journal of the American Medical Association* 275, no. 3 (1996), pp. 217–23; Al-Rodhan, 'Meta-Geopolitics of Pandemics'.

82. See S.L. Pimm *et al.*, 'The Future of Biodiversity', *Science* 269, no. 5222 (1995), p. 347.

83. A.D. Barnosky *et al.*, 'Approaching a State Shift in Earth's Biosphere', *Nature* 486, no. 7401 (2012), pp. 52–58.

84. D. Pamlin and S. Armstrong, *Global Challenges: 12 Risks that Threaten Human Civilisation: The Case for a New Category of Risks* (Stockholm: Global Challenges Foundation, 2015), p. 79.

85. Al-Rodhan, '3 Disruptive Frontier Risks that Could Strike by 2040'.

86. N.R.F. Al-Rodhan, 'A Neurophilosophy of Fake News, Disinformation and Digital Citizenship', *Blog of the American Philosophical Association*, 25 August 2020.

87. J. Schell, *The Fate of the Earth* (New York: Alfred A. Knopf, 1982).

88. Al-Rodhan, 'A Neurophilosophy of Two Technological Game-Changers'.

89. N.R.F. Al-Rodhan, 'Inevitable Transhumanism? How Emerging Strategic Technologies Will Affect the Future of Humanity', ETH Zürich Center for Strategic Studies, 29 October 2013.

90. N.R.F. Al-Rodhan, *Emotional Amoral Egoism: A Neurophilosophy of Human Nature and Motivations*, 2nd edn (Cambridge: Lutterworth Press, forthcoming 2021), ch. 4.5.1.

91. N.R.F. Al-Rodhan, *Sustainable History and Human Dignity: A Neurophilosophy of History and the Future of Civilisation*, 2nd edn (Cambridge: Lutterworth Press, forthcoming 2021), ch. 17.3.

92. Al-Rodhan, 'Major Transformative Technologies and the Five Dimensions of Global Security'.

93. G. Wilson, 'Minimizing Global Catastrophic and Existential Risks from Emerging Technologies through International Law', *Virginia Environmental Law Journal* 31, no. 2 (2013), pp. 307–64.

94. A. Kelle, 'Ensuring the Security of Synthetic Biology: Towards a 5P Governance Strategy', *Systems and Synthetic Biology* 3, no. 85 (2009), pp. 85–90; H. Bernauer *et al.*, 'Technical Solutions for Biosecurity in Synthetic Biology', *Industry Association Synthetic Biology* (2008), pp. 1–19.

95. However, see some of the suggestions in M.S. Garfinkel *et al.*, 'Synthetic Genomics: Options for Governance', *Industrial Biotechnology* 3, no. 4 (2007), pp. 333–65.
96. Ibid.
97. N.R.F. Al-Rodhan, 'Quantum Computing and Global Security', *Geneva Centre for Security Policy*, 20 February 2015.
98. Al-Rodhan, *Emotional Amoral Egoism*, ch. 2.5.
99. Lauren, Craig and George, *Force and Statecraft*, p. xv.
100. *Encyclopedia Britannica*, 'Geopolitics', by D.H. Deudney, 12 June 2013.

3. Rethinking Geopolitics

1. K. Dodds, *Geopolitics: A Very Short Introduction*, 3rd edn (Oxford: Oxford University Press, 2019), p. 4.
2. J.J. Grygiel, *Great Powers and Geopolitical Change* (Baltimore: Johns Hopkins University Press, 2006), p. 15.
3. S. Guzzini (ed.), *The Return of Geopolitics in Europe?: Social Mechanisms and Foreign Policy Identity Crisis* (Cambridge: Cambridge University Press, 2012), p. 1.
4. Table compiled from the following sources: L.K.D. Kristof, 'The Origins and Evolution of Geopolitics', *Journal of Conflict Resolution* 4, no. 1 (1960), pp. 15–51; S.B. Cohen, *Geopolitics of the World System* (New York: Rowman & Littlefield, 2003); Dodds, *Geopolitics*; C. Flint, *Introduction to Geopolitics*, 3rd edn (London: Routledge, 2017); G. Sloan, *Geopolitics, Geography and Strategic History* (London: Routledge, 2018); J. Black, *Geopolitics and the Quest for Dominance* (Bloomington, IN: Indiana University Press, 2016); Guzzini (ed.), *The Return of Geopolitics in Europe?* (Cambridge Studies in International Relations) (Cambridge: Cambridge University Press, 2012); Grygiel, *Great Powers and Geopolitical Change* (Baltimore, Maryland: John Hopkins University Press, 2006).
5. E.L. Frost, 'Globalization and National Security: A Strategic Agenda', in R.L. Kugler and E. Frost (eds), *Global Century: Globalization and National Security* (Washington, DC: National Defense University Press, 2001), p. 37; see also S. Dalby, *Anthropocene Geopolitics: Globalization, Security, Sustainability* (Ottawa: University of Ottawa Press, 2020); Y. Kumar, *Geopolitics in the Era of Globalisation: Mapping an Alternative Global Future* (New York: Routledge, 2021).
6. P.R. Faber, 'Thinking about Geography: Some Competing Geopolitical Models for the 21st Century', Academic Research Branch, NATO Defense College, Rome, Research Paper no. 15 (February 2005), p. 3.
7. Ibid.
8. Ibid.
9. Ibid.

10. S.G. Brooks, *Producing Security: Multinational Corporations, Globalization, and the Changing Calculus of Conflict* (Princeton, NJ: Princeton University Press, 2011), p. 14.

11. Faber, 'Thinking about Geography: Some Competing Geopolitical Models for the 21st Century', 3.

12. Ibid., 3.

13. I. Kant, 'Perpetual Peace: A Philosophical Proposal', in I. Kant, *Kant's Principles of Politics, including his Essay on Perpetual Peace: A Contribution to Political Science*, trans. W. Hastie (Edinburgh: T. & T. Clark, 1891).

14. M. Kuus and K. Dodds, *The Routledge Research Companion to Critical Geopolitics* (London: Routledge, 2016), p. 5.

15. Dodds, *Geopolitics*, p. 44.

16. G.Ó. Tuathail, *Critical Geopolitics: The Politics of Writing Global Space* (Minneapolis: University of Minnesota Press, 1996).

17. G.Ó. Tuathail, 'Problematizing Geopolitics: Survey, Statesmanship and Strategy', *Transactions of the Institute of British Geographers* 19, no. 3 (1994), p. 259.

18. Tuathail, 'Problematizing Geopolitics', p. 269.

19. Dodds, *Geopolitics*, pp. 44–45.

20. Ibid.

21. Kuus and Dodds, *The Routledge Research Companion to Critical Geopolitics*, p. 75.

22. Ibid.

23. See, for example, R.T. Robin, *The Making of the Cold War Enemy: Culture and Politics in the Military-Intellectual Complex* (Princeton, NJ: Princeton University Press, 2003).

24. Kristof, 'The Origins and Evolution of Geopolitics', p. 45.

25. Dodds, *Geopolitics*, pp. 45–46; J. Dittmer and D. Bos, *Popular Culture, Geopolitics, and Identity* (London: Rowman & Littlefield, 2019), p. xiii.

26. Dittmer and Bos, *Popular Culture*, p. xiii.

27. Robert A. Saunders and Vlad Strukov (eds), *Popular Geopolitics: Plotting an Evolving Interdiscipline* (Abingdon: Routledge, 2018), p. 1.

28. G. Kemp and R.E. Harkavy, *Strategic Geography and the Changing Middle East* (Washington, DC: Brookings Institution Press, 1997), p. 8.

29. Ibid., p. 9.

30. Ibid., pp. 8–9.

31. Ibid., p. 9.

32. See, for example, A. Gamlen, *Human Geopolitics: States, Emigrants, and the Rise of Diaspora Institutions* (Oxford: Oxford University Press, 2019); F. Galgano and E.J. Palka (eds), *Modern Military Geography* (Abingdon: Routledge, 2011); G.L. Clark, M.P. Feldman, M.S. Gertler and D. Wójcik (eds), *The New Oxford Handbook of Economic Geography* (Oxford: Oxford University Press, 2018).

33. Nayef Al-Rodhan, 'Meta-Geopolitics: The Relevance of Geopolitics in the Digital Age', *E-international Relations*, 25 May 2014.
34. Grygiel, *Great Powers and Geopolitical Change*, pp. 3–5.
35. See D.E. Streusand, 'Geopolitics versus Globalization', in S.W.J. Tancredi (ed.), *Globalization and Maritime Power* (Washington, DC: National Defence University Press, 2002).
36. *Encyclopedia Britannica*, 'September 11 Attacks: United States [2001]', by P.L. Bergen, last updated 10 September 2020.
37. T. Friedman, *The Lexus and the Olive Tree: Understanding Globalization*, rev. edn (New York: Anchor Books, 2000), p. 250.
38. Streusand, 'Geopolitics versus Globalization'.
39. Kristof, 'The Origins and Evolution of Geopolitics', p. 19. Emphasis in original.
40. Streusand, 'Geopolitics versus Globalization'.

4. *Meta-Geopolitics* and the Seven Dimensions of State Power

1. F.M. Sempa, 'Halford Mackinder's Last View of the Round World', *The Diplomat*, 23 March 2015.
2. G.J. Ikenberry, 'An Agenda for Liberal International Renewal', in M.A. Flournoy and S. Brimley (eds), *Finding our Way: Debating American Grand Strategy* (Washington, DC: Center for a New American Security, 2008), p. 47.
3. Ibid.
4. Ibid., p. 50.
5. Ibid.
6. Ibid., p. 58.
7. V. Kapuria-Foreman, 'Population and Growth Causality in Developing Countries', *Journal of Developing Areas* 29, no. 4 (1995), pp. 531–32.
8. C.B. Keely, 'Demographic Developments and Security', in M.E. Brown (ed.), *Grave New World: Security Challenges in the 21st Century* (Washington, DC: Georgetown University Press, 2003), p. 201.
9. Ibid.
10. D.E. Bloom, D. Canning and G. Fink, 'Implications of Population Aging for Economic Growth', National Bureau of Economic Research, Working Paper 16705 (January 2011), p. 3.
11. See Eurostat, 'Ageing Europe: Statistics on Population Developments', last updated July 2020; World Health Organisation, 'Aging and Health', accessed 24 July 2021,; E. D'Ambrogio, 'Japan's Ageing Society', European Parliamentary Research Service Briefings, December 2020.
12. R. Jackson, 'The Global Retirement Crisis', *The Geneva Papers on Risk and Insurance: Issues and Practice* 27, no. 4 (2002), pp. 500–1.

13. Ibid., pp. 507–8.
14. Ibid., pp. 490–91.
15. N. Howe and R. Jackson, 'Rising Populations Breed Rising Powers', *Financial Times*, 9 February 2007,.
16. Ibid.
17. S. Liou, 'Chinese Immigration to Russia and Its Non-traditional Security Impact', *East Asia* 34 (2017), pp. 271–86; E. Kogan, 'A Ticking Bomb? Chinese Immigration to Russia's Far East', *European Security and Defence*, 14 May 2019.
18. National Academies of Sciences, Engineering and Medicine, *The Growth of World Population: Analysis of the Problems and Recommendations for Research and Training* (Washington DC: The National Academic Press, 1963), pp. 17–19.
19. Howe and Jackson, 'Rising Populations Breed Rising Powers'.
20. J. Parkin Daniels, '"Everything Is Collapsing": Colombia Battles Third Covid Wave amid Social Unrest', *The Guardian*, 22 June 2021.
21. W. Easterly, J. Ritzen and M. Woolcock, 'Social Cohesion, Institutions, and Growth', *Economics and Politics* 18, no. 2 (2006), p. 107.
22. Ibid.
23. Ibid., p. 112.
24. Ibid., p. 117.
25. Ibid., p. 120.
26. Ibid.
27. I. Yasaveev, 'Not an Epidemic, but a Global Problem: The Authorities' Construction of HIV/AIDS in Russia', *Medicine (Baltimore)* 99, no. 21 (2020).
28. See UNICEF, 'HIV and AIDS'.
29. Easterly, Ritzen and Woolcock, 'Social Cohesion, Institutions, and Growth', p. 120.
30. P.W. Singer, 'AIDS and International Security', *Survival* 44, no. 1 (2002), p. 148.
31. See R.A. Atun and S. Fitzpatrick, *Advancing Economic Growth: Investing in Health* (London: Chatham House, 2005), p. 7.
32. Ibid.
33. A. Illmer, 'North Korean Propaganda Changes Its Tune', BBC News, 23 June 2018.
34. See M. Kneuer, 'Autocratic Regimes and Foreign Policy', *Oxford Research Encyclopedias*, 26 September 2017, https://doi.org/10.1093/acrefore/9780190228637.013.392.
35. See Channing Mavrellis, *Transnational Crime and the Developing World* (Washington, DC: Global Financial Integrity, 2017), pp. 3–21; J.J.F. Forest, 'Globalization and Transnational Crime', *E-International Relations*, 16 September 2020.
36. D. Kaufmann, 'What the Pandemic Reveals about Governance, State Capture, and Natural Resources', Brookings Institution, 10 July 2020.

37. S. Atrache, 'Lebanon Needs Help to Cope with Huge Refugee Influx', International Crisis Group, 19 September 2016.
38. Q. Wright, 'Design for a Research Project on International Conflicts and the Factors Causing Their Aggravation or Amelioration', *Western Political Quarterly* 10, no. 2 (1957), pp. 263–75.
39. Ibid., pp. 268–69.
40. N.R.F. Al-Rodhan and S. Kuepfer, *Stability of States: The Nexus between Transnational Threats, Globalization, and Internal Resilience* (Geneva: Slatkine, 2007), p. 25.
41. Ibid.
42. N. Ferguson, 'What is Power?', *Hoover Digest*, no. 2 (2003), n.p.
43. Ibid.
44. Ibid.
45. J.A. Goldstone and J. Ulfelder, 'How to Construct Stable Democracies', *Washington Quarterly* 28, no. 1 (2004–5), p. 16.
46. See P.H. Baker, 'Conflict Resolution: A Methodology for Assessing Internal Collapse and Recovery', in C. Pumphrey and R. Schwartz-Barcott (eds), *Armed Conflict in Africa* (Lanham, MD: Scarecrow Press, 2003).
47. Ibid.
48. N. Donovan, M. Smart, M. Moreno-Torres, J.O. Kiso and G. Zachariah, 'Countries at Risk of Instability: Risk Factors and Dynamics of Instability', Prime Minister's Strategy Unit Background Paper, February 2005, p. 3.
49. See *Encyclopedia Britannica*, 'Failed State', by N.H. Barma, 17 May 2016.
50. P.J. Garrity, 'Interests and Issues: Perspectives on Future Challenges to US Security', in S.A. Cambone (ed.), *A New Structure for National Security Policy Planning* (Washington, DC: Center for Strategic and International Studies, 1998), p. 101.
51. Z.M. Awdel, N.M. Odel and W.F. Saadi, 'The Rise of the Globalization and Its Effects on the Autonomy of State and Political Economy', *Journal of Critical Reviews* 7, no. 6 (2020), pp. 998–1000.
52. Oxfam International, 'Brazil: Extreme Inequality in Numbers' (accessed 6 October 2021).
53. K. Rowlingson, *Does Income Inequality Cause Health and Social Problems?* (York: Joseph Rowntree Foundation, 2011), p. 5; B. Keeley, *Income Inequality: The Gap between Rich and Poor* (Paris: OECD Publishing, 2015), pp. 32–35.
54. T. Mitrova, 'Russia's Energy Strategy', Atlantic Council Eurasia Center, July 2019, pp. 1–2.
55. C. Cravens, 'The Nationalization of Iranian Oil', *Commodities, Conflict, and Cooperation* (Fall 2016 & Winter 2017).
56. B. Puranen and O. Widenfalk, 'The Rentier State: Does Rentierism Hinder Democracy', in M. Moaddel (ed.), *Values and Perceptions of the*

Islamic and Middle Eastern Publics (New York: Palgrave Macmillan, 2007), p. 160.

57. Al-Rodhan and Kuepfer, *Stability of States*, p. 27.

58. Organization for Security and Economic Co-operation in Europe, *Best-Practice Guide for a Positive Business and Investment Climate* (Vienna: OSCE, 2006), p. 50.

59. Ibid., p. 17.

60. Z. Drabek and W. Payne, 'The Impact of Transparency on Foreign Direct Investment', *Journal of Economic Integration* 17, no. 4 (2002), pp. 778–79.

61. See D. Yergin, 'Ensuring Energy Security', *Foreign Affairs* 82, no. 2 (2006), pp. 71–72; World Bank, 'Access to Energy Is at the Heart of Development', 18 April 2018.

62. M. Gross, 'Latin America's Resources: Blessing or Curse?,' *Current Biology* 24, no. 6 (2014), pp. 209.

63. R. Mills and F. Alhashemi, *Resource Regionalism in the Middle East and North Africa: Rich Lands, Neglected People* (Washington, DC: The Brookings Institution, 2018), pp. 4–6, https://www.brookings.edu/research/resource-regionalism-in-the-middle-east-and-north-africa-rich-lands-neglected-people/.

64. J. Cavanagh and J. Mander, 'World Bank, IMF Turned Poor Third World Nations into Loan Addicts', *CCPA Monitor* (July-August 2003), pp. 19–21.

65. Al-Rodhan, *The Five Dimensions of Global Security*, p. 49.

66. L. Maizland, 'China's Fight against Climate Change and Environmental Degradation', Council on Foreign Relations, Backgrounder, 19 May 2021.

67. European Environment Agency, 'Growth without Economic Growth', Briefing, 11 Jan 2021.

68. E.R. Peterson, *Addressing Our Global Water Future*, Center for Strategic and International Studies with Sandia National Laboratories (Washington, DC: CSIS, 2005).

69. J.K. Griffiths, 'Waterborne Diseases', in W.C. Cockerham and S.R. Quah (eds), *International Encyclopedia of Public Health*, 2nd edn (Amsterdam: Elsevier, 2016), pp. 388–89.

70. Peterson, *Addressing Our Global Water Future*.

71. S. Glynn, 'Turkey Is Reportedly Depriving Hundreds of Thousands of People of Water', *Open Democracy*, 14 June 2021.

72. S. Waslekar, 'Water Is More than a Strategic Resource: We Need to Acknowledge That', World Economic Forum and Project Syndicate, 26 January 2017.

73. S.D. Donner and S. Webber, 'Obstacles to Climate Change Adaptation Decisions: A Case Study of Sea-Level Rise and Coastal Protection Measures in Kiribati', *Sustainability Science* 9, no. 3 (2014), pp. 331–45.

74. J.J. Chen and V. Mueller, 'Climate Change Is Making Soils Saltier, Forcing Many Farmers to Find New Livelihoods', *The Conversation*, 29 November 2018.

75. A. Dupont, 'The Strategic Implications of Climate Change', *Survival* 50, no. 3 (2008), p. 36.

76. Ibid., p. 39.

77. H. Breitenbauch, K.S. Kristensen and J. Groesmeyer, 'Military and Environmental Challenges in the Arctic', Carnegie Europe, 28 November 2019.

78. R. Gosnell, 'Caution in the High North: Geopolitical and Economic Challenges of the Arctic Maritime Environment', *War on the Rocks*, 25 June 2018.

79. Y. Sun, 'Defining the Chinese Threat in the Arctic', Arctic Institute, Center for Circumpolar Security Studies, 7 April 2020.

80. E. Fischer, 'Disaster Response: The Role of a Humanitarian Military', *Army Technology*, 25 July 2011.

81. C.-A. Hofmann and L. Hudson, 'Military Responses to Natural Disasters: Last Resort or Inevitable Trend', *Humanitarian Exchange* 44 (2009), pp. 29–31.

82. C. Bluth, 'Norms and International Relations: The Anachronistic Nature of Neo-realist Approaches', POLIS Working Paper no. 12, February 2004, https://www.researchgate.net/profile/Christoph-Bluth /publication/239566016_Norms_and_International_Relations_The _anachronistic_nature_of_neo-realist_approaches/links/549c3de00cf2d6 581ab482c9/Norms-and-International-Relations-The-anachronistic -nature-of-neo-realist-approaches.pdf

83. K. Naumann *et al.*, *Towards a Grand Strategy for an Uncertain World: Renewing Transatlantic Partnership* (Lunteren, Netherlands: Noaber Foundation, 2007).

84. L. Maizland, 'China's Repression of Uyghurs in Xinjiang', Council on Foreign Relations, Backgrounder, 1 March 2021.

85. J.-M. Versluis and J. de Lange, 'Rising Crime Rate, Low Prosecution Rates: How Law Enforcement in SA Has All but Collapsed', *City Press/ News 24*, 21 October 2019.

86. K. Anggoro, 'Transnational Security Concerns, Defence Modernization and Security Cooperation in Southeast Asia', *Dialogue + Cooperation* 3 (2003), p. 25.

87. R. Godson, 'Transnational Crime, Corruption, and Security', in Brown, *Grave New World*, p. 262.

88. Statista, 'Countries with the Highest Military Spending Worldwide in 2020 (in Billion US Dollars)', https://www.statista.com/statistics/262742 /countries-with-the-highest-military-spending/ (accessed 4 August 2021).

89. C. Taylor, 'Renewables Could Displace Fossil Fuels to Power the World by 2050, Report Claims', CNBC, 23 April 2021.

90. I. Ozturk, *Energy Dependency and Security: The Role of Efficiency and Renewable Energy Sources*, Working Paper E-37113-PAK-1 (London: International Growth Centre, 2014; B. Terzic, Energy Independence and Security: A Reality Check, Deloitte Center for Energy Solutions (Westlake, TX: Deloitte University Press, 2013).

91. Power Technology, 'Power Plays: The Role of Energy in Modern Geopolitics', 26 April 2018.

92. O. Odgaard and J. Delman, 'China's Energy Security and Its Challenges towards 2035', *Energy Policy* 71 (August 2014), pp. 107–17.

93. Y. Trofimov, 'The European Union Is Punching Below Its Weight in World Affairs', *Wall Street Journal*, 17 December 2019, https://www.wsj .com/articles/the-european-union-is-punching-below-its-weight-in -world-affairs-11576578603; A. Moravcsik, 'Europe Is Still a Superpower', *Foreign Policy*, 13 April 2017.

94. Moravcsik, 'Europe is Still a Superpower'.

95. Ferguson, 'What is Power?'

96. M. Hindley, 'World War I Changed America and Transformed Its Role in International Relations', *Humanities* 38, no. 3 (2017), n.p.; D. Frum, 'The Real Story of How America Became an Economic Superpower', *The Atlantic*, 24 December 2014.

97. N.R.F. Al-Rodhan, 'The Meta-Geopolitics of Geneva 1815–2015', ETH Zürich Center for Security Studies, 26 February 2015.

98. Permanent Mission of Switzerland to the United Nations Office, 'Facts and Figures about International Geneva', https://www.eda.admin.ch /missions/mission-onu-geneve/en/home/geneve-international/faits-et -chiffres.html.

99. A. Dreher and S. Voigt, 'Does Membership in International Organisations Increase Governments' Credibility? Testing the Effect of Delegating Power', CESifo Working Paper Series no. 2285 (2008), pp. 31–32.

100. M. Groff and J. Lorik, 'Strengthening the Rules-Based Global Order: The Case for an International Rule of Law Package', Stimson, 14 September 2020.

101. L. Goczek, E. Witkowska and B. Witkowski, 'How Does Education Quality Affect Economic Growth', *Sustainability* 13, no. 11 (2021), pp. 1–2.

102. S. Polyzos and D. Tsiotas, 'The Contribution of Transport Infrastructures to the Economic and Regional Development', *Theoretical and Empirical Researches in Urban Development* 15, no. 1 (2020), pp. 4–7.

103. S.A. Kocs, 'Explaining the Strategic Behaviour of States: International Law and System Structure', *International Studies Quarterly* 38, no. 4 (1994), pp. 539–40.

104. A.K. Sen, 'A Rising China Has Pacific Islands in Its Sights: US Lawmakers Seek Ways to Deepen Engagement with a Critical Region',

United States Institute for Peace, 23 July 2020; J. Pryke, 'The Risks of China's Ambitions in the South Pacific', Brookings Institution, 20 July 2020.
105. Ferguson, 'What is Power?'.
106. Lauren, Craig and George, *Force and Statecraft*, pp. 246–47.

5. Statecraft and Neurophilosophy

1. J. Bickle, *The Oxford Handbook of Philosophy and Neuroscience* (Oxford: Oxford University Press, 2009), p. 3.
2. L. Zmigrod and M. Tsakiris, 'Computational and Neurocognitive Approaches to the Political Brain: Key Insights and Future Avenues for Political Neuroscience', *Philosophical Transactions of the Royal Society B* 376, no. 1822.
3. See J. Bijsterbosch *et al.*, 'Challenges and Future Directions for Representations of Functional Brain Organization', *Nature Neuroscience* 23, no. 12 (2020), pp. 1484–95.
4. For a general overview, see M. Malecka, 'Knowledge, Behaviour, and Policy: Questioning the Epistemic Presuppositions of Applying Behavioural Science in Public Policymaking', *Synthese*, 5 February 2021.
5. Al-Rodhan, *Emotional Amoral Egoism*, ch. 3.
6. A. Shackman and T. Wager, 'The Emotional Brain: Fundamental Questions and Strategies for Future Research', *Neuroscience Letters*, no. 693 (6 March 2019), pp. 68–74.
7. Al-Rodhan, *Emotional Amoral Egoism*, ch. 3.
8. E.A. Phelps *et al.*, 'Emotion and Decision Making: Multiple Modulatory Neural Circuits', *Annual Review of Neuroscience* 37 (2014), pp. 263–87.
9. N.R.F. Al-Rodhan, 'A Neurophilosophy of Human Nature: Emotional Amoral Egoism and the Five Motivators of Humankind', *Blog of the American Philosophical Association*, 4 April 2019; N.R.F. Al-Rodhan, 'Predisposed Tabula Rasa', *The Oxford University Politics Blog*, 15 May 2015.
10. Al-Rodhan, *Emotional Amoral Egoism*, ch. 3.0.
11. I. Persson and J. Savulescu, 'The Moral Importance of Reflective Empathy', *Neuroethics* 11, no. 2 (2018), pp. 183–93.
12. J. Decety and J.M. Cowell, 'Friends or Foes: Is Empathy Necessary for Moral Behavior?', *Perspectives on Psychological Science* 9, no. 4 (2014), pp. 525–37.
13. Al-Rodhan, *Emotional Amoral Egoism*, ch. 3.1.
14. Ibid.
15. Ibid., ch. 4.0.
16. S. Chaudoin, H.V. Milner, X. Pang, 'International Systems and Domestic Politics: Linking Complex Interactions with Empirical Models in International Relations', *International Organization* 69, no. 2 (2015), pp. 275–309.

17. H. Shinoda, 'The Politics of Legitimacy in International Relations: A Critical Examination of NATO's Intervention in Kosovo', *Alternatives* 25, no. 4 (2000), pp. 532–33.

18. J. Cockayne, *State Fragility, Organised Crime and Peacebuilding: Towards a More Strategic Approach*, NOREF Report, (Oslo: Norwegian Centre for Conflict Resolution, 2011), pp. 1–2.

19. N.R.F. Al-Rodhan, 'Proposal of a Dignity Scale for Sustainable Governance', *The Oxford University Politics Blog*, 29 January 2016.

20. Ibid.

21. Al-Rodhan, *Sustainable History and Human Dignity*, ch. 7.2.

22. Ibid.

23. Ibid.

24. Al-Rodhan, *Emotional Amoral Egoism*, ch. 4.1.

25. N.R.F. Al-Rodhan, 'The "Sustainable History" Thesis: A Guide for Regulating Trans- and Post-Humanism', *E-International Relations*, 24 April 2018, https://www.e-ir.info/2018/04/24/the-sustainable-history -thesis-a-guide-for-regulating-trans-and-post-humanism.

26. A. Wyne, 'The Need to Think More Clearly about "Great-Power Competition"', RAND, 11 February 2019.

27. N.R.F. Al-Rodhan, *Symbiotic Realism: A Theory of International Relations in an Instant and an Interdependent World* (Berlin: LIT, 2007), pp. 9–10.

28. E.A. Heinze and B.J. Jolliff, 'Idealism and Liberalism', in J.T. Ishiyama and M. Breuning (eds), *21st Century Political Science: A Reference Handbook* (London: SAGE Publications, 2011), Pt III, p. 319–26.

29. G. Pinson and C. Morel Journel (eds), *Debating the Neoliberal City* (London: Routledge, 2017), p. 160.

30. Al-Rodhan, *Symbiotic Realism*, pp. 9–10.

31. D. Jacobi and A. Freyberg-Inan (eds), *Human Beings in International Relations* (Cambridge: Cambridge University Press, 2015), p. 14.

32. N.P. Monteiro and K.G. Ruby, 'IR and the False Promise of Philosophical Foundations', *International Theory* 1, no. 1 (2009), p. 16.

33. Ibid., pp. 16–17.

34. Ibid., p. 26.

35. Ibid., p. 27.

36. K.N. Waltz, *Theory of International Politics*, 1st edn (New York: McGraw-Hill, 1979), p. 124.

37. Monteiro and Ruby, 'IR and the False Promise of Philosophical Foundations', pp. 28–29.

38. Ibid., p. 30.

39. Ibid., pp. 16–17.

40. Ibid., p. 24.

41. Jacobi and Freyberg-Inan, *Human Beings in International Relations*, p. 14.

42. Ibid., p. 10.

43. Monteiro and Ruby, 'IR and the False Promise of Philosophical Foundations', pp. 32–34.

44. Ibid., p. 18.
45. Ibid., pp. 42–44.
46. Al-Rodhan, *Symbiotic Realism*, pp. 9–10.
47. C. Elman and M. Jensen (eds), *The Realism Reader* (New York: Routledge, 2014), p. 236.
48. V. Navarro, *Neoliberalism, Globalization, and Inequalities: Consequences for Health and Quality of Life* (London: Routledge, 2020), p. 1.
49. Ibid.
50. Ibid.
51. F.N. Faria, *The Evolutionary Limits of Liberalism: Democratic Problems, Market Solutions and the Ethics of Preference Satisfaction* (Cham: Palgrave Macmillan, 2019), p. 2
52. Navarro, *Neoliberalism, Globalization, and Inequalities*, p. 1.
53. Al-Rodhan, *Symbiotic Realism*, pp. 9–10.
54. Ibid, p. 11.
55. Ibid., p. 15.
56. Ibid., p. 12.
57. Ibid., p. 78.
58. Ibid., pp. 85–87.
59. Ibid., pp. 119, 120–21.
60. N.R.F. Al-Rodhan, 'The Emotional Amoral Egoism of States', *The Oxford University Politics Blog*, 25 June 2015.
61. Ibid.
62. Sources: M.B. Steger and R.K. Roy, *Neoliberalism: A Very Short Introduction* (Oxford: Oxford University Press, 2021); R.H. Jackson, G. Sørensen and J. Møller, *Introduction to International Relations: Theories and Approaches*, 7th edn (Oxford: Oxford University Press, 2019); D. Jacobi and A. Freyberg-Inan (eds), *Human Beings in International Relations* (Cambridge: Cambridge University Press, 2015); M. Griffiths (ed.), *Encyclopedia of International Relations and Global Politics* (New York: Routledge, 2013); M. Zehfuss, *Constructivism in International Relations: The Politics of Reality* (Cambridge: Cambridge University Press, 2002); J. Haynes, P. Hough, S. Malik and L. Pettiford, *World Politics: International Relations and Globalisation in the 21st Century* (London: Sage, 2017).
63. Y. Ariffin, J.-M. Coicaud and V. Popovski (eds), *Emotions in International Politics: Beyond Mainstream International Relations* (Cambridge: Cambridge University Press, 2015), p. 1.
64. See J. Mercer, 'Feeling Like a State: Social Emotion and Identity', *International Theory* 6, no. 3 (2014), pp. 515–35.
65. See A. Lerner, 'What's It Like to Be a State? An Argument for State Consciousness', *International Theory* 13, no. 2 (2021), pp. 260–86.
66. Mercer, 'Feeling Like a State: social emotion and identity', p. 530.

67. Lerner, 'What's It Like to Be a State? An Argument for State Consciousness'.

68. Al-Rodhan, 'The Emotional Amoral Egoism of States'.

69. Ibid.

70. N.R.F. Al-Rodhan, 'A Neurophilosophy of Fear-Induced Pre-Emptive Aggression and Pseudo-Altruism', *Blog of the American Philosophical Association*, 4 August 2020.

71. Al-Rodhan, 'The Emotional Amoral Egoism of States'.

72. Ibid.

73. R. Markwica, *Emotional Choices: How the Logic of Affect Shapes Coercive Diplomacy* (Oxford: Oxford University Press, 2018), p. 47.

74. Ibid., p. 49.

75. Ibid., p. 10.

76. Al-Rodhan, 'The Emotional Amoral Egoism of States'.

77. N.R.F. Al-Rodhan, 'Strategic Culture and Pragmatic National Interest', *Global Policy*, 22 July 2015.

78. Ibid., p. 14.

79. R. Cooper, 'The New Liberal Imperialism', *The Guardian*, 7 April 2002.

80. G. Allison, 'The Impact of Globalization on National and International Security', in J.S. Nye Jr and J.D. Donahue (eds), *Governance in a Globalizing World* (Washington, DC: Brookings Institution Press, 2000), p. 76.

81. D.M. Snow, *National Security for a New Era: Globalization and Geopolitics*, 2nd edn (New York: Pearson Longman, 2007), p. 381.

82. V. Ferraro, 'Globalizing Weakness: Is Global Poverty a Threat to the Interests of States?', *Environmental Change and Security Program Report*, no. 9 (2003), p. 14.

83. United Nations, United Nations Charter, 1945.

84. Al-Rodhan, *The Three Pillars of Sustainable National Security in a Transnational World*, pp. 77–112.

85. Ibid.

86. Al-Rodhan, *The Five Dimensions of Global Security*.

87. Ibid.

88. D.S. Reveron, N.K. Gvosdev and J.A. Cloud (eds), *The Oxford Handbook of US National Security* (Oxford: Oxford University Press, 2018), p. 1.

89. Ibid.

90. Al-Rodhan, *Sustainable History and Human Dignity*, ch. 12.2.

91. Ibid.

92. Ibid.

93. Al-Rodhan, *The Five Dimensions of Global Security*, pp. 11–12.

94. Reveron, Gvosdev and Cloud (eds), *The Oxford Handbook of US National Security*.

95. L. Axworthy, 'Human Security and Global Governance: Putting People First', *Global Governance*, no. 7 (2001), p. 19.

96. S. Tadjbakhsh and A. Chenoy, *Human Security: Concepts and Implications* (New York: Routledge, 2007), p. 3.

97. J. Matlary, 'Much Ado about Little: The EU and Human Security', *International Affairs* 84, no. 1 (2008), pp. 135–36.

98. M. Martin and T. Owen, *Routledge Handbook of Human Security* (New York: Routledge, 2014), p. 2.

99. International Commission on Intervention and State Sovereignty, *The Responsibility to Protect: Research, Bibliography and Background: Supplementary Volume to the Report of the International Commission on Intervention and State Sovereignty* (Ottawa: International Development Research Centre, 2001), p. 11.

100. Matlary, 'Much Ado about Little', pp. 135–37.

101. Study Group on Europe's Security Capabilities, 'A Human Security Doctrine for Europe: The Barcelona Report', presented to the EU High Representative for Common Foreign and Security Policy, Javier Solana, Barcelona, 15 September 2004.

102. Ibid., p. 139.

103. UN Trust Fund for Human Security, 'What Is Human Security?', https://www.un.org/humansecurity/what-is-human-security (accessed 10 May 2021).

104. Al-Rodhan, *The Five Dimensions of Global Security*, pp. 45–46.

105. N.R.F. Al-Rodhan, *Sustainable History and the Dignity of Man* (Münster: LIT, 2009), p. 325.

106. Al-Rodhan, *The Five Dimensions of Global Security*, pp. 46–47.

107. Al-Rodhan, *The Five Dimensions of Global Security*, see especially 'Environmental Security'.

108. M.T. Klare, 'Global Warming Battlefields: How Climate Change Threatens Security', *Current History* 106 (November 2007), p. 355.

109. K. Sudmeier-Rieux *et al.*, *Ecosystems, Livelihoods and Disasters: An Integrated Approach to Disaster Risk Management*, Ecosystem Management Series no. 4 (Gland: IUCN, 2006.

110. World Bank, 'Economics of Adaptation to Climate Change', 6 June 2011.

111. Al-Rodhan, *Sustainable History and Human Dignity*, ch. 12.2.

112. Ibid.

113. K. Levy, S.M. Smith and E.J. Carlton, 'Climate Change Impacts on Waterborne Diseases: Moving toward Designing Interventions', *Current Environmental Health Reports* 5, no. 2 (2018), pp. 272–82.

114. Al-Rodhan, *Sustainable History and Human Dignity*, ch. 12.2.

115. Ibid.

116. Ibid.

117. Ibid.
118. Ibid.
119. Ibid.
120. Al-Rodhan, *The Five Dimensions of Global Security*, p. 73; S. Croucher, *Globalization and Belonging: The Politics of Identity in a Changing World* (Lanham, MD: Rowman & Littlefield, 2018), p. 2.
121. Al-Rodhan, *The Five Dimensions of Global Security*, p. 13.
122. Al-Rodhan, *Emotional Amoral Egoism*, ch. 4.3.3.
123. Ibid.
124. K.M. Flückiger, 'Xenophobia, Media Stereotyping, and Their Role in Global Insecurity', in N.R.F. Al-Rodhan (ed.), *Policy Briefs on the Transcultural Aspects of Security and Stability* (Berlin: LIT, 2006), pp. 21–22.
125. Al-Rodhan, *Emotional Amoral Egoism*, ch. 4.4.3.
126. A.G. Stolberg, *How Nation-States Craft National Security Strategy Documents* (Carlisle, PA: Strategic Studies Institute, US Army War College, 2013), p. 11.
127. J.S. Lantis, 'Strategic Culture: From Clausewitz to Constructivism', *Strategic Insights* 4, no. 10 (October 2005), p. 2.
128. J.S. Lantis, 'Strategic Culture: From Clausewitz to Constructivism', in J.L. Johnson, K.M. Kartchner and J.A. Larsen (eds), *Strategic Culture and Weapons of Mass Destruction: Culturally Based Insights into Comparative National Security Policymaking* (New York: Palgrave Macmillan, 2003), p. 34.
129. Ibid.
130. Al-Rodhan, 'The Emotional Amoral Egoism of States'.
131. Ibid.
132. Al-Rodhan, 'Strategic Culture and Pragmatic National Interest'.
133. J.Y. Chiao *et al.*, 'Theory and Methods in Cultural Neuroscience', *Social Cognitive and Affective Neuroscience* 5, nos 2–3 (2010), p. 356.
134. D. Coch, K.W. Fischer and G. Dawson (eds), *Human Behavior, Learning, and the Developing Brain: Typical Development* (New York: The Guilford Press, 2007), p. 19.
135. Ibid.
136. See Al-Rodhan, *Emotional Amoral Egoism*, ch. 4.5.8.
137. Al-Rodhan, 'Strategic Culture and Pragmatic National Interest'.
138. N.R.F. Al-Rodhan, 'The "Ocean Model of Civilization", Sustainable History Theory, and Global Cultural Understanding', *The Oxford University Politics Blog*, 1 June 2017,.
139. Al-Rodhan, *Symbiotic Realism*, p. 91.
140. Al-Rodhan, *The Three Pillars of Sustainable National Security in a Transnational World*, p. 160.

6. Just Power

1. R.L. Armitage and J.S. Nye Jr, *CSIS Commission on Smart Power* (Washington, DC: CSIS, 2007).
2. J. True, 'Soft Power or Smart Power? Flipping Australia's White Paper', Australian Institute of International Affairs, 27 November 2017.
3. Thucydides, *History of the Peloponnesian War*, p. 151.
4. C. Nederman, 'Niccolò Machiavelli', *The Stanford Encyclopedia of Philosophy* (Summer 2019 edition).
5. T. Hobbes, *Leviathan*, ed. C.B. MacPherson (Aylesbury: Hazell, Watson & Viney Ltd., 1972 [1651]), p. 161.
6. H. Bull, 'Hobbes and the International Anarchy', *Social Research* 48, no. 4 (Winter 1981), pp. 717–719.
7. J.S. Nye Jr, *Power in the Global Information Age: From Realism to Globalization* (New York: Routledge, 2004), p. 128.
8. Kissinger, *Diplomacy*, p. 79.
9. P. Ramsey, 'Force and Political Responsibility', in E.W. Lefever (ed.), *Ethics and World Politics: Four Perspectives* (Baltimore: Johns Hopkins University Press, 1972), p. 72.
10. J. G. Ruggie, 'What Makes the World Hang Together? Neo-utilitarianism and the Social Constructivist Challenge', *International Organization* 52, no. 4 (Autumn 1998), p. 856.
11. Ibid., p. 869.
12. Ibid., pp. 856–57.
13. Ibid., pp. 855–56.
14. Ibid., p. 882.
15. D. Gavel, 'Joseph Nye on Smart Power', Harvard Kennedy School, 3 July 2008.
16. Armitage and Nye, 'CSIS Commission on Smart Power'.
17. Gavel, 'Joseph Nye on Smart Power'.
18. Armitage and Nye, 'Stop Getting Mad, America'.
19. Armitage and Nye, 'CSIS Commission on Smart Power', p. 1.
20. A. Choudhary, 'Global Justice', *Global Encyclopedia of Public Administration, Public Policy, and Governance*, 6 July 2018; see also G. Brock, 'Global Justice', *The Stanford Encyclopedia of Philosophy* (Winter 2021 edition).
21. Choudhary, 'Global Justice'; Brock, 'Global Justice'.
22. Nye, *Power in the Global Information Age*, p. 124.
23. Al-Rodhan, *Emotional Amoral Egoism*, pp. 189–90.
24. Al-Rodhan, *The Five Dimensions of Global Security*, p. 94.
25. Ibid., p. 95.
26. Ibid.
27. Geneva Academy RULAC online portal, 'Use of Force', last updated 6 February 2017, https://www.rulac.org/legal-framework/use-of-force.
28. Al-Rodhan, *The Five Dimensions of Global Security*, p. 96.

29. Pew Research Center, 'Religion and American Foreign Policy: Prophetic, Perilous, Inevitable', 5 February 2003.

30. N.R.F. Al-Rodhan and L. Watanabe (eds), *A Proposal for Inclusive Peace and Security* (Geneva: Slatkine, 2007), pp. 86–90.

31. J. Yoo, 'Marcus Tullius Cicero, De Officiis', Hoover Institution, 6 February 2019.

32. As paraphrased in R. Hoag, 'The Recourse to War as Punishment: A Historical Theme in Just War Theory', *Studies in the History of Ethics*, no. 2 (2006), p. 4.

33. BBC, Religions, 'Judaism and War'," www.bbc.co.uk/religion (accessed on 13 November 2008).

34. Ibid.

35. J. O'Donnell, 'St. Augustine', *Encyclopaedia Britannica*, 9 November 2021.

36. BBC, Ethics, 'Holy Wars' https://www.bbc.co.uk/ethics/war/religious /holywar.shtml (accessed 30 June 2021).

37. Ibid.

38. BBC, Religions, 'Islam and War', www.bbc.co.uk/religion (accessed on 13 November 2008).

39. Ibid.

40. BBC, Religions, 'Jihad'," www.bbc.co.uk/religion (accessed on 13 November 2008).

41. Ibid.

42. Ibid.

43. BBC, Religions, 'Hinduism and War', www.bbc.co.uk/religion (accessed on 13 November 2008).

44. B. Crisher, 'Altering *Jus ad Bellum*: Just War Theory in the 21st Century and the 2002 National Security Strategy of the United States', *Critique: A Worldwide Journal of Politics* (Spring 2005), p. 3.

45. H. Grotius, *De iure praedae commentaries*, ch. 3, cited in J. Miller, 'Hugo Grotius', *The Stanford Encyclopedia of Philosophy* (Spring 2021 edition).

46. Crisher, 'Altering *Jus ad Bellum*', p. 4.

47. Avalon Project, 'The Covenant of the League of Nations (including amendments adopted to December 1924'.

48. Avalon Project, 'Charter of the United Nations, 26 June 1945'.

49. M. Walzer, *Just and Unjust Wars: A Moral Argument with Historical Illustrations*, 3rd edn (New York: Basic Books, 2000).

50. Ibid., p. 54.

51. Ibid., pp. 80–85.

52. Crisher, 'Altering *Jus ad Bellum*', p. 5.

53. Global Centre for the Responsibility to Protect, 'What Is R2P?'.

54. G.F. Kennan, *American Diplomacy, 1900–1950* (Chicago: University of Chicago Press, 1951), pp. 101–2.

55. C.A.J. Coady, *The Ethics of Armed Humanitarian Intervention*, Peaceworks No. 45 (Washington, DC: United States Institute of Peace, 2002), pp. 15–16.

56. Ibid., p. 16.
57. Walzer, *Just and Unjust Wars*, p. 106.
58. F. Tesón, *Humanitarian Intervention: An Inquiry into Law and Morality* (New York: Brill, 2005), p. 15.
59. Ibid.
60. S. Hoffmann, *World Disorders: Troubled Peace in the Post-Cold War Era* (Lanham, MD: Rowman & Littlefield, 1998), pp. 161–64.
61. Coady, 'The Ethics of Armed Humanitarian Intervention', p. 21.
62. M. Walzer, 'Just and Unjust Occupations', *Dissent*, Winter 2004.
63. B. Orend, 'Justice after War', *Ethics & International Affairs* 16, no. 1 (2002), pp. 43–56.
64. Ibid., p. 55.
65. Ibid.
66. J. Mandle, *Global Justice* (Cambridge: Polity Press, 2006), p. 106.
67. W. Byanyima, 'The Shocking Truth about Inequality Today', World Economic Forum, 21 January 2019.
68. N. Yonzan *et al.*, 'Is COVID-19 Increasing Global Inequality?', *Data Blog* (World Bank), 7 October 2021.
69. UN Development Programme, *Human Development Report 1998* (New York: Oxford University Press, 1998), p. 30.
70. C. Jones, *Global Justice: Defending Cosmopolitanism* (Oxford: Oxford University Press, 2001), p. 2.
71. J.H. Carens, 'Aliens and Citizens: The Case for Open Borders', in W. Kymlicka (ed.), *The Rights of Minority Cultures* (Oxford: Oxford University Press, 1995), p. 332.
72. T. Nagel, 'The Problem of Global Justice', *Philosophy and Public Affairs* 33, no. 2 (2005), p. 118.
73. Ibid.
74. M. Walzer, *Thick and Thin: Moral Argument at Home and Abroad* (Notre Dame, IN: University of Notre Dame Press, 1994), pp. 21–40.
75. See J. Rawls, *A Theory of Justice*, rev. edn (Oxford: Oxford University Press, 1999).
76. Mandle, *Global Justice*, p. 102.
77. Ibid., p. 132.
78. Oxfam International, *Rigged Rules and Double Standards: Trade, Globalisation, and the Fight against Poverty* (Oxford: Oxfam, 2002), p. 5.
79. Nagel, 'The Problem of Global Justice', p. 143.
80. See UN Office for Disarmament Affairs, 'Arms Trade'.
81. D. Drezner, 'How Smart are Smart Sanctions?', *International Studies Review*, no. 5 (2003), pp. 107–10,.
82. Al-Rodhan, *The Five Dimensions of Global Security*.
83. Ibid., p. 107.
84. Ibid., p. 108.

85. Ibid., p. 109.

86. Ibid., pp. 110–11.

87. Ibid., p. 112.

88. Ibid., pp. 113–14.

89. Al-Rodhan, *Symbiotic Realism*, p. 11.

90. D. Held, 'Violence, Law and Justice in a Global Age', *Constellations* 9, no. 1 (2002), pp. 74–88.

91. Ibid.

7. The Concept of Reconciliation Statecraft

1. Al-Rodhan, *Symbiotic Realism*, p. 117.

2. A. Kamguian, 'Universal Rights vs Group Rights', International Humanist and Ethical Union, 6 July 2005, via the Internet Archive Wayback Machine, https://web.archive.org/web/20070623192107/http://www.iheu.org/node/1691.

3. UN OHCHR, Convention on the Elimination of All Forms of Discrimination against Women, ratified 18 December 1979, entered into force 3 September 1981, 1249 UNTS 13.

4. UN OHCHR, Convention on the Rights of the Child, ratified 20 November 1989, entered into force 2 September 1990, 1577 UNTS 3.

5. UN OHCHR, Declaration on the Rights of Disabled Persons, A/RES/3447 (XXX), 9 December 1975.

6. R. Cohen-Almagor, 'Between Individual Rights and Group Rights', *Academicus International Scientific Journal* 18 (February 2018), pp. 10–14.

7. M.J. Kerski, 'Threats and Opportunities for Advancing the Major Global Interests of the United States', National Defense University, National War College, Washington, DC, 2000, pp. 2–3.

8. Snow, *National Security for a New Era*, p. 381.

9. A. Wolfers, *Discord and Collaboration: Essays on International Politics* (Baltimore: Johns Hopkins University Press, 1962), p. 150.

10. Allison, 'The Impact of Globalization on National and International Security', p. 76.

11. R. Minshull, *Regional Geography: Theory and Practice* (New York: Routledge, 2017), p. 13.

12. J.D. Parker, 'The Spillover Effects of the Syrian Civil War', in H. Moodrick-Even Khen, N.T. Boms and S. Ashraph (eds), *The Syrian War: Between Justice and Political Reality* (Cambridge: Cambridge University Press, 2020), pp. 198–216.

13. F. Georgie, 'The Role of Racism in the European "Migration Crisis": A Historical Materialist Perspective', in V. Satgar (ed.), *Racism after Apartheid: Challenges for Marxism and Anti-Racism* (Johannesburg: Wits University Press, 2019), pp. 96–97.

14. B. Buzan, *People, States and Fear: The National Security Problem in International Relations* (Brighton: Wheatsheaf, 1983), p. 106.
15. B. Buzan and O. Wæver, *Regions and Powers: The Structure of International Security* (Cambridge: Cambridge University Press, 2003), p. 45.
16. UNEP, *Global Environment Outlook - GEO-6: Summary for Policymakers* (Cambridge: Cambridge University Press, 2019), p. 21.
17. A. Carpenter and A.G. Kostianoy (eds), *Oil Pollution in the Mediterranean Sea: Part I: The International Context* (Cham: Springer Nature Switzerland, 2019), p. 135.
18. European Council, *European Security Strategy: A Secure Europe in a Better World* (Brussels: European Communities, 2009)p. 7, https://www.consilium.europa.eu/media/30823/qc7809568enc.pdf.
19. Ibid., p. 8.
20. J. Beiser-McGrath, 'Targeting the Motivated? Ethnicity and Pre-emptive Use of Government Repression', *Swiss Political Science Review* 25, Issue 3 (2019), pp. 203–4.
21. R. Brody, 'The Future of French Cinema', *New Yorker*, 2 January 2013.
22. UN OHCHR, International Covenant on Economic, Social and Cultural Rights, adopted 16 December 1966, came into force 23 March 1976, 999 UNTS 171.
23. Al-Rodhan, *Symbiotic Realism*.
24. Al-Rodhan, 'The "Ocean Model of Civilization"'.
25. D. Ayton-Shenker, 'The Challenge of Human Rights and Cultural Diversity', United Nations Background Note, March 1995.
26. UN Department of Economic and Social Affairs, 'The 17 Goals', https://sdgs.un.org/goals (accessed 30 June 2021).
27. United Nations, United Nations Treaty Collection, https://treaties.un.org (accessed 30 June 2021).
28. UN Department of Economic and Social Affairs, 'The 17 Goals'.
29. M.K. Mishra, 'Sustainable Development: Linking Economy and Environment in the Era of Globalization', Working Paper, ZBW – Leibniz Information Centre for Economics, Kiel, Hamburg (2020), pp. 3–5, 7.
30. G.W. Bush, 'The National Security Strategy of the United States', White House, September 2002.
31. Kerski, 'Threats and Opportunities for Advancing the Major Global Interests of the United States', p. 9.
32. I.L. Claude Jr, 'Swords into Ploughshares: The Problems and Progress of International Organization', in J.N. Moore (ed.), *National Security Law* (Durham, NC: Carolina Academic Press, 1990), p. 45.
33. Ibid.
34. See M. Cipollina and L. Salvatici, 'On the Effects of EU Trade Policy: Agricultural Tariffs Still Matter', *European Review of Agricultural Economics* 47, no. 4 (2020), pp. 1369–73.

35. WTO, 'Regionalism: Friends or Rivals?', Understanding the WTO: Cross-Cutting and New Issues, https://www.wto.org/english/thewto_e /whatis_e/tif_e/bey1_e.htm (accessed 13 January 2022).

36. Ibid.

37. F. Harvey, 'Major Climate Changes Inevitable and Irreversible – IPCC's Starkest Warning Yet,' *The Guardian*, 9 August 2021.

38. K. Klubnikin and D. Causey, 'Environmental Security: Metaphor for the Millennium', *Seton Hall Journal of Diplomacy and International Relations* 3, no. 2 (2002), p. 117.

39. M. Eghdami and A.P. Barros, 'Deforestation Impacts on Orographic Precipitation in the Tropical Andes', *Front. Environ. Sci.*, 20 November 2020.

40. R.T. Watson *et al.*, 'Land Use, Land-Use Change and Forestry', Intergovernmental Panel on Climate Change Special Report (Cambridge: Cambridge University Press, 2000).

41. D. Carrington, 'Plummeting Insect Numbers "Threaten Collapse of Nature"', *The Guardian*, 10 February 2019.

42. K. Pavid, 'Aspirin, Morphine and Chemotherapy: The Essential Medicines Powered by Plants', Natural History Museum, 19 February 2021, https://www.nhm.ac.uk/discover/essential-medicines -powered-by-plants.html.

43. Al-Rodhan, *Symbiotic Realism*, p. 12.

44. A.M. Ghilarov, 'Ecosystem Functioning and Intrinsic Value of Biodiversity', *Oikos* 90(2) (2000), pp. 408–12.

45. I.D. Cresswell, H. Murphy H, 'Biodiversity: Importance of biodiversity', in *Australia State of the Environment 2016* (Canberra: Australian Government Department of the Environment and Energy, 2016), https:// soe.environment.gov.au/theme/biodiversity/topic/2016/importance -biodiversity.

46. H. Golden, 'Makah Tribe in US Hopes for Rights to Resume Sacred Tradition of Gray Whale Hunting', *The Guardian*, 12 November 2021.

47. Canadian Seal Hunt, 'WWF Defends Pro Sealing Stance', 22 April 2006, https://www.canadiansealhunt.com/wwf.html#:~:text=WWF's%20 approach%20is%20designed%20to,is%20of%20the%20utmost%20 importance.

48. WWF, 'Seals', https://www.worldwildlife.org/species/seals (accessed 12 January 2021).

49. Canadian Seal Hunt, 'WWF Defends Pro Sealing Stance'.

50. Ibid.

51. Al-Rodhan, *Emotional Amoral Egoism*, ch. 5.

52. Ibid., ch. 3.

53. National Archives, 'Extract from the Official Account of the Bomber Command by Arthur Harris, 1945', http://www.nationalarchives.gov.uk /education/heroesvillains/g1/cs3/g1cs3s1.htm (accessed 12 January 2021).

54. History.com Editors, 'Bombing of Dresden', 7 June 2019, https://www
    .history.com/topics/world-war-ii/battle-of-dresden.
55. J.-M. Coicaud and N.J. Wheeler, 'Introduction: The Changing Ethics of
    Power beyond Borders', in J.-M. Coicaud and N.J. Wheeler (eds),
    *National Interest and International Solidarity: Particular and Universal
    Ethics in International Life* (New York: United Nations University Press,
    2008), p. 3.
56. Ibid., p. 5.
57. Ibid.
58. UN News, 'WHO Chief Warns against COVID-19 "Vaccine
    Nationalism", Urges Support for Fair Access', 18 August 2020.
59. Coicaud and Wheeler, 'Introduction', p. 6.
60. A. Budd, 'Gramsci's Marxism and International Relations', *International
    Socialism* 2, no. 114 (10 April 2007).
61. Coicaud and Wheeler, 'Introduction', p. 2.
62. Ibid.
63. Ibid., p. 7.
64. Ibid., p. 8.
65. J.W. Meiser, 'Introducing Liberalism in International Relations Theory',
    E-International Relations, 18 February 2018.
66. Coicaud and Wheeler, 'Introduction', p. 9.
67. I. Kant, 'On the Agreement between Politics and Morality According to
    the Transcendental Concept of Public Rights', in I. Kant, *Kant: Political
    Writings*, 2nd edn, ed. H.S. Reiss (Cambridge: Cambridge University
    Press, 1991), pp. 125–30.
68. Coicaud and Wheeler, 'Introduction', p. 9.
69. Al-Rodhan, *Symbiotic Realism*, p. 14.
70. Al-Rodhan, *The Five Dimensions of Global Security*.
71. Al-Rodhan, *The Three Pillars of Sustainable National Security in a
    Transnational World*.
72. Ibid., p. 160.
73. Al-Rodhan and Watanabe (eds), *A Proposal for Inclusive Peace and
    Security*.
74. Ibid., p. 125.
75. Ibid., p. 126.
76. Coicaud and Wheeler, 'Introduction', p. 11.
77. K. Sikkink, 'Transnational Politics, International Relations Theory, and
    Human Rights', *Political Science and Politics* 31, no. 3 (1998), p. 519.

8. Case Studies: Geopolitical Realities and Dilemmas of Twenty-Seven Selected States

1. Since the end of the White Australia policy in 1973, Australia has pursued an official policy of multiculturalism and has welcomed a large and continuing flow of immigrants from across the world, with the largest number in the twenty-first century coming from Asia. Net migration, which normally increases by about 60,000 every three months, has led to a steady increase in the Australian population. This trend came to a halt in 2020 when Australia shut its international borders to non-Australians and non-residents to avoid the spread of COVID-19 with what has, so far, been a successful strategy. With a decrease of 34,804 people, the Australian population has shrunk for the first time since the First World War. See G. Jericho, 'Closed Borders and Fear of the Future: Australia's Population Shrank during the Pandemic', *The Guardian*, 20 March 2021; W. Haseltine, 'What Can We Learn from Australia's Covid-19 Response?', *Forbes*, 24 March 2021; J. Fang and E. Handley, 'When Will Skilled Migrants Return to Australia? Not for Another Year, Government Says', ABC News, 12 May 2021.

2. Despite its economic reliance on migrants, Australia faces serious challenges in terms of discrimination, particularly towards its indigenous population. At the 2016 census, 649,171 people (2.8 per cent of the total population) identified as being indigenous (Aboriginal Australians and Torres Strait Islanders). Indigenous Australians are significantly over-represented in the criminal justice system, with Aboriginal and Torres Strait Islander people comprising 28 per cent of Australia's adult prison population, but just three per cent of the national population. Australian Human Rights Commission, 'Race Discrimination', https://humanrights.gov.au/our-work/race-discrimination; P. Karp, 'Australia Urged to Adopt Plan to Fight "Resurgence of Racism"', *The Guardian*, 16 March 2021; Australian Bureau of Statistics, '2016 Census Community Profile', 23 October 2017; Australian Bureau of Statistics, 'Census of Population and Housing: Reflecting Australia, Stories from the Census, 2016', 28 June 2017,; Human Rights Watch, 'World Report 2020: Australia – Events of 2019', https://www.hrw.org/world-report/2020/country-chapters/australia #2c9b66 (Accessed 30 June 2020).

3. Excellent public-private hybrid health-care system. Australian Government Department of Health, 'The Australian Health System', last updated 7 August 2019; D. Scott, 'Two Sisters. Two Different Journeys through Australia's Health Care System', *Vox*, 15 January 2020.

4. Australia has adopted hostile policies towards asylum seekers. Its offshore asylum-seeker detention facilities are especially criticised as violating human rights law and international conventions on the

treatment of refugees and asylum seekers. See E. Pearson, 'Seven Years of Suffering for Australia's Asylum Seekers, Refugees', Human Rights Watch, 16 July 2020; Australian Human Rights Commission, 'Asylum Seekers and Refugees', https://humanrights.gov.au/our-work/rights-and -freedoms/publications/asylum-seekers-and-refugees#detention (accessed 30 June 2021); R. Manne, 'Treatment of Asylum Seekers in Australia', La Trobe University, 5 March 2018.

5. It is involved in multiple free trade agreements, including the landmark Regional Comprehensive Economic Partnership (RCEP), signed in 2020, which builds on Australia's existing free trade compacts in the Asia-Pacific region. Australian participation will improve export access and supply chain opportunities for Australian businesses in fourteen Indo-Pacific countries. Regional Comprehensive Economic Partnership, 'RCEP: A New Trade Agreement that Will Shape Global Economics and Politics', https://rcepsec.org/2020/11/26/rcep-a-new-trade-agreement -that-will-shape-global-economics-and-politics (accessed 25 June 2021); Australian Government, Australian Trade and Investment Commission, 'Australia Signs World's Largest Free Trade Agreement', 26 November 2020.

6. Australia is so rich in natural resources, it is heavily reliant on mining and fossil fuels, with its primary energy consumption being dominated by coal (around 40 per cent), oil (34 per cent) and gas (22 per cent). Coal accounts for about 75 per cent of Australia's electricity generation, followed by gas (16 per cent), hydro (five per cent) and wind (around two per cent). This reliance on fossil fuels for energy is closely linked to Australia's slowness to take steps to combat the climate crisis and with its unwillingness to make specific promises at the international level regarding the reduction of greenhouse gas emissions, particularly when compared with other developed countries and their commitment to the Paris Agreement. Climate Action Tracker, 'Australia', updated 15 September 2021, https:// climateactiontracker.org/countries/australia; Australian Government, Geoscience Australia, 'Energy – Overview', https://www.ga.gov.au /scientific-topics/energy/basics (accessed 8 August 2021).

7. Eastern Australia is one of the most fire-prone regions of the world, and its predominant eucalyptus forests have evolved to thrive on the phenomenon of bushfire. Fire can, nonetheless, cause significant property damage and loss of both human and animal life. Bushfires have killed approximately 800 people in Australia since 1851 and billions of animals. The 2019–20 bushfires alone are estimated to have led to the deaths of at least 33 people and over three billion animals. T. Burgess *et al.*, *Black Summer: Australian Newspaper Reporting on the Nation's Worst Bushfire Season* (Melbourne: Monash University Climate Change Communication Research Hub, 2020; K. Tolhurst, 'It's 12 Months since the Last Bushfire Season Began, but Don't Expect the Same This Year', *The Conversation*, 10 June 2020; A. Spring and C. Earl,

'Australia's Biodiversity at Breaking Point – a Picture Essay', *The Guardian*, 15 May 2019; Convention on Biological Diversity, 'Australia – Main Details', https://www.cbd.int/countries/profile/?country=au (accessed 30 June 2021).

8. Science and Technology Australia, 'Australia Can't Afford to Lose R&D Investment in Recovery', 27 March 2020, https://scienceand technologyaustralia.org.au/australia-cant-afford-to-lose-rd-investment -in-recovery; Committee for Sydney, 'Australia Lags the Developed World on Research and Development: It's Time to Catch Up', 27 August 2020.

9. C. Lane, 'Top Universities in Australia 2021', QS Top Universities, 26 May 2021.

10. K. Ziesing, '2021 Defence Budget at a Glance', *Australian Defence Magazine*, 11 May 2021.

11. J. Saballa, 'Australian Military to Establish New $7 Billion Space Division', *The Defence Post*, 20 May 2021.

12. Over the past decade, China has more aggressively pushed its maritime claims in the South China Sea – an approach that goes against the maritime and sovereign rights of the five Southeast Asian littoral states. China's aggressive approach has become a greater concern in Australia's relations with China, the United States, Southeast Asian littoral states, and ASEAN, since China began its artificial island-building campaign in the Spratlys in 2013. M. Cook, *Australia's South China Sea Challenges*, Lowy Institute Policy Brief (Sydney: Lowy Institute for International Policy, 2021); G. Crossley and K. Needham, 'China Suspends Economic Dialogue with Australia as Relations Curdle', Reuters, 5 May 2021; Al Jazeera, 'China-Australia Tensions Explained in 500 Words', 1 December 2020.

13. B. Scott, 'Five Eyes: Blurring the Lines between Intelligence and Policy', *The Interpreter* (Lowy Institute), 27 July 2020.

14. Brazil has one of the highest levels of income inequality in the world. Strong socio-cultural prejudice hampers socio-economic mobility. The average income of Afro-Brazilians, who make up 55 per cent of the population, is less than half the average income of the white population. Poverty in Brazil remains widespread. A third of the population in São Paulo and Rio de Janeiro live in slums. There is also great discrimination towards black and indigenous Brazilians. Brazil Institute and P. Martins, 'Despite Gains, Black Brazilians Remain Underrepresented in Politics', Wilson Center, 24 February 2021; Brazil Institute, 'Pandemic to Worsen Brazil's Troubling School Dropout Rates', Wilson Center, 30 October 2020; Oxfam International, 'Brazil: Extreme Inequality in Numbers', (accessed 20 July 2021); A. Salata, 'Race, Class and Income Inequality in Brazil: A Social Trajectory Analysis', *SciELO Brasil* 63, no. 3 (2020), p. 3; CEJIL, 'Brazil: Respect for the Rights of Indigenous Peoples Is Fundamental to Environmental

Conservation', 11 February 2020; E. Telles, 'Racial Discrimination and Miscegenation: The Experience in Brazil', UN Chronicle, https://www .un.org/en/chronicle/article/racial-discrimination-and-miscegenation -experience-brazil (Accessed 30 June 2021); R. Tsavvko Garcia, 'Diversity in Brazil Is Still Just an Illusion', Al Jazeera, 22 October 2020.

15. The 1988 constitution considers access to medicine a human right, and the vast majority of Brazilians in need of public health care receive it. Brazil Institute, 'Healthcare Inequality and the COVID-19 Pandemic in Brazil', Wilson Center, 4 June 2020; R.H.M. Pereira *et al.*, 'Geographic Access to COVID-19 Healthcare in Brazil Using a Balanced Float Catchment Area Approach', *Social Science and Medicine* 273 (March 2021), pp. 1–12.

16. Despite a persistent spread of malaria and dengue, as well as recurring waves of the Zika virus following the major outbreak in 2015–16, Brazil has been quite successful in terms of containing the spread of HIV/ AIDS. In 2018, there were around 900,000 people living with HIV in Brazil, an increase of 21 per cent compared to 2010, with 66 per cent having access to treatment. Key populations are disproportionately affected by HIV in Brazil. Transgender people are estimated to have an HIV prevalence rate of 30 per cent, gay men and other men who have sex with men, 18.3 per cent, people who inject drugs, 5.9 per cent and prisoners, 4.5 per cent. E.M. de Carvalho *et al.*, '*Aedes aegypti*: The Main Enemy of Public Health in Brazil: Challenges and Perspective for Public Health', IntechOpen, 27 November 2019; X. Casas, 'New Zika Cases in Brazil Overshadowed by Covid-19', Human Rights Watch, 28 May 2020; UNAIDS, 'Brazil', https://www.unaids.org/en/20191011_country_focus _Brazil (accessed 30 June 2021).

17. Despite the fact that over the past couple of decades significant progress has been made towards strengthening the rule of law, Brazil is nonetheless regarded as one of the most corrupt countries in the world and has been plagued by multiple corruption scandals, the most recent of which is 'Operation Car Wash'. This concerns the investigation, authorised by the Brazilian Supreme Court, of 48 current and former legislators, including former presidents Luiz Inácio Lula da Silva and Dilma Rousseff, in March 2016. G. Lorenzon, 'Corruption and the Rule of Law: How Brazil Strengthened Its Legal System', CATO Institute, Policy Analysis no. 827, 20 November 2017; D. Mello, 'Brazil Still Seen among Most Corrupt Countries', Agência Brasil, 24 January 2021.

18. Brazil exports a variety of commodities, ranging from soya to iron ore, that are in high demand on the world market, especially among the rising economies in Asia, but is not too heavily reliant on a single export commodity or a single purchaser. Commodity.com, 'Brazil's Economy: Foreign Trade Figures Reveal Why They're a Major Global Player', 7 April 2021, https://commodity.com/data/brazil.

19. Not only is Brazil one of the only countries in the world to be in control of the full nuclear cycle, but it is also the world's ninth-largest economy, with a GDP of US$1.84 trillion in 2019, down from US$2.6 trillion in 2011. Although it entered a recession in 2014, which was worsened by the increasingly burdensome public debt (98.94 per cent of GDP in 2020), it has a mixed economy and abundant natural resources. World Bank, 'GDP: Brazil', https://data.worldbank.org/indicator/NY.GDP. MKTP.CD?locations=BR (accessed 30 June 2021); Statista, 'Brazil: National Debt from 2016 to 2026 in Relation to Gross Domestic Product', 19 October 2021, https://www.statista.com/statistics/271041 /national-debt-of-brazil-in-relation-to-gross-domestic-product-gdp; Brazil Institute, 'Worst. GDP. Ever. What Does the Future Hold for Brazil?', Wilson Center, 16 September 2020.

20. In the 2000s significant deposits of oil were discovered in Brazil's deep coastal waters, in addition to large reserves already known, making Brazil is the world's eighth-largest oil producer. Until 1997, the government-owned Petróleo Brasileiro S.A. (Petrobras) had a monopoly on oil, but since then more than fifty oil companies have engaged in oil exploration. Foundation for Economic Education, 'Brazil's Disastrous Attempt to Re-nationalize Oil Production', 19 October 2016.

21. Despite the fact that Brazil has recently pledged to reduce its greenhouse gas emissions, it is one of the largest emitters in the world and current president Jair Bolsonaro has adopted agricultural policies which go against global efforts to tackle the climate crisis, including punishing environmental and human rights defenders and refusing to join the Latin American Escazú Climate Agreement. J. Timperley, 'The Carbon Brief Profile: Brazil', 7 March 2018; A. Prusa and B. Vasconcelos Cimatti, 'Too Hot: The Threat to Amazon Biodiversity', Argentina Project, Wilson Center, 21 May 2021; Brazil Institute, 'Brazil among Notable Absences in Latin America's Escazú Climate Agreement', Wilson Center, 24 May 2021; R.A. Butler, 'Amazon Destruction', Mongabay, 4 December 2020.

22. In the past four decades, one fifth of the Amazon rainforest, which is not only the largest carbon sink in the world, but also home to ten per cent of global biodiversity, has been cut down. Land clearances to win land for cattle farms and to plant soya beans are the most common causes of deforestation, along with illegal logging and mining. S. Margulis, *Causes of Deforestation of the Brazilian Amazon*, World Bank Working Paper no. 22 (Washington, DC: World Bank, 2004), p. 29.

23. In 2008, Brazil began to build two new hydroelectric dams on the Madeira River that were supposed to generate up to eight per cent of the country's electricity. As predicted by those that opposed their construction, the rising water levels caused by the dams have in turn resulted in the displacement of many local residents, who have been seriously uprooted from their lifestyles, livelihoods and cultures. The dams have also had a

substantial negative impact on local wildlife, by decreasing fish stocks, among other deleterious outcomes. S. Cunningham, 'Santo Antônio Mega-Dam on Brazil's Madeira River Disrupts Local Lives', Mongabay, 3 December 2018; R.M. Almeida *et al.*, 'Hydropeaking Operations of Two Run-of-River Mega-Dams Alter Downstream Hydrology of the Largest Amazon Tributary', *Frontiers in Environmental Science* 8, no. 120 (22 July 2020), pp. 1–11; R.E. Santos *et al.*, 'Damming Amazon Rivers: Environmental Impacts of Hydroelectric Dams on Brazil's Madeira River According to Local Fishers' Perception', *Ambio* (A Journal of the Human Environment) 49, no. 10 (2020), pp. 1612–28.

24. The education system perpetuates social stratification in Brazil. Although basic education is universal, it is of poor quality. Almost seven per cent of Brazilians are illiterate and nearly 30 per cent are considered functionally illiterate. Only 70 per cent of Brazilians between fifteen and nineteen are in school, and only sixteen per cent complete university. Although university tuition is free, only students who are wealthy enough to afford private education are usually able to pass the entrance exams; hence, government investment in higher education serves mostly the rich, thus perpetuating income inequality. Few Afro-Brazilians attend university, as they are often from poor backgrounds and thus unable to get the necessary high-quality secondary education to prepare themselves for the university entry exams. However, thanks to the growth of the formal sector, an export boom, lower inflation and increased government handouts to the poor, the wealth gap has started to narrow, with poverty decreasing. Over the past decade, progress has also been made towards improving the quality of Brazilian universities and to making them more accessible. Macrotrends, 'Brazil Literacy Rate 1980–2021' (accessed 30 June 2021),; Statista, 'Percentage of Population Deemed Functionally Literate in Brazil from 2007 to 2018' (accessed 30 June 2021); Brazil Institute, 'Pandemic to Worsen Brazil's Troubling School Dropout Rates'; WENR, 'Education in Brazil', 14 November 2019.

25. Despite the fact that Brazil spends less than one per cent of GDP on R&D, it is nonetheless at the forefront of the region in terms of investment in R&D by the private sector, which has spurred significant growth in medium-sized and high-tech firms. C.W. Thurston, 'Brazil Emerges as Regional R&D Center', *Coatings World*, 13 March 2020; A. Tedeneke, 'Brazil's Small and Medium-Sized Entreprises Join Fourth Industrial Revolution', 7 November 2019; OECD, *SME and Entrepreneurship Policy in Brazil 2020*, OECD Studies on SMEs and Entrepreneurship (Paris: OECD, 2020).

26. Brazil's Embraer is the third-largest aeroplane manufacturer in the world and leads the sector in Latin America. It is also the main producer of sugar cane-based ethanol. A side effect of this mass production of

ethanol, however, is that the production of the necessary sugar cane is one of the driving causes of deforestation in Brazil. D.C. Zacharias, 'Brazilian Offshore Oil Exploration Areas: An Overview of Hydrocarbon Pollution', *Revista Ambiente & Agua* 15, no. 5 (2020), pp. 1–20; M.O. de Souza Dias *et al.*, 'Sugarcane Processing for Ethanol and Sugar in Brazil', *Environmental Development* 15 (2015), pp. 35–51; Aerospace Meetings Brazil, 'The Aerospace Industry in Brazil', http://brazil.bciaerospace.com/index.php/en/am-brazil/aerospace-industry-in-brazil (accessed 30 June 2021).

27. Statista, 'Crimes and Violence in Brazil: Statistics and Facts', 14 September 2021, https://www.statista.com/topics/7017/crime-and-violence-in-brazil; US Department of State, Overseas Security Advisory Council, 'Brazil 2020 Crime and Safety Report: Rio de Janeiro', 13 May 2020.

28. Bolsonaro has expressed support for the potential development of nuclear submarines, in stark contrast to Brazil's sponsorship of the 2017 Treaty on the Prohibition of Nuclear Weapons. As a signatory to the Nuclear Non-Proliferation Treaty, Brazil can enrich uranium only for civilian purposes, such as for the production of nuclear power.
L. Bandarra, 'Brazilian Nuclear Policy under Bolsonaro: No Nuclear Weapons but a Nuclear Submarine', *Bulletin of the Atomic Scientists*, 12 April 2019; World Nuclear Association, 'Nuclear Power in Brazil', updated August 2021.

29. C. Meacham, 'Why Does US-Brazil Defense Cooperation Matter?', CSIS, 1 December 2015.

30. China is the most populous country in the world. World Bank, 'World Development Indicators: Population Dynamics', http://wdi.worldbank.org/table/2.1 (accessed 30 June 2021).

31. In 1979, the Chinese government introduced legislation to curb population growth. This effort is popularly known as the one-child policy, though the legislation which was in place until 2016 was much more complex. As a result of the one-child policy and the Chinese tradition of male inheritance, there is currently a national gender imbalance, with 30 million more men than women. Sex-selective abortion, though illegal, is thought to be a widespread practice. The shortage of women in China has negative consequences for Chinese society as a whole. Some experts speculate that the rise in mental health problems among men can be attributed to the fact that an increasing number of young men are unable to find a wife and start a family. Moreover, China has seen increased incidents of kidnapping and trafficking of women for marriage, as well as a rise in the number of prostitutes – which may in turn lead to a higher incidence of HIV infection. K. Sotamayor, 'The One-Child Policy Legacy on Women and Relationships in China', Independent Lens, 5 February 2020; H. Barr, 'China's Bride Trafficking Problem', Human Rights Watch, 31 October 2019; V. Ni, 'China Announces Three-Child

Limit in Major Policy Shift', *The Guardian*, 31 May 2021; Avert, 'HIV and AIDS in China', https://www.avert.org/professionals/hiv-around-world/asia-pacific/china (accessed 7 July 2021).

32. *Newsletter for the European Union*, 'Internal Migration in China', 25 February 2019.

33. Millions of rural migrants face serious discrimination in cities, where rural people are generally looked down upon and treated as second-class citizens. Rural migrants are also usually not given access to urban housing or public schools for their children. Both the influx of rural labourers into cities and the expansion of city boundaries are leading to clashes between urban dwellers and peasants in the countryside. Land seizures in rural areas to build suburban homes for wealthy city dwellers have been reported. *The Economist*, 'Many Chinese Suffer Discrimination Based on Their Regional Origin', 11 April 2019.

34. The vast majority of health facilities are in urban areas, which leaves many rural residents without easy access to medical care. V.M. Qin *et al.*, 'Rural and Urban Differences in Health System Performance among Older Chinese Adults: Cross-Sectional Analysis of a National Sample', *BMC Health Services Research* 20, no. 1 (2020), pp. 1–14.

35. Vascular disease and cancer have become the leading causes of death among Chinese adults. J. He *et al.*, 'Major Causes of Death among Men and Women in China', *New England Journal of Medicine*, 353, no. 11 (October 2005), pp. 1124–34.

36. China accounts for one out of six suicides in the world. In the past couple of decades, however, it went from having one of the highest suicide rates to one of the lowest. R. Yu *et al.*, 'Factors Associated with Suicide Risk among Chinese Adults: A Prospective Cohort Study of 0.5 Million Individuals', *PLOS Medicine* 18, no. 3 (2021), p. e1003545; Jie Zhang, 'The Gender Ratio of Chinese Suicide Rates: An Explanation in Confucianism', *Sex Roles: A Journal of Research* 70, nos 3–4 (2014), pp. 146–54; A.G. Bhaya, 'China Leads the World in Suicide Prevention', CGTN, 10 September 2019.

37. World Economic Forum, 'How the One-Party State May Shape Our Future', 2 August 2019.

38. For the most part, social protest in China takes the form of localised protests revolving around a single issue of discontent or distress. Frequent reasons for protests are market-based price adjustments for basic necessities, rural migration, land confiscation, uneven distribution of wealth and investment, air and water pollution and corruption. A sense that local officials are corrupt and the justice system weak discourages people from addressing their concerns through regular channels. Y. Li, 'A Zero-Sum Game? Repression and Protest in China', *Government and Opposition* 54, no. 2 (April 2019), pp. 309–35; W. Freeman, 'The Accuracy of China's "Mass Incidents"', *Financial Times*, 2 March 2010.

39. Although there have always been high levels of corruption in China, it is still unclear whether the country has grown so rapidly *because of* or *despite* corruption. Y. Huang, 'The Truth about Chinese Corruption', Carnegie Endowment for International Peace, 29 May 2015.

40. In order to maintain political stability and control, the government has adopted numerous policies and pieces of legislation which have been criticised as violating human rights, including freedom of expression and assembly. Human Rights Watch, 'World Report 2021: China – Events of 2020', https://www.hrw.org/world-report/2021/country-chapters/china-and-tibet (Accessed 30 June 2021).

41. J. Gunter, 'Uyghur Imams Targeted in China's Xinjiang Crackdown', BBC News, 13 May 2021; BBC News, 'Who Are the Uyghurs and Why Is China Being Accused of Genocide?', 21 June 2021.

42. State Council of the People's Republic of China, '2020: China's GDP Expands by 2.3% to Top 101.6 Trillion Yuan', 19 January 2021, http://english.www.gov.cn/news/videos/202101/19/content_WS60064cecc6d0f725769441ba.html. China is also the world's largest exporter and second-largest importer of goods. See World Bank, 'Exports of Goods and Services', accessed 30 June 2021, https://data.worldbank.org/indicator/BX.GSR.GNFS.CD; International Trade Center, 'Trade Map', 9 July 2021.

43. FTI Consulting, 'The Impact of Covid-19 on the Construction Industry in China', 19 August 2020.

44. Y. Chen, P. Luo and T. Chang, 'Urbanization and the Urban-Rural Income Gap in China: A Continuous Wavelet Coherency Analysis', *Sustainability* 12, no. 19 (2020), pp. 1–14.

45. The downside of China's rapid economic development and growth is large-scale environmental pollution and degradation. It has quickly become the world's largest emitter of greenhouse gases. Nonetheless, over the past ten years the previously severe levels of air pollution have started to decline. BBC News, 'Report: China Emissions Exceed All Developed Nations Combined', 7 May 2021.

46. Almost all of the country's waterways are polluted, and half of the population has no access to safe drinking water. T. Ma *et al.*, 'Pollution Exacerbates China's Water Scarcity and Its Regional Inequality', *Nature Communications* 11, no. 650 (2020), pp. 1–9; D. Tingting, 'In China, the Water You Drink Is as Dangerous as the Air You Breathe', *The Guardian*, 2 June 2017.

47. Maizland, 'China's Fight against Climate Change and Environmental Degradation'.

48. Despite these challenges in the environmental sector, over the past couple of decades China has spent increasing amounts of its budget on scientific and technological research. This has led it to become second only to the United States in developing new technologies. With a top-down approach, the government invests large sums in R&D across

multiple sectors, with the aim of driving economic wealth through science and technological innovation. S. Shead, 'China's Spending on R&D Hits a Record $378 Billion', CNBC, 1 March 2021; A. Kharpal, 'China Spending on Research and Development to Rise 7% Per Year in Push for Major Tech Breakthroughs', CNBC, 4 March 2021; R.P. Suttmeier, 'How China Is Trying to Invent the Future as a Science Superpower', *Scientific American*, 9 July 2021; J. Ekrem, 'China's Historic Rise in Science and Tech Stirs Criticism', *ScienceBusiness*, 6 April 2020.

49. China became the third country to launch a human into space in 2003 and is one of the leading countries in the space sector. In April 2021, it also launched modules for a new space station which, if operational as planned in 2022, would become the second existing space station to orbit the Earth. Importantly, although China has declared peaceful intentions towards space, it has also invested heavily in infrastructure designed to secure both economic and military advantages. Not only does it carry out numerous tests involving the launch and destruction of satellites, but it also has what is essentially a *de facto* 'space force'. Space .com, 'China's Space Program', https://www.space.com/topics/china -space-program (accessed 30 June 2021); BBC News, 'China Launches First Module of New Space Station', 29 April 2021; E.B. Kania, 'China Has a "Space Force". What Are Its Lessons for the Pentagon?', *Defense One*, 29 September 2018; L. Zivitski, 'China Wants to Dominate Space, and the US Must Take Countermeasures', *DefenseNews*, 23 June 2020.

50. In addition to being one of the leading states in the context of space militarisation, China plays an important military role within its region. Its long borders have always led to boundary disputes with its neighbours, including over its control and militarisation of the South China Sea. G. Austin, 'How Did the South China Dispute Begin and Where Is It Headed?', Scroll.in, 29 July 2020; BBC News, 'South China Sea Dispute: China's Pursuit of Resources "Unlawful", Says US,' 14 July 2020; Cook, 'Australia's South China Sea Challenges'; Z. Keck, 'China's Newest Maritime Dispute', *The Diplomat*, 20 March 2014; K. Vaswani, 'The Sleepy Island Indonesia Is Guarding from China', BBC News, 20 October 2014.

51. H. Davidson, 'US Official Warns China against "Catastrophic" Move on Taiwan', *The Guardian*, 7 July 2021.

52. Since the extensive borders also contribute to energy-security concerns, such as those stemming from the US domination of the Strait of Malacca, China has also invested heavily in developing oil and gas pipelines along friendly routes which fall outside the control of the US. S. Zheng, 'China Targets Energy Security as Risks from US Rivalry Grow', *South China Morning Post*, 9 March 2021; Jian Zhang, *China's Energy Security: Prospects, Challenges and Opportunities*, CNAPS Visiting Fellow Working Paper (Washington, DC: Brookings Institution, 2011).

53. Ministry of Foreign Affairs of the People's Republic of China, 'China's Policies on Asia-Pacific Security Cooperation', January 2017.

54. In 2020, Egypt's population was 102.3 million, making it the most populous country in North Africa, the Middle East and the Arab world. See WorldOmeter, 'Egypt Population', https://www.worldometers.info /world-population/egypt-population (accessed 19 July 2021).

55. US Department of State, Bureau of Near Eastern Affairs, 'Background Note: Egypt', March 2008.

56. The official poverty rate was 29.7 per cent in the 2019/20 fiscal year. See VOA News, 'Egypt: A Third of Population Lives in Poverty', 30 July 2019.

57. Immunisation against the most common infectious diseases is extensive, as is access to healthcare. Center for Global Health and Development, 'Egypt's Health Care System', https://cghd.org/index.php /global-health-partnerships-and-solutions/profiles/43-egypts-health -care-system (accessed 30 June 2021).

58. In 2020, the infant mortality rate was about 14.6 out of 1,000 live births and 20.3 within children under five, whereas the maternal mortality rate is 37 per 100,000 live births. Macrotrends, 'Egypt's Infant Mortality Rate 1950–2021', https://www.macrotrends.net/countries/EGY/egypt /infant-mortality-rate (accessed 30 June2021).

59. A state of emergency was declared upon the assassination of President Anwar Sadat in 1981, which led to the election of President Hosni Mubarak. In March 2007, a series of constitutional amendments approved by parliament and a popular referendum (boycotted by the opposition) replaced the emergency laws. Although the government argued that these powers were necessary to fight terrorism, critics said that the changed constitution continued to grant the president emergency-style powers, allowing him to circumvent judicial authorities under the pretext of national security. In January 2011, widespread protests began against the Mubarak government. A month later, the military assumed power and dissolved the parliament. In the following month, a parliamentary election was held for the first time since 1981 and Mohamed Morsi was elected president in June 2012, supported by the Muslim Brotherhood. Violent protests broke out in December 2012 when Morsi sought to immunise his decrees from challenge. Following a wave of discontent, the military removed Morsi from power in a *coup d'état* in July 2013. After a transition period, Marshal Abdel Fattah El-Sisi was elected president of Egypt in 2014 in a landslide victory. He was re-elected in 2018, facing no serious opposition. In 2019, a series of constitutional amendments were approved by the parliament and by a referendum, further increasing the president's and the military's power. See M. Asser, 'Egypt: A Permanent Emergency?', BBC News, 27 March 2007; Human Rights Watch, 'World Report 2020: Egypt – Events of 2019', https://www.hrw

.org/world-report/2020/country-chapters/egypt (Accessed 20 July 2021).

60. It has one of the largest and most diversified economies of the Middle East, based on agriculture, media, petroleum imports, natural gas and tourism, and the second-largest economy in Africa, with a GDP of US$303 billion in 2019. Statistica, 'African Countries with the Highest Gross Domestic Product (GDP) in 2020', https://www.statista.com /statistics/1120999/gdp-of-african-countries-by-country (accessed 12 July 2021); World Bank, 'GDP: Egypt', https://data.worldbank.org /indicator/NY.GDP.MKTP.CD?locations=EG (accessed 30 June 2021).

61. One of the factors which most heavily contribute to the economic conditions in Egypt is its unstable political environment, which has led to a progressive fall in foreign investment. P. Kingsley, 'Egypt "Suffering Worst Economic Crisis since 1930s"', *The Guardian*, 16 May 2013.

62. Human intervention has also contributed to environmental degradation and high levels of pollution. B. Larsen, *Arab Republic of Egypt: Cost of Environmental Degradation: Air and Water Pollution* (Washington, DC: World Bank, 2019).

63. The extremely dry and desert climate is heavily reliant on the Nile, its only water source, and faces frequent droughts, as well as flash floods and earthquakes. N. El-Sayed, 'Nile River: Extreme Droughts and Heavy Rains', *Nature Middle East*, 15 May 2017.

64. The literacy rate is 71.1 per cent but contains a difference of more than ten per cent between the male and female populations. UNESCO Institute of Statistics, 'Literacy Rate, Adult Male: Egypt, Arab Republic', September 2021, https://data.worldbank.org/indicator/SE.ADT.LITR .MA.ZS?locations=EG.

65. It is also one of the leaders in the region in terms of R&D investment. J. Ekrem, 'Aiming High: Egypt Strives to Boost Its R&D Performance', *ScienceBusiness*, 16 June 2020.

66. Crisis 24, 'Egypt Country Report', https://crisis24.garda.com/insights -intelligence/intelligence/country-reports/egypt (accessed 1 July 2021).

67. Ibid.; B. Zollner, 'Surviving Repression: How Egypt's Muslim Brotherhood Has Carried On', Carnegie Middle East Center, 11 March 2019.

68. J. Harchaoui, *Why Turkey Intervened in Libya* (Washington DC: Foreign Policy Research Institute, 2020), pp. 6–7.

69. This has particularly contributed to the strained relations between Egypt and other powerful states in the region, specifically Turkey and Iran. D. Esfandiyari, 'Iran and Egypt: A Complicated Tango', EUISS, 18 October 2012.

70. BBC News, 'Profile: Arab League – Timeline', 5 November 2013.

71. A. Bloch and I. Saber, 'What's Driving the Conflict in the Eastern Mediterranean', *Lawfare*, 25 January 2021; M. Colombo, 'Mutual

Reassurance: Why Europe Should Support Talks between Egypt and Turkey', European Council on Foreign Relations, 14 January 2021.

72. 2020 also saw the escalation of the dispute between Egypt and Ethiopia surrounding the Grand Ethiopian Renaissance Dam, which Egypt sees as an existential threat since it may significantly reduce the amount of water Egypt receives from the Nile. J.M. Mbaku, 'The Controversy over the Grand Ethiopian Renaissance Dam', Brookings Institution, 5 August 2020.

73. Not only do all EU countries have a very high Human Development Index, according to the UNDP, but they also have excellent public health care systems, which are giving rise to increasing health care costs for member states. One element contributing to the costs of health care is the ageing population. European Commission, '2018 Ageing Report: Policy Challenges for Societies', 25 May 2018.

74. The EU is a political and economic union which, over the past 50 years, has grown to include 27 member states and a population of about 447 million. An internal single market, which aims to ensure the free movement of people, goods, services and capital, has been established through a standardised system of laws that apply in all member states in those matters which have been deemed to fall under the competency of the EU. This has enabled the EU to enact legislation in justice and home affairs and to maintain common policies on trade, agriculture, fisheries and regional development. European Commission, 'Policies', https://ec.europa.eu/info/policies_en (accessed 15 November 2021).

75. The main issue lies in the fact that the EU currently lacks strong leadership and a common constitution. Furthermore, the current generation of European leaders did not live through the carnage of the Second World War and thus lack the zeal and idealism of the EU's founders, who wished to create an integrated political union among former enemy states to prevent future wars on the continent. Moreover, political decisions in Brussels are mostly taken on the basis of unanimity. As member states often fail to agree on a common policy, many policies implemented remain vague and indecisive. The EU's decision-making process allows for little public participation, giving rise to what is perceived as a serious democratic deficit. Informal negotiations within policy-making bodies allow for little transparency. See Jensen, 'The Democratic Deficit of the European Union'.

76. The electorates in many EU states feel alienated from EU institutions and are increasingly susceptible to the nationalist rhetoric of populist politicians at home, advocating tough anti-immigration measures and putting narrow national interests ahead of the well-being of the Union. Moreover, the populations of EU member states still base their concepts of nationhood and national identity on ethnicity. It is this same rhetoric that led the United Kingdom to renounce its membership of the EU

following a referendum in 2016. J. Dennison and N. Carl, 'The Ultimate Causes of Brexit: History, Culture and Geography', London School of Economics British Politics and Policy Blog, 18 July 2016.

77. The EU's economy is one of its biggest strengths but simultaneously one of its biggest weaknesses. In 2021 alone, the EU had generated a nominal GDP of around US$17.1 trillion, constituting approximately eighteen per cent of global nominal GDP and the second-largest net wealth in the world after the US. Nineteen of the EU member states are also part of the Eurozone. In 2016, unemployment in the EU stood at 8.9 per cent while inflation was at 2.2 per cent, and the account balance was at −0.9 per cent of GDP. There is a significant economic imbalance, however, between the wealthier states in the EU and the poorer ones, which is one of the main sources of internal disagreements about common economic policies. Over the past couple of decades, the EU has faced multiple recessions, with economic stagnation often being attributed to over-regulation and the large welfare-state structures of many member states. See T.M. Andersen *et al.*, 'The Welfare State after the Great Recession', *Intereconomics* 47, no. 4 (2012), pp. 200–5.

78. When the European Economic Community was first founded in 1957, it had no environmental policy. Legislation has since been introduced, however, extending to all areas of environmental protection, including air pollution, water quality, waste management, nature conservation, and the control of chemicals, industrial hazards, and biotechnology, making environmental policy a core area of European politics. Despite this, ozone and particulate matter remain a problem. European Environment Agency, 'Air Pollution', 23 November 2020, https://www .eea.europa.eu/themes/air/air-quality-management/improving-europe -s-air-quality/improving-europe-s-air-quality/intro.

79. Since member states continue to rely heavily on fossil fuels for energy, greenhouse gas emissions are significant, with the EU emitting 9.1 per cent of the global total in 2017. For this reason, mitigating climate change has become one of the top priorities of EU environmental policy, with the EU having set a target of zero GHG emission by 2050 under the European Green Deal. European Commission, 'EU Climate Action and the European Green Deal', https://ec.europa.eu/clima/policies/eu -climate-action_en (accessed 30 June 2021).

80. The excellent provision of education has given rise to a highly skilled labour force. OECD, 'Employment by Education Level', https://data .oecd.org/emp/employment-by-education-level.htm (accessed 30 June 2021).

81. Although the EU invests relatively little in R&D (2.19 per cent of GDP) compared to the six per cent of GDP spent on R&D in the United States, it is nonetheless one of the world leaders in science and technology, including in space programmes. Eurostat, 'R&D Expenditure at 2.19% of GDP in 2019', 27 November 2021.

82. The new EU Security Union Strategy for the period from 2020 to 2025 was laid out by the European Commission on 24 July 2020, aimed at ensuring European security, both in the physical and digital world and across all parts of society. Balancing internal and external security, the Commission identified key areas of focus, which include: organised crime; terrorism and the prevention of violent radicalisation; resilience of critical infrastructures and public spaces; cybercrime, including fighting child sexual abuse; law enforcement cooperation and information exchange; research and innovation. Organised crime and corruption are estimated to present between €218 and €282 billion in economic loss annually. Terrorism and radicalisation, both by Islamist extremists, as well as by far right and far left extremists, are also perceived as a significant security threat. In this regard, on 9 December 2020, the Commission put forward a specific new Counter Terrorism Agenda aimed at anticipating, preventing, protecting and responding to terrorist threats. According to the Commission, the Europol mandate should also be strengthened to enable the agency to better support national law enforcement authorities with information, analysis and expertise, and to facilitate cross-border police cooperation and terrorism-related investigations. Cooperation and information sharing are especially important if member states are effectively to tackle the rise in increasingly sophisticated cybercrime. Research and innovation are therefore also seen as a key component of an effective European security strategy. European Commission, 'Communication from the Commission on the EU Security Union Strategy', COM (2020) 605, 24 July 2020.

83. In terms of foreign policy and diplomacy, the main strength of the EU lies in soft power. Through its enlargement policy, the EU has been enormously successful at promoting peaceful democratisation in prospective member states, starting with Spain in the 1970s. S. Grimm, 'Democracy Promotion and the European Union', Research Network External Democracy Promotion Wire, 15 January 2019.

84. EU foreign policy is often paralysed, however, as the individual national interests of member states do not converge. EU members' short-term economic interests sometimes contradict the EU's agreed-upon, long-term foreign-policy objectives, which often makes EU foreign policy highly inconsistent and thus hurts the EU's reputation as a reliable partner abroad. L. Schuette, 'Should the EU Make Foreign Policy Decisions by Majority Voting?', Centre for European Reform, 15 May 2019.

85. According to the EU, however, only in a well-ordered global system governed by international law can the EU rest securely. A key priority of EU diplomacy is the strengthening of the UN. It also promotes more inclusive international financial and economic institutions, such as the WTO. See European Council, 'European Security Strategy: A Secure Europe in a Better World', p. 9.

86. N. Burns, 'Brexit Is a Challenge Shared by the UK, the EU and the US', *The Security Times*, February 2020.

87. Causes of disagreement between the EU and their partners in the US, particularly in relation to China, are increasing. D. Whineray, '5 Reasons Why US-Europe Tensions Will Grow in the 2020s – and How to Stop It', Carnegie Endowment for International Peace, 16 January 2020.

88. The EU fears Russia's military capacities, but it needs Russia for regional stability as well as for energy security. European Commission, High Representative of the Union for Foreign Affairs and Security Policy, 'Joint Communication to the European Parliament, the European Council and the Council on EU-Russia Relations: Push Back, Constrain and Engage', JOIN (2021) 20, 16 June 2021, pp. 1–2.

89. N. Kapoor, 'Russia-EU Relations: The End of a Strategic Partnership', *ORF Issue Brief*, no. 451 (March 2021), p. 3.

90. France has a total population of around 68 million (as of July 2021). France stands out among developed countries in general, and European countries in particular, for its relatively high rate of natural population growth. Although, as of January 2021, the fertility rate had declined slightly to 1.84 children per woman, below the replacement rate of 2.1, it was responsible for almost all natural population growth via birth in the European Union in 2006. Nevertheless, in line with the rest of the EU, France's population is ageing, with about a fifth of French people being 65 years old or older. Statista, 'Total Population of France from 1982 to 2021, in Millions', https://www.statista.com/statistics/459939 /population-france/ (accessed 30 July 2021).

91. In its 2000 assessment of world health-care systems, the World Health Organization found that France's universal health-care system provided the 'close to best overall health care' in the world. This health-care system is costly, however; France spends 11.2 per cent of its 2018 GDP on it. World Health Organization, 'World Health Organization Assesses the World's Health Systems', 7 February 2000; Statista, 'Total Expenditure on Health as a Percentage of Gross Domestic Product (GDP) in France from 1980 to 2019', https://www.statista.com /statistics/429197/healthcare-expenditure-as-a-share-of-gdp-in-france /(accessed 30 July 2021).

92. Due to large-scale immigration over the past century and a half, with France accepting about 200,000 legal immigrants annually, it has a vastly multicultural population. Moreover, it is among the top five asylum recipients in the world, with 100,412 applications in 2017 aloneA. Kalt *et al.*, 'Asylum Seekers, Violence and Health: A Systematic Review of Research in High-Income Host Countries', *American Journal of Public Health* 103, no. 3 (2013), pp. e30–e42; Asylum Information Database, 'Country Report: France', 2017 update, https://asylumineurope.org/wp -content/uploads/2018/02/report-download_aida_fr_2017update.pdf.

93. Large-scale immigration has not come without its challenges and is a particularly contentious issue in twenty-first-century France, as demonstrated by the debates surrounding religious freedoms, and especially those of Muslim communities, which France has sought to curb on the basis of its constitutional secularism. Wilson Center, 'Secularism and Islam in France', 16 June 2021.

94. This is especially the case in Algeria (archives, nuclear waste etc.). J.-M. Collin and P. Bouveret, 'Radioactivity under the Sand: The Waste from French Nuclear Tests in Algeria', Heinrich Böll Stiftung Foundation, July 2020.

95. Marine Le Pen, leader of the extreme right Front National, placed second in the 2017 French presidential elections. G. Aisch, M. Bloch, K.K.R. Lai and B. Morenne, 'How France Voted', *The New York Times*, 7 May 2017; C. Belot, 'Disentangling Varieties of French Nationalism: Why Does It Matter', *French Politics* 19, no. 4 (2021), pp. 1–32.

96. A member of the G7 (Group of Seven) leading industrialised countries, France is the world's seventh-largest economy by nominal GDP, which currently stands at US$2.93 trillion (in 2021). It also ranks fourth in the world in terms of aggregate household wealth. A. Shorrocks, J. Davies and R. Lluberas, *Global Wealth Report*, 10th edn (Zürich: Credit Suisse, 2019).

97. Santander, 'France: Foreign Investment', https://santandertrade.com/en /portal/establish-overseas/france/foreign-investment (accessed 30 July 2021).

98. Embassy of France in the Caribbean, 'France, Europe's Leading Agricultural Power', https://lc.ambafrance.org/1-France-Europe -s-leading (accessed 30 June 2021).

99. Despite the fact that it is one of the most industrialised countries in the world, due to its heavy investment in nuclear power, which now accounts for 70 per cent of its electricity production, France is the smallest emitter of carbon dioxide among the G7 and only the nineteenth in the world, behind less populous states such as Australia. France's main electricity generation and distribution company, Électricité de France, is also one of the world's largest producers of electricity, accounting for 20 per cent of the EU's electricity in 2018, primarily from nuclear power. The heavy reliance on nuclear has had a positive impact on French GHG emissions and has resulted in less pollution, but the French state is not encouraging investment in renewable energies. IAEA Power Reactor Information System, 'France', https://pris.iaea.org/PRIS/CountryStatistics/CountryDetails. aspx?current=FR (accessed 7 January 2018); Ministère de l'Écologie, de l'Énergie, du Développement durable et de la Mer (France), *Repères: Chiffres clés du transport: Édition 2010* (Key Transportation Figures: 2010 Edition) (La Défense: 2010), via the Internet Archive Wayback Machine, https://web.archive.org/web/20100601124351/http:/www

.developpement-durable.gouv.fr/IMG/pdf/Chiffres_transport-pdf.pdf;
World Nuclear Association, 'Nuclear Power in France', January 2021,
http://www.world-nuclear.org/information-library/country-profiles
/countries-a-f/france.aspx; UN Environmental Indicators,
'Greenhouse Gas Emissions', July 2010, via the Internet Archive
Wayback Machine, https://web.archive.org/web/20100310190132/http:/
unstats.un.org/unsd/environment/air_co2_emissions.htm; Morgane
Remy, 'CO$_2$: La France moins pollueuse grâce au nucléaire' (CO$_2$:
France Pollutes Less Thanks to Nuclear Energy), *L'Usine Nouvelle*, 18
June 2010; Ambassade de France en Chine, 'L'énergie nucléaire en
France' (Nuclear Energy in France), 7 January 2008, via the Internet
Archive Wayback Machine, https://web.archive.org/
web/20100701211529/http:/www.ambafrance-cn.org/L-energie-
nucleaire-en-France.html.

100. Not only was France one of the first countries to create an environment
ministry, in 1971, but, according to the 2018 Environmental
Performance Index, France was the second-most environmentally
conscious country in the world (after Switzerland). Climate Change
Post, 'Climate Change: France', https://www.climatechangepost.com
/france/climate-change (accessed 2 June 2021),; Ambassade de France en
Chine, 'L'énergie nucléaire en France'; Yale University, '2018 EPI
Results', 23 July 2019, epi.envirocenter.yale.edu.

101. In 2018, the Programme for International Student Assessment
coordinated by the OECD ranked France's education as below the
OECD average. One of the sources of criticism of the French education
system lies in the divide between public universities and the prestigious
and selective *grandes écoles*, which are seen as encouraging elitism, since
they produce many, if not most, of France's high-ranking civil servants,
CEOs and politicians. Compare Your Country, 'PISA 2018', http://www
.compareyourcountry.org/pisa/country/fra?lg=en (accessed 30
June 2021),; M. Bartnik, 'Boursiers: Les grandes écoles dans la
tourmente' (Scholarship Students: Elite Schools in Crisis), *Le Figaro*, 8
January 2010.

102. EY, 'How Can Europe Reset the Investment Agenda Now to Rebuild Its
Future?', 28 May 2020.

103. The Bloomberg Innovation Index ranked France among the ten most
innovative countries in the world. Since the Middle Ages, France has
been a major contributor to scientific and technological achievement
and today is a major member of CERN, as well as the home of
Minatec, Europe's leading nanotechnology research centre. UNESCO
Institute of Statistics, 'How Much Does Your Country Invest in R&D?',
accessed 18 June 2021; M. Jamrisko and W. Lu, 'Germany Breaks
Korea's Six-Year Streak as Most Innovative Nation', AITRIZ, 18
January 2018.

104. After the former USSR and the US, France was the third nation to launch its own space satellite. France Diplomatie, 'France at the Heart of the Rosetta Space Mission: A Unique Technological Challenge', 22 May 2015, via the Internet Archive Wayback Machine, https://web. archive.org/web/20150522152217/http:/www.diplomatie.gouv.fr/en /french-foreign-policy-1/scientific-diplomacy/events-7867/article /france-at-the-heart-of-the-rosetta.

105. Not only is it a leader in civilian nuclear technology, but France is also a nuclear power, and has the third-largest nuclear weapons arsenal in the world. *Business Insider*, 'The 17 Countries Generating the Most Nuclear Power', 6 March 2014; Federation of American Scientists, 'Status of World Nuclear Forces', 18 June 2015, via the Internet Archive Wayback Machine, https://web.archive.org/web /20150618103342/http:/fas.org/issues/nuclear-weapons/status-world -nuclear-forces.

106. The French armed forces are the largest in the EU and among the largest in the world. France is also the fifth-biggest military spender in the world after the United States, China, Saudi Arabia and India, with an annual military expenditure in 2020 of US$52.7 billion, or 2.1 per cent of its GDP. N. Tian *et al.*, *Trends in World Military Expenditure, 2020* (Stockholm: SIPRI, 2021).

107. Although it has signed and ratified the Comprehensive Nuclear Test Ban Treaty (CTBT) and acceded to the Nuclear Non-Proliferation Treaty, France is a nuclear power and relies on nuclear deterrence in complete independence. In its arsenal, it has both submarines armed with nuclear ballistic missiles and medium-range air-to-ground missiles with nuclear warheads. CTBTO Preparatory Commission, 'Status of Signature and Ratification', http://www.ctbto.org/the-treaty/status-of -signature-and-ratification.

108. World Economic Forum, 'Global Arms Sales Captured in Four Charts', 18 December 2018.

109. B. Sussman, 'The List: Best and Worst Countries for Cybersecurity', Secure World Expo, 13 November 2019.

110. France considers terrorism a major security threat and has been victim to numerous terrorist attacks, including the November 2015 jihadist attacks in Paris, which left 130 dead and 350 wounded. France Diplomatie, 'Terrorism: France's International Action' https://www .diplomatie.gouv.fr/en/french-foreign-policy/security-disarmament-and -non-proliferation/terrorism-france-s-international-action/ (accessed 30 June 2021) ; BBC News, 'Paris Attacks: France Remembers Night of Terror amid Jihadist Threat', 13 November 2020.

111. Being one of the five permanent members of the UN Security Council, an official nuclear-weapons state and a member of both the EU and NATO, France remains a great power in global affairs. French foreign

policy after the Second World War has been largely shaped by its membership in the European Union, which it helped to found and of which it has become one of the two most influential driving forces, alongside Germany. A. Gazeau-Secret, 'Francophonie et diplomatie d'influence' (French-speaking Countries and Influence Diplomacy), *Géoéconomie*, no. 55 (2010), pp. 39–56; J.S. Levy, *War in the Modern Great Power System 1495–1975* (Lexington: University of Kentucky, 2014 [1983]), p. 29;.

112. France is one of the largest donors (in absolute terms) of development aid in the world. Donor Tracker, 'France', 30 June 2021, https://donortracker.org/country/france.

113. France also retains strong political and economic influence in its former African colonies, to which it supplies economic aid and troops for peacekeeping missions and military support. J. Bender, 'France's Military Is All over Africa', *Business Insider*, 22 January 2015.

114. Germany had a population of over 83 million in 2019. World Bank, 'Population, Total: Germany', https://data.worldbank.org/indicator/SP .POP.TOTL?locations=DE (accessed 30 June 2021).

115. Germany's fertility rate of 1.51 children born per woman (2019 estimate) is below the replacement rate of 2.1 and is one of the lowest fertility rates in the world. The infant mortality rate is also very low (3.2 per 1,000 live births in 2019). World Bank, 'Fertility Rate: Germany', https://data .worldbank.org/indicator/SP.DYN.TFRT.IN?locations=DE (accessed 30 June 2021).

116. Germany has the world's oldest universal health-care system, dating from Bismarck's social legislation of the 1880s. According to the World Health Organization, its health-care system was 77 per cent government-funded as of 2013. In 2014, Germany spent 11.3 per cent of its GDP on health care. Life expectancy in Germany is 80.19 years. European Observatory on Health Care Systems, 'Health Care Systems in Transition: Germany', 2000, p. 8, https://apps.who.int/iris/bitstream /handle/10665/108301/HiT-de-2000-eng.pdf?sequence=9&isAllowed=y; World Bank, 'Health Expenditure, Total (% of GDP)', 1 January 2016, http://data.worldbank.org/indicator/SH.XPD.TOTL.ZS; World Bank, 'Life Expectancy at Birth, Total (Years) – Germany', https://data .worldbank.org/indicator/SP.DYN.LE00.IN?locations=DE (accessed 30 June 2021).

117. In 2019, the principal cause of death was cardiovascular disease, at 37 per cent. Obesity in Germany has been increasingly cited as a major health issue, with a 2014 study showing that 52 per cent of the adult German population was overweight or obese. World Health Organization, 'Germany Country Health Profile 2019'; Eurostat, 'Overweight and Obesity – BMI statistics', https://ec.europa.eu/eurostat /statistics-explained/index.php/Overweight_and_obesity_-_BMI _statistics (accessed 14 March 2020).

118. After the United States, Germany is the second most popular immigration destination in the world, with 18.6 million people (22.5 per cent) of the country's residents being of immigrant or partially immigrant descent in 2016. As of 2018, Germany also ranks fifth among EU countries in terms of the percentage of migrants in the country's population, at 12.9 per cent. Federal Statistical Office of Germany, 'Bevölkerung mit Migrationshintergrund um 8,5 % gestiegen', 1 August 2017, https://www.destatis.de/DE/Presse/Pressemitteilungen /2017/08/PD17_261_12511.html; UN Department of Economic and Social Affairs, 'International Migration Report 2015', September 2016 https://www.un.org/en/development/desa/population/migration /publications/migrationreport/docs/MigrationReport2015.pdf; OECD, 'Foreign Population', https://data.oecd.org/migration/foreign -population.htm#indicator-chart (accessed 9 March 2020).

119. In the 2017 German federal election, the right-wing populist Alternative for Germany, known for its strong anti-immigration rhetoric, gained enough votes to attain representation in the parliament for the first time. DW, 'Germany's Political Parties – What You Need to Know', 5 October 2021; J. Stone, 'German Elections: Far-Right Wins MPs for First Time in Half a Century', *The Independent*, 24 September 2017.

120. Germany has a social market economy with a highly skilled labour force, a low level of corruption and a high level of innovation. It is the world's third-largest exporter and third-largest importer of goods, and has the largest economy in Europe, which is also the world's fourth-largest economy by nominal GDP (US$3.86 trillion in 2019). In addition, it has the fourth-lowest unemployment rate in Europe, which, according to Eurostat, amounts to 3.2 per cent as of January 2020. In 2017, according to the International Monetary Fund, the country accounted for 28 per cent of the Eurozone economy. Transparency International, 'Corruption Perceptions Index 2020', accessed 30 June 2020, https://www.transparency.org/en/cpi/2020/index/; K. Schwab (ed.), *The Global Competitiveness Report 2018* (Geneva: World Economic Forum, 2018), p. 11; World Bank, 'GDP: Germany', https://data.world bank.org/indicator/NY.GDP.MKTP.CD?locations=DE (accessed 30 June 2021); Eurostat, 'Unemployment Statistics', https://ec.europa.eu /eurostat/statistics-explained/index.php/Unemployment_statistics (accessed 30 June 2021); International Monetary Fund, 'Germany: Spend More at Home', 7 July 2017.

121. Germany is the birthplace of the automobile and its automotive industry is regarded as one of the most competitive and innovative in the world. It is also the fourth largest by production. C. Randall, 'CAM Study Reveals: German Carmakers Are Most Innovative', Electrive, 10 December 2019; International Organization of Motor Vehicle Manufacturers, '2017 Production Statistics', http://www.oica.net /category/production-statistics.

122. In 2015, Germany was the world's seventh-largest consumer of energy and produced an average of two per cent of the total global of annual greenhouse gas emissions. Germany intends to shut down all of its nuclear power stations by 2022, which in the year 2000 had a 29.5 per cent share of the power generation mix, down to 11.4 per cent in 2020. Because of this, Germany now meets the country's power demands using 40 per cent renewable sources. K. Appunn, 'The History behind Germany's Nuclear Phase-Out', Clean Energy Wire, 9 March 2021.

123. Germany is committed to the Paris Agreement and several other treaties promoting biodiversity, low emission standards and water management. It is also known for having one the highest household recycling rates in the world – at around 65 per cent. M. Eddy, 'Germany Passes Climate-Protection Law to Ensure 2030 Goals', *New York Times*, 15 November 2019; WaterLex, 'Legal Country Mapping: Germany', 6 July 2018, http://humanright2water.org/wp-content/uploads/2020/07 /WL-Country-Mapping-Germany.pdf; Climate Action, 'Germany Is the World's Leading Nation for Recycling', 11 December 2017.

124. Although the education is generally of excellent quality, Germany experiences some important inequities in educational outcomes, with socio-economically disadvantaged students being much less likely to gain a tertiary qualification. According to an OECD report, Germany was the world's third leading destination for international study in 2014. OECD, 'Education Policy Outlook: Germany', June 2020, https://www .oecd.org/education/policy-outlook/country-profile-Germany-2020.pdf, pp. 3, 7–9; A. Krause-Pilatus and S. Schüller, 'Evidence and Persistence of Education Inequality in an Early Tracking System: The German Case', IZA Discussion Paper no. 8545 (October 2014); T. Pitman and H. Forsyth, 'Should We Follow the German Way of Free Higher Education?', *The Conversation*, 17 March 2014; L. Bridgestock, 'The Growing Popularity of International Study in Germany', QS TopUniversities, 23 February 2016.

125. Research and development efforts form an integral part of the German economy, with Germany ranking fourth globally in terms of the number of science and engineering research papers published in 2018. Federal Ministry of Education and Research (Germany), 'Federal Report on Research and Innovation 2020',https://www.datenportal.bmbf.de/portal /en/bufi.html ; N. McCarthy, 'The Countries Leading the World in Scientific Research', World Economic Forum, 13 January 2020.

126. German Aerospace Center, 'Germany Invests 3.3 Billion Euro in European Space Exploration and Becomes ESA's Largest Contributor', 28 November 2019.

127. In absolute terms, German military expenditure is the eighth highest in the world. In 2018, however, military spending was at $49.5 billion, only about 1.2 per cent of the country's GDP and well below the NATO target of two per cent. Tian *et al.*, *Trends in World Military Expenditure, 2018*;

A. Macias, 'Trump Approves Plan to Withdraw 9,500 U.S. Forces from
Germany', CNBC, 30 June 2020; IHS Jane's 360, 'Germany to Increase
Defence Spending', 2 July 2015, via the Internet Archive Wayback
Machine, https://web.archive.org/web/20150705180905/http:/www
.janes.com/article/52745/germany-to-increase-defence-spending.

128. As of 2017, the German military had about 3,600 troops stationed in
foreign countries as part of international peacekeeping forces.
Bundeswehr, 'Einsatzzahlen – die Stärke der deutschen Kontingente',
18 August 2017, http://club.bruxelles2.eu/wp-content/uploads/2016/04
/Chiffres-Opex-2016-@DE160422.pdf; International Insider, 'Germany
Extends Unified Armed Forces Mission in Mali', 1 June 2020, https://
internationalinsider.org/germany-extends-unified-armed-forces-mission
-in-mali.

129. Germany has played an influential role in the European Union since its
inception and has maintained a strong alliance with France and all
neighbouring countries since 1990. It promotes the creation of a more
unified European political, economic and security apparatus.; J. Freed,
'The Leader of Europe? Answers an Ocean Apart', *New York Times*, 4
April 2008,; Die Bundesregierung, *Shaping Globalization – Expanding
Partnerships – Sharing Responsibility: A Strategy Paper by the German
Government* (Berlin: Federal Foreign Office, 29 March 2020).

130. Cultural ties and economic interests have crafted a bond between
Germany and the US resulting in a bilateral policy trajectory known as
Atlanticism. US Department of State, 'U.S. Relations with Germany', 21
June 2021, https://www.state.gov/u-s-relations-with-germany; US
Embassy in Berlin, 'U.S.-German Economic Relations Factsheet',
May 2006, via the Internet Archive Wayback Machine, https://web
.archive.org/web/20110511123309/http:/germany.usembassy.gov
/germany/img/assets/9336/econ_factsheet_may2006.pdf.

131. The development policy of Germany is an independent area of foreign
policy. The German government sees development policy as a joint
responsibility of the international community and for this reason it was
the world's second-biggest aid donor in 2019 after the United States.
A-K. Hornidge and I. Scholz, 'Seven Principles to Guide German
Development Policy', The Current Column of the German Development
Institute, 10 May 2021; A. Green, 'Germany, Foreign Aid, and the
Elusive 0.7%', Devex, 8 August 2019.

132. The Nord Stream 2 gas pipeline from Russia to Germany, currently
under construction, is putting Germany at risk of sanctions from the
US, in addition to the companies involved in the project. J. Wettengel,
'Gas Pipeline Nord Stream 2 Links Germany to Russia, but Splits
Europe', Clean Energy Wire Factsheet, 9 September 2021, https://www
.cleanenergywire.org/factsheets/gas-pipeline-nord-stream-2-links
-germany-russia-splits-europe; J. Stern, 'Germany Will Never Back
Down on Its Russian Pipeline', *Foreign Policy*, 25 February 2021.

133. World Bank, 'Population, Total: India', https://data.worldbank.org
/indicator/SP.POP.TOTL?locations=IN (accessed 30 June 2021); World
Bank, 'Population Growth: India', https://data.worldbank.org/indicator
/SP.POP.GROW?locations=IN (accessed 30 June 2021).

134. Around 2.79 million individuals are diagnosed with tuberculosis in
India annually, according to data from 2016. According to the World
Health Organisation's 2017 World Malaria Report, India's malaria
surveillance system ranks among the worst in the world. Health Issues
India, 'Infectious Diseases in India', https://www.healthissuesindia.com
/infectious-diseases (accessed 30 June 2021); TB Facts, 'How Many
People Have TB in India', https://tbfacts.org/tb-statistics-india (accessed
30 June 2021).

135. Between the years 1990 and 2016, Indians recorded a 50 per cent
increase in heart disease and stroke. The number of people with diabetes
has increased 2.5 times, from 26 million in 1990 to 65 million in 2016.
In the same period, the number of chronic lung disease cases in India
has almost doubled, from 28 million to 55 million. The contribution of
cancers to total health loss in India has also doubled between 1990 to
2016. Scroll, 'India Latest Health Scorecard: More Heart Disease, a Surge
in Diabetes and a Rising Suicide Rate', 16 September 2018, https://scroll
.in/pulse/894452/india-latest-health-scorecard-more-heart-disease-a
-surge-in-diabetes-and-a-rising-suicide-rate.

136. By 2019, the infant mortality rate had decreased to 28.3 per 1,000 live
births. The maternal mortality ratio stood at 143 per 100,000 live births
in 2017. UN Inter-agency Group for Child Mortality Estimation,
'Mortality Rate, Infant: India', https://data.worldbank.org/indicator/SP
.DYN.IMRT.IN?locations=IN (accessed 30 June 2021); World Bank,
'Maternal Mortality Ratio: India', https://data.worldbank.org/indicator
/SH.STA.MMRT.NE?locations=IN (accessed 30 June 2021).

137. A. Kasthuri, 'Challenges to Healthcare in India', *Indian Journal of
Community Medicine* 43, no. 3 (2018), pp. 141–43.

138. Though illegal, the caste system is still observed in many rural areas and
has experienced a sort of revival with the rise of Hindu nationalism in
the past several decades.

139. The lowest caste, the Dalit ('untouchables'), which make up about 25 per
cent of India's total population, still face widespread discrimination.
Although India has implemented a series of affirmative action measures
to increase the representation of lower-caste members in higher-skilled
jobs and universities, social discrimination against the lower classes
continues to plague Indian society and hurts India's social cohesion.
India's approximately two hundred million Muslims (the country's
largest minority group) have also faced discrimination in employment,
education and the political system. G. Subramanyam, 'In India, Dalits

Still Feel Bottom of the Caste Ladder', NBC News, 13 September 2020; P. Sur, 'Under India's Caste System, Dalits Are Considered Untouchable. The Coronavirus Is Intensifying That Slur', CNN, 16 April 2020; L. Maizland, 'India's Muslims: An Increasingly Marginalized Population', Council on Foreign Relations, Backgrounder, 20 August 2020; Human Rights Watch, 'Shoot the Traitors: Discrimination Against Muslims under India's New Citizenship Policy', 9 April 2020.

140. M. Vaishnav, 'The Decay of Indian Democracy: Why India No Longer Ranks among the Lands of the Free', *Foreign Affairs*, 18 March 2021; S. Dhume, 'Is India Still a Democracy? The Answer Isn't So Clear', *Wall Street Journal*, 15 April 2021.

141. The Hindu-nationalist Bharatiya Janata Party (BJP) is one of the two major political parties in India, along with the Indian National Congress. It wants India to become a Hindu, rather than a secular, state as the current constitution defines it. If that transpires, non-Hindus may come to feel excluded from the political process, which could lead to ethnic violence. In 2014, the BJP, led by Narendra Modi, became the first political party since 1984 to win a majority and govern without the support of other parties. More importantly, India's independent judiciary helps to protect the constitution of the pluralist nation. NDTV, 'Election Results 2014: Narendra Modi Wins India. BJP and Allies Cross 300 Seats', 17 May 2014.

142. World Bank, 'GDP: India', https://data.worldbank.org/indicator/NY .GDP.MKTP.KD?locations=IN (accessed 30 June 2021); World Bank, 'GDP Growth: India', https://data.worldbank.org/indicator/NY.GDP .MKTP.KD.ZG?locations=IN (accessed 30 June 2021).

143. The service sector makes up 55.6 per cent of GDP, the industrial sector 26.3 per cent and the agricultural sector 18.1 per cent. The technology industry, comprising both IT services and business process outsourcing, has increased its contribution to India's GDP from 1.2 per cent in 1998 to 7.7 per cent in 2017. NASSCOM, 'The IT-BPM Industry in India 2017: Strategic Review' https://nasscom.in/knowledge-center/publications /it-bpm-industry-india-2017-strategic-review.

144. M. Aslany, 'The Indian Middle Class, Its Size, and Urban-Rural Variations', *Contemporary South Asia* 27, no. 2 (2019), pp. 196–213; S. Mohapatra, 'Pre-Budget Ground Reality: The Indian Middle Class under Modi 1.0 and 2.0', *Economic Times*, 23 January 2021.

145. In 2019, the poverty line reduced further to about 2.7 per cent and India no longer holds the position of the nation with the largest population in poverty. It has around 84 million people living in extreme poverty which makes up about six per cent of its total population, as of May 2021. World Data Lab, 'World Poverty Clock', https://worldpoverty.io (accessed 14 July 2021); J. Slater, 'India Is No Longer Home to the Largest Number of Poor People in the World. Nigeria Is', *Washington Post*, 14 July 2021.

146. International Labour Organization, 'Informal Economy in South Asia', 14 July 2021; R. Deb, 'Covid-19: An Opportunity to Redesign India's Formal-Informal Economy Dynamics', Observer Research Foundation, 15 October 2020.

147. India's external debt was US$563.5 billion at the end of December 2020. Government of India, 'India's Quarterly External Debt Report for Quarter Ending December 2020', https://dea.gov.in/sites/default/files /Report%20on%20India%27s%20External%20Debt%20as%20at%20 end-December%202020.pdf; S&P Global, 'India's Infrastructure Push Needs New Model, Strong State Support to Succeed', 12 April 2021, https://www.spglobal.com/marketintelligence/en/news-insights/latest -news-headlines/india-s-infrastructure-push-needs-new-model-strong -state-support-to-succeed-63343927.

148. India has low per capita emissions of greenhouse gases, but the country as a whole is the third-largest greenhouse gas producer, after China and the United States. Of the thirty most polluted cities in the world in 2019, twenty-one were in India. India suffers from large-scale environmental pollution as a result of rapid economic growth – a formidable challenge for a country with a high population density whose economy relies heavily on the country's natural resources. Fifty-one per cent of pollution is caused by the industrial pollution, 27 per cent by vehicles, 17 per cent by crop burning. International Energy Agency, 'CO$_2$ Emissions from Fuel Combustion: Highlights: 2011 Edition', https://selectra.co.uk /sites/default/files/pdf/co2highlights.pdf; H. Regan, '21 of the World's 30 Cities with the Worst Air Pollution Are in India', CNN, 25 February 2020.

149. The Air (Prevention and Control of Pollution) Act was passed in 1981 to regulate air pollution but has failed to reduce it because of poor enforcement of the rules. In 2019, India launched a 'National Clean Air Programme' with a tentative national target of a 20 to 30 per cent reduction in fine particulate pollutant concentrations by 2024. Other environmental initiatives include a 1,600-kilometre-long and five-kilometre-wide Great Green Wall of Aravalli ecological corridor, along the Aravalli range from Gujarat to Delhi, which will also connect to the Shivalik hill range with the planting of 1.35 billion new native trees over ten years. N. Gokhale, 'India's 40-Year-Old Law to Combat Air Pollution Languishes as the Crisis Intensifies', *Mongabay*, 10 November 2020; India Environmental Portal, 'National Clean Air Programme', 10 January 2019, http://www.indiaenvironmentportal.org.in/content /460562/national-clean-air-programme-ncap; *Indian Express*, 'Want Govt to Build 1,600 km Green Wall along Aravalli, Says Activist', 24 December 20.

150. India's extensive use of groundwater has resulted in rapidly decreasing water tables and has already led to extreme shortages in some of India's most populated regions, with as many as 256 of 700 districts reporting

critical or over-exploited groundwater levels as of 2017. S. Snyder, 'Water in Crisis: India', The Water Project, https://thewaterproject.org/water-crisis/water-in-crisis-india (accessed 14 July 2021); M. Nathan, 'India's Water Crisis: The Seen and Unseen', DownToEarth, 19 March 2021, https://www.downtoearth.org.in/blog/water/india-s-water-crisis-the-seen-and-unseen-76049; M.R. Hota, 'India's Water Crisis: Is There a Solution?', *Financial Express*, 23 September 2021.

151. In India's higher education system, a significant number of seats are reserved under affirmative action policies for the historically disadvantaged. In recent decades India's improved education system is often cited as one of the main contributors to its economic development. World Bank, 'Literacy Rate: India', https://data.worldbank.org/indicator/SE.ADT.LITR.ZS?locations=IN (accessed 30 June 2021).

152. The Indian Space Research Organisation (ISRO) is one of six government space agencies in the world which possess full launch capabilities, deploy cryogenic engines, launch extraterrestrial missions and operate large fleets of artificial satellites. T. Narasimhan, 'ISRO on Cloud Nine as India Joins "Cryo Club"', *Business Standard*, 7 January 2014; B. Harvey, H.H.F. Smid and T. Pirard, *Emerging Space Powers: The New Space Programs of Asia, the Middle East and South-America* (Chichester: Springer Science & Business Media, 2011), p. 144.

153. With a strength of over 1.4 million active personnel, it is the world's second-largest military force. It also has the third-largest defence budget in the world.; *News18*, '20% Sailor Shortage in Navy, 15% Officer Posts Vacant in Army, Nirmala Sitharaman Tells Parliament', 27 December 2017; Global Security, 'India – Army', 6 January 2016, http://www.globalsecurity.org/military/world/india/army.htm; N. Tian *et al.*, *Trends in World Military Expenditure, 2019* (Stockholm: SIPRI, 2020); *Economic Times*, 'India and China Increase Their Nuclear Arsenal Even as the Global Number Goes Down', 2 December 2020.

154. The Line of Control is a military control line between the Indian- and Pakistani-controlled parts of the former princely state of Jammu and Kashmir and serves as the *de facto* border. Council on Foreign Relations, 'Global Conflict Tracker: Conflict between India and Pakistan', https://www.cfr.org/global-conflict-tracker/conflict/conflict-between-india-and-pakistan (accessed 30 June 2021).

155. In 2000, the two countries signed a Declaration of Strategic Partnership that formalised their cooperation in the military field. Originally, the Indo-Russian strategic partnership has been built on five major components: politics, defence, civil nuclear energy, anti-terrorism co-operation and space. However, more recently, an additional economic component has grown in importance. M.B. Alam, 'Contextualising India-Russia Relations', *World Affairs: The Journal of International Issues* 23(1), pp. 53.

156. Two-way trade between the longstanding economic and strategic rivals stood at $77.7 billion last year. The root cause is an ill-defined, 3,440km-long disputed border, which has led to many armed clashes over the years. See Karthikeyan Sundaram and Archana Chaudhary, 'China Back as India's Top Trade Partner even as Relations Sour', *Economic Times*, 23 February 2021.

157. Indonesia's population was 270.6 million people as of 2019. World Bank, 'Population, Total: Indonesia', https://data.worldbank.org/indicator/SP .POP.TOTL?locations=ID (accessed 30 June 2021).

158. Indonesia has about 1,340 recognised ethnic groups. Statistics Indonesia, 'Mengulik Data Suku di Indonesia' (Analysis of Tribal Data in Indonesia), https://www.bps.go.id/news/2015/11/18/127/mengulik -data-suku-di-indonesia.html (accessed 29 July 2021).

159. Most hospitals are in urban areas. Moreover, according to data from the World Bank, in Indonesia, in 2019, there were 0.5 physicians per 1,000 people and 3.8 nurses and midwives per 1,000 people. In 2019, however, the country put in place the largest system of universal health care in the world. World Bank, 'Physicians (per 1,000 people) – Indonesia', https://data.worldbank.org/indicator/SH.MED.PHYS.ZS?locations=ID (accessed 13 January 2022); World Bank, 'Nurses and Midwives (per 1,000 people) – Indonesia', https://data.worldbank.org/indicator/ SH.MED.NUMW.P3?locations=ID (accessed 13 January 2022); I.N. Sutarsa, A.W. Prastyani and R. Al Adawiyah, 'Raising National Health Insurance Premiums Doesn't Solve Indonesia's Health-Care Problems: This Is What Needs to Be Done', *The Conversation*, 11 June 2020.

160. New cases of HIV in Indonesia have risen from 7,000 per year in 2006 to 48,000 per year in 2017, giving rise to one of the world's fastest-growing HIV epidemics. P. Riono and S.J. Challacombe, 'HIV in Indonesia and in Neighbouring Countries and Its Social Impact', *Oral Diseases* 26, no. S1 (30 August 2020), pp. 28–33; G. Cairns, 'Indonesia: Tackling HIV in One of the World's Fastest Growing Epidemics', Aidsmap, 4 September 2018; M. Fox, 'Dengue: Modified Mosquitoes Reduce Dengue Cases by 77% in Indonesia Experiment', CNN, 10 June 2021.

161. Since riots that brought down long-time dictator Suharto, Indonesia has become a democracy. More power has been given to local governments and direct presidential elections were held for the first time in 2004. K. Evans, 'Guide to the 2019 Indonesia Elections', Australia Indonesia Center, 2019, http://australiaindonesiacentre.org/wp-content /uploads/2019/08/Guide-to-the-2019-Presidential-Elections-Kevin -Evans.pdf; S.D. Harijanti and T. Lindsey, 'Indonesia: General Elections Test the Amended Constitution and the New Constitutional Court', *International Journal of Constitutional Law* 4, no. 1 (2006.

162. The Executive Summary of the US Department of State '2020 Country Reports on Human Rights Practices: Indonesia' states that 'significant human rights issues included: unlawful or arbitrary killings; reports of torture by police; arbitrary arrest or detention; political prisoners; restrictions on free expression, the press, and the internet, including censorship and the existence of criminal libel laws; interference with the freedom of peaceful assembly; serious acts of corruption; lack of investigation of and accountability for violence against women; crimes involving violence or threats of violence against lesbian, gay, bisexual, transgender, and intersex persons; and the existence of laws criminalizing consensual same-sex sexual conduct between adults'. Amnesty International, 'Indonesia 2020', https://www.amnesty.org/en/countries/asia-and-the-pacific/indonesia/report-indonesia (accessed 30 June 2021); US Department of State, '2020 Country Reports on Human Rights Practices: Indonesia', https://www.state.gov/reports/2020-country-reports-on-human-rights-practices/Indonesia.

163. Indonesia is the only G20 member state in Southeast Asia and has the largest economy in the region. It is classified as a newly industrialised country. According to a 2021 estimate, it is the world's sixteenth-largest economy by nominal GDP. World Bank, 'GDP Growth: Indonesia', https://data.worldbank.org/indicator/NY.GDP.MKTP.KD.ZG?locations=ID (accessed 30 June 2021).

164. T. Wijaya and S. Nursamsu, 'The Trouble with Indonesia's Infrastructure Obsession', *The Diplomat*, 9 January 2020.

165. According to the International Energy Agency, Indonesia was the world's tenth-largest natural gas producer in 2009. It was one of the top oil exporters in the 1990s, but has seen a significant decline over the past few years. International Energy Agency, , *Key World Energy Statistics 2010* (Paris: OECD Publishing, 2010); F. Ungku, 'Indonesia's New Law to Take Years to Reverse Oil and Gas Output Slump', Reuters, 24 February 2020.

166. World Atlas, 'How Many Islands Are There in Indonesia?', https://www.worldatlas.com/articles/how-many-islands-does-indonesia-have.html (accessed 9 August 2021).

167. Indonesia's large and growing population and rapid industrialisation are giving rise to serious environmental issues, which are often given a low priority. These issues include the destruction of peatlands, large-scale illegal deforestation (causing extensive haze across parts of Southeast Asia), over-exploitation of marine resources, air pollution, garbage management, and reliable water and wastewater services, which all contribute to Indonesia's low ranking in the 2020 Environmental Performance Index. The country is one of the world's major CO_2

emitters. Yale University, '2020 Environmental Performance Index: Country Profile: Indonesia', 9 June 2020, https://epi.yale.edu/sites /default/files/files/IDN_EPI2020_CP.pdf; H. Ritchie and M. Roser, 'Indonesia: CO_2 Country Profile', Our World in Data, https:// ourworldindata.org/co2/country/indonesia (accessed 30 June 2021).

168. The government spends about 3.6 per cent of GDP (2015) on education. The decentralisation reforms in the post-Suharto era, however, have affected education financing. Local governments, and no longer the central government, are now responsible for education expenses, which has led to wide discrepancies between poorer and wealthier regions. UNESCO Institute of Statistics, 'Indonesia', http://uis.unesco.org/en /country/id (accessed 10 August 2021); World Bank, 'Literacy Rate: Indonesia', https://data.worldbank.org/indicator/SE.ADT.LITR .ZS?locations=ID (accessed 30 June 2021); A. Rosser, 'Beyond Access: Making Indonesia's Education System Work', Lowy Institute for International Policy, 21 February 2018.

169. Many graduates from Indonesia's leading universities find themselves ill-prepared to enter the job market or have to take on jobs that do not match their skills and education. Matching university curricula with skills requirements in the job market will be necessary to improve the situation. International Labour Organisation, 'Bridging Indonesia's Skills Gap through Partnership between Industry – Vocational Education and Training', 26 June 2019.

170. Indonesian troops have regularly been implicated in the mistreatment of civilians in the two restless provinces of Papua and Aceh. S. Widianto, 'Indonesian Military Says Troops Suspected of Killing 2 Papuan Civilians', Reuters, 14 July 2021.

171. Global Security, 'Indonesia: Foreign Relations', https://www.global security.org/military/world/indonesia/forrel.htm (accessed 30 June 2021).

172. Indonesia, a secular state with a Muslim majority, is a member of the Organisation of the Islamic Conference but counts itself as a moderate Islamic country that maintains ties with Israel. M.Z. Rakhmat, 'The Quiet Growth in Indonesia-Israel Relations', *The Diplomat*, 11 March 2015.

173. According to a 2019 estimate, 24.6 per cent of Iranians are under fifteen years of age. Today, the fertility rate has dropped to 2.1 children per woman. World Bank, 'Population Ages 0–14: Iran', https://data .worldbank.org/indicator/SP.POP.0014.TO.ZS?locations=IR (accessed 30 June 2021); World Bank, 'Fertility Rate: Iran, Islamic Rep.', accessed 30 June 2021, https://data.worldbank.org/indicator/SP.DYN.TFRT. IN?locations=IR (accessed 30 June 2021).

174. Although Iran has not yet fully achieved universal health coverage, health care is recognised as a constitutional right in Iran and is largely free, with the government increasing its health-care expenditure to 8.7 per cent out of a GDP of $1.64 trillion by 2017. I.L. Graticola, '8 Facts

about Healthcare in Iran', The Borgen Project, 1 October 2020; L.
Doshmangir *et al.*, 'Iran Health Insurance System in Transition: Equity
Concerns and Steps to Achieve Universal Health Coverage',
International Journal for Equity in Health, 20 (2021), pp. 1–14.

175. Iran has high levels of consumption of opium derivatives and other
addictive substances. A.A. Noorbala *et al.*, 'Evaluation of Drug and
Alcohol Abuse in People Aged 15 Years and Older in Iran', *Iranian
Journal of Public Health* 49, no. 10 (2020), pp. 1940–46, https://doi
.org/10.18502/ijph.v49i10.4697.

176. *Arab Times*, 'Poor Infrastructure an Obstacle to Development in Iran
Football', 22 December 2020.

177. Although reformists won the 2020 elections, new elections in 2021 put
in place hard-line conservative Ebrahim Raisi, a staunch opponent of
Western values. P. Wintour, 'Raisi's Election Victory Raises Difficulties
as Iran Nuclear Deal Talks Resume', *The Guardian*, 20 June 2021.

178. Amnesty International, 'Iran 2020', https://www.amnesty.org/en
/countries/middle-east-and-north-africa/iran/report-iran; Human Rights
Watch, 'World Report 2021: Iran – Events of 2020', https://www.hrw.org
/world-report/2021/country-chapters/iran (accessed 20 July 2021).

179. Iran had a GDP of about US$454 billion in 2018. Economic sanctions
against the country, however, such as the embargo against Iranian crude
oil, have systematically injured its economy. Since 1979, the US and other
countries have applied various economic, trade, scientific and military
sanctions against Iran, most often using UNSC resolutions as a legal
basis. In 2015, an agreement was reached between Iran and the UN's five
permanent members for a framework, the so-called 'nuclear deal' that,
once finalised and implemented, would lift most of the sanctions in
exchange for limits on Iran's nuclear programmes, extending for at least
ten years. In 2018, however, the US withdrew from the agreement and
numerous sanctions were reinstated. World Bank, 'GDP: Iran', https://
data.worldbank.org/indicator/NY.GDP.MKTP.CD?locations=IR
(accessed 30 June 2021); K. Robinson, 'What Is the Iran Nuclear Deal?',
Council on Foreign Relations, Backgrounder, 18 August 2021.

180. In 2020, the unemployment rate stood at eleven per cent. The main
causes of the high unemployment rate are rapid population growth and
restrictive labour policies. The lowering of the minimum wage has
enabled the decrease in unemployment, despite economic stagnation.
Statista, 'Iran: Unemployment Rate from 1999 to 2020', https://www
.statista.com/statistics/294305/iran-unemployment-rate (accessed 30
June 2021); S. Rajabi, 'Unemployment in Iran a Problem with Political
and Social Dimensions', *Iran Focus*, 17 May 2021.

181. Iran is an 'energy superpower' and is second in the world for natural gas
reserves and fourth for proven crude oil reserves. The economy is
centred primarily on its hydrocarbon, agricultural and service sectors,
as well as a noticeable state presence in the manufacturing and financial

services. Although Iran is relatively diversified for an oil-exporting country, economic activity and government revenues still rely on oil revenues and have, therefore, been volatile. A comprehensive strategy of market-based reforms was adopted by the government for its 20-year economic vision and five-year development plan for the years 2016/17 to 2021/22. This is based on three pillars: the development of a resilient economy, progress in science and technology and the promotion of cultural excellence. The reform of state-owned enterprises and of the financial and banking sectors, and the allocation and management of oil revenues are all considered to be priorities. World Bank, 'Islamic Republic of Iran', 30 March 2021, https://www.worldbank.org/en /country/iran/overview; US Congress, *Energy and the Iranian Economy: Hearing before the Joint Economic Committee*, Senate Hearing 109–720, 25 July 2006 (Washington, DC: US Government Printing Office, 2007.

182. The US sanctions in 2018 triggered inflation. World Bank, 'Islamic Republic of Iran'.

183. I. Emadodin, T. Reinsch and F. Taube, 'Drought and Desertification in Iran', *Hydrology* 6, no. 3 (2019), p. 66; M.T. Sheykhi, 'Population Surge Threatens Water Supply in Iran', Water World, 1 April 2003.

184. J.P. Rafferty, '9 of the Biggest Oil Spills in History', Encyclopedia Britannica, https://www.britannica.com/list/9-of-the-biggest-oil-spills-in-history; World Bank, 'Islamic Republic of Iran'.

185. The December 2003 earthquake in the city of Bam killed about 26,000 people, for instance. C.S. Oliveira *et al.*, *Assessing and Managing Earthquake Risk: Geo-scientific and Engineering Knowledge for Earthquake Risk Mitigation: Developments, Tools, Techniques* (Dordrecht, Netherlands: Springer, 2006), p. 445.

186. United Nations, 'Status of Treaties, United Nations Framework Convention on Climate Change', in United Nations Treaty Collection, https://treaties.un.org (accessed 20 November 2019).

187. G. Farjadi, A. Amini, and P. Alaedini, 'Employment of Highly Educated Labor Force', in P. Alaedini and M.R. Razavi (eds), *Industrial, Trade, and Employment Policies in Iran* (Cham: Springer, 2018), pp. 247–67.

188. Low investment in R&D. UNESCO Institute of Statistics, 'Iran (Islamic Republic of)', http://uis.unesco.org/en/country/ir?theme=science -technology-and-innovation (accessed 30 June 2021); *Financial Tribune*, 'Boosting R&D Investment Vital for Economic Growth', 18 December 2017.

189. M. Suleman, 'What's Going on at the Iran-Pakistan Border?', *The Diplomat*, 23 April 2021; A. Karami, 'Iran Struggles with Border Security', AL-Monitor, 18 February 2016.

190. The most violent protests since the 1979 revolution were those that took place in November 2019; they were brutally repressed by the government. S. Maloney, 'Iranian Protesters Strike at the Heart of the Regime's

Revolutionary Legitimacy', Brookings Institution, 19 November 2019; Amnesty International, 'Iran: More Than 100 Protesters Believed to Be Killed as Top Officials Give Green Light to Crush Protests', 19 November 2019; F. Fassihi and R. Gladstone, 'With Brutal Crackdown, Iran Is Convulsed by Worst Unrest in 40 Years', *New York Times*, 3 December 2019.

191. With some 523,000 active-duty forces and another 350,000 reserves, Iran has the largest standing military in the Middle East. Iran's defence budget in 2018 was more than US$13 billion, behind regional foes such as Saudi Arabia, which spent some US$70 billion, and Israel, at US$18.5 billion, and far behind the United States, which spent more than $700 billion. Its large tank force is, however, mostly made up of older and completely outdated models. D. Stavljanin and P. Baumgartner, 'Persian Might: How Strong Is Iran's Military?', Radio Free Europe, 9 January 2020; US Department of Defense, 'Iran Military Power Report Statement', 19 November 2019, https://www.defense.gov/Newsroom /Releases/Release/Article/2021009/iran-military-power-report-statement; Center for Strategic and International Studies, 'Iran's Military and Nuclear Capabilities', https://www.csis.org/programs/burke-chair -strategy/iran/irans-military-and-nuclear-capabilities (accessed 30 June 2021).

192. On 3 January 2020, the Revolutionary Guard General Qasem Soleimani was assassinated by the United States in Iraq, which considerably heightened the existing tensions between the two countries. C. Clary and C. Talmadge, 'The US-Iran Crisis Has Calmed Down – But Things Won't Ever Go Back to How They Were Before', Brookings Institution, 17 January 2020; Council on Foreign Relations, 'US Relations with Iran, 1953–2021', https://www.cfr.org/timeline/us-relations-iran-1953-2021 (accessed 30 June 2021).

193. Iran supplies these militias with missiles and drones. Feierstein, 'Iran's Role in Yemen and Prospects for Peace'; Feltman, 'Hezbollah: Iran's Most Successful Export'; D. Kenner, 'Why Israel Fears Iran's Presence in Syria?', *The Atlantic*, 22 July 2018.

194. US Congressional Research Service, 'Iran's Foreign and Defense Policies', 11 January 2021, pp. 2–4.

195. Not much has changed in the Iranian system since the revolution in 1979. Although progress has been made, the country has never moved past the revolution to adopt the characteristics of a traditional state. M. Fisher, 'Iran's System Keeps Its Grip, Despite the Chaos (or Because of It)', *New York Times*, 20 June 2021; A. Fathollah-Nejad, 'Four Decades Later, Did the Iranian Revolution Fulfil Its Promises?', Brookings Institution, 11 July 2019.

196. M. Kabalan, 'Sectarian Conflicts in the Middle East Can Be Resolved', Al Jazeera, 10 October 2018.

197. Iran has a strong commitment to the Organisation of Islamic Cooperation (OIC) and the Non-Aligned Movement. Organisation of Islamic Cooperation, 'Member States', https://www.oic-oci.org/states /?lan=en (accessed 30 June 2021); P. Jacomino, 'Iranian President Says Non-Aligned Movement States Must Unite against Unilateralism', Radio Havana Cuba, 8 February 2017, https://www.radiohc.cu/pt/noticias /internacionales/120997-iranian-president-says-non-aligned-movement -states-must-unite-against-unilateralism.

198. Iran has observer status in the Shanghai Cooperation Organization and aspires to membership of this body. It is an ally and supporter of China. J.M. Dorsey, 'Iran Signals Membership of China's Shanghai Cooperation Organization', *Arabian Post*.

199. Council on Foreign Relations, 'US Relations with Iran'.

200. A. Vatanka, 'Russia, Iran, and Economic Integration on the Caspian', *Middle East Institute*, 17 August 2020; A. Khoshnood, 'Iran-Russia Ties: Never Better but Maybe Not Forever?', *Middle East Institute*, 12 February 2020.

201. *Middle East Monitor*, 'Ex-adviser to UAE Crown Prince Compares Iran's "Occupation" of Gulf Islands to Israel Occupation', 5 January 2021.

202. Statistica, 'Israel: Total Population from 2016 to 2026', https://www .statista.com/statistics/526560/total-population-of-israel (accessed 30 June 2021); Jewish Virtual Library, 'Vital Statistics: Latest Population Statistics for Israel (2020)', https://www.jewishvirtuallibrary.org /latest-population-statistics-for-israel.

203. The largest minority is that of Palestinian Arabs, who comprise 21.1 per cent of the population in early 2021. Since Israel derives its identity from its Jewishness, however, it is difficult for Arab citizens to fit into the country's cultural and political mainstream. They also suffer from official discrimination. Arab communities in Israel receive fewer state resources, and poor communities do not receive sufficient development aid. Public schools for Israeli Arabs remain underfunded. Moreover, Israeli Arabs are underrepresented in the public sector. Jewish Virtual Library, 'Vital Statistics: Latest Population Statistics for Israel'; Amnesty International, 'Israel and Occupied Palestinian Territories 2020', https:// www.amnesty.org/en/location/middle-east-and-north-africa/israel-and -occupied-palestinian-territories/report-israel-and-occupied-palestinian -territories/ (accessed 12 January 2022); Human Rights Watch, 'Israel: Discriminatory Land Policies Hem in Palestinians', 12 May 2020; R. Al Sanah, J. Bsoul and T. Habjouqa, '"The Illusion of Citizenship Has Gone": Israel's Arabs Look to the Future', *The Economist*, 19 May 2021.

204. D. Sheen, 'Black Lives Do Not Matter in Israel', Al Jazeera, 29 March 2018; J. Marlowe, 'Israel's Mizrahi Activists Are Fighting the Racist Nation-State Law', *The Nation*, 27 May 2021.

205. Elections over the past couple of decades repeatedly led to unstable coalition governments dominated by right-wing conservative parties. R. Eglash, 'After Three Elections and Political Deadlock, Israel Finally

Swears in New Government', *Washington Post*, 17 May 2020; M. Elsana, 'Historic Change: Arab Political Parties Are Now Legitimate Partners in Israel's Politics and Government', *The Conversation*, 11 June 2021; O. Holmes, 'New Israeli Coalition Government Seeks to Put an End to Netanyahu Era', *The Guardian*, 12 June 2021; O. Holmes, 'Israeli Coalition Ousts Netanyahu as Prime Minister after 12 Years', *The Guardian*, 13 June 2021.

206. L. Beehner, 'Israel and the Doctrine of Proportionality', Council on Foreign Relations, Backgrounder, 13 July 2006.

207. In 2019, Israel had a GDP of US$394.7 and ranked twentieth in the 2018 Global Competitiveness Index. Leading exports include machinery and equipment, software, cut diamonds, agricultural products, chemicals, and textiles and apparel, which reached a total of US$60.6 billion. In 2019, high-tech products made up 23 per cent of Israeli manufactured exports. World Bank, 'GDP: Israel', https://data.worldbank.org/indicator /TX.VAL.TECH.MF.ZS?locations=IL (accessed 30 June 2021); World Bank, 'High-Technology Exports: Israel', https://data.worldbank.org /indicator/NY.GDP.MKTP.CD?locations=IL (accessed 30 June 2021); Schwab (ed.), *The Global Competitiveness Report 2018*; US Central Intelligence Agency, 'Israel', *The World Factbook*, updated 5 November 2021, https://www.cia.gov/the-world-factbook/countries /israel; Observatory of Economic Complexity, 'Israel: Exports', OEC World, https://oec.world/en/profile/country/isr (accessed 30 June 2021).

208. The Oslo peace process in the 1990s gave Israel a remarkable economic boost. Its export market became bigger as more countries loosened restrictions on Israeli imports, and Israel was able to attract large amounts of foreign investment. Since joining the OECD in 2010, Israel's economy has consistently been growing faster than that of the other member states. This growth has been unequal, however, and has left sectors of the population as well as businesses behind. C. Springfield, 'Accounting for Israel's Economic Boom', *International Banker*, 6 June 2018; S. Solomon, 'From 1950s Rationing to Modern High-Tech Boom: Israel's Economic Success Story', *Times of Israel*, 18 April 2018; E. Halon, 'Israel's Economic Growth Has Left Most People Behind: Study', *Jerusalem Post*, 20 February 2020, https://www.jpost.com/israel-news /israels-economic-growth-has-left-most-people-behind-618152.

209. In 2019, Israel had the highest military expenditure per capita in the world. Tian *et al.*, *Trends in World Military Expenditure, 2019*, p. 3.

210. Water used to be the most pressing environmental issue for Israel. Resources are limited, while demand by a growing population and growing industry is rising. Some of Israel's water sources have also become seriously polluted by agricultural fertilisers and industrial waste. Through the use of technologies and water management strategies, however, Israel is becoming a 'water superpower' in the Middle East. P. Marin *et al.*, *Water Management in Israel: Key*

Innovations and Lessons Learned for Water Scarce Countries, Water Global Practice Technical Paper (Washington, DC: World Bank, 2017), pp. 17–32; D. Fisch, 'Israel's Environmental Problems', *Palestine-Israel Journal of Politics, Economics and Culture* 5, no. 1 (1998); A. Rosenbaum, 'Is Israel's Scarcity of Water a Blessing in Disguise?', *Jerusalem Post*, 7 January 2021; M. Weiss, 'How Israel Used Desalination to Address Its Water Shortage', *Irish Times*, 18 July 2019.

211. Industrial development and rapid population growth have taken their toll on Israel's environment. Deforestation, the disappearance of natural habitats, natural-resource scarcity and industrial pollution are common problems in modern Israel. D. Ben-Shaul, 'Israel Environment and Nature: Environmental Issues', Jewish Virtual Library, https://www .jewishvirtuallibrary.org/environmental-issues-in-israel (accessed 30 June 2021).

212. UNESCO Institute of Statistics, 'Israel', http://uis.unesco.org/en /country/il (accessed 30 June 2021); OECD, 'Israel', https://gpseducation .oecd.org/CountryProfile?primaryCountry=ISR&treshold=10&topic =EO (accessed 30 June 2021).

213. Jewish Virtual Library, 'Education in Israel: Adult Education', https:// www.jewishvirtuallibrary.org/adult-education-in-israel (accessed 30 June 2021).

214. Overall, Israel has a highly skilled population. Its booming tech sectors do, however, suffer from a lack of skilled workers, leading Israeli companies to fill these jobs with migrant labour. Israel has the highest fertility rate of all OECD countries. Nowadays, nearly 30 per cent of the population in Israel is under fifteen years of age, which is far above the European average, for example. Meanwhile, while the number of older people will grow, they will not make up as high a proportion of the total population as in other industrialised countries. OECD, 'OECD Job Strategy: Israel', https://www.oecd.org/israel/jobs-strategy-ISRAEL-EN. pdf (accessed 30 June 2021); L. Tress, 'High Tech Workforce Growing but Lacks Skilled Employees, Report Says', *Times of Israel*, 27 February 2020; *Jerusalem Post*, 'Israel Has a Lot of Children. Is This a Problem and What Should We Do?', 10 March 2021; Population Reference Bureau, 'Israel's Demography Has a Unique History', 9 January 2014.

215. Compared to Europe, for instance, the percentage of migrants in Israel who have completed education and possess university degrees is significantly higher. A. Razin, 'Israel's Immigration Story: Winners and Losers', National Bureau of Economic Research, Working Paper no. 24283, February 2018, pp. 10–12.

216. At 4.95 per cent of its GDP in 2018, Israel that year spent the highest percentage of GDP in the world on research and development, most of which went into computer systems, cybersecurity, AI and medical research. It also has one of the highest number of start-ups in the world. World Bank, 'R&D Expenditure: Israel', https://data.worldbank.org

/indicator/GB.XPD.RSDV.GD.ZS?locations=IL (accessed 30 June 2021); *Financial Times*, 'How Israel Is Leading the World in R&D', 8 February 2017; T. Beeri, 'Start-Up Nation: Israel Spends Most Money in the World on R&D – World Economic Forum', *Jerusalem Post*, 5 November 2020.

217. Most countries agree that Israel has occupied the West Bank, including East Jerusalem, and the Gaza Strip since the end of the Six-Day War in 1967. Today, as a result of the Oslo Accords, direct authority over the West Bank is formally divided between Israel and the Palestinian Authority. In practice, however, Israel retains essential control over the entire territory. The Gaza Strip saw the withdrawal of the Israeli ground forces in 2005, as part of a unilateral disengagement plan. Nonetheless, Israel continues to be recognised as the occupying power in the Gaza strip due to the degree of control it continues to exercise over the territory. Geneva Academy RULAC online portal, 'Military Occupation of Palestine by Israel', last updated 19 May 2021, https://www.rulac.org/browse/conflicts/military-occupation-of-palestine-by-israel#collapse 1accord.

218. In 2019, the United States provided Israel with US$3.8 billion in military aid. J.M. Sharp, 'US Foreign Aid to Israel', US Congressional Research Service, updated 16 November 2020.

219. Israel neither denies nor confirms possession of nuclear weapons, but it is estimated that Israel possesses about 80 to 400 nuclear warheads. It is not a signatory to the Nuclear Non-Proliferation Treaty and is theoretically free to develop nuclear weapons. By remaining ambiguous about its status, Israel can deter possible aggressors without the imposition of sanctions by the international community, which is unable to provide full proof of Israel's nuclear weapons programme. Many experts agree, however, that Israel's nuclear ambitions have triggered the proliferation of chemical, biological and possibly nuclear weapons programmes in several Middle Eastern countries. In principle, Israel supports the vision of a nuclear-free Middle East but only after 'comprehensive security' has been achieved and WMD programmes in Arab states have been fully dismantled. H.M. Kristensen and R.S. Norris, 'Israeli Nuclear Weapons, 2014', *Bulletin of the Atomic Scientists* 70, no. 6 (2014), pp. 97–115; Arms Control Association, 'Nuclear Weapons: Who Has What at a Glance', October 2021, https://www.armscontrol.org/factsheets/Nuclear weaponswhohaswhat;.

220. In May 2021, amidst rising tensions, a new Israel-Palestine crisis flared up, with protests in Israel that escalated into rocket attacks from Gaza and airstrikes by Israel. The reciprocal attacks were halted following a ceasefire requested by the UNSC. A positive resolution of the decades-long conflict seems unlikely, however. Some experts suggest that the two-state solution is losing traction, due to Israeli territorial annexations

and the recent clashes. Internal political divisions within Palestine also remain a challenge to peaceful negotiation. K. Robinson, 'What Is US Policy on the Israeli-Palestinian Conflict?', Council on Foreign Relations, Backgrounder, 27 May 2021; Atlantic Council, 'Experts React: What's Next after the Israel-Hamas Ceasefire?', 20 May 2021; D.J. Wilcox, 'The Israeli-Palestinian Peace Process: Lessons from Oslo', *E-International Relations*, 14 September 2020.

221. According to the Japanese Statistics Bureau, in 2018, foreigners made up only about 2.2 per cent of the population. The Japanese, long isolated from the rest of the world, share a deep-rooted sense of ethnic homogeneity and superiority. T. Jones, 'Racism in Japan: A Conversation with Anthropology Professor John G. Russell', *Tokyo Weekender*, 19 October 2020; D. Arudou, *Embedded Racism: Japan's Visible Minorities and Racial Discrimination* (Lanham, MD: Lexington Books, 2015).

222. In 2019, 91.7 per cent of the Japanese population lived in cities. Statista, 'Japan: Degree of Urbanization from 2010 to 2020', https://www.statista .com/statistics/270086/urbanization-in-japan (accessed 30 June 2021); Trading Economics, 'Japan: Employment in Agriculture', https:// tradingeconomics.com/japan/employment-in-agriculture-percent-of -total-employment-wb-data.html (accessed 30 June 2021).

223. Overall life expectancy in Japan was nearly 84.4 years in 2019. A diet rich in fish and rice is seen as a contributing factor for this long life expectancy. World Bank, 'Life Expectancy at Birth, Total (Years) – Japan', https://data.worldbank.org/indicator/SP.DYN.LE00.IN?locations=JP (accessed 30 June 2021); S. Tsugane, 'Why Has Japan Become the World's Most Long-Lived Country: Insights from a Food and Nutrition Perspective', *European Journal of Clinical Nutrition* 75 (2021), pp. 921–28.

224. Japan has had universal health coverage for sixty years. The health-care system is in large part financed by insurance premiums, subsidised by public funds. World Bank, 'Universal Health Coverage for Inclusive and Sustainable Development', https://www.worldbank.org/en/topic/health /publication/universal-health-coverage-for-inclusive-sustainable -development (accessed 30 June 2021).

225. The Liberal Democratic Party has ruled the country for most of the post-war era, either on its own or as part of a coalition. Yoshihide Suga succeeded Shinzo Abe as prime minister in 2020 in the most recent government to be led by the party. See M. Solis, 'Japan's Democratic Renewal and the Survival of the Liberal Order', Brookings Institution, 22 January 2021.

226. According to a 2018 poll conducted in Japan by the Pew Research Center, 62 per cent of the population believe that no matter who wins, the situation in Japan will not change significantly. Japan's democracy suffers from political disengagement, however. In 2017, voter turnout stood at only 53.7 per cent. The democracy index compiled by the

Economist Intelligence Unit captures this lack of vitality of the Japanese democracy. Although in 2019, Japan ranked number 24, with high marks on electoral process, pluralism, and civil liberties, it had low scores in the categories of political participation and culture. This latter indicator also measures citizen engagement in politics and the number of female politicians, which are both weak spots for Japan. See Solis, 'Japan's Democratic Renewal'; *Economist* Intelligence Unit, 'Democracy Index 2020: In Sickness and in Health?'.

227. With a GDP of over US$5 trillion in 2020, Japan's economy is third in size globally, behind only the US and China. Statista, 'Japan GDP in Current Prices from 1986 to 2006', https://www.statista.com /statistics/263578/gross-domestic-product-gdp-of-japan (accessed 30 June 2021); World Bank, 'GDP: Japan', https://data.worldbank.org /indicator/NY.GDP.MKTP.CD?locations=JP (accessed 30 June 2021).

228. AFE East Asia, Columbia University, 'Economy and Trade Factsheet: Basic Points about Japan's Economy and Trading Patterns', http://afe .easia.columbia.edu/japan/japanworkbook/economics/factshe.htm (accessed 30 June 2021).

229. V. Argy and L. Stein, *The Japanese Economy* (London: Palgrave Macmillan, 1997), pp. 57–72.

230. In 2020, Japan had a low unemployment rate of around 2.4 per cent and, in 2019, its labour force consisted of 67 million workers. In 2018, however, around 15.4 per cent of the population was living below the poverty line. At more than a thousand trillion yen, Japan has the highest ratio of public debt to GDP than any other country, with national debt at 256 per cent relative to GDP as of 2020. Statista, 'Poverty Rate in Japan from 1991 to 2018', https://www.statista.com /statistics/1172622/japan-poverty-rate (accessed 30 June 2021); Statista, 'Japan: National Debt from 2016 to 2026 in Relation to GDP', accessed 30 June 2021, https://www.statista.com/statistics/267226/japans -national-debt-in-relation-to-gross-domestic-product-gdp (accessed 30 June 2021).

231. Japan's earthquakes are caused by at least three tectonic plates that rub against each other. Japan experiences one-fifth of the world's earthquakes. On 11 March 2011, an earthquake of 9.0 Richter-scale magnitude took place off of the north-eastern coast of Japan. It was the strongest ever recorded in the country and triggered a tsunami up to 30 metres high that washed up to five kilometres inland. Not only did this result in massive loss of life (nearly 20,000 people died), environmental devastation and infrastructural damage, but the tsunami also damaged several nuclear power plants, triggering the Fukushima nuclear disaster. UN Environment Programme, 'Great East Japan Earthquake and Tsunami', https://www.unep.org/explore-topics/disasters-conflicts /where-we-work/japan/great-east-japan-earthquake-and-tsunami (accessed 30 June 2021).

232. Kagoshima, Fukuoka, Osaka, Tokyo and Okayama all experience high levels of air pollution. The number of deaths linked to air pollution exposure has risen continuously since 2010; it reached 42.6 thousand in 2019, making Japan one of the countries with the highest number of deaths attributable to air pollution exposure. International Association for Medical Assistance to Travellers, 'Japan: Air Pollution', https://www.iamat.org/country/japan/risk/air-pollution (accessed 30 June 2021); Statista, 'Number of Deaths Attributable to Air Pollution in Japan between 2010 and 2019', https://www.statista.com/statistics/935022/number-deaths-air-pollution-japan (accessed 30 June 2021).

233. Although Japan used to have the largest science and technology industry in the world, over the past couple of decades it has faced increasing competition from states such as the US and China, among others. As of 2018, industry accounts for about 30 per cent of Japan's GDP. According to the Statistics Bureau of Japan, in 2019, the R&D expenditure share of GDP remained at 3.5 per cent. Open Access Government, 'How Can Japan Remain a World Competitor in Science and Technology?', 23 September 2020; Statista, 'Japan: Distribution of GDP across Economic Sectors from 2008 to 2018', https://www.statista.com/statistics/270093/distribution-of-gross-domestic-product-gdp-across-economic-sectors-in-japan (accessed 30 June 2021).

234. Japan consistently finishes among the first places in the OECD surveys that compare fifteen-year-olds' abilities in reading, mathematics and science. OECDevelopment, *Reviews of National Policies for Education: Education Policy in Japan: Building Bridges towards 2030* (Paris: OECD Publishing, 2018); OECD, 'Education at a Glance 2019: Japan', https://www.oecd.org/education/education-at-a-glance/EAG2019_CN_JPN.pdf.

235. Japan has a long-standing space programme and is becoming NASA's largest partner in relation to space exploration. Although traditionally Japan expressed its intentions to use space for entirely peaceful uses, the past few years have seen a shift towards the development of space capacities for defence purposes. N.V. Patel, 'Why Japan is Emerging as NASA's Most Important Space Partner', *MIT Technology Review*, 22 July 2020; A. Vijayakumar, 'Japan's Rise as a Space Power', *Japan Times*, 28 January 2020; L. Fatton, 'Is Japan Entering the New Space Race?,' *East Asia Forum*, 20 February 2020.

236. In addition, the constitution limits defence expenditure to one per cent of GDP. In 2021, however, the ruling party expressed the intention to scrap that limit and increase military spending. The country maintains a small self-defence force. *Encyclopedia Britannica*, 'Self-Defense Force: Japanese Armed Force', April 2011; World Bank, 'Military Expenditure: Japan', https://data.worldbank.org/indicator/MS.MIL.XPND.GD.ZS?locations=JP (accessed 30 June 2021); J. Kobara, 'Japan to Scrap 1% GDP Cap on Defense Spending: Minister Kishi', Nikkei Asia, 20 May 2021.

237. Since the end of the Cold War, some Japanese have been starting to doubt US determination to continue to guarantee Japanese security and have been calling for a stronger national defence force. This desire for stronger defence capabilities has increased over the past couple of decades due to the growing military power of China and North Korea. Ministry of Foreign Affairs of Japan, 'Japan-US Security Treaty', https://www.mofa.go.jp/region/n-america/us/q&a/ref/1.html (accessed 30 June 2021); L. Maizland and B. Xu, 'The US-Japan Security Alliance', Council on Foreign Relations, Backgrounder, 22 August 2019.

238. Japan has several unresolved disputes over islands occupied and administered by regional Second World War enemies. A resolution of the disputes seems unlikely in the near future. These disputes could seriously poison Japan's relations with Russia, China and South Korea. R.P. Pedrozo, 'International Law and Japan's Territorial Disputes', *Review of Island Studies*, 6 February 2018; J. Ryall, 'Japan's Territorial Disputes: China, South Korea, Russia and More', *SCMP*, 26 February 2021; A. Dudden, 'Japanese Territorial Disputes and the Legacy of Empire', *Oxford Research Encyclopedia of Asian History*, 29 July 2019; Ministry of Foreign Affairs of Japan, 'Japanese Territory Q&A', https://www.mofa.go.jp/territory/page1we_000007.html (accessed 30 June 2021).

239. Japan has not done enough to apologise and compensate for the crimes it committed as an aggressor state against China and South Korea before and during the Second World War. Controversies remain about Japanese history books that ignore Japanese atrocities, as well as Japan's refusal to pay compensation for former Korean sex slaves. C.H. Park, *The Three Enduring Legacies of the Pacific War in East Asia* (Washington, DC: Wilson Center, 2020); M. Shin, 'Conflict between South Korea and Japan Surges Again with Court's "Comfort Women" Decision', *The Diplomat*, 26 January 2021; B. Stokes, 'Hostile Neighbors: China vs. Japan', Pew Research Center, 13 September 2016.

240. Donor Tracker, 'Japan', 15 July 2021, https://donortracker.org/country/japan.

241. Together with Germany, Brazil and India, Japan aspires to gain a permanent seat with veto power on the UN Security Council. Its bid has so far been unsuccessful. China opposes Japan's accession as a permanent Security Council member. C. Yang, 'Japan's Dream for UN Security Council Seat Crushed by Its Historical Mirages', *Global Times*, 26 September 2020; UN General Assembly, 'Committee on Contributions', https://www.un.org/en/ga/contributions/honourroll.shtml (accessed 30 June 2021); Ministry of Foreign Affairs of Japan, 'Japan's Foreign Policy to Promote National and Worldwide Interests', 2017, https://www.mofa.go.jp/policy/other/bluebook/2017/html/chapter3/c030105.html.

242. The population is about 60 per cent Kazakh, a quarter Russian, and includes various minorities, notably Germans and Ukrainians. Embassy of the Republic of Kazakhstan, 'Ethnic Groups', https://kazakhembus. com/about-kazakhstan/culture/ethnic-groups (accessed 30 June 2021).

243. Following the collapse of the Soviet Union, Kazakhstan lost almost two million people (mostly Russians and Germans returning to their homelands). Today, immigration is offsetting emigration. Due to its economy and to the weakening of Russia's in the wake of the 2014 Ukraine conflict, the country attracts migrants from poorer neighbouring states, especially Uzbekistan, Kyrgyzstan and Tajikistan and, to a lesser degree, Russia and China. K. Sharifzoda, 'Why Is Kazakhstan a Growing Destination for Central Asian Migrant Workers?', *The Diplomat*, 13 June 2019; S. Calderone, 'Kazakhstan is Central Asia's Migration Outlier', Eurasianet, 3 May 2018.

244. Kazakhstan is attempting to shift to a universal health-care system. A 2020 reform, the Compulsory Social and Medical Insurance programme, aims to reduce out-of-pocket expenses (the cost of care that patients are responsible for), which made up 45.14 per cent of Kazakhstan's total health spending in 2014. Nevertheless, although funding has steadily grown over the past decade, health-care financing in Kazakhstan is still very limited, making up only 3.1 per cent of its GDP in 2017, in comparison with the global average of 9.89 per cent. A.M. Vanderveen, 'Healthcare in Kazakhstan: Problems and Solutions', The Borgen Project, 17 August 2020; Official Information Source of the Prime Minister of the Republic of Kazakhstan, 'Review of Kazakhstan's Healthcare System: Results of 2020 and Plans for 2021', 1 March 2021, https://www.primeminister.kz/en/news/reviews/review-of-kazakhstans -healthcare-system-Results-of-2020-and-plans-for-20215968.

245. Life expectancy in Kazakhstan has been steadily increasing, going from 63.5 years in 1995 to nearly 73.2 in 2019. Similarly, the infant mortality rate has decreased from 44.8 per 1,000 live births in 1995 to 9.3 in 2019. According to the World Health Organization, however, although the government has adopted numerous bans to address the issue, Kazakhstan still has the highest alcohol consumption rate in Central Asia. World Bank, 'Mortality Rate: Kazakhstan', https://data.worldbank .org/indicator/SP.DYN.IMRT.IN?locations=KZ (accessed 30 June 2021); World Bank, 'Life Expectancy at Birth, Total (Years) – Kazakhstan', https://data.worldbank.org/indicator/SP.DYN.LE00.IN?locations=KZ (accessed 30 June 2021); R. Amanbekova, 'Alcohol Consumption in Central Asia', *Central Asian Bureau for Analytical Reporting*, 9 March 2020; M. Neufeld *et al.*, 'Alcohol Control Policies in Former Soviet Union Countries: A Narrative Review of Three Decades of Policy Changes and Their Apparent Effects', *Drug and Alcohol Review* 40, no. 3 (2020), pp. 350–67; HealthData, 'Kazakhstan', http://www.healthdata .org/kazakhstan (accessed 30 June 2021); International Association for

Medical Assistance to Travellers, 'Kazakhstan', https://www.iamat.org /country/kazakhstan/risk/tuberculosis (accessed 30 June 2021); A. Davis *et al.*, 'Risks for Tuberculosis in Kazakhstan: Implications for Prevention', *International Journal of Tuberculosis and Lung Disease* 21, no. 1 (2017), pp. 86–92.

246. Kazakhstan provides free anti-retroviral therapy for everyone who is infected with HIV, which has enabled it to slow down the epidemic. UNAIDS, 'Kazakhstan', https://www.unaids.org/en/regionscountries /countries/kazakhstan (accessed 30 June 2021); US Embassy and Consulate in Kazakhstan, 'Kazakhstan Has the Highest Percent of Awareness among People Living with HIV in Central Asia', https:// kz.usembassy.gov/hiv-awareness (accessed 30 June 2021); USAID, 'Eliminating HIV', 1 December 2020, https://www.usaid.gov/kazakhstan /success-stories/dec-2020-eliminating-hiv.

247. Kazakhstan is a democratic, secular, constitutional, unitary republic. It was led by Nursultan Nazarbayev from 1991 to 2019. When he resigned, he was succeeded by Kassym-Jomart Tokayev. The president has the power to veto legislation that has been passed by the parliament and leads the armed forces. BBC News, 'Kazakh Leader Resigns after Three Decades', 19 March 2019; O. Auyezov, 'Kazakhstan's Leader Nazarbayev Resigns after Three Decades in Power', *U.S. News*, 19 March 2019, https://www.usnews.com/news/world/articles/2019-03-19/president-of -kazakhstan-nursultan-nazarbayev-resigns.

248. In the December 2005 elections, incumbent President Nursultan Nazarbayev (in office since 1990) won another seven-year term, receiving 90 per cent of the popular vote. OSCE observers declared that the elections were seriously flawed. A 2007 parliamentary amendment removed term limits for the presidency. The ruling party has been able to render opposition parties ineffective through new parliamentary election rules such as banning electoral blocs and requiring parties to win at least seven per cent of the vote in order to win parliamentary seats. In the August 2007 parliamentary elections, Nazarbayev's Nur Otan party won all electable parliamentary seats. Although the OSCE has seen some progress in the context of the January 2021 elections, in 2020, Freedom House rated Kazakhstan as a 'consolidated authoritarian regime', on the grounds that freedom of speech is not respected and that Kazakhstan's electoral laws do not provide for free and fair elections. Organization for Security and Economic Co-operation in Europe, 'Presidential Election, 4 December 2005', https://www.osce.org/odihr /elections/kazakhstan/eoms/presidential_2005; Organization for Security and Economic Co-operation in Europe, 'Parliamentary Elections, 18 August 2007', https://www.osce.org/odihr/elections/57937 (accessed 30 June 2021); Freedom House, 'Kazakhstan: Nations in Transit 2020 Country Report', https://freedomhouse.org/country /kazakhstan/nations-transit/2020 (accessed 30 June 2021).

249. Kazakhstan has an estimated GDP of US$187.8 billion in 2021. Supported by rising oil output and prices, Kazakhstan's economy grew at an average of eight per cent per year until 2013, before suffering a slowdown in 2014 and 2015 and settling at 4.5 per cent in 2019. It was also the first former Soviet republic to repay all of its debt to the International Monetary Fund, seven years ahead of schedule. Statista, 'Kazakhstan: GDP in Current Prices from 1996 to 2026', https://www .statista.com/statistics/436143/gross-domestic-product-gdp-in- kazakhstan (accessed 30 June 2021); World Bank, 'GDP Growth: Kazakhstan', https://data.worldbank.org/indicator/NY.GDP.MKTP.KD .ZG?locations=KZ (accessed 30 June 2021); International Monetary Fund, 'IMF Executive Board Concludes 2013 Article IV Consultation with the Republic of Kazakhstan', 14 August 2013, https://www.imf.org /external/np/sec/pr/2013/pr13308.htm; US Department of State, 'Kazakhstan Profile', https://2009-2017.state.gov/outofdate/bgn /kazakhstan/47484.htm (accessed 30 June 2021).

250. Kazakhstan's rate of foreign investment was growing steadily until 2008. With the 2008–9 financial crisis, however, it plummeted. It recovered until 2016, before crashing again. World Bank, 'FDI: Kazakhstan', https://data.worldbank.org/indicator/BX.KLT.DINV.WD.GD.ZS ?locations=KZ (accessed 30 June 2021); Global Economy, 'Kazakhstan: Foreign Direct Investment', https://www.theglobaleconomy.com/ Kazakhstan/Foreign_Direct_Investment (accessed 30 June 2021).

251. From 2008 to 2017, the poverty rate decreased from twelve per cent to 2.5. Similarly, unemployment decreased from 13.5 per cent in 1999 to 4.5 per cent in 2020. Trade relations and a significant increase in GDP per capita are the main reasons for the reduction in poverty and unemployment. Statista, 'Poverty Headcount Ratio in Kazakhstan from 2007 to 2017', https://www.statista.com/statistics/818364/poverty -headcount-ratio-in-kazakhstan (accessed 30 June 2021); Statista, 'Kazakhstan: Unemployment Rate from 1999 to 2020', https://www .statista.com/statistics/436179/unemployment-rate-in-kazakhstan (accessed 30 June 2021); M. Thomas, 'Poverty in Kazakhstan Is Like a Small Business', The Borgen Project, 6 August 2020.

252. Kazakhstan has twelve per cent of the world's uranium resources and in 2009 became the world's leading uranium producer, with almost 28 per cent of world production. In 2019, Kazakhstan produced 43 per cent of the world's uranium. World Nuclear Association, 'Uranium and Nuclear Power in Kazakhstan', https://world-nuclear.org/information -library/country-profiles/countries-g-n/kazakhstan.aspx (accessed 30 June 2021).

253. A. Genova, 'This Is What Nuclear Weapons Leave in Their Wake', *National Geographic*, 28 December 2017.

254. S. Nurtazin *et al.*, 'Quality of Drinking Water in the Balkhash District of Kazakhstan's Almaty Region', *Water* 12, no. 2 (2020), pp. 1–14; G. DeLorenzo, 'Water Quality in Kazakhstan', The Borgen Project, 21 June 2017.

255. Y. Hu, Y. Han and Y. Zhang, 'Land Desertification and Its Influencing Factors in Kazakhstan', *Journal of Arid Environments* 180 (September 2020), n.p.; F. Alakbarov, 'Water-Related Pollution Matters. Just Look at the Aral Sea', *Jerusalem Post*, 12 August 2017; T. Austin Wæhler and E. Sveberg Dietrichs, 'The Vanishing Aral Sea: Health Consequences of an Environmental Disaster', *Tidsskriftet*, 3 October 2017.

256. In Kazakhstan's major cities, air pollution exceeds the WHO standards of safety and has led to an increase in associated illnesses, including up to 6,000 premature deaths each year. See OECD Green Growth Studies, *Addressing Industrial Air Pollution in Kazakhstan* (Paris: OECD Publishing, 2019).

257. Only 2.6 per cent of GDP was spent on education in 2018. World Bank, 'Government Expenditure on Education: Kazakhstan', https://data .worldbank.org/indicator/SE.XPD.TOTL.GD.ZS?locations=KZ (accessed 30 June 2021); UNESCO Institute of Statistics, 'Kazakhstan', http://uis .unesco.org/en/country/kz?theme=education-and-literacy (accessed 30 June 2021); OECD, *OECD Reviews of School Resources: Kazakhstan 2015* (Paris: OECD Publishing, 2015).

258. Despite government policies to strengthen innovation in the country, in 2018, only 0.12 per cent of GDP was spent on R&D. Insufficient funding and issues of implementation have caused these policies to fail. World Bank, 'R&D Expenditure: Kazakhstan', https://data.worldbank.org /indicator/GB.XPD.RSDV.GD.ZS?locations=KZ (accessed 14 August 2021); M. Saiymova *et al.*, 'The Knowledge-Based Economy and Innovation Policy in Kazakhstan: Looking at Key Practical Problems', *Academy of Strategic Management Journal* 17, no. 6 (2018), n.p.

259. Since it sits between the two major powers of Russia and China, Kazakhstan has adopted a foreign policy of 'multi-vector diplomacy', which has enabled it to maintain stable and good relations with both countries. R. Vanderhill, S.F. Joireman and R. Tulepbayeva, 'Between the Bear and the Dragon: Multivectorism in Kazakhstan as a Model Strategy for Secondary Powers', *International Affairs* 96, no. 4 (2020), pp. 975–93; I. Akylbayev and B.Y.S. Wong, 'What Kazakhstan Can Teach about Medium-State Diplomacy', *Foreign Policy*, 4 May 2021.

260. Although Kazakhstan's defence costs were US$1.22 billion in 2007, they only made up 1.2 per cent of its GDP, a relatively low ratio which progressively decreased to 1.06 per cent in 2019. In 2019–20, however, Kazakhstan ramped up its defence programme, on the basis of

growing regional and national security threats. Statista, 'Kazakhstan: Ratio of Military Spending to Gross Domestic Product (GDP) from 2009 to 2019', https://www.statista.com/statistics/810452/ratio-of -military-expenditure-to-gross-domestic-product-gdp-kazakhstan (accessed 30 June 2021); K. Altynbayev, 'Eyeing "Plenty of Threats", Kazakhstan Ramps up Defence Spending', *Caravanserai*, 15 May 2019; A. Ashimov, 'Kazakhstan to Modernise Armed Forces' Weaponry in Defence-Spending Plan', *Caravanserai*, 14 February 2020.

261. According to the government of Kazakhstan, the main threats to its national and regional security stem from the instability in Afghanistan and encompass terrorism, extremism, drug trafficking, transnational crime and illegal migration. Altynbayev, 'Eyeing "Plenty of Threats", Kazakhstan Ramps up Defence Spending'.

262. The two countries have had a military cooperation agreement since 1994. This was updated and strengthened in 2020. R. Rousseau, 'Kazakhstan's Strategic and Military Relations with Russia', *Diplomatic Courier*, 20 July 2011; Radio Free Europe, 'Russia, Kazakhstan Replace Decades-Old Military Cooperation Agreement', 16 October 2020; *Army Technology*, 'Russia and Kazakhstan Sign Military Cooperation Agreement', 19 October 2020.

263. A. Zhupankhan, K. Tussupova and R. Berndtsson, 'Water in Kazakhstan, a Key in Central Asian Water Management', *Hydrological Sciences Journal* 63, no. 5 (2018), pp. 752–62; New Defence Order Strategy, 'Russian-Kazakh Military Cooperation Agreement', https:// dfnc.ru/en/vtc/russian-kazakh-military-cooperation-agreement (accessed 30 June 2021).

264. N. Yau, 'Tracing the Chinese Footprints in Kazakhstan's Oil and Gas Industry', *The Diplomat*, 12 December 2020; A. Nurjanov, 'EU, Kazakhstan Intend to Deepen Energy Ties', *Caspian News*, 30 March 2021; K. Rapoza, '"Strategic Competition": US Looks to Kazakhstan to Expand Ties', *Forbes*, 25 April 2021.

265. Kazakhstan, Kyrgyzstan and Uzbekistan established the Central Asian Union in 1994; Tajikistan joined in 1998. Over the past 20 years, however, the countries have grown apart from one another. It was not until Uzbekistan's shift toward greater regional cooperation that Central Asian integration started to gain traction again. As Kazakhstan has repeatedly argued, in the face of external influences, Central Asia should be able to make its own decisions about what is best for the region, which is plagued by overlapping initiatives that are often ineffective and serve external actors' economic and political interests. J. Lee, A. Asiryan and M. Butler, 'Integration of the Central Asian Republics: The ASEAN Example', *E-International Relations*, 17 September 2020; S.F. Starr, 'Is This Central Asia's ASEAN Moment?', *The Diplomat*, 5 December 2019.

266. According to the UN, Lithuania has the second-fastest shrinking population in the world after Lebanon. The Lithuanian population in 2019 (just under 2.8 million) constituted only 74.6 per cent of what it had been in 1991. It is estimated that over the next five years, Lithuania's population will decrease at an annual rate of one per cent. High levels of emigration, low birth rates and high rates of suicide are some of the causes of the population decrease. World Bank, 'Population, Total: Lithuania', https://data.worldbank.org/indicator/SP.POP.TOTL?locations=LT (accessed 30 June 2021); European Commission, 'Lithuania: Population: Demographic Situation, Languages and Religions', 31 March 2021, https://eacea.ec.europa.eu/national-policies/eurydice/content/population -demographic-situation-languages-and-religions-44_en; J. Bakaite, 'LRT FACTS. Is Lithuania the world's fastest-shrinking country?', *LRT*, 5 October 2020.

267. The number of immigrants, especially from Belarus and Ukraine, has been increasing. For the first time in years, the number of immigrants is exceeding that of emigrants (more than 43,000 immigrants in 2020). European Commission, 'Lithuania'.

268. 28.3 per cent of the population is at risk of poverty or social exclusion, well above the EU average of 21.9 per cent. The income of the richest 20 per cent of the population is also 7.1 times higher than the income of the poorest 20 per cent, compared to 5.17 times on average across the EU. V. Budzinauskas, 'Despite Positive Changes, Social Problems Persist in Lithuania – EU Commission', *LRT*, 27 February 2021; World Inequality Database, 'Lithuania', https://wid.world/country/lithuania (accessed 30 June 2021); EAPN Lithuania, 'Poverty and Social Exclusion in Lithuania 2018', pp. 2–3; OECD, 'Lithuania Economic Snapshot: Economic Forecase Summary (May 2021)', https://www .oecd.org/economy/lithuania-economic-snapshot (accessed 22 July 2021).

269. The overall health of the Lithuanian population remains among the worst in the EU. Life expectancy at birth was 75.8 years in 2017, more than five years below the EU average (80.9 years). Lifestyle-related risk factors account for more than half of all deaths in Lithuania. Although on the decline, alcohol consumption is higher than in any other EU country. Moreover, in 2014, one in five adults reported smoking on a daily basis. In 2017, seventeen per cent of adults were obese, a higher proportion than the EU average of fifteen per cent. The country's death rate is also increasing and stood at nearly fourteen per cent in 2019. Underfunding of the health system undermines accessibility and equity, with Lithuania spending much less on health than the EU as a whole, both in absolute terms and as a share of GDP. Furthermore, only two thirds of health expenditure is publicly financed, compared with the EU average of 79 per cent. OECD/European Observatory on Health Systems and Policies, *Lithuania: Country Health Profile 2019: State of Health in*

the EU (Paris: OECD Publishing and European Observatory on Health Systems and Profiles, Brussels, 2019), p. 3; Budzinauskas, 'Despite Positive Changes, Social Problems Persist in Lithuania – EU Commission'; World Bank, 'Death Rate: Lithuania', https://data .worldbank.org/indicator/SP.DYN.CDRT.IN?locations=LT (accessed 30 June 2021).

270. A. Grigas, 'Lithuania's New Government: Women-Led Coalition Wins Confidence in Difficult Times', *Atlantic Council*, 30 October 2020.

271. Lithuania had a GDP of US$29.6 billion in 2019. It was the first country to declare independence from the Soviet Union in 1990 and, through the implementation of numerous liberal reforms, it rapidly moved from centrally planned to a market economy. The high growth rates it enjoyed after joining the European Union led to the notion of a 'Baltic Tiger'. The financial crisis in 2008–9 triggered a deep recession in the country which was successfully overcome through harsh austerity. World Bank, 'GDP: Lithuania', https://data.worldbank.org/indicator/NY.GDP.MKTP. CD?locations=LT (accessed 30 June 2021); World Bank, 'GDP Growth: Lithuania', https://data.worldbank.org/indicator/NY.GDP.MKTP.KD .ZG?locations=LT (accessed 30 June 2021); *Financial Times*, 'Lithuania Rules out Devaluation', 18 November 2009, https://www.ft.com/content /692bf806-5bef-11de-aea3-00144feabdc0.

272. The 2017 budget resulted in a 0.5 per cent surplus, with the gross debt stabilising at around 40 per cent of GDP. OECD, *OECD Economic Surveys: Lithuania 2018* (Paris: OECD Publishing, 2018).

273. Euronews, 'Lithuania Votes: Centre-Right Opposition Wins Second Round of Legislative Elections', 26 October 2020.

274. Around 95 per cent of all foreign direct investment in Lithuania comes from EU countries. Sweden is the largest investor, accounting for 20 to 30 per cent of all FDI in Lithuania. FDI into Lithuania spiked in 2017, reaching its highest-ever recorded number of green-field investment projects, making Lithuania the country with the third-highest average job value of investment projects, after Ireland and Singapore. Lietuvos Bankas Eurosistema, 'Tiesioginės užsienio investicijos Lietuvoje pagal šalį', 9 January 2018, https://web.archive.org/web/20180109194528 /https:/www.lb.lt/lt/tiesiogines-uzsienio-investicijos-lietuvoje-pagal -sali-1; J. Dencik and R. Spee, *Global Location Trends – 2018 Annual Report: Getting Ready for Globalization 4.0*, July 2018, IBM Institute for Business Value, p. 7.

275. Lithuania has the highest mortality rate from exposure to air pollution in the OECD. Transport and energy are the main sources of emissions and pollution, followed by agriculture and industry. Environmental performance has improved since the mid-2000s, however. H. Blöchliger and S. Strumskyte, 'Greening Lithuania's Growth', OECD Economics Department, Working Paper no. 1667, 23 April 2021, p. 3.

276. Ibid.

277. The fiscal stimulus package approved in March 2020, which amounts to around ten per cent of GDP, has boosted investment programmes with an environmental goal, including the Climate Action Programme. About fifteen per cent of the total is dedicated to improving energy efficiency, promoting renewable energy and enhancing the competitiveness and reliability of the energy sector. Blöchliger and Strumskyte, 'Greening Lithuania's Growth'.

278. Lithuania figures among the moderate innovators group in the International Innovation Index and ranks fifteenth among EU countries. Lasers and biotechnology are the flagship fields of the Lithuanian science and high-tech industry. The Lithuanian femtosecond laser system, Šviesos konversija (Light Conversion), has 80 per cent of market share worldwide and is used in DNA research, ophthalmological surgeries, the nanotech industry and scientific research. Similarly, the Vilnius University Laser Research Center has developed one of the most powerful femtosecond lasers in the world, used mainly to treat oncological diseases. Moreover, Lithuanian biochemist Virginijus Šikšnys is one of the inventors of the CRISPR-Cas9 gene-editing tool. Between 2011 and 2016, yearly growth of Lithuania's biotech and life science sector was 22 per cent. Lietuvos mokslo taryba (Lithuanian Science Council), 'Lietuvos ekonomikos ilgalaikio konkurencingumo iššūkiai' (Challenges to the Long-Term Competitiveness of the Lithuanian Economy), 2015, https://www.lmt.lt/data/public/uploads /2016/09/ekonomikos-moksliniu-tyrimu-programos-rekomendacijos. pdf, p. 18 ; European Commission, 'European Innovation Scoreboard 2021',21 June 2021; European Commission, 'Lithuania, a Leading Light in Laser Technology – Digital Single Market', 14 September 2012, via the Internet Archive Wayback Machine, https://web.archive.org /web/20180110175105/https:/ec.europa.eu/digital-single-market/en/news /lithuania-leading-light-laser-technology; Delfi, 'Daugiausiai inovacijų lietuviai sukūrė gyvybės mokslų srityje', 14 September 2017, https:// www.delfi.lt/partnerio-turinys/lietuvos-amziaus-inovacijos/daugiausiai -inovaciju-lietuviai-sukure-gyvybes-mokslu-srityje.d?id=75754757; Light Conversion, 'Light Conversion – About Us', 5 February 2018, http://lightcon.com/about-us.html; Delfi, 'Įgyvendinta svajonė sukėlė perversmą pasaulinėje lazerių rinkoje', 25 August 2017, https://www .delfi.lt/partnerio-turinys/lietuvos-amziaus-inovacijos/igyvendinta -svajone-sukele-perversma-pasaulineje-lazeriu-rinkoje.d?id=75532853; Delfi, 'Lietuviai sukūrė vieną galingiausių lazerių pasaulyje', 31 August 2017, https://www.delfi.lt/partnerio-turinys/lietuvos-amziaus -inovacijos/lietuviai-sukure-viena-galingiausiu-lazeriu-pasaulyje .d?id=75607431; G. Guglielmi, 'Million-Dollar Kavli Prize Recognizes Scientist Scooped on CRISPR', *Nature*, updated 4 June 2018; Flanders Investment and Trade Market Survey, 'Life Science and Biotech Industry in Lithuania', December 2016, p. 2.

279. Republic of Lithuania, 'Programme of the Eighteenth Government of the Republic of Lithuania', Resolution no. XIV-72, 11 December 2020.

280. In 2019, 55 per cent of 25 to 34 year-olds had a tertiary degree in Lithuania, as compared to the OECD average of 45 per cent. In 2017, however, Lithuania only invested a total of US$6,652 per student compared to the US$11,231 OECD average. This represents only 3.4 per cent of GDP, below the OECD 4.9 per cent average. UNESCO Institute of Statistics, 'Lithuania', http://uis.unesco.org/country/LT (accessed 30 June 2021); T. Franco, 'Education in Lithuania', The Borgen Project, 8 November 2017; OECD, 'Education GPS: Lithuania', 2020, https://gpseducation.oecd.org/CountryProfile?primaryCountry=LTU&treshold=10&topic=EO.

281. Grigas, 'Lithuania's New Government'.

282. Ministry of National Defence, Republic of Lithuania, 'Lithuanian Armed Forces Continue Contributing to International Operations', 23 January 2021, https://kam.lt/en/news_1098/current_issues/lithuanian_armed_forces_continue_contributing_to_international_operations.html.

283. World Bank, 'Military Expenditure (% of GDP), Lithuania, 1993–2019', https://data.worldbank.org/indicator/MS.MIL.XPND.GD.ZS?locations=LT (accessed 30 June 2021).

284. Ministry of National Defence, Republic of Lithuania, 'NATO', https://kam.lt/en/international_cooperation_1089/nato_1282.html (accessed 30 June 2021).

285. The NATO Energy Security Centre of Excellence is located in Vilnius, Lithuania. NATO Energy Security, 'Centres of Excellence', https://enseccoe.org/en/about/6 (accessed 30 June 2021).

286. Lithuania is one of the countries in the Baltic region most critical of Belarus and has offered refuge to many of its political dissidents. Tensions between the two countries are on the rise in mid-2021, not only because of the arrest of Belarusian journalist Raman Pratasevich through the forced landing in Belarus of a plane en route to Lithuania by Belarusian forces, but also because of an influx of illegal immigrants, which Lithuania claims Belarus is deliberately redirecting into its territory. Following Pratasevich's arrest, the Lithuanian government took a leadership role in establishing sanctions against Belarus. T. Wesolowsky, 'Lithuania Says Lukashenka Is Flooding Baltic State's Border with Migrants', Radio Free Europe, 18 June 2021; *Baltic Times*, 'EU to Discuss Serious Sanctions Unless Minsk Releases Pratasevich – Lithuanian President', 24 May 2021; L. Harding and A. Roth, 'Raman Pratasevich: The Belarus Journalist Captured by a Fighter Jet', *The Guardian*, 25 May 2021.

287. S. Lau, 'Lithuania Pulls out of China's "17 + 1" Bloc in Eastern Europe', Politico, 21 May 2021.

288. Despite a recent decrease of poverty in Mexico, income inequality remains significant. This inequality principally comes from labour income inequality, in which education levels play a determining role.

The trend has been mitigated, however, by government social transfers. See F. Lambert and H. Park, 'Income Inequality and Government Transfers in Mexico', IMF Working Paper, WP/19/148, 11 July 2019, p. 1; F. Lambert, 'How Mexico's Social Spending Reduced Poverty and Income Inequality', IMF Diálogo a Fondo, https://blog-dialogoafondo .imf.org/?page_id=11901 (accessed 18 June 2021).

289. The Mexican Constitution recognises the right to autonomy but some states' local legislation limits this right. Access to education, employment and fair treatment before states' jurisdictions is limited due to systemic discrimination. See UN Office of the High Commissioner for Human Rights, 'Advancing Indigenous Peoples' Rights in Mexico', https://www.ohchr.org/en/NewsEvents/Pages/IndigenousPeoplesRights InMexico.aspx (accessed 18 June 2021).

290. World Bank, 'Life Expectancy at Birth, Total (Years) – Mexico', https:// data.worldbank.org/indicator/SP.DYN.LE00.IN?locations=MX (accessed 18 June 2021).

291. This is the rate for the year 2018. Cardiovascular diseases are the most frequent cause of death. Diabetes and cancer are also very frequent. See World Health Organization, 'Mexico', 2018, https://www.who.int/nmh /countries/mex_en.pdf (accessed 18 June 2021).

292. Since September 2020, the beginning of the political campaign, some 100 political assassinations have occurred, tarnishing the democratic process and illustrating a greater trend of insecurity. See K. Suarez, R. Romo, J. Berlinger, 'Mexico's President Loses Grip on Power in Mid-Term Elections Marred by Violence', CNN World, 7 June 2021.

293. Transparency International, 'Mexico', https://www.transparency.org/en /countries/mexico (accessed 30 June 2021).

294. By gross domestic product (GDP) prior to the COVID-19 pandemic. See World Bank, 'Gross Domestic Product 2019', https://databank. worldbank.org/data/download/GDP.pdf (accessed 18 June 2021).

295. In 2019, the total sum of trade in goods between the two countries accounted for US$614.5 billion. Whenever there is an economic downturn or recession in the United States, demand for Mexican goods will naturally decline. See US Department of State, Bureau of Western Hemisphere Affairs, 'US Relations with Mexico: Bilateral Relations Fact Sheet', 16 September 2021, https://www.state.gov/u-s-relations-with -mexico.

296. Mexico is one of the largest producers of oil worldwide and the fourth largest in the Americas after Brazil. Most of the exports are transferred to the United States (nine per cent of US crude oil imports) and Europe. See US Energy Information Administration, 'Country Analysis Executive Summary: Mexico', 30 November 2020.

297. In February 2021, these remittances reached a record number and should be sustained by the United States economic growth and fiscal stimulus package. See Reuters, 'Remittances to Mexican Families Rise to Record High for February', 5 April 2021.

298. Mexico lost 662 kha of forest between 2002 and 2020, mostly in the regions of Campeche, Chiapas, Quintana Roo, Yucatan and Veracruz. This is primarily the result of industrial activities and this deforestation endangers indigenous people and contributes to global warming. See Global Forest Watch, 'Mexico', https://www.globalforestwatch.org /dashboards/country/MEX (accessed 18 June 2021).

299. See World Bank, 'Literacy Rate: Mexico', 2018, https://data.worldbank .org/indicator/SE.ADT.LITR.ZS?locations=MX (accessed 30 June 2021).

300. Mexico spends only 0.4 per cent of GDP on R&D. The business sector plays a small role in innovation, which is mostly in the hands of the higher-education and government sectors. Productivity has slowed down as a result of low R&D investment, the slow spread of ICT and slow job creation. See UNESCO Institute of Statistics, 'How Much Does Your Country Invest in R&D?'

301. Mexico has the second-highest share of public spending on education among OECD countries. Access to secondary education has improved but paths from secondary to tertiary education are still difficult to navigate. See OECD, 'Education at a Glance 2019: Mexico', https://www .oecd.org/education/education-at-a-glance/EAG2019_CN_MEX.pdf.

302. Between 1990 and 2015, 1.4 million Mexicans with higher education degrees left the country. See Oxford Analytica, 'Mexico's Brain Drain to Continue Unabated', *Expert Briefings*, 2018.

303. The 2018 rate of intentional homicides was 29 per 100,000 people, while the OECD average was five per 100,000. See World Bank, 'Intentional Homicides', https://data.worldbank.org/indicator/VC.IHR.PSRC .P5?locations=MX (accessed 18 June 2021).

304. The United States estimates that 90 per cent of the cocaine entering the country passes through the Mexico/US border. The drug traffickers are violent and engage in kidnappings, murder or other extortion attempts. See United Nations Office on Drugs and Crime, 'Mexico, Central America and the Caribbean', https://www.unodc.org/unodc/en/drug -trafficking/mexico-central-america-and-the-caribbean.html (accessed 18 June 2021); BBC News, 'How Dangerous Is Mexico?', 18 February 2020.

305. Besides the Zapatistas in Chiapas, a small group called EPR garnered national attention when they bombed fuel pipelines in 2007 and allied with other social protests in the country in 2013. See P. Corcoran, 'How Mexico's EPR Insurgents Have Changed Course', InSight Crime, 23 October 2013.

306. Upon taking office in December 2006, President Felipe Calderon launched an offensive against drugs cartels. Some 25,000 federal troops were dispatched to areas where drugs gangs are most active, especially near the US border. Battles were fought between the gangs and federal

troops and among the gangs themselves. These battles caused 2,500 deaths in 2007. This strategy led to the creation of smaller, more violent groups when former leaders were removed; results have been limited. See *The Economist*, 'No Country for Old Men', 24 January 2008; Council on Foreign Relations, 'Mexico's Long War: Drugs, Crime and Cartels', Backgrounder, 26 February 2021.

307. Mexico is considered a hotspot of human trafficking. Its victims include young men forced to work for drugs cartels and women forced into prostitution in the United States. See C. Murray, 'Mexico Human Trafficking Cases Rise by a Third but Many States Found Lagging', Reuters, 22 January 2020.

308. The three countries joined together to create the world's largest free trade area in 1994, NAFTA. This was replaced by USMCA, which came into effect in 2020. E. Beaulieu and D. Klemen, 'You Say USMCA or T-MEC and I Say CUSMA: The New NAFTA – Let's Call the Whole Thing On', *School of Public Policy Publications SPP Briefing Paper* 13, no. 7 (2020), n.p.; Office of the United States Trade Representative, 'United States-Mexico-Canada Agreement', https://ustr.gov/trade -agreements/free-trade-agreements/united-states-mexico-canada -agreement (accessed 1 October 2018).

309. The current crisis more specifically concerns the co-regulation of Central American migration in the United States following tense relations with the previous Trump administration. See J. Abdalla, 'Biden to Broaden US-Mexican Relations, Keep Immigration at Top', Al Jazeera, 12 March 2021.

310. The fertility rate in 2019 was 5.3 children per woman. See World Bank, 'Fertility Rate: Nigeria', https://data.worldbank.org/indicator/SP.DYN. TFRT.IN?locations=NG (accessed 30 June 2021).

311. See US Department of State, Office of International Religious Freedom, '2018 Report on International Religious Freedom: Nigeria', https://www .state.gov/reports/2018-report-on-international-religious-freedom /nigeria.

312. The northern states are majority-Muslim, the south majority-Christian. See J. Campbell, 'Conflict in Nigeria is More Complicated than "Christians vs. Muslims"', Council on Foreign Relations, 1 May 2019.

313. See Human Rights Watch, '"You Pray for Death": Trafficking of Women and Girls in Nigeria', 27 August 2019.

314. The country has among the worst health indicators in the African continent. Nigeria notably suffers from poor access to health services for women and girls. See World Bank, 'Life Expectancy at Birth, Total (Years) – Nigeria', https://data.worldbank.org/indicator/SP.DYN.LE00. IN?locations=NG (accessed 19 June 2021); USAID, 'Global Health Nigeria', updated 12 July 2021, https://www.usaid.gov/nigeria/global-health.

315. USAID, 'Global Health Nigeria'.

316. Nigeria has had a democratic constitution since 1999. Despite progress, citizens' participation in institutions remains limited. Distribution of power and resources remain challenges. S. Obaji, 'Nigeria Is Not a Failed State, but It Has Not Delivered Democracy for Its People', *The Conversation*, 19 November 2020.

317. Half of the government's revenue comes from oil. See Reuters, 'UPDATE 2-Nigeria's Government Expects Economy to Contract by 3.4% in 2020', 5 May 2020.

318. Nigeria ranks 149 out of 180 on Transparency International's 'Corruption Perceptions Index 2020'.

319. The Covid-19 pandemic exacerbated the situation and food security is also threatened. See World Bank, 'Poverty and Equity Brief: Nigeria', April 2021, https://databank.worldbank.org/data/download/poverty /987B9C90-CB9F-4D93-AE8C-750588BF00QA/AM2020/Global _POVEQ_NGA.pdf.

320. Despite recent billion-dollar investments introduced by President M. Buhari to build railways and other infrastructure, critics highlight the lack of investment in the south and the lack of transparency. See N. Munshi, 'Nigeria Infrastructure Splurge to Boost Economy', *Financial Times*, 17 February 2021.

321. J. Monye and O. Abang, 'Taxing the Informal Sector – Nigeria's Missing Goldmine', Bloomberg Tax, 15 October 2020.

322. This is a slight improvement from previous years. See Federal Ministry of Water Resources, Government of Nigeria, National Bureau of Statistics and UNICEF, *Water, Sanitation, Hygiene: National Outcome Routine Mapping 2019* (November 2020), https://www.unicef.org /nigeria/reports/water-sanitation-hygiene-national-outcome-routine -mapping-2019.

323. See Global Forest Watch, 'Nigeria', https://www.globalforestwatch.org /dashboards/country/NGA (accessed 20 June 2021).

324. It is estimated that in Lagos alone, air pollution caused 11,200 premature deaths in 2018. See K. Kemper and S. Chaudhuri, 'Air Pollution: A Silent Killer in Lagos', World Bank Blogs, 3 September 2020.

325. Women are particularly affected, with just a literacy rate of only 52.7 per cent. See UNESCO Institute of Statistics, 'Nigeria', http://uis.unesco.org /en/country/ng (accessed 20 June 2021).

326. Reforms not fully implemented, resources poorly used and high level of illiteracy. See O.O.S. Ekundayo, 'Education in Nigeria Is in a Mess from Top to Bottom: Five Things That Can Fix It', *The Conversation*, 26 March 2019.

327. Nigeria's Human Development Index value was 0.539 in 2019. See UNDP, *The Next Frontier: Human Development and the Anthropocene: UNDP Human Development Report 2020* (New York: UNDP, 2020), p. 1.

328. Resentment in the oil-rich Niger Delta is fuelled by the impoverished and discontented local population, who do not benefit from their region's resource wealth. Kidnappings of foreign workers are common, as are attacks on oil installations and police stations. Some armed militant groups even perpetrate killings. In 2019, more than a thousand deaths were recorded. See Pind Foundation, *Niger Delta Annual Conflict Report: January to December 2020*, https://pindfoundation.org/niger-delta-annual-conflict-report-january-december-2020; J. Campbell, 'Significant Rise of Insecurity in the Niger Delta through 2019', Council on Foreign Relations, 26 February 2020.

329. See Swissinfo, 'Major Drug Trafficking Network Busted in Zurich', 3 December 2020.

330. Nigeria helped set up the Economic Community of West Africa and held the chair of the African Union in 2005–6. It has taken leading roles in the resolution of conflicts in Liberia, Sierra Leone and Sudan. The rise of corruption and its own security challenges made the spread of its influence more complex. See S. Folarin, 'Nigeria Was Once an Indisputable Leader in Africa: What Happened?', *The Conversation*, 24 May 2020.

331. Pakistan is the world's fifth-most populous country with a population of 224.9 million (2021) and has the world's second-largest Muslim population. The urban population is growing by two per cent a year, posing great developmental and managerial challenges. World Population Review, 'Pakistan Population 2021', https://worldpopulationreview.com/countries/pakistan-population (accessed 9 August 2021); World Bank, 'Population Growth: Pakistan', https://data.worldbank.org/indicator/SP.POP.GROW?locations=PK (accessed 30 June 2021).

332. In 2019, the number of refugees in Pakistan was about 1.4 million, the majority of which came from neighbouring Afghanistan. Over the past ten years Pakistan has seen a decrease in the previously extremely high number of internally displaced persons. World Bank, 'Refugee Population by Country or Territory of Asylum: Pakistan', https://data.worldbank.org/indicator/SM.POP.REFG?locations=PK (accessed 30 June 2021); UN Office of the High Commissioner for Human Rights, 'Pakistan', https://www.unhcr.org/pakistan.html (accessed 30 June 2021); Internal Displacement Monitoring Centre, 'Pakistan', https://www.internal-displacement.org/countries/pakistan (accessed 30 June 2021).

333. Baluchistan is rich in resources and has a strategically important location on Pakistan's north-western border, yet it is rather poor and underdeveloped. Unrest in the region escalated in the early 2000s. Militants in the province demanded economic and political autonomy, which Islamabad refused to grant. Although government attempts to repress the insurgency and silence militants were initially counterproductive and only fuelled resentment and alienation among

the Baluchs, the insurgency has, since then, decreased in intensity. Z. Hussain, 'The Battle for Balochistan', *Dawn*, 25 April 2013; Associated Press, 'US Declares Pakistan's Separatist Baluchistan Liberation Army as Terrorist Group', *Indian Express*, 3 July 2019, https://indianexpress .com/article/pakistan/us-declares-pakistans-separatist-baluchistan -liberation-army-as-terrorist-group-5812092.

334. Life expectancy at birth was 67.2 years in 2019, while infant mortality per 1,000 live births in 2019 was 55.7 (down from 84.4 in 2000). World Bank, 'Life Expectancy at Birth, Total (Years) – Pakistan', https://data .worldbank.org/indicator/SP.DYN.LE00.IN?locations=PK (accessed 30 June 2021); World Bank, 'Mortality Rate: Pakistan', https://data .worldbank.org/indicator/SP.DYN.IMRT.IN?locations=PK (accessed 30 June 2021).

335. The government spends only about 2.6 per cent of its GDP on health, and most health services are run by the private sector, to which only the well-off have access. Nearly 40 per cent of all deaths in Pakistan are caused by communicable diseases. Many others die from diseases that could be prevented through vaccines, such as polio. B. Shaikh, 'Private Sector in Health Care Delivery: A Reality and Challenge in Pakistan', *Journal of Ayub Medical College Abbottabad* 27, no. 2 (2015), pp. 496–98; Z. Kurji, 'Analysis of the Health Care System of Pakistan: Lessons Learnt and Way Forward', *Journal of Ayub Medical College Abbottabad* 28, no. 3 (2016), pp. 601–4; S. Javed *et al.*, 'Patients' Satisfaction and Public and Private Sectors' Health Care Service Quality in Pakistan: Application of Grey Decision Analysis Approaches', *International Journal of Health Planning and Management* 34, no. 1 (30 August 2018), pp. 168–82; World Bank, 'Pakistan', https://data.worldbank.org/ indicator/SH.DTH.NCOM.ZS?locations=PK (accessed 30 June 2021); US Centers for Disease Control, 'Global Health Pakistan', accessed 30 June 2021, https://www.cdc.gov/globalhealth/countries/pakistan/default .htm (accessed 30 June 2021).

336. Currently, nearly two million people are infected with the virus. Factors contributing to rising infection rates are high-risk behaviour among intravenous drugs users and unsafe practices among sex workers. The WHO and UNAIDS have classified Pakistan as a high-risk country for HIV infection. UNAIDS, 'Pakistan', https://www.unaids.org/en /regionscountries/countries/pakistan (accessed 30 June 2021); A. Latif, 'Pakistan Sitting on a Ticking AIDS Bomb', *Pakistan Tribune*, 6 October 2006, https://web.archive.org/web/20080111121613/http:/www .paktribune.com/news/index.shtml?156327.

337. Although the periods 1958–71, 1977–88 and 1999–2008 saw military coups that resulted in the imposition of martial law and military commanders who governed as *de facto* presidents, in 2013, the country moved into a

democratic transition. S.P. Cohen, *The Idea of Pakistan* (Washington, DC: Brookings Institution Press, 2004); The World, 'Historic Election Marks Transition in Pakistan', PRX/WGBH, 14 May 2013.

338. Transparency International, 'Corruption Perceptions Index 2020'.

339. Pakistan is South Asia's second-largest economy, with a GDP of 278 billion in 2019. Although the growth rate plummeted to 0.98 per cent in 2019 from 5.8 in 2018, it is predicted to resume at a rate of around five per cent. World Bank, 'GDP: Pakistan', https://data.worldbank.org/indicator /NY.GDP.MKTP.CD?locations=PK (accessed 30 June 2021); World Bank, 'GDP Growth: Pakistan', https://data.worldbank.org/indicator/NY.GDP .MKTP.KD.ZG?locations=PK (accessed 30 June 2021); WIO News, 'Pakistan Will Achieve 5 Per Cent GDP in Next Fiscal: Finance Minister', 24 May 2021, https://www.wionews.com/south-asia/pakistan-will-achieve-5-per-cent-gdp-growth-in-next-fiscal-finance-minister-387073.

340. *Express Tribune*, 'Liberalisation: The Case for a Free Market in Pakistani Agriculture', 9 December 2012.

341. Pakistan is one of the largest producers of natural commodities in the world. Despite the fact that the structure of the Pakistani economy has changed from a mainly agricultural to a strong service base, as of 2019, agriculture accounted for 22 per cent of GDP. Bureau of Statistics, Government of Pakistan, 'Agriculture Statistics', accessed 30 June 2021, https://www.pbs.gov.pk/content/agriculture-statistics (accessed 30 June 2021).

342. According to the World Bank, poverty in Pakistan fell from 64.3 per cent in 2001 to 24.3 per cent in 2015. World Bank, 'Poverty Headcount Ratio at National Poverty Lines: Pakistan', https://data.worldbank.org /indicator/SI.POV.NAHC?locations=PK (accessed 30 June 2021).

343. The earthquake which occurred on 8 October 2005 killed over 87,000 people and left millions homeless. Earthquake Engineering Research Institute, 'The Kashmir Earthquake of October 8, 2005: Impacts in Pakistan', ReliefWeb, 28 February 2006.

344. Pakistan's deforestation rate is the second highest in Asia. J. Shahid, 'Pakistan's Deforestation Rate Second Highest in Asia: WWF', *DAWN*, 15 August 2020; R. Jabeen, 'The Green Emergency: Deforestation in Pakistan', World Bank Blogs, 22 May 2019.

345. Pakistan may reach absolute water scarcity by 2040. *Business Standard*, 'Water Crisis Looms Large in Pakistan, May Face Absolute Scarcity by 2040', 22 March 2021.

346. Currently, Pakistan has the world's second-highest number of out-of-school children with an estimated 22.8 million children aged five to sixteen not attending school, representing 44 per cent of the total population in this age group. Although Pakistan has increased its expenditure on education to 2.8 per cent of GDP, it is still well below

UNICEF's four per cent target. Reforms are taking place to address the poor quality of the education system and the number of out-of-school children. UNICEF Pakistan, 'Education', https://www.unicef.org /pakistan/education (accessed 30 June 2021); A. Khamis, 'Teacher Education in Pakistan', in K.G. Karris and C.C. Wolhuter (eds), *International Handbook on Teachers Education World-Wide: Issues and Challenges* (Nicosia, Cyprus: HM Studies, 2019), pp. 675–92; R. Hunter, 'Education in Pakistan', WENR, 25 February 2020.

347. World Bank, 'Literacy Rate: Pakistan', https://data.worldbank.org /indicator/SE.ADT.LITR.ZS?locations=PK (accessed 30 June 2021).

348. Although both Pakistan and India have maintained a fragile ceasefire since 2003, they nonetheless regularly exchange fire across the contested border, known as the Line of Control, accusing each other of violating the ceasefire and claiming to be shooting in response to attacks. Border skirmishes that began in late 2016 and continued into 2018 killed dozens and displaced thousands of civilians on both sides. In February 2019, an attack on a convoy of Indian paramilitary forces in Indian-controlled Kashmir killed at least 40 soldiers. The attack, claimed by Pakistani militant group Jaish-e-Mohammad, was the deadliest attack in Kashmir in three decades. This led India to conduct airstrikes, to which Pakistan responded with its own in rapid escalation. Council on Foreign Relations, 'Global Conflict Tracker: Conflict between India and Pakistan'; Center for Arms Control and Non-Proliferation, 'History of India and Pakistan', 26 November 2019, https://armscontrolcenter.org /history-of-conflict-in-india-and-pakistan.

349. Center for Arms Control and Non-Proliferation, 'Fact Sheet: Pakistan's Nuclear Inventory', March 2021, https://armscontrolcenter.org /pakistans-nuclear-capabilities.

350. Council on Foreign Relations, 'Global Conflict Tracker: Conflict between India and Pakistan'; H. Janjua, 'Pakistan Faces Dilemma over Trade Ties with India', DW, 5 April 202100.

351. Pakistan is a major non-NATO ally as part of the ongoing War on Terror and a leading recipient of aid from the US. Between 2002 and 2013, it received US$26 billion in economic and military aid and sales of military equipment. Pakistan also has strong military and economic relations with China, which were strengthened by the 2015 launch of the China-Pakistan Economic Corridor. B.O. Riedel, *Avoiding Armageddon: America, India, and Pakistan to the Brink and Back* (Washington, DC: Brookings Institution Press, 2013), pp. 170, 216; H.T. Boon and G.K.H. Ong, 'Military Dominance in Pakistan and China–Pakistan Relations', *Australian Journal of International Affairs* 75, no. 1 (2021), pp. 80–102; K. Adeney and F. Boni, 'How China and Pakistan Negotiate', Carnegie Endowment for International Peace, 24 May 2021.

352. Russia's population growth rate decreased steadily from 1985 (0.7 per cent) to an all-time low in 2002 when it reached a negative rate of −0.46 per cent. After a period of slow increase in population growth, which peaked at a positive rate of 2.1 per cent in 2014, it has started falling again, becoming negative once more in 2018. Under both low and medium growth-rate prediction models, the Russian population is estimated to continue to decline. In 2019, the birth rate stood at 1.5, though the life-expectancy rate increased steadily from 65 years in 2003 to 73 in 2019, reflecting significant improvements in health conditions in the country, according to the World Bank. World Bank, 'Population Growth: Russian Federation', https://data.worldbank.org/indicator/SP. POP.GROW?locations=RU (accessed 30 June 2021); Statista, 'Population Projection for Russia 2021–2036, by Scenario', https://www.statista.com /statistics/1009186/russia-population-projection-by-scenario (accessed 30 June 2021); World Bank, 'Life Expectancy at Birth, Total (Years) – Russian Federation', https://data.worldbank.org/indicator/SP.DYN.LE00. IN?locations=RU (accessed 30 June 2021); World Bank, 'Russia among Global Top Ten Improvers for Progress Made in Health and Education, Says World Bank Report', 16 September 2020.

353. The Russian government is facing a dramatic population decline in the Far East and the north which it is seeking to tackle through incentives for the rural population to refrain from relocating. A. Sheludkov, J. Kamp and D. Müller, 'Decreasing Labor Intensity in Agriculture and the Accessibility of Major Cities Shape the Rural Population Decline in Postsocialist Russia', *Eurasian Geography and Economics* 62, no. 4 (2021), pp. 481–506; Statista, 'Internal Migration in Russia from 2009 to 2019', https://www.statista.com/statistics/1009980/internal-migration -russia-by-federal-district (accessed 30 June 2021); D. Shapiro and N. Yefimova-Trilling, 'Russian Population Decline in Spotlight Again', *Russia Matters*, 13 September 2019.

354. Despite Russia's universal health care, many people do not have access to sufficient medical treatment. Poor health care stems from a lack of governmental funding. More than 17,500 Russian villages and towns have no medical infrastructure and salaries for doctors and nurses are very low. In addition, the Russian government plans to cut its health-care budget further by 33 per cent, bringing it down to US$5.8 billion a year. Presently Russia only spends 5.3 per cent of its GDP on health care, significantly less than the global average of ten per cent. Underfunding contributed to a severe drugs shortage problem in 2019. In 2017, the leading causes of death were ischemic heart disease, stroke, Alzheimer's disease, cardiomyopathy, cirrhosis and lung cancer. A. Sharudenko, '10 Facts about Healthcare in the Russian Federation', The Borgen Project, 18 June 2020; Statista, 'Healthcare in Russia:

Statistics and Facts', 22 April 2021, https://www.statista.com/topics
/4824/health-care-in-russia.

355. Russia is facing an HIV/AIDs epidemic but so far has failed to effectively
address the problem, relying on moral arguments rather than good
practices. In 2018 alone, AIDS took the lives of 37,000 people across
Russia, with the rate of new infections rising by between ten and fifteen
per cent a year, according to the World Health Organization. A much
more successful result has been achieved in the state's attempts to
address alcoholism in the country. I. Yasaveev, 'Not an Epidemic, but a
Global Problem: The Authorities' Construction of HIV/AIDS in Russia',
Medicine (Baltimore) 99, no. 21 (2020); M. Bennetts, 'The Epidemic
Russia Doesn't Want to Talk About', Politico, 11 May 2020; Avert, 'HIV
and AIDS in Russia', https://www.avert.org/professionals/hiv-around
-world-eastern-europe-central-asia/russia (accessed 30 June 2021); J.
Cohen, 'Russia's HIV/AIDS Epidemic Is Getting Worse, Not Better',
Science, 11 June 2018; *Lancet*, 'Russia's Alcohol Policy: A Continuing
Success Story', 394, no. 10205 (5 October 2019), P1205.

356. The growth of xenophobia in Russia has been widely reported. Victims
of violent xenophobic attacks have included: students, immigrants and
refugees from Africa, Asia, the Middle East and Latin America; ethnic
minorities from the Caucasus and Central Asia; Jews; and Roma.
According to human rights groups, the government does not do enough
to prevent and aggressively prosecute racially inspired attacks and
discrimination, but rather often uses them as a tool of political
legitimation. Human Rights Watch, 'World Report 2021: Russia – Events
of 2020', https://www.hrw.org/world-report/2021/country-chapters
/russia#aff61a (accessed 20 July 2021); M.A. Kingsbury, 'Beyond
Attitudes: Russian Xenophobia as a Political Legitimation Tool',
E-International Relations, 30 April 2017.

357. Civil liberties restrictions, arbitrary arrests and abuses against Jehovah's
Witnesses and members of the LGBTIQ+ community are on the rise.
Amnesty International, 'Russian Federation', https://www.amnesty.org
/en/countries/europe-and-central-asia/russian-federation (accessed 30
June 2021); Human Rights Watch, 'World Report 2021: Russia – Events
of 2020'.

358. Russia has a long history of corruption. Anti-corruption efforts often
turn into forms of political repression and do not go to the root of the
problem. Transparency International, 'Russia', https://www.transparency
.org/en/countries/russia# (accessed 30 June 2021); S. Kaspe, 'Opinion:
The Political Meanings and Uses of Russian Corruption', Geopolitical
Intelligence Services, 30 April 2021.

359. Russia is the world's eleventh-largest economy in terms of GDP, which
stood at 1.7 trillion in 2019 following a period of recovery after the 2008
global financial crisis. Russia has some of the world's largest oil and gas
deposits and contains over 30 per cent of the world's natural resources,

making it an 'energy superpower'. In 2016, the oil-and-gas sector accounted for 36 per cent of federal budget revenues. Russia's heavy dependence on energy exports, however, leaves its economy highly vulnerable to price fluctuations in the energy market. World Bank, 'GDP: Russia', https://data.worldbank.org/indicator/NY.GDP.MKTP .CD?locations=RU (accessed 30 June 2021); K.M. Korabik, 'Russia's Natural Resources and Their Economic Effects', Penn State College of Earth and Mineral Sciences, 1 December 1997, via the Internet Archive Wayback Machine, https://web.archive.org/web/20190720062114 /https://www.ems.psu.edu/~williams/russia.htm; M. Russell, 'The Russian Economy: Will Russia Ever Catch Up?', European Parliamentary Research Service Publications Office, 11 March 2015; Harvard University Press, 'The Future of Russia as an Energy Superpower', 20 November 2017, https://harvardpress.typepad.com/hup_publicity /2017/11/future-of-russia-as-energy-superpower-thane-gustafson.html; US Energy Information Administration, 'Russia – Analysis', 31 October 2017.

360. Mitrova, 'Russia's Energy Strategy'; Petro Online, 'Why Does Russia Want to Nationalise Its Oil and Gas Industry?', 9 July 2016, https://www .petro-online.com/news/fuel-for-thought/13/breaking-news/why-does -russia-want-to-nationalise-its-oil-and-gas-industry/39472.

361. Russia's unemployment has decreased from thirteen per cent in 1999 to 4.4 per cent in 2020. Statista, 'Russia: Unemployment Rate from 1999 to 2020', https://www.statista.com/statistics/263712/unemployment-in -russia (accessed 30 June 2021).

362. According to official regulatory data, in 2018, 35 to 60 per cent of drinking water reserves in Russia failed to meet safety standards, with 40 per cent of surface water and seventeen per cent of spring water being undrinkable. In total, by 2018, eleven million Russians did not have access to safe drinking water. This is the result of a deteriorated water supply infrastructure and pollution. K. Ritter, 'Pollutants and Heavy Metals Taint Moscow's Water Supply', Circle of Blue, 12 April 2018; O. Primin, 'Clean Water of Russia: Problems and Solutions', *IOP Conference Series: Materials Science and Engineering* 365, no. 2 (2018); S. Bramlett, 'Driven by Industry: Water Pollution in Russia from Coast to Coast', The Borgen Project, 13 March 2018.

363. According to a 2016 OECD estimate, 54 per cent of Russia's 25 to 64 year-olds have attained a tertiary education. This places Russia in second place for the highest attainment of tertiary education among 35 OECD member countries. OECD, 'Education at a Glance 2016: Russian Federation', https://read.oecd-ilibrary.org/education/education-at-a -glance-2016/russian-federation_eag-2016-76-en#page1.

364. R&D investment in Russia in 2019 stood at only one per cent of GDP. Seventy per cent of the funding comes from public sources and much of it is utilised by public research institutes, leaving the private sector

lagging far behind. Statista, 'Russia: GDP Spent on R&D', https://www
.statista.com/statistics/461754/share-of-gdp-expenditure-on-research
-and-development-russia (accessed 30 June 2021); A. Sanghi and S.
Yusuf, 'Russia's Uphill Struggle with Innovation', World Bank, 17
September 2018.

365. Even in a sector in which Russia used to be at the forefront, such as
aerospace, its level of innovation is insufficient. Although Russia's
near-space exploration and its rocket engines are still among the most
powerful and reliable, Russia lags behind in terms of deep-space
exploration and the development of reusable launch vehicles. Sanghi
and Yusuf, 'Russia's Uphill Struggle with Innovation'.

366. V. Mau, 'Russia's Human Capital Challenge', OECD, 2013, https://www
.oecd.org/russia/russias-human-capital-challenge.htm; N. Alekseeva,
N. Antoshkova and V. Vasilenok, 'The Potential of Human Capital's
Development in Russia in the Digital Age', *Atlantis Highlights in
Computer Science* (September 2019), pp. 9–12.

367. According to Russia's Academy of Sciences, the number of scientists
who emigrate every year from Russia is five times higher now than it
was before President Putin returned to the presidency in 2012. This is
due to a weakened economy and especially to political repression. J.E.
Herbst and S. Erofeev, 'The Putin Exodus: The New Russian Brain
Drain', Atlantic Council, 21 February 2019; M. Bennetts, 'Russia's Brain
Drain Soars as Scientists Flee "Spy Mania"', *The Times*, 22 April 2021,
https://www.thetimes.co.uk/article/russia-brain-drain-scientists-flee
-spy-mania-vladimir-putin-wbbrknzkc.

368. In 2014, Russia took control of the Ukraine region of Crimea and
subsequently declared its annexation, claiming that this was supported
by the local population through a referendum. The pro-Russian protests
in the Donbas region which followed escalated into a war between the
Ukrainian government and the Russian-backed separatist forces of the
self-declared Donetsk and Luhansk People's Republics. These actions
were heavily condemned by the international community, leading the
members of what was, at the time, the G8 to suspend Russia's
membership. As will be explored in more depth in the Appendix, the
tensions that lasted for over eight years led Russia to ionvade Ukraine on
24 Fenruary 2022. Council on Foreign Relations, 'Global Conflict
Tracker: Conflict in Ukraine',https://www.cfr.org/global-conflict-tracker
/conflict/conflict-ukraine (accessed 30 June 2021).

369. Russia is pursuing a 'spheres of influence' strategy in foreign policy; this
is the basis for its military intervention in Syria. M. Yacoubian, 'What is
Russia's Endgame in Russia?' United States Institute of Peace, 16
February 2021.

370. Russia also has interests in the Mediterranean, which it is seeking to protect through its involvement in the Libyan civil war. Center for Strategic and International Studies, 'Exploiting Chaos: Russia in Libya', 23 September 2021; D. Yachyshen, 'Russia Now Has a Position in Libya. What Next?', Foreign Policy Research Institute, 23 November 2020; S. Ramani, 'Russia's Strategic Transformation in Libya: A Winning Gambit?', RUSI, Commentary, 28 April 2021.

371. European Parliament, 'Russia', https://www.europarl.europa.eu /factsheets/en/sheet/177/russia (accessed 30 June 2021).

372. About 24.8 per cent of Saudi Arabia's population is under 15 years old, although its birth rate is declining (2.3 per cent in 2019) and its population of 34.3 million (2019) is expected to grow to almost 40 million by 2025. World Bank, 'Population Ages 0–14: Saudi Arabia', https://data.worldbank.org/indicator/SP.POP.0014.TO.ZS?locations=SA (accessed 30 June 2021); World Bank, 'Population, Total: Saudi Arabia', https://data.worldbank.org/indicator/SP.POP.TOTL?locations=SA (accessed 30 June 2021); World Bank, 'Fertility Rate: Saudi Arabia', https://data.worldbank.org/indicator/SP.DYN.TFRT.IN?locations=SA.

373. J. Al Tamimi, 'Saudis Back Women's Role in Public Life', *Gulf News*, 28 May 2014.

374. Helped by the oil boom, the government has invested in a modern health-care system and successfully reduced the number of deaths caused by preventable or treatable diseases. Saudis thus have a relatively high life expectancy of 75.1 years. At the same time, however, the country has seen significant increases in cases of cardiovascular disease, diabetes and cancer. World Bank, 'Life Expectancy at Birth, Total (Years) – Saudi Arabia', https://data.worldbank.org/indicator /SP.DYN.LE00.IN?locations=SA (accessed 30 June 2021); S. Tyrovolas *et al.*, 'The Burden of Disease in Saudi Arabia 1990–2017: Results from the Global Burden of Disease Study 2017', *The Lancet* 4, no. 5, May 2020.

375. In 2005, Saudi Arabia allowed municipal elections to be held. The elections were a first step on the way to liberal reforms in the country, with significant steps towards social and economic renewal of Saudi Arabia being taken by the Crown Prince Mohammed bin Salman in 2019, through a national program known as Vision 2030. King Faisal Center for Research and Islamic Studies, 'Vision 2030 and Reform in Saudi Arabia: Facts and Figures, April 2015–April 2021', May 2021.

376. Saudi Arabia is one of the top 20 economies in the world and is hence part of the G20. Saudi Arabia possesses about seventeen per cent of the world's oil reserves. The oil and gas sector accounts for about 50 per cent of GDP and about 70 per cent of export earnings. OPEC, 'Saudi Arabia',

https://www.opec.org/opec_web/en/about_us/169.htm (accessed 30
June 2021); Statista, 'Distribution of Oil and Non-Oil Revenue in Saudi
Arabia in 2020', https://www.statista.com/statistics/1154249/saudi
-arabia-oil-and-non-oil-revenue-share (accessed 30 June 2020).

377. A. Puri-Mirza, 'Banking Industry in Saudi Arabia – Statistics and Facts',
Statista, 17 December 2020.

378. Investment in the growth of the private sector is part of the Vision 2030
plan. Oxford Business Group, 'More Private Sector Participation to
Stimulate Growth in Saudi Arabia Industry', in *The Report: Saudi
Arabia 2018* (OBG, 2018).

379. Saudi Arabia's unemployment rate is not particularly high (the official
unemployment rate in 2020 was 5.86 per cent) but it is building a series
of large economically powerful cities to increase employment as part of
the Vision 2030 plan.

380. As of 2008, roughly two thirds of workers employed in Saudi Arabia
were foreigners, with a high of 90 per cent in the private sector. In
January 2014, the Saudi government had lowered the 90 per cent rate,
doubling the number of Saudi citizens working in private sector
employment to 1.5 million compared to the ten million foreign
expatriates working in the kingdom. K.E. House, *On Saudi Arabia: Its
People, Past, Religion, Fault Lines – and Future* (Eldon, MO: Knopf,
2012), p. 157; Reuters, 'Saudi Arabia Doubles Private Sector Jobs in
30-Month Period', 19 January 2014.

381. This includes a significant investment in future advanced technology
as well as in the new city, Neom, with a planned US$500-billion
investment. Moreover, the country is developing its tourism sector on
both land and sea with high sustainability standards. *Neom News*,
'Neom Saudi Arabia', http://neomsaudicity.net (accessed 30
June 2021).

382. Focal Line Solar, 'Saudi Arabia Is Getting Serious about Green Energy',
30 June 2021.

383. Lack of rain and perennial rivers, as well as depleting underground
water resources, makes water scarcity a significant challenge. C.
Bradbury, 'Water Crisis in Saudi Arabia', The Borgen Project, 10
July 2020; E. DeNicola *et al.*, 'Climate Change and Water Scarcity:
The Case of Saudi Arabia', *Annals of Global Health* 81, no. 3 (2015),
pp. 342–53.

384. Saudi Arabia is leading the green revolution in the Middle East. The
country notably aims to plant 50 billion trees. L. Steffen, 'Saudi Arabia
Plans to Cut Emissions by 60% by Planting 50 Billion Trees', *Intelligent
Living*, 6 May 2021.

385. Saudi Arabia spends 8.8 per cent of its GDP on education, compared
with the global average of 4.6 per cent. Public education is open and free
to every Saudi citizen, and the literacy rate is 97 per cent for males and

77.8 per cent for females (2017). The curriculum in Saudi Arabia is moving towards the critical-thinking skills needed in the modern labour market. *Arab News*, 'Saudi Arabia Most Improved Economy for Business', 29 May 2019; World Bank, 'Literacy Rate: Saudi Arabia (Males)', https://data.worldbank.org/indicator/SE.ADT.LITR. MA.ZS?locations=SA (accessed 30 June 2021); World Bank, 'Literacy Rate: Saudi Arabia (Females)', https://data.worldbank.org/indicator/SE .ADT.LITR.FE.ZS?locations=SA (accessed 30 June 2021); OECD, *Reviews of National Policies for Education: Education in Saudi Arabia* (Paris: OECD Publishing, 2020).

386. The investment is leading to an exponential growth in research centres. KSA Ministry of Education, 'R&D in the Kingdom', https://rdo.moe.gov .sa/en/AbouttheProgram/Pages/RandDintheKingdom.aspx (accessed 30 June 2020).

387. In 2019, the Vision 2030 programme saw the implementation of reforms aimed at the overhaul of the country's curricula to better prepare its workforce. University scholarships have also enabled around 200,000 Saudis to attend major global universities. Oxford Business Group, 'Educational Reforms to Improve Teaching Quality in Saudi Arabia', in *The Report: Saudi Arabia 2020* (OBG, 2020); *Arab News*, 'Scholarship Students Abroad Promote Vision 2030', 26 May 2016.

388. Saudi Arabia is determined to maintain its pre-eminent position on the peninsula *vis-à-vis* Iran. It feels challenged by Iran's nuclear ambitions and the country's sponsorship of Shia militants in Iraq, Palestine (via Hamas) and Lebanon (via Hezbollah) and it is seeking to counterbalance Iran's influence in the Muslim world. J. Marcus, 'Why Saudi Arabia and Iran are Bitter Rivals', BBC News, 16 September 2019.

389. In 2015, Saudi Arabia started a military intervention in Yemen leading a coalition of nine countries from West Asia and North Africa in response to calls from the president of Yemen Abdrabbuh Mansur Hadi for military support after he was ousted by the Houthi rebel movement.

390. In 2019, Saudi Arabia became the third-largest donor to UNRWA, having donated US$800 million since 1994. The Saudi development fund has also provided support to maintain Palestinian refugee camps in different countries. Y. Farouk, 'Saudi Arabia: Aid as a Primary Foreign Policy Tool', Carnegie Endowment for International Peace, 9 June 2020.

391. As the custodian of Islam's holy places, Saudi Arabia not only attracts millions of Muslim pilgrims every year, it also reinforces the country's role as a leader of the Islamic world and as a defender of Islamic interests in the world. *Encyclopedia Britannica*, 'Hajj', 15 November 2021.

392. K. Alkhathlan, D. Gately and M. Javid, 'Analysis of Saudi Arabia's Behavior within OPEC and the World Oil Market', *Science Direct* 64 (2014), pp. 209–25.

393. US Department of State, 'U.S. Relations with Saudi Arabia', 15 December 2020, https://www.state.gov/u-s-relations-with-saudi-arabia/.

394. Saudi Arabia was one of the states behind the 2002 Arab Peace Initiative. See J. Kostiner, 'Saudi Arabia and the Arab-Israeli Peace Process: The Fluctuation of Regional Coordination', *British Journal of Middle Eastern Studies* 36, no. 3 (2009), pp. 417–29.

395. South Africa has the highest number of people infected with HIV/AIDS in the world, with 20 per cent of the global total. The epidemic reduced life expectancy in South Africa from 63.4 in 1991 to 53.4 in 2004. Since then, it has increased to 64.1 in 2019. In 2019, nineteen per cent of the population was HIV-positive. The government has slowed down the pandemic through deliberate policies and has provided free anti-retroviral drugs, but this is not enough to contain the crisis. World Bank, 'Life Expectancy at Birth, Total (Years) – South Africa', https://data.worldbank.org/indicator/SP.DYN.LE00.IN?locations=ZA (accessed 30 June 2021); S.M. Allinder and J. Fleischman, 'The World's Largest HIV Epidemic in Crisis: HIV in South Africa', CSIStudies, 2 April 2019; S. Satoh and E. Boyer, 'HIV in South Africa', *The Lancet* 394, no. 10197 (10 August 2019), p. 467; Avert, 'HIV and AIDS in South Africa', https://www.avert.org/professionals/hiv-around-world/sub-saharan-africa/south-africa (accessed 30 June 2021).

396. A large wealth gap between the white minority and the black majority has always existed in South Africa (in 2000–1, the average income of white households was nine times higher than that of the average black household). Today, however, there are increasing divisions among blacks as well because of the emergence of a small but rapidly growing black middle class. Inequality manifests itself through a skewed income distribution, unequal access to opportunities and regional disparities. International Monetary Fund, 'Six Charts Explain South Africa's Inequality', 30 January 2020; Republic of South Africa, 'How Unequal is South Africa?', 4 February 2020, http://www.statssa.gov.za/?p=12930.

397. Since the end of apartheid in 1994, South Africa has had fair and peaceful national elections, and a democratic culture has become entrenched within society. The country has achieved relative racial peace due to post-apartheid reconciliation efforts and the maintenance of a pluralist political system. Yet the country's fragile democratic system is threatened by widespread social and economic inequality. J. Campbell, 'South Africa', Council on Foreign Relations, https://www.cfr.org/expert-brief/south-africa(accessed 12 January 2022); S. Friedman, 'South Africa Remains a Nation of Insiders and Outsiders, 27 Years after Democracy', *The Conversation*, 25 April 2021.

398. There are slow but ongoing efforts to tackle corruption, which has been a constant feature of South African political life for much of the past 350 years. C. Vandome and J. Hamill, 'South Africa: A First Shot at

Corruption', Chatham House, 19 May 2021; S. Friedman, 'How Corruption in South Africa Is Deeply Rooted in the Country's Past and Why That Matters', *The Conversation*, 28 August 2020.

399. South Africa's GDP, which stood at US$351.4 billion in 2019 and US$282.59 in 2020, is the third-largest economy in Africa after Nigeria and Egypt. It is the only African state that is part of the G20. South Africa has a comparative advantage in the production of agriculture, mining and manufacturing products relating to these sectors, making its formal economy solid and competitive. In 2016, the top five challenges for South Africa's economy were inefficient government bureaucracy, restrictive labour regulations, a shortage of skilled workers for some high-tech industries, political instability and corruption, whilst the country's banking sector was rated as a strongly positive feature of the economy. World Bank, 'GDP: South Africa', accessed 30 June 2021, https://data. worldbank.org/indicator/NY.GDP.MKTP.CD?locations=ZA (accessed 30 June 2021); Statista, 'African Countries with the Highest Gross Domestic Product (GDP) in 2020', accessed 30 June 2021, https://www.statista.com/ statistics/1120999/gdp-of-african-countries-by-country (accessed 30 June 2021); International Monetary Fund, 'World Economic Outlook Database', https://www.imf.org/en/Publications/SPROLLs/world-economic-outlook-databases#sort=%40imfdate%20descending (accessed June 2021); K. Schwab (ed.), *The Global Competitiveness Report 2015–2016* (Geneva: World Economic Forum, 2015).

400. Almost half of the South African population lives in poverty and the unemployment rate has risen to 32.6 per cent in the first quarter of 2021. A. Bittar, '5 Facts about Poverty in South Africa', The Borgen Project, 14 August 2020; Trading Economics, 'South Africa Unemployment Rate', https://tradingeconomics.com/south-africa/unemployment-rate (accessed 30 June 2021); Statista, 'South Africa: Unemployment Rate from Q1 2019 to Q1 2020, by Population Group', https://www.statista .com/statistics/1129481/unemployment-rate-by-population-group-in-south-africa (accessed 30 June 2021).

401. South Africa has been suffering from severe electricity shortages in recent years, which has interrupted mining activities and has also led to economic losses for small businesses and farmers. The government largely halted the construction of new power stations in the 1980s, but it has since changed strategy through programmes such as the 2,000-megawatt Risk Mitigation Independent Power Producer Procurement Programme, which encompasses various gas, wind and solar projects. H. Winkler, 'Why South Africa's Electricity Blackouts Are Set to Continue for the Next Five Years', *The Conversation*, 30 March 2021; S. Mfundza Miller and M. Muller, 'South Africa's Energy Crisis Has Triggered Lots of Ideas: Why Most Are Wrong', *The Conversation*, 22 January 2020.

402. This is due to the fact that coal and wood are major sources of heat and energy in South Africa. However, through the 2019 Integrated Resource Plan, which sets out a long-term diversification of energy sources by 2030, South Africa aims to reduce the carbon footprint of the energy sector while meeting growing energy demand and ensuring a socio-economically just transition. The plan sees no new coal plants being built after 2030 and four-fifths of capacity closed by 2050. H. Ritchie and M. Roser, 'South Africa: CO_2 Country Profile', Our World in Data, https://ourworldindata.org/co2/country/south-africa (accessed 30 June 2021); International Energy Agency, 'South Africa', https://www.iea.org/countries/south-africa (accessed 30 June 2021); Carbon Brief, 'The Carbon Brief Profile: South Africa', 15 October 2018; Climate Action Tracker, 'South Africa', https://climateactiontracker.org/countries/south-africa (accessed 30 June 2021).

403. South Africa is regarded as the clean-energy trailblazer of the African continent. N. Okonjo-Iweala, 'Africa Can Play a Leading Role in the Fight against Climate Change', Brookings Institution, 8 January 2020.

404. Large-scale mining activities in South Africa release large amounts of toxic heavy metals, including arsenic, cadmium, copper, cobalt, zinc and uranium, into the country's groundwater and river systems. Insufficient public sanitation infrastructure further compounds the lack of safe water. M.C.C. Musingafi and T. Tom, 'Fresh Water Sources Pollution: A Human Related Threat to Fresh Water Security in South Africa', *Journal of Public Policy and Governance* 1, no. 2 (2014), pp. 72–81; A.L.K. Abia, 'River of Bacteria: A South African Study Pinpoints What's Polluting the Water', *The Conversation*, 24 November 2020.

405. Republic of South Africa, 'South Africa's Updated Draft Nationally Determined Contribution (NDC) Launched', 30 March 2021, https://www.environment.gov.za/mediarelease/creecy_indc2021draftlaunch_climatechangecop26.

406. Many well-educated, mostly White South African professionals are emigrating to other English-speaking Western states, a process that has greatly accelerated since the end of apartheid, due to both push and pull factors (millions have emigrated since 1994). V.H. Mlambo and T. Cotties Adetiba, 'Brain Drain and South Africa's Socioeconomic Development: The Waves and Its Effects', *Journal of Public Affairs* 19, no. 4 (2019), p. e1942; B. Mfeka, 'Brain Drain Is Another Threat to Economic Reforms and Recovery', IOL News, 14 October 2020; BusinessTech, 'South Africa's Emigration Problem – No One Knows How Big the Brain Drain Really Is', 23 May 2019.

407. Black South Africans have a huge education deficit, a legacy of the 40-year apartheid period. Although over the past ten years the overall illiteracy rate in South Africa has been brought down to only thirteen per cent of the adult population, the quality of education in poorer, rural

areas remains low. Since the end of apartheid, the government has invested a lot of money in education (6.5 per cent of its GDP in 2019). Education reforms geared towards creating a unitary educational system that provides quality education to people of all races are ongoing. South Africa has a range of very good universities, as well as technical and teacher-training colleges, yet low numbers of South Africans of university age are in tertiary education. Despite the fact that black South Africans represent the majority of the young adult population, as of 2019, only fourteen per cent of blacks aged eighteen to 29 were enrolled at a higher education institution in South Africa, compared to the 57 per cent of whites. World Bank, 'Literacy Rate: South Africa', https://data .worldbank.org/indicator/SE.ADT.LITR.ZS?locations=ZA (accessed 30 June 2021); Amnesty International, 'South Africa: Broken and Unequal Education Perpetuating Poverty and Inequality', 11 February 2020; UNESCO Institute of Statistics, 'South Africa', http://uis.unesco.org/en /country/za (accessed 30 June 2021); World Bank, 'Government Expenditure on Education, Total (% of GDP) – South Africa', https:// data.worldbank.org/indicator/SE.XPD.TOTL.GD.ZS?locations=ZA (accessed 30 June 2021); N.P. Mncayi, 'South African Graduates May Be Mostly Employed, but Skills and Jobs Often Don't Match', *The Conversation*, 13 April 2021; E.N. Tjønneland, 'Crisis at South Africa's Universities – What Are the Implications for Future Cooperation with Norway?', *CMI Brief* 16, no. 3 (2017).

408. South Africa's crime rate, often attributed to the social and economic inequality in the country, is among the highest in the world (it is rivalled only by Venezuela and Papua New Guinea). On average, there are around 58 murders per day in South Africa. BusinessTech, 'South Africa Crime Stats 2020: Everything You Need to Know', 31 July 2020; World Population Review, 'Crime Rate by Country 2021', https:// worldpopulationreview.com/country-rankings/crime-rate-by-country (accessed 30 June 2021); J. Felix, 'Crime Mostly Affects Poor SA Communities – Researcher', *Eyewitness News*, 14 September 2019.

409. South Africa has been a major advocate for restructuring the UN Security Council and is seeking a permanent seat on it. As one of the wealthiest and most developed African states, the country acts as an advocate for the interests of the African continent within the international community. H. Isilow, 'S. Africa Demands More African Representation at UNSC', Anadolu Agency, 22 September 2020.

410. South Africa has contributed to the resolution of conflicts in the Democratic Republic of Congo, Sudan, Burundi, Rwanda and the Ivory Coast. The country took a leading role in setting up the African Union in 2001. South Africa has considerable soft-power capabilities. First, it boasts the most developed and second-biggest economy on the continent and thus can use economic incentives as a foreign policy tool. Second, the country enjoys considerable status and respect within the

international community as a relatively stable multiparty, multiracial and multicultural democracy in Africa, having undergone a peaceful political transformation in 1994. C. Hendricks and N. Majozi, 'South Africa's International Relations: A New Dawn?', *Journal of African and Asian Studies* 56, no. 1 (2021), pp. 64–78.

411. Over the past three decades, the number of foreign residents in South Korea has increased at an exponential rate, significantly changing the demographic landscape of the country. In 2019, the population of registered foreigners in South Korea stood at around 1.27 million, having grown from about 919,000 in 2010 and only 50,000 in 1990. This demographic change has brought the risk of social tensions and the need for integration of foreigners, which the government has sought to address through labour regulations and assimilation policies. Statista, 'Population of Registered Foreigners in South Korea from 2010 to 2019', 5 March 2021, https://www.statista.com/statistics/1068529/south-korea-registered-foreigners-number; M. Kim-Bossard, 'Challenging Homogeneity in Contemporary Korea: Immigrant Women, Immigrant Laborers, and Multicultural Families', *Education about Asia* 23, no. 2 (Fall 2018), pp. 38–41; Korea.net, 'Becoming a Society That Respects Cultural Diversity', https://www.korea.net/AboutKorea/Society/Transformation-Multicultural-Society (accessed 30 June 2021); T. Lim, 'The Road to Multiculturalism in South Korea', *Georgetown Journal of International Affairs*, 10 October 2017.

412. With 516 people per square kilometre in 2020, the country has one of the world's highest population densities. Statista, 'Population Density in South Korea from 2000 to 2020', 15 June 2021, https://www.statista.com/statistics/756232/south-korea-population-density; World Bank, 'Population, Total: Republic of Korea', https://data.worldbank.org/indicator/SP.POP.TOTL?locations=KR (accessed 30 June 2021).

413. The fertility rate in 2019 was 0.9, the lowest among OECD countries, down from over six in 1960. Combined with a life expectancy of 83.2 years in 2019, this has led to the rapid ageing of the population. World Bank, 'Fertility Rate: Republic of Korea', https://data.worldbank.org/indicator/SP.DYN.TFRT.IN?locations=KR (accessed 30 June 2021); OECD, 'Fertility Rates', https://data.oecd.org/pop/fertility-rates.htm (accessed 30 June 2021); World Bank, 'Life Expectancy at Birth, Total (Years) – Republic of Korea', https://data.worldbank.org/indicator/SP.DYN.LE00.IN?locations=KR (accessed 30 June 2021).

414. The rate of urbanisation has consistently been over 81 per cent since 2009. Statista, 'South Korea: Urbanization from 2010 to 2020', 6 July 2021, https://www.statista.com/statistics/455905/urbanization-in-south-korea.

415. Environmental pollution and poor sanitation cause significant health problems in South Korea. According to a 2017 survey, about 51 per cent of respondents suffered from more than three diagnosed chronic

diseases. More than 80 per cent of deaths in South Korea are linked to chronic illnesses such as cancer and heart disease. Statista, 'Share of Elderly People Suffering from Diagnosed Chronic Diseases in South Korea in 2017, by Number of Diseases', https://www.statista.com/statistics/944213/south-korea-seniors-with-chronic-conditions-by-number-of-diseases (accessed 30 June 2021); Institute for Health Metrics and Evaluation, 'South Korea', http://www.healthdata.org/south-korea (accessed 30 June 2021); L. Dayeong, '81% of Deaths in Korea Caused by Chronic Illnesses', *Korea Herald*, 20 August 2015.

416. Suicide is the leading cause of death among teenagers in Korea, which also has the highest suicide rate overall in the OECD. Student surveys have shown that poor grades and fears of failure are major causes of suicide. D. Mani and S. Trines, 'Education in South Korea', WENR, 16 October 2018.

417. The main two political parties in South Korea are the liberal Democratic Party of Korea (DPK) and the conservative People Power Party (PPP). During the 2020 parliamentary elections, the outgoing Democratic Party and its satellite, the Platform Party, won a landslide victory, taking 60 per cent of the seats between them, gaining the three fifths super-majority required to fast-track government procedures. The conservative alliance led by the United Future Party won only 103 seats, the worst conservative result since 1960. M. Jae-in, 'South Korea's Governing Party Wins Election by a Landslide', Al Jazeera, 16 April 2020.

418. Calculated by 2021 GDP estimates. In 2019, South Korea's GDP stood at US$1.65 trillion. International Monetary Fund, 'Projected GDP Ranking', April 2021, https://statisticstimes.com/economy/projected-world-gdp-ranking.ph.

419. South Korea's export-oriented policies are one of the most important factors of its economic success and have led to it becoming the world's seventh-largest exporter of goods and the ninth-largest importer. In 2019, trade represented almost 76.7 per cent of its GDP. World Bank, 'Trade in Percent of GDP: Republic of Korea', https://data.worldbank.org/indicator/NE.TRD.GNFS.ZS?locations=KR (accessed 30 June 2021); Observatory of Economic Complexity, 'South Korea', https://oec.world/en/profile/country/kor (accessed 18 November 2021); Santander, 'South Korea Foreign Trade in Figures', https://santandertrade.com/en/portal/analyse-markets/south-korea/foreign-trade-in-figures (accessed 30 June 2021); S. Moon, 'Decrease in the Growth of Domestic Demand in Korea', Korea Institute for International Economic Policy, December 2015.

420. As Asia's fourth-largest economy, South Korea exported goods worth over US$136 billion to China in 2019, comprising a quarter of its total exports. The past few years, however, have seen a decrease in Korea's investment in China because it has been caught in the crossfire of the

US-China trade war. C.M. Lee, 'South Korea Is Caught between China and the United States', Carnegie Endowment for International Peace, 21 October 2020; H. Jianguo, 'Cooperation with China Crucial to South Korean Economy', *Global Times*, 4 August 2020; F. Bermingham and L. Jeong-ho, 'One of China's Most Successful Investors Is Quietly Leaving', *inkstonebusiness*, 10 July 2019, https://www.inkstonenews.com/business /samsung-and-other-south-korean-companies-leave-china-sets-example -western-firms-fleeing-trade-war/article/3018033.

421. Income per capita nearly doubled in South Korea in 2020 compared to 2009. While poverty rates have significantly decreased since the 1970s, poverty in South Korea is still present, with two major groups experiencing poverty in South Korea today: the non-regular workers; and the elderly. About fifteen per cent of South Koreans were living in poverty in 2013. Social assistance is scarce and few qualify for it. Despite significant economic success, social spending is extremely low in South Korea at 12.2 per cent of GDP compared with an OECD average of 20 per cent in 2019, one of the lowest in the OECD. CEIC, 'South Korea Household Income Per Capita', https://www.ceicdata.com/en/indicator /korea/annual-household-income-per-capita (accessed 30 June 2021); Y.J. Yi, 'History of Poverty in South Korea', The Borgen Project, 25 February 2020; Human Rights Measurement Initiative, 'Data in Action: Spotlights on South Korea', https://humanrightsmeasurement.org /country-spotlights/data-in-action-spotlight-on-south-korea (accessed 30 June 2021); OECD, 'Social Spending', https://data.oecd.org/socialexp /social-spending.htm (accessed 30 June 2021).

422. Irregular jobs are temporary and offer few training opportunities and career prospects. According to the latest data from Statistics Korea, in 2018, nearly five million South Koreans were engaged in forms of irregular work, out of total workforce of just over 26.4 million. J. Cho, G. Kim and T. Kwon, 'Employment Problems with Irregular Workers in Korea: A Critical Approach to Government Policy', *Pacific Affairs* 81, no. 3 (2008), pp. 407–26; H. Morris, 'For Irregular Workers, Korea's Labor Market Embeds Unfairness', *Asia Times*, 21 February 2018, https://asiatimes.com/2018/02/irregular-workers-koreas-labor-market -embeds-unfairness.

423. Urban air pollution affects the health of South Korean city dwellers, who constitute a vast majority of South Koreans. According to the World Health Organization, in 2019, Korea experienced the worst air quality of any of the 35 richest countries. In 2015, South Korea was also the world's thirteenth-largest greenhouse gas emitter. US International Trade Administration, 'South Korea – Country Commercial Guide', updated 13 August 2021, https://www.trade.gov/knowledge-product/korea-air -pollution-control; IQAir, 'Air Quality in South Korea', updated 24 November 2021, https://www.iqair.com/south-korea; J. Gabbatiss, 'The Carbon Brief Profile: South Korea', 6 April 2020.

424. South Korea has one of the highest proportions of people between 25 and 34 years of age to have completed some form of tertiary education, at 70 per cent in 2018. The country was placed second among OECD countries for math skills among teenagers in 2005. South Korea places a lot of value and cultural and national importance on education and believes that investments in education have been key to the country's rapid and successful economic development in the past four decades. South Korea's literacy rate was 98 per cent in 2019. Mani and Trines, 'Education in South Korea'; OECD, *Lessons from PISA for Korea* (Paris: OECD Publishing, 2014), p. 190; Index Mundi, 'South Korea Literacy', https://www.indexmundi.com/south_korea/literacy.html (accessed 30 June 2021).

425. South Korea is a global innovation leader, ranking second in Bloomberg's 2020 Innovation Index. This is thanks to its high level of R&D investment and to it being a leader in both the 'fourth industrial revolution' and in the digital banking sector. L. Dayton, 'How South Korea Made Itself a Global Innovation Leader', *Nature*, 28 May 2020; K. Cagape, 'Why the Korean IT Industry Is One of the Best in the World', TECHINASIA, 16 May 2017.

426. OECD, 'Reducing the Gap between Skill Supply and Demand in Korea', https://www.oecd-ilibrary.org/sites/dfe47455-en/index.html?itemId =/content/component/dfe47455-en (accessed 30 June 2021).

427. The Korean War ended in 1953 without a peace agreement. In April 2018, however, the two countries signed the Panmunjom Declaration for Peace, Prosperity and Unification of the Korean Peninsula. According to the declaration, both governments agreed to cooperate on officially ending the Korean War and the Korean conflict. They also agreed to begin a new era of national reconciliation, peace, reunification and prosperity and improvements to inter-Korean communication and relations, with the declaration agreeing that both sides would 'make active efforts to seek the support and cooperation of the international community for the denuclearization of the Korean peninsula'. Nevertheless, in 2020, North Korea carried out a series of provocations against South Korea, including the demolition of the Inter-Korean Liaison Office, raising tensions once more. South Korean Ministry of Foreign Affairs, 'Panmunjom Declaration for Peace, Prosperity and Unification of the Korean Peninsula', 11 September 2018, http://www.mofa.go.kr/eng/brd/m_5478/view.do?seq=319130&srchFr =&srchTo=&srchWord=&srchTp=&multi_itm_seq=0&itm_seq_1 =0&itm_seq_2=0&company_cd=&company_nm=&page=1&titleNm=; Crisis 24, 'South Korea Country Report', https://crisis24.garda.com /insights-intelligence/intelligence/country-reports/south-korea (accessed 30 June 2021).

428. About 28,500 US troops remain in South Korea. The US also has a strong military presence in the nearby Pacific region, including in Japan.

US Congressional Research Service, 'South Korea: Background and US Relations', 26 May 2021.

429. North Korea remains a significant military threat to South Korea. The country has one of the largest military forces in the world, the majority of which are deployed in an offensive mode along the Demilitarized Zone between the two Koreas. J. Kim, 'China and Regional Security Dynamics on the Korean Peninsula', in C.M. Lee and K. Botto (eds), Korea Net Assessment: Politicized Security and Unchanging Strategic Realities (Washington, DC: Carnegie Endowment for International Peace, 2020), pp. 55–65; K. Min-Seok, 'The State of the North Korean Military', in Lee and Botto (eds), Korea Net Assessment.

430. Lee, 'South Korea Is Caught between China and the United States'; F. Nicolas, 'The Economic Pillar of Korea's New Southern Policy: Building on Existing Assets', *Asie.Visions*, no. 120, Ifri, February 2021.

431. Challenges include recent tax cuts for businesses and a reduction in welfare programmes, even though health, education and elderly care are supported. See N. Sanandaji, 'So Long, Swedish Welfare State?', *Foreign Policy*, 5 September 2018.

432. 82.5 years in 2018. See OECD Better Life Initiative, 'How's Life in Sweden?', 2020, https://www.oecd.org/sweden/Better-Life-Initiative -country-note-Sweden.pdf.

433. 10.90 per cent of the GDP in 2018. See World Bank, 'Current Health Expenditure: Sweden', https://data.worldbank.org/indicator/SH.XPD .CHEX.GD.ZS?locations=SE (accessed 20 June 2021).

434. For decades, Sweden has been governed by the traditional left and right parties. The emergence of a populist party is thus surprising and could trigger significant challenges for forming a government in 2021. See R. Milne, 'Sweden's Government on Brink ahead of No-Confidence Vote', *Financial Times*, 17 June 2021.

435. Growth of 4.3 per cent is predicted for 2021. See OECD, 'Swedish Economic Snapshot - Swedish Economic Forecast Summary (December 2021)', https://www.oecd.org/economy/sweden-economic -snapshot/ (accessed 13 January 2022).

436. According to the OECD data for the second quarter of 2021, 74.1 per cent for people of working age; the OECD average is 66.9 per cent and the EU average is 67.5 per cent. See OECD, 'Employment Rate (Indicator)', 2021, https://doi.org/10.1787/1de68a9b-en (accessed on 13 September 2021).

437. Mostly in the creative and technological domains.

438. Exposure to outdoor air pollution is generally lower than the OECD average.

439. Investments by both the public and private sectors.

440. Sweden's mean PISA score is 499 and its student skills in science are highlighted.

441. Sweden has had a welcoming immigration policy but this is contested by the rise of populism in the country.

442. Though Sweden is leading in R&D as well as employing most of its citizens in technological or creative jobs, this trend is accompanied by a natural rise in cyber vulnerabilities. The Swedish police describe this challenge as one of the major security risks for the country. See L. Roden, 'The Four Big Security Challenges Facing Sweden Today', *The Local*, 16 March 2017.

443. Sweden has a tradition of neutrality which it notably followed during the Second World War. See NATO Slovenija, 'Neutral European Countries: Austria, Sweden, Finland, Ireland', http://nato.gov.si/eng /topic/national-security/neutral-status/neutral-countries (accessed 21 June 2021).

444. Sixth-largest financial donor to the UN system. See Government Offices of Sweden, 'Sweden and the UN in Figures', 29 June 2018, https://www .government.se/government-policy/sweden-and-the-un/sweden-and-the -un-in-figures.

445. Notably in the EU's COVID-19 recovery plan conditions, where it advocates for loans rather than grants to states in need. See Euractiv, 'Sweden and Denmark Step Out of the Shadows as EU's Frugals', 10 July 2020.

446. See US Department of State, Overseas Security Advisory Council, 'Switzerland 2020 Crime and Safety Report: Bern', 31 July 2020.

447. See World Bank, 'Life Expectancy at Birth, Total (Years) – Switzerland', https://data.worldbank.org/indicator/SP.DYN.LE00.IN?locations=CH (accessed 21 June 2021).

448. See World Bank, 'Current Health Expenditure: Switzerland', https:// data.worldbank.org/indicator/SH.XPD.CHEX.GD.ZS?locations=CH (accessed 21 June 2021).

449. See World's Top Exports, 'World's Top Export Countries', https://www .worldstopexports.com/worlds-top-export-countries (accessed 21 June 2021).

450. Switzerland is attractive for the banking sector because of its central location, political stability, low inflation, excellent financial-services infrastructure and strict bank-secrecy laws. Money-laundering, however, has tarnished its image and scandals continue to emerge despite the introduction of strong anti-money-laundering laws. See K. Romy, 'Banking Secrecy Remains a Business Model for Swiss Banks', Swissinfo.ch, 5 February 2021.

451. More than 150 per cent of GDP in 2015. See OECD, 'Switzerland: Trade and Investment Statistical Note', 2017.

452. See Federal Office for the Environment (Switzerland), 'Air Quality in Switzerland', 18 June 2021, https://www.bafu.admin.ch/bafu/en/home /topics/air/info-specialists/air-quality-in-switzerland.html.

453. The country's stable political environment and efficient infrastructure provide ideal conditions for excellence in research and academia. Education is decentralised and ranks among the best systems worldwide. See V. Ung-Kono, '10 Facts about Education in Switzerland', The Borgen Project, 17 July 2016.

454. Some 3.2 per cent of GDP goes into R&D, of which the private sector contributes the largest part. See UNESCO Institute of Statistics, 'How Much Does Your Country Invest in R&D?.'

455. Federal Intelligence Service (Switzerland), 'Switzerland's Security 2020', https://www.newsd.admin.ch/newsd/message/attachments/63415.pdf.

456. Switzerland's post-Cold War security policy is based on the premise that actively cooperating with friendly states and international organisations to promote international peace and security will reduce the possibility that Switzerland will suffer from the negative effects of instability and war. See State Secretariat for Economic Affairs (Switzerland), 'Swiss International Cooperation', 5 March 2021, https://www.seco -cooperation.admin.ch/secocoop/en/home/strategy/focus/international -cooperation.html.

457. See NATO Slovenija, 'Neutral European Countries'.

458. The Swiss-EU institutional agreement was not signed, following a decision by the Federal Council on 26 May 2021. See Federal Department of Foreign Affairs (Switzerland), 'No Signing of Swiss-EU Institutional Agreement', 26 May 2021, https://www.eda.admin.ch/eda /en/fdfa/fdfa/aktuell/newsuebersicht/2021/05/institutionelles -abkommen-kein-abschluss.html.

459. Sixth-largest financial donor to the UN system. See Government Offices of Sweden, 'Sweden and the UN in Figures'.

460. Turkey's annual population growth rate is 1.49 per cent (2019 estimate). In 2007, Turkey's population was a little over 71 million. In 2020, it reached 84.17 million and it has been estimated that it will grow to almost 90 million by 2025. World Bank, 'Population Growth: Turkey', https://data.worldbank.org/indicator/SP.POP.GROW?locations=TR (accessed 30 June 2021); Statista, 'Total Population of Turkey 2016 to 2026', https://www.statista.com/statistics/263753/total-population-of -turkey (accessed 30 June 2021).

461. In 2002, Turkey's health-care system was plagued by inefficiencies and dissatisfaction, with an infant mortality rate of 26.1 per 1,000 live births and less than two thirds of the population with health insurance. This resulted in unequal health-care access among different population groups. The Health Transformation Programme led by the Turkish government since 2003 has contributed to improving the health-care system and making it more financially accessible, which enabled the rate of health-care access for the Turkish population to reach 98 per cent in 2012, resulting in visible improvements in health outcomes. Not only did infant mortality rates halve, but life expectancy grew to 74 years.

Health care is still underfunded, however, with only 4.7 per cent of GDP spent on the sector in 2019, well below the global average of 9.5 per cent in 2018. World Bank, 'Turkey: Transforming Health Care for All', 27 April 2018, https://www.worldbank.org/en/about/partners/brief /turkey-transforming-health-care-for-all; Statista, 'Total Health Expenditure as Share of GDP in Turkey from 2000 to 2019', https:// www.statista.com/statistics/893497/health-expenditure-as-share-of -gdp-in-turkey (accessed 30 June 2021); World Bank, 'Current Health Expenditure: Turkey', https://data.worldbank.org/indicator/SH.XPD .CHEX.GD.ZS?locations=TR (accessed 30 June 2021).

462. Turkey has drawn harsh criticism from the international community, and especially the EU, for not fully respecting the rights of minority ethnic groups in Turkey, in particular, those of the Kurds, who comprise about fifteen to 20 per cent of Turkey's population. The use of the Kurdish language as the primary language of instruction is prohibited even today in both public and private schools. Minority Rights Group, 'Kurds', https://minorityrights.org/minorities/kurds-2 (accessed 30 June 2021).

463. Turkey faces high levels of violence against women. It controversially withdrew from the Istanbul Convention (Council of Europe Convention on Preventing and Combating Violence against Women and Domestic Violence), which provides a roadmap for the elimination of gender-based violence against women and girls, in 2021. F. Basar and N. Demirci, 'Domestic Violence against Women in Turkey', *Pakistan Journal of Medical Sciences* 34, no. 3 (May-June 2018); K. Genç, 'Turkey Withdraws from Treaty on Violence against Women', *The Lancet* 397, no. 10283 (April 2021), https://www.thelancet.com/journals/lancet /article/PIIS0140-6736(21)00837-0/fulltext; Amnesty International, 'Turkey: Women across the World Demand Reversal of Decision to Quit Gender-Based Violence Treaty', 10 May 2021.

464. Between 1923 and 2018, Turkey was a parliamentary representative democracy. A referendum in 2017 approved the adoption of a presidential system which gives President Recep Tayyip Erdogan complete control of the executive, including the power to issue decrees, appoint his own cabinet and so on. A unicameral parliament, called the Grand National Assembly of Turkey, exercises legislative authority in the country. Although the judiciary is formally independent from the executive and the legislature, the constitutional changes that came into effect with the referendums in 2007, 2010 and 2017 gave larger powers to the president and the ruling party to appoint or dismiss judges and prosecutors. This has contributed to allegations that Erdogan's government is becoming increasing authoritarian. *The Economist*, 'Recep Tayyip the First: Erdogan Inaugurates a New Political Era in Turkey', 28 June 2018; C. Morris, 'Turkey Elections: How Powerful Will the Next Turkish President Be?', BBC News, 22 June 2018; Z. Yilmaz and

B.S. Turner, 'Turkey's Deepening Authoritarianism and the Fall of Electoral Democracy', *British Journal of Middle Eastern Studies* 46, no. 5 (2019), pp. 691–98; B. Burak, 'Turkey's Authoritarian Slide and Political Decay', *International Policy Digest*, 14 February 2021.

465. Since it came to power in 2002, Erdogan's Justice and Development Party (the APK), which strongly denies it is Islamist, has been accused of adopting increasingly anti-secular policies, progressively distancing Turkey from the EU. J. Wang and B. Wang, 'Turkish Islamic Movement after Conservatives in Power', *Asian Journal of Middle Eastern and Islamic Studies* 12, no. 2 (2017), pp. 55–68; *Encyclopedia Britannica*, 'Justice and Development Party', 12 November 2021; *Encyclopedia Britannica*, 'Turkey', by M.E. Yapp and J.C. Dewdney, 21 November 2021; Global Security, 'Justice and Development Party (AKP) Adalet ve Kalkinma Parti (AKP)', https://www.globalsecurity.org/military/world /europe/tu-political-party-akp.htm (accessed 30 June 2021); A. Simsek, 'Support for Muslim Brotherhood Isolates Turkey', DW, 21 August 2013; Ö. Taşpınar, 'Turkey: The New Model?', Brookings Institution, 25 April 2012.

466. The most significant problem stalling Turkey's democratic progress and drawing wide criticism from human rights agencies and the EU is the treatment of its Kurdish minority, whose minority status is not recognised by Turkey.

467. Turkey's human rights record has been the subject of much controversy and international condemnation and is one of the major obstacles to the country's accession to the EU. Between 1959 and 2011, the European Court of Human Rights issued more than 2,400 judgements against Turkey for human rights violations on issues such as Kurdish rights, women's rights, LGBTQI+ rights and media freedom. H. Merkezi, 'Turkey Ranks First in Violations in between 1959–2011', English Bianet, 15 May 2012; European Court of Human Rights, 'Annual Report 2014 of the European Court of Human Rights, Council of Europe'; European Parliament, Human Rights Sub-Committee, 'Human Rights in Turkey: Still a Long Way to Go to Meet Accession Criteria', 26 October 2010, https://www.europarl.europa.eu/news/lv/press-room/20101025IPR90072 /human-rights-in-turkey-still-a-long-way-to-go-to-meet-accession -criteria.

468. Since 1984, the Kurdistan Workers' Party (PKK) has been involved in a conflict with the Turkish government (with ceasefires in 1999–2004 and 2013–15). The PKK has various objectives, including an independent Kurdish state, autonomy and increased human rights for Kurds within Turkey. E. Lust (ed.), *The Middle East* (Washington, DC: CQ Press, 2019), p. 37; R. Onursal, 'Why the Kurdish Conflict in Turkey Is So Intractable', *The Conversation*, 18 October 2019; M. Hoffman, 'The State of the Turkish-Kurdish Conflict', *Center for American Progress*, 12 August 2019.

469. With a GDP of US$648.44 billion in 2020, Turkey is the world's twentieth-largest economy. According to the World Bank, the middle-class population in Turkey rose from eighteen to 41 per cent of the population between 1993 and 2010 and unemployment in Turkey was 13.6 per cent in 2019. It has a very unstable and fluctuating GDP growth rate, however. It stood at −4.8 per cent in 2009 following the financial crisis, 11.2 per cent in 2011 during a period of intense growth and economic reforms, but was only 0.9 per cent in 2019. Statista, 'The 20 Countries with the Largest Gross Domestic Product in 2020', 16 June 2021, https://www.statista.com/statistics/268173/countries-with-the-largest-gross-domestic-product-gdp; World Bank, 'New World Bank Report Looks at Turkey's Rise to the Threshold of High-Income Status and the Challenges Remaining', 10 December 2014; World Bank, 'Unemployment: Turkey', https://data.worldbank.org/indicator/SL.UEM.TOTL.ZS?locations=TR (accessed 30 June 2021); World Bank, 'GDP Growth: Turkey', https://data.worldbank.org/indicator/NY.GDP.MKTP.KD.ZG?locations=TR (accessed 30 June 2021).

470. Turkey borders several countries and regions that hold huge reserves of fossil fuels. The TurkStream pipeline, for instance, carries Russian gas into Europe, bypassing Ukraine, with whom Russia has an ongoing conflict. I. Berk and S. Schulte, 'Turkey's Role in Natural Gas – Becoming a Transit Country?', EWI Working Paper, no. 17/01, January 2017; J. Bauomy, 'TurkStream: Europe Needs Gas and Russia Has It – The Story behind That New Pipeline', euronews, 8 January 2020; O. Astakhova and C. Sezer, 'Turkey, Russia Launch TurkStream Pipeline Carrying Gas to Europe', Reuters, 8 January 2020.

471. O. Torul and O. Oztunali, 'On Income and Wealth Inequality in Turkey', *Central Bank Review* 18, no. 3 (2018), p. 96.

472. Turkey has the largest informal sector size (relative to GDP) among OECD members along with Mexico, amounting to about 25 to 30 per cent of official GDP. Although the size of the informal sector has declined significantly since the 1980s, it still constitutes a large section of the economy and acts as a barrier for growth, technological advancement and the efficiency of public finance. O.E. Atesagaoglu, C. Elgin and O. Oztunali, 'TFP Growth in Turkey Revisited: The Effect of Informal Sector', *Central Bank Review* 17, no. 1 (2017), pp. 11–17.

473. The Turkish pharmaceutical industry ranks seventh in Europe and sixteenth in the world in terms of market size. Turkey should therefore make the most of this opportunity to become a key services and pharma products supplier for neighbouring regions, with a total export potential of US$8 billion. The potential of the industry stems from its high-tech manufacturing capability, its capacity to enter the global competition with its geographical location and relatively reasonable cost structure. Moreover, since it does not have any problems of sustainability, the pharmaceutical sector is regarded as having key strategic importance for

Turkey by policy makers and is often included in incentive packages. Nevertheless, the sector still faces challenges in terms of foreign trade deficit and insufficient funding for R&D. ERAI, 'The Pharmaceutical Industry in Turkey – 1', 6 May 2021; L. Jafari and L. Stancu, *Turkey Pharmaceuticals and Biopharmaceuticals 2020* (London: Global Business Reports, 2020).

474. European Environment Agency, 'Turkey – Industrial Pollution Profile 2020', 14 September 2020, https://www.eea.europa.eu/themes/industry /industrial-pollution/industrial-pollution-country-profiles-2020/turkey.

475. Water supplies are critically low in certain areas of the country. Suwanu Europe, 'Water Scarcity Increases in Turkey', 19 January 2021.

476. In October 2020, for instance, a magnitude 7.0 earthquake, originating in the Aegean Sea and followed by a tsunami, hit the province of Izmir, in Turkey, causing widespread damage to the country's third-largest city. More than 116 people died and over 1,000 were injured. Thousands of families lost their homes. T. Meyers, 'Responding to Turkey's Devastating Earthquake', *Direct Relief*, 7 December 2021, https:// reliefweb.int/report/turkey/responding-turkey-s-devastating -earthquake.

477. Although it has increased significantly since it measured less than 0.8 per cent in 2008 (aided also by a support package adopted in 2016), Turkey's investment in R&D is still very low. Trading Economics, 'Turkey – Research and Development Expenditure', July 2021, https:// tradingeconomics.com/turkey/research-and-development-expenditure -percent-of-gdp-wb-data.html; UNCTAD, Investment Policy Hub, 'Turkey Introduced a New R&D Support Package', 1 March 2016.

478. Although Turkey has made considerable improvements in educational performance over recent years, not all students have equal access to good quality and engaging education. OECD, 'Education Policy Outlook: Turkey', June 2020, https://www.oecd.org/turkey/country -profile-Turkey-2020.pdf, pp. 3, 8.

479. The Turkish government is fighting a reasonably successful war against drug trafficking. It is making similar but less successful efforts to address human trafficking. M. Tosun, 'Turkey Deals Heavy Blow to Drug Trafficking in 2020', Anadolu Agency, 3 January 2021; M.N. Erdogan, 'Turkey: Drug Trade, Organized Crime Hit Hard in 2020', Anadolu Agency, 7 January 2021; US Department of State, Office to Monitor and Combat Trafficking in Persons, '2020 Trafficking in Persons Report: Turkey', https://www.state.gov/reports/2020-trafficking -in-persons-report/turkey; Council of Europe, 'Strengthening the Human Rights Protection of Migrants and Victims of Human Trafficking in Turkey', https://www.coe.int/en/web/ankara/streng thening-the-human-rights-protection-of-migrants-and-victims-of -human-trafficking-in-turkey (accessed 30 June 2021); T. Ismayilzada,

'Tackling Human Trafficking in Turkey', The Borgen Project, 29 March 2021.

480. Turkey provides military support to the Tripoli-based Government of National Accord. Harchaoui, *Why Turkey Intervened in Libya*; D. Lepeska, 'Turkey Can Play a Constructive Role in Libya. But Will It?', *N OPINION*, https://www.thenationalnews.com/opinion/comment/turkey-can-play-a-constructive-role-in-libya-but-will-it-1.1232326 (accessed 30 June 2021).

481. Since the beginning of the Arab Spring in 2011, Turkey has supported the Syrian rebels trying to overturn Assad's regime. In 2016, it sent troops into Syria to fight Islamic State. D.L. Phillips, 'The Truth about Turkey's Role in Syria', Columbia University Institute for the Study of Human Rights, 1 March 2021, http://www.humanrightscolumbia.org/news/truth-about-turkey%E2%80%99s-role-syria.

482. International Crisis Group, 'Rising Tensions in the Eastern Mediterranean', 13 July 2021.

483. G. Dalay, 'Turkey, Europe, and the Eastern Mediterranean: Charting a Way out of the Current Deadlock', Brookings Institution, 28 January 2021.

484. Turkey officially became a candidate for membership in 1999 and accession negotiations started in 2005. The EU has stated, however, that the negotiations will not progress until Turkey agrees to apply the Additional Protocol of the Ankara Association Agreement to Cyprus. European Commission, 'Turkey', 30 June 2021, https://ec.europa.eu/neighbourhood-enlargement/countries/detailed-country-information/turkey_en.

485. Although the relationship has suffered over the past few years, Turkey remains a strong US and NATO partner. G. Aybet, 'Turkey-US Relations: Where Now?', RUSI, Commentary, 30 April 2021, https://rusi.org/explore-our-research/publications/commentary/turkey-us-relations-where-now; US Department of State, 'U.S. Relations with Turkey', 20 January 2021, https://www.state.gov/u-s-relations-with-turkey.

486. This is an improvement but is still much lower than the OECD average of 80 years. See World Bank, 'Life Expectancy at Birth, Total (Years) – Ukraine', https://data.worldbank.org/indicator/SP.DYN.LE00.IN?locations=UA (accessed 2 June 2021).

487. Despite being the third-lowest European country in terms of inequalities, inequalities between urban and rural areas remain. See World Bank, 'In Ukraine, Labor, Taxation, and Social Policies Must Be Upgraded to Address Rising Inequality, Says World Bank', 25 September 2018.

488. This is below its European neighbours. See WHO Europe, 'Budgetary Space for Health in Ukraine', Health Policy Paper Series no. 20/01, July 2020, p. 1.

489. K.G. Ilinova, 'Foreign and Domestic Policy of Ukraine at the Present Stage', *Post-Soviet Issues* 5, no. 1 (2018), pp. 89–100.

490. The European Union is close to the government and Russia has a strong influence on Eastern regions. See ibid.

491. M. Minakov, 'Ukraine's Political Agenda for the First Half of 2021', Focus Ukraine, 22 January 2021.

492. 112.UA International, 'EBRD Improves Prediction of Growth of Ukraine's Economy for 2021', 29 June 2021.

493. S. Commander, N. Isachenkova and Y. Rodionova, 'A Model of the Informal Economy with an Application to Ukraine', *IZA*, 21 September 2009.

494. World Bank, 'Unemployment: Ukraine', https://data.worldbank.org /indicator/SL.UEM.TOTL.ZS?locations=UA (accessed 22 June 2021).

495. International Association for Medical Assistance to Travellers, 'Ukraine General Health Risks: Air Pollution', 16 April 2020, https://www.iamat .org/country/ukraine/risk/air-pollution#.

496. Mitigated by the COVID-19 pandemic, but still high. One of the main factors is the coal industry. See Climate Action Tracker, 'Ukraine', 30 July 2020, https://climateactiontracker.org/countries/ukraine.

497. Ministry of Education and Science of Ukraine, 'Science in Ukraine', https://mon.gov.ua/eng/science/nauka/nauka-v-ukrayini (accessed 22 June 2021).

498. UNESCO Institute of Statistics, 'How Much Does Your Country Invest in R&D?'

499. Ibid.

500. Crimea was annexed by Russia in 2014. See L. Peter, 'Is Russia Going to War with Ukraine and Other Questions', BBC News, 13 April 2021.

501. S. Lain, 'Russia Piles Up the Pressure on Ukraine', RUSI, Commentary, 6 April 2021, https://rusi.org/commentary/russia-piles-pressure-ukraine.

502. This includes information warfare. See T. Kuzio, 'Russia Is Quietly Occupying Ukraine's Information Space', Atlantic Council, 27 June 2020.

503. O. Goncharenko, 'Rising EU-Russia Tensions Are Good News for Ukraine', Atlantic Council, 11 February 2021.

504. Over the last two decades, Ukraine became increasingly close to both toe EU and NATO, and expressed its ambition to join both organisations. As is expanded upon in the Appendix, this shifted the country away from its previous status as a 'buffer zone' between Russia and Europe. Ilinova, 'Foreign and Domestic Policy of Ukraine'.

505. Long-term improvements in life expectancy and mortality in the UK have stalled and are falling behind other high-income countries, with life expectancy stuck at about 81 years since 2013. Meanwhile, the difference between the health of people living in the best- and worst-off communities is widening. Health Foundation, 'Top Line Facts on the

Big Issues in Health and Social Care', 9 December 2019; World Bank, 'Life Expectancy at Birth, Total (Years) – United Kingdom', https://data .worldbank.org/indicator/SP.DYN.LE00.IN?locations=GB (accessed 30 June 2021); Care Quality Commission, *The State of Health Care and Adult Social Care in England 2019/20*, HC 799 (London: Care Quality Commission, 2020).

506. The UK has an alarmingly high level of income inequality compared to other developed countries. The richest fifth had an income more than twelve times the amount earned by the poorest fifth. In the period leading up to financial year ending (FYE) March 2020, income inequality steadily increased to 36.3 per cent, according to estimates from the Household Finances Survey. This was the highest reported measure of income inequality over the ten-year period leading up to FYE 2020. Equality Trust, 'The Scale of Economic Inequality in the UK', https://www.equalitytrust.org.uk/scale-economic-inequality-uk (accessed 30 June 2021); J. O'Neill, 'Household Income Inequality, UK: Financial Year Ending 2020', Office for National Statistics, 21 January 2021, https://www.ons.gov.uk/peoplepopulationandcommunity /personalandhouseholdfinances/incomeandwealth/bulletins/household incomeinequalityfinancial/financialyearending2020.

507. According to recent statistics, unemployment in 2019 was four per cent among white Britons and seven per cent among minority groups combined, reaching the respective rates of ten and nineteen per cent for people aged sixteen to 24. According to the Equality and Human Rights Commission, black workers in the UK with degrees earn 23.1 per cent less on average than white workers. Rates of prosecution and sentencing for black people are also three times higher than for white people. Whereas only 8.3 per cent of white people in the UK live in overcrowded accommodation, the percentage is 30.9 per cent for Pakistani or Bangladeshi people, and 26.8 per cent in the case of black people. The Equality and Human Rights Commission also found that 35.7 per cent of ethnic minorities were more likely to live in poverty compared with 17.2 per cent of white people. Equality and Human Rights Commission, 'Race Report Statistics', https://www.equalityhumanrights.com/en /race-report-statistics (accessed 30 June 2021); P. Walker and N. Parveen, 'Racial Disparities in the UK: Key Findings of the Report – and What Its Critics Say', *The Guardian*, 31 March 2021.

508. After the Second World War, employment opportunities in the UK abounded, and people from all over the Commonwealth came to the country to help fill the labour shortage. Hundreds of thousands of refugees fleeing the creation of Communist regimes in Eastern Europe also found a new home in the UK. Despite gradual restrictions on immigration, the UK continues to remain a country with high numbers of immigrants, with approximately 6.2 million people of non-British

nationality living in the UK in 2019 and 9.5 million people who were born abroad. K. Lowe, 'Five Times Immigration Changed the UK', BBC News, 20 January 2020.

509. The UK voted to leave the European Union in a 2016 referendum. Since then, a large part of domestic political focus has been on identifying a path for the separation and on reconstructing internal political unity. Brexit has contributed to worsening internal relations between the countries of the UK. Following Brexit, Scotland has called for a second referendum on its independence from the UK. G. Atkins *et al.*, *Barriers to Delivering New Domestic Policies* (London: Institute for Fiscal Studies, 2019); US Congressional Research Service, 'The United Kingdom: Background, Brexit, and Relations with the United States', 16 April 2021, pp. 2–5.

510. The Conservatives' approach to immigration has drawn a lot of criticism in recent years. From the 2018 deportation and removal of some Windrush migrants and their families to the new immigration law adopted in 2021 which is based on a points system and would exclude many of the categories who previously immigrated to the UK, the Conservative government is demonstrating a shift in the UK's traditionally migration-friendly policies. Gov.uk, 'New Immigration System: What You Need to Know', https://www.gov.uk/guidance/new-immigration-system-what-you-need-to-know (accessed 30 June 2021); T. Brooks, 'Priti Patel's Immigration Reform Is a Confusing Mess That Will Leave Us Worse Off', *The Independent*, 29 May 2021.

511. The UK has one of the most globalised economies in the world, and in 2019 it was the fifth-largest exporter in the world and the fifth-largest importer. The UK is also one of the biggest countries in terms of both inward and outward investment. Brexit came into force in 2021, in 2020, the UK's trade with the European Union accounted for 49 per cent of the country's exports and 52 per cent of its imports. Statista, 'The 20 Countries with the Largest Gross Domestic Product in 2020';;; M. Ward, 'Statistics on UK-EU Trade', House of Commons Library Research Briefing, 10 November 2020.

512. D. Reid, 'New York Stretches Lead over London as the World's Top Financial Center, Survey Shows', CNBC, 19 September 2019.

513. Britain's aerospace industry is the second-largest national aerospace industry in the world, and its pharmaceutical industry is also among the largest. Although the country has been a net importer of oil since 2005, its economy is boosted by North Sea oil and gas production; with reserves estimated at 2.8 billion barrels in 2016. ADS Group, 'Industry Facts and Figures 2017: A Guide to the UK's Aerospace, Defence, Security & Space Sectors', 12 June 2017, https://www.adsgroup.org.uk/facts/facts-figures-2017; A. Monaghan, 'Pharmaceutical Industry Drives British Research and Innovation', *The Guardian*, 22 April 2014; US Central Intelligence Agency, 'Crude Oil – Proved Reserves', *The World Factbook*, https://www.cia.gov/the-world-factbook/field/crude-oil

-proved-reserves/country-comparison; UK Department for Business, Energy and Industrial Strategy, 'Crude Oil and Petroleum: Production, Imports and Exports 1890 to 2020', 29 July 2021, https://www.gov.uk /government/statistical-data-sets/crude-oil-and-petroleum-production -imports-and-exports.

514. Air pollution today remains the single biggest environmental threat to health in the UK, shortening the lives of approximately 40,000 people a year through heart or lung problems. Environment Agency (United Kingdom), 'State of the Environment: Health, People and the Environment', updated 23 July 2021, https://www.gov.uk/government /publications/state-of-the-environment/state-of-the-environment -health-people-and-the-environment; R. Frost, '5 Sustainability Issues Affecting UK', Acre, 9 July 2018.

515. Although levels have risen globally, the UK's emissions of all greenhouse gases have been falling steadily over the past 30 years, with British emissions at 57 per cent of their 1990 levels in 2018. Institute for Government, 'UK Net Zero Target', https://www .instituteforgovernment.org.uk/explainers/net-zero-target (accessed 30 June 2021).

516. Four of the ten best universities in the world are in the UK. Although there is a national system for student loans, university tuition fees in England are higher than in all OECD countries and economies except the United States. Among OECD countries, the United Kingdom spends the fourth highest proportion of its GDP on primary to tertiary educational institutions. According to the Equality and Human Rights Commission's Race Report, however, just six per cent of black school leavers attended an elite university, compared with twelve per cent of mixed and Asian school leavers and eleven per cent of white school leavers. Equality and Human Rights Commission, 'Race Report Statistics'; OECD, 'Education at a Glance 2019: United Kingdom', https:// www.oecd.org/education/education-at-a-glance/EAG2019_CN_GBR .pdf; UNESCO Institute of Statistics, 'United Kingdom of Great Britain and Northern Ireland', http://uis.unesco.org/country/GB (accessed 30 June 2021); UniversityRankings.ch, 'QS World University Rankings 2021', https://www.universityrankings.ch/results/QS/2021.

517. The UK was ranked fifth on the Global Innovation Index 2019. UK Department of International Trade, 'UK Innovation', https://www.great .gov.uk/international/content/about-uk/why-choose-uk/uk-innovation (accessed 30 June 2021).

518. In the UK in 2018, total expenditure on R&D was £37.1 billion, the equivalent of 1.7 per cent of GDP. The government has set the target for total R&D investment at 2.4 per cent of GDP by 2027. The business sector is responsible for twice was much R&D investment as the government. C. Rhodes, G. Hutton and M. Ward, 'Research and Development Spending', House of Commons Library Research Briefing, 16 March 2021; UK Department for Business, Energy and Industrial

Strategy, 'UK Research and Development Roadmap', updated 21
January 2021, https://www.gov.uk/government/publications/
uk-research-and-development-roadmap/uk-research-and-development
-roadmap.

519. MI5 considers these to the three biggest threats to British national
security. UK MI5, 'FAQ about MI5', https://www.mi5.gov.uk/faq
/what-are-the-biggest-current-threats-to-national-security (accessed 30
June 2021); Centre for the Protection of National Infrastructure, 'Threat
Landscape', updated 31 March 2021, https://www.cpni.gov.uk/threat
-landscape.

520. Although in 2019 the UK spent only 2.1 per cent of its GDP on defence,
it is the overall fourth-largest spender in the world on military. BBC
News, 'What Is Happening to the Size of the Army?', 22 March 2021,;
Statista, 'Defense Spending UK 2021', https://www.statista.com
/statistics/298490/defense-spending-united-kingdom-uk (accessed 30
June 2021).

521. The United Kingdom's nuclear arsenal currently includes a stockpile of
approximately 225 warheads. Of these, up to 120 are operationally
available for deployment on four ballistic missile submarines. In 2021,
however, the government announced the UK would increase its
stockpile ceiling to up to 260 warheads. H.M. Kristensen and M. Korda,
'United Kingdom Nuclear Weapons, 2021', *Bulletin of Atomic Scientists*
77, no. 3 (May 2021), pp. 153–58; K. Reif and S. Bugos, 'UK to Increase
Cap on Nuclear Warhead Stockpile', Arms Control Association,
April 2021.

522. In March 2021, the UK government said China is in 'a state of ongoing
non-compliance' with the Sino-British Joint Declaration, a treaty signed
by the two countries that guarantees Hong Kong's rights and freedoms
after the city was handed back to Beijing in 1997. J. Curtis, J. Lunn and
M. Ward, 'The UK-China Relationship', House of Commons Library
Research Briefing, 14 September 2020; R. Olsen, 'UK Says China
Breached Hong Kong Handover Treaty for Third Time', *Forbes*, 14
March 2021.

523. Disparities are linked to long-standing inequities in health outcomes
and access to care, education, employment and economic status. Black
people report being subjected to many forms of police abuse, including
non-lethal force, arbitrary arrests and detentions, and harassment, at
significantly higher rates than white people. Similar abuse takes place
against Native Americans, who are killed by the police at even higher
rates than black people. Although about half of all murder victims in the
US are black; in 2019, nearly 80 per cent of new death sentences were
imposed in cases involving victims who were white. Of the executions in
2019, 73 per cent involved cases with only white victims. The racial
disparities are even more obvious if one looks at cases involving white
defendants and black victims. In the 2019 Survey of Consumer
Finances, white families have the highest level of both median and mean

family wealth, with black families' median and mean wealth being less than fifteen per cent that of white families. Some lawmakers in the United States have tried to ensure that a larger proportion of African Americans are represented in universities and leading job positions through affirmative-action programmes, but this is politically contested and has been weakened by the courts. Human Rights Watch, 'World Report 2021: United States – Events of 2020', https://www.hrw.org /world-report/2021/country-chapters/united-states (accessed 20 July 2021); Statista, 'Number of Prisoners on Death Row in the United States in 2019, by Race', https://www.statista.com/statistics/629895 /number-of-death-row-inmates-by-race-us (accessed 30 June 2021); Death Penalty Information Center, 'DPIC Analysis: Racial Disparities Persisted in US Death Sentences and Executions in 2019', 21 January 2020; N. Bhutta *et al.*, 'Disparities in Wealth by Race and Ethnicity in the 2019 Survey of Consumer Finances', Federal Reserve Notes, 28 September 2020; K. McIntosh *et al.*, 'Examining the Black-White Wealth Gap', Brookings Institution, 27 February 2020; J. Chen, 'Vanderbilt Researcher Finds that Supreme Court Ban on Race-Conscious College Admissions Would Restrict the Pipeline of Future Leaders', Vanderbilt University Research News, 10 June 2021.

524. Nearly 40 million Americans live below the official poverty line. The poverty rate in the United States varies widely across different ethnic groups, with about 18.8 per cent of the black population with an income below the poverty line in 2019 compared with only 7.3 per cent of the white (non-Hispanic) people. Statista, 'Poverty Rate in the United States from 1990 to 2019', https://www.statista.com/statistics/200463/us -poverty-rate-since-1990 (accessed 30 June 2021); Poverty USA, 'The Population of Poverty USA', https://www.povertyusa.org/facts (accessed 30 June 2021).

525. The United States spends more than other countries on health care (nearly twice as much as the OECD average) without obtaining better health outcomes. The US has a health-care system that largely consists of private providers and private insurance, but over the past few years a higher share of health-care funding has been provided by government. 34 per cent of Americans received their health care via government insurance or direct public provision in 2018. Although in 2020 only fifteen per cent of Americans had neither private nor government health insurance, many people still face large and variable out-of-pocket health-care costs. As a result, despite the fact that the quality of health care is excellent for those who can afford it, the United States has one of the worst health profiles in the developed world, with high rates of untreated diabetes and high blood pressure. R. Nunn, J. Parsons and J. Shambaugh, 'A Dozen Facts about the Economics of the US Health-Care System', Brookings Institution, 10 March 2020; S. Duckett, 'How the US Health-Care System Works – and How Its Failures Are Worsening the Pandemic', *The Conversation*, 18 November 2020; Centers for Disease

Control and Prevention, 'Leading Causes of Death', https://www.cdc
.gov/nchs/fastats/leading-causes-of-death.htm (accessed 30 June 2021);
A. Barrell, 'Which Diseases Cause the Most Death in the US?', *Medical
News Today*, 25 June 2020.

526. Following the one-term administration of Republican President Donald
Trump, the Democrats won the majority in both the House of
Representatives and the Senate during the November 2020 elections.
S. Lewis, 'Joe Biden Breaks Obama's Record for Most Votes Ever Cast
for a US Presidential Candidate', CBS, 7 December 2020.

527. US GDP in 2019 was US$21.4 trillion. World Bank, 'GDP: United States',
https://data.worldbank.org/indicator/NY.GDP.MKTP.CD?locations=US
(accessed 20 June 2021); Statista, 'The 20 Countries with the Largest
Gross Domestic Product (GDP) in 2020'.

528. Statista, 'United States National Debt from 2016 to 2026', https://www
.statista.com/statistics/262893/national-debt-in-the-united-states
(accessed 30 June 2021).

529. China overtook the United States' leading position in 2006. To date,
the US has contributed more to human-caused climate change than
any other nation. The US is also the top producer and consumer of
both oil and natural gas and has the world's second-largest fleet of
coal-fired power plants. Climate change is a highly divisive issue in US
politics and the Republic Party has repeatedly blocked any form of
comprehensive government action. The Republican government led by
Donald Trump also left the Paris Agreement, which President Joe
Biden immediately re-joined upon taking office in 2021. J. Gabbatiss,
'The Carbon Brief Profile: United States', 22 April 2021; US White
House, 'Fact Sheet: President Biden Sets 2030 Greenhouse Gas
Pollution Reduction Target Aimed at Creating Good-Paying Union
Jobs and Securing US Leadership on Clean Energy Technologies', 22
April 2021.

530. According to the American Lung Association, 135 million Americans
are breathing unhealthy air. N. Lee, '135 Million Americans Are
Breathing Unhealthy Air, American Lung Association Says', CNBC, 22
April 2021.

531. K.A. Borden and S.L. Cutter, 'Spatial Patterns of Natural Hazards
Mortality in the United States', *International Journal of Health
Geographics* 7, no. 64 (2008), pp. 1–13.

532. *Newsville Times*, 'Drought in the Western United States Sets a 122-Year
Record', 23 July 2021.

533. According to the American Association for the Advancement of Science,
in 2020, the United States was ranked tenth in research and
development intensity (a measure of R&D investment as a percentage of
a nation's GDP) but continued to lead in total research and development
spending. American Association for the Advancement of Science, 'A
Snapshot of US R&D Competitiveness: 2020 Update', 22 October 2020,

https://www.aaas.org/news/snapshot-us-rd-competitiveness-2020
-update.

534. Five of the world's top ten universities are in the United States.
UniversityRankings.ch, 'QS World University Rankings 2021'.

535. Private schools often provide a better education than public schools, and
there are great differences in the quality of public schools across the
country. As schools are financed through property taxes, public schools
in wealthy neighbourhoods usually have more resources available and
are able to attract better teachers, thus often offering a better education
to students. Disadvantaged students in the US are two-and-a-half times
more likely to be low performers in exams than their more-advantaged
counterparts. There are long-standing concerns about the decline in the
overall quality of American schools compared to public schools in other
developed countries. C. Turner, 'America's Schools Are "Profoundly
Unequal," Says US Civil Rights Commission', NPR, 11 January 2018;
American University School of Education, 'What the US Education
System Needs to Reduce Inequality', 11 July 2018.

536. B. Jones, 'How US-China Tensions Could Hamper Development Efforts',
World Economic Forum, 16 September 2020; Al Jazeera, 'Amid
Tensions, US and Russia Hold "Substantive" Arms Talks', 28 July 2021.

537. Following decades of tensions with North Korea, and the United States'
military support of South Korea, progress was made towards
denuclearisation when President Trump and Kim Jong Un met in 2018.
Unfortunately, since then little progress has been made in practice.
Although the relationship between the US and Iran seemed to be
improving with the signing of the nuclear deal in 2015, Trump's
withdrawal from the deal and the imposition of new sanctions on Iran
in 2018, followed by the US assassination of Iranian General Soleimani
in 2020, pushed tensions between the two countries to a new high.
Council on Foreign Relations, 'US Relations with Iran'; Council on
Foreign Relations, 'Global Conflict Tracker: North Korea Crisis', https://
www.cfr.org/global-conflict-tracker/conflict/north-korea-crisis
(accessed 30 June 2021); R. Einhorn, 'The Key Choices Now Facing the
Biden Administration on North Korea', Brookings Institution, 30
March 2021.

538. For a long time, the US sought a solution to the Israel-Palestine conflict
that would result in two states. The Trump administration diverged
from this objective, however, when it recognised Jerusalem as sole
capital of Israel, accepted its annexation of the Golan Heights and
expressed absolute support for Israel's actions. These actions were
subjected to harsh criticism from other states. The resurgence of
violence between Israel and Palestine in May 2021 further exacerbated
the criticism when the US repeatedly stopped the UN Security Council
from issuing a resolution requesting a ceasefire and expressed support
for Israel's attacks against Palestinians. Robinson, 'What Is US Policy on

the Israeli-Palestinian Conflict?'; C. Newton, 'A History of the US Blocking UN Resolutions against Israel', Al Jazeera, 19 May 2021.

9. Case Studies: Geostrategic Imperatives and Future Trajectories of Twenty-Seven Selected States

1. Australia should adopt programmes which focus on training the police force to not adopt racial biases towards indigenous people and Torres Strait Islanders in the context of law enforcement. It should also prioritise the adoption of social and economic policies to bridge the gap between white Australians and indigenous peoples and to punish racial discrimination in education and the work environment. Australia should also adopt a national anti-racism framework designed to address the increasing racism, particularly towards people of colour and Muslims. See Australian Human Rights Commission, 'Australia Needs a National Anti-Racism Framework', 16 March 2021, https://humanrights .gov.au/about/news/speeches/australia-needs-national-anti-racism -framework; UN Office of the High Commissioner for Human Rights, 'Committee on the Elimination of Racial Discrimination Examines Australia's Report', 28 November 2017, https://www.ohchr.org/en /NewsEvents/Pages/DisplayNews.aspx?NewsID=22460&LangID=E.

2. Australia has one of the highest public health-care expenditures per capita in the OECD. In 2018, it spent over 9.2 per cent of its GDP on health care, over two per cent more than it spent 20 years ago. For Australia's excellent health-care system to remain financially sustainable, the government must continue to support its public-private hybrid approach, which can provide health care at a high standard while not increasing its cost for the state. See World Bank, 'Current Health Expenditure: Australia', https://data.worldbank.org/indicator/SH.XPD .CHEX.GD.ZS?locations=AU (accessed 20 July 2021); Australian Institute of Health and Welfare, *Australia's Health Expenditure: An International Comparison* (Canberra: AIHW, 2019), pp. 2–3.

3. Australia must immediately eliminate indefinite offshore detention for asylum seekers in accordance with international recommendations. Asylum seekers should also be granted free legal assistance and the possibility of applying for permanent residency. Not only should those in detention be granted family reunification rights, but the right of children to an education should also be guaranteed. Eliminating offshore detention would be economically advantageous, since it presently costs more than AU$1 billion a year. See Kaldor Centre for International Refugee Law, 'Factsheet: The Cost of Australia's Asylum and Refugee Policies: A Source Guide', University of South Wales, 1 June 2020; Australian Human Rights Commission, 'Asylum Seekers and

Refugees'; UN Office of the High Commissioner for Human Rights, 'Monitoring Asylum in Australia', https://www.unhcr.org/asylum-in-australia.html (accessed 20 July 2021).

4. Australia should increase trade with members of the Regional Comprehensive Economic Partnership and ratify more free-trade agreements. Regional Comprehensive Economic Partnership, 'RCEP: A New Trade Agreement That Will Help Shape Global Economics and Politics'.

5. It is also estimated that a total trade war with China would cost Australia six per cent of its GDP. R. Tyers and Y. Zhou, 'An All-Out Trade War with China Would Cost Australia 6% of GDP', *The Conversation*, 30 November 2020.

6. The latest Intergenerational Report of the Migration Council of Australia estimates that the Australian population will almost double from 24 million today to 40million by 2055. The modelling shows that GDP will fall and wage growth will slow. Although the government assumes net overseas migration will remain stable at 215,000 people per year, the modelling says Australia needs 250,000 migrants a year to boost the economy by $1.6 trillion by 2050. Migrants also fill jobs in sectors such as agriculture that Australians alone cannot. No Borders Law Group, 'Australia Needs 250,000 New Migrants a Year: Study', https://www.noborders-group.com/news/australia-needs-more-migrants (accessed 20 July 2021); A. Boucher and R. Breunig, 'We Need to Restart Immigration Quickly to Drive Economic Growth. Here's One Way to Do It Safely', *The Conversation*, 15 October 2020.

7. Australia has the capacity to become a regional exporter of renewable energy. This shift would not only combat climate change; it would strengthen the Australian economy. F. Ueckerdt *et al.*, *Australia's Power Advantage: Energy Transition and Hydrogen Export Scenarios: Insights from the Australian-German Energy Transition Hub* (Melbourne and Potsdam: Energy Transition Hub, September 2019), p. 3.

8. A. Prytz, 'COVID-Recovery Budget Needs to Invest in Public Education, Says Union', *The Age*, 30 August 2020.

9. If Australia is to withstand China's economic and political influence, it must not only strengthen its ties with other historic Chinese rivals in the region, including first and foremost Japan and Indonesia, as well as the other members of ASEAN, but also work towards a peaceful solution to its own tensions with China. K. Johnson and J. Detsch, 'Australia Draws a Line on China', *Foreign Policy*, 4 May 2021; R. Taylor, 'What Can Australia Do about China? Ask Our Neighbours', *Business News*, 8 December 2020.

10. The 2014–15 recession ended Brazil's streak of poverty reduction, and poverty rates started to rise once more. Severe inequalities remain, in which the richest six per cent of Brazilians have the same wealth as half of the poorest. It is therefore necessary to address structural causes of

inequality, such as the unfair tax system or insufficient investments in social policies. See World Bank, 'Poverty and Equity Brief: Brazil', April 2020, https://databank.worldbank.org/data/download /poverty/33EF03BB-9722-4AE2-ABC7-AA2972D68AFE/Global _POVEQ_BRA.pdf; Oxfam International, 'Brazil: Extreme Inequality in Numbers'.

11. In Brazil, most of the country's arable land is owned by a few wealthy families. This situation not only perpetuates economic inequality, it also leads to social tensions in the countryside, including actions by the Movement of Landless Rural Workers, which is demanding land redistribution. *Encyclopedia Britannica*, 'Landless Workers Movement', by T. McCowan, 22 November 2016.

12. J.E.R. Vieira Filho and A. Fornazier, 'Agricultural Productivity: Closing the Gap between Brazil and the United States', *Cepal Review* 118 (2016), p. 205.

13. In 2011, the Brazilian government developed a plan to improve its transportation network and boost its economy. Since this comes at a high cost, however, in terms of investment, the government will most likely have to re-direct money from some of its high welfare-state expenditures. Placing fewer hurdles on businesses will also promote investment. Moreover, an easier and more efficient taxation system will ease burdens on businesses and make it more efficient for the government to collect taxes. See C.V. Plaza *et al.*, 'Economic and Environmental Location of Logistics Integration Centers: The Brazilian Soybean Transportation Case', *TOP: An Official Journal of the Spanish Society of Statistics and Operations Research* 28, no. 3 (2020), pp. 749–71.

14. Although Brazil benefits strongly at the economic level from its oil and sugar-cane-based ethanol exports and domestic use, it must invest in the development of renewable and green energy. This is necessary if Brazil is to curb its greenhouse gas emissions and slow the deforestation of the Amazon rainforest. Indeed, not only is the Amazon a precious resource for the biosphere, but its destruction will have negative implications beyond Brazil's borders. Providing a range of incentives to stop people from clearing new land, implementing land reform and creating jobs in labour-intensive industries may be some measures that Brasilia can take in addition to stricter law enforcement. See R.A. Butler, 'Amazon Conservation: How to Save the Rainforest', *Mongabay*, 1 April 2019.

15. The Madeira dams have already started to have a negative environmental and social impact at the local level. The government must therefore take steps to develop adaptation and mitigation programmes to address the risk of floods and displacement. It must also provide compensation to the fishermen whose sources of income and nourishment have been depleted by the creation of the dams.

16. For more information on incentives for investment in R&D, see OECD, Directorate for Science Technology and Innovation, 'R&D Tax Incentives: Brazil, 2019', December 2019, https://www.oecd.org/sti/rd-tax-stats-brazil.pdf, p. 2.

17. Improving the quality of primary education and making secondary and college education more available to the poor will also be important to reducing inequalities. See M. Raiser, 'Brazil Can Improve Education by Copying Its Own Successes', Brookings Institution, 6 March 2018; World Bank, *Inequality and Economic Development in Brazil*, World Bank Country Study (Washington, DC: World Bank 2004); L. Fulton, 'Coca Conflict: Brazil's Impending War on Drugs', *Harvard International Review* 29, no. 2 (2007), p. 7.

18. The urban slums, especially those in São Paulo, remain fertile ground for organised gangs dealing in cocaine and other narcotics. Brazil's challenge is to devise effective programmes to reduce widespread urban poverty and fight organised crime in a systematic way. R. Muggah, 'Lessons from Organised Crime Task Forces: Brazil and Beyond', Global Initiative, 16 October 2017.

19. O. Stuenkel, 'Latin America Is Too Polarised to Help Stabilize Bolivia', *Foreign Policy*, 13 November 2019.

20. F.H. Cardoso *et al.*, 'Brazil's Foreign Policy Today Is a Violation of Its Own Constitution', *The Wire*, 13 May 2020; M. Gomes Saraiva and A. de Mello e Silva, 'Between Political Crisis and COVID-19: Bolsonaro's Foreign Policy', *E-International Relations*, 2 June 2020.

21. K.E. Lehmann, 'Can Brazil Lead? The Breakdown of Brazilian Foreign Policy and What It Means for the Region', *Rising Powers Quarterly* 2, no. 2 (2017), p. 128; C. Felter, D. Renwick and A. Chatzky, 'Mercosur: South America's Fractious Trade Block', Council on Foreign Relations, Backgrounder, 10 July 2019.

22. Due to the country's one-child policy, which ran until 2016, the lack of females and rising lifespan, Chinese society is ageing, which could pose an increased burden on social relations and the country's economy. Old people will have to receive support from the government or their adult children. Either measure would reduce net savings and investment. VOA News, 'In Fast-Aging China, Elder Care Costs Loom Large', 23 May 2021.

23. This could be achieved by implementing programmes for integration and implementing legislation which prohibits discrimination in the employment sector on these grounds. See C. Chuanyi and C. Xiaoli, 'Changing the Policy Paradigm on Chinese Migrant Workers', in E.P. Mendes and S. Srighanthan (eds), *Confronting Discrimination and Inequality in China: Chinese and Canadian Perspectives* (Ottawa: University of Ottawa Press, 2009), pp. 99–128.

24. The environmental degradation cost in China increased from 511 billion yuan to 1,892 billion yuan from 2004 to 2017, but its share in the GDP decreased from 3.05 per cent to 2.23 per cent. G. Ma *et al.*,

'The Valuation of China's Environmental Degradation from 2004 to 2017', *Environmental Science and Ecotechnology* 1 (2020), pp. 1–10.

25. The farming and food-growing policies currently in force in China are a major impediment to increasing economic prosperity in rural areas. The Chinese government currently restricts diversification of farm products and instead forces farmers to grow mostly wheat and rice. The reasoning behind this policy is that Beijing does not want to import any significant amount of these staples to meet domestic demand. Sales of these grains are not profitable for farmers, however. Beijing's failure to address rural economic stagnation will only further increase the wealth disparities between rural and urban areas. A. Donley, 'Report: China to Be Nearly Self-Sufficient in Wheat, Rice by 2025', World-Grain.com, 26 May 2021.

26. A. Gilder *et al.*, 'How China's Financial Liberalization Can Unlock New Opportunities', EY, 7 November 2019.

27. The Chinese government must invest more in the private sector and reduce its control over it. L. Wei, 'China's Xi Ramps up Control of Private Sector: "We Have No Choice but to Follow the Party"', *Wall Street Journal*, 10 December 2020; C. Desheng, 'President: Promote Healthy Development of Private Sector', *China Daily*, 17 September 2020.

28. China has become one of the rising stars of global innovation. Some argue, however, that this will only be sustainable if China adopts a more open innovation system which finds a balance between development based on absorbing foreign technology and participating in the open global innovation system. Until now, China has been able to learn from the open global innovation system, while protecting its key strategic industries, 'indigenising' the technologies and becoming increasingly more technologically autonomous. With these two goals becoming more incompatible, China must dismantle the barriers that shelter some domestic firms from foreign multinationals. This would simultaneously stimulate the incentive to innovate on the part of Chinese enterprises, boost their productivity by enhancing market competition and overcome a major source of tension with its trading partners. Only an industrially mature China, which recognises that globalisation also confers many advantages, can match other open advanced economies. D. Medvedev, M. Piatkowski and S. Yusuf, 'Will China Become a Global Innovation Champion? Keeping the Global Innovation System Open Will Be Key', World Bank Blogs, 14 May 2020.

29. Although many solutions to the South China Sea dispute have been proposed, taking into account the unlikelihood of all ASEAN countries agreeing on exactly one political or legal strategy and, even if this were to occur, China not retaliating economically, the only solution may lie in compromise, with all parties accepting some limit to the influence they exercise over the area and to the resources they are allowed to extract or

fish. W. Kusuma, A.C. Kurnia and R.A. Agustian, 'South China Sea: Conflict, Challenge and Solution', *Lampung Journal of International Law* 3, no. 1 (2021), pp. 57–59.

30. Unemployment can turn into a significant social problem in Egypt. Most unemployed are young, well-educated and usually not from a poor background. Their expectations for an interesting and well-paying job are often thwarted. It is in the formal private sector where most new jobs would need to be created. See World Bank, 'Unemployment, Youth Total: Egypt', https://data.worldbank.org/indicator/SL.UEM.1524 .ZS?locations=EG (accessed 20July 2021); World Bank, 'Egypt: Job Creation for Better Livelihoods', 22 February 2021.

31. In 2017, a national survey in Egypt found that approximately 1.6 million children between the ages of twelve to seventeen were working, often for no pay. Estimates of NGOs were significantly higher, however. Poverty is the main cause for children having to work. Working children are often subject to abuse and usually perform less well in school. In 2019, Egypt made a moderate advancement in efforts to eliminate the worst forms of child labour through the adoption of new legislation and policies. See US Bureau of International Labor Affairs, '2019 Findings on the Worst Forms of Child Labor', https://www.dol.gov/sites/dolgov/files/ILAB /child_labor_reports/tda2019/Egypt.pdf, pp. 1–2; International Labour Organisation, 'The ILO Project Will Contribute to the Elimination of Child Labour in Egypt's Cotton Supply Chain', 17 June 2019;

32. World Bank, '45 Million Egyptians to Benefit from Improvements to the Public Health System', 27 June 2018.

33. In 2019, the Egyptian government passed constitutional amendments that arguably consolidate authoritarian rule, including those that undermine the judiciary's dwindling independence and expand the military's power to intervene in political life. Human Rights Watch, 'World Report 2020: Egypt – Events of 2019'.

34. Making cuts in the public sector and fostering private-sector development is a key measure in the economic reform programme which is to be implemented by 2025. However, slimming down the public sector, a necessary prerequisite to reducing the budget deficit, may prove to be an unsustainable policy for the government, since it might counteract ongoing measures to reduce unemployment. A. Emam, 'Egypt Struggles with Bloated Public Sector', *Arab Weekly*, 18 November 2018.

35. In 2020, total domestic debt was over 90 per cent of GDP. To reduce the fiscal deficit and public domestic debt, the government will need to make some painful spending cuts. Rather than adopt a radical policy of austerity as it has done over the past few years, the Egyptian government should focus on reducing military spending. The process of privatisation which has also been ongoing since the fall of Mubarak will also have to be continued. M. Mandour, 'Sisi's Debt Crisis', Carnegie Endowment for International Peace, 20 November 2018.

36. The country is prone to rising inflation as the money stock increases with capital inflows. Inflation peaked at 23.54 per cent in 2017 but has rapidly decreased to 4.79 per cent in 2021. Statista, 'Egypt – Inflation Rate from 1986 to 2026 (Compared to the Previous Year)', https://www.statista.com/statistics/377354/inflation-rate-in-egypt (accessed 20 July 2021).

37. The potential for job creation lies in the formal private sector. Formality has also been shown to raise productivity, wages and working conditions. Egypt is currently underutilising its many young, well-educated people. It is important that the country create the necessary economic conditions to make sure that their human skills can be put to good use to help the national economy grow and develop.

38. There are two main deficiencies in the Egyptian education system. First, free, compulsory basic education needs to be made available to everyone to increase general literacy rates in the country. Second, secondary and post-secondary curricula need to focus on the skills that are most in demand in the job market. See L. Loveluck, 'Education in Egypt: Key Challenges', Chatham House, Background Paper, March 2012, p. 3.

39. Since the removal from power of President Morsi, Egypt has seen a surge in terrorist attacks (as many as 100 per month in 2015 and at least a 3,000 per cent increase since 2011) by an increasing range of terrorist groups and in more and more locations (extending beyond their original focus in North Sinai). A. Pauwels, 'Preventing Terrorism in the South', EUISS, Brief no. 6, 8 March 2017, pp. 1–4; D.A. Winter *et al.*, 'The Role of Sub-National Authorities from the Mediterranean Region in Addressing Radicalisation and Violent Extremism of Young People', European Committee of the Regions (2017), https://cor.europa.eu/en/engage/studies/Documents/Radicalisation-Violent-Extremism-Young%20People.pdf, p. 13.

40. Despite the intervention of the African Union to try to find a sustainable compromise between Egypt and Ethiopia's interests, the situation has yet to move past the present deadlock. Tensions are, instead, continuously increasing and may lead to a military conflict. O. Marbot, 'Egypt-Ethiopia: "Dam of Discord" Continues to Pressure Relations', *Africa Report*, 6 May 2021; A.L. Wahba, 'Egypt Asks for UN Help in Long-Running Ethiopian Dam Dispute', Bloomberg, 12 June 2021.

41. A. Melcangi, 'Egypt Recalibrated Its Strategy in Libya Because of Turkey', Atlantic Council, 1 June 2021; A. Aydintasbas *et al.*, 'Cooling-off: How Europe Can Help Stabilise the Middle East', European Council on Foreign Relations, Commentary, 18 June 2021.

42. A stronger EU will also require integrating foreigners into European society by promoting multiculturalism and cosmopolitanism. Policies must be adopted to eliminate inequalities and xenophobia towards immigrants, especially in education and the workplace. Measures to promote integration must be balanced with the objectives of the EU

Security Strategy, and not be forfeit by prejudice and blanket anti-Islamic policies to combat terrorism or by policies that target asylum seekers and refugees. See European Network Against Racism, 'Racism Plays a Key Role in Migrants Exclusion and Violation of Rights in the European Union', 2 May 2017.

43. Politicians in member states need to make it clear to voters that EU membership and enlargement are beneficial to their countries. It is possible that, after the EU's economy has been reinvigorated and the COVID-19 pandemic overcome, people will be more sympathetic towards the political union. Measures to strengthen legitimacy of and support for the Union could include increasing transparency in EU institutions by formalising the policy-making process and providing citizens with easier access to EU institutions. See H. Hofmann and P. Leino-Sandberg, 'An Agenda for Transparency in the EU', *European Law Blog*, 23 October 2019.

44. For the well-being of the EU and its citizens, it is important to create more jobs to reduce the unemployment rate, to promote economic growth and to pay for Europe's increasingly ageing population. To speed up job creation, EU governments need to make their labour markets more flexible. Moreover, governments need to cut some of their high welfare-state expenditures. Governments will also need to unconditionally accept the EU's single-market principle and competition policies. The EU must find ways to convince member states and their electorates that a union-wide free market will be to the long-term benefit of everyone. W. Eichhorst, P. Marx and C. Wehner, 'Labor Market Reforms in Europe: Towards More Flexicure Labor Markets?', *Journal for Labour Market Research* 51, no. 3 (2017), pp. 1–2.

45. The promotion of innovation in clean technologies will help to reduce air and water pollution in Europe and will help Europe to become a leading producer of these technologies in the future, providing a further boost to the economy. See M. Farmer, 'EU Energy Policy: World-Leading, Insufficient, or Both?', Power Technology, 20 April 2021.

46. In 2000, the EU set the goal of increasing R&D investment to three per cent of GDP for its member states. As stated above, the EU has yet to meet this target. Unfortunately, innovation is still dealt with by member states on a national basis, so cooperation is imperative to speed up the process of innovation. Brussels could facilitate cooperation by setting up European innovation centres where scientists from industry and academia could meet. The EU can also encourage investments by the private sector by creating a more favourable climate for innovation and entrepreneurship. See F. Zubascu, 'Funding Synergies to Nudge EU Countries Closer to 3% R&D Spending Target by 2030', *Science Business*, 1 March 2021, https://sciencebusiness.net /news/funding-synergies-nudge-eu-countries-closer-3-rd-spending -target-2030.

47. Renewable energy use on a larger scale would also reduce the EU's energy dependence on Russia. Currently, over 27 per cent of the EU's oil imports and 41 per cent of its natural gas imports come from Russia. The EU is too dependent on oil supplies from Russia, which Russia could easily exploit to further its own interests. EU member states need to cooperate more closely to counteract Russian attempts to make the EU even more dependent on Russian energy. The EU's challenge is to increase Western investments in the oil- and natural-gas-rich Caspian region and build pipelines that go through the Black Sea and Turkey, thus circumventing Russia as a transit country. Eurostat, 'From Where Do We Import Energy?', https://ec.europa.eu/eurostat/cache/infographs /energy/bloc-2c.html (accessed 20 July 2021).

48. In addition to continuing to motivate bordering states to become solid liberal democracies by holding out the prospect of EU membership, the EU should also place more importance on developing a common foreign policy towards states which are not considered future EU members. The European Security Strategy recognises that violent conflict and weak state institutions enable organised crime to flourish in neighbouring states and make the EU less secure. The EU has a self-interest in strengthening ties with neighbouring countries and providing incentives for those states to develop into more prosperous, democratic and stable entities. Unfortunately, the EU's member states often have different strategic priorities regarding the EU neighbourhood and developing consistent policies towards the various troubled regions along the EU's periphery remains a challenge to be worked out. See F. Fabbri, F. McNamara and K. Bamberg, 'Competing Priorities at the EU's External Border', European Policy Centre, 28 December 2018, p. 3.

49. As an economic powerhouse, the EU still needs to translate its economic might into political leverage on the world stage. It could focus on strengthening its role as a leader on climate change and international development, for example. A prerequisite for the EU to increase its political leverage, however, would be that EU member states develop a common and coherent EU foreign policy, capable of addressing challenges including that of illegal migrants and asylum seekers. *The Economist*, 'How to Manage the Migrant Crisis', 6 February 2016.

50. France must increase its education, employment and social initiatives for integrating immigrants into the mainstream of society. This will require recognising cultural differences and allowing forms of religious expression in schools. See A. Escafré-Dublet, 'Mainstreaming Immigrant Integration Policy in France: Education, Employment, and Social Cohesion Initiatives', Migration Policy Institute, August 2014; OECD, *Working Together for Local Integration of Migrants and Refugees in Paris* (Paris: OECD Publishing, 2018), p. 100; European Union Agency for Fundamental Rights, *Integration of Young Refugees in the EU: Good Practices and Challenges* (Luxemburg: Publications Office of

the European Union, 2019); S. Gohir, 'The Veil Ban in Europe: Gender Equality or Gendered Islamophobia?', *Georgetown Journal of International Affairs* 16, no. 1 (2015), pp. 27–28.

51. Ethnic profiling is a well-documented practice carried out by the French police and mainly targets black and Arab members of society. See Human Rights Watch, 'France: End Systemic Police Discrimination'.

52. The COVID-19 Recovery Plan is France's opportunity to prioritise investment in the green transition. Proposed measures include boosting investment in ecological and digital transformation. So far, the government has pledged €30 billion towards the thermal renovation of buildings, the decarbonisation of industry, green hydrogen, cleaner transport and transformation of the agricultural sector. See Ministère de l'Europe et des Affaires Étrangères (France), 'France Relance Recovery Plan: Building the France of 2030', https://www.diplomatie.gouv.fr/en /french-foreign-policy/economic-diplomacy-foreign-trade/promoting -france-s-attractiveness/france-relance-recovery-plan-building-the -france-of-2030 (accessed 21 July 2021); J. Franks *et al.*, 'Five Charts on France's Policy Priorities to Navigate the COVID-19 Crisis', International Monetary Fund, 19 January 2021.

53. In 2020, the French government announced it would make no new decisions on nuclear power until 2022, while aiming to reduce the share of nuclear energy in France's total energy supply to 50 per cent from its current 70 per cent by 2035. Although nuclear energy does not produce the same greenhouse gas emissions as fossil fuels, and France has been praised for its successful storage and disposal practices, storage and disposal of radioactive waste may become a serious issue in coming decades. France should therefore gradually shift its reliance on fossil fuels to renewable energies that do not require the same dangerous storage and disposal and increase its recycling practices. See Nuclear Engineering International, 'France to Decide on New Nuclear Build after 2022', 14 January 2020; A. Farngoul, 'France's Love Affair with Nuclear Power Will Continue, but Change Is Afoot', CNBC, 10 March 2021; Power Technology, 'Managing Nuclear Waste in France: The Long and Short Game', 2 May 2018; S. Krikorian, 'France's Efficiency in the Nuclear Fuel Cycle: What Can "Oui" Learn?', International Atomic Energy Agency, 4 September 2019.

54. France and Germany are the two countries who have done the most to back the European Green Deal and proposed measures such as a carbon tax levy to speed up the EU's green transition and the achievement of the net-zero target. See K. Abnett, 'Germany, France Throw Weight behind EU's "Green" Recovery Plan', Reuters, 19 May 2020, https://www.reuters.com/article/us-eu-recovery-climate- idUSKBN22V1ZB.

55. France is already leading the EU in terms of innovation, despite tough regulatory requirements. Increasing investment in the R&D and technology sectors would give France a further push towards increasing its competitiveness on the global level. EU Today, 'France Is Spearheading EU Tech Innovation', 29 February 2020.

56. Although France has taken significant steps toward disarmament – including halving its warhead total since its Cold War peak and no longer deploying nuclear weapons on its aircraft carrier, it continues to possess the third-largest nuclear arsenal in the world. See Arms Control Association, 'Arms Control and Proliferation Profile: France', July 2019, https://www.armscontrol.org/factsheets/franceprofile.

57. European Commission, 'A Counter-Terrorism Agenda for the EU: Anticipate, Prevent, Protect, Respond', COM (2020) 795, 9 December 2020.

58. Since cyber security is also a major security threat for the country, France should strengthen its 2015 Cyber Security Strategy and increase investment in digital technologies in both the public and private sector. See Ministère de l'Europe et des Affaires Étrangères (France), 'France and Cyber Security', https://www.diplomatie.gouv.fr/en/french-foreign -policy/security-disarmament-and-non-proliferation/fight-against -organized-criminality/cyber-security (accessed 21 July 2021).

59. France is the only EU country with a permanent seat on the UNSC. See H. Vincze, 'One Voice, but Whose Voice? Should France Cede Its UN Security Council Seat to the EU?', Foreign Policy Research Institute, 20 March 2019.

60. Africa is the main beneficiary of French development aid. However, France should continue to reduce the use of loans as a means of providing development aid, thus reducing its direct influence over its former colonies. Ministère de l'Europe et des Affaires Étrangères (France), 'Development Assistance', https://www.diplomatie.gouv.fr/en /french-foreign-policy/development-assistance (accessed 21 July 2021); N. Cornelissen, '5 Facts about France's Foreign Aid', The Borgen Project, 10 November 2020.

61. N. Michel, 'Colonialism: "France Has to Acknowledge the Contradictions in Its History", Ayrault', *Africa Report*, 6 July 2020.

62. Algerian researchers estimate that thousands of Algerians have suffered the effects of nuclear radiation across the Algerian Sahara caused by France's seventeen atmospheric and underground nuclear tests in the 1960s, and many of the sites are yet to be decontaminated. See A. Bryant, 'Algeria: 60 Years On, French Nuclear Tests Leave Bitter Fallout', DW, 13 February 2020; F. Alilat, 'Algeria: France Urged to Reveal Truth about Past Nuclear Tests', *Africa Report*, 10 September 2020.

63. Since Germany's population is rapidly ageing, and health issues such as obesity are increasing in frequency, it is predicted that the cost of health care in Germany will increase. The government should

therefore invest in health awareness programmes and encourage its citizens to engage in physical activity and eat healthily. The combined effect of these measures will contribute to reducing the incidence of disease linked to obesity and old age and control the rising cost of health care. It is also expected that Germany's old-age dependency ratio will rise to 57 per cent in 2050 from 32 per cent currently. The country has stated that it will gradually raise the retirement age from 65 to 67 years by 2031. This will not be sufficient. See S. Dallmeyer, P. Wicker and C. Breuer, 'How an Aging Society Affects the Economic Costs of Inactivity in Germany: Empirical Evidence and Projections', *European Review of Aging and Physical Activity* 14 (2017), pp. 1–9; F. Winnekens, 'Global Aging 2016: German Reforms Start to Tackle to Cost of Aging', S&P Global, 12 January 2016; Reuters, 'Germany's Scholz Rejects Further Hike of Retirement Age to 68', 8 June 2021.

64. Despite its history of immigration, Germany never adopted a coherent strategy or policy of integration. The German National Action Plan on Integration, adopted in March 2021 during an Integration Summit, foresees a five-stage integration process which involves accompanying migrants from before they arrive in Germany right through to active participation in society via work and civic engagement. The plan has been criticised, however, for failing to address the need for the 'inclusion' of migrants already residing in Germany, and not going to the root of social exclusion, which is also financial. See J.E. Chemin and A.K. Nagel, 'Integration Policies, Practices and Experiences: Germany Country Report', Respond Migration, Working Paper Series 5, Paper 2020/51 (2020).

65. Although recent surveys have shown a decrease in public support for populist rhetoric, the growth in anti-migrant and anti-Muslim speech following the 2015 refugee crisis demonstrates that pro-active measures should be taken by the government to combat racist public discourse. See J. Gedmin, 'Right-Wing Populism in Germany: Muslims and Minorities after the 2015 Refugee Crisis', Brookings Institution, 24 July 2019; DW, 'Populism in Germany Declines Sharply, Says Bertelsmann Study', 3 September 2020.

66. In 2020, Germany announced a shift from its long-standing austerity policies with a large COVID-19 stimulus package. Estimates predict that this will enable the German economy to quickly recover from the coronavirus pandemic and to pave the way for a general shift in economic policy in the EU. This, however, should not remain a one-off. A shift in its approach to economics will enable Germany to maintain its place as one of the largest economies in the world. See S. Amaro, 'The Coronavirus Crisis Has Changed the German Mindset – and This Matters for Markets', CNBC, 6 July 2020.

67. In addition to becoming a world leader in the production of electric vehicles, Germany is providing numerous incentives to encourage its citizens to purchase electric cars and has a strategy to cut greenhouse gas emissions. As a ruling by the German Constitutional Court in 2021 held, however, Germany's Climate Action Plan was not enough. The government accepted the ruling and stated that it would set more ambitious plans. See K. Appunn, F. Eriksen and J. Wettengel, 'Germany's Greenhouse-Gas Emissions and Energy Transition Targets', Clean Energy Wire, 16 July 2021; Reuters, 'Germany Sets Tougher CO_2 Emission Reduction Targets after Top Court Ruling', 5 May 2021.

68. Since socio-economic backgrounds in Germany, as well as immigration status, determine the likelihood of remaining in long-term education and attainment rates, the government should invest in programmes to encourage people from lower socio-economic backgrounds and immigrants to progress to higher education. It could also increase the number of scholarships and funding for poorer families, as well as courses to enable migrant children to catch up with the German system. Segregation between schools at an early age on the basis of academic performance should also be removed. See OECD, 'Education Policy Outlook: Germany', pp. 7–9.

69. M. Eddy, 'Far-Right Terrorism Is No. 1 Threat, Germany Is Told after Attack', *New York Times*, 29 December 2020.

70. Germany is facing an increasing number of hackings and cyber attacks, as well as data breaches. As Germany's cyber security authority has stated, this is a growing threat to the democratic stability in the country since it could impact the legitimacy of elections. See J. Delcker, 'Cyber Threat Looms Large over German Election', *DW*, 25 May 2021, .

71. M. Karnitschnig, 'What Merkel Wants', *Politico*, 25 June 2020; *The Economist*, 'Germany is Doomed to Lead Europe', 27 June 2020.

72. More efficient surveillance systems must be put in place to monitor the spread of these diseases.

73. Human Rights Watch, 'India: Government Policies, Actions Target Minorities', 19 February 2021.

74. K.S. Venkatachalam, 'Destroy India's Caste System before It Destroys India', *The Diplomat*, 4 August 2016.

75. India's challenge is to modify its highly restrictive labour regulations for the purpose of enlarging the job market in labour-intensive industries, which is also a great way to absorb the 90 million new job-market entrants India is expecting over the next ten years. See I. Dhasmana, 'India Will Need to Find Jobs for Additional 90 Mn, Says McKinsey Report', *Business Standard*, 26 August 2020.

76. Investment in infrastructure is necessary to sustain the development of the Indian economy, as is the privatisation of some select public-sector services. It is estimated that India should invest up to US$777.73 billion by 2022 in infrastructure for sustainable development in the country.

See S. Agarwal, 'Infrastructure Sector Crucial for India's Economic
Growth, but These Roadblocks Need to Be Managed', *Financial Express*;
World Bank, 'World Bank in India: India Overview', https://www
.worldbank.org/en/country/india/overview#2 (accessed 21 July 2021).

77. Deregulation of the agricultural sector is necessary for the adoption of
more innovative practices and to enable the movement of produce.
However, the reforms proposed by the government in 2020 to deregulate
the sector have found strong opposition in the farmers themselves, who
argue that this process will hand the source of their livelihoods to large
corporations and increase the cost of food. A balance must therefore be
found between the two competing needs. See R. Chandra, 'Need to
Deregulate Indian Agriculture', Business World, 16 December 2020,
http://www.businessworld.in/article/Need-to-Deregulate-Indian
-Agriculture/16-12-2020-354240; S. Ruparelia, 'India's Farmers Are
Right to Protest against Agricultural Reforms', *The Conversation*, 24
January 2021.

78. N. Kumar and R. Rani, 'Regional Disparities in Social Development;
Evidence from States and Union Territories of India', *South Asian Survey*
26, no. 1 (2019), pp. 2–3; S. Balasubramanian, R. Kumar and P.
Loungani, 'Sustaining India's Growth Miracle Requires Increased
Attention to Inequality of Opportunity', *Vox EU*, 12 March 2021.

79. India is a net importer with a trade deficit of US$15.24 billion in
April 2021, which increased by 120.34 per cent over the trade deficit of
US$6.92 billion in April 2020. See K. Suneja, 'Record Growth in April
Exports, Trade Deficit Swells to $15.24 Billion', *Economic Times*, 3
May 2021.

80. India is committed to having 40 per cent of its installed capacity from
non-fossil fuel sources by 2030, by which it aims to achieve a renewable
target of 175 GW by 2022 and 450 GW by 2030. Hydroelectric power
will represent a significant amount of this renewable energy.
Nevertheless, India must be conscious of the potential environmental
impact of the dams and hydropower stations. See A.K. Verma, 'India's
True Hydropower Potential Remains Untapped', *The Hindu Business
Line*, 14 May 2020; J.P. Casey, 'Hydropower and Geopolitics: Winners
and Losers in the Indian Sub-Continent', Power Technology, 6
April 2021.

81. See M. Matto, 'India's Water Crisis: The Clock Is Ticking', Down to
Earth, 21 June 2019; *Economic Times*, 'Times Water Summit 2020: It's
Still Not Late in Saving India from Becoming a Waterless Country If We
Start Acting Now!', 30 November 2020.

82. Close ties with the United States would help counterbalance the
growing predominance of China. Furthermore, an alliance with the
United States would improve India's odds of receiving its coveted
permanent seat on the UN Security Council. It is not certain, however,
whether India will choose to become a close US ally. Perhaps gaining

reliable access to natural gas, which will necessitate a closer
relationship with Russia and Iran, will rank higher among India's
short-term priorities than the development of its civilian nuclear-
energy production with the help of the United States. Furthermore,
there is opposition to forging closer ties with the United States from
within India. Indian businessmen involved in rapidly growing trade
with China would like to see their government pursue closer ties with
the latter. Entering into growing competition with China as a result of
closer ties with the United States is a risk that India might not want to
take. The pursuit of a looser partnership with the United States that is
based on a few shared interests, especially energy issues and climate
change, might be the best option for India to pursue. A further
consequence of a closer relationship with the United States might also
be increased US involvement in finding a solution to the Kashmir
conflict, which India has so far insisted is a purely internal matter. See
K. Li, 'China and India Trade Competition and Complementary
Analysis of the "Belt and Road" Background', *Modern Economy* 9 no. 7
(2018), pp. 1213–14; V. Gokhale, 'The Road from Galwan: The Future of
India-China Relations', Carnegie India, 10 March 2021; US Department
of State, Office of the Spokesperson, 'US-India Joint Statement on
Launching the US-India Climate and Clean Energy 2030 Partnership',
22 April 2021.

83. India is determined to find new sources of natural gas, which may lead
    to a strategic relationship with Russia and China at the expense of closer
    cooperation with the United States. Oil and gas have become an
    increasingly important feature in the Indo-Russian relationship, while
    trade ties and strategic interests dominate India's relationship with
    China. At the same time, India has a lot to win, from both an economic
    and a military-strategic perspective, from close relations with the
    United States. Balancing these different interests wisely without
    alienating either party will be a difficult task for India's foreign-policy
    elite in the decades to come. See S.S. Kulkarni and A. Pimpalkhare,
    'India's Import Diversification Strategy for Natural Gas: An Analysis of
    Geopolitical Implications', Observer Research Foundation, Issue Brief
    no. 330, 6 December 2019, pp. 6, 9–10.

84. Rapid decentralisation accompanied the post-Suharto era, and this also
    greatly affected the health-care system. Keeping up high standards in
    the health-care system through good governance will be a major
    challenge. Although the universal health-care system became fully
    active in 2019, much remains to be done to ensure that people, especially
    the poor, have equitable and inexpensive access to the health care they
    need. See Sutarsa *et al.*, 'Raising National Health Insurance Premiums
    Doesn't Solve Indonesia's Health-Care Problems: This Is What Needs to
    Be Done'.

85. Tailored public health approaches that address context-specific challenges must be adopted to contain the HIV epidemic. Indonesia must also confront structural barriers and the heterogeneity of the epidemic itself. See K. Gedela *et al.*, 'Getting Indonesia's HIV Epidemic to Zero? One Size Doesn't Fit All', *International Journal of STD and AIDS* 32, no. 3 (2021), pp. 290–99.

86. Child malnutrition remains a serious health issue in Indonesia. Even before COVID-19, Indonesia faced high levels of malnutrition. In 2018, close to three in ten children under five years of age were stunted while one in ten were wasted. Indonesia's maternal mortality rate remains high, standing at 305 per 100,000 in 2015. See UNICEF Indonesia, 'Nutrition', https://www.unicef.org/indonesia/nutrition (accessed 21 July 2021); K.P. Karana, 'Indonesia: Number of Malnourished Children Could Increase Sharply due to COVID-19 Unless Swift Action Is Taken', UNICEF Indonesia, 30 June 2020; S. Ahmed and J. Fullerton, 'Challenges of Reducing Maternal and Neonatal Mortality in Indonesia: Ways Forward', *International Journal of Gynecology and Obstetrics* 144, no. S1 (2019), pp. 1–3.

87. Several issues need to be addressed and improved in Indonesian democratic reforms. Rooting out corruption and making both the central and local governments more accountable and effective are one set of measures. Ensuring the legitimacy and accountability of local authorities through direct elections by citizens is also essential to protect the democratic gains Indonesia has made over the past 20 years. See S. Jaffrey, 'Is Indonesia Becoming a Two-Tier Democracy?', Carnegie Endowment for International Peace, 23 January 2020; B. Bland, 'Politics in Indonesia: Resilient Elections, Defective Democracy', Lowy Institute for International Policy, 10 April 2019.

88. The official unemployment rate hovers at around 4.8 per cent, having halved since 2007. The rapid process of urbanisation which characterises Indonesia has meant that the unemployment in urban areas is significantly higher than in rural zones. Women also face higher unemployment rates than men, particularly in the formal sector. The rapidly growing population in Indonesia and the high number of young people risk inverting the downward trend in unemployment rates. See Statista, 'Indonesia: Unemployment Rate from 1999 to 2020', https://www.statista.com/statistics/320129/unemployment-rate-in-indonesia (accessed 21 July 2021); Indonesia Investments, 'Unemployment in Indonesia', https://www.indonesia-investments.com/finance /macroeconomic-indicators/unemployment/item255 (accessed 21 July 2021).

89. Both points have been top priorities for the government over the past two decades. See J. Blank, 'How the (Once) Most Corrupt Country in the World Got Clean(er)', *The Atlantic*, May 2019.

90. Indonesia has recently announced the relocation of the country's capital from the island of Java to the island of Borneo. Java's limited sustainability is evident from extreme deforestation, biodiversity loss, intense road traffic and high pollution, and Jakarta is not only one of the most densely populated cities in the world, but also one of the most threatened by climate change. See P. Van de Vuurst and L.E. Escobar, 'Perspective: Climate Change and the Relocation of Indonesia's Capital to Borneo', *Frontiers in Earth Science* 8 (2020), p. 2.

91. Most forest fires are caused by humans. Public campaigns to convince the population of the devastating long-term effects (including global warming and loss of biodiversity) that forest fires are causing will be crucial. See D. Dunne, 'The Carbon Brief Profile: Indonesia', 27 March 2019.

92. Contaminated water is to blame for the high occurrence of waterborne diseases. See UNICEF Indonesia, 'Water, Sanitation and Hygiene', https://www.unicef.org/indonesia/water-sanitation-and-hygiene (accessed 21 July 2021).

93. Many Indonesian university graduates are trained in subjects that are not in demand in the job market. Meanwhile, many jobs remain unfilled because the country lacks people with the necessary skills to do them. See International Labour Organisation, 'Bridging Indonesia's Skills Gap through Partnership between Industry – Vocational Education and Training',.

94. Following the Bali attacks of 2002, Indonesia set up two new anti-terrorism units: one specialises in intelligence-gathering, while the other is a well-trained anti-terrorism squad. These units have been quite effective at combating terrorism in the country, yet the terrorist threat is far from over, as demonstrated by the second bombing in Bali in 2005 and by the one in Jakarta in 2009. Although significant progress has been made over the past 20 years in terms of training and efficiency of the anti-terrorism units, as well as in sentencing people found guilty of terrorism, any new laws adopted must not lead to human rights violations and unjust arrests. See United Nations Office on Drugs and Crime, 'Indonesia: Terrorism Prevention', https://www.unodc.org/indonesia/en/issues/terrorism-prevention.html (accessed 21 July 2021); US Department of State, Bureau of Counterterrorism, 'Country Reports on Terrorism 2019: Indonesia', https://www.state.gov/reports/country-reports-on-terrorism-2019/indonesia (accessed 21 July 2021); M. Haripin, C.H. Anindya and A. Priamariszki, 'The Politics of Counter-Terrorism in Post-Authoritarian States: Indonesia's Experience, 1998–2018', *Defense and Security Analysis* 36, no. 3 (2020), pp. 275–99.

95. As one of the countries with the highest number of internet users in the world, in 2018, Indonesia had more than 200 million cyber attacks. To deal with this security threat, the government has issued regulations and set up a number of institutions in the defence ministry

and national police force. This is not enough, however. Indonesia must not only strengthen its cyber legal framework, but also heavily invest in its digital security systems and industry. See T. Chairil, 'Cybersecurity for Indonesia: What Needs to Be Done?', *The Conversation*, 9 May 2019.

96. In order to keep the population stable, the fertility rate should remain at about 2.1, not 1.8 as it was in 2017. Population growth would bring both economic advantages and disadvantages, since it might boost the economy but is unlikely to be sustainable in the long term. See P. Dérer, 'The Iranian Miracle: The Most Effective Family Planning Program in History?', The Overpopulation Project, 21 March 2019; A.B. Solomon, 'Inside Iran: Iran's Demographic Problem', *Jerusalem Post*, 25 January 2014, https://www.jpost.com/features/front-lines/inside-iran -irans-demographic-problem-339246.

97. Invest in job creation in the private sector. See Statista, 'Iran'.

98. Over half of Iran's college graduates are women, but only 17.9 per cent of them were employed in the workforce in 2019. COVID-19 has only worsened their disproportionate unemployment rates. See World Bank, 'Labor Force Participation Rate, Female (% of Female Population Ages 15+) (Modeled ILO Estimate) – Iran, Islamic Rep.', https://data.world bank.org/indicator/SL.TLF.CACT.FE.ZS?locations=IR (accessed 21 July 2021); R. Burkova, '"It's a Men's Club": Discrimination against Women in Iran's Job Market', Human Rights Watch, 25 May 2017; N. Chamlou, 'COVID-19 Depressed Women's Employment Everywhere, and More So in Iran', Atlantic Council, 29 April 2021.

99. In 2017, only 0.8 per cent of Iran's GDP went to R&D, which is far below the global average of nearly 2.3 in 2018. See UNESCO Institute of Statistics, 'Iran (Islamic Republic of)'; *Financial Tribune*, 'Boosting R&D Investment Vital for Economic Growth'.

100. See Global Initiative against Transnational Organised Crime, *Under the Shadow: Illicit Economies in Iran*, Research Report (Geneva: GI-TOC, 2020), pp. 8–9.

101. Starting with groups such as Hezbollah in Lebanon and the Houthis in Yemen, Iran must stop supporting terrorist actions in the Middle East aimed at destabilising the region. See F. Gardner, 'Iran's Network of Influence in Mid-East "Growing"', BBC News, 7 November 2019.

102. Violence against Arabs in Israel has been on the rise recently as the police have not only overlooked abuses against them, but also physically abused them themselves. See Amnesty International, 'Israel and Occupied Palestinian Territories 2020'; Human Rights Watch, 'Israel'; Al-Sanah, Bsoul and Habjouqa, '"The Illusion of Citizenship Has Gone"'.

103. See J. Banish, 'Education in Israel: The Arab-Jewish Divide', The Borgen Project, 21 January 2019; D. Zaken, 'Push to Revamp Education Funding Falls Flat in Israel', Al-Monitor, 20 July 2020.

104. Despite its developed and robust economy, Israel still suffers from widespread poverty. Over 23 per cent of Israelis live in poverty. Most seriously hit are Arab-Israelis, 35 per cent of whom live below the poverty line. In 2018, Israel also had the highest number of children living in poverty in the OECD, with a whopping 22.2 per cent. See Statista, 'Proportion of Children Living in Poverty in OECD Countries in 2018', https://www.statista.com/statistics/264424/child-poverty-in-oecd-countries (accessed 22 July 2021); *Jerusalem Post*, 'About Two Million Israelis Live Below the Poverty Line – Report', 22 January 2021; X. Gonikberg, 'Efforts to Reduce Poverty in Israel', The Borgen Project, 15 September 2020.

105. Due to several years of droughts and the country's general geographic predicament, Israel has to confront the fact that there is just not enough fresh water in the country to supply its population. Besides water conservation, Israel will have to come up with cheap ways of desalinating seawater to increase water supply. Several projects to generate cheap energy to desalinate seawater are underway, among them the building of solar-energy plants and a power plant that generates energy from ocean waves. See Marin *et al.*, *Water Management in Israel*; Rosenbaum, 'Is Israel's Scarcity of Water a Blessing in Disguise?'.

106. The water level of the Dead Sea, a major tourist destination due to the mineral richness of its water, is decreasing by three to five feet per year. The reason for this is that the Jordan River, which flows into the Dead Sea, carries less and less water (in fact, less than one twentieth of the water it carried a few decades ago), as much of its water is being directed into Israeli, Jordanian and Palestinian towns and settlements. See J. Hammer, 'The Dying of the Dead Sea', *Smithsonian Magazine*, October 2005; Y. Schwartz, 'Can Israel and Jordan Cooperate to Save the Dying Dead Sea?', *National Geographic*, 6 December 2018.

107. A positive resolution of the decades-long conflict seems unlikely. Some experts suggest that the two-state solution is losing traction, because of Israeli territorial annexations and the recent clashes in May. Moreover, internal political divisions within Palestine also remain a challenge to peaceful negotiation. See Robinson, 'What is US Policy on the Israeli-Palestinian Conflict?'; Wilcox, 'The Israeli-Palestinian Peace Process: Lessons from Oslo'.

108. This should be done along the 1967 borders which existed prior to the land grabs of Arab territory by Israelis. See N. Ahmed, 'Remembering the 2002 Arab Peace Initiative', *Middle East Monitor*, 28 March 2021.

109. See A.D. Miller, 'How Israel and the Arab World Are Making Peace without a Peace Deal', Carnegie Endowment for International Peace, 27 May 2020; S. Mabon, 'Israel-Palestine Conflict: Why Gulf Leaders Are Staying Quiet – For Now', *The Conversation*, 17 May 2021.

110. It is estimated that the number of people aged 65 years or older in Japan will increase from about 36.2 million people in 2020 to almost 36.8 million people by 2025. By contrast, the number of children, as well as the working-age population, is predicted to shrink. The growing number of pensioners puts enormous strains on the public pension system. See Statista, 'Population of Japan from 1995 to 2019 with a Forecast until 2025, by Age Group', https://www.statista.com/statistics /612575/japan-population-age-group (accessed 22 July 2021); *The Economist*, 'Japan's Pension Problems are a Harbinger of Challenges Elsewhere', 9 July 2019.

111. As Japan's workforce is shrinking, the country will increasingly have to rely on immigrant workers to maintain economic growth and finance the pension system. According to one estimate, Japan would need to admit seventeen million new immigrants by 2050 to maintain the size of its current workforce. Japanese society, however, might resent growing immigration due to common, deep-rooted prejudices against foreigners, especially from other parts of Asia, so integration of foreign workers will prove to be a major social challenge. See M. Pollmann and N. Yashiro, 'Resolved: Japan Has Not Done Enough to Bolster Immigration', CSIS, *Debating Japan* 3, no. 6 (2020), n.p.; M. Gelin, 'Japan Radically Increased Immigration – and No One Protested', *Foreign Policy*, 23 June 2020.

112. Gender equality remains very low in Japan. Women continue to face massive discrimination in the workplace, including wage discrimination. Closing the gender equality gap requires including women at all levels of the workforce, including boardrooms and politics. See K. Yamaguchi, 'Japan's Gender Gap', *Finance and Development* 56, no. 1 (2019), p. 27; J. Ryall, 'Japan's "Appalling" Gender Equality Record Puts Spotlight on Sexism', DW, 5 April 2021; M. Eda, 'Why Closing Japan's Gender Gap Will Be Achieved with Equality from the Top', World Economic Forum, 30 March 2021.

113. To end *de facto* one-party rule in Japan, the Japanese would need to foster a more active civil society and ordinary citizens would need to play a more active part in political deliberations and challenge the incumbents – this way, elections in Japan could become more competitive. The introduction of public hearings, referenda and public participation in instituting regulations would add to a more vibrant and more democratic political culture in Japan. See M. Tsubogo, 'The Role of Civil Society and Participatory Governance in Japanese Democracy', *Japanese Political Science Review* 2 (2014), pp. 39–61.

114. With gross public debt at 256 per cent of GDP, the highest among OECD countries, Japan needs to trim its high annual budget deficits, especially in view of its rapidly ageing population. From 56.9 per cent in 2020, the old-age dependency ratio is expected to rise to 88.4 per cent of the working population in 2050. Although this may increase recession,

Japan will also have to increase taxes and reduce public spending. See *Economic Times*, 'Japan's Debt Mountain: How Is It Sustainable?', 10 June 2020; H. Tran, 'Do Deficits Matter? Japan Shows They Do', Atlantic Council, 6 July 2020.

115. Japan has been fighting deflation for over two decades now. Land prices and bank lending continue to fall, so putting a stop to further deflation will be crucial. See M. Fujikawa, 'In Japan, They're Still Worried about Deflation Not Inflation', *Wall Street Journal*, 19 March 2021.

116. In 2018, Japan was the third-largest emitter of greenhouse gases, with its plans for decarbonisation being significantly set back following the 2011 Fukushima nuclear disaster, which pushed Japan towards the use of fossil fuels. In 2020, however, newly elected Prime Minister Yoshihide Suga pledged to cut Japan's greenhouse gas emissions to net zero by 2050. In 2021, the government also pledged to cut emissions by 46 per cent compared to 2013 levels by 2030. See J. Timperley, 'The Carbon Brief Profile: Japan', 25 June 2018; K. Takenaka, Y. Takemoto and Y. Obayashi, 'Japan Vows Deeper Emission Cuts as Biden Holds Climate Summit', Reuters, 22 April 2021.

117. Increasingly there are debates inside Japan about whether Japan's pacifist constitution needs to be amended to allow for a stronger military so that Japan can wean itself away from the US military umbrella. Japan is also beginning to doubt America's determination to protect it, given that the country's geopolitical value has declined since the end of the Cold War. North Korea's hostile posture and nuclear tests have given these questions increased urgency. Japan's neighbours, however, are fearful of and oppose Japanese rearmament. See *Encyclopedia Britannica*, 'Self-Defense Force: Japanese Armed Force'; Kobara, 'Japan to Scrap 1% GDP Cap on Defence Spending: Minister Kishi'.

118. See T. Siripala, 'US and Japan Name China as Threat to International Order', *The Diplomat*, 17 March 2021.

119. Japan has to import all of its oil and natural gas from abroad and is therefore highly vulnerable to any cuts in supply. Following the Fukushima nuclear disaster in 2011, Japan has had to move away from nuclear power and invest in other energy sources. It has therefore signed an oil-sharing agreement with ASEAN countries. Since the only sustainable long-term option for energy security is renewable energy sources, however, Japan must increase investment in this sector. This will help the country to fulfil its emission reduction targets. See International Energy Agency, 'Japan 2021: Energy Policy Review', March 2021; T. Tsuji, 'Japan Targets Vietnam for First ASEAN Oil-Sharing Deal', *Financial Times*, 26 April 2021; X. Zhihai, 'Rethinking Japan's Energy Security 8 Years after Fukushima', *The Diplomat*, 21 March 2019.

120. Despite their political divisions, China is Japan's biggest export buyer, with purchasing rates of more than 20 per cent of the total of Japanese exports. Strengthening trade ties may help to assuage military and security threats. See Nikkei Asia, 'China Passes US as Top Japanese Export Buyer, Topping 20%', 22 January 2021.

121. Building and cultivating strong ties with these countries will help Japan to pose a counterweight to rising Chinese predominance in Southeast, South and Northeast Asia.

122. See Park, *The Three Enduring Legacies of the Pacific War in East Asia*; Shin, 'Conflict between South Korea and Japan Surges Again with Court's "Comfort Women" Decision'.

123. Although Kazakhstan is currently a peaceful country, its ethnic diversity and the growing economic disparities among its population are leading to an increase in social tensions, which manifested in widespread protests across 2018, 2019 and 2020 and the resignation of former President Nursultan Nazarbayev. The government can help to avoid such a development by curtailing corruption, instituting good social programmes for the less fortunate and aiming economic policy at a more equitable distribution of the country's wealth. See Reuters, 'Dozens Detained in Rare Kazakhstan Independence Day Protests', 16 December 2019.

124. For Kazakhstan to achieve the goals it has set for itself in the health sector, it must continue to construct new facilities and to purchase new equipment. It must also increase funding for medical training programmes in order to sustain its growing health-care workforce. See Vanderveen, 'Healthcare in Kazakhstan'.

125. Connected with drugs abuse is an increase in HIV/AIDS infections and drug-related crimes. The knowledge-based approach to substance use and HIV prevention, which has been mostly used in Kazakhstan, does not equip at-risk adolescents with risk reduction skills. Kazakhstan also recognises the traditionally high suicide rates in the country as a public threat. Although overall suicide rates in the country have decreased over the past decade, the child suicide rate remains very high. See L. Ismalyilova and A. Terlikbayeva, 'Building Competencies to Prevent Youth Substance Use in Kazakhstan: Mixed Methods Findings from a Pilot Family-Focused Multimedia Trial', *Journal of Adolescent Health* 63, no. 3 (2018), pp. 301–12; Central Asian Bureau for Analytical Reporting, 'Pandemic and Suicide Issues in Kazakhstan: Prevention Strategies', 22 February 2021; World Bank, 'Suicide Mortality Rate (Per 100,000 Population) – Kazakhstan', https://data .worldbank.org/indicator/SH.STA.SUIC.P5?locations=KZ (accessed 22 July 2021).

126. Despite the government's adoption of an anti-corruption strategy in 2015, Kazakhstan ranked 94th out of 180 countries for corruption, according to Transparency International's 'Corruption Perceptions

Index 2020'; A. Mukashev, 'How Is the Fight against Corruption in Kazakhstan Taking Place?', Central Asian Bureau for Analytical Reporting, 28 May 2020.

127. In 2018, the government adopted the 'Seven Pillars of Justice Strategy', which encompassed large, sweeping reforms to the country's system of adopting judges, with the aim of increasing their independence and selecting them according to their expertise. To this date, this has been considered a successful endeavour. Kazakhstan must therefore continue to implement this judicial system and not return to a system which undermines accountability through the political appointment of judges. See T. Donakov, 'Kazakhstan – Building a Fair and Impartial Judicial System Fit for the Modern Age', *New Jurist*, 27 May 2019.

128. Kazakhstan's economic growth is currently too dependent on the oil and mining industries. To insulate the economy from external shocks, the government must continue to promote economic diversification. Although Kazakhstan's oil and gas industry is extremely lucrative, global reliance on fossil fuels will decrease over the coming decades with the aim of reducing greenhouse gases and slowing climate change. If it is to remain competitive, Kazakhstan must develop other sectors, focusing on products and technologies that will be sustainable in the long term. See World Bank, *Kazakhstan: The Challenge of Economic Diversification amidst Productivity Stagnation: Country Economic Update Fall 2018* (Washington, DC: World Bank, 2018).

129. Over the past two decades Kazakhstan has been trying to establish itself as the major financial hub in Central Asia. The most significant step in this direction was taken in 2018 through the inauguration of the Astana International Financial Centre in the capital, which also includes Kazakhstan's second stock exchange, the first one being in the city of Almaty. See J. Lam, 'Kazakhstan: Central Asia's Global Financial Hub', HKTDC Research, 31 July 2019; K. Rapoza, 'Kazakhstan Opens Astana International Financial Center in Hopes to Become Eurasian Financial Hub', *Forbes*, 26 June 2018.

130. Over the past couple of years, almost 60 per cent of investment projects in Kazakhstan have been related to non-extractive sectors, including manufacturing, transportation, trade and financial and insurance services. Despite this, the past few years have seen an overall decrease in foreign investment. The government must adopt measures to improve the investment climate, digitise and modernise current legislation. See B. Sartbayev, 'Kazakhstan Aims to Become a Destination for Global Investment', *Foreign Policy*, https://foreignpolicy.com/sponsored /kazakhstan-aims-to-become-a-destination-for-global-investment (accessed 22 July 2021).

131. Kazakhstan has successfully reduced the percentage of its population living in poverty over the past two decades by raising employment rates and real wages. This reduction is dependent, however, on the financial

situation of the country and, therefore, on oil, as demonstrated in 2016 and 2020 when oil prices dropped and poverty and inequality rates increased once more. There are also large wealth gaps between urban and rural areas and among the different regions. The country also lacks a sizeable middle class. One measure the government can take to increase its middle class is to encourage the development of small and medium-sized enterprises. This in turn will require foreign direct investment and a stronger education system which can enable social mobility. See World Bank, 'Poverty and Equity Brief: Kazakhstan', April 2021, https://databank.worldbank.org/data/download/poverty/987B9C90-CB9F-4D93-AE8C-750588BF00QA/AM2020/Global_POVEQ_KAZ.pdf; N. Hodges, 'Cautious Hope: Top 10 Facts about Poverty in Afghanistan', The Borgen Project, 3 October 2018, https://borgenproject.org/cautious-hope-top-10-facts-about-poverty-in-kazakhstan.

132. According to a 2019 report by Kazakhstan's National Academy of Sciences, the 'non-observed economy' was equivalent to 22 to 27 per cent in Kazakhstan. According to a 2018 working paper by the International Monetary Fund, however, Kazakhstan's informal sector equates to 39 per cent of its GDP. Migrant workers comprise a substantial part of the informal workforce. See T.K. Bekzhanova and A.B. Temirova, 'Non-observed Economy as Part of the Developing Economy', *Reports of the International Academy of Sciences of the Republic of Kazakhstan* 2, no. 324 (2019), p. 215; L. Medina and F. Schneider, 'Shadow Economies around the World: What Did We Learn over the Last 20 Years?', IMF Working Paper no. 18/17, January 2018; International Federation for Human Rights, 'Invisible and Exploited in Kazakhstan: The Plight of Kyrgyz Migrant Workers and Members of Their Families', FIDH Report no. 713a, June 2018, p. 18.

133. Kazakhstan's focus on the formation of an environmentally friendly economy is enshrined in the concept approved in 2013 on its transition to a 'green economy'. To implement the ambitious goals of the concept, which include meeting 50 per cent of its energy needs through renewable sources by 2050, Kazakhstan has adopted a number of laws and by-laws (on energy conservation and energy efficiency, support for renewable energy sources etc.). The government is also relying on mechanisms and instruments of economic incentive. Another measure concerns the adoption of a national report to assess the main socially significant environmental problems, the implementation of state policy in the field of the environment and the use of natural resources. See E. Abakhanov, 'New Environmental Code of Kazakhstan: Expectations and Prospects', Central Asian Bureau for Analytical Reporting, 6 April 2020.

134. Although the oil industry is one of the biggest strengths of Kazakhstan's economy, the government must adopt strict environmental regulations for the expansion of its fossil fuel sector, with the aim of reducing greenhouse gas emissions and reducing environmental damage.

135. In 2020, USAID launched its Regional Water and Vulnerable Environment Program, aimed at promoting stability, economic prosperity and healthy ecosystems in Central Asia by addressing critical water, energy and agriculture sector linkages. It also focuses on addressing vulnerabilities to climate change. See USAID, 'New USAID Program to Strengthen Transboundary Water Cooperation in Central Asia', 30 September 2020.

136. OECD, *Reforming Kazakhstan: Progress, Challenges and Opportunities* (Paris: OECD Publishing, 2017), p. 121.

137. Besides nuclear weapons facilities, the country also had Soviet-era biological weapons production and storage plants on its territory. Trilateral cooperation from 1996 to 2012 among the United States, Kazakhstan and Russia enhanced security and surveillance and sealed off boreholes, tunnels and other infrastructure previously used by the Soviets for nuclear tests. Kazakhstan has also taken steps to secure biological weapons facilities from both natural and man-made threats. The country must continue to monitor these structures and carry out maintenance to ensure that they do not become a serious security threat. See A.C. Weber and C.L. Parthemore, 'Lessons from Kazakhstan', Belfer Center for Science and International Affairs, January 2017.

138. Kazakhstan's borders remain porous and underpaid border guards are susceptible to corruption. Kazakhstan is a major transit country for drugs trafficked from Afghanistan to consumer markets in Russia and Europe. See S.V. Golunov and R.N. McDermott, 'Border Security in Kazakhstan: Threats, Policies and Future Challenges', *Journal of Slavic Military Studies* 18, no. 1 (2005), pp. 31–58.

139. On 18 August 2018 the five countries bordering the Caspian Sea (Russia, Iran, Azerbaijan, Kazakhstan and Turkmenistan) signed the Convention on the Legal Status of the Caspian Sea, a new convention to regulate the use of the Caspian Sea and its resources.

140. Since announcing the withdrawal of its troops from Afghanistan, the US has expressed its interest in establishing military bases in Central Asia in countries such as Kazakhstan. The Kazakh government must be careful not to anger Russia and China if it is to maintain peace and security in the region. See W.A. Sanchez, 'The Future of US-Kazakhstan Relations', *Georgetown Journal of International Affairs*, 28 May 2010.

141. In order to address the challenge presented by a rapidly decreasing population, Lithuania should provide its citizens with incentives to discourage them from emigrating and provide financial and social support to young families in order to increase the birth rate. The government should simplify immigration procedures to further boost the level of immigrants to the country, particularly skilled ones. Since mental health problems and high suicide rates are also a contributing factor, the government should introduce programmes for mental

well-being and make all mental support and therapy free. See European Commission, Eurydice, 'Lithuania – Population: Demographic Situation, Languages and Religions', 31 March 2021.

142. One of the groups which must suffer from income inequality and severe poverty is old-age pensioners. Lithuania should raise pensions by reforming the tax system to increase taxes on wealthier sections in the population and provide financial support for lower-income families, especially those with children. See OECD, 'Lithuania Economic Snapshot'; Budzinauskas, 'Despite Positive Changes, Social Problems Persist in Lithuania – EU Commission'; EAPN Lithuania, 'Report: Poverty and Social Exclusion in Lithuania 2018', pp. 2–3.

143. Lithuania should increase the number of programmes designed to tackle alcoholism, as well as smoking. Funding for health care should also be increased. See OECD/European Observatory on Health Systems and Policies, *Lithuania: Country Health Profile 2019: State of Health in the EU*, p. 3.

144. The female-led coalition is set to bring competence, experience, and stability. Their initial focus should be on meeting domestic public expectations within the constraints of budget resources. However, it will likely also have to address economic and social reforms as well as foreign policy challenges, particularly in the context of the country's tense relations with Belarus. See Grigas, 'Lithuania's New Government'.

145. According to the OECD, following the COVID-19 crisis one of the government's priorities should be the integration of less-skilled workers into the labour market. This would not only reduce inequality, but it would also further boost the economy. See OECD, 'Lithuania Economic Snapshot'.

146. Lithuania's government has set up regional development as one of its highest policy priorities. Presently, municipal governments account for only 33 per cent of public investment in Lithuania. Since municipal public investment can attract private domestic and foreign direct investment, foster growth and improve the well-being of all residents, the government should increase funding in this regard. See OECD, 'Lithuania Economic Snapshot'.

147. Lithuania's booming biotech industry is driving its economic recovery from the coronavirus pandemic. Increasing investment in the sector will make it a leading force of the Lithuanian economy.

148. Lithuania does not tax environmentally damaging activities enough. Indeed, it sets no CO_2 tax, has one of the lowest excise duties on motor fuel, petrol and diesel in the OECD and has one of the largest 'diesel differential', the gap in the price of diesel versus unleaded petrol. Lithuania also provides among the highest subsidies to fossil fuels. Only in 2020 did the country introduce a purchase tax for passenger vehicles which takes emissions into account. The country therefore ought to increase fossil fuel taxes and remove subsidies, if it is to reach its

ambitious environmental and climate-management objectives and the
net-zero carbon emission target by 2050. See Blöchlinger and
Strumskyte, 'Greening Lithuania's Growth', p. 3.

149. Although the Lithuanian government has allocated fifteen per cent of its
2020 stimulus package to renewable energy and energy efficiency, and
adopted policies aimed at achieving net zero by 2020, the processes must
be mainstreamed and simplified, rather than having over two hundred
concurrent projects. See ibid., p. 6.

150. The Lithuanian government hopes to maintain the country's growth in
the science and biotechnology sector, with the aim of becoming one of
the leading countries in the life sciences in the Central and Eastern
European region by 2030. For this reason, it set out a strategy in 2018 to
increase the GDP contribution of the industry from two to five per cent
over the next decade. In addition to increasing investment in this sector,
the government should set out clear policy objectives and strengthen
ties between research institutions, universities and governmental
bodies. See A. Irwin-Hunt, 'The "Golden-Age" of Lithuanian Life
Sciences', FDi Intelligence, 19 April 2021.

151. See UNESCO Institute of Statistics, "Lithuania: Education and Literacy,"
accessed 22 July 2021, http://uis.unesco.org/country/LT; Franco,
"Education in Lithuania"; OECD, 'Lithuania – Overview of the Education
System (EAG 2020)', https://gpseducation.oecd.org/CountryProfile?prima
ryCountry=LTU&treshold=10&topic=EO (accessed 22 July 2021).

152. Cyber attacks will increase in number, but so will disinformation,
xenophobia and outside surveillance, all of which have the potential to
destabilise Lithuania. The Lithuanian intelligence forces perceive China
as a particular threat in this regard. Lithuania will therefore have to
increase its investment in cyber security and work to combat the spread
of disinformation across all platforms. Strengthening its ties to the EU
and NATO will also provide it with increased protection from both
Russia and China. See State Security Department of the Republic of
Lithuania and Defence Intelligence Security Service under the Ministry
of National Defence, *National Threat Assessment 2021* (Vilnius: State
Security Department of Lithuania, 2021), pp. 12–14; Crisis 24,
'Lithuania Country Report', https://crisis24.garda.com/insights
-intelligence/intelligence/country-reports/lithuania (accessed 22
July 2021); L. Kojala, 'Baltic Security: The Same Challenges Remain,
Even during a Pandemic', Foreign Policy Research Institute, 28
May 2020.

153. The Lithuanian energy grids used to be closely connected to Russia's.
Although steps have already been taken jointly by Lithuania and the EU
to reduce this dependence, more must be done to ensure that Russia
cannot influence Lithuanian decisions by its control over its energy
sources. See ibid.

154. The current spending level is already slightly above two per cent and has almost quadrupled in nominal terms to reach more than US$1 billion in 2020, with Lithuania's government committing to increasing defence spending every year for the next decade, reaching at least 2.5 per cent of GDP by 2030. The commitment may need to be raised further, however, in light of the increasing threat presented by Russia and China.

155. In this regard, by taking charge of the EU's relations with Belarus, Lithuania can also establish itself as a political and diplomatic power within the organisation and not just the Baltic region.

156. Currently about 42 per cent live in poverty. See World Bank, 'Poverty and Equity Brief: Mexico', April 2020, https://databank.worldbank.org /data/download/poverty/33EF03BB-9722-4AE2-ABC7-AA2972D68AFE /Global_POVEQ_MEX.pdf.

157. In 2020, the unemployment level was 4.71 per cent of the total workforce. See World Bank, 'Unemployment: Mexico', https://data .worldbanks.org/indicator/SL.UEM.TOTL.ZS?locations=MX (accessed 18 June 2021).

158. Currently, the demand is increasing domestically and Mexico relies (as net importer) on the US supply. See US Energy Information Administration, 'Country Analysis Executive Summary: Mexico'.

159. Doing so will provide increased revenue for the government to spend on human resources, including education and health. In May 2021, 22.6 million people worked in the informal sector, notably as a result of the economic impact of the COVID-19 pandemic. See Reuters, 'Mexico Loses 12 Million Jobs, Workers in Informal Sector Grow', 30 June 2020.

160. Only by increasing human capital, productivity and growth can Mexico create sufficient new jobs to absorb the increasing demand. See ibid.

161. Total R&D spending was 0.4 per cent of GDP in 2020 with most spending in universities and the government sector. Spending in the business sector accounts for almost $2 million.

162. Reuters, 'Mexico Loses 12 Million Jobs, Workers in Informal Sector Grow'.

163. According to a 2018 US Central Intelligence Agency report, drugs cartels are in control of 20 per cent of Mexican territory. The number of homicides and disappearances has reached record numbers. See M.B. Sheridan, 'Violent Criminal Groups are Claiming More Territory', *Washington Post*, 29 October 2020.

164. It is currently threatened by an attempt by the president's coalition to implement laws that will threaten the constitution and balance of power. See J.M. Vivanco, 'López Obrador Threatens Judicial Independence', Human Rights Watch, 26 April 2021.

165. Fifty-five per cent of undocumented migrants in the United States were born in Mexico. Their situation is often precarious and the Immigration and Customs Enforcement Agency was recently accused

of human rights violations. See E. Nieblas-Bedolla, 'Legalisation of Undocumented Immigrants in the USA', *The Lancet* 397, no. 10268 (2021), pp. 25–26.

166. Especially in a context of immigration crisis between Central America and the United States, where Mexico plays a mitigation role. See Abdalla, 'Biden to Broaden US-Mexican Relations, Keep Immigration at Top'.

167. See USAID, 'Global Health Nigeria'.

168. Nigeria needs to increase government spending on health, which is currently under four per cent of GDP and thus one of the lowest rates on the continent. Hospitals will need to have better medical equipment and their personnel need to be better trained. See USAID, 'Global Health Nigeria'; World Bank, 'Current Health Expenditure: Nigeria', https:// data.worldbank.org/indicator/SH.XPD.CHEX.GD.ZS?locations=NG (accessed 20 June 2021).

169. This would include, among other measures: increasing pressure on the terrorist group Boko Haram; better training of security forces; better law enforcement and mechanisms to fight discrimination based on religion or ethnicity; taking measures to protect women from abuse, traffickers and genital mutilation; and fighting corruption, which can help to fuel intimidation and violence against political opponents and provide money to buy votes and weapons. See Amnesty International, 'Nigeria 2020', 20 June 2021, https://www.amnesty.org/en/countries /africa/nigeria/report-nigeria; UNICEF, 'Take Action to Eliminate Female Genital Mutilation by 2030', 6 February 2019.

170. Transparency International, 'Corruption Perceptions Index 2020'.

171. Among these goals is to eradicate poverty and hunger as well as ensure good health and quality education. The UN Development Programme assists the country in this process. See UNDP Nigeria, 'Sustainable Development Goals', https://www.ng.undp.org/content /nigeria/en/home/sustainable-development-goals.html (accessed 20 June 2021).

172. Ibid.

173. Nigeria, and particularly its poor residents, will be hard hit by climate change, which is expected to lead to droughts, floods and soil degradation. See M. Yahya, 'Nigeria Must Lead on Climate Change', UNDP, 4 October 2019.

174. Reforms must be introduced and strictly followed to ensure more school enrolment and fight the high illiteracy rate. More funding should be allocated to this cause. Special attention should be given to women and girls' access to education. See Ekundayo, 'Education in Nigeria Is in a Mess from Top to Bottom'.

175. Nigeria has been very active in this organisation and is currently working on implementing common tariffs among member states. See ECOWAS, 'Directors General of Customs in the Region Hold Meeting on Common External Tariff', 21 November 2019, https://www.ecowas.

int/directors-general-of-customs-in-the-region-hold-meeting-on
-common-external-tariff.

176. To improve social conditions, Pakistan will have to free up more money
to spend on health care, education and infrastructure. This could be
done by decreasing military expenditure, since Pakistan's military
expenditure as a percentage of GDP is the highest in the region and has
continued to increase over the past ten years. See Statista, 'Pakistan:
Ration of Military Spending to Gross Domestic Product (GDP) from
2009 to 2019', https://www.statista.com/statistics/810540/ratio-of
-military-expenditure-to-gross-domestic-product-gdp-pakistan
(accessed 22 July 2021); Lopes da Silva *et al.*, *Trends in World Military
Expenditure, 2020.*

177. Pakistan's population will continue to grow rapidly, so devising
population policies and finding ways to reduce unemployment and
poverty will be key challenges. See A. Goujon, A. Wazir and N. Gailey,
'Pakistan: A Population Giant Falling behind Its Demographic
Transition', *Population and Societies* 576, no. 4 (2020), pp. 1–4.

178. According to the *State of Food Security and Nutrition in the World*
report for 2020, the prevalence of undernourishment in Pakistan is 12.3
per cent; an estimated 26 million people in Pakistan are undernourished
or suffer from food insecurity. Many of these are children. Poverty and
the rise in food prices are one reason for widespread food insecurity in
the country. To tackle the problem, Pakistan will have to improve rural
infrastructure to promote increased production of food staples and
increase food imports. See FAO, IFAD, UNICEF, WFP and World
Health Organization, *The State of Food Security and Nutrition in the
World 2020: Transforming Food Systems for Affordable Healthy Diets*
(Rome: FAO, 2020), p. 169; Q. uz-Zaman, 'Low Earnings and
Agricultural Neglect Push Pakistan into Food Insecurity', Eco-Business,
14 December 2020.

179. 17.7 million people in Pakistan currently live without clean water. See
Water Aid, 'Pakistan', https://www.wateraid.org/where-we-work
/pakistan (accessed 22 July 2021); A. Sharma, '10 Facts about Sanitation
in Pakistan', The Borgen Project, 21 March 2020.

180. Some foreign policy experts have suggested that there might be a coup
in Pakistan which would propel the country into severe instability and
chaos. As long as moderate political parties remain strong and the
secular military maintains its dominant position in the country,
however, an extremist coup seems unlikely. Nevertheless, as a result of
the many competing forces in Pakistan, the country faces large
challenges ahead in securing its domestic political situation and turning
into a stable democracy. Efforts should be made to reduce the influence
of the military in politics and to ensure that democratic principles and
norms are applied in practice and not just in theory. See F. Bibi, S.
Jameel and S.U. Jalal, 'What Is Democracy? Challenges for Democracy

in Pakistan', *Global Political Review* 3, no. 1 (2018), pp. 66–67; M. Singh, 'The Curious Case of Pakistan's Democracy', Global Risks Insights, 20 September 2018.

181. Pakistan is striving to improve its ranking as the slowest for infrastructure expansion in the region, according to the World Bank, through a US$2.4 billion government investment in 2021 for highways, power and transportation. This is in addition to projects worth billions of dollars, funded by the World Bank, Asian Development Bank (ADB), Gulf Cooperation Council countries, the Japan International Cooperation Agency (JICA) and the US$56 billion China-Pakistan Economic Corridor (CPEC). The latter, however, has been criticised for the high debt burden it will place on Pakistan. A balance must be found between the need to boost the economy and development and increasing national debt. See N. Mathews, 'Pakistan Invests in Infrastructure, but Many Obstacles Stand in the Way of Construction', *Engineering News Record*, 13 April 2021; M. Javid, 'Public and Private Infrastructure Investment and Economic Growth in Pakistan: An Aggregate and Disaggregate Analysis', *Sustainability* 11, no. 12 (2019).

182. The rapid melting of the Himalayan glaciers, on whose waters hundreds of millions of South Asians depend, is a very serious security threat for Pakistan. To maximise its domestic water resources, Pakistan will have to invest in its water infrastructure and clean up polluted water sources. See P. Sleet, 'Water Resources in Pakistan: Scarce, Polluted and Poorly Governed', Future Directions International, 31 January 2019.

183. A 2007 World Bank report singles out air and water pollution as the two most important environmental challenges facing Pakistan. If Pakistan fails to tackle these problems effectively, its economic growth potential will be seriously jeopardised. Today, environmental pollution is already costing the country at least US$2.3 billion every year. Resource degradation and diseases and premature mortality due to water and air pollution account for much of these costs. Setting quality standards for water and air and fostering public and private investments in technology and infrastructure that help reduce pollution will be important steps for Pakistan to ensure the country's future well-being. See M. Sharma, 'Environmental Degradation Draining Pakistan's Economy', Down to Earth, 16 July 2014; R. Khalid, 'Air Pollution Causes 50pc of Environmental Degradation Cost', *News International*, 13 November 2019, https://www.thenews.com.pk/print/554881-air-pollution-causes-50pc-of-environmental-degradation-cost.

184. See M. Nawaz and G. Naeem, *Coastal Hazard Early Warning Systems in Pakistan: Gap Analysis* (Oxford: Oxfam GB, 2016), pp. 24–27.

185. See Pakistan Alliance for Girls Education, 'Education Budget of Pakistan', accessed 22 July 2021, https://page.org.pk/education-budget-of-pakistan (accessed 22 July 2021).

186. Peace and stability in Kashmir and Afghanistan, as well as victory in the war on terrorism, can only be achieved with the help of Pakistan. See Belfer Center for Science and International Affairs, 'South Asia Week: Pakistan's Role in Regional Stability', 25 April 2016; *News International*, 'Pakistan's Pivotal Role in Regions' Peace, Security: Foreign Minister', 17 October 2019, https://www.thenews.com.pk/latest/542436-pakistan-playing-pivotal-role-in-region-s-peace-security-fm.

187. Both countries should comply with ceasefire decisions and avoid escalation. See Council on Foreign Relations, 'Conflict between India and Pakistan'.

188. The Russian government is increasing the number of programmes which address family planning and providing financial support to young families to try and encourage an increase in birth rates. See L. Palveleva and R. Coalson, 'Echoes of War and Collapse: Russia's Demographic Decline as Small 1990s Generation Comes of Age', Radio Free Europe/Radio Liberty, 12 January 2020.

189. Some of the incentives being used currently to discourage internal migration include free land in the Arctic. Measures should focus on the creation of new jobs in those areas and the improvement of the local infrastructure, health-care system and access to education. See N.V. Mkrtchyan, 'Migration in Rural Areas of Russia: Territorial Differences', *Population and Economics* 3, no. 1 (2019), pp. 39–51; Sheludkov, Kamp and Müller, 'Decreasing Labor Intensity in Agriculture'.

190. See Kaspe, 'Opinion: The Political Meanings and Uses of Russian Corruption'.

191. See World Bank, 'Greater Productivity, Investment in People Can Put Russia Back on Path to Sustainable and Inclusive Growth', 12 January 2017.

192. Russia must prevent a growing economic gap between booming metropolitan centres (especially Moscow and St Petersburg) and the rest of the country, as it may hurt social cohesion. See V. Agibalova *et al.*, 'Rural-Urban Segregation: A Special Case of Researching Monetary Income of the Population', *International Journal of Innovation, Creativity and Change* 14, no. 9 (2020), p. 375; S.K. Wegren, 'Rural Inequality in Post-Soviet Russia', *Problems of Post-Communism* 61, no. 1 (2014), pp. 52–64.

193. According to the World Bank, the laws on foreign investment must be simplified in order to encourage investors to place their money in Russia and boost growth despite the sanctions imposed by the West after the annexation of Crimea in 2014. See A. Ostroukh and A. Marrow, 'World Bank Tells Russia: Simplify Laws to Draw Foreign Investment', Reuters, 25 March 2021.

194. Increasing numbers of Russian citizens are willing to contribute to environmental efforts through campaigning and activism. Not only do they lack access to policy-making processes, however, they are also often

targeted by the police, labelled 'foreign agents' and arrested. See
A. Davydova, 'Environmental Activism in Russia: Strategies and
Prospects', CSIS, 3 March 2021; D. Aitkhozhina, 'Environmental Work
Can Be Undesirable in Russia', Human Rights Watch, 14 January 2021.

195. Modernise Russia without resorting to authoritarianism.

196. For more information on how Russia and Ukraine can reconcile their
interests, see the Appendix.

197. Russia's aggressive rhetoric, far-reaching territorial claims and resource
exploration have done little to improve its diplomatic position there
vis-à-vis the other Arctic states; Russia has only antagonised them. See
E. Rumer, R. Sokolsky and P. Stronsky, 'Russia in the Arctic – A Critical
Examination', Carnegie Endowment for International Peace, Paper, 29
March 2021.

198. See Neom, 'Neom: An Accelerator of Human Progress', https://www
.neom.com/en-us (accessed 28 July 2021).

199. This economic strategy is included in the Vision 2030 programme.
There are already not enough jobs for Saudi nationals in Saudi Arabia
and, with its young population and high birth rate, the demand for jobs
will only increase. See Oxford Business Group, 'More Private Sector
Participation to Stimulate Growth in Saudi Arabia Industry'.

200. Measures which could be adopted include legislating to ensure that
wages paid by the private sector are comparable to those paid by the
public sector and that private-sector employees should be given the
same social benefits.

201. Saudi Arabia's cyber-security market is expected to grow at a
compounded annual rate of 16.59 per cent between 2018 and 2023,
representing the largest market in the Middle East. As part of the
country's Vision 2030 development plan, Saudi Arabia announced a
relatively modest US$2.1 billion investment in its space programme.
Some estimate that its space industry could generate more than US$1
trillion annually by 2040. See A. Alwazir and J. Dichter, 'USSABC
Economic Brief: Saudi Arabia's Emergence in Cyber Technology',
US-Saudi Arabian Business Council, January 2020, p. 1; C.W. Dunne,
'Arab Space Programs Level Up', Arab Center Washington, DC, 30
April 2021, http://arabcenterdc.org/policy_analyses/arab-space
-programs-level-up.

202. See King Abdullah University of Science and Technology, 'KAUST',
https://www.kaust.edu.sa/en (accessed 28 July 2021).

203. Over the past decade, Saudi Arabia has significantly reduced female
unemployment rates, decreasing from 32 per cent in 2018 to 24 in 2020.
Although Saudi women make up 55.8 per cent of graduates (2019), they
make up only 33 per cent of the labour force, which is, nonetheless, an
extremely positive improvement from the sixteen-per-cent labour force
participation rate that prevailed in 2000. By encouraging more women
to work, Saudi Arabia could increase its skilled labour force. See
S. Gomez Tamayo, J. Koettl and N. Rivera, 'The Spectacular Surge of

the Saudi Female Labor Force', Brookings Institution, 21 April 2021;
A. Puri-Mirza, 'Share of Female Graduates Saudi Arabia 2010–2019',
Statista, 16 March 2021; World Bank, 'Labor Force Participation Rate,
Female (% of Population Ages 15+) (Modeled ILO Estimate) – Saudi
Arabia', https://data.worldbank.org/indicator/SL.TLF.CACT.
FE.ZS?locations=SA (accessed 22 July 2021).

204. Saudi Arabia plays a crucial mediating role in the Israeli-Palestinian
conflict. As a leading member of the Arab League, it supports an
independent Palestine alongside Israel in accordance with the pre-1967
borders. See E. Marteu, 'Saudi Arabia and the Israel-Palestine Conflict:
Between a Rock and a Hard Place', *The Conversation*, 24 June 2018.

205. See S. Al-Sarhan, 'Saudi Arabia, the Natural Leader of the Muslim
World', *Arab News*, 4 February 2021.

206. The disease has also had a negative effect on economic development and
growth, resulting from lower public and private savings, rising health
costs and the shortened lifespan of many skilled and trained workers.
Besides launching aggressive prevention campaigns, the government
needs to increase the coverage of its free anti-retroviral-medication
programme for HIV/AIDS patients (which presently covers about 70 per
cent of the infected population), especially in more remote, poorer areas
of the country. The high incidence of rape in South Africa, a common
way for women to contract the virus, also needs to be addressed through
better law-enforcement measures. One controversial measure which is
currently being implemented by the South African government involves
holding rapists accountable for passing on HIV up to three years after
the rape. See UNAIDS, 'South Africa', https://www.unaids.org/en
/regionscountries/countries/southafrica (accessed 22 July 2021);
N. Abrahams *et al.*, 'Increase in HIV Incidence in Women Exposed
to Rape', *AIDS* 35, no. 4 (2021), pp. 633–42; M. Malan, 'How Rape
Survivors' Long-term Risk of HIV Infection Can Lead to Heavier
Sentences for Rapists', *News 24*, 1 December 2020.

207. Although South African President Cyril Ramaphosa is treating
corruption as a serious issue and trying to combat it through both law
and policy, he is facing opposition within his own party, which hampers
efforts and undermines the effectiveness of the results. See D. Bernstein
and N. Shaw, 'Anti-Corruption in South Africa', *Global Compliance
News*, https://www.globalcompliancenews.com/anti-corruption/anti
-corruption-in-south-africa-2 (accessed 22 July 2021); M. Magome,
'South Africa's President Fights Own Party over Corruption', AP News,
19 February 2021.

208. In 1994, about 87 per cent of the farmland in South Africa was in the
hands of around 60,000 white farmers and the government, while the
nineteen million black South Africans living in rural areas cultivated
the remaining thirteen per cent. By 2004, land reform programmes run
by the new ANC government had been able to redistribute only 3.4 per
cent of the country's agricultural land, with 72 per cent of it still in the

hands of whites in 2017. In 2020, the government of South Africa announced plans to redistribute 700,000 hectares of farmland to black farmers. This redistribution, however, is likely to face the same deficiencies as the redistribution policies adopted in the first 20 years since the end of apartheid. As before, the government does not want to reduce agricultural efficiency by giving the land to people with insufficient farming experience. Instead, through the selection process and the use of specific training programmes which focus on modern farming technologies, the government's redistribution programme seems aimed at creating a small class of black commercial farmers. In March 2021 the government also announced the creation of a special Land Court to help unblock land redistribution and address ownership issues. See C. Clark, 'South Africa Confronts a Legacy of Apartheid: Why Land Reform Is a Key Issue in the Upcoming Election', *The Atlantic*, 3 May 2019; B. Cousins, 'Problematic Assumptions Raise Questions about South Africa's New Land Reform Plan', *The Conversation*, 26 October 2020; Reuters, 'South Africa Plans Special Court to Help Unblock Land Redistribution', 1 March 2021.

209. South Africa must improve the education system to increase the number of people with in-demand skills and encourage foreign investment if it is to reduce its exceedingly high unemployment rates. See GroundUp, 'Why Is South Africa's Unemployment Rate So High?', *Daily Maverick*, 14 February 2019; Santander, 'South Africa: Foreign Investment', https://santandertrade.com/en/portal/establish-overseas/south-africa/foreign-investment (accessed 22 July 2021).

210. The flagship Black Economic Empowerment Act, launched in 2003 under the government of Thabo Mbeki, was an ambitious attempt to close the gap and improve black participation in the economy through affirmative action. It has yet to achieve the desired results, however. In 2019, black ownership in companies across the economy was just 29 per cent, compared to 25 per cent in 2018 and 32 per cent in 2016. No sector of the economy has more than 50 per cent black ownership in large entities, with historically white-dominated sectors of the South African economy, such as finance (25 per cent) and agriculture (twelve per cent), particularly resistant to change. See D. Thomas, 'Is South African Transformation Dead?', *African Business*, 1 September 2020; J. Cotterill and C. Bruce-Lockhart, 'Black South Africans Lose Out as Economic Divide Bites', *Financial Times*, 2 May 2019; International Monetary Fund, 'Six Charts Explain South Africa's Inequality'.

211. This will imply drastically reducing water pollution caused, for example, by the mining industry. Moreover, the government needs to address overfishing to maintain the progress made over the past ten years in the recovery of endangered species such as abalone and linefish. See S.E. Kerwatch, 'Are South African Linefishes Recovering and What Makes

Them Prone to Overexploitation?', *African Journal of Marine Science* 42, no. 3 (2020), pp. 361–73; M.-L. Antoni, 'In South Africa, Abalone Farming Goes for Gold', Global Seafood Alliance, 22 October 2018.

212. See Okonjo-Iweala, 'Africa Can Play a Leading Role in the Fight against Climate Change'.

213. The government will need to come up with active measures to increase incentives for its educated elite to stay in the country and to encourage the diaspora to return. Effectively addressing the many social ills is one way to do so. Technology may also provide a strong instrument to combat brain drain. The government therefore should invest in tech start-ups and research. See Mlambo and Cotties Adetiba, 'Brain Drain and South Africa's Socioeconomic Development'.

214. While South Africa has a very high crime rate, its law enforcement seems highly inefficient and its rehabilitation programme ineffective. Few of the crimes committed lead to arrest or prosecution, but the improvement of economic and social conditions (especially inequality and unemployment) is expected to reduce the prevalence of crime. See J.-M. Versluis and J. de Lange, 'Rising Crime Rate, Low Prosecution Rates'; BusinessTech, 'South Africa Crime Stats 2020'; Felix, 'Crime Mostly Affects Poor SA Communities – Researcher'.

215. South Korea must shift away from assimilation policies towards ones which encourage multiculturalism. See Kim-Bossard, 'Challenging Homogeneity in Contemporary Korea', p. 38; Lim, 'The Road to Multiculturalism in South Korea'.

216. These include the high cost of education, lack of childcare facilities and the lack of family-friendly employment conditions. See H. Bak, 'Low Fertility in South Korea', in A. Farazmand (ed.), *Global Encyclopedia of Public Administration, Public Policy, and Governance* (Cham: Springer, 2019), pp. 3–5.

217. Since 2000, South Korea's health-care expenditure has doubled from four per cent of GDP to eight per cent in 2019. South Korea's national health insurance needs to provide its services in more cost-effective ways. Further opening up some health services to private competition might be one way to go. Moreover, the government should develop programmes to address the high incidence of chronic disease, which, if left to grow at the present rate, will have an increasingly burdensome financial impact on the health-care system. See Statista, 'South Korea's National Health Expenditure as a Percent of GDP from 2000 to 2019', https://www.statista.com/statistics/647320/health-spending-south-korea (accessed 23 July 2021); K. Heo *et al.*, 'A Critical Juncture in Universal Healthcare: Insights from South Korea's COVID-19 Experience for the United Kingdom to Consider', *Humanities and Social Sciences Communications* 8 (2021), pp. 2–3; OECD, *OECD Reviews of Public Health: Korea: A Healthier Tomorrow* (Paris: OECD Publishing, 2020), pp. 57–58.

218. The bribery and political scandal in late 2016 and early 2017 that led to the impeachment of President Park Geun-hye demonstrated how weak leadership generated a political leadership vacuum. The government should be attentive to the need for public consensus and should operate within established legislative mechanisms that ensure public accountability. See S.A. Snyder, 'Introduction', in S.A. Snyder *et al.*, *Domestic Constraints on South Korea's Foreign Policy* (New York: Council on Foreign Relations, 2018), pp. 1–2.

219. Employment protection laws for regular workers are very rigid, as are the social security obligations imposed on companies. As a result, companies increasingly employ irregular workers who receive lower salaries and have little job protection and limited social security benefits. This development not only increases income inequalities, it also hurts productivity, as firms make few investments in training their irregular labour force. To promote an increase in regular employment, employment regulations for regular workers need to be made more flexible and the government should ensure that social security is accessible to all, irrespective of employment. See Choo, Kim and Kwon, 'Employment Problems with Irregular Workers in Korea'; S. Denney, 'Number of Irregular Workers Continue to Rise in South Korea', *The Diplomat*, 10 November 2015.

220. In 2019, around 53 per cent of the female population in South Korea aged fifteen years and older was participating in the labour force. The female labour force participation rate in South Korea has risen steadily in recent years but is still far below the average for the member countries of the OECD, contributing to labour shortages in some sectors. See Statista, 'Female Labor Participation Rate in South Korea from 2003 to 2020', https://www.statista.com/statistics/641654/south-korea-female -labor-force-participation-rate (accessed 23 July 2021); World Bank, 'Labor Force Participation Rate, Female (% of Population Ages 15+) (Modeled ILO Estimate) – Korea, Rep.', https://data.worldbank.org /indicator/SL.TLF.CACT.FE.ZS?locations=KR (accessed 23 July 2021).

221. Foreign workers are primarily employed by small and medium-sized enterprises, especially in the manufacturing sector, where they comprise ten per cent of employment, up from less than one per cent in the early 2000s. Attracting more foreign workers would help reduce labour shortages in some sectors and thus increase productivity and growth. See M. Stokes, 'Migrants Are Doing the Jobs South Koreans Sneer At', *Foreign Policy*, 28 January 2021; A. Kuhn, 'As Workforce Ages, South Korea Increasingly Depends on Migrant Labor', NPR, 2 June 2021; OECD, 'Korea Should Adapt Its Migration Programmes to Ensure Continued Success in the Face of Expected Challenges', 28 February 2019; S.-C. Jeon, 'Foreign Workers in the Korean Labour Market: Current Status and Policy Issues', BIS Paper no. 100, 13 February 2019, pp. 209–11.

222. In 2020, South Korea imported 95 per cent of its energy needs from overseas, with more than 40 per cent coming from coal. The third Energy Master Plan up to 2040, adopted in June 2019, aims to increase the renewable electricity share to 20 per cent by 2030 and 30 to 35 per cent by 2040, up from only three per cent in 2017. Furthermore, South Korea's 2020 Green New Deal aims to achieve net zero emissions and to accelerate the transition towards a low-carbon and green economy, and is the first commitment of its kind in East Asia. Korea must therefore increase investment in renewable energies and provide individual citizens with incentives to reduce fossil fuel emissions. See J.-H. Lee and J. Woo, 'Green New Deal Policy of South Korea: Policy Innovation for a Sustainability Transition', *Sustainability* 12, no. 23 (2020), pp. 1–3; Korea Energy Economics Institute, *Energy Info Korea* (Ulsan: Korea Energy Economics Institute, 2018), p. 6.

223. South Korea heavily adopted nuclear power to reduce emissions from fossil fuel power plants; however, the country is now facing a significant nuclear waste storage problem. See B. Smith, 'South Korea: Environmental Issues, Policies and Clean Technology', AZO Clean Tech, 9 July 2015; Sustainable Governance Indicators, 'Environmental Policies', https://www.sgi-network.org/2018/South_Korea/Environmental_Policies (accessed 23 July 2021).

224. In 2020, taking lessons at private institutes was the most popular method of after-school education in South Korea with around 37.7 per cent of Korean students attending such institutes. To make education more equitable, the government should reform the education system in such a way that private tutoring will no longer be necessary for students to achieve top results. P.T. Hultberg, 'Costs and Benefits of After School Tutoring Programs: The South Korean Case', *International Journal of Social Economics* 48, no. 6 (2021), pp. 862–77; Statista, 'Private Education Rate of Students in South Korea in 2020, by Type of Tutoring', https://www.statista.com/statistics/1043943/south-korea-private-education-participation-rate-by-tutoring-type (accessed 23 July 2021).

225. Since education is one of the main causes, the government should focus on reducing competitiveness and mental pressure on students. Moreover, English language teaching is generally highly prioritised in Korea, and competence in English is highly important for employment prospects, university admissions and social status. Previous governments have suggested making English the main language of instruction in schools. However, the craze for learning English in both the public and private education system became so intense that in 2018 the Korean government banned the teaching of English prior to third grade, on the grounds that it was detrimental to the Korean language and Korean culture. The government should promote bilingualism without detracting from the history and culture of Korea if it is to

maintain social cohesion. See Mani and Trines, 'Education in South Korea'.

226. See Dayton, 'How South Korea Made Itself a Global Innovation Leader'.

227. The proportion of the population of working age was 73.1 per cent in 2015. It is, however, projected to decline to 63.1 per cent in 2030 and to reach only 49.7 per cent in 2060. This will put an immense burden on social spending and halt economic growth. The country needs to take measures to facilitate the participation of women in the labour market (through more family-friendly work arrangements and by providing more childcare facilities) and of older people by raising the retirement age. Although the government has announced plans to raise the retirement age from 60 to 65 years in 2022, this is not nearly sufficient to address the decreasing labour force. The government should also simplify immigration procedures in order to increase the percentage of young migrants working in the country. See T. Eck, 'South Korea's Demographic Deficit', *The Interpreter* (Lowy Institute), 31 August 2018; Pulse, 'S. Korea to Raise Retirement Age Revision as Official Agenda Next Year', 15 April 2021.

228. Although North Korea has gone against the principles of the Panmunjom Declaration for Peace, Prosperity and Unification of the Korean Peninsula by continuing to carry out weapons tests and minor attacks against South Korea, the South Korean government should refrain from retaliating, in order to avoid a military escalation. Rather, it should focus on diplomacy and make use of both countries' relationships with China to engage in pro-active discussions. This is especially important for the successful denuclearisation of North Korea. See USIP China-North Korea Senior Study Group, *China's Role in North Korea Nuclear and Peace Negotiations* (Washington, DC: United States Institute of Peace, 2019), pp. 8–12; J. Kim, 'China and Regional Security Dynamics on the Korean Peninsula'.

229. South Korea should strengthen its military ties with the US while not antagonising China and destabilising the region. A reconciliation process to address the grievances and crimes committed during the war should also be fostered and regarded as a priority. See US Congressional Research Service, 'South Korea: Background and US Relations'; S.A. Snyder, 'The US-South Korea Summit: A Relationship Restored?', Council on Foreign Relations, 25 May 2021.

230. South Korea has successfully negotiated free trade agreements with the United States, the EU and the ASEAN countries. The conclusion of RCEP in 2020 (the largest free trade agreement in the world), in particular, will help to regulate growing regional competition from China and protect Korea's trade capacities. It will also strengthen Korea's diplomatic ties with all other regional powers. See Australian Government, Department of Foreign Affairs and Trade, 'Regional

Comprehensive Economic Partnership', https://www.dfat.gov.au/trade/agreements/not-yet-in-force/rcep (accessed 23 July 2021).

231. Despite being an international model, the welfare state is in crisis, notably due to reforms favouring the private sector and the rise of extremist groups. See Sanandaji, 'So Long, Swedish Welfare State?'

232. Far-right groups have introduced a feeling of suspicion and tensions between citizens and migrants. The welcoming and responsible Swedish could suffer from these fear-induced reflexes and this could significantly challenge social cohesion. See ibid.

233. The current global political crisis, the COVID-19 pandemic and internal dynamics have reinforced populist ideas, notably through disinformation on social media. This trend could limit the current government's attempt to establish a coalition and make Sweden's governance highly complex. See Milne, 'Sweden's Government on Brink ahead of No-Confidence Vote'.

234. Sweden plans to fulfil 100 per cent of its electricity needs from renewable sources in 2040. See International Renewable Energy Agency, *Innovative Solutions for 100% Renewable Power in Sweden* (Masdar City: IRENA, with the Swedish Energy Agency, 2020).

235. Sweden's plans and actions could inspire other countries and should be at the centre of its international strategy. See ibid.

236. Decentralised and funded for children and adults, including vocational education. See European Commission Eurydice, 'Sweden: Organisation of the Education System and its Structure', 1 January 2020.

237. Sweden is an ally of NATO member states and tensions with Russia impact the security situation in the Baltic Sea. See S. Johnson, 'Sweden Beefs up Baltic Sea Forces amid Regional Tensions', Reuters, 26 August 2020.

238. This is especially necessary given the pandemic and the need for greater solidarity. See Euractiv, 'Sweden and Denmark Step Out of the Shadows as EU's Frugals'.

239. Minority groups including Tamils, Albanians, Jews, Muslims and Yenish nomads have been discriminated against in Switzerland and there have been incidents of racismwhich may have been incited or at least encouraged by the xenophobic discourse spread by a far-right party. See Federal Department of Home Affairs (Switzerland), 'Which Foreigners Face the Most Discrimination?', https://www.edi.admin.ch/edi/en/home/fachstellen/frb/FAQ/welche-gruppen-von-auslaendern--innen-werden-am-meisten-diskrimi.html#context-sidebar (accessed 21 June 2021).

240. Switzerland faces the challenge of having to support a growing number of retirees with a smaller number of workers paying into the pension scheme. An ageing population combined with a low birth rate will also create labour-force shortages. Switzerland will have to come up with

ways to increase the labour-force participation of people over 55. See OECD, *OECD Economic Surveys: Switzerland 2019* (Paris: OECD Publishing, 2019), ch. 2.

241. Improving the market environment for fair competition on the national level among health insurance companies, health-care services and drugs companies is one measure that Switzerland should consider. See *The Local*, 'How Switzerland Wants to Reduce Healthcare Costs', 26 August 2020.

242. This can be supported through a strong engagement in humanitarian affairs and the maintenance of Geneva as a diplomatic hub *par excellence*. See Federal Department of Foreign Affairs (Switzerland), 'Humanitarian Diplomacy', 23 March 2021, https://www.eda.admin.ch /eda/en/home/foreign-policy/human-rights/humanitarian-policy.html; Permanent Mission of Switzerland to the United Nations Office, 'Facts and Figures about International Geneva'.

243. In particular, implementing the new Swiss Soil Strategy. See Federal Office for the Environment (Switzerland), 'Soil: In Brief', 8 May 2020, https://www.bafu.admin.ch/bafu/en/home/topics/soil/in-brief.html #2005132307.

244. 'The country is campaigning for a seat on the UN Security Council, but taking on that role will clash with some fundamental tenets of Swiss foreign policy': See S. Fillion, 'The End of Swiss Neutrality', *Foreign Policy*, 15 January 2021.

245. As illustrated by the recent Putin-Biden Summit. See F. Gsteiger, 'Biden-Putin Summit: Why Geneva?', Swissinfo, 4 June 2021.

246. If Turkey's already large population continues to grow at its current rate, the country could experience a major demographic crisis, leading to high youth unemployment and domestic instability. Education and health-care facilities would need to be rapidly expanded. Moreover, Turkey would need to aggressively promote the creation of new jobs to absorb the growing number of new labour-market entrants. However, if the country is able to slow population growth, maintain a relatively constant age balance and create new job opportunities for its young population, it may be able to achieve significant economic progress.

247. HIV cases in the country have increased by 465 per cent in the past ten years. At present, the rates of HIV infection are low but steadily on the rise. The rise in cases can be at least partially linked to the increase in intravenous drugs use and prostitution. See B. Mete *et al.*, 'HIV Care in Istanbul, Turkey: How Far Is It from the UNAIDS 90-90-90 Targets?', *International Journal of STD and AIDS* 30, no. 13 (2019), pp. 1298–1303.

248. Turkey should re-affirm itself as a secular state if it is to remain internally stable and protect its relationship with the EU, US and NATO. See K. Senvic, R.W. Hood Jr and T.J. Coleman III, 'Secularism in Turkey', 2017, pp. 2–9, https://www.researchgate.net

/publication/322962600_Secularism_in_Turkey; B. Stanicek, 'Hagia Sophia: Turkey's Secularism under Threat', European Parliamentary Research Service, PE 652.026, July 2020, pp. 1–2; M. Akyol, 'Turkey's Troubled Experiment with Secularism', The Century Foundation, 25 April 2019.

249. While Turkey is justified in prosecuting violent acts, it will need to address some of the PKK's legitimate grievances, demands and aspirations and work towards a political compromise that would offer the PKK enough incentives to renounce violence. First and foremost, Ankara will need to reverse discriminatory policies against the Kurds and grant them a certain autonomy without jeopardising Turkey's national unity and security.

250. Atesagaoglu, Elgin and Oztunali, 'TFP Growth in Turkey Revisited'.

251. Turkey must continue to invest in strategies to address water shortages. See Ministry of Foreign Affairs (Turkey), 'Turkey's Policy on Water Issues', https://www.mfa.gov.tr/turkey_s-policy-on-water-issues.en.mfa (accessed 23 July 2021).

252. Tensions in the region have been rising because of Turkey's direct military intervention against the Kurds in Northern Iraq. See D. Jones, 'Turkey-Iran Tensions Rise as Ankara Expands Operations in Iraq', VOA News, 2 March 2021, https://www.voanews.com/middle-east /turkey-iran-tensions-rise-ankara-expands-operations-iraq.

253. Especially Iraq, Libya and Syria. See J. Barigazzi and H. von der Burchard, 'EU Ministers and Borrell Urge Turkey to Stop Interfering in Libya', *Politico*, 7 January 2020.

254. Inequalities between rural and urban areas remain significant and should be addressed Given Russia's growing influence in the information domain, it might be easy to stoke up resentment and national disunity. If Moscow and the centralised governance system were to lose influence social cohesion in Russia would suffer. World Bank, 'In Ukraine, Labor, Taxation, and Social Policies Must Be Upgraded to Address Rising Inequality, Says World Bank'.

255. This is essential to maintain cohesion and citizens' engagement in political processes. See Kuzio, 'Russia Is Quietly Occupying Ukraine's Information Space'.

256. The informal economy reduces the state's income and does not protect citizens from unemployment. Fair and sustainable opportunities should be created. See Minakov, 'Ukraine's Political Agenda for the First Half of 2021'.

257. Published in 2020 but not implemented. See Climate Action Tracker, 'Ukraine'.

258. This industry is responsible for the high level of emissions but the government has a limited exit strategy. It has become essential to move away from it, given its impact on the air pollution level and citizens' health.

259. Ukraine spends a significant amount of its budget on the education system and this should be continued. See G. Beviglia, '8 Facts about Education in Ukraine', The Borgen Project, 18 July 2019.

260. Ibid.

261. For more information on how Ukraine can sustainably resolve the crisis with Russia, see the Appendix.

262. Investment needs to be directed towards health care. Stronger measures are needed to ensure that the government is held to account for the health of the population, for instance through the adoption of a legislative framework. See Health Foundation, 'Top Line Facts on the Big Issues in Health and Social Care'.

263. See O'Neill, 'Household Income Inequality'; Equality Trust, 'The Scale of Economic Inequality in the UK'.

264. The Commission on Race and Ethnic Disparities was asked by Prime Minister Boris Johnson to determine how best to tackle ethnic disparities within employment, health care, the criminal justice system and education. The Commission's report was highly criticised for arguing that geography, family influence, socio-economic background, culture and religion have a more significant impact on life chances than the existence of racism in the UK. In one of the most controversial sections of the report, the Commission argued that education has been the single most emphatic success story of the British ethnic minority experience, where children from many ethnic communities largely do as well as or better than white pupils, in stark contrast to the numbers of admissions to the most prestigious British universities and to the high rate of racist incidents recorded. In light of all the criticism towards the report and all of the contradictory evidence, the government should commission a new report, with the aim of identifying the key challenges and solutions to the racial inequality which undeniably exists in the UK. See J. Cameron-Chileshe, 'Campaigners Accuse UK Racial Inequality Report of Complacency', *Financial Times*, 1 April 2021; Walker and Parveen, 'Racial Disparities in the UK: Key Findings of the Report – and What Its Critics Say'.

265. Following Brexit, the government will have to prioritise domestic unity if it is to maintain stability within the country as well as its political standing abroad. See B. Peabody, 'Brexit Is Probably the United Kingdom's Death Knell', *Foreign Policy*, 3 February 2021.

266. According to the Office for National Statistics, following the UK's exit from the EU single market in January 2021, goods exports to the EU fell 40.7 per cent from December 2020 and imports dropped 28.8 per cent. See D. Kirka, 'UK Trade with EU Plunges after Brexit, Hurting Economy', AP News, 12 March 2021.

267. Public borrowing was £19.1 billion in February 2021, the highest figure since 1993. The Office for Budget Responsibility previously forecast public borrowing would reach £355 billion in 2020/21 (equal to seventeen per cent of GDP). See M. Ward, 'Economy in March 2021:

Post-Brexit Trade Data and Consumer Confidence', House of Commons Library Insight, 26 March 2021.

268. The government also set a legally binding midway target to cut the country's greenhouse gas emissions 78 per cent by 2035 compared to 1990 levels, which amounts to a 60 per cent reduction from today's levels, and might be the strongest legally binding target in the world. The government has adopted a number of policies in this regard. For example, all companies listed in the UK are now required to report their carbon emissions in their annual report and there are higher penalties for environmental offences. The government is also providing financial incentives for the adoption of green technologies to companies that use renewable energy to generate heat, and enacting energy-saving methods in the workplace. However, for the emission reduction targets to be reached, be it in 2035 or 2050, the government will have to do more, including doubling the UK's renewable energy capacity over the next five years and installing carbon capture technologies on new gas power plants. See Environment Agency (United Kingdom), 'State of the Environment'; P. Forster, 'UK Target to Cut Emissions 78% by 2035 Is World-Leading – But to Hit It, Action Is Needed Now', *The Conversation*, 22 April 2021; B. Smith, 'United Kingdom: Environmental Issues, Policies and Clean Technology', AZO Clean Tech, 9 June 2015.

269. The government should reduce its contributions to private education and increase them to state schools. Moreover, the government should develop programmes to raise the performance of schools in lower-income neighbourhoods and invest more in those that are underperforming in order to achieve equality within the system. Finally, affirmative action steps should also be taken to increase the number of black, Asian and minority ethnic and working-class students in elite universities. See C. Alexander and W. Shankley, '5 Ethnic Inequalities in the State Education System in England', in B. Byrne *et al.* (eds), *Ethnicity and Race in the UK: State of the Nation* (Bristol: Bristol University Press, 2020), pp. 93–96.

270. If the UK is to remain competitive in terms of innovation, it must significantly increase its R&D investment. Increasing economic productivity and prosperity through new products, services and jobs will also help transform British public services. See UK Department for Business, Energy and Industrial Strategy, 'UK Research and Development Roadmap'.

271. The space industry is one of the UK's fastest-growing sectors, worth £16.8bn in 2019. R&D investment in space technologies now sits at £702m, up eighteen per cent and five times the national average intensity. In terms of transformative technologies, by 2020 the UK was spending around 1.67 per cent of GDP on R&D into nanotechnology, and over 101 companies were operating in the UK nanotechnology market. See know.space, *Size and Health of the UK Space Industry 2020:*

Summary Report for the UK Space Agency (May 2021), p. 3; S. Moore, 'Nanotechnology in the United Kingdom Market Report', AZO Nano, 10 January 2020.

272. In March 2021, the UK government published a report titled, *Global Britain in a Competitive Age: The Integrated Review of Security, Defence, Development and Foreign Policy*, which laid out a new 'full spectrum' approach to the UK's cyber security capabilities, which are designed to improve the country's defences and deter potential attackers. Under this plan, the UK government plans to invest £24 billion in cyber security and the armed forces. See L. Irwin, 'UK Emphasises Cyber Security in New Foreign Policy Strategy', IT Governance, 18 March 2021, https://www.itgovernance.co.uk/blog/uk-emphasises-cyber-security-in-new-foreign-policy-strategy; A. Scroxton, 'UK Plans "Full Spectrum" Approach to National Cyber Security', *Computer Weekly*, 15 March 2021.

273. The UK government's 2021 decision to increase the country's nuclear arsenal prompted concern around the world and raised questions about the UK's commitment to its nuclear disarmament obligations under the Nuclear Non-Proliferation Treaty (NPT). The UK should, instead, promote non-proliferation by setting an example and progressively reducing its nuclear arsenal. See Kristensen and Korda, 'United Kingdom Nuclear Weapons, 2021'; Reif and Bugos, 'UK to Increase Cap on Nuclear Weapons Stockpile'.

274. In June 2021, the UK signed its first completely new trade deal post-Brexit, with Australia. See UK Government, 'UK Agrees Historic Trade Deal with Australia', 15 June 2021; T. Heron and G. Siles-Brugge, 'The UK-Australia Trade Deal Is Not Really about Economic Gain – It's about Demonstrating Post-Brexit Sovereignty', *The Conversation*, 18 June 2021.

275. China is a very important trading partner of the UK. Although Five Eyes and NATO increasingly see China as a threat, the UK will have to find a balance between the two competing needs if it is to protect its economy as well as its diplomatic alliances. The same applies to Russia, with whom diplomatic relations have reached a standstill. See Curtis, Lunn and Ward, 'The UK-China Relationship'; D. Trenin, 'UK Security Review: Implications for Russia', Carnegie Moscow Center, 2 April 2021.

276. Medical costs are currently growing at a high rate. Moreover, the ageing population increases overall demand for medical treatment. In other words, the United States needs to find ways to make health-care delivery more efficient, while maintaining high quality standards. Measures should also be taken to provide easier access to health insurance for the uninsured. Overall costs could be lowered by setting caps on treatment and equalising the cost of the same procedure irrespective of the care-site. See Committee for a Responsible Federal Budget, 'Three Ways

to Lower Health Care Costs', 23 February 2021; R. Tomlin, 'Four Ways to Reduce Healthcare Costs', *Medical Economics*, 11 February 2020.

277. Social security programmes will soon run out of money, with Medicare expected to exhaust its reserves in 2026, and most others by 2035. Due to the increasing number of old and retired people, the government will need to find ways to make its social security system sustainable over the long run. Some of the possible ways to achieve this are increasing the retirement age (which currently stands between 66 and 67 years), reducing replacement rates for high earners and raising the ceiling on earnings subject to social security taxes. To balance public finances, the US government will also need to find ways to increase its revenue. See US Congressional Research Service, 'The Social Security Retirement Age', 8 January 2021, p. 2; L. Konish, 'Bipartisan Plan to Fix Social Security Draws Criticism', CNBC, 20 April 2021.

278. The United States has about 10.5 to twelve million illegal immigrants (which amount to approximately 3.2 to 3.6 per cent of the total population), most of them entering the country by crossing the US-Mexico border. Many illegal immigrants find employment in American industry and agriculture, and they have become an indispensable labour resource for many American enterprises. Illegal immigrants often fill jobs that many believe US citizens would not take, or would take only for higher wages. President Joe Biden has made sweeping reform proposals for the immigration system, including an earned roadmap to citizenship for undocumented individuals and family reunification. More broadly speaking, however, the immigration system should be expanded to include more avenues for legal migration, including to short-term jobs. Stronger partnerships should also be established with countries such as Mexico, Guatemala, Honduras and El Salvador to address the root causes of high numbers of illegal immigrants into the US. See E. Kamarck and C. Stenglein, 'How Many Undocumented Immigrants Are in the United States and Who Are They?', Brookings Institution, 12 November 2019; US White House, 'Fact Sheet: President Biden Sends Immigration Bill to Congress as Part of His Commitment to Modernise Our Immigration System', 20 January 2021.

279. All industries try to influence political decisions in the US through lobbying on a large scale. See Statista, 'Leading Lobbying Industries in the United States in 2020, by Total Lobbying Spending', https://www .statista.com/statistics/257364/top-lobbying-industries-in-the-us (accessed 24 July 2021).

280. The American Jobs Plan announced by President Joe Biden is an important step in this direction. It proposes a series of large strategic investments that have the potential to increase productivity growth, create high-quality jobs and foster a transition to a 100-per-cent clean-energy future. See A. Vinelli and C.E. Weller, 'The Path to Higher,

More Inclusive Economic Growth and Good Jobs', Center for American Progress, 27 April 2021; US White House, 'Fact Sheet: The American Jobs Plan', 31 March 2021; A. Vinelli and C.E. Weller, 'Move Fast and Think Big: 7 Key Principles for the Economic Package America Needs Now', Center for American Progress, 4 February 2021.

281. In 2021, President Joe Biden announced a new target for the United States to achieve a 50 to 52 per cent reduction from 2005 levels in economy-wide net greenhouse gas pollution in 2030. Biden aims to create a carbon pollution-free power sector by 2035 and a net-zero emissions economy by no later than 2050. Since the US has the largest nuclear and the second-largest renewable capacity in the world, it has the potential to achieve this goal if it sets itself clear targets and enforces them on the private sector through carbon emission taxes. See US White House, 'Fact Sheet: President Biden Sets 2030 Greenhouse Gas Pollution Reduction Target'; Gabbatiss, 'The Carbon Brief Profile: The United States'.

282. A highly educated workforce is crucial for a country to remain on top in the global economy. Many US high-school graduates are not prepared for employment or college. Academic standards, curricula and examinations in primary and secondary schools are less demanding than in many other developed countries, which is one of the key reasons for the underperformance of US students in international tests. Implementing high learning objectives and assessment standards on the national level and providing incentives for states to make their school curricula more demanding are measures that the next administration should consider. Funding for public education should also be distributed more equally. See American University School of Education, 'What the US Education System Needs to Reduce Inequality'.

283. In 2020, of the total American population only 37.6 per cent of males and 38.3 per cent of females had completed tertiary education. To increase the average level of education of the workforce, the United States has to take measures to increase the number of university graduates. For one, students need to be better prepared academically to enter and complete college, which is a task that needs to be addressed at the elementary- and high-school level. For another, many students able to succeed at the university level drop out due to a lack of financial resources. Rather than increase student-loan limits, the government should work to reduce the cost of higher education in the US. Indeed, student debt has more than doubled over the past two decades, with 43 million borrowers owing nearly US$1.6 trillion altogether in federal student loans at the end of 2020. Additional private loans bring this total to about US$1.7 trillion. The issue of student loans is at the centre of political discussions now, with some calling for cancellation or forgiveness of student debt. This would be a potentially destabilising

political move and the Democratic Party has yet to adopt a joint position on this. See Statista, 'Percentage of the US Population Who Have Completed Four Years of College or More from 1940 to 2020, by Gender', https://www.statista.com/statistics/184272/educational-attainment-of-college-diploma-or-higher-by-gender (accessed 24 July 2021); A. Siripurapu and M. Speier, 'Is Rising Student Debt Harming the US Economy?', Council on Foreign Relations, 13 April 2021; D. Looney, D. Wessel and K. Yilla, 'Who Owes All That Student Debt? And Who'd Benefit If We Were Forgiven?', Brookings Institution, 28 January 2020.

284. Deloitte, '2020 US and Global Life Sciences Outlook: Creating New Value: Building Blocks for the Future', https://www2.deloitte.com/us/en/pages/life-sciences-and-health-care/articles/us-and-global-life-sciences-industry-trends-outlook.html (accessed 24 July 2021).

285. See J. Stock, M. Daniel and T. Goldstein, 'Partnerships Are Our Best Weapon in the Fight against Cybercrime. Here's Why', World Economic Forum, 21 January 2020, https://www.weforum.org/agenda/2020/01/partnerships-are-our-best-weapon-in-the-fight-against-cybercrime-heres-why; D. Manky, 'The Hard Truth and Good News about the Fight against Cybercrime', Forbes, 17 May 2021, https://www.forbes.com/sites/fortinet/2021/05/17/the-hard-truth-and-good-news-about-the-fight-against-cybercrime/?sh=6437115519b5; A. Peters and A. Hindocha, 'US Global Cybercrime Cooperation: A Brief Explainer', Third Way, 26 June 2020.

286. Even-handed mediation and support of a fair solution of the Arab-Israeli conflict would be a way to achieve this. See S.M. Walt, 'It's Time to End the "Special Relationship" with Israel', Foreign Policy, 27 May 2021, https://foreignpolicy.com/2021/05/27/its-time-to-end-the-special-relationship-with-israel.

287. The two-state solution provides a viable option for a Palestinian state with borders coinciding with those existing in 1967 and is in line with UN resolutions and international law as well as the Arab Peace Plan of 2002. See Z. Beauchamp, 'In Defence of the Two-State Solution', Vox, 26 May 2021; I. Goldenberg, 'Biden Can Keep the Two-State Solution Alive', Foreign Affairs, 21 June 2021.

288. The Biden administration is going to have to make several critical choices concerning its foreign policy approach towards North Korea. The most important of these choices is between two fundamentally different approaches: ramping up pressure to compel it to make the 'strategic choice' to abandon its nuclear weapons capabilities completely and in a relatively short period of time; or, alternatively, pursuing denuclearisation as a long-term process to be achieved in phases without gaining a near-term commitment on when that goal will eventually be fulfilled. Both these options will be challenging, especially since, although North Korean

leader Kim Jong Un has expressed the intention to engage in dialogue with the US, he has also reiterated his commitment to the nuclear programme. See Einhorn, 'The Key Choices Now Facing the Biden Administration on North Korea'; Associated Press, 'North Korea's Kim Vows to Be Ready for Confrontation with the US', NPR, 18 June 2021.

289. From the standpoint of 2021, it remains unclear what US-Iran relations will look like in the next couple of years. Although President Biden has stated that he intends to re-join the nuclear deal, the election in June 2021 in Iran of Raisi, who is known for his opposition to western ideals, may further destabilise relations between the two countries. The US should do everything possible to seek a diplomatic resolution to the increasing tensions and treat the finding of an agreement on nuclear as a priority. See *World Politics Review*, 'What Comes Next in the Standoff between the US and Iran?', 29 October 2021.

290. This is necessary to make sure that outer space remains secure and sustainable for humanity as a whole now and in the future. R. Pillai Rajagopalan, 'The Outer Space Treaty: Overcoming Space Security Governance Challenges', Council on Foreign Relations, 23 February 2021; P. Lewis, 'Create a Global Code of Conduct for Outer Space', Chatham House, 12 June 2019, https://www.chathamhouse .org/2019/06/create-global-code-conduct-outer-space.

10. The Tripwire Pivotal Corridor and its Geopolitical Significance

1. Z. Brzezinski, *The Grand Chessboard: American Primacy and Its Geostrategic Imperatives* (New York: Basic Books, 1997), p. 41.
2. Ibid.
3. Source: National Geographic Maps, appears with alteration, published in the first edition of the book.
4. N. Megoran, 'Revisiting the "Pivot": The Influence of Halford Mackinder on Analysis of Uzbekistan's International Relations', *Geographical Journal* 70, December 2004.
5. R. Chase, E. Hill and P. Kennedy, *The Pivotal States: A New Framework for US Policy in the Developing World* (New York: W.W. Norton & Company, 1998).
6. UNCTAD, *Review of Maritime Transport 2020* (New York: UNCTAD, 2020), p. 35.
7. US Energy Information Administration, 'The Strait of Hormuz Is the World's Most Important Oil Transit Chokepoint', 20 June 2019.
8. US Energy Information Administration, 'The Bab el-Mandeb Strait Is a Strategic Route for Oil and Natural Gas Shipments', 27 August 2019.

9. US Energy Information Administration, 'The Suez Canal and SUMED Pipeline are Critical Chokepoints for Oil and Natural Gas Trade', 23 July 2019.

10. BBC News, 'Egypt's Suez Canal Blocked by Huge Container Ship', 24 March 2021.

11. US Energy Information Administration, 'The Danish and Turkish Straits Are Critical to Europe's Crude Oil and Petroleum Trade', 18 August 2017.

12. A.E. Levite and B. Tertrais, 'What Might the Middle East Look by 2025?', *CERI Strategy Papers*, 20 May 2008.

13. World Bank, 'Population Growth: Europe and Central Asia', https://data .worldbank.org/indicator/SP.POP.GROW?locations=Z7 (accessed 9 June 2021)

14. World Bank, 'Unemployment: Europe and Central Asia', 2020, https:// data.worldbank.org/indicator/SL.UEM.TOTL.ZS?locations=MX-Z7.

15. European Union Agency for Fundamental Rights, 'Facing the Challenges of Migrant Integration', 3 March 2017.

16. See Z. Beauchamp, 'Rwanda's Genocide – What Happened, Why It Happened, and How It Still Matters', Vox, 10 April 2014; J. Maron, 'What Led to the Genocide against the Tutsi in Rwanda?', Canadian Museum for Human Rights, https://humanrights.ca/story/what-led-to -the-genocide-against-the-tutsi-in-rwanda (accessed 27 July 2021).

17. Geneva Academy RULAC online portal, 'Military Occupation of Palestine by Israel'.

18. Hoffman, 'The State of the Turkish-Kurdish Conflict'.

19. O. Karasapan and S. Shah, 'Why Syrian Refugees in Lebanon Are a Crisis within a Crisis', Brookings Institution, 15 April 2021; UN Office of the High Commissioner for Human Rights, 'Refugees and Asylum Seekers in Turkey', https://www.unhcr.org/tr/en/refugees-and-asylum -seekers-in-turkey (accessed 30 June 2021).

20. T. Naff, *Water in the Middle East: Conflict or Cooperation?* (New York: Routledge, 2020), p. 5.

21. M. Duyar, 'Analysis: Israel's Most Powerful Tool in Persuading Jordan: "Water Problem"', Anadolu Agency, 8 June 2021; M. Zeitoun and M. Dajani, 'Israel Is Hoarding the Jordan River – It's Time to Share', *The Conversation*, 19 December 2019.

22. R. Aviram, A. Hindi and S.A. Hammour, *Coping with Water Scarcity in the Jordan River Basin* (New York: The Century Foundation, 2020).

23. B. Keynoush, 'Water Scarcity Could Lead to the Next Major Conflict between Iran and Iraq', Middle East Institute, 18 March 2021.

24. Ibid.

25. W. Abtew and S.B. Dessu, *The Grand Ethiopian Renaissance Dam on the Blue Nile* (Cham: Springer Nature, 2019), p. 5.

26. Marbot, 'Egypt-Ethiopia'.

27. Mbaku, 'The Controversy over the Grand Ethiopian Renaissance Dam'; Wahba, 'Egypt Asks for UN Help in Long-Running Ethiopian Dam Dispute'.
28. Abtew and Dessu, *The Grand Ethiopian Renaissance Dam on the Blue Nile*, pp. 103–4.
29. World Bank, 'Helping India Overcome Its Water Woes', 9 December 2019.
30. R.M. DeConto *et al.*, 'The Paris Climate Agreement and Future Sea-Level Rise from Antarctica', *Nature* 593 (2021), pp. 83–89.
31. J. Brigham-Grette and A. Dutton, 'Antarctica Is Headed for a Climate Tipping Point by 2060, with Catastrophic Melting If Carbon Emissions Aren't Cut Quickly', *The Conversation*, 17 May 2019.
32. Ibid.
33. Z. Cormier, 'Antarctica, the New Hot Real Estate', *Toronto Star*, 18 November 2007, http://www.thestar.com/News/Ideas/article/277390.
34. RANE Worldview, powered by Stratfor, 'The Strategic Importance of the Caspian Sea', 19 May 2014; US Energy Information Administration, 'Oil and Petroleum Products Explained: Where Our Oil Comes From', 8 April 2021; S.M. Houshialsadat, 'The Role of the Persian Gulf's Natural Gas Reserves for the European Union's Energy Security' (PhD diss., Durham University, 2013), http://etheses.dur.ac.uk/7751.
35. S. Gross, 'Why Are Fossil Fuels So Hard to Quit?', Brookings Institution, June 2020.
36. Kemp and Harkavy, *Strategic Geography and the Changing Middle*, p. 110.
37. A. Di Paola, J. Lee and B. Wingfield, 'Middle East Petro-States' Reliance on China Surges with Covid-19', Al Jazeera, 3 June 2020.
38. N. Chestney, 'Analysis: Gas Faces Existential Crisis in Climate Wary Europe', *Reuters*, 14 May 2021.
39. S. Blank, *India's Energy Options in Central Asia*, SASSI Research Report 12 (London: SASSI, 2007), pp. 3–13.
40. G. Bahgat, 'Maritime Security in the Persian Gulf', *Middle East Policy* 26, no. 4 (2019), p. 67.
41. M. Connell, 'Operation Sentinel Protects Gulf Shipping', The Iran Primer, 2 September 2020.
42. Ibid.
43. J. Bunyard, 'What a New Naval Vessel Says about Iran's Ambitions at Sea', Newlines Institute for Strategy and Policy, 16 June 2021.
44. US Energy Information Administration, 'Oil and Natural Gas Production Is Growing in Caspian Sea Region', 11 September 2013.
45. P. Kubicek, 'Energy Politics and Geopolitical Competition in the Caspian Basin', *Journal of Eurasian Studies* 4(2) (2013), pp. 171–180.

46. R.E. Hoagland, 'The United States in the Caspian Region: A Reliable Partner', Caspian Policy Center, 10 August 2020, https://www.caspian policy.org/research/articles/the-united-states-in-the-caspian-region-a -reliable-partner-11656.

47. N. Aliyev, 'Russia's Military Capabilities in the Caspian', CACI, 21 February 2019.

48. R. Weitz, 'Continuity and Change in US Policies Towards the Caspian Region', MEI, 2 April 2020.

49. M. Bryza, 'The Greater Caspian Region: A New Silk Road, With or Without a New Belt', Atlantic Council, 29 February 2020.

50. WorldOMeter, 'Russia Oil', https://www.worldometers.info/oil/russia-oil (accessed 24 June 2021).

51. V. Kutcherov et al., 'Russian Natural Gas Exports: An Analysis of Challenges and Opportunities', Energy Strategy Reviews, 30 (2020), pp. 1–10.

52. Z. Agayev, 'BP's Caspian Sea Project Emerges as Russia's Rival for European Gas Market', World Oil, 31 December 2020; F. Sassi, 'What the "Power of Siberia" Tells Us about China-Russia Relations', The Diplomat, 7 December 2019.

53. BBC News, 'Ukraine Crisis: Russia Halts Has Supplies to Kiev', 16 June 2014.

54. C. Weaver, 'Russia Cuts Gas Supplies to Belarus', Financial Times, 21 June 2020, https://www.ft.com/content/a94728f8-7d21-11df-8845 -00144feabdc0.

55. Sassi, 'What the "Power of Siberia" Tells Us about China-Russia Relations'; Agayev, 'BP's Caspian Sea Project Emerges as Russia's Rival for European Gas Market'.

56. D.M. Herszenhorn, 'In Nord Stream 2 Fight, Ukraine Gives EU Taste of Its Own Bureaucracy', Politico, 26 July 2021.

57. K. Skinner and R.A. Berman, 'Biden's Surrender to Merkel on Nord Stream 2', Foreign Policy, 26 July 2021.

58. Ibid.

59. Reuters Staff, 'Russia Begins TurkStream Gas Flows to Greece, North Macedonia, Reuters, 5 January 2020; Gazprom, 'Supplies of Russian Gas to Hungary and Croatia Via New Route Commences, 1 October 2021.

60. A. Borunda, 'Arctic Summer Ice Could Disappear as Early as 2035', National Geographic, 13 August 2020.

61. F. Macdonald, 'This Map Shows All the Claims on the Arctic Seafloor', Science Alert, 18 August 2015, https://www.sciencealert.com/this-map -shows-all-country-s-claims-on-the-arctic-seafloor.

62. Convention on the Law of the Sea, ratified10 December 1982, came into force 16 November 1994, 1833 UNTS 397, Art. 57.

63. Port Technology International Team, 'Is the Arctic Route the Future of Shipping?', Port Technology, 5 November 2018; R.C. Rasmussen, 'An Emerging Strategic Geometry – Thawing Chokepoints and Littorals in the Arctic', Center for International Maritime Security, 3 June 2020.

64. Australian Government, Department of Agriculture, Water and the Environment, Australian Antarctic Programme, 'Antarctic Territorial Claims', https://www.antarctica.gov.au/about-antarctica/law-and-treaty /history/antarctic-territorial-claims (accessed 24 June 2021).

65. K. Dodds, 'In 30 Years the Antarctic Treaty Becomes Modifiable, and the Fate of a Continent Could Hang in the Balance', *The Conversation*, 12 July 2018.

66. United Nations, 'Resolving Israel-Palestinian Conflict "Key to Sustainable Peace" in the Middle East: Guterres', 4 February 2021, https://news.un.org/en/story/2020/02/1056722.

67. K. Katzman, 'Iran-Iraq Relations', US Congressional Research Service, 13 August 2010, Summary.

68. US Institute of Peace, 'The Current Situation in Iraq', Fact Sheet, 4 August 2020.

69. T. Craig Jones, 'America, Oil and War in the Middle East', *The Journal of American History* 99(1) (2012), pp. 208–218.

70. Al-Rodhan and Kuepfer, *Stability of States*, p. 51.

71. BBC News, 'Iran Nuclear Deal: US Joins Vienna Talks Aimed at Reviving Accord', 6 April 2021.

72. A. Lewis, 'Libya's Divisions', Reuters, 14 September 2018.

73. *Arab Weekly*, 'Cracks Emerging in Libya's Veneer of National Unity,' 12 May 2021.

74. Al Jazeera, 'Libya Militias Rake in Millions in European Migration Funds: AP', 31 December 2019.

75. United Nations, 'The Sahel: Land of Opportunities', 29 June 2018, https://www.un.org/africarenewal/sahel.

76. Centre for Humanitarian Dialogue, *Agropastoral Mediation in the Sahel Region of Mali, Niger and Burkina Faso* (Geneva: Centre for Humanitarian Dialogue, 2019).

77. M. Tran, 'Mali: A Guide to the Conflict', *The Guardian*, 16 January 2013.

78. *Defense Post*, 'After Eight Years of Mali Campaign, France Seeks Exit Strategy', 6 January 2021.

79. UNHCR, 'Syria Refugee Crisis', https://www.unrefugees.org /emergencies/syria/ (accessed 30 June 2021).

80. P. Wintour, 'Yemen Civil War: The Conflict Explained', *The Guardian*, 20 June 2019.

81. K. Robinson, 'Yemen's Tragedy: War, Stalemate, and Suffering', Council on Foreign Relations, Backgrounder, 5 February 2021.

82. World Food Programme, 'Yemen Emergency', https://www.wfp.org /emergencies/yemen-emergency (accessed 30 June 2021).

83. World Food Programme, 'Somalia', https://www.wfp.org/countries /somalia (accessed 30 June 2021).

84. FAO, 'UN Continues Support to Fight Desert Locust in Somalia amid COVID-19 Response', 1 May 2020.

85. Brzezinski, *The Grand Chessboard*, p. 128.

86. Cornell and Sultan, 'The Caspian Connection'.

87. Ibid.

88. World Atlas, 'The Ethnic Groups of Afghanistan', https://www .worldatlas.com/articles/ethnic-groups-of-afghanistan.html (accessed 24 June 2021).

89. Cornell and Sultan, 'The Caspian Connection'.

90. Brzezinski, *The Grand Chessboard*.

91. Ibid.

92. Faber, 'Thinking about Geography', p. 7.

93. L. Ventura, 'Poorest Countries in the World in 2021', *Global Finance*, 21 May 2021; A. Koop, 'Mapped: The 25 Poorest Countries in the World', *Visual Capitalist*, 22 April 2021.

94. T. Shelton, 'Taliban Taking Back Territory as Australian and US Forces Prepare to Leave Afghanistan by September', ABC News, 18 June 2021; F. Qazizai and D. Hadid, 'The Taliban Are Getting Stronger in Afghanistan as US and NATO Forces Exit', NPR, 5 June 2021.

95. V. Felbab-Brown, 'Drugs, Security, and Counternarcotics Policies in Afghanistan', Brookings Institution, 29 October 2020.

96. A. Boudet, 'The Issue of Drug Trafficking from Afghanistan in Central Asia and Proposed Solutions', *Russian International Affairs Council*, 5 May 2016.

97. UN Office of the High Commissioner for Human Rights, 'Refugees in Iran', https://www.unhcr.org/ir/refugees-in-iran (accessed 30 June 2021).

98. A. Latif, 'Afghan Refugees in Pakistan Pin Hopes on US Pullout', Anadolu Agency, 21 April 2021.

99. Amnesty International, 'Afghanistan: Country's Four Million Internally Displaced Need Urgent Support amid Pandemic', 30 March 2021.

100. Ibid.

101. E. Carll, 'An Afghanistan at Peace Could Connect South and Central Asia', Atlantic Council, 18 May 2011.

102. I. Kiesow and N. Norling, 'The Rise of India: Problems and Opportunities', Central Asia-Caucasus Institute and Silk Road Studies Program, John Hopkins University-SAIS, January 2007.

103. *Encyclopedia Britannica*, 'Kashmir', 11 November 2021.

104. E. Blackmore, 'The Kashmir Conflict: How Did It Start?', *National Geographic*, 2 March 2019.

105. O.B. Toon *et al.*, 'Rapidly Expanding Nuclear Arsenals in Pakistan and India Portend Regional and Global Catastrophe', *Science Advances* 5, no. 10 (2 October 2019.

106. United Nations, 'Loss of Autonomy in Indian-Administered Jammu and Kashmir Threatens Minorities' Rights – UN Independent Experts', 18 February 2021.
107. M.A. Soloshcheva, 'The Uyghur Terrorism: Phenomenon and Genesis', *Iran & the Caucasus* 21, no. 4 (2017), pp. 416–17.
108. K. Mehta, 'Locating Xinjiang in China's Eurasian Ambitions', Observer Research Foundation, Occasional Paper, 25 September 2018.
109. Maizland, 'China's Repression of Uyghurs in Xinjiang'.
110. See, for example, UN OHCHR, 'China: UN Experts Deeply Concerned by Alleged Detention, Forced Labour of Uyghurs', 29 March 2021.
111. J. Yeung, J. Griffiths and N. Gan, 'The US Is Sanctioning Chinese Officials over Alleged Abuse of Uyghurs in Xinjiang. Here's What You Need to Know' CNN, 25 March 2021.
112. J. Berlinger, 'North Korea, Syria and Myanmar among Countries Defending China's Actions in Xinjiang', CNN, 15 July 2019.
113. Y.A. Adeto, 'State Fragility and Conflict Nexus: Contemporary Security Issues in the Horn of Africa', *African Journal of Conflict Studies* 19, no. 1 (2019), p. 15; M.M. Abshir, 'Ethiopia, Eritrea, Somalia, Djibouti: The Constant Instability in the Horn of Africa', *Africa Report*, 20 April 2021; A.D. Beyene, 'The Horn of Africa and the Gulf: Shifting Power Plays in the Red Sea', *Africa Report*, 16 November 2020.
114. UNHCR, 'Somalia Refugee Crisis Explained', https://www.unrefugees .org/news/somalia-refugee-crisis-explained (accessed 24 June 2021).
115. Fund for Peace, 'Fragile States Index 2018', 24 April 2018.
116. Adeto, 'State Fragility and Conflict Nexus', p. 16.
117. Al Jazeera, 'Ethiopia's Massive Nile Dam Explained', 8 July 2021.
118. D. Kopp, 'Opinion: Deadly Effects of Rwandan Genocide Still Felt Today', DW, 6 April 2014; K. Ighobor, 'Work in Progress for Africa's Remaining Conflict Hotspots', *Africa Renewal*, 23 December 2019.
119. European Commission, 'Humanitarian Aid: Over €34 Million in African Great Lakes Region', 18 September 2019.
120. Ibid.; UN Office for the Coordination of Humanitarian Affairs, 'Regional Outlook for the Horn of Africa and Great Lakes Region: January-March 2017', 24 February 2017.
121. US Department of State, Overseas Security Advisory Council, 'Democratic Republic of the Congo 2019 Crime and Safety Report', 4 April 2019.
122. S.G. Borgerson, 'Arctic Meltdown: The Economic and Security Implications of Global Warming', *Foreign Affairs* 87, no. 2 (March/ April 2008).
123. M. Bennett, 'The Arctic Shipping Route No One's Talking About', *Maritime Executive*, 8 May 2019.
124. E. Levick, 'The Drawbacks of Arctic Shipping', Global Risk Insights, 8 February 2018.

125. Ibid.; G. Gricius, 'Geopolitical Implications of New Arctic Shipping Lanes', *The Arctic Institute*, 18 March 2021; J. Murphy, 'Is the Arctic Set to Become a Main Shipping Route?', BBC News, 1 November 2018.

126. Port Technology, 'Is the Arctic Route the Future of Shipping?'

127. Rasmussen, 'An Emerging Strategic Geometry'.

128. *Scientific American*, 'Without a Treaty to Share the Arctic, Greedy Countries Will Destroy It', 1 December 2017.

129. Ibid.

130. J. Fu and D. Jiang, 'Canada's Sovereignty over the Northwest Passage', *ARCGIS*, 5 January 2020; D. Steinfeld, 'The US-Canada Northwest Passage Dispute', *Brown Political Review*, 8 April 2020.

131. Chase, Hill and Kennedy, *The Pivotal States*.

132. Ibid., pp. 6–7.

133. Brzezinski, *The Grand Chessboard*, pp. 134–35.

134. Ibid., p. 135.

135. Naumann *et al.*, 'Towards a Grand Strategy for an Uncertain World', p. 58.

136. M. Levitt, 'Hezbollah's Regional Activities in Support of Iran's Proxy Networks', Middle East Institute, 26 July 2021, pp. 4–7.

137. Feierstein, 'Iran's Role in Yemen and Prospects for Peace'.

138. I. Levy, 'How Iran Fuels Hamas Terrorism', Washington Institute for Near East Policy, *Policy Watch 3494*, 1 June 2021.

139. International Institute for Strategic Studies, *Iran's Networks of Influence in the Middle East* (London: International Institute for Strategic Studies, 2019), pp. 121–25.

140. A. Vohra, 'Iran is Trying to Convert Syria to Shiism', *Foreign Policy*, 15 March 2021.

141. A. Bilgic, 'Biden and the Iran Nuclear Deal: What to Expect from the Negotiations', *The Conversation*, 22 February 2021.

142. A. Cordesman, 'Iran's Support of the Hezbollah in Lebanon', CSIS, 15 July 2006.

143. Bahgat, 'Maritime Security in the Persian Gulf'.

144. Connell, 'Operation Sentinel Protects Gulf Shipping'; Bunyard, 'What a New Naval Vessel Says about Iran's Ambitions at Sea'.

145. BBC News, 'Iranian "Spy Ship" Damaged by Explosion in Red Sea', 7 April 2021.

146. W. Figueroa, 'China-Iran Relations: The Myth of Massive Investment', *The Diplomat*, 6 April 2021.

147. Ibid.

148. Ibid.

149. See Statista, 'Proportion of Children Living in Poverty in OECD Countries in 2018'; *Jerusalem Post*, 'About Two Million Israelis Live Below the Poverty Line – Report'.

150. Springfield, 'Accounting for Israel's Economic Boom'; Solomon, 'From 1950s Rationing to Modern High-Tech Boom'; E. Halon, 'Israel's Economic Growth Has Left Most People Behind: Study'.

151. Geneva Academy RULAC online portal, 'Military Occupation of Palestine by Israel'.

152. Beehner, 'Israel and the Doctrine of Proportionality'.

153. Amnesty International, 'Israel and Occupied Palestinian territories 2020'; BBC News, 'Israel Strikes in Gaza after Fire Balloons Launched', 16 June 2021.

154. Amnesty International, 'Israel and Occupied Palestinian Territories 2020'.

155. Ibid.; Al Sanah *et al.*, '"The Illusion of Citizenship Has Gone"'.

156. Sheen, 'Black Lives Do Not Matter in Israel'; Marlowe, 'Israel's Mizrahi Activists Are Fighting the Racist Nation-State Law'.

157. Elsana, 'Historic Change: Arab Political Parties Are Now Legitimate Partners in Israel's Politics and Government'.

158. Marin *et al.*, *Water Management in Israel*.

159. C. Newton, 'A History of the US Blocking UN Resolutions against Israel'.

160. E. Schewe, 'Settlements and the Israel-Palestine Conflict: Background Reading', *JSTOR Daily*, 19 May 2019, https://daily.jstor.org/israeli -settlement-palestine-background-readings/.

161. Al Jazeera, 'Israeli Settlements Amount to "War Crime", UN Expert', 9 July 2021.

162. 'Statement of ICC Prosecutor, Fatou Bensouda, Respecting an Investigation of the Situation in Palestine', International Criminal Court, 3 March 2021.

163. D. Newman, 'Borders and Conflict Resolution', in T.M. Wilson and H. Donnan (eds), *A Companion to Border Studies* (Hoboken, NJ: John Wiley & Sons, 2012), pp. 252.

164. See Miller, 'How Israel and the Arab World Are Making Peace Without a Peace Deal'.

165. Organisation of Islamic Cooperation, 'History', https://www.oic-oci.org /page/?p_id=52&p_ref=26&lan=en (accessed 24 June 2021).

166. Kemp and Harkavy, *Strategic Geography and the Changing Middle*, pp. 76–77.

167. Economic Cooperation Foundation, 'Saudi (Arab) Peace Initiative (2002)', 23 March 2002, https://ecf.org.il/issues/issue/167.

168. J. Feierstein, 'Saudi Arabia: Liberalization, not Democratization', American Foreign Service Association, *Foreign Service Journal* (May 2018).

169. Neom News, 'Neom Saudi Arabia'.

170. King Abdullah University of Science and Technology, 'KAUST'.

171. Bradbury, 'Water Crisis in Saudi Arabia'; DeNicola *et al.*, 'Climate Change and Water Scarcity'.

172. World Bank, 'Population Ages (0–14): Saudi Arabia'.
173. V. Godinho, 'Two-Thirds of Saudi Arabia's Population Is under the Age of 35', Gulf Business, 10 August 2020.
174. House, *On Saudi Arabia*, p. 157.
175. KSA Vision 2030, 'Vision 2030: A Sustainable Saudi Vision', https://www.vision2030.gov.sa (accessed 30 June 2021).
176. EG 24 News, 'Is Turkey Closing the Bosphorus and Dardanelles Straits to Russia?', 28 February 2020.
177. S. Cagaptay and N. Gencsoy, 'Startup of the Baku-Tbilisi-Ceyhan Pipeline: Turkey's Energy Role', Policy Watch no. 998, Washington Institute for Near East Policy, 27 May 2005; K. Kirişci, *Turkey's Foreign Policy in Turbulent Times*, Chaillot Paper no. 92 (Paris: EUISS, 2006), p. 86.
178. Kirişci, *Turkey's Foreign Policy in Turbulent Times*.
179. Institute for Security and Development Policy, 'Turkey's Kurdish Conflict: 2015 to Present: Backgrounder', December 2016, https://ethz .ch/content/dam/ethz/special-interest/gess/cis/center-for-securities -studies/resources/docs/ISDP-Turkeys-Kurdish-Conflict-2015-Present .pdf, p. 2.
180. Global Security, 'Kurdistan – Turkey', https://www.globalsecurity.org /military/world/war/kurdistan-turkey.htm (accessed 24 November 2021).
181. Human Rights Watch, 'World Report 2020: Turkey', https://www.hrw .org/world-report/2020/country-chapters/turkey (accessed 13 January 2022).
182. VOA News, 'Turkish Operation Increases Conflict among Kurds in Iraq', 21 June 2021; *Encyclopedia Britannica*, 'Turkey'; S. Glynn, 'Turkey's Invasion of Northern Iraq Could Lead to Kurdish Civil War', *Open Democracy*, 2 July 2021.
183. Glynn, 'Turkey's Invasion of Northern Iraq Could Lead to Kurdish Civil War'.
184. G. Tol, 'Viewpoint: Why Turkey Is Flexing Its Muscles Abroad', BBC News, 16 October 2020.
185. Akyol, 'Turkey's Troubled Experiment with Secularism'.
186. *The Economist*, 'Recep Tayyip the First'.
187. *The Economist*, 'The Turkish Train Crash', 2 December 2006, p. 34.
188. J. Gorvett, 'Greece is Making a Comeback in the Eastern Mediterranean', *Foreign Policy*, 24 May 2021; DW, 'Greece, Turkey Agree to Work on Relationship', 31 May 2021.
189. DW, 'Turkey Extends Controversial Mediterranean Gas Exploration', 25 October 2020.
190. G. Tol and Y. Işık, 'Turkey-NATO Ties Are Problematic, but There Is One Bright Spot', Middle East Institute, 16 February 2021.
191. A. Got, 'Turkey's Crisis with the West: How a New Low in Relations Risks Paralyzing NATO', *War on the Rocks*, 19 November 2020.
192. Al Jazeera, 'Purchase of S-400 a "Done Deal", Turkey Tells US', 24 March 2021.

193. A. Macias, 'US Sanctions Turkey over Purchase of Russian S-400 Missile System', CNBC, 14 December 2020.
194. Al Jazeera, 'Purchase of S-400 a "Done Deal", Turkey Tells US'.
195. A. Baghdassarian, 'Congressional Recognition of the Armenian Genocide – 104 Years of Denial', *Harvard Human Rights Journal* 34, no. 1 (2021), n.p.
196. T. de Waal, 'What Next after the US Recognition of the Armenian Genocide?' Carnegie Europe, 30 April 2021.
197. R.E. Ebel, 'The Geopolitics of Russian Energy', CSIS, 21 July 2009.
198. S. Cordey, *Cyber Influence Operations: An Overview and Comparative Analysis* (Zürich: ETH Zürich Center for Security Studies, 2019); T. Summers, 'How the Russian Government Used Disinformation and Cyber Warfare in 2016 Elections – An Ethical Hacker Explains', *The Conversation*, 27 July 2018.
199. BBC News, 'Russia Offers Free Land to Stop Arctic Depopulation', 16 July 2020.
200. GeoHistory, 'Nationalist Thought in Contemporary Russia', 3 September 2013.
201. J. Polaniy, 'How Many Minutes to Midnight? A High-Level Panel Convenes to Check the State of the "Doomsday Clock' in R. Braun, R. Hinde, D. Krieger, H. Kroto and S. Milne (eds), *Joseph Rotblat: Visionary for Peace* (London: Wiley, 2007)
202. S. Peterson, 'Russia, Iran Harden against West', *Christian Science Monitor*, 18 October 2007, http://www.csmonitor.com/2007/1018/p06s02-woeu.html.
203. J. Matters, 'Biden and Putin's First Meeting Won't Reset US Relations with Russia', *The Conversation*, 15 June 2021.
204. L. Harding, 'What We Know about Russia's Interference in the US Election', *The Guardian*, 16 December 2016.
205. *Moscow Times*, 'Council of Europe Urges Russia to Release Navalny Immediately', 21 June 2021.
206. P. Kirby, 'Why has Russia Invaded Ukraine and What does Putin Want?', BBC News, 9 March 2022.
207. I. Berman, 'Slouching toward Eurasia?', *Perspective* 12, no. 1 (September-October 2001), https://www.ilanberman.com/5947/slouching-toward-eurasia.
208. Ibid.
209. A. Dugin, *The Basics of Geopolitics*, cited in C. Clover, 'Will the Russian Bear Roar Again?', *Financial Times*, 2 December 2000, http://eurasia.com.ru/eng/ft.html.
210. Schwab (ed.), *The Global Competitiveness Report 2015–2016*.
211. Schwab (ed.), *The Global Competitiveness Report 2018*.
212. Y.H. Lun, K.H. Lai and T.C.E. Cheng, *Shipping and Logistics Management* (London: Springer, 2010), p. 14.

213. Ibid.

214. *Economic Times*, 'Piracy Pushes Ship Owners to Opt for Cape of Good Hope', 23 November 2008.

215. M. Chatin and G. Gallarotti, *Emerging Powers in International Politics: The BRICS and Soft Power* (Abingdon: Routledge, 2018), p. 5.

216. H. Besada, 'Enduring Political Divides in South Africa', Centre for International Governance Innovation, Technical Paper no. 3, 1 April 2007, pp. 10–11.

217. Bittar, '5 Facts about Poverty in South Africa'.

218. Ritchie and Roser, 'South Africa: CO$_2$ Country Profile'.

219. Abia, 'River of Bacteria'.

220. WorldOMeter, 'Egypt Population'.

221. World Bank, 'GDP: Egypt'.

222. K. Robinson, 'The Arab Spring at Ten Years: What's the Legacy of the Uprisings?', Council on Foreign Relations, 3 December 2020.

223. M. Saied, 'Spotlight on Egypt to Help Mediate with Hamas', *Al-Monitor*, 18 May 2021.

224. Nuclear Threat Initiative, 'Pakistan', https://www.nti.org/countries /pakistan/ (accessed 29 November 2021).

225. World Bank, 'Refugee Population by Country or Territory of Asylum: Pakistan'.

226. World Bank, 'Literacy Rate: Pakistan', https://data.worldbank.org /indicator/SE.ADT.LITR.ZS?locations=PK (accessed 24 June 2021).

227. *Business Standard*, 'Water Crisis Looms Large in Pakistan, May Face Absolute Scarcity by 2040'.

228. Shaikh, 'Private Sector in Health Care Delivery'.

229. World Bank, 'Life Expectancy at Birth, Total (Years) – Pakistan'.

230. N.R.F. Al-Rodhan, G.P Herd and L. Watanabe, *Critical Turning Points in the Middle East, 1915–2015* (Hampshire: Palgrave Macmillan, 2011).

231. See, for example, P. Mangold, *Superpower Intervention in the Middle East* (Abingdon: Routledge Revivals, 2013), p. 9.

232. World Bank, 'China Product Exports and Imports to Middle East and North Africa 2019'.

233. Y. Xu, *China, Africa and Responsible International Engagement* (New York: Routledge, 2017), p. xxvii.

234. C. Lovotti *et al.* (eds), *Russia in the Middle East and North Africa: Continuity and Change* (Abingdon: Routledge, 2020), p. 2.

235. J.B. Alterman, 'Russia, the United States, and the Middle East', CSIS, 21 July 2017.

236. Ibid.

237. A.H. Cordesman, 'America's Failed Strategy in the Middle East: Losing Iraq and the Gulf', CSIS, 2 January 2020.

238. Kemp and Harkavy, *Strategic Geography and the Changing Middle East*, p. 330.

239. M. Ottaway and S. Mair, 'States at Risk and Failed States: Putting Security First', Carnegie Endowment for International Peace and German Institute for International and Security Affairs, Policy Outlook, September 2004.
240. Al-Rodhan, *Emotional Amoral Egoism*, ch. 4.
241. Ibid.
242. See Al-Rodhan, *Symbiotic Realism*, esp. p. 119.
243. Al-Rodhan, *Sustainable History and Human Dignity,* introduction.
244. See Al-Rodhan, *Symbiotic Realism*, esp. p. 119.
245. Al-Rodhan, *Emotional Amoral Egoism*, ch. 4.4.9.
246. Al-Rodhan, *Sustainable History and Human Dignity,* ch. 15.5.

11. The Future State of the World and the Way Forward

1. E. Parrado *et al.*, 'What are Frontier Risks and How Can We Prepare for Them?', World Economic Forum, 2 June 2021.
2. Al-Rodhan, '3 Disruptive Frontier Risks that Could Strike by 2040'.
3. N.R.F. Al-Rodhan, *Meta-Geopolitics of Outer Space: An Analysis of Space Power, Security and Governance* (Basingstoke: Palgrave Macmillan, 2012).
4. Al-Rodhan, '3 Disruptive Frontier Risks that Could Strike by 2040'.
5. Ibid.
6. M. Weinzierl, 'Space, the Final Economic Frontier', *Journal of Economic Perspectives* 32, no. 2 (2018), 173–92.
7. N.R.F. Al-Rodhan, 'Weaponization and Outer Space Security," *Global Policy Journal*, 12 March 2018.
8. Z. Abbany, 'Modern Spy Satellites in an Age of Space Wars', DW, 25 August 2020; M. Wolverton, 'Contesting the High Ground', *Mechanical Engineering* 141, no. 7 (July 2019), p. 55.
9. M.P. Gleason and P.L. Hays, 'Getting the Most Deterrent Value from US Space Forces', Center for Space Policy and Strategy, October 2020, p. 2; M. Krepon and J. Thompson (eds), *Anti-Satellite Weapons, Deterrence and Sino-American Space Relations* (Washington, DC: Stimson Center, 2013), pp. 18–19.
10. M. Sheehan, *The International Politics of Space* (New York: Routledge, 2007), p. 93.
11. Ibid.
12. J. Harper, 'Special Report: Pentagon Reexamining Space-Based Interceptors', *National Defense Magazine*, 22 April 2019.
13. T.M. Blatt, 'Anti-Satellite Weapons and the Emerging Space Arms Race', *Harvard International Review*, 26 May 2020.
14. Harper, 'Special Report: Pentagon Reexamining Space-Based Interceptors'.
15. N.R.F. Al-Rodhan, 'In Space, Either We All Win, or We All Lose', *Parliament Magazine*, 28 October 2020.

16. Ibid.
17. C. Gohd, 'Everyone Wants a Space Force – but Why?', Space.com, 11 September 2020.
18. Arms Control Association, 'The Outer Space Treaty at a Glance', October 2020, https://www.armscontrol.org/factsheets/outerspace.
19. J. Harper, 'Special Report: Would Space-Based Interceptors Spark a New Arms Race?', *National Defense Magazine*, 24 April 2019.
20. Al-Rodhan, '3 Disruptive Frontier Risks that Could Strike by 2040'.
21. Al-Rodhan, 'Weaponization and Outer Space Security'.
22. Al-Rodhan, 'In Space, Either We All Win, or We All Lose'.
23. UN Office for Outer Space Affairs, Treaty on Principles Governing the Activities of States in the Exploration and Use of Outer Space.
24. Al-Rodhan, '3 Disruptive Frontier Risks that Could Strike by 2040'.
25. *Oxford Dictionary of Phrase and Fable*, 'Artificial Intelligence'.
26. Al-Rodhan, *Emotional Amoral Egoism*, ch. 2.5.
27. Al-Rodhan, 'Major Transformative Technologies and the Five Dimensions of Global Security'.
28. Ibid.
29. S. Kalantzakos, 'Rare Earths, the Climate Crisis, and Tech-Imperium', London School of Economics, *Blogs*, 24 March 2021.
30. Al-Rodhan, 'Major Transformative Technologies and the Five Dimensions of Global Security'.
31. IBM, 'What Is Quantum Computing?', https://www.ibm.com/quantum -computing/what-is-quantum-computing (accessed 30 July 2021).
32. Al-Rodhan, 'Major Transformative Technologies and the Five Dimensions of Global Security'.
33. J. O'Brien, 'How Quantum Computing Could Be One of the Most Innovative Climate Change Solutions', World Economic Forum, 17 December 2019.
34. Al-Rodhan, 'Major Transformative Technologies and the Five Dimensions of Global Security'.
35. K. Kitchen and B. Drexel, 'Quantum Computing: A National Security Primer', American Enterprise Institute, April 2021.
36. Ibid.
37. Al-Rodhan, 'Neuromorphic Computers: What Will They Change'.
38. D. Strukov *et al.*, 'Building Brain-Inspired Computing', *Nature Communications* 10 (2019), p. 2.
39. Ibid., p. 4.
40. Al-Rodhan, 'Major Transformative Technologies and the Five Dimensions of Global Security'.
41. Al-Rodhan, 'Neuromorphic Computers: What Will They Change'.
42. Al-Rodhan, 'Meta-Geopolitics of Pandemics'.
43. Al-Rodhan, '3 Disruptive Frontier Risks that Could Strike by 2040'.
44. B. Jeffs, 'A Clinical Guide to Viral Haemorrhagic Fevers: Ebola, Marburg and Lassa', *Tropical Doctor* 36, no. 1 (2006), pp. 1–4.

45. See World Health Organization, 'Factsheet 99 on Rabies', 17 May 2021, https://www.who.int/news-room/fact-sheets/detail/rabies.

46. See B. Arroll, 'Common Cold', *BMJ Clinical Evidence* PMCID: PMC3275147, PMID: 21406124 (2011) (2011), pp. 1–27.

47. Z. Car *et al.*, 'Modeling the Spread of COVID-19 Infection Using a Multilayer Perceptron', *Computational and Mathematical Methods in Medicine* 2020, Article ID 5714714 (2020), pp. 1–10.

48. See US Department of Health and Human Services, Centers for Disease Control and Prevention, 'HIV in the United States: The Stages of Care', November 2014.

49. Al-Rodhan, 'Meta-Geopolitics of Pandemics'.

50. Riley *et al.*, 'Slum Health', p. 2.

51. P. Wintour and J. Borger, 'Trump Attacks China over COVID "Plague" as Xi Urges Collaboration in Virus Fight', *The Guardian*, 22 September 2020.

52. R. Jacobsen, 'Top Researchers Are Calling for a Real Investigation into the Origin of COVID-19', *MIT Technology Review*, 13 May 2021.

53. K. Schaeffer, 'A Look at the Americans Who Believe There Is Some Truth to the Conspiracy Theory That COVID-19 Was Planned', Pew Research Center, 24 July 2020, https://www.pewresearch.org/fact-tank/2020/07/24/a-look-at-the-americans-who-believe-there-is-some-truth-to-the-conspiracy-theory-that-covid-19-was-planned.

54. Al-Rodhan, 'Meta-Geopolitics of Pandemics'.

55. Al-Rodhan, 'A Neurophilosophy of Two Technological Game-Changers'. See also M. El Karoui *et al.*, 'Future Trends in Synthetic Biology – A Report', *Frontiers in Bioengineering and Biotechnology* 7 (2019), p. 1.

56. M.J. Poznansky, *Saved by Science: The Hope and Promise of Synthetic Biology* (Toronto: ECW Press, 2020), p. 1.

57. Ibid., p. 2.

58. See M.-S. Roell and M.D. Zurbriggen, 'The Impact of Synthetic Biology for Future Agriculture and Nutrition', *Current Opinion in Biotechnology* 61 (2020), pp. 102–9.

59. Al-Rodhan, 'A Neurophilosophy of Two Technological Game-Changers'; P. Nouvel, 'De la biologie synthétique à l'homme synthétique' (From Synthetic Biology to Synthetic Man), *Comptes rendus biologies* 338, nos 8–9 (2015), pp. 559–65.

60. Nouvel, 'De la biologie synthétique à l'homme synthétique', p. 561.

61. B. Lemma, 'CRISPR Dreams: The Potential for Gene Editing', *Harvard International Review* 40, no. 1 (2019), pp. 6–7.

62. D. Perrin, 'Nobel Prize for CRISPR Honors Two Great Scientists – And Leaves out Many Others', *The Conversation*, 8 October 2020.

63. H. Frangoul *et al.*, 'CRISPR-Cas9 Gene Editing for Sickle Cell Disease and β-Thalassemia', *New England Journal of Medicine*, 5 December 2020, p. 8.

64. E. Dolgin, 'Synthetic Biology Speeds Vaccine Development', *Nature*, 28 September 2020.

65. G.J. Macdonald, 'Vaccine Makers Could Benefit from Synthetic Biology', *Genetic Engineering & Biotechnology News*, 29 June 2021.

66. J. Li *et al.*, 'Advances in Synthetic Biology and Biosafety Governance', p. 2.

67. Wickiser *et al.*, 'Engineered Pathogens and Unnatural Biological Weapons'.

68. Al-Rodhan, 'A Neurophilosophy of Governance of Artificial Intelligence and Brain-Computer Interface'; Drew, 'The Ethics of Brain-Computer Interfaces'.

69. J.J. Daly and R. Sitaram, 'BCI Therapeutic Applications for Improving Brain Function', in J. Wolpaw and E.W. Wolpaw (eds), *Brain-Computer Interfaces: Principles and Practice* (New York: Oxford University Press, 2012), pp. 351–62.

70. S. Aas and D. Wasserman, 'Brain-Computer Interfaces and Disability: Extending Embodiment, Reducing Stigma?', *Journal of Medical Ethics* 42, no. 1 (2016), p. 37.

71. A.P. Alivisatos *et al.*, 'Neuroscience: The Brain Activity Map', *Science* 339, no. 6125 (2013), pp. 1284–85.

72. Drew, 'The Ethics of Brain-Computer Interfaces'.

73. Ibid.

74. Ibid.

75. Ibid.

76. Ibid.

77. Ibid.

78. L. Pycroft *et al.*, 'Brainjacking: Implant Security Issues in Invasive Neuromodulation', *World Neurosurgery* 92 (2016), pp. 454–62; Al-Rodhan, "A Neurophilosophy of Governance of Artificial Intelligence and Brain-Computer Interface."

79. J. Pugh *et al.*, 'Brainjacking in Deep Brain Stimulation and Autonomy', *Ethics and Information Technology* 20 (2018), pp. 220–21.

80. L. Pycroft, 'Brainjacking – A New Cyber-Security Threat', *The Conversation*, 23 August 2016.

81. D. Carrington, 'Climate Crisis "Unequivocally" Caused by Human Activities, Says IPCC Report,' *The Guardian*, 9 August 2021.

82. See Intergovernmental Panel on Climate Change, *Climate Change 2014*.

83. The World Bank has estimated that the cost of adapting to 2°C climate change would be in the order of US$70 billion to US$100 billion a year, see World Bank, 'Economics of Adaptation to Climate Change'.

84. See Intergovernmental Panel on Climate Change, *Climate Change 2014*.

85. J. Podesta and P. Ogden, 'The Security Implications of Climate Change', *Washington Quarterly* 31, no. 1 (2007–8), p. 116.

86. Pamlin and Armstrong, *Global Challenges: 12 Risks that Threaten Human Civilisation*, p. 63.
87. Patz *et al.*, 'Global Climate Change and Emerging Infectious Diseases', pp. 217–23; Al-Rodhan, 'Meta-Geopolitics of Pandemics'.
88. A. Panda, 'Climate Change, Displacement, and Managed Retreat in Coastal India', Migration Policy Institute, 22 May 2020.
89. World Bank, 'Curbing Desertification in China', 4 July 2019; A. Gupta, 'How Communities in China Helped Keep Desertification at Bay', Down to Earth, 5 September 2019.
90. A. Randall, 'Climate Change Driving Migration into China's Vulnerable Cities', Climate and Migration Coalition (Accessed 30 July 2021).
91. H. Haider, *Climate Change in Nigeria: Impacts and Responses*, K4D Helpdesk Report 675 (Brighton: Institute of Development Studies, 2019), p. 2.
92. D. Sabaghi, 'The Middle East Looks to Innovate Its Way out of a Water Crisis', *World Politics Review*, 14 April 2021.
93. A. Parshotam, 'Sliding towards Disaster: Migration in European African Relations', SAIIA, 18 October 2018.
94. C. Baczynska, 'Factbox: EU Divisions over Migration to Resurface under New Plan', *Reuters*, 23 September 2020.
95. United Nations, 'Unprecedented Impacts of Climate Change Disproportionately Burdening Developing Countries, Delegate Stresses, as Second Committee Concludes General Debate', 8 October 2019.
96. J. Sachs, 'The New Geopolitics', *Scientific American*, 22 May 2006.
97. Global Network Against Food Crises and Food Security Information Network, 'Global Report on Food Crises 2021: In Brief', https://docs.wfp.org/api/documents/WFP-0000127413/download/?_ga=2.113993218.468372453.1625057045-1996012570.1625057045 (accessed 30 July 2021), p. 1.
98. Ibid., p. 3.
99. Ibid., pp. 3–4.
100. C. Madramootoo (ed.), *Emerging Technologies for Promoting Food Security: Overcoming the World Food Crisis* (Cambridge: Woodhead Publishing, 2015).
101. D. Bereuter and D. Glickman, *Stability in the 21st Century: Global Food Security for Peace and Prosperity* (Chicago: Chicago Council for Global Affairs, 2017).
102. World Vision, 'Global Water Crisis: Facts, FAQs, and How to Help', 16 April 2021.
103. World Wildlife Fund, 'Water Scarcity', https://www.worldwildlife.org/threats/water-scarcity (accessed 30 July 2021).
104. International Atomic Energy Agency, 'Nuclear Desalination', https://www.iaea.org/topics/non-electric-applications/nuclear-desalination (accessed 30 July 2021); J. Conca, 'How 1,500 Nuclear-Powered Water Desalination Plants Could Save the World from Desertification', *Forbes*, 14 July 2019.

105. C. Pascual, 'The Geopolitics of Energy: From Security to Survival', Brookings Institution, January 2008.

106. World Wildlife Fund, 'Six Ways Loss of Arctic Ice Impacts Everyone', https://www.worldwildlife.org/pages/six-ways-loss-of-arctic-ice-impacts -everyone (accessed 30 July 2021).

107. P. Wadhams, *A Farewell to Ice: A Report from the Arctic* (Oxford: Oxford University Press, 2017), p. 3.

108. J.-L. Chen *et al.*, 'Variation of Sea Ice and Perspectives of the Northwest Passage in the Arctic Ocean', *Advances in Climate Change Research*, 15 February 2021.

109. Bennett, 'The Arctic Shipping Route No One's Talking About'.

110. C. Kissane and A. Varga, 'Russia's Drilling in the Arctic Is a Threat to the World – and to Itself', *World Politics Review*, 9 July 2020.

111. Gosnell, 'Caution in the High North'.

112. A. Tugushev, 'The Porto Franco Regime in Canadian and Russian Sea Ports as an Instrument of Socio-Economic Development in the Arctic', The Arctic Institute, 9 June 2020.

113. US Congressional Research Service, 'Changes in the Arctic: Background and Issues for Congress', Report Prepared for Members of Committees and Congress, 16 June 2021, p. 15.

114. G. Faulconbridge, 'Russian Sub Plants Flag Under North Pole', Reuters, 2 August 2007.

115. Naval Technology, 'Royal Canadian Navy Receives Delivery of Second AOPS Patrol Ship', 16 July 2021.

116. K. Calamur, 'Denmark Claims Part of the Arctic, including the North Pole', NPR, 15 December 2014; M. Jacobsen, 'Denmark's Strategic Interests in the Arctic: It's the Greenlandic Connection, Stupid!', The Arctic Institute Center for Circumpolar Security Studies, 4 May 2016.

117. UN Division for Ocean Affairs and the Law of the Sea, 'Commission on the Limits of the Continental Shelf (CLCS): Outer Limits of the Continental Shelf beyond 200 Nautical Miles from the Baselines: Submissions to the Commission: Submission by the Kingdom of Norway', 20 August 2009, https://www.un.org/Depts/los/clcs_new /submissions_files/submission_nor.htm.

118. Sun, 'Defining the Chinese Threat in the Arctic'.

119. The Arctic Council, 'About the Arctic Council', https://arctic-council. org/en/about (accessed 30 July 2021).

120. Macdonald, 'This Map Shows All the Claims on the Arctic Seafloor';.

121. The Arctic Council, 'About the Arctic Council'.

122. A. Singh Verma, 'A Case for the United States' Ratification of UNCLOS', *Diplomatist*, 2 May 2020.

123. J.D. Carlson *et al.*, 'Scramble for the Arctic', *The SAIS Review of International Affairs* 33(2) (2013), pp. 28–38.

124. S. Satei, 'The Legal Status of the Northwest Passage: Canada's Jurisdiction or International Law in Light of Recent Developments in Arctic Shipping Regulation?', in L.P. Hildebrand, L.W. Brigham and T.M. Johansson (eds), *Sustainable Shipping in a Changing Arctic* (Cham: Springer, 2018), pp. 241–52.
125. R. Falk, 'The Waning of the State and the Waxing of Cyberworld', in J. Kurbalija (ed.), *Modern Diplomacy* (Msida, Malta: Mediterranean Academy of Diplomatic Studies, 1998), p. 229.
126. Ibid., p. 230.
127. Ibid.
128. Ibid., p. 231.
129. S. Rejali and Y. Heiniger, 'The Role of Digital Technologies in Humanitarian Law, Policy and Action: Charting a Path Forward', *International Review of the Red Cross* 913 (March 2021).
130. BBC News, 'US Election 2020: How to Spot Disinformation?', https://www.bbc.com/news/av/world-us-canada-54518196 (accessed 30 July 2021).
131. Al-Rodhan, 'A Neurophilosophy of Fake News, Disinformation and Digital Citizenship'.
132. Kastener and Wohlforth, 'A Measure Short of War'.
133. Ibid.
134. R. Oloruntoba, 'Cyber Attacks Can Shut Down Critical Infrastructure. It's Time to Make Cyber Security Compulsory', *The Conversation*, 27 May 2021.
135. World Economic Forum, 'Wild Wide Web', https://reports.weforum.org/global-risks-report-2020/wild-wide-web (accessed 30 June 2021).
136. N.R.F. Al-Rodhan, 'Cyber Security and Space Security', *Space Review*, 26 May 2020.
137. Ibid.
138. Ibid.
139. Ibid.
140. N.R.F. Al-Rodhan, 'Global Navigation Satellite Systems: A Symbiotic Realist Paradigm', *Space Review*, 15 February 2021.
141. Ibid.
142. Ibid.
143. N. Brzica, 'Understanding Contemporary Asymmetric Threats', *Croatian International Relations Review* 24, no. 83 (2018), pp. 34–51.
144. Al-Rodhan, 'A Neurophilosophy of Fake News, Disinformation and Digital Citizenship'.
145. Bluth, 'Norms and International Relations', p. 7.
146. Schell, *The Fate of the Earth*.
147. Reif and Bugos, 'UK to Increase Cap on Nuclear Warhead Stockpile'.
148. Ibid.
149. C. Quinn, 'Tehran and Washington Signal Slow Going for Nuclear Deal', *Foreign Policy*, 30 July 2021, https://foreignpolicy.com/2021/07/30/iran-nuclear-deal-raisi-sanctions.

150. N.R.F. Al-Rodhan, 'Hypersonic Missiles and Global Security', *The Diplomat*, 13 November 2015.
151. Ibid.
152. Ibid.
153. N.R.F. Al-Rodhan, 'COVID-19 Has Shown the World Is Not Prepared for Potential Bioweapons', CAPX, 2 September 2020.
154. Al-Rodhan, 'A Neurophilosophy of Two Technological Game-Changers'.
155. N.R.F. Al-Rodhan, *The Politics of Emerging Strategic Technologies: Implications for Geopolitics, Human Enhancement and Human Destiny* (London: Palgrave Macmillan, 2011), p. 178.
156. See M. More, 'On Becoming Posthuman', *Free Inquiry* 14, no. 4 (1994), pp. 38–41.
157. Al-Rodhan, 'Inevitable Transhumanism?'
158. N.R.F. Al-Rodhan, 'Free Will in the Age of Neuromodulation', *Philosophy Now*, no. 127 (2018).
159. Ibid.
160. N.R.F. Al-Rodhan, 'Neurophilosophy and Transhumanism', *Blog of the American Philosophical Association*, 19 February 2019.
161. N. Bostrom, 'Transhumanist Values', *Review of Contemporary Philosophy* 4, nos 1–2 (2005), pp. 87–101.
162. Ibid., p. 137.
163. Al-Rodhan, 'A Neurophilosophy of Two Technological Game-Changers'.
164. Al-Rodhan, *Emotional Amoral Egoism*, ch. 3.6.2.
165. See, for example, P. Pettit, 'The Globalized Republican Ideal', *Global Justice and Non-Domination* 9, no. 1 (2016), pp. 47–68.
166. S.I. Hay *et al.*, 'Big Data Opportunities for Global Infectious Disease Surveillance', *PLOS Medicine* 10, no. 4 (2013), pp. 1–4.
167. A. Thompson, 'How Governments Use Big Data to Violate Human Rights', *The Conversation*, 13 January 2019.
168. Al-Rodhan, *Sustainable History and Human Dignity*, ch. 17.3.
169. Al-Rodhan, *Emotional Amoral Egoism*, ch. 4.5.4.
170. FDR Group and PEN America, 'Chilling Effects: NSA Surveillance Drives US Writers to Self-Censor', 12 November 2013.
171. N.R.F. Al-Rodhan, 'The Social Contract 2.0: Big Data and the Need to Guarantee Privacy and Civil Liberties', *The Oxford University Politics Blog*, 22 September 2014.
172. F. d'Agostino, G. Gaus and J. Thrasher, 'Contemporary Approaches to the Social Contract', in *The Stanford Encyclopedia of Philosophy* (Winter 2021 edition), E.N. Zalta (ed.), forthcoming.
173. Al-Rodhan, 'The Social Contract 2.0'.
174. Al-Rodhan, *Emotional Amoral Egoism*, ch. 4.5.4.
175. R. Jackson and N. Howe, *The Graying of the Great Powers: Demography and Geopolitics in the 21st Century* (Washington, DC: CSIS, 2008), p. 185.

176. Center for Global Development, 'Global Demographic Trends', https://www.cgdev.org/page/global-demographic-trends (accessed 30 June 2021); B. Quillin, 'Changing Global Demographics: The Certain Future', *BBVA*, 14 October 2019.

177. J. Tilley, 'Hard Evidence: Do We Become More Conservative with Age?', *The Conversation*, 4 October 2015.

178. W.H. Frey, 'What the 2020 Census Will Reveal about America: Stagnating Growth, an Aging Population, and Youthful Diversity', Brookings Institution, 11 January 2021; H. Alas, 'The Rise of African Nations' Populations', *US News*, 24 December 2020.

179. S. Repucci and A. Slipowitz, 'Freedom in the World 2021: Democracy under Siege', Freedom House, 2021; Freedom House, 'New Report: The Global Decline in Democracy Has Accelerated', 3 March 2021.

180. United Nations, 'World Population Projected to Reach 9.8 Billion in 2050, and 11.2 Billion in 2100', 21 June 2017; J. Vespa, L. Medina and D.M. Armstrong, 'Demographic Turning Points for the United States: Population Projections for 2020 to 2060', US Census Bureau, February 2020; W.H. Frey, 'The US Will Become "Minority White" in 2045, Census Projects', Brookings Institution, 14 March 2018.

181. C. Bell, *The End of the Vasco da Gama Era: The Next Landscape of World Politics*, Lowy Institute Paper 21 (Sydney: Lowy Institute for International Policy, Australia, 2007), p. 11.

182. World Bank, 'Population Growth: Russian Federation'; Statista, 'Population Projection for Russia 2021–2036, by Scenario'; World Bank, 'Life Expectancy at Birth, Total (Years) – Russian Federation'.

183. See Case Study 3A: China.

184. National Intelligence Council, 'Global Trends 2025: A Transformed World', November 2008, www.dni/nic/NIC_2025_project.html, p. 16.

185. UN Women, 'Facts and Figures: Economic Empowerment', https://www.unwomen.org/en/what-we-do/economic-empowerment/facts-and-figures (accessed 30 June 2021); World Bank, 'Girls' Education', https://www.worldbank.org/en/topic/girlseducation (accessed 30 June 2021).

186. National Intelligence Council, 'Global Trends 2025', p. 16.

187. Bell, *The End of the Vasco da Gama Era*, p. 11.

188. G.J. Ikenberry, M. Mastanduno and W.C. Wohlforth, *International Relations Theory and the Consequences of Unipolarity* (Cambridge: Cambridge University Press, 2011), p. 221.

189. J.S., Jr, Nye, 'The Future of American Power: Dominance and Decline in Perspective,' *Foreign Affairs* 89(6), 2010, p. 3.

190. P. Zhenqiang, 'The US-Europe-China Triangle in an Increasingly Multipolar World', Konrad Adenauer Stiftung, January 2006.

191. B. Jones, 'China and the Return of Great Power Strategic Competition', Brookings Institution, February 2020.

192. J. Blanchette, 'Xi's Gamble: The Race to Consolidate Power and Stave off Disaster', *Foreign Affairs*, July/August 2021.

193. J.S. Roy, 'Leadership in a Multipolar World: Can the United States Influence Cooperation between China and Russia?', *National Bureau of Asian Research*, 8 April 2018.

194. Matters, 'Biden and Putin's First Meeting Won't Reset US Relations with Russia'.

195. J. Diamond, 'Russian Hacking and the 2016 Election: What You Need to Know', CNN, 16 December 2016.

196. Roy, 'Leadership in a Multipolar World'.

197. Ibid.

198. Ibid.

199. A. Macias, 'List of Countries with Nuclear Weapons', CNBC, 16 March 2018.

200. Bell, *The End of the Vasco da Gama Era*, pp. 15–16.

201. *Encyclopedia Britannica*, 'Concert of Europe', 22 February 2016.

202. Pew Research Center, 'The Future of World Religions: Population Growth Projections, 2010–2050', 2 April 2015.

203. A. Mansour, 'Education and Development in Islamic World', 6 March 2020.

204. N.R.F. Al-Rodhan, *The Role of the Arab-Islamic World in the Rise of the West: Implications for Contemporary Trans-Cultural Relations* (London: Palgrave Macmillan, 2012).

205. K. Kaiser, 'Human Rights: A Western Policy Tool?', Belfer Center for Science and International Affairs, 5 December 2018.

206. P. Khanna, 'Here Comes the Second World', *Prospect*, no. 146 (2008), p. 60.

207. Ibid., p. 61.

208. R. Bernal-Meza and L. Xing (eds), *China-Latin America Relations in the 21st Century: The Dual Complexities of Opportunities and Challenges* (Cham: Palgrave Macmillan, 2020), p. 2.

209. M. Cook, 'ASEAN-Australia Relations: The Suitable Status Quo', Lowy Institute for International Policy, 6 August 2018.

210. Khanna, 'Here Comes the Second World', p. 62.

211. K. Whiting, 'An Expert Explains: What is RCEP, the World's Biggest Trade Deal?', World Economic Forum, 18 May 2021.

212. F. Zakaria, 'The Future of American Power: How America Can Survive the Rise of the Rest', *Foreign Affairs* 87, no. 3 (2008), pp. 18–43.

213. See L. Kamel (ed.), *The Frailty of Authority: Borders, Non-State Actors and Power Vacuums in a Changing Middle East* (Rome: Edizioni Nuova Cultura, 2017).

214. R.N. Haass, 'The Age of Nonpolarity: What Will Follow US Dominance', *Foreign Affairs* 87, no. 3 (2008).

215. Z. Rodionova, 'World's Largest Corporations Make More Money than Most Countries on Earth Combined', *The Independent*, 13 September 2016; A. Levy, 'Google Is Even More Influential than You Think', CNBC, 12 May 2015.

216. Haass, 'The Age of Nonpolarity'.
217. P. Spoonley, 'Far-Right Extremists Still Threaten New Zealand, a Year on from the Christchurch Attacks', *The Conversation*, 10 March 2020.
218. C. Cadwalladr and E. Graham-Harrison, 'Revealed: 50 Million Facebook Profiles Harvested for Cambridge Analytica in Major Data Breach', *The Guardian*, 17 March 2018; A. Hern, 'Cambridge Analytica: How Did It Turn Clicks into Votes?', *The Guardian*, 6 May 2018.
219. *Encyclopedia Britannica*, 'East India Company', 12 February 2021; W. Dalrymple, 'The East India Company: The Original Corporate Raiders', *The Guardian*, 4 March 2015.
220. N. Reiff, '10 Biggest Oil Companies', *Investopedia*, 10 September 2020.
221. UNESCO, 'Non-Governmental Organizations, Centres of Expertise and Research Institutes', https://ich.unesco.org/en/ngo-centers-and -institutions-00329 (accessed 30 June 2021).
222. Funds for NGOs, 'How Marketing and Communication Strategies Can Help NGOs Achieve Fundraising Success', https://www.fundsforngos .org/civil-society-2/how-can-marketing-communications-strategies -help-ngos-achieve-fundraising-success (accessed 30 June 2021).
223. US National Intelligence Council, 'Nonstate Actors: Impact on International Relations and Implications for the United States', 23 August 2007, https://fas.org/irp/nic/nonstate_actors_2007.pdf.
224. I. Ejaz, B.T. Shaikh and N. Rizvi, 'NGOs and Government Partnership for Health Systems Strengthening: A Qualitative Study Presenting Viewpoints of Government, NGOs and Donors in Pakistan', *BMC Health Services Research* 11, no. 122 (2011), pp. 1–7.
225. G. Sørensen, *The Transformation of the State: Beyond the Myth of Retreat* (London: Palgrave, 2004), p. 142.
226. See Case Studies 3A: China and 18A: Russian Federation.
227. Al-Rodhan, *Sustainable History and Human Dignity,* introduction.
228. Al-Rodhan, *Emotional Amoral Egoism*, ch. 4.4.9.

Appendix Understanding the Conflict between Russia and Ukraine

1. *Encyclopedia Britannica*, 'The Crisis in Crimea and Eastern Ukraine' (accessed 10 March 2022).
2. P. Kirby, 'Why Has Russia Invaded Ukraine and What Does Putin Want?', *BBC*, 9 March 2022.
3. Kirby, ibid; K. Volker, 'The (Russian) Empire Strikes Back', CEPA, 10 January 2022; D. Cohen, 'Romney: Putin Can't Be Allowed to Rebuild the Soviet Union', *Politico*, 16 January 2022.
4. J.J. Mearsheimer, 'Why Ukraine Is The West's Fault?', University of Chicago Alumni Weekend, Presentation of 4 June 2015, available at https://www.youtube.com/watch?v=JrMiSQAGOS4.
5. D. Fried, 'Putin's "Denazification" Claim Shows He Has No Case Against Ukraine', *Politico*, 1 March 2022.

6. J. Rankin, K. Willsher and L. Harding, 'Putin Accuses NATO of Ignoring Russia's Concerns As Ukraine Crisis Simmers', *The Guardian*, 28 January 2022.

7. L.D. Johnson, 'United Nations Response Options to Russia's Aggression: Opportunities and Rabbit Holes', *Just Security*, 1 March 2022.

8. S. Pifer, 'Why Care About Ukraine and the Budapest Memorandum', *Brookings*, 5 December 2019.

9. A. Khan, 'Is Russia Committing War Crimes By Bombing Hospitals in Ukraine?', *Al Jazeera*, 10 March 2022.

10. G. Kessler, 'The Iraq War and WMDs: An Intelligence Failure or a White House Spin?', *The Washington Post*, 22 March 2019.

11. E. MacAskill and J. Borger, 'Iraq War Was Illegal and Breached UN Charter, Says Annan', *The Guardian*, 16 September 2004.

12. J. Martyns Okeke, 'Why NATO Intervention in Libya Is Not a Victory for Responsibility to Protect', Institute for Security Studies, 10 April 2012.

13. Council on Foreign Relations Editors, 'Iran's Revolutionary Guards', Council on Foreign Relations Backgrounder, last updated 6 May 2019.

14. H. Hassan, 'The True Origins of ISIS', *The Atlantic*, 30 November 2018.

15. Mearsheimer, 'Why Ukraine Is The West's Fault?'.

16. G. Sauvage, 'Did NATO "Betray" Russia by Expanding to the East?', *France24*, 30 January 2022; P. Wintour, 'Russia's Belief in NATO "Betrayal" - and Why It Matters Today', *The Guardian*, 12 January 2022.

17. Wintour, ibid.

18. Ibid.

19. Associated Press, 'Vladimir Putin criticised NATO's Presence in Eastern Europe, says "They Played Us"', The Economic Times, 2 February 2022, available at https://economictimes.indiatimes.com/news/international/world-news/vladimir-putin-criticises-natos-presence-in-eastern-europe-says-they-played-us/videoshow/89287473.cms?from=mdr; Reuters Staff, 'Putin Criticises NATO Expansion as Alliance Holds London Summit, *Reuters*, 3 December 2019.

20. Mearsheimer, 'Why Ukraine Is The West's Fault?'.

21. T. Galen Carpenter, 'Many Predicted NATO Expansion Would Lead to War. Those Warnings Were Ignored', *The Guardian*, 28 February 2022.

22. T. L. Friedman, 'Foreign Affairs; Now A Word From Y', *The New York Times*, 2 May 1998.

23. Ibid.

24. Ibid.

25. Ibid; R.T. Davies, 'Kennan's Consistency', *The New York Times*, 10 May 1998.

26. *NATO Bucharest Summit Declaration, Issued by the Heads of State and Government Participating in the Meeting of the North Atlantic Council in Bucharest on 3 April 2008* (Bucharest: 2008), Para 23; available at https://www.nato.int/cps/en/natolive/official_texts_8443.htm.

27. Mearsheimer, 'Why Ukraine Is The West's Fault?'.

28. Ibid.
29. Ibid.
30. Ibid.
31. Ibid.
32. A. Cura, 'Boundary Claims of Separatists in Ukraine Could Hint At Extent of Russian Intervention', *AA*, 24 February 2022.
33. P. Dickinson, 'How Ukraine's Orange Revolution Shaped Twenty-First Century Politics', *Atlantic Council*, 22 November 2020.
34. Mearsheimer, 'Why Ukraine Is The West's Fault?'.
35. J.J. Mearsheimer, 'Why the Ukraine Crisis is the West's Fault: The Liberal Delusions That Provoked Putin', *Foreign Affairs*, Vol. 93(5), 2014, pp. 77-78.
36. Ibid, p. 77.
37. Ibid.
38. Mearsheimer, 'Why Ukraine Is The West's Fault?'.
39. N.R.F. Al-Rodhan, 'The "Emotional" Amoral Egoism of States', *The Montréal Review*, May 2015.
40. See Chapter 5 and N.R.F. Al-Rodhan, 'A Neuro-Philosophy of Global Order: The Case for Symbiotic Realism, Multi-Sum Security and Just Power', *Blog of the American Philosophical Association*, 23 May 2019.
41. BBC, 'Ukraine: What Sanctions Are Being Imposed Against Russia?', *BBC*, 9 March 2022; M. Bělin and J. Hanousek, 'Making Sanctions Bite: The EU-Russian Sanctions of 2014', *VOX EU/ CEPR*, 29 April 2019.
42. J. Beale, 'Ukraine: Are Arms Shipments From the West Making a Difference?', *BBC*, 8 March 2022.
43. BBC, 'Ukraine: What Sanctions Are Being Imposed Against Russia?', ibid.
44. European Commission, 'Ukraine: EU Agrees to Extend the Scope of Sanctions on Russia and Belarus, European Commission, 9 March 2022.
45. M. Shields and S. Koltroiwtz, 'Neutral Swiss Join EU Sanctions Against Russia in Break With Past,' *Reuters*, 28 February 2022.
46. BBC, 'Ukraine: What Sanctions Are Being Imposed Against Russia?'.
47. A. Palazzo, 'EU to Ban Russian Flights in Effort to Further Isolate Putin', *TIME*, 27 February 2022; D. Koenig, Z. Miller and C. Rugaber, 'President Biden Bans Russian Planes from US Airspace', *TIME*, 1 March 2022.
48. L. Kayali, 'RT France Challenges EU Ban Before Court', *Politico*, 8 March 2022; A. Sherman, 'Russia-backed Cable News Station RT America Shuts Down Operations Immediately Amid Ukraine Invasion', *CNBC*, 3 March 2022.
49. C. Baldi, 'L'Università Bicocca Cancella il Corso di Paolo Nori Su Dostoevskij. Lo Scrittore in Lacrime: "E' Censura". Poi il Dietrofront Dell'Ateneo', *La Stampa*, 2 Marzo 2022.
50. J. Clinton and S. Butler, 'IKEA Closes All Stores Amid Exodus of Western Firms', *The Guardian*, 3 March 2022.

51. K. Buchholz, 'Which European Countries Depend on Russian Gas?,' *Statista*, 24 February 2022; E. Krukowska and A. Nardelli, 'EU Aims to Cut Russia Gas Dependence by Almost 80% This Year', *Bloomberg*, 7 March 2022.

52. BBC, 'Ukraine Conflict: Petrol At Fresh Record as Oil and Gas Prices Soar', *BBC*, 8 March 2022.

53. Z. Weise, 'Germany Shelves Nord Stream 2 Pipeline', *Politico*, 22 February 2022.

54. S. Munir Khasru, 'Ukraine War: Asia Caught in Rip Tide of Power Polarisation and Sanctions Chaos,' *South China Morning Post*, 28 February 2022.

55. M. Nichols and H. Pamuk, 'Russia Vetoes UN Security Council Action on Ukraine as China Abstains', *Reuters*, 26 February 2022.

56. Al Jazeera, 'UN Resolution Against Ukraine Invasion: Full Text', *Al Jazeera*, 3 March 2022.

57. A. Roth, S. Walker, J. Rankin and J. Borger, 'Putin Signals Escalation As He Puts Russia's Nuclear Force On High Alert', *The Guardian*, 28 February 2022.

58. Khan, 'Is Russia Committing War Crimes By Bombing Hospitals in Ukraine?'.

59. B. Plett Usher,' Ukraine Conflict: Why Biden Won't Send Troops to Ukraine', *BBC*, 25 February 2022.

60. N. Dhanesha, 'How To Think About the Risk of Nuclear War, According to Three Experts', *Vox*, 27 February 2022.

61. BBC, 'How Many Refugees Have Fled Ukraine and Where Are They Going?', *BBC*, 10 March 2022.

62. Jurist Staff, 'Ukraine Dispatch: "The Infrastructure of Several Cities Has Been Destroyed"', *Jurist*, 2 March 2022.

63. The Economist, 'The Rouble's Collapse Compounds Russia's Isolation', *The Economist*, 28 February 2022.

64. S. Aleksashenko, 'How Much Damage Will Sanctions Do to Russia?,' *Al Jazeera*, 3 March 2022.

65. As discussed during the GCSP Staff and Fellows Briefing on 9 March 2022, held under Chatham House Rules.

66. Ibid.

67. D. Cave, 'The War in Ukraine Holds a Warning for the World Order', *New York Times*, 4 March 2022.

68. C. Michaelsen, 'What Are Sanctions, Do They Ever Work – And Could They Stop Russia's Invasion of Ukraine?', *The Conversation*, 27 February 2022.

69. As discussed during the GCSP Staff and Fellows Briefing on 9 March 2022, held under Chatham House Rules.

70. N.R.F. Al-Rodhan, 'Reconciliation Statecraft: Eight Competing Principal Interests, *Global Policy*, 1 February 2018.

71. Al-Rodhan, 'A Neuro-Philosophy of Global Order: The Case for Symbiotic Realism, Multi-Sum Security and Just Power'.

Bibliography

112.UA International, 'EBRD Improves Prediction of Growth of Ukraine's Economy for 2021', 29 June 2021

Aas, S., and D. Wasserman, 'Brain-Computer Interfaces and Disability: Extending Embodiment, Reducing Stigma?', *Journal of Medical Ethics* 42, no. 1 (2016), pp. 37–40

Abakhanov, E., 'New Environmental Code of Kazakhstan: Expectations and Prospects', Central Asian Bureau for Analytical Reporting, 6 April 2020

Abbany, Z., 'Modern Spy Satellites in an Age of Space Wars', *DW*, 25 August 2020

Abdalla, J., 'Biden to Broaden US-Mexican Relations, Keep Immigration at Top', Al Jazeera, 12 March 2021

Abia, A.L.K., 'River of Bacteria: A South African Study Pinpoints What's Polluting the Water', *The Conversation*, 24 November 2020

Abnett, K., 'Germany, France Throw Weight behind EU's "Green" Recovery Plan', Reuters, 19 May 2020, https://www.reuters.com/article/us-eu-recovery -climate-idUSKBN22V1ZB

Abrahams, N., S. Mhlongo, K. Dunkle, E. Chirwa, C. Lombard, S. Seedat, A.P. Kengne *et al.*, 'Increase in HIV Incidence in Women Exposed to Rape', *AIDS* 35, no. 4 (2021), pp. 633–42

Abshir, M.M., 'Ethiopia, Eritrea, Somalia, Djibouti: The Constant Instability in the Horn of Africa', *Africa Report*, 20 April 2021

Abtew, W., and S.B. Dessu, *The Grand Ethiopian Renaissance Dam on the Blue Nile* (Cham: Springer Nature, 2019)

Adeney, K., and F. Boni, 'How China and Pakistan Negotiate', Carnegie Endowment for International Peace, 24 May 2021

Adeto, Y.A., 'State Fragility and Conflict Nexus: Contemporary Security Issues in the Horn of Africa', *African Journal of Conflict Studies* 19, no. 1 (2019)

ADS Group, 'Industry Facts and Figures 2017: A Guide to the UK's Aerospace, Defence, Security and Space Sectors', 12 June 2017, https://www .adsgroup.org.uk/facts/facts-figures-2017

Aerospace Meetings Brazil 2018, 'The Aerospace Industry in Brazil', http://
brazil.bciaerospace.com/index.php/en/am-brazil/aerospace-industry-in
-brazil (accessed 30 June 2021)

AFE East Asia, Columbia University, 'Economy and Trade Factsheet: Basic
Points about Japan's Economy and Trading Patterns', http://afe.easia
.columbia.edu/japan/japanworkbook/economics/factshe.htm (accessed 30
June 2021)

Agarwal, S., 'Infrastructure Sector Crucial for India's Economic Growth,
but These Roadblocks Need to Be Managed', *Financial Express*, 20
February 2021

Agayev, Z., 'BP's Caspian Sea Project Emerges as Russia's Rival for European
Gas Market', World Oil, 31 December 2020

Agibalova, V., S. Buntovski, A. Khachirov, A. Osipova and E. Drannikova,
'Rural-Urban Segregation: A Special Case of Researching Monetary Income
of the Population', *International Journal of Innovation, Creativity and
Change* 14, no. 9 (2020), pp. 367–77

Ahmed, N., 'Remembering the 2002 Arab Peace Initiative', *Middle East
Monitor*, 28 March 2021

Ahmed, S., and J. Fullerton, 'Challenges of Reducing Maternal and Neonatal
Mortality in Indonesia: Ways Forward', *International Journal of Gynecology
and Obstetrics* 144, no. S1 (2019), pp. 1–3

Aisch, G., M. Bloch, K.K.R. Lai and B. Morenne, 'How France Voted', *The
New York Times*, 7 May 2017

Aitkhozhina, D., 'Environmental Work Can Be Undesirable in Russia',
Human Rights Watch, 14 January 2021Akylbayev, I., and B.Y.S. Wong,
'What Kazakhstan Can Teach about Medium-State Diplomacy', *Foreign
Policy*, 4 May 2021

Akyol, M., 'Turkey's Troubled Experiment with Secularism', The Century
Foundation, 25 April 2019

Alakbarov, F., 'Water-Related Pollution Matters. Just Look at the Aral Sea',
Jerusalem Post, 12 August 2017

Alam, M.B., 'Contextualising India-Russia Relations', *World Affairs: The
Journal of International Issues* 23(1), pp. 48–59

Alas, H., 'The Rise of African Nations' Populations', *US News*, 24
December 2020

Alekseeva, N., N. Antoshkova and V. Vasilenok, 'The Potential of Human
Capital's Development in Russia in the Digital Age', *Atlantis Highlights in
Computer Science* (September 2019), pp. 9–12

Alexander, C., and W. Shankley, '5 Ethnic Inequalities in the State Education
System in England', in B. Byrne, C. Alexander, O. Khan, J. Nazroo and W.
Shankley (eds), *Ethnicity and Race in the UK: State of the Nation* (Bristol:
Bristol University Press, 2020), pp. 93–125

Alilat, F., 'Algeria: France Urged to Reveal Truth about Past Nuclear Tests',
Africa Report, 10 September 2020

Alivisatos, A.P., M. Chun, G.M. Church, K. Deisseroth, J.P. Donoghue, R.J. Greenspan, P.L. McEuen *et al.*, 'Neuroscience: The Brain Activity Map', *Science* 339, no. 6125 (2013), pp. 1284–85

Aliyev, N., 'Russia's Military Capabilities in the Caspian', CACI, 21 February 2019

Al Jazeera, 'Amid Tensions, US and Russia Hold "Substantive" Arms Talks', 28 July 2021

Al Jazeera, 'China-Australia Tensions Explained in 500 Words', 1 December 2020, https://www.aljazeera.com/economy/2020/12/1/australia -china-tensions-explained-in-500-words

Al Jazeera, 'Ethiopia's Massive Nile Dam Explained', 8 July 2021

Al Jazeera, 'Israeli Settlements Amount to "War Crime", UN Expert', 9 July 2021

Al Jazeera, 'Libya Militias Rake in Millions in European Migration Funds: AP', 31 December 2019

Al Jazeera, 'Purchase of S-400 a "Done Deal", Turkey Tells US', 24 March 2021

Alkhathlan, K., D. Gately and M. Javid, 'Analysis of Saudi Arabia's Behavior within OPEC and the World Oil Market', *Science Direct* 64 (2014), pp. 209–25

Allinder, S.M., and J. Fleischman, 'The World's Largest HIV Epidemic in Crisis: HIV in South Africa', Center for International and Strategic Studies, 2 April 2019

Allison, G., 'The Impact of Globalization on National and International Security', in J.S. Nye Jr and J.D. Donahue (eds), *Governance in a Globalizing World* (Washington, DC: Brookings Institution Press, 2000), pp. 72–85

Almeida, R.M., S.K. Hamilton, E.J. Rosi, N. Barros, C.R.C. Doria, A.S. Flecker, A.S. Fleischmann *et al.*, 'Hydropeaking Operations of Two Run-of-River Mega-Dams Alter Downstream Hydrology of the Largest Amazon Tributary', *Frontiers in Environmental Science* 8, no. 120 (22 July 2020), pp. 1–11

Al-Rodhan, N.R.F., *Emotional Amoral Egoism: A Neurophilosophy of Human Nature and Motivations*, 2nd edn (Cambridge: Lutterworth Press, forthcoming 2021)

Al-Rodhan, N.R.F., *Meta-Geopolitics of Outer Space: An Analysis of Space Power, Security and Governance* (Basingstoke: Palgrave Macmillan, 2012)

Al-Rodhan, N.R.F., *Sustainable History and Human Dignity: A Neurophilosophy of History and the Future of Civilisation*, 2nd edn (Cambridge: Lutterworth Press, forthcoming 2021)

Al-Rodhan, N.R.F., *Sustainable History and the Dignity of Man* (Münster: LIT, 2009)

Al-Rodhan, N.R.F., *Symbiotic Realism: A Theory of International Relations in an Instant and an Interdependent World* (Berlin: LIT, 2007)

Al-Rodhan, N.R.F., *The Five Dimensions of Global Security: Proposal for a Multi-sum Security Principle* (Berlin: LIT, 2007)

Al-Rodhan, N.R.F., *The Politics of Emerging Strategic Technologies: Implications for Geopolitics, Human Enhancement and Human Destiny* (London: Palgrave Macmillan, 2011)

Al-Rodhan, N.R.F., *The Role of the Arab-Islamic World in the Rise of the West: Implications for Contemporary Trans-Cultural Relations* (London: Palgrave Macmillan, 2012)

Al-Rodhan, N.R.F., *The Three Pillars of Sustainable National Security in a Transnational World* (Berlin: LIT, 2008)

Al-Rodhan, N.R.F., '3 Disruptive Frontier Risks that Could Strike by 2040', World Economic Forum, 18 December 2020

Al-Rodhan, N.R.F., 'A Neurophilosophy of Fake News, Disinformation and Digital Citizenship', *Blog of the American Philosophical Association*, 25 August 2020

Al-Rodhan, N.R.F., 'A Neurophilosophy of Fear-Induced Pre-Emptive Aggression and Pseudo-Altruism', *Blog of the American Philosophical Association*, 4 August 2020

Al-Rodhan, N.R.F., 'A Neurophilosophy of Governance of Artificial Intelligence and Brain-Computer Interface', *Blog of the American Philosophical Association*, 1 June 2020

Al-Rodhan, N.R.F., 'A Neurophilosophy of Human Nature: Emotional Amoral Egoism and the Five Motivators of Humankind', *Blog of the American Philosophical Association*, 4 April 2019

Al-Rodhan, N.R.F., 'A Neurophilosophy of Two Technological Game-Changers: Synthetic Biology and Superintelligence', *Blog of the American Philosophical Association*, 29 June 2020

Al-Rodhan, N.R.F., 'COVID-19 Has Shown the World Is Not Prepared for Potential Bioweapons', CAPX, 2 September 2020

Al-Rodhan, N.R.F., 'Cyber Security and Space Security', *Space Review*, 26 May 2020

Al-Rodhan, N.R.F., 'Free Will in the Age of Neuromodulation', *Philosophy Now*, no. 127 (2018)

Al-Rodhan, N.R.F., 'Global Navigation Satellite Systems: A Symbiotic Realist Paradigm', *Space Review*, 15 February 2021

Al-Rodhan, N.R.F., 'Hypersonic Missiles and Global Security', *The Diplomat*, 13 November 2015

Al-Rodhan, N.R.F., 'Inevitable Transhumanism? How Emerging Strategic Technologies Will Affect the Future of Humanity', ETH Zürich Center for Security Studies, 29 October 2013

Al-Rodhan, N.R.F., 'In Space, Either We All Win, or We All Lose', *Parliament Magazine*, 28 October 2020

Al-Rodhan, N.R.F., 'Major Transformative Technologies and the Five Dimensions of Global Security', *Oxford Political Review*, 23 June 2020, http://oxfordpoliticalreview.com/2020/06/23/major-transformative -technologies-and-the-five-dimensions-of-security

Al-Rodhan, N.R.F., 'Meta-Geopolitics of Pandemics: The Case of COVID-19', *Global Policy*, 8 May 2020

Al-Rodhan, N.R.F., 'Meta-Geopolitics: The Relevance of Geopolitics in the Digital Age', *E-International Relations*, 25 May 2014

Al-Rodhan, N.R.F., 'Neuromorphic Computers: What Will They Change?', *Global Policy*, 18 February 2016

Al-Rodhan, N.R.F., 'Neurophilosophy and Transhumanism', *Blog of the American Philosophical Association*, 19 February 2019

Al-Rodhan, N.R.F., 'Predisposed Tabula Rasa', *The Oxford University Politics Blog*, 15 May 2015

Al-Rodhan, N.R.F., 'Proposal of a Dignity Scale for Sustainable Governance', *The Oxford University Politics Blog*, 29 January 2016

Al-Rodhan, N.R.F., 'Quantum Computing and Global Security', *Geneva Centre for Security Policy*, 20 February 2015

Al-Rodhan, N.R.F., 'Reconciliation Statecraft: Eight Competing Principal Interests', ETH Zürich Center for Security Studies, 7 February 2018

Al-Rodhan, N.R.F., 'Strategic Culture and Pragmatic National Interest', *Global Policy*, 22 July 2015

Al-Rodhan, N.R.F., 'The "Ocean Model of Civilization", Sustainable History Theory, and Global Cultural Understanding', *The Oxford University Politics Blog*, 1 June 2017

Al-Rodhan, N.R.F., 'The Emotional Amoral Egoism of States', *The Oxford University Politics Blog*, 25 June 2015

Al-Rodhan, N.R.F., 'The Meta-Geopolitics of Geneva 1815–2015', ETH Zürich Center for Security Studies, 26 February 2015

Al-Rodhan, N.R.F., 'The Social Contract 2.0: Big Data and the Need to Guarantee Privacy and Civil Liberties', *The Oxford University Politics Blog*, 22 September 2014

Al-Rodhan, N.R.F., 'The "Sustainable History" Thesis: A Guide for Regulating Trans- and Post-Humanism', *E-International Relations*, 24 April 2018, https://www.e-ir.info/2018/04/24/the-sustainable-history-thesis-a-guide-for-regulating-trans-and-post-humanism

Al-Rodhan, N.R.F., 'Weaponization and Outer Space Security', *Global Policy Journal*, 12 March 2018

Al-Rodhan, N.R.F., 'What Will Space Look Like in 2021?', *Space Review*, 11 January 2021, https://www.thespacereview.com/article/4103/1

Al-Rodhan, N.R.F., and L. Watanabe (eds), *A Proposal for Inclusive Peace and Security* (Geneva: Slatkine, 2007)

Al-Rodhan, N.R.F., G.P Herd and L. Watanabe, *Critical Turning Points in the Middle East, 1915–2015* (Hampshire: Palgrave Macmillan, 2011)

Al-Rodhan, N.R.F., and S. Kuepfer, *Stability of States: The Nexus between Transnational Threats, Globalization, and Internal Resilience* (Geneva: Slatkine, 2007)

Al Sanah, R., J. Bsoul and T. Habjouqa, '"The Illusion of Citizenship Has Gone": Israel's Arabs Look to the Future', *The Economist 1843 Magazine*, 19 May 2021

Al-Sarhan, S., 'Saudi Arabia, the Natural Leader of the Muslim World', *Arab News*, 4 February 2021

Al Tamimi, J., 'Saudis Back Women's Role in Public Life', *Gulf News*, 28 May 2014

Alterman, J.B., 'Russia, the United States, and the Middle East', CSIS, 21 July 2017

Altynbayev, K., 'Eyeing "Plenty of Threats", Kazakhstan Ramps up Defence Spending', *Caravanserai*, 15 May 2019

Alwazir, A., and J. Dichter, 'USSABC Economic Brief: Saudi Arabia's Emergence in Cyber Technology', US-Saudi Arabian Business Council, January 2020

Amanbekova, R., 'Alcohol Consumption in Central Asia', Central Asian Bureau for Analytical Reporting, 9 March 2020

Amaro, S., 'The Coronavirus Crisis Has Changed the German Mindset – and This Matters for Markets', CNBC, 6 July 2020

American Association for the Advancement of Science, 'A Snapshot of US R&D Competitiveness: 2020 Update', 22 October 2020, https://www.aaas .org/news/snapshot-us-rd-competitiveness-2020-update

American University School of Education, 'What the US Education System Needs to Reduce Inequality', 11 July 2018

Amnesty International, 'Afghanistan: Country's Four Million Internally Displaced Need Urgent Support amid Pandemic', 30 March 2021

Amnesty International, 'Indonesia 2020', https://www.amnesty.org/en /countries/asia-and-the-pacific/indonesia/report-indonesia (accessed 30 June 2021)

Amnesty International, 'Iran 2020', https://www.amnesty.org/en/countries /middle-east-and-north-africa/iran/report-iran

Amnesty International, 'Iran: More than 100 Protesters Believed to Be Killed as Top Officials Give Green Light to Crush Protests', 19 November 2019

Amnesty International, 'Israel and Occupied Palestinian Territories 2020', https://www.amnesty.org/en/location/middle-east-and-north-africa /israel-and-occupied-palestinian-territories/report-israel-and-occupied -palestinian-territories/ (accessed 12 January 2022).

Amnesty International, 'Nigeria 2020', https://www.amnesty.org/en /countries/africa/nigeria/report-nigeria (accessed 20 June 2021)

Amnesty International, 'Russian Federation', https://www.amnesty.org /en/countries/europe-and-central-asia/russian-federation (accessed 30 June 2021)

Amnesty International, 'South Africa: Broken and Unequal Education Perpetuating Poverty and Inequality', 11 February 2020

Amnesty International, 'Turkey: Women across the World Demand Reversal of Decision to Quit Gender-Based Violence Treaty', 10 May 2021

Andersen, T.M., G. Basso, C. Degryse, M. Dolls, W. Eichhorst, A.C. Hemerijck, T. Leoni *et al.*, 'The Welfare State after the Great Recession', *Intereconomics* 47, no. 4 (2012), pp. 200–29

Anggoro, K., 'Transnational Security Concerns, Defence Modernization and Security Cooperation in Southeast Asia', *Dialogue + Cooperation* 3 (2003), pp. 25–28

Antoni, M.-L., 'In South Africa, Abalone Farming Goes for Gold', Global Seafood Alliance, 22 October 2018

Appunn, K., 'The History behind Germany's Nuclear Phase-Out', Clean Energy Wire, 9 March 2021

Appunn, K., F. Eriksen and J. Wettengel, 'Germany's Greenhouse-Gas Emissions and Energy Transition Targets', Clean Energy Wire, 16 August 2021

Arab News, 'Saudi Arabia Most Improved Economy for Business', 29 May 2019

Arab News, 'Scholarship Students Abroad Promote Vision 2030', 26 May 2016

Arab Times, 'Poor Infrastructure an Obstacle to Development in Iran Football', 22 December 2020

Arab Weekly, 'Cracks Emerging in Libya's Veneer of National Unity', 12 May 2021

Arctic Council, 'About the Arctic Council', https://arctic-council.org/en /about (accessed 30 July 2021)

Argy, V., and L. Stein, *The Japanese Economy* (London: Palgrave Macmillan, 1997)

Ariffin, Y., J.-M. Coicaud and V. Popovski (eds), *Emotions in International Politics: Beyond Mainstream International Relations* (Cambridge: Cambridge University Press, 2015)

Armitage, R.L., and J.S. Nye Jr, *CSIS Commission on Smart Power* (Washington, DC: CSIS, 2007)

Armitage, R.L., and J.S. Nye Jr, 'Stop Getting Mad, America. Get Smart', *Washington Post*, 9 December 2007

Arms Control Association, 'Arms Control and Proliferation Profile: France', July 2019, https://www.armscontrol.org/factsheets/franceprofile

Arms Control Association, 'Nuclear Weapons: Who Has What at a Glance', October 2021, https://www.armscontrol.org/factsheets /Nuclearweaponswhohaswhat

Arms Control Association, 'The Outer Space Treaty at a Glance', October 2020, https://www.armscontrol.org/factsheets/outerspace

Army Technology, 'Russia and Kazakhstan Sign Military Cooperation Agreement', 19 October 2020

Arroll, B., 'Common Cold', *BMJ Clinical Evidence* PMCID: PMC3275147, PMID: 21406124 (2011), pp. 1–27

Arudou, D., *Embedded Racism: Japan's Visible Minorities and Racial Discrimination* (Lanham, MD: Lexington Books, 2015)

Ashimov, A., 'Kazakhstan to Modernise Armed Forces' Weaponry in Defence-Spending Plan', *Caravanserai*, 14 February 2020

Aslany, M., 'The Indian Middle Class, Its Size, and Urban-Rural Variations', *Contemporary South Asia* 27, no. 2 (2019), pp. 196–213

Asser, M., 'Egypt: A Permanent Emergency?', BBC News, 27 March 2007

Associated Press, 'North Korea's Kim Vows to Be Ready for Confrontation with the US', NPR, 18 June 2021

Associated Press, 'US Declares Pakistan's Separatist Baluchistan Liberation Army as Terrorist Group', *Indian Express*, 3 July 2019, https://indianexpress .com/article/pakistan/us-declares-pakistans-separatist-baluchistan -liberation-army-as-terrorist-group-5812092

Astakhova, O., and C. Sezer, 'Turkey, Russia Launch TurkStream Pipeline Carrying Gas to Europe', Reuters, 8 January 2020

Asylum Information Database, 'Country Report: France', 2017 update, https://asylumineurope.org/wp-content/uploads/2018/02/report -download_aida_fr_2017update.pdf

Atesagaoglu, O.E., C. Elgin and O. Oztunali, 'TFP Growth in Turkey Revisited: The Effect of Informal Sector', *Central Bank Review* 17, no. 1 (2017), pp. 11–17

Atkins, G., A. Cheung, J. Marshall and G. Tetlow, *Barriers to Delivering New Domestic Policies* (London: Institute for Fiscal Studies, 2019)

Atlantic Council, 'Experts React: What's Next after the Israel-Hamas Ceasefire?', 20 May 2021

Atrache, S., 'Lebanon Needs Help to Cope with Huge Refugee Influx', International Crisis Group, 19 September 2016

Atun, R.A., and S. Fitzpatrick, *Advancing Economic Growth: Investing in Health* (London: Chatham House, 2005)

Austin, G., 'How Did the South China Dispute Begin and Where Is It Headed?', Scroll.in, 29 July 2020

Australian Bureau of Statistics, '2016 Census Community Profile', 23 October 2017

Australian Bureau of Statistics, 'Census of Population and Housing: Reflecting Australia, Stories from the Census, 2016', 28 June 2017, https://www.abs .gov.au/ausstats/abs@.nsf/Lookup/by%20Subject/2071.0~2016~Main%20 Features~Aboriginal%20and%20Torres%20Strait%20Islander%20 Population%20Data%20Summary~10

Australian Government, Australian Institute of Health and Welfare, *Australia's Health Expenditure: An International Comparison* (Canberra: AIHW, 2019), pp. 2–3

Australian Government, Australian Trade and Investment Commission, 'Australia Signs World's Largest Free Trade Agreement', Australian Government, 26 November 2020, https://www.austrade.gov.au/news/latest -from-austrade/2020-latest-from-austrade/australia-signs-worlds-largest -free-trade-agreement

Australian Government, Department of Agriculture, Water and the Environment, Australian Antarctic Program, 'Antarctic Territorial Claims', https://www.antarctica.gov.au/about-antarctica/law-and-treaty/history/antarctic-territorial-claims (accessed 24 June 2021)

Australian Government, Department of Foreign Affairs and Trade, 'Regional Comprehensive Economic Partnership', https://www.dfat.gov.au/trade/agreements/not-yet-in-force/rcep (accessed 23 July 2021)

Australian Government, Department of Health, 'The Australian Health System', last updated 7 August 2019

Australian Government, Geoscience Australia, 'Energy – Overview', https://www.ga.gov.au/scientific-topics/energy/basics (accessed 8 August 2021)

Australian Human Rights Commission, 'Asylum Seekers and Refugees', https://humanrights.gov.au/our-work/rights-and-freedoms/publications/asylum-seekers-and-refugees#detention (accessed 30 June 2021)

Australian Human Rights Commission, 'Australia Needs a National Anti-Racism Framework', 16 March 2021. https://humanrights.gov.au/about/news/speeches/australia-needs-national-anti-racism-framework

Australian Human Rights Commission, 'Race Discrimination', https://humanrights.gov.au/our-work/race-discrimination (accessed 26 June 2021)

Auyezov, O., 'Kazakhstan's Leader Nazarbayev Resigns after Three Decades in Power', *U.S. News*, 19 March 2019, https://www.usnews.com/news/world/articles/2019-03-19/president-of-kazakhstan-nursultan-nazarbayev-resigns

Avalon Project, The Covenant of the League of Nations (including amendments adopted to December 1924)

Avalon Project, Charter of the United Nations, 26 June 1945

Avert, 'HIV and AIDS in China', https://www.avert.org/professionals/hiv-around-world/asia-pacific/china (accessed 7 July 2021)

Avert, 'HIV and AIDS in Russia', https://www.avert.org/professionals/hiv-around-world/eastern-europe-central-asia/russia (accessed 30 June 2021)

Avert, 'HIV and AIDS in South Africa', https://www.avert.org/professionals/hiv-around-world/sub-saharan-africa/south-africa (accessed 30 June 2021)

Aviram, R., A. Hindi and S.A. Hammour, *Coping with Water Scarcity in the Jordan River Basin* (New York: The Century Foundation, 2020)

Awdel, Z.M., N.M. Odel and W.F. Saadi, 'The Rise of the Globalization and Its Effects on the Autonomy of State and Political Economy', *Journal of Critical Reviews* 7, no. 6 (2020), pp. 998–1000

Axworthy, L., 'Human Security and Global Governance: Putting People First', *Global Governance*, no. 7 (2001), pp. 19–23

Aybet, G., 'Turkey-US Relations: Where Now?' RUSI, Commentary, 30 April 2021, https://rusi.org/explore-our-research/publications/commentary/turkey-us-relations-where-now

Aydintasbas, A., J. Barnes-Dacey, C. Bianco, H. Lovatt and T. Megerisi, 'Cooling-off: How Europe Can Help Stabilise the Middle East', European Council on Foreign Relations, Commentary, 18 June 2021

Aykol, M., *Turkey's Troubled Experiment with Secularism* (New York: The Century Foundation, 2019), https://tcf.org/content/report/turkeys-troubled-experiment-secularism/?agreed=1

Ayton-Shenker, D., 'The Challenge of Human Rights and Cultural Diversity', United Nations, Background Note, March 1995

Baczynska, C., 'Factbox: EU Divisions over Migration to Resurface under New Plan', Reuters, 23 September 2020

Baghdassarian, A., 'Congressional Recognition of the Armenian Genocide – 104 Years of Denial', *Harvard Human Rights Journal* 34, no. 1 (2021), n.p.

Bahgat, G., 'Maritime Security in the Persian Gulf', *Middle East Policy* 26, no. 4 (2019), pp. 67–78

Bak, H., 'Low Fertility in South Korea', in A. Farazmand (ed.), *Global Encyclopedia of Public Administration, Public Policy, and Governance* (Cham: Springer, 2019), pp. 1–11

Bakaite, J., 'LRT FACTS: Is Lithuania the World's Fastest-Shrinking Country?', *LRT*, 5 October 2020

Baker, P.H., 'Conflict Resolution: A Methodology for Assessing Internal Collapse and Recovery', in C. Pumphrey and R. Schwartz-Barcott (eds), *Armed Conflict in Africa* (Lanham, MD: Scarecrow Press, 2003)

Balasubramanian, S., R. Kumar and P. Loungani, 'Sustaining India's Growth Miracle Requires Increased Attention to Inequality of Opportunity', *Vox EU*, 12 March 2021

Baldwin, D., *Economic Statecraft* (Princeton, NJ: Princeton University Press, 1985)

Baltic Times, 'EU to Discuss Serious Sanctions Unless Minsk Releases Pratasevich – Lithuanian President', 24 May 2021

Bandarra, L., 'Brazilian Nuclear Policy under Bolsonaro: No Nuclear Weapons but a Nuclear Submarine', *Bulletin of the Atomic Scientists*, 12 April 2019

Banish, J., 'Education in Israel: The Arab-Jewish Divide', The Borgen Project, 21 January 2019

Barigazzi, J., and H. von der Burchard, 'EU Ministers and Borrell Urge Turkey to Stop Interfering in Libya', *Politico*

Barnett, T.P.M., *The Pentagon's New Map: War and Peace in the Twenty-First Century* (New York: Berkley Books, 2004)

Barnosky, A.D., E.A. Hadly, J. Bascompte, E.L. Berlow, J.H. Brown, M. Fortelius, W.M. Getz *et al.*, 'Approaching a State Shift in Earth's Biosphere', *Nature* 486, no. 7401 (2012), pp. 52–58

Barr, H., 'China's Bride Trafficking Problem', Human Rights Watch, 31 October 2019, https://www.hrw.org/news/2019/10/31/chinas-bride-trafficking-problem

Barrell, A., 'Which Diseases Cause the Most Death in the US?', *Medical News Today*, 25 June 2020

Bartnik, M., 'Boursiers: Les grandes écoles dans la tourmente' (Scholarship Students: Elite Schools in Crisis), *Le Figaro*, 8 January 2010

Basar, F., and N. Demirci, 'Domestic Violence against Women in Turkey', *Pakistan Journal of Medical Sciences* 34, no. 3 (May-June 2018), pp. 660–65

Bauomy, J., 'TurkStream: Europe Needs Gas and Russia Has It – The Story behind That New Pipeline', euronews, 8 January 2020

BBC, Ethics, 'Holy Wars', https://www.bbc.co.uk/ethics/war/religious/holywar.shtml (accessed 30 June 2021)

BBC, Religions, 'Hinduism and War', www.bbc.co.uk/religion (accessed on 13 November 2008)

BBC, Religions, 'Islam and War', www.bbc.co.uk/religion (accessed on 13 November 2008)

BBC, Religions, 'Jihad', www.bbc.co.uk/religion (accessed on 13 November 2008)

BBC, Religions, 'Judaism and War', www.bbc.co.uk/religion (accessed on 13 November 2008)

BBC News, 'China Launches First Module of New Space Station', 29 April 2021

BBC News, 'Egypt's Suez Canal Blocked by Huge Container Ship', 24 March 2021

BBC News, 'How Dangerous Is Mexico?', 18 February 2020, https://www.bbc.co.uk/news/world-latin-america-50315470

BBC News, 'Iran Nuclear Deal: US Joins Vienna Talks Aimed at Reviving Accord', 6 April 2021

BBC News, 'Iranian "Spy Ship" Damaged by Explosion in Red Sea', 7 April 2021

BBC News, 'Israel Strikes in Gaza after Fire Balloons Launched', 16 June 2021, https://www.bbc.com/news/world-middle-east-57492745

BBC News, 'Kazakh Leader Resigns after Three Decades', 19 March 2019

BBC News, 'Paris Attacks: France Remembers Night of Terror amid Jihadist Threat', 13 November 2020

BBC News, 'Profile: Arab League – Timeline', 5 November 2013

BBC News, 'Report: China Emissions Exceed All Developed Nations Combined', 7 May 2021

BBC News, 'Russia Offers Free Land to Stop Arctic Depopulation', 16 July 2020

BBC News, 'South China Sea Dispute: China's Pursuit of Resources "Unlawful", Says US', 14 July 2020

BBC News, 'Ukraine Crisis: Russia Halts Gas Supplies to Kiev', 16 June 2014

BBC News, 'US Election 2020: How to Spot Disinformation', https://www.bbc.com/news/av/world-us-canada-54518196 (accessed 30 June 2021)

BBC News, 'What Is Happening to the Size of the Army?', 22 March 2021

BBC News, 'Who Are the Uyghurs and Why Is China Being Accused of Genocide?' 21 June 2021

Beauchamp, Z., 'In Defence of the Two-State Solution', *Vox*, 26 May 2021

Beauchamp, Z., 'Rwanda's Genocide – What Happened, Why It Happened, and How It Still Matters', *Vox*, 10 April 2014

Beaulieu, E., and D. Klemen, 'You Say USMCA or T-MEC and I Say CUSMA: The New NAFTA – Let's Call the Whole Thing On' *School of Public Policy Publications SPP Briefing Paper* 13, no. 7 (2020), n.p.

Beehner, L., 'Israel and the Doctrine of Proportionality', Council on Foreign Relations, Backgrounder, 13 July 2006

Beeri, T., 'Start-Up Nation: Israel Spends Most Money in the World on R&D – WEF', *Jerusalem Post*, 5 November 2020

Beiser-McGrath, J., 'Targeting the Motivated? Ethnicity and Pre-emptive Use of Government Repression', *Swiss Political Science Review* 25, Issue 3 (2019), pp. 203–25

Bekzhanova, T.K., and A.B. Temirova, 'Non-observed Economy as Part of the Developing Economy', *Reports of the International Academy of Sciences of the Republic of Kazakhstan* 2, no. 324 (2019), pp. 215–22

Belfer Center for Science and International Affairs, 'South Asia Week: Pakistan's Role in Regional Stability', 25 April 2016

Bell, C., *The End of the Vasco da Gama Era: The Next Landscape of World Politics*, Lowy Institute Paper 21, (Sydney: Lowy Institute for International Policy, 2007)

Belot, C., 'Disentangling Varieties of French Nationalism: Why Does It Matter?', *French Politics* 19, no. 4 (2021), pp. 1–32

Bender, J., 'France's Military Is All over Africa', *Business Insider*, 22 January 2015

Bennett, M., 'The Arctic Shipping Route No One's Talking About', *Maritime Executive*, 8 May 2019

Bennetts, M., 'Russia's Brain Drain Soars as Scientists Flee "Spy Mania"', *The Times*, 22 April 2021, https://www.thetimes.co.uk/article/russia-brain -drain-scientists-flee-spy-mania-vladimir-putin-wbbrknzkc

Bennetts, M., 'The Epidemic Russia Doesn't Want to Talk About', *Politico*, 11 May 2020

Ben-Shaul, D., 'Israel Environment and Nature: Environmental Issues', Jewish Virtual Library, https://www.jewishvirtuallibrary.org/environmental -issues-in-israel (accessed 30 June 2021)

Bereuter, D., and D. Glickman, *Stability in the 21st Century: Global Food Security for Peace and Prosperity* (Chicago: Chicago Council on Global Affairs, 2017), https://www.thechicagocouncil.org/research/report/stability -21st-century-global-food-security-peace-and-prosperity

Berk, I., and S. Schulte, 'Turkey's Role in Natural Gas – Becoming a Transit Country?', EWI Working Paper, no. 17/01, January 2017

Berlinger, J., 'North Korea, Syria and Myanmar among Countries Defending China's Actions in Xinjiang', CNN, 15 July 2019

Berman, I., 'Slouching toward Eurasia?', *Perspective* 12, no. 1 (September-October 2001), https://www.ilanberman.com/5947/slouching-toward -eurasia

Bermingham, F., and L. Jeong-ho, 'One of China's Most Successful Investors Is Quietly Leaving', *inkstonebusiness*, 10 July 2019, https://www

.inkstonenews.com/business/samsung-and-other-south-korean-companies
-leave-china-sets-example-western-firms-fleeing-trade-war/article/3018033

Bernal-Meza, R., and L. Xing (eds), *China–Latin America Relations in the 21st Century: The Dual Complexities of Opportunities and Challenges* (Cham: Palgrave Macmillan, 2020)

Bernauer, H., J.W. Christopher, M. Deininger, P. Fischer, K. Habermeier, S. Heumann, H. Maurer *et al.*, 'Technical Solutions for Biosecurity in Synthetic Biology', *Industry Association Synthetic Biology* (2008), pp. 1–19

Bernstein, D., and N. Shaw, 'Anti-corruption in South Africa', *Global Compliance News*, https://www.globalcompliancenews.com/anti-corruption/anti-corruption-in-south-africa-2 (accessed 22 July 2021)

Besada, H., 'Enduring Political Divides in South Africa', Centre for International Governance Innovation, Technical Paper no. 3, 1 April 2007

Beviglia, G., '8 Facts about Education in Ukraine', The Borgen Project, 18 July 2019

Beyene, A.D., 'The Horn of Africa and the Gulf: Shifting Power Plays in the Red Sea', *Africa Report*, 16 November 2020

Bhaya, A.G., 'China Leads the World in Suicide Prevention', CGTN, 10 September 2019

Bhutta, N., A.C. Chang, L.J. Dettling and J.W. Hsu, with assistance from J. Hewitt, 'Disparities in Wealth by Race and Ethnicity in the 2019 Survey of Consumer Finances', Federal Reserve Notes, 28 September 2020

Bibi, F., S. Jameel and S.U. Jalal, 'What Is Democracy? Challenges for Democracy in Pakistan', *Global Political Review* 3, no. 1 (2018), pp. 66–75

Bickle, J., *The Oxford Handbook of Philosophy and Neuroscience* (Oxford: Oxford University Press, 2009)

Bijsterbosch, J., S.J. Harrison, S. Jbabdi, M. Woolrich, C. Beckmann, S. Smith and E.P. Duff, 'Challenges and Future Directions for Representations of Functional Brain Organization', *Nature Neuroscience* 23, no. 12 (2020), pp. 1484–95

Bilgic, A., 'Biden and the Iran Nuclear Deal: What to Expect from the Negotiations', *The Conversation*, 22 February 2021

Bittar, A., '5 Facts about Poverty in South Africa', The Borgen Project, 14 August 2020

Black, J., *Geopolitics and the Quest for Dominance* (Indiana: Indiana University Press, 2016)

Blackmore, E., 'The Kashmir Conflict: How Did It Start?', *National Geographic*, 2 March 2019

Blanchette, J., 'Xi's Gamble: The Race to Consolidate Power and Stave Off Disaster', *Foreign Affairs*, July/August 2021

Bland, B., 'Politics in Indonesia: Resilient Elections, Defective Democracy', Lowy Institute for International Policy, 19 April 2019

Blank, J., 'How the (Once) Most Corrupt Country in the World Got Clean(er)', *The Atlantic*, May 2019

Blank, S., *India's Energy Options in Central Asia*, SASSI Research Report 12 (London: SASSI, 2007),

Blatt, T.M., 'Anti-Satellite Weapons and the Emerging Space Arms Race', *Harvard International Review*, 26 May 2020

Bloch, A., and I. Saber, 'What's Driving the Conflict in the Eastern Mediterranean', *Lawfare*, 25 January 2021

Blöchliger, H., and S. Strumskyte, 'Greening Lithuania's Growth', OECD Economics Department, Working Paper no. 1667, 23 April 2021

Bloom, D.E., D. Canning and G. Fink, 'Implications of Population Aging for Economic Growth', National Bureau of Economic Research, Working Paper 16705 (January 2011), p. 3

Bluth, C., 'Norms and International Relations: The Anachronistic Nature of Neo-realist Approaches', POLIS Working Paper no. 12, February 2004 https://www .researchgate.net/profile/Christoph-Bluth/publication/239566016_Norms _and_International_Relations_The_anachronistic_nature_of_neo-realist _approaches/links/549c3de00cf2d6581ab482c9/Norms-and-International -Relations-The-anachronistic-nature-of-neo-realist-approaches.pdf

Boon, H.T., and G.K.H. Ong, 'Military Dominance in Pakistan and China–Pakistan Relations', *Australian Journal of International Affairs* 75, no. 1 (2021), pp. 80–102

Borden, K.A., and S.L. Cutter, 'Spatial Patterns of Natural Hazards Mortality in the United States', *International Journal of Health Geographics* 7, no. 64 (2008), pp. 1–13

Borgerson, S.G., 'Arctic Meltdown: The Economic and Security Implications of Global Warming', *Foreign Affairs* 87, no. 2 (March/April 2008), pp. 63–77

Borunda, A., 'Arctic Summer Ice Could Disappear as Early as 2035', *National Geographic*, 13 August 2020

Bostrom, N., 'Transhumanist Values', *Review of Contemporary Philosophy* 4, nos. 1–2 (2005), pp. 87–101

Boucher, A., and R. Breunig, 'We Need to Restart Immigration Quickly to Drive Economic Growth. Here's One Way to Do It Safely', *The Conversation*, 15 October 2020

Boudet, A., 'The Issue of Drug Trafficking from Afghanistan in Central Asia and Proposed Solutions', *Russian International Affairs Council*, 5 May 2016

Bradbury, C., 'Water Crisis in Saudi Arabia', The Borgen Project, 20 July 2020

Bramlett, S., 'Driven by Industry: Water Pollution in Russia from Coast to Coast', The Borgen Project, 13 March 2018

Brazil Institute, 'Brazil among Notable Absences in Latin America's Escazú Climate Agreement', Wilson Center, 24 May 2021

Brazil Institute, 'Healthcare Inequality and the COVID-19 Pandemic in Brazil', Wilson Center, 4 June 2020

Brazil Institute, 'Pandemic to Worsen Brazil's Troubling School Dropout Rates', Wilson Center, 30 October 2020

Brazil Institute, 'Worst. GDP. Ever. What Does the Future Hold for Brazil?', Wilson Center, 16 September 2020

Brazil Institute and P. Martins., 'Despite Gains, Black Brazilians Remain Underrepresented in Politics', Wilson Center, 24 February 2021

Breitenbauch, H., K.S. Kristensen and J. Groesmeyer, 'Military and Environmental Challenges in the Arctic', Carnegie Europe, 28 November 2019

Bridgestock, L., 'The Growing Popularity of International Study in Germany', QS TopUniversities, 23 February 2016

Brigham-Grette, J., and A. Dutton, 'Antarctica Is Headed for a Climate Tipping Point by 2060, with Catastrophic Melting If Carbon Emissions Aren't Cut Quickly', *The Conversation*, 17 May 2019

Brock, G., 'Global Justice', *The Stanford Encyclopedia of Philosophy* (Winter 2021 edition)

Brody, R., 'The Future of French Cinema', *New Yorker*, 2 January 2013

Brooks, S.G., *Producing Security: Multinational Corporations, Globalization, and the Changing Calculus of Conflict* (Princeton, NJ: Princeton University Press, 2005)

Brooks, T., 'Priti Patel's Immigration Reform Is a Confusing Mess That Will Leave Us Worse Off', *The Independent*, 29 May 2021

Brown, M.E., (ed.), *Grave New World: Security Challenges in the 21st Century* (Washington DC: Georgetown University Press, 2003)

Bryant, A., 'Algeria: 60 Years On, French Nuclear Tests Leave Bitter Fallout', DW, 13 February 2020

Bryza, M., 'The Greater Caspian Region: A New Silk Road, With or Without a New Belt', Atlantic Council, 29 February 2020

Brzezinski, Z., *The Grand Chessboard: American Primacy and Its Geostrategic Imperatives* (New York: Basic Books, 1997)

Brzica, N., 'Understanding Contemporary Asymmetric Threats', *Croatian International Relations Review* 24, no. 83 (2018), pp. 34–51

Budd, A., 'Gramsci's Marxism and International Relations', *International Socialism* 2, no. 114 (10 April 2007)

Budzinauskas, V., 'Despite Positive Changes, Social Problems Persist in Lithuania – EU Commission', *LRT*, 27 February 2021

Bull H., 'Hobbes and the International Anarchy', *Social Research* 48, no. 4 (Winter 1981),

Bundeswehr (German Federal Army), 'Einsatzzahlen – die Stärke der deutschen Kontingente', 18 August 2017, http://club.bruxelles2.eu/wp-content/uploads/2016/04/Chiffres-Opex-2016-@DE160422.pdf

Bunyard, J., 'What a New Naval Vessel Says about Iran's Ambitions at Sea', Newlines Institute for Strategy and Policy, 16 June 2021

Burak, B., 'Turkey's Authoritarian Slide and Political Decay', *International Policy Digest*, 14 February 2021

Burgess, T., J.R. Burgmann, S. Hall, D. Holmes and E. Turner, *Black Summer: Australian Newspaper Reporting on the Nation's Worst Bushfire Season*

(Melbourne: Monash University Climate Change Communication Research Hub, 2020)

Burkova, R., '"It's a Men's Club": Discrimination against Women in Iran's Job Market', Human Rights Watch, 25 May 2017

Burns, N., 'Brexit Is a Challenge Shared by the UK, the EU and the US', *The Security Times*, February 2020

Bush, G.W., 'The National Security Strategy of the United States', White House, September 2002

Business Insider, 'The 17 Countries Generating the Most Nuclear Power', 6 March 2014

Business Standard, 'Water Crisis Looms Large in Pakistan, May Face Absolute Scarcity by 2040', 22 March 2021

BusinessTech, 'South Africa Crime Stats 2020: Everything You Need to Know', 31 July 2020

BusinessTech, 'South Africa's Emigration Problem – No One Knows How Big the Brain Drain Really Is', 23 May 2019

Butler, R.A., 'Amazon Destruction', Mongabay, 4 December 2020

Butler, R.A., 'How to Save the Rainforest', *Mongabay*, 1 April 2019

Buzan, B., *People, States and Fear: The National Security Problem in International Relations* (Brighton: Wheatsheaf, 1983)

Buzan, B., and O. Wæver, *Regions and Powers: The Structure of International Security* (Cambridge: Cambridge University Press, 2003)

Byanyima, W., 'The Shocking Truth about Inequality Today', World Economic Forum, 21 January 2019

Cadwalladr, C., and E. Graham-Harrison, 'Revealed: 50 Million Facebook Profiles Harvested for Cambridge Analytica in Major Data Breach', *The Guardian*, 17 March 2018

Cagape, K., 'Why the Korean IT Industry Is One of the Best in the World', TECHINASIA, 16 May 2017

Cagaptay, S., and N. Gencsoy, 'Startup of the Baku-Tbilisi-Ceyhan Pipeline: Turkey's Energy Role', Policy Watch no. 998, Washington Institute for Near East Policy, 27 May 2005

Cairns, G., 'Indonesia: Tackling HIV in One of the World's Fastest Growing Epidemics', Aidsmap, 4 September 2018

Calamur, K., 'Denmark Claims Part of the Arctic, including the North Pole', NPR, 15 December 2014

Calderone, S., 'Kazakhstan is Central Asia's Migration Outlier', Eurasianet, 3 May 2018

Cameron-Chileshe, J., 'Campaigners Accuse UK Racial Inequality Report of Complacency', *Financial Times*, 1 April 2021

Campbell, J., 'Conflict in Nigeria is More Complicated than "Christians vs. Muslims"', Council on Foreign Relations, 1 May 2019

Campbell, J., 'South Africa', Council on Foreign Relations, https://www.cfr.org/expert-brief/south-africa (accessed 12 January 2022)

Campbell, J., 'Significant Rise of Insecurity in the Niger Delta through 2019, Council on Foreign Relations, 26 February 2020

Canadian Polar Commission, *International Polar Year Canadian Science Report: Highlights* (Ottawa: Canadian Polar Commission, 2012)

Canadian Seal Hunt, 'WWF Defends Pro Sealing Stance', 22 April 2006, https://www.canadiansealhunt.com/wwf.html#:~:text=WWF's%20 approach%20is%20designed%20to,is%20of%20the%20utmost%20 importance.

Car, Z., S. Baressi Šegota, N. Anđelić, I. Lorencin and V. Mrzljak, 'Modeling the Spread of COVID-19 Infection Using a Multilayer Perceptron', *Computational and Mathematical Methods in Medicine* 2020, Article ID 5714714 (2020), pp. 1–10

Carbon Brief, 'The Carbon Brief Profile: South Africa', 15 October 2018

Cardoso, F.H., A.N. Ferreira, C. Amorim, C. Lafer, F. Rezek, J. Serra, R. Ricupero and H. Kalout, 'Brazil's Foreign Policy Today Is a Violation of Its Own Constitution', *The Wire*, 13 May 2020

Care Quality Commission, *The State of Health Care and Adult Social Care in England 2019/20*, HC 799 (London: Care Quality Commission, 2020)

Carens, J.H., 'Aliens and Citizens: The Case for Open Borders', in W. Kymkicka (ed.), *The Rights of Minority Cultures* (Oxford: Oxford University Press, 1995), pp. 331–49

Carll, E., An Afghanistan at Peace Could Connect South and Central Asia', Atlantic Council, 18 May 2011

Carpenter, A., and A.G. Kostianoy (eds), *Oil Pollution in the Mediterranean Sea: Part I: The International Context* (Cham: Springer Nature Switzerland, 2019)

Carrington, D., 'Climate Crisis "Unequivocally" Caused by Human Activities, Says IPCC Report', *The Guardian*, 9 August 2021

Carrington, D., 'Plummeting Insect Numbers "Threaten Collapse of Nature"', *The Guardian*, 10 February 2019

Carlson, J.D., C. Hubach, J. Long, K. Minteer and S. Young, 'Scramble for the Arctic', *The SAIS Review of International Affairs* 33(2) (2013), pp. 21–43

Carvalho, E.M. de, S.S. Valverde and J.A.H. Muñoz, '*Aedes aegypti*: The Main Enemy of Public Health in Brazil: Challenges and Perspective for Public Health', IntechOpen, 27 November 2019

Casas, X., 'New Zika Cases in Brazil Overshadowed by Covid-19', Human Rights Watch, 28 May 2020

Casey, J.P., 'Hydropower and Geopolitics: Winners and Losers in the Indian Sub-Continent', Power Technology, 6 April 2021

Cavanagh, J., and J. Mander, 'World Bank, IMF Turned Poor Third World Nations into Loan Addicts', *CCPA Monitor* (July-August 2003), pp. 19–21

CEIC, 'South Korea Household Income Per Capita', https://www.ceicdata .com/en/indicator/korea/annual-household-income-per-capita (accessed 30 June 2021)

CEJIL, 'Brazil: Respect for the Rights of Indigenous Peoples Is Fundamental to Environmental Conservation', 11 February 2020

Center for Arms Control and Non-Proliferation, 'Fact Sheet: Pakistan's Nuclear Inventory', March 2021, https://armscontrolcenter.org/pakistans-nuclear-capabilities

Center for Arms Control and Non-Proliferation, 'History of India and Pakistan', 26 November 2019, https://armscontrolcenter.org/history-of-conflict-in-india-and-pakistan

Center for Global Development, 'Global Demographic Trends', https://www.cgdev.org/page/global-demographic-trends (accessed 30 June 2021)

Center for Global Health and Development, 'Egypt's Healthcare System', https://cghd.org/index.php/global-health-partnerships-and-solutions/profiles/43-egypts-health-care-system (accessed 30 June 2021)

Center for Strategic and International Studies, 'Exploiting Chaos: Russia in Libya', 23 September 2021

Center for Strategic and International Studies, 'Iran's Military and Nuclear Capabilities', https://www.csis.org/programs/burke-chair-strategy/iran/irans-military-and-nuclear-capabilities (accessed 30 June 2021)

Central Asian Bureau for Analytical Reporting, 'Pandemic and Suicide Issues in Kazakhstan: Prevention Strategies', 22 February 2021

Centre for Humanitarian Dialogue, *Agropastoral Mediation in the Sahel region of Mali, Niger and Burkina Faso* (Geneva: Centre for Humanitarian Dialogue, 2019)

Centre for the Protection of National Infrastructure, 'Threat Landscape', updated 31 March 2021, https://www.cpni.gov.uk/threat-landscape

Chairil, T., 'Cybersecurity for Indonesia: What Needs to Be Done?', *The Conversation*, 9 May 2019

Chamlou, N., 'COVID-19 Depressed Women's Employment Everywhere, and More So in Iran', Atlantic Council, 29 April 2021

Chandra, R., 'Need to Deregulate Indian Agriculture', Business World, 16 December 2020, http://www.businessworld.in/article/Need-to-Deregulate-Indian-Agriculture/16-12-2020-354240

Chase, R., E. Hill and P. Kennedy, *The Pivotal States: A New Framework for US Policy in the Developing World* (New York: W.W. Norton & Company, 1998)

Chatin, M., and G. Gallarotti, *Emerging Powers in International Politics: The BRICS and Soft Power* (Abingdon: Routledge, 2018)

Chaudoin, S., H.V. Milner and X. Pang, 'International Systems and Domestic Politics: Linking Complex Interactions with Empirical Models in International Relations', *International Organization* 69, no. 2 (2015), pp. 275–309

Chemin, J.E., and A.K. Nagel, 'Integration Policies, Practices and Experiences: Germany Country Report', Respond Migration, Working Paper Series 5, Paper 2020/51 (2020

Chen, J., 'Vanderbilt Researcher Finds that Supreme Court Ban on Race-Conscious College Admissions Would Restrict the Pipeline of Future Leaders', Vanderbilt University Research News, 10 June 2021

Chen, J.J., and V. Mueller, 'Climate Change Is Making Soils Saltier, Forcing Many Farmers to Find New Livelihoods', *The Conversation*, 29 November 2018

Chen, J.-L., S.-C. Kang, J.-M. Guo, M. Xu and Z.-M. Zhang, 'Variation of Sea Ice and Perspectives of the Northwest Passage in the Arctic Ocean', *Advances in Climate Change Research*, 15 February 2021

Chen, Y., P. Luo and T. Chang, 'Urbanization and the Urban-Rural Income Gap in China: A Continuous Wavelet Coherency Analysis', *Sustainability* 12, no. 19 (2020), pp. 1–14

Chestney, N., 'Analysis: Gas Faces Existential Crisis in Climate Wary Europe', *Reuters*, 14 May 2021

Chiao, J.Y., A.R. Hariri, T. Harada, Y. Mano, N. Sadato, T.B. Parrish and T. Iidaka, 'Theory and Methods in Cultural Neuroscience,' *Social Cognitive and Affective Neuroscience* 5, nos 2–3 (2010), pp. 356–61

Cho, J., G. Kim and T. Kwon, 'Employment Problems with Irregular Workers in Korea: A Critical Approach to Government Policy', *Pacific Affairs* 81, no. 3 (2008), pp. 407–26

Choudhary, A., 'Global Justice', *Global Encyclopedia of Public Administration, Public Policy, and Governance*, 6 July 2018

Chuanyi, C., and C. Xiaoli, 'Changing the Policy Paradigm on Chinese Migrant Workers', in E.P. Mendes and S. Srighanthan (eds), *Confronting Discrimination and Inequality in China: Chinese and Canadian Perspectives* (Ottawa: University of Ottawa Press, 2009), pp. 99–128

Cipollina, M., and L. Salvatici, 'On the Effects of EU Trade Policy: Agricultural Tariffs Still Matter', *European Review of Agricultural Economics* 47, no. 4 (2020), pp. 1367–1401

Clark, C., 'South Africa Confronts a Legacy of Apartheid: Why Land Reform Is a Key Issue in the Upcoming Election', *The Atlantic*, 3 May 2019

Clark, G.L., M.P. Feldman, M.S. Gertler and D. Wójcik (eds), *The New Oxford Handbook of Economic Geography* (Oxford: Oxford University Press, 2018)

Clary, C., and C. Talmadge, 'The US-Iran Crisis Has Calmed Down – But Things Won't Ever Go Back to How They Were Before', Brookings Institution, 13 September 2020

Claude, I.L., Jr, 'Swords into Ploughshares: The Problems and Progress of International Organization', in J.N. Moore (ed.), *National Security Law* (Durham, NC: Carolina Academic Press, 1990), pp. 42–46

Claude, I.L., Jr, 'Theoretical Approaches to National Security and World Order', in J.N. Moore (ed.), *National Security Law* (Durham, NC: Carolina Academic Press, 1990), pp. 3–14

Climate Action Tracker, 'Australia', updated 15 September 2020, https://climateactiontracker.org/countries/australia

Climate Action Tracker, 'South Africa', https://climateactiontracker.org
/countries/south-africa (accessed 30 June 2021)

Climate Action Tracker, 'Ukraine', 30 July 2020, https://climateactiontracker
.org/countries/ukraine

Climate Action, 'Germany Is the World's Leading Nation for Recycling', 11
December 2017

Climate Change Post, 'Climate Change: France', https://www.climatechange
post.com/france/climate-change (accessed 2 June 2021),

Coady, C.A.J., The Ethics of Armed Humanitarian Intervention, Peaceworks
No. 45 (Washington, DC: United States Institute of Peace, 2002)

Coch, D., K.W. Fischer and G. Dawson (eds), *Human Behavior, Learning, and
the Developing Brain: Typical Development* (New York: The Guilford Press,
2007)

Cockayne, J., State Fragility, Organised Crime and Peacebuilding: Towards
a More Strategic Approach, NOREF Report (Oslo: Norwegian Centre for
Conflict Resolution, 2011), pp. 1–2

Codevilla, A., *Informing Statecraft: Intelligence for a New Century* (New York:
Free Press, 2002)

Cohen-Almagor, R., 'Between Individual Rights and Group Rights,'
Academicus International Scientific Journal 18 (February 2018), pp. 9–25

Cohen, B.J., *Currency Statecraft: Monetary Rivalry and Geopolitical Ambition*
(Chicago: Chicago University Press, 2019)

Cohen, J., 'Russia's HIV/AIDS Epidemic Is Getting Worse, Not Better',
Science, 11 June 2018

Cohen, S.B., *Geopolitics of the World System* (New York: Rowman &
Littlefield, 2003)

Cohen, S.P., *The Idea of Pakistan* (Washington, DC: Brookings Institution
Press, 2004)

Coicaud, J.-M., and N.J. Wheeler, 'Introduction: The Changing Ethics of
Power beyond Borders', in J.-M. Coicaud and N.J. Wheeler (eds), *National
Interest and International Solidarity: Particular and Universal Ethics in
International Life* (New York: United Nations University Press, 2008),
pp. 1–24

Collin, J.-M., and P. Bouveret, 'Radioactivity under the Sand: The Waste from
French Nuclear Tests in Algeria', Heinrich Böll Stiftung, July 2020

Colombo, M., 'Mutual Reassurance: Why Europe Should Support Talks
between Egypt and Turkey', European Council on Foreign Relations, 14
January 2021

Commander, S., N. Isachenkova and Y. Rodionova, 'A Model of the Informal
Economy with an Application to Ukraine', *IZA*, 21 September 2009

Committee for a Responsible Federal Budget, 'Three Ways to Lower Health
Care Costs', 23 February 2021

Committee for Sydney, 'Australia Lags the Developed World on Research and
Development: It's Time to Catch Up', 27 August 2020

Commodity.com, 'Brazil's Economy: Foreign Trade Figures Reveal Why They're a Major Global Player', 7 April 2021, https://commodity.com/data/brazil

Compare Your Country, 'PISA 2018'

Conca, J., 'How 1,500 Nuclear-Powered Water Desalination Plants Could Save the World from Desertification', *Forbes*, 14 July 2019

Connell, M., 'Operation Sentinel Protects Gulf Shipping', The Iran Primer, 2 September 2020

Convention on Biological Diversity, 'Australia – Main Details'

Cook, M., 'ASEAN-Australia Relations: The Suitable Status Quo', Lowy Institute for International Policy, 6 August 2018

Cook, M., *Australia's South China Sea Challenges*, Lowy Institute Policy Brief (Sydney: Lowy Institute for International Policy, 2021)

Cooper, R., 'The New Liberal Imperialism', *The Guardian*, 7 April 2002

Corcoran, P., 'How Mexico's EPR Insurgents Have Changed Course', InSight Crime, 23 October 2013

Cordesman, A.H., 'America's Failed Strategy in the Middle East: Losing Iraq and the Gulf', CSIS, 2 January 2020

Cordesmann, A.H., 'Iran's Support of the Hezbollah in Lebanon', CSIS, 15 July 2006

Cordey, S., *Cyber Influence Operations: An Overview and Comparative Analysis* (Zürich: ETH Zürich Center for Security Studies, 2019)

Cormier, Z., 'Antarctica, the New Hot Real Estate', *Toronto Star*, 18 November 2007, http://www.thestar.com/News/Ideas/article/277390

Cornelissen, N., '5 Facts about France's Foreign Aid', The Borgen Project, 10 November 2020

Cornell, S.E., and M. Sultan, 'The Caspian Connection: The New Geopolitics of Central Eurasia', Caspian Brief, Cornell Caspian Consulting, December 2000, http://www.cornellcaspian.com/pub/0011centraleurasia.html

Cortright, D., 'Positive Inducements in International Statecraft', *Fraser Forum*, 2 May 2000 (based on a paper of the same title commissioned by the Fraser Institute)

Cortright, D., and G.A. Lopez, 'Carrots, Sticks and Cooperation: Economic Tools of Statecraft', in B.R. Rubin (ed.), *Cases and Strategies for Preventive Action* (Century Foundation Press, 1998) Cotterill, J., and C. Bruce-Lockhart, 'Black South Africans Lose Out as Economic Divide Bites', *Financial Times*, 2 May 2019

Council of Europe, 'Strengthening the Human Rights Protection of Migrants and Victims of Human Trafficking in Turkey', https://www.coe.int/en/web/ankara/strenghtening-the-human-rights-protection-of-migrants-and-victims-of-human-trafficking-in-turkey (accessed 30 June 2021)

Council on Foreign Relations, 'Global Conflict Tracker: Conflict between India and Pakistan', ,https://www.cfr.org/global-conflict-tracker/conflict/conflict-between-india-and-pakistan (accessed 30 June 2021)

Council on Foreign Relations, 'Global Conflict Tracker: Conflict in Ukraine', https://www.cfr.org/global-conflict-tracker/conflict/conflict-ukraine (accessed 30 June 2021)

Council on Foreign Relations, 'Global Conflict Tracker: North Korea Crisis', https://www.cfr.org/global-conflict-tracker/conflict/north-korea-crisis (accessed 30 June 2021)

Council on Foreign Relations, 'Mexico's Long War: Drugs, Crime and Cartels', Backgrounder, 26 February 2021

Council on Foreign Relations, 'US Relations with Iran, 1953–2021', https://www.cfr.org/timeline/us-relations-iran-1953-2021 (accessed 30 June 2021)

Cousins, B., 'Problematic Assumptions Raise Questions about South Africa's New Land Reform Plan', *The Conversation*, 26 October 2020

Craig Jones, T., 'America, Oil and War in the Middle East', *The Journal of American History* 99(1) (2012), pp. 208–218

Cravens, C., 'The Nationalisation of Iranian Oil', *Commodities, Conflict, and Cooperation* (Fall 2016 & Winter 2017)

Cresswell I.D., H. Murphy H, 'Biodiversity: Importance of biodiversity', in *Australia State of the Environment 2016* (Canberra: Australian Government Department of the Environment and Energy, 2016), https://soe.environment.gov.au/theme/biodiversity/topic/2016/importance-biodiversity.

Crisher, B., 'Altering *Jus ad Bellum*: Just War Theory in the 21st Century and the 2002 National Security Strategy of the United States', *Critique: A Worldwide Journal of Politics* (Spring 2005), pp. 1–30

Crisis 24, 'Egypt Country Report', https://crisis24.garda.com/insights-intelligence/intelligence/country-reports/egypt (accessed 1 July 2021)

Crisis 24, 'Lithuania Country Report', https://crisis24.garda.com/insights-intelligence/intelligence/country-reports/lithuania (accessed 22 July 2021)

Crisis 24, 'South Korea Country Report', https://crisis24.garda.com/insights-intelligence/intelligence/country-reports/south-korea (accessed 30 June 2021)

Crossley, G., and K. Needham, 'China Suspends Economic Dialogue with Australia as Relations Curdle', Reuters, 5 May 2021

Croucher, S., *Globalization and Belonging: The Politics of Identity in a Changing World* (Lanham, MD: Rowman & Littlefield, 2018)

CTBTO Preparatory Commission, 'Status of Signature and Ratification', http://www.ctbto.org/the-treaty/status-of-signature-and-ratification

Cunningham, S., 'Santo Antônio Mega-Dam on Brazil's Madeira River Disrupts Local Lives', Mongabay, 3 December 2018

Curtis, J., J. Lunn and M. Ward, 'The UK-China Relationship', House of Commons Library Research Briefing, 14 September 2020

D'Agostino, F., G. Gaus and J. Thrasher, 'Contemporary Approaches to the Social Contract', *The Stanford Encyclopedia of Philosophy* (Winter 2021 edition), E.N. Zalta (ed.), forthcoming

Dalay, G., 'Turkey, Europe, and the Eastern Mediterranean: Charting a Way out of the Current Deadlock', Brookings Institution, 28 January 2021

Dalby, S., *Anthropocene Geopolitics: Globalization, Security, Sustainability* (Ottawa: University of Ottawa Press, 2020)

Dallmeyer, S., P. Wicker and C. Breuer, 'How an Aging Society Affects the Economic Costs of Inactivity in Germany: Empirical Evidence and Projections', *European Review of Aging and Physical Activity* 14 (2017), pp. 1–9

Dalrymple, W., 'The East India Company: The Original Corporate Raiders', *The Guardian*, 4 March 2015

Daly, J.J., and R. Sitaram, 'BCI Therapeutic Applications for Improving Brain Function', in J. Wolpaw and E.W. Wolpaw (eds), *Brain-Computer Interfaces: Principles and Practice* (New York: Oxford University Press, 2012), pp. 351–62

D'Ambrogio, E., 'Japan's Ageing Society', European Parliamentary Research Service Briefings, December 2020

Daniels, J.P., '"Everything Is Collapsing": Colombia Battles Third Covid Wave amid Social Unrest', *The Guardian*, 22 June 2021

Davidson, H., 'US Official Warns China against "Catastrophic" Move on Taiwan', *The Guardian*, 7 July 2021

Davis, A., A. Terlikbayeva, A. Aifah, S. Hermosilla, Z. Zhumadilov, E. Berikova, S. Rakhimova *et al.*, 'Risks for Tuberculosis in Kazakhstan: Implications for Prevention', *International Journal of Tuberculosis and Lung Disease* 21, no. 1 (2017), pp. 86–92

Davydova, A., 'Environmental Activism in Russia: Strategies and Prospects', Center for Strategic and International Studies, 3 March 2021

Dayeong, L., '81% of Deaths in Korea Caused by Chronic Illnesses', *Korea Herald*, 20 August 2015

Dayton, L., 'How South Korea Made Itself a Global Innovation Leader', *Nature*, 28 May 2020

Death Penalty Information Center, 'DPIC Analysis: Racial Disparities Persisted in US Death Sentences and Executions in 2019', 21 January 2020

Deb, R., 'Covid-19: An Opportunity to Redesign India's Formal-Informal Economy Dynamics', Observer Research Foundation, 15 October 2020

Decety, J., and J.M. Cowell, 'Friends or Foes: Is Empathy Necessary for Moral Behavior?', *Perspectives on Psychological Science* 9, no. 4 (2014), pp. 525–37

DeConto, R.M., D. Pollard, R.B. Alley, I. Velicogna, E. Gasson, N. Gomez, S. Sadai *et al.*, 'The Paris Climate Agreement and Future Sea-Level Rise from Antarctica', *Nature* 593 (2021), pp. 83–89

Defense Post, 'After Eight Years of Mali Campaign, France Seeks Exit Strategy', 6 January 2021

Delcker, J., 'Cyber Threat Looms Large over German Election', *DW*, 25 May 2021

Delfi, 'Daugiausiai inovacijų lietuviai sukūrė gyvybės mokslų srityje', 14 September 2017, https://www.delfi.lt/partnerio-turinys/lietuvos

-amziaus-inovacijos/daugiausiai-inovaciju-lietuviai-sukure-gyvybes
-mokslu-srityje.d?id=75754757

Delfi, 'Įgyvendinta svajonė sukėlė perversmą pasaulinėje lazerių rinkoje',
25 August 2017, https://www.delfi.lt/partnerio-turinys/lietuvos-amziaus
-inovacijos/igyvendinta-svajone-sukele-perversma-pasaulineje-lazeriu
-rinkoje.d?id=75532853

Delfi, 'Lietuviai sukūrė vieną galingiausių lazerių pasaulyje', 31 August 2017,
https://www.delfi.lt/partnerio-turinys/lietuvos-amziaus-inovacijos
/lietuviai-sukure-viena-galingiausiu-lazeriu-pasaulyje.d?id=75607431

Deloitte, '2020 US and Global Life Sciences Outlook: Creating New Value:
Building Blocks for the Future', https://www2.deloitte.com/us/en/pages
/life-sciences-and-health-care/articles/us-and-global-life-sciences-industry
-trends-outlook.html (accessed 24 July 2021)

DeLorenzo, G., 'Water Quality in Kazakhstan', The Borgen Project, 21
June 2017

Dencik, J., and R. Spee, *Global Location Trends – 2018 Annual Report:
Getting Ready for Globalization 4.0*, July 2018, IBM Institute for Business
Value, p. 7

DeNicola, E., O.S. Aburizaiza, A. Siddique, A. Siddique, H. Khwaja and D.O.
Carpenter, 'Climate Change and Water Scarcity: The Case of Saudi Arabia',
Annals of Global Health 81, no. 3 (2015), pp. 342–53

Denney, S., 'Number of Irregular Workers Continue to Rise in South Korea',
The Diplomat, 10 November 2015

Dennison, J., and N. Carl, 'The Ultimate Causes of Brexit: History, Culture
and Geography', London School of Economics British Politics and Policy
blog, 18 July 2016

Dérer, P., 'The Iranian Miracle: The Most Effective Family Planning Program
in History?', The Overpopulation Project, 21 March 2019

Desheng, C., 'President: Promote Healthy Development of Private Sector',
China Daily, 17 September 2020

Dhasmana, I., 'India Will Need to Find Jobs for Additional 90 Mn, Says
McKinsey Report', *Business Standard*, 26 August 2020

Dhume, S., 'Is India Still a Democracy? The Answer Isn't So Clear', *Wall Street
Journal*, 15 April 2021

Diamond, J., 'Russian Hacking and the 2016 Election: What You Need to
Know', CNN, 16 December 2016

Die Bundesregierung, *Shaping Globalization – Expanding Partnerships –
Sharing Responsibility: A Strategy Paper by the German Government*
(Berlin: Federal Foreign Office, 29 March 2020)

Di Paola, A., J. Lee and B. Wingfield, 'Middle East Petro-States' Reliance on
China Surges with Covid-19', Al Jazeera, 3 June 2020

Dittmer, J., and D. Bos, *Popular Culture, Geopolitics, and Identity* (London:
Rowman & Littlefield, 2019)

Dodds, K., *Geopolitics: A Very Short Introduction*, 3rd edn (Oxford: Oxford
University Press, 2019)

Dodds, K., 'In 30 Years the Antarctic Treaty Becomes Modifiable, and the Fate of a Continent Could Hang in the Balance', *The Conversation*, 12 July 2018

Dolgin, E., 'Synthetic Biology Speeds Vaccine Development', *Nature*, 28 September 2020

Donakov, T., 'Kazakhstan – Building a Fair and Impartial Judicial System Fit for the Modern Age', *New Jurist*, 27 May 2019

Donley, A., 'Report: China to Be Nearly Self-Sufficient in Wheat, Rice By 2025', World-Grain.com, 26 May 2021

Donner, S.D., and S. Webber, 'Obstacles to Climate Change Adaptation Decisions: A Case Study of Sea-Level Rise and Coastal Protection Measures in Kiribati', *Sustainability Science* 9, no. 3 (2014), pp. 331–45

Donor Tracker, 'France', 30 June 2021, https://donortracker.org/country/france

Donor Tracker, 'Japan', 15 July 2021, https://donortracker.org/country/japan

Donovan, N., M. Smart, M. Moreno-Torres, J.O. Kiso and G. Zachariah, 'Countries at Risk of Instability: Risk Factors and Dynamics of Instability', Prime Minister's Strategy Unit Background Paper, February 2005, p. 3

Dorsey, J.M., 'Iran Signals Membership of China's Shanghai Cooperation Organization', *Arabian Post*

Doshmangir, L., M. Bazyar, A. Rashidian and V.S. Gordeev, 'Iran Health Insurance System in Transition: Equity Concerns and Steps to Achieve Universal Health Coverage', *International Journal for Equity in Health*, 20 (2021), pp. 1–14

Drabek, Z., and W. Payne, 'The Impact of Transparency on Foreign Direct Investment', *Journal of Economic Integration* 17, no. 4 (2002), pp. 777–810

Dreher, A., and S. Voigt, 'Does Membership in International Organisations Increase Governments' Credibility? Testing the Effect of Delegating Power', CESifo Working Paper Series no. 2285 (2008)

Drew, L., 'The Ethics of Brain-Computer Interfaces', *Nature* 571 (2019), pp. S19–S21

Drezner, D., 'How Smart are Smart Sanctions?', *International Studies Review*, no. 5 (2003), pp. 107–10

Duckett, S., 'How the US Health-Care System Works – and How Its Failures Are Worsening the Pandemic', *The Conversation*, 18 November 2020

Dudden, A., 'Japanese Territorial Disputes and the Legacy of Empire', *Oxford Research Encyclopedia of Asian History*, 29 July 2019

Dugin, A., *The Basics of Geopolitics*, cited in C. Clover, 'Will the Russian Bear Roar Again?', *Financial Times*, 2 December 2000, http://eurasia.com.ru/eng/ft.html

Dunne, C.W., 'Arab Space Programs Level Up', Arab Center Washington DC, 30 April 2021, http://arabcenterdc.org/policy_analyses/arab-space-programs-level-up

Dunne, D., 'The Carbon Brief Profile: Indonesia', 27 March 2019

Dupont, A., 'The Strategic Implications of Climate Change', *Survival* 50, no. 3 (2008), pp. 29–54

Duyar, M., 'Analysis: Israel's Most Powerful Tool in Persuading Jordan: "Water Problem"', Anadolu Agency, 8 June 2021

DW, 'Germany's Political Parties – What You Need to Know, 5 October 2021

DW, 'Greece, Turkey Agree to Work on Relationship', 31 May 2021

DW, 'Populism in Germany Declines Sharply, Says Bertelsmann Study', 3 September 2020

DW, 'Turkey Extends Controversial Mediterranean Gas Exploration', 25 October 2020

EAPN Lithuania, 'Poverty and Social Exclusion in Lithuania 2018'

Earthquake Engineering Research Institute, 'The Kashmir Earthquake of October 8, 2005: Impacts in Pakistan', ReliefWeb, 28 February 2006

Easterly, W., J. Ritzen and M. Woolcock, 'Social Cohesion, Institutions, and Growth', *Economics and Politics* 18, no. 2 (2006), pp. 103–20

Ebel, R.E., 'The Geopolitics of Russian Energy', Center for Strategic and International Studies, 21 July 2009

Eck, T., 'South Korea's Demographic Deficit', *The Interpreter* (Lowy Institute), 31 August 2018

Economic Cooperation Foundation, 'Saudi (Arab) Peace Initiative (2002)', 23 March 2002, https://ecf.org.il/issues/issue/167

Economic Times, 'India and China Increase Their Nuclear Arsenal Even as the Global Number Goes Down', 2 December 2020

Economic Times, 'Japan's Debt Mountain: How Is It Sustainable?', 10 June 2020

Economic Times, 'Piracy Pushes Ship Owners to Opt for Cape of Good Hope', 23 November 2008

Economic Times, 'Times Water Summit 2020: It's Still Not Late in Saving India from Becoming a Waterless Country If We Start Acting Now!', 30 November 2020

Economist Intelligence Unit, 'Democracy Index 2020: In Sickness and in Health?'

Economist, The, 'Germany is Doomed to Lead Europe', 27 June 2020

Economist, The, 'Japan's Pension Problems are a Harbinger of Challenges Elsewhere', 9 July 2019

Economist, The, 'How to Manage the Migrant Crisis', 6 February 2016

Economist, The, 'Many Chinese Suffer Discrimination Based on Their Regional Origin', 11 April 2019

Economist, The, 'No Country for Old Men', 24 January 2008

Economist, The, 'Recep Tayyip the First: Erdogan Inaugurates a New Political Era in Turkey', 28 June 2018

Economist, The, 'The Turkish Train Crash', 2 December 2006

ECOWAS, 'Directors General of Customs in the Region Hold Meeting on Common External Tariff', 21 November 2019, https://www.ecowas.int

/directors-general-of-customs-in-the-region-hold-meeting-on-common
-external-tariff

Eda, M., 'Why Closing Japan's Gender Gap Will Be Achieved with Equality from the Top', World Economic Forum, 30 March 2021

Eddy, M., 'Far-Right Terrorism Is No. 1 Threat, Germany Is Told after Attack', *New York Times*, 29 December 2020

Eddy, M., 'Germany Passes Climate-Protection Law to Ensure 2030 Goals', *New York Times*, 15 November 2019

EG 24 News, 'Is Turkey Closing the Bosphorus and Dardanelles Straits to Russia?', 28 February 2020

Eghdami, M. and A.P. Barros, 'Deforestation Impacts on Orographic Precipitation in the Tropical Andes', *Front. Environ. Sci.*, 20 November 2020

Eglash, R., 'After Three Elections and Political Deadlock, Israel Finally Swears in New Government', *Washington Post*, 17 May 2020

Eichhorst, W., P. Marx and C. Wehner, 'Labor Market Reforms in Europe: Towards More Flexicure Labor Markets?', *Journal for Labour Market Research* 51, no. 3 (2017), pp. 1–17

Einhorn, R., 'The Key Choices Now Facing the Biden Administration on North Korea', Brookings Institution, 30 March 2021

Ejaz, I., B.T. Shaikh and N. Rizvi, 'NGOs and Government Partnership for Health Systems Strengthening: A Qualitative Study Presenting Viewpoints of Government, NGOs and Donors in Pakistan', *BMC Health Services Research* 11, no. 122 (2011), pp. 1–7

Ekrem, J., 'Aiming High: Egypt Strives to Boost Its R&D Performance', *ScienceBusiness*, 16 June 2020

Ekrem, J., 'China's Historic Rise in Science and Tech Stirs Criticism', *ScienceBusiness*, 6 April 2020

Ekundayo, O.O.S., 'Education in Nigeria Is in a Mess from Top to Bottom: Five Things That Can Fix It', *The Conversation*, 26 March 2019

El Karoui, M., M. Hoyos-Flight and L. Fletcher, 'Future Trends in Synthetic Biology – A Report', *Frontiers in Bioengineering and Biotechnology* 7 (2019), pp. 1–8

Elman, C., and M. Jensen (eds), *The Realism Reader* (New York: Routledge, 2014)

Elsana, M., 'Historic Change: Arab Political Parties Are Now Legitimate Partners in Israel's Politics and Government', *The Conversation*, 11 June 2021

El-Sayed, N., 'Nile River: Extreme Droughts and Heavy Rains', *Nature Middle East*, 15 May 2017

Emadodin, I., T. Reinsch and F. Taube, 'Drought and Desertification in Iran', *Hydrology* 6, no. 3 (2019), 66 (1–12)

Emam, A., 'Egypt Struggles with Bloated Public Sector', *Arab Weekly*, 18 November 2018

Embassy of France in the Caribbean, 'France, Europe's Leading Agricultural Power', https://lc.ambafrance.org/1-France-Europe-s-leading (accessed 30 June 2021)

Embassy of the Republic of Kazakhstan, 'Ethnic Groups', https://kazakhembus.com/about-kazakhstan/culture/ethnic-groups (accessed 30 June 2021)

Encyclopedia Britannica, 'Concert of Europe', 22 February 2016

Encyclopedia Britannica, 'East India Company', 12 February 2021.

Encyclopedia Britannica, 'Failed State', by N.H. Barma, 17 May 2016

Encyclopedia Britannica, 'Geopolitics', by D.H. Deudney, 12 June 2013

Encyclopedia Britannica, 'Hajj', 15 November 2021

Encyclopedia Britannica, 'Justice and Development Party', 12 November 2021

Encyclopedia Britannica, 'Kashmir', 11 November 2021

Encyclopedia Britannica, 'Landless Workers Movement', by T. McCowan, 22 November 2016

Encyclopedia Britannica, 'Self-Defense Force: Japanese Armed Force', 21 April 2011

Encyclopedia Britannica, 'September 11 Attacks: United States [2001]', by P.L. Bergen, 10 September 2020

Encyclopedia Britannica, 'Turkey', by M.E. Yapp and J.C. Dewdney, 21 November 2021

Environment Agency (United Kingdom), 'State of the Environment: Health, People and the Environment', updated 23 July 2021, https://www.gov.uk/government/publications/state-of-the-environment/state-of-the-environment-health-people-and-the-environment

Equality and Human Rights Commission, 'Race Report Statistics', https://www.equalityhumanrights.com/en/race-report-statistics (accessed 30 June 2021)

Equality Trust, 'The Scale of Economic Inequality in the UK', https://www.equalitytrust.org.uk/scale-economic-inequality-uk (accessed 30 June 2021)

ERAI, 'The Pharmaceutical Industry in Turkey – 1', 6 May 2021

Erdogan, M.N., 'Turkey: Drug Trade, Organized Crime Hit Hard in 2020', Anadolu Agency, 7 January 2021

Escafré-Dublet, A., 'Mainstreaming Immigrant Integration Policy in France: Education, Employment, and Social Cohesion Initiatives', Migration Policy Institute, August 2014

Esfandiyari, D., 'Iran and Egypt: A Complicated Tango', EUISS, 18 October 2012

Euractiv, 'Sweden and Denmark Step Out of the Shadows as EU's Frugals', 10 July 2020

Euronews, 'Lithuania Votes: Centre-Right Opposition Wins Second Round of Legislative Elections', 26 October 2020

European Commission, '2018 Ageing Report: Policy Challenges for Societies', 25 May 2018

European Commission, 'A Counter-Terrorism Agenda for the EU: Anticipate, Prevent, Protect, Respond', COM (2020) 795, 9 December 2020

European Commission, 'Communication from the Commission on the EU Security Union Strategy', COM (2020) 605, 24 July 2020

European Commission, 'EU Climate Action and the European Green Deal', https://ec.europa.eu/clima/policies/eu-climate-action_en (accessed 30 June 2021)

European Commission, 'European Innovation Scoreboard 2021', 21 June 2021

European Commission, Eurydice, 'Lithuania – Population: Demographic Situation, Languages and Religions', 31 March 2021

European Commission, Eurydice, 'Sweden: Organisation of the Education System and its Structure', 1 January 2020

European Commission, High Representative of the Union for Foreign Affairs and Security Policy, 'Joint Communication to the European Parliament, the European Council and the Council on EU-Russia Relations: Push Back, Constrain and Engage', JOIN (2021) 20, 16 June 2021

European Commission, 'Humanitarian Aid: Over €34 Million in African Great Lakes Region', 18 September 2019

European Commission, 'Lithuania, a Leading Light in Laser Technology – Digital Single Market', 14 September 2012, via the Internet Archive Wayback Machine, https://web.archive.org/web/20180110175105/https:/ec.europa.eu/digital-single-market/en/news/lithuania-leading-light-laser-technology

European Commission, 'Lithuania: Population: Demographic Situation, Languages and Religions', 31 March 2021, https://eacea.ec.europa.eu/national-policies/eurydice/content/population-demographic-situation-languages-and-religions-44_en

European Commission, 'Policies', https://ec.europa.eu/info/policies_en (accessed 15 November 2021)

European Commission, 'Turkey', 30 June 2021, https://ec.europa.eu/neighbourhood-enlargement/countries/detailed-country-information/turkey_en

European Council, *European Security Strategy: A Secure Europe in a Better World* (Brussels: European Communities, 2009)https://www.consilium.europa.eu/media/30823/qc7809568enc.pdf

European Court of Human Rights, 'Annual Report 2014 of the European Court of Human Rights, Council of Europe'

European Environment Agency, 'Air Pollution', 23 November 2020, https://www.eea.europa.eu/themes/air/air-quality-management/improving-europe-s-air-quality/improving-europe-s-air-quality/intro

European Environment Agency, 'Growth without Economic Growth', Briefing, 11 Jan 2021

European Environment Agency, 'Turkey – Industrial Pollution Profile 2020', 14 September 2020, https://www.eea.europa.eu/themes/industry/industrial-pollution/industrial-pollution-country-profiles-2020/turkey

European Network Against Racism, 'Racism Plays a Key Role in Migrants Exclusion and Violation of Rights in the European Union', 2 May 2017

European Observatory on Health Care Systems, 'Health Care Systems in Transition: Germany', 2000, https://apps.who.int/iris/bitstream/handle /10665/108301/HiT-de-2000-eng.pdf?sequence=9&isAllowed=y

European Parliament, Human Rights Sub-Committee, 'Human Rights in Turkey: Still a Long Way to Go to Meet Accession Criteria', 26 October 2010, https://www.europarl.europa.eu/news/lv/press-room/20101025IPR90072/human-rights-in-turkey-still-a-long-way-to-go -to-meet-accession-criteria

European Parliament, 'Russia', https://www.europarl.europa.eu/factsheets/en /sheet/177/russia (accessed 30 June 2021)

European Union Agency for Fundamental Rights, *Integration of Young Refugees in the EU: Good Practices and Challenges* (Luxemburg: Publications Office of the European Union, 2019)

European Union Agency for Fundamental Rights, 'Facing the Challenges of Migrant Integration', 3 March 2017

Eurostat, 'Ageing Europe: Statistics on Population Developments', last updated July 2020

Eurostat, 'From Where Do We Import Energy?' https://ec.europa.eu/eurostat /cache/infographs/energy/bloc-2c.html (accessed 20 July 2021)

Eurostat, 'Overweight and Obesity – BMI statistics', https://ec.europa.eu /eurostat/statistics-explained/index.php/Overweight_and_obesity_-_BMI _statistics (accessed 14 March 2020)

Eurostat, 'R&D Expenditure at 2.19% of GDP in 2019', 27 November 2021

Eurostat, 'Unemployment Statistics', https://ec.europa.eu/eurostat /statistics-explained/index.php/Unemployment_statistics (accessed 30 June 2021)

EU Today, 'France Is Spearheading EU Tech Innovation', 29 February 2020

Evans, K., 'Guide to the 2019 Indonesia Elections', Australia Indonesia Center, 2019, http://australiaindonesiacentre.org/wp-content/uploads/2019/08 /Guide-to-the-2019-Presidential-Elections-Kevin-Evans.pdf

Express Tribune, 'Liberalisation: The Case for a Free Market in Pakistani Agriculture', 9 December 2012

EY, 'How Can Europe Reset the Investment Agenda Now to Rebuild Its Future?', 28 May 2020

Fabbri, F., F. McNamara and K. Bamberg, 'Competing Priorities at the EU's External Border', European Policy Centre, 28 December 2018

Faber, P.R., 'Thinking about Geography: Some Competing Geopolitical Models for the 21st Century', Academic Research Branch, NATO Defense College, Rome, Research Paper no. 15 (February 2005), pp. 4–5

Falk, R., 'The Waning of the State and the Waxing of Cyberworld', in J. Kurbalija (ed.), *Modern Diplomacy* (Msida, Malta: Mediterranean Academy of Diplomatic Studies, 1998)

Fang, J., and E. Handley, 'When Will Skilled Migrants Return to Australia? Not for Another Year, Government Says', ABC News (Australia), 11 May 2021

Faria, F.N., *The Evolutionary Limits of Liberalism: Democratic Problems, Market Solutions and the Ethics of Preference Satisfaction* (Cham: Palgrave Macmillan, 2019)

FAO, IFAD, UNICEF, WFP and World Health Organization, *The State of Food Security and Nutrition in the World 2020: Transforming Food Systems for Affordable Healthy Diets* (Rome: FAO, 2020)

FAO, 'UN Continues Support to Fight Desert Locust in Somalia amid COVID-19 Response', 1 May 2020

Farjadi, G., A. Amini and P. Alaedini, 'Employment of Highly Educated Labor Force', in P. Alaedini and M.R. Razavi (eds), *Industrial, Trade, and Employment Policies in Iran* (Cham: Springer, 2018), pp. 247–67

Farmer, M., 'EU Energy policy: World-Leading, Insufficient, or Both?', Power Technology, 20 April 2021

Farngoul, A., 'France's Love Affair with Nuclear Power Will Continue, but Change Is Afoot', CNBC, 10 March 2021

Farouk, Y., 'Saudi Arabia: Aid as a Primary Foreign Policy Tool', Carnegie Endowment for International Peace, 9 June 2020

Fassihi, F., and R. Gladstone, 'With Brutal Crackdown, Iran Is Convulsed by Worst Unrest in 40 Years', *New York Times*, 3 December 2019

Fatollah-Nejad, A., 'Four Decades Later, Did the Iranian Revolution Fulfil Its Promises?', Brookings Institution, 11 July 2019

Fatton, L., 'Is Japan Entering the New Space Race?', *East Asia Forum*, 20 February 2020

Faulconbridge, G., 'Russian Sub Plants Flag Under North Pole', Reuters, 2 August 2007

FDR Group and PEN America, 'Chilling Effects: NSA Surveillance Drives US Writers to Self-Censor', 12 November 2013

Fearon, J.D., 'Domestic Politics, Foreign Policy, and Theories of International Relations', *Annual Review of Political Science* 1 (1998), pp. 289–313

Federal Department of Foreign Affairs (Switzerland), 'No Signing of Swiss-EU Institutional Agreement', 26 May 2021, https://www.eda.admin .ch/eda/en/fdfa/fdfa/aktuell/newsuebersicht/2021/05/institutionelles -abkommen-kein-abschluss.html

Federal Department of Foreign Affairs (Switzerland), 'Humanitarian Diplomacy', 23 March 2021, https://www.eda.admin.ch/eda/en/home /foreign-policy/human-rights/humanitarian-policy.html

Federal Department of Home Affairs (Switzerland), 'Which Foreigners Face the Most Discrimination?', https://www.edi.admin.ch/edi/en/home /fachstellen/frb/FAQ/welche-gruppen-von-auslaendern--innen-werden-am -meisten-diskrimi.html#context-sidebar (accessed 21 June 2021)

Federal Intelligence Service (Switzerland), 'Switzerland's Security 2020', https://www.newsd.admin.ch/newsd/message/attachments/63415.pdf

Federal Ministry of Education and Research (Germany), 'Federal Report on Research and Innovation 2020',https://www.datenportal.bmbf.de/portal/en/bufi.html

Federal Ministry of Water Resources, Government of Nigeria, National Bureau of Statistics and UNICEF, *Water, Sanitation, Hygiene: National Outcome Routine Mapping 2019* (November 2020), https://www.unicef.org/nigeria/reports/water-sanitation-hygiene-national-outcome-routine-mapping-2019

Federal Office for the Environment (Switzerland), 'Air Quality in Switzerland', 18 June 2021, https://www.bafu.admin.ch/bafu/en/home/topics/air/info-specialists/air-quality-in-switzerland.html

Federal Office for the Environment (Switzerland), 'Soil: In Brief', 8 May 2020, https://www.bafu.admin.ch/bafu/en/home/topics/soil/in-brief.html#2005132307

Federal Statistical Office of Germany, 'Bevölkerung mit Migrationshintergrund um 8,5 % gestiegen', 1 August 2017, https://www.destatis.de/DE/Presse/Pressemitteilungen/2017/08/PD17_261_12511.html

Federation of American Scientists, 'Status of World Nuclear Forces', 18 June 2015, via the Internet Archive Wayback Machine, https://web.archive.org/web/20150618103342/http:/fas.org/issues/nuclear-weapons/status-world-nuclear-forces

Feierstein, G.M., 'Iran's Role in Yemen and Prospects for Peace', Middle East Institute, 6 December 2018

Feierstein, J., 'Saudi Arabia: Liberalization, not Democratization', American Foreign Service Association, *Foreign Service Journal* (May 2018)

Felbab-Brown, V., 'Drugs, Security, and Counternarcotics Policies in Afghanistan', Brookings Institution, 29 October 2020

Felix, J., 'Crime Mostly Affects Poor SA Communities', *Eyewitness News*, 14 September 2019

Felter, C., D. Renwick and A. Chatzky, 'Mercosur: South America's Fractious Trade Block', Council on Foreign Relations, Backgrounder, 10 July 2019

Feltman, J., 'Hezbollah: Iran's Most Successful Export', Brookings Institution, 17 January 2019

Ferguson, N., 'What is Power?', *Hoover Digest*, no. 2 (2003), n.p.

Ferraro, V., 'Globalizing Weakness: Is Global Poverty a Threat to the Interests of States?', *Environmental Change and Security Program Report*, no. 9 (2003), pp. 12–19

Figueroa, W., 'China-Iran Relations: The Myth of Massive Investment', *The Diplomat*, 6 April 2021

Fillion, S., 'The End of Swiss Neutrality', *Foreign Policy*, 15 January 2021

Financial Times, 'How Israel Is Leading the World in R&D', 8 February 2017

Financial Times, 'Lithuania Rules out Devaluation', 18 November 2009, https://www.ft.com/content/692bf806-5bef-11de-aea3-00144feabdc0

Financial Tribune, 'Boosting R&D Investment Vital for Economic Growth', 18 December 2017

Fisch, D., 'Israel's Environmental Problems', *Palestine-Israel Journal of Politics, Economics and Culture* 5, no. 1 (1998)

Fischer, E., 'Disaster Response: The Role of a Humanitarian Military', *Army Technology*, 25 July 2011

Fisher, M., 'Iran's System Keeps Its Grip, Despite the Chaos (or Because of It)', *New York Times*, 20 June 2021

Flanders Investment and Trade Market Survey, 'Life Science and Biotech Industry in Lithuania', December 2016

Flint, C., *Introduction to Geopolitics*, 3rd edn (London: Routledge, 2017)

Flückiger, K.M., 'Xenophobia, Media Stereotyping, and Their Role in Global Insecurity', in N.R.F. Al-Rodhan (ed.), *Policy Briefs on the Transcultural Aspects of Security and Stability* (Berlin: LIT, 2006)

Focal Line Solar, 'Saudi Arabia Is Getting Serious about Green Energy', 30 June 2021

Folarin, S., 'Nigeria Was Once an Indisputable Leader in Africa: What Happened?', *The Conversation*, 24 May 2020

Forest, J.J.F., 'Globalization and Transnational Crime', *E-International Relations*, 16 September 2020

Forster, P., 'UK Target to Cut Emissions 78% by 2035 Is World-Leading – But to Hit It, Action Is Needed Now', *The Conversation*, 22 April 2021

Foundation for Economic Education, 'Brazil's Disastrous Attempt to Re-nationalize Oil Production', 19 October 2016

Fox, M., 'Dengue: Modified Mosquitoes Reduce Dengue Cases by 77% in Indonesia Experiment', CNN, 10 June 2021

France Diplomatie, 'France at the Heart of the Rosetta Space Mission: A Unique Technological Challenge', 22 May 2015, via the Internet Archive Wayback Machine. https://web.archive.org/web/20150522152217/http:/www.diplomatie.gouv.fr/en/french-foreign-policy-1/scientific-diplomacy/events-7867/article/france-at-the-heart-of-the-rosetta

France Diplomatie, 'Terrorism: France's International Action', https://www.diplomatie.gouv.fr/en/french-foreign-policy/security-disarmament-and-non-proliferation/terrorism-france-s-international-action (accessed 30 June 2021)

France en Chine, Ambassade de, 'L'énergie nucléaire en France' (Nuclear Energy in France), 7 January 2008, via the Internet Archive Wayback Machine, https://web.archive.org/web/20100701211529/http:/www.ambafrance-cn.org/L-energie-nucleaire-en-France.html

Franco, T., 'Education in Lithuania', The Borgen Project, 8 November 2017

Frangoul, H., D. Altshuler, M. D. Cappellini, Y.-S. Chen, J. Domm, B.K. Eustace, J. Foell, J. de la Fuente *et al.*, 'CRISPR-Cas9 Gene Editing for Sickle Cell Disease and β-Thalassemia', *New England Journal of Medicine*, 5 December 2020

Franks, J., B. Gruss, M. Patnam and S. Weber, 'Five Charts on France's Policy Priorities to Navigate the COVID-19 Crisis', International Monetary Fund, 19 January 2021

Freed, J., 'The Leader of Europe? Answers an Ocean Apart', *New York Times*, 4 April 2008, https://www.nytimes.com/2008/04/04/world/europe/04iht -poll.4.11666423.html

Freedom House, 'Kazakhstan: Nations in Transit 2020 Country Report', https://freedomhouse.org/country/kazakhstan/nations-transit/2020 (accessed 30 June 2021)

Freedom House, 'New Report: The Global Decline in Democracy Has Accelerated', 3 March 2021

Freeman, W., 'The Accuracy of China's "Mass Incidents"', *Financial Times*, 2 March 2010

Frey, W.H., 'The US Will Become "Minority White" in 2045, Census Projects', Brookings Institution, 14 March 2018

Frey, W.H., 'What the 2020 Census Will Reveal about America: Stagnating Growth, an Aging Population, and Youthful Diversity', Brookings Institution, 11 January 2021

Friedman, S., 'How Corruption in South Africa Is Deeply Rooted in the Country's Past and Why That Matters', *The Conversation*, 28 August 2020

Friedman, S., 'South Africa Remains a Nation of Insiders and Outsiders, 27 Years after Democracy', *The Conversation*, 25 April 2021

Friedman, T., *The Lexus and the Olive Tree: Understanding Globalization*, rev. edn (New York: Anchor Books, 2000)

Frost, E.L., 'Globalization and National Security: A Strategic Agenda', in R.L. Kugler and E. Frost (eds), *Global Century: Globalization and National Security* (Washington, DC: National Defense University Press, 2001), pp. 35–74

Frost, R., '5 Sustainability Issues Affecting UK', Acre, 9 July 2018

Frum, D., 'The Real Story of How America Became an Economic Superpower', *The Atlantic*, 24 December 2014

FTI Consulting, 'The Impact of Covid-19 on the Construction Industry in China', 19 August 2020

Fu, J., and D. Jiang, 'Canada's Sovereignty over the Northwest Passage', *ARCGIS*, 5 January 2020

Fujikawa, M., 'In Japan, They're Still Worried about Deflation Not Inflation', *Wall Street Journal*, 19 March 2021

Fulton, L., 'Coca Conflict: Brazil's Impending War on Drugs', *Harvard International Review* 29, no. 2 (2007)

Fund for Peace, 'Fragile States Index 2018', 24 April 2018

Funds for NGOs, 'How Marketing and Communication Strategies Can Help NGOs Achieve Fundraising Success', https://www.fundsforngos.org /civil-society-2/how-can-marketing-communications-strategies-help-ngos -achieve-fundraising-success (accessed 30 June 2021)

Gabbatiss, J., 'The Carbon Brief Profile: South Korea', 6 April 2020

Gabbatiss, J., 'The Carbon Brief Profile: The United States', 22 April 2021

Galgano, F., and E.J. Palka (eds), *Modern Military Geography* (Abingdon: Routledge, 2011)

Gamlen, A., *Human Geopolitics: States, Emigrants, and the Rise of Diaspora Institutions* (Oxford: Oxford University Press, 2019)

Gardner, F., 'Iran's Network of Influence in Mid-East "Growing"', BBC News, 7 November 2019

Garfinkel, M.S., D. Endy, G.L. Epstein and R.M. Friedman, 'Synthetic Genomics: Options for Governance', *Industrial Biotechnology* 3, no. 4 (2007), pp. 333–65

Garner, R., P. Ferdinand and S. Lawson, *Introduction to Politics* (Oxford: Oxford University Press, 2020)

Garrity, P.J., 'Interests and Issues: Perspectives on Future Challenges to US Security', in S.A. Cambone (ed.), *A New Structure for National Security Policy Planning* (Washington, DC: Center for Strategic and International Studies, 1998), p. 91ff.

Gavel, D., 'Joseph Nye on Smart Power', Harvard Kennedy School, 3 July 2008

Gazeau-Secret, A., 'Francophonie et diplomatie d'influence' (French-speaking Countries and Influence Diplomacy), *Géoéconomie*, no. 55 (2010), pp. 39–56

Gazprom, 'Supplies of Russian Gas to Hungary and Croatia Via New Route Commences, 1 October 2021

Gedela, K., D.N. Wirawan, F.S. Wignall, H. Luis, T.P. Merati, E. Sukmaningrum and I. Irwanto, 'Getting Indonesia's HIV Epidemic to Zero? One Size Doesn't Fit All', *International Journal of STD and AIDS* 32, no. 3 (2021), pp. 290–99

Gedmin, J., 'Right-Wing Populism in Germany: Muslims and Minorities after the 2015 refugee crisis', Brookings Institution, 24 July 2019

Gelin, M., 'Japan Radically Increased Immigration – and No One Protested', *Foreign Policy*, 23 June 2020

Genç, K., 'Turkey Withdraws from Treaty on Violence against Women', *The Lancet* 397, no. 10283 (April 2021), https://www.thelancet.com/journals/lancet/article/PIIS0140-6736(21)00837-0/fulltext

Geneva Academy RULAC online portal:

'Military Occupation of Palestine by Israel', last updated 19 May 2021, https://www.rulac.org/browse/conflicts/military-occupation-of-palestine-by-israel#collapse1accord

'Use of Force', last updated 6 February 2017, https://www.rulac.org/legal-framework/use-of-force

Genova, A., 'This Is What Nuclear Weapons Leave in Their Wake', *National Geographic*, 28 December 2017

GeoHistory, 'Nationalist Thought in Contemporary Russia', 3 September 2013

Georgie, F., 'The Role of Racism in the European "Migration Crisis": A Historical Materialist Perspective', in V. Satgar (ed.), *Racism after Apartheid: Challenges for Marxism and Anti-Racism* (Johannesburg: Wits University Press, 2019), pp. 96–117

German Aerospace Center, 'Germany Invests 3.3 Billion Euro in European Space Exploration and Becomes ESA's Largest Contributor', 28 November 2019

Ghilarov, A.M., 'Ecosystem Functioning and Intrinsic Value of Biodiversity', *Oikos* 90(2) (2000), pp. 408–12

Gilder, A., J. Chan, A. Jiang and L.-M. Chew, 'How China's Financial Liberalization Can Unlock New Opportunities', EY, 7 November 2019

Glass, L.-M., and J. Newig, 'Governance for Achieving the Sustainable Development Goals: How Important Are Participation, Policy Coherence, Reflexivity, Adaptation and Democratic Institutions?,' *Early System Governance* 2 (2019)

Gleason, M.P., and P.L. Hays, 'Getting the Most Deterrent Value from US Space Forces', Center for Space Policy and Strategy, October 2020

Global Centre for the Responsibility to Protect, 'What is R2P?'

Global Economy, 'Kazakhstan: Foreign Direct Investment', https://www .theglobaleconomy.com/Kazakhstan/Foreign_Direct_Investment (accessed 30 June 2021)

Global Forest Watch, 'Mexico', https://www.globalforestwatch.org /dashboards/country/MEX (accessed 18 June 2021)

Global Forest Watch, 'Nigeria', https://www.globalforestwatch.org /dashboards/country/NGA (accessed 20 June 2021)

Global Initiative against Transnational Organised Crime, *Under the Shadow: Illicit Economies in Iran*, Research Report (Geneva: GI-TOC, 2020)

Global Network Against Food Crises and Food Security Information Network, 'Global Report on Food Crises 2021: In Brief', https:// docs.wfp.org/api/documents/WFP-0000127413/download/?_ga =2.113993218.468372453.1625057045-1996012570.1625057045 (accessed 30 July 2021)

Global Security, 'India – Army', 6 January 2016, http://www.globalsecurity .org/military/world/india/army.htm

Global Security, 'Indonesia: Foreign Relations', https://www.globalsecurity .org/military/world/indonesia/forrel.htm (accessed 30 June 2021)

Global Security, 'Justice and Development Party (AKP) Adalet ve Kalkinma Parti (AKP)', https://www.globalsecurity.org/military/world/europe/tu -political-party-akp.htm (accessed 30 June 2021)

Global Security, 'Kurdistan – Turkey', https://www.globalsecurity.org /military/world/war/kurdistan-turkey.htm (accessed 24 November 2021)

Glynn, S., 'Turkey Is Reportedly Depriving Hundreds of Thousands of People of Water', *Open Democracy*, 14 June 2021

Glynn, S., 'Turkey's Invasion of Northern Iraq Could Lead to Kurdish Civil War', *Open Democracy*, 2 July 2021

Goczek, L., E. Witkowska and B. Witkowski, 'How Does Education Quality Affect Economic Growth?', *Sustainability* 13, no. 11 (2021), pp. 1–22

Godinho, V., 'Two-Thirds of Saudi Arabia's Population Is under the Age of 35', Gulf Business, 10 August 2020

Godson, R., 'Transnational Crime, Corruption, and Security', in Brown, *Grave New World*, pp. 259–78

Gohd, C., 'Everyone Wants a Space Force – but Why?', Space.com, 11 September 2020

Gohir, S., 'The Veil Ban in Europe: Gender Equality or Gendered Islamophobia?', *Georgetown Journal of International Affairs* 16, no. 1 (2015), pp. 24–33

Gokhale, N., 'India's 40-Year-Old Law to Combat Air Pollution Languishes as the Crisis Intensifies', *Mongabay*, 10 November 2020

Gokhale, V., 'The Road from Galwan: The Future of India-China Relations', Carnegie India, 10 March 2021

Golden, H., 'Makah Tribe in US Hopes for Rights to Resume Sacred Tradition of Gray Whale Hunting', *The Guardian*, 12 November 2021

Goldenberg, I., 'Biden Can Keep the Two-State Solution Alive', *Foreign Affairs*, 21 June 2021

Goldstone, J.A., and J. Ulfelder, 'How to Construct Stable Democracies', *Washington Quarterly* 28, no. 1 (2004–5), pp. 7–20

Golunov, S.V., and R.N. McDermott, 'Border Security in Kazakhstan: Threats, Policies and Future Challenges', *Journal of Slavic Military Studies* 18, no. 1 (2005), pp. 31–58

Gomes Saraiva, M., and A. de Mello e Silva, 'Between Political Crisis and COVID-19: Bolsonaro's Foreign Policy', *E-International Relations*, 2 June 2020

Gomez Tamayo, S., J. Koettl and N. Rivera, 'The Spectacular Surge of the Saudi Female Labor Force', Brookings Institution, 21 April 2021

Goncharenko, O., 'Rising EU-Russia Tensions Are Good News for Ukraine', Atlantic Council, 11 February 2021

Gonikberg, X., 'Efforts to Reduce Poverty in Israel', The Borgen Project, 15 September 2020

Gorvett, J., 'Greece is Making a Comeback in the Eastern Mediterranean', *Foreign Policy*, 24 May 2021

Gosnell, R., 'Caution in the High North: Geopolitical and Economic Challenges of the Arctic Maritime Environment, *War on the Rocks*, 25 June 2018

Got, A., 'Turkey's Crisis with the West: How a New Low in Relations Risks Paralyzing NATO', *War on the Rocks*, 19 November 2020

Goujon, A., A. Wazir and N. Gailey, 'Pakistan: A Population Giant Falling behind Its Demographic Transition', *Population and Societies* 576, no. 4 (2020), pp. 1–4

Government Offices of Sweden, 'Sweden and the UN in Figures', 29 June 2018, https://www.government.se/government-policy/sweden-and -the-un/sweden-and-the-un-in-figures

Government of India, 'India's Quarterly External Debt Report for Quarter Ending December 2020', https://dea.gov.in/sites/default/files/Report%20 on%20India%27s%20External%20Debt%20as%20at%20end-December%20 2020.pdf

Government of Pakistan, Pakistan Bureau of Statistics, 'Agriculture Statistics', https://www.pbs.gov.pk/content/agriculture-statistics (accessed 30 June 2021)

Gov.uk, 'New Immigration System: What You Need to Know', https://www.gov.uk/guidance/new-immigration-system-what-you-need-to-know (accessed 30 June 2021)

Graticola, I.L., '8 Facts about Healthcare in Iran', The Borgen Project, 1 October 2020

Green, A., 'Germany, Foreign Aid, and the Elusive 0.7%', Devex, 8 August 2019

Gricius, G., 'Geopolitical Implications of New Arctic Shipping Lanes', *The Arctic Institute*, 18 March 2021

Griffiths, J.K., 'Waterborne Diseases', in W.C. Cockerham and S.R. Quah (eds), *International Encyclopedia of Public Health*, 2nd edn (Amsterdam: Elsevier, 2016)

Griffiths, M. (ed.), *Encyclopedia of International Relations and Global Politics* (New York: Routledge, 2013)

Grigas, A., 'Lithuania's New Government: Women-Led Coalition Wins Confidence in Difficult Times', *Atlantic Council*, 30 October 2020

Grimm, S., 'Democracy Promotion and the European Union', Research Network External Democracy Promotion Wire, 15 January 2019

Groff, M., and J. Lorik, 'Strengthening the Rules-Based Global Order: The Case for an International Rule of Law Package', Stimson, 14 September 2020

Gross, M., 'Latin America's Resources: Blessing or Curse?,' *Current Biology* 24, no. 6 (2014)

Gross, S., 'Why Are Fossil Fuels So Hard to Quit?', Brookings Institution, June 2020

GroundUp, 'Why Is South Africa's Unemployment Rate So High?', *Daily Maverick*, 14 February 2019

Grygiel, J.J., *Great Powers and Geopolitical Change* (Baltimore: Johns Hopkins University Press, 2006)

Gsteiger, F., 'Biden-Putin Summit: Why Geneva?', Swissinfo, 4 June 2021

Guglielmi, G., 'Million-Dollar Kavli Prize Recognizes Scientist Scooped on CRISPR', *Nature*, updated 4 June 2018

Gunter, J., 'Uyghur Imams Targeted in China's Xinjiang Crackdown', BBC News, 13 May 2021

Gupta, A., 'How Communities in China Helped Keep Desertification at Bay', Down to Earth, 5 September 2019

Guzzini, S., (ed.), *The Return of Geopolitics in Europe?: Social Mechanisms and Foreign Policy Identity Crisis* (Cambridge: Cambridge University Press, 2012)

Haass, R.N., 'The Age of Nonpolarity: What Will Follow US Dominance', *Foreign Affairs* 87, no. 3 (2008)

Haider, H., *Climate Change in Nigeria: Impacts and Responses*, K4D Helpdesk Report 675 (Brighton: Institute of Development Studies, 2019)

Halon, E., 'Israel's Economic Growth Has Left Most People Behind: Study', *Jerusalem Post*, 20 February 2020, https://www.jpost.com/israel-news /israels-economic-growth-has-left-most-people-behind-618152

Hammer, J., 'The Dying of the Dead Sea', *Smithsonian Magazine*, October 2005

Harchaoui, J., *Why Turkey Intervened in Libya* (Washington, DC: Foreign Policy Research Institute, 2020)

Harding, L., 'What We Know about Russia's Interference in the US Election', *The Guardian*, 16 December 2016

Harding, L., and A. Roth, 'Raman Pratasevich: The Belarus Journalist Captured by a Fighter Jet', *The Guardian*, 25 May 2021

Harijanti, S.D., and T. Lindsey, 'Indonesia: General Elections Test the Amended Constitution and the New Constitutional Court', *International Journal of Constitutional Law* 4, no. 1 (2006), pp. 138–150

Haripin, M., C.H. Anindya and A. Priamariszki, 'The Politics of Counter-Terrorism in Post-Authoritarian States: Indonesia's Experience, 1998–2018', *Defense and Security Analysis* 36, no. 3 (2020), pp. 275–99

Harper, J., 'Special Report: Pentagon Reexamining Space-Based Interceptors', *National Defense Magazine*, 22 April 2019

Harper, J., 'Special Report: Would Space-Based Interceptors Spark a New Arms Race?', *National Defense Magazine*, 24 April 2019

Harvard University Press, 'The Future of Russia as an Energy Superpower', 20 November 2017, https://harvardpress.typepad.com/hup_publicity/2017/11 /future-of-russia-as-energy-superpower-thane-gustafson.html

Harvey, B., H.H.F. Smid and T. Pirard, *Emerging Space Powers: The New Space Programs of Asia, the Middle East and South-America* (Chichester: Springer Science & Business Media, 2011)

Harvey, F., 'Major Climate Changes Inevitable and Irreversible – IPCC's Starkest Warning Yet', *The Guardian*, 9 August 2021

Haseltine, W., 'What Can We Learn from Australia's Covid-19 Response?', *Forbes*, 24 March 2021

Hay, S.I., D.B. George, C.L. Moyes and J.S. Brownstein, 'Big Data Opportunities for Global Infectious Disease Surveillance', *PLOS Medicine* 10, no. 4 (2013), pp. 1–4

Haynes, J., P. Hough, S. Malik and L. Pettiford, *World Politics: International Relations and Globalisation in the 21st Century* (London: Sage, 2017)

He, J., D. Gu, X. Wu, K. Reynolds, X. Duan, C. Yao, J. Wang et al., 'Major Causes of Death among Men and Women in China', *New England Journal of Medicine*, 353, no. 11 (October 2005), pp. 1124–34

HealthData, 'Kazakhstan', http://www.healthdata.org/kazakhstan (accessed 30 June 2021)

Health Foundation, 'Top Line Facts on the Big Issues in Health and Social Care', 9 December 2019

Health Issues India, 'Infectious Diseases in India', https://www.healthissues india.com/infectious-diseases (accessed 30 June 2021)

Heinze, E.A., and B.J. Jolliff, 'Idealism and Liberalism', in J.T. Ishiyama and M. Breuning (eds), *21st Century Political Science: A Reference Handbook* (London: SAGE Publications, 2011), Pt III, pp. 319–26

Held, D., 'Violence, Law and Justice in a Global Age', *Constellations* 9, no. 1 (2002), pp. 74–88

Hendricks, C., and N. Majozi, 'South Africa's International Relations: A New Dawn?', *Journal of African and Asian Studies* 56, no. 1 (2021), pp. 64–78

Heo, K., K. Jeong, D. Lee and Y. Seo, 'A Critical Juncture in Universal Healthcare: Insights from South Korea's COVID-19 Experience for the United Kingdom to Consider', *Humanities and Social Sciences Communications* 8 (2021), pp. 1–9

Herbst, J.E., and S. Erofeev, 'The Putin Exodus: The New Russian Brain Drain', Atlantic Council, 21 February 2019

Hern, A., 'Cambridge Analytica: How Did It Turn Clicks into Votes?', *The Guardian*, 6 May 2018

Heron, T., and G. Siles-Brugge, 'The UK-Australia Trade Deal Is Not Really about Economic Gain – It's about Demonstrating Post-Brexit Sovereignty', *The Conversation*, 18 June 2021

Herszenhorn, D.M., 'In Nord Stream 2 Fight, Ukraine Gives EU Taste of Its Own Bureaucracy', *Politico*, 26 July 2021

Hindley, M., 'World War I Changed America and Transformed Its Role in International Relations', *Humanities* 38, no. 3 (2017), n.p.

History.com Editors, 'Bombing of Dresden', 7 June 2019, https://www.history .com/topics/world-war-ii/battle-of-dresden

Hoag, R., 'The Recourse to War as Punishment: A Historical Theme in Just War Theory', *Studies in the History of Ethics*, no. 2 (2006), pp. 1–28

Hoagland, R.E., 'The United States in the Caspian Region: A Reliable Partner', Caspian Policy Center, 10 August 2020, https://www.caspianpolicy.org /research/articles/the-united-states-in-the-caspian-region-a-reliable -partner-11656

Hobbes, T., *Leviathan*, ed. C.B. MacPherson (Aylesbury: Hazell, Watson & Viney Ltd., 1972 [1651])

Hodges, N., 'Cautious Hope: Top 10 Facts about Poverty in Afghanistan', The Borgen Project, 3 October 2018, https://borgenproject.org/cautious-hope -top-10-facts-about-poverty-in-kazakhstan

Hoffman, M., 'The State of the Turkish-Kurdish Conflict', *Center for American Progress*, 12 August 2019

Hoffmann, S., *World Disorders: Troubled Peace in the Post-Cold War Era* (Lanham, MD: Rowman & Littlefield, 1998)

Hofmann, C.-A., and L. Hudson, 'Military Responses to Natural Disasters: Last Resort or Inevitable Trend', Humanitarian *Exchange* 44 (2009), pp. 29–31

Hofmann, H., and P. Leino-Sandberg, 'An Agenda for Transparency in the EU', *European Law Blog*, 23 October 2019

Holmes, O., 'Israeli Coalition Ousts Netanyahu as Prime Minister after 12 Years', *The Guardian*, 13 June 2021

Holmes, O., 'New Israeli Coalition Government Seeks to Put an End to Netanyahu Era', *The Guardian*, 12 June 2021

Hornidge, A-K., and I. Scholz, 'Seven Principles to Guide German Development Policy', The Current Column of the German Development Institute, 10 May 2021

Hota, M.R., 'India's Water Crisis: Is There a Solution?', *Financial Express*, 23 September 2021

House, K.E., *On Saudi Arabia: Its People, Past, Religion, Fault Lines – and Future* (Eldon, MO: Knopf, 2012)

Houshialsadat, S.M., 'The Role of the Persian Gulf's Natural Gas Reserves for the European Union's Energy Security', (PhD diss., Durham University, 2013), http://etheses.dur.ac.uk/7751

Howe, N., and R. Jackson, 'Rising Populations Breed Rising Powers', *Financial Times*, 9 February 2007, https://www.ft.com/content/6c0ed452-b7b0-11db-bfb3-0000779e2340

Hu, Y., Y. Han and Y. Zhang, 'Land Desertification and Its Influencing Factors in Kazakhstan', *Journal of Arid Environments* 180 (September 2020), n.p.

Huang, Y., 'The Truth about Chinese Corruption', Carnegie Endowment for International Peace, 29 May 2015

Hultberg, P.T., 'Costs and Benefits of After School Tutoring Programs: The South Korean Case', *International Journal of Social Economics* 48, no. 6 (2021), pp. 862–77

Human Rights Measurement Initiative. "Data in Action: Spotlights on South Korea." Accessed 30 June 2021. https://humanrightsmeasurement.org/country-spotlights/data-in-action-spotlight-on-south-korea

Human Rights Watch, 'France: End Systemic Police Discrimination', 27 January 2021

Human Rights Watch, 'India: Government Policies, Actions Target Minorities', 19 February 2021

Human Rights Watch, 'Israel: Discriminatory Land Policies Hem in Palestinians', 12 May 2020

Human Rights Watch, 'Shoot the Traitors: Discrimination Against Muslims under India's New Citizenship Policy', 9 April 2020

Human Rights Watch, 'World Report 2020: Australia – Events of 2019', https://www.hrw.org/world-report/2020/country-chapters/australia#2c9b66 (Accessed 30 June 2020)

Human Rights Watch, 'World Report 2020: Egypt – Events of 2019', https://www.hrw.org/world-report/2020/country-chapters/egypt (Accessed 20 July 2021)

Human Rights Watch, 'World Report 2021: China – Events of 2020', https://www.hrw.org/world-report/2021/country-chapters/china-and-tibet (Accessed 30 June 2021)

Human Rights Watch, 'World Report 2021: Iran – Events of 2020'. https://www.hrw.org/world-report/2021/country-chapters/iran (accessed 20 July 2021)

Human Rights Watch, 'World Report 2021: Russia – Events of 2020' https://www.hrw.org/world-report/2021/country-chapters/russia#aff61a (accessed 20 July 2021)

Human Rights Watch, 'World Report 2020: Turkey', https://www.hrw.org/world-report/2020/country-chapters/turkey (accessed 13 January 2022)

Human Rights Watch, 'World Report 2021: United States – Events of 2020' https://www.hrw.org/world-report/2021/country-chapters/united-states (accessed 20 July 2021)

Human Rights Watch, '"You Pray for Death": Trafficking of Women and Girls in Nigeria', 27 August 2019

Hunter, R., 'Education in Pakistan', WENR, 25 February 2020

Hussain, Z., 'The Battle for Balochistan', *Dawn*, 25 April 2013

IBM, 'What Is Quantum Computing?', https://www.ibm.com/quantum-computing/what-is-quantum-computing (accessed 30 July 2021)

Ighobor, K., 'Work in Progress for Africa's Remaining Conflict Hotspots', *Africa Renewal*, 23 December 2019

IHS Jane's 360, 'Germany to Increase Defence Spending', 2 July 2015, via the Internet Archive Wayback Machine, https://web.archive.org/web/20150705180905/http:/www.janes.com/article/52745/germany-to-increase-defence-spending

Ikenberry, G.J., 'An Agenda for Liberal International Renewal', in M.A. Flournoy and S. Brimley (eds), *Finding our Way: Debating American Grand Strategy* (Washington, DC: Center for a New American Security, 2008), pp. 45–59

Ikenberry, G.J., 'Review: *Statecraft: Strategies for a Changing World*, by Margaret Thatcher', *Foreign Affairs*, September/October 2002

Ikenberry, G.J., M. Mastanduno and W.C. Wohlforth, *International Relations Theory and the Consequences of Unipolarity* (Cambridge: Cambridge University Press, 2011)

Ilinova, K.G., 'Foreign and Domestic Policy of Ukraine at the Present Stage', *Post-Soviet Issues* 5, no. 1 (2018), pp. 89–100

Illmer, A., 'North Korean Propaganda Changes Its Tune', BBC News, 23 June 2018

Index Mundi, 'South Korea Literacy', https://www.indexmundi.com/south_korea/literacy.html (accessed 30 June 2021)

India Environmental Portal, 'National Clean Air Programme', 10 January 2019, http://www.indiaenvironmentportal.org.in/content/460562/national-clean-air-programme-ncap

Indian Express, 'Want Govt to Build 1,600 km Green Wall along Aravalli, Says Activist', 24 December 2019

Indonesia Investments, 'Unemployment in Indonesia', https://www.indonesia
-investments.com/finance/macroeconomic-indicators/unemployment
/item255 (accessed 21 July 2021)

Institute for Government, 'UK Net Zero Target', https://www.institutefor
government.org.uk/explainers/net-zero-target (accessed 30 June 2021)

Institute for Health Metrics and Evaluation. "South Korea." Accessed 30
June 2021. http://www.healthdata.org/south-korea

Institute for Security and Development Policy, 'Turkey's Kurdish Conflict:
2015 to Present: Backgrounder', December 2016, https://ethz.ch/content
/dam/ethz/special-interest/gess/cis/center-for-securities-studies/resources
/docs/ISDP-Turkeys-Kurdish-Conflict-2015-Present.pdf

Intergovernmental Panel on Climate Change (IPCC), *Climate Change 2014:
Synthesis Report: Contribution of Working Groups I, II and III to the Fifth
Assessment Report of the Intergovernmental Panel on Climate Change*, ed.
R.K. Pachauri and L.A. Meyer (Geneva: IPCC, 2015)

Internal Displacement Monitoring Centre, 'Pakistan', https://www.internal
-displacement.org/countries/pakistan (accessed 30 June 2021)

International Association for Medical Assistance to Travellers, 'Ukraine
General Health Risks: Air Pollution', 16 April 2020, https://www.iamat.org
/country/ukraine/risk/air-pollution#

International Association for Medical Assistance to Travellers, 'Japan:
Air Pollution', https://www.iamat.org/country/japan/risk/air-pollution
(accessed 30 June 2021)

International Association for Medical Assistance to Travellers, 'Kazakhstan',
https://www.iamat.org/country/kazakhstan/risk/tuberculosis (accessed 30
June 2021)

International Atomic Energy Agency (IAEA), 'Nuclear Desalination', https://
www.iaea.org/topics/non-electric-applications/nuclear-desalination
(accessed 30 July 2021)

International Atomic Energy Agency Power, Reactor Information System,
'France', https://pris.iaea.org/PRIS/CountryStatistics/CountryDetails
.aspx?current=FR (accessed 8 January 2018)

International Commission on Intervention and State Sovereignty, *The
Responsibility to Protect: Research, Bibliography and Background:
Supplementary Volume to the Report of the International Commission on
Intervention and State Sovereignty* (Ottawa: International Development
Research Centre, 2001)

International Criminal Court, 'Statement of ICC Prosecutor, Fatou Bensouda,
Respecting an Investigation of the Situation in Palestine,' 3 March 2021

International Crisis Group, 'Rising Tensions in the Eastern Mediterranean',
13 July 2021

International Energy Agency, 'CO$_2$ Emissions from Fuel Combustion:
Highlights: 2011 Edition', https://selectra.co.uk/sites/default/files/pdf
/co2highlights.pdf

International Energy Agency, 'Japan 2021: Energy Policy Review', March 2021

International Energy Agency, *Key World Energy Statistics 2010* (Paris: OECD Publishing, 2010)International Energy Agency, 'South Africa', https://www .iea.org/countries/south-africa (accessed 30 June 2021)

International Federation for Human Rights, 'Invisible and Exploited in Kazakhstan: The Plight of Kyrgyz Migrant Workers and Members of Their Families', FIDH Report no. 713a, June 2018

International Insider, 'Germany Extends Unified Armed Forces Mission in Mali', 1 June 2020, https://internationalinsider.org/germany-extends -unified-armed-forces-mission-in-mali/International Institute for Strategic Studies, *Iran's Networks of Influence in the Middle East* (London: International Institute for Strategic Studies, 2019)

International Labour Organization, 'Informal Economy in South Asia', 14 July 2021

International Labour Organisation, 'Bridging Indonesia's Skills Gap through Partnership between Industry – Vocational Education and Training', 26 June 2019

International Labour Organisation, 'The ILO Project Will Contribute to the Elimination of Child Labour in Egypt's Cotton Supply Chain', 17 June 2019

International Monetary Fund, 'Germany: Spend More at Home', 17 July 2017

International Monetary Fund, 'IMF Executive Board Concludes 2013 Article IV Consultation with the Republic of Kazakhstan', 14 August 2013, https:// www.imf.org/external/np/sec/pr/2013/pr13308.htm

International Monetary Fund, 'Projected GDP Ranking', April 2021, https:// statisticstimes.com/economy/projected-world-gdp-ranking.ph

International Monetary Fund, 'Six Charts Explain South Africa's Inequality', 30 January 2020

International Monetary Fund, 'World Economic Outlook Database', https://www.imf.org/en/Publications/SPROLLs/world-economic-outlook -databases#sort=%40imfdate%20descending (accessed 30 June 2021)

International Organization of Motor Vehicle Manufacturers, '2017 Production Statistics', http://www.oica.net/category/production-statistics

International Renewable Energy Agency, *Innovative Solutions for 100% Renewable Power in Sweden* (Masdar City: IRENA, with the Swedish Energy Agency, 2020)

International Trade Center, 'Trade Map', 9 July 2021

IQAir, 'Air Quality in South Korea', updated 24 November 2021, https://www .iqair.com/south-korea

Irwin-Hunt, A., 'The "Golden-Age" of Lithuanian Life Sciences', FDi Intelligence, 19 April 2021

Irwin, L., 'UK Emphasises Cyber Security in New Foreign Policy Strategy', IT Governance, 18 March 2021, https://www.itgovernance.co.uk/blog/uk -emphasises-cyber-security-in-new-foreign-policy-strategy

Isilow, H., 'S. Africa Demands More African Representation at UNSC', Anadolu Agency, 22 September 2020

Ismalyilova, L., and A. Terlikbayeva, 'Building Competencies to Prevent Youth Substance Use in Kazakhstan: Mixed Methods Findings from a Pilot Family-Focused Multimedia Trial', *Journal of Adolescent Health* 63, no. 3 (2018), pp. 301–12

Ismayilzada, T., 'Tackling Human Trafficking in Turkey', The Borgen Project, 29 March 2021

Jabeen, R., 'The Green Emergency: Deforestation in Pakistan', World Bank Blogs, 22 May 2019

Jackson, R., 'The Global Retirement Crisis', *The Geneva Papers on Risk and Insurance: Issues and Practice* 27, no. 4 (2002), pp. 486–511

Jackson, R., and N. Howe, *The Graying of the Great Powers: Demography and Geopolitics in the 21st Century* (Washington, DC: CSIS, 2008)

Jackson, R.H., G. Sørensen and J. Møller, *Introduction to International Relations: Theories and Approaches*, 7th edn (Oxford: Oxford University Press, 2019)

Jacobi, D., and A. Freyberg-Inan (eds), *Human Beings in International Relations* (Cambridge: Cambridge University Press, 2015)

Jacobsen, M., 'Denmark's Strategic Interests in the Arctic: It's the Greenlandic Connection, Stupid!', The Arctic Institute, 4 May 2016

Jacobsen, R., 'Top Researchers Are Calling for a Real Investigation into the Origin of COVID-19', *MIT Technology Review*, 13 May 2021

Jacomino, P., 'Iranian President Says Non-Aligned Movement States Must Unite against Unilateralism', Radio Havana Cuba, 8 February 2017, https://www.radiohc.cu/pt/noticias/internacionales/120997-iranian-president-says-non-aligned-movement-states-must-unite-against-unilateralism

Jae-in, M., 'South Korea's Governing Party Wins Election by a Landslide', Al Jazeera, 16 April 2020

Jafari, L., and L. Stancu, *Turkey Pharmaceuticals and Biopharmaceuticals 2020* (London: Global Business Reports 2020)

Jaffrey, S., 'Is Indonesia Becoming a Two-Tier Democracy?', Carnegie Endowment for International Peace, 23 January 2020

Jamrisko, M., and W. Lu, 'Germany Breaks Korea's Six-Year Streak as Most Innovative Nation', AITRIZ, 18 January 2018

Janjua, H., 'Pakistan Faces Dilemma over Trade Ties with India', DW, 5 April 2021

Javed, S., S. Liu, A. Mahmoudi and M. Nawaz, 'Patients' Satisfaction and Public and Private Sectors' Health Care Service Quality in Pakistan: Application of Grey Decision Analysis Approaches', *International Journal of Health Planning and Management* 34, no. 1 (30 August 2018), pp. 168–82

Javid, M., 'Public and Private Infrastructure Investment and Economic Growth in Pakistan: An Aggregate and Disaggregate Analysis', *Sustainability* 11, no. 12 (2019), pp. 1–22

Jeffs, B., 'A Clinical Guide to Viral Haemorrhagic Fevers: Ebola, Marburg and Lassa', *Tropical Doctor* 36, no. 1 (2006), pp. 1–4

Jensen, T., 'The Democratic Deficit of the European Union', *Living Reviews in Democracy*, March 2009

Jeon, S.-C., 'Foreign Workers in the Korean Labour Market: Current Status and Policy Issues', BIS Paper no. 100, 13 February 2019

Jericho, G., 'Closed Borders and Fear of the Future: Australia's Population Shrank during the Pandemic', *The Guardian*, 20 March 2021

Jerusalem Post, 'About Two Million Israelis Live Below the Poverty Line – Report', 22 January 2021

Jerusalem Post, 'Israel Has a Lot of Children. Is This a Problem and What Should We Do?', 10 March 2021

Jewish Virtual Library, 'Education in Israel: Adult Education', https://www .jewishvirtuallibrary.org/adult-education-in-israel (accessed 30 June 2021)

Jewish Virtual Library, 'Vital Statistics: Latest Population Statistics for Israel (2020)', https://www.jewishvirtuallibrary.org/latest-population-statistics -for-israel

Jianguo, H., 'Cooperation with China Crucial to South Korean Economy', *Global Times*, 4 August 2020

Johnson, K., and J. Detsch, 'Australia Draws a Line on China', *Foreign Policy*, 4 May 2021

Johnson, S., 'Sweden Beefs up Baltic Sea Forces amid Regional Tensions', Reuters, 26 August 2020

Jones, B., 'China and the Return of Great Power Strategic Competition', Brookings Institution, February 2020

Jones, B., 'How US-China Tensions Could Hamper Development Efforts', World Economic Forum, 16 September 2020

Jones, C., *Global Justice: Defending Cosmopolitanism* (Oxford: Oxford University Press, 2001)

Jones, D., 'Turkey-Iran Tensions Rise as Ankara Expands Operations in Iraq', VOA News, 2 March 2021, https://www.voanews.com/middle-east/turkey -iran-tensions-rise-ankara-expands-operations-iraq

Jones, T., 'Racism in Japan: A Conversation with Anthropology Professor John G. Russell', *Tokyo Weekender*, 19 October 2020

Kabalan, M., 'Sectarian Conflicts in the Middle East Can Be Resolved', Al Jazeera, 10 October 2018

Kahin, A.R., and G.M. Kahin, *Subversion as Foreign Policy: The Secret Eisenhower and Dulles Debacle in Indonesia* (New York: New Press, 1995)

Kaiser, K., 'Human Rights: A Western Policy Tool?', Belfer Center for Science and International Affairs, 5 December 2018

Kalantzakos, S., 'Rare Earths, the Climate Crisis, and Tech-Imperium', London School of Economics, *Blogs*, 24 March 2021

Kaldor Centre for International Refugee Law, 'Factsheet: The Cost of Australia's Asylum and Refugee Policies: A Source Guide', University of South Wales, 1 June 2020

Kalt, A., M. Hossein, L. Kiss and C. Zimmerman, 'Asylum Seekers, Violence and Health: A Systematic Review of Research in High-Income Host Countries', *American Journal of Public Health* 103, no. 3 (2013), pp. e30–e42

Kamarck, E., and C. Stenglein, 'How Many Undocumented Immigrants Are in the United States and Who Are They?', Brookings Institution, 12 November 2019

Kamel, L., (ed.), *The Frailty of Authority: Borders, Non-State Actors and Power Vacuums in a Changing Middle East* (Rome: Edizioni Nuova Cultura, 2017)

Kamguian, A., 'Universal Rights vs Group Rights', International Humanist and Ethical Union, 6 July 2005, via the internet archive Wayback Machine, https://web.archive.org/web/20070623192107/http://www.iheu.org/node/1691

Kania, E.B., 'China Has a "Space Force". What Are Its Lessons for the Pentagon?', *Defense One*, 29 September 2018

Kant, I., *Kant: Political Writings*, 2nd edn, ed. H.S. Reiss (Cambridge: Cambridge University Press, 1991)

Kant, I., *Kant's Principles of Politics, including his Essay on Perpetual Peace: A Contribution to Political Science*, trans, by W. Hastie (Edinburgh: T. & T. Clark, 1891)

Kapoor, N., 'Russia-EU Relations: The End of a Strategic Partnership', *ORF Issue Brief*, no. 451 (March 2021)

Kapuria-Foreman, V., 'Population and Growth Causality in Developing Countries', *Journal of Developing Areas* 29, no. 4 (1995), pp. 531–40

Karami, A., 'Iran Struggles with Border Security', AL-Monitor, 18 February 2016

Karana, K.P., 'Indonesia: Number of Malnourished Children Could Increase Sharply due to COVID-19 Unless Swift Action Is Taken', UNICEF Indonesia, 30 June 2020

Karasapan, O., and S. Shah, 'Why Syrian Refugees in Lebanon Are a Crisis within a Crisis', Brookings Institution, 15 April 2021

Karnitschnig, M., 'What Merkel Wants', *Politico*, 25 June 2020

Karp, P., 'Australia Urged to Adopt Plan to Fight "Resurgence of Racism"', *The Guardian*, 16 March 2021

Kaspe, S., 'Opinion: The Political Meanings and Uses of Russian Corruption', Geopolitical Intelligence Services, Reports, 30 April 2021

Kasthuri, A., 'Challenges to Healthcare in India', *Indian Journal of Community Medicine* 43, no. 3 (2018), pp. 141–43

Kastner, J., and W.C. Wohlforth, 'A Measure Short of War: The Return of Great-Power Subversion', *Foreign Affairs*, July/August 2021

Katzman, K., 'Iran-Iraq Relations', US Congressional Research Service, 13 August 2010

Kaufmann, D., 'What the Pandemic Reveals about Governance, State Capture, and Natural Resources', Brookings Institution, 10 July 2020

Keck, Z., 'China's Newest Maritime Dispute', *The Diplomat*, 20 March 2014

Keeley, B., *Income Inequality: The Gap between Rich and Poor* (Paris: OECD Publishing, 2015)

Keely, C.B., 'Demographic Developments and Security', in Brown (ed.), *Grave New World*, pp. 197–212

Kelle, A., 'Ensuring the Security of Synthetic Biology: Towards a 5P Governance Strategy', *Systems and Synthetic Biology* 3, no. 85 (2009), pp. 85–90

Kemp, G., and R.E. Harkavy, *Strategic Geography and the Changing Middle East* (Washington, DC: Brookings Institution Press, 1997)

Kemper, K., and S. Chaudhuri, 'Air Pollution: A Silent Killer in Lagos', World Bank Blogs, 3 September 2020

Kennan, G.F., *American Diplomacy, 1900–1950* (Chicago: University of Chicago Press, 1951)

Kenner, D., 'Why Israel Fears Iran's Presence in Syria?', *The Atlantic*, 22 July 2018

Kerimray, A., B. Kenessov and F. Karaca, 'RETRACTED ARTICLE: Trends and Health Impacts of Major Urban Air Pollutants in Kazakhstan', *Journal of the Air & Waste Management Association* 24, no. 1 (2020), pp. 1331–47

Kerski, M.J., 'Threats and Opportunities for Advancing the Major Global Interests of the United States', National Defense University, National War College, Washington, DC, 2000

Kerwatch, S.E., 'Are South African Linefishes Recovering and What Makes Them Prone to Overexploitation?', *African Journal of Marine Science* 42, no. 3 (2020), pp. 361–73

Keynoush, B., 'Water Scarcity Could Lead to the Next Major Conflict between Iran and Iraq', Middle East Institute, 18 March 2021

Khalid, R., 'Air Pollution Causes 50pc of Environmental Degradation Cost', *News International*, 13 November 2019, https://www.thenews.com.pk /print/554881-air-pollution-causes-50pc-of-environmental-degradation-cost

Khamis, A., 'Teacher Education in Pakistan', in K.G. Karris and C.C. Wolhuter (eds), *International Handbook on Teachers Education World-Wide* (Nicosia, Cyprus: HM Studies, 2019), pp. 675–92

Khanna, P., 'Here Comes the Second World', *Prospect*, no. 146 (2008), pp. 13–17

Kharpal, A., 'China Spending on Research and Development to Rise 7% Per Year in Push for Major Tech Breakthroughs', CNBC, 4 March 2021

Khoshnood, A., 'Iran-Russia Ties: Never Better but Maybe Not Forever?', *Middle East Institute*, 12 February 2020

Kiesow, I., and N. Norling, 'The Rise of India: Problems and Opportunities', Central Asia-Caucasus Institute and Silk Road Studies Program, John Hopkinks University-SAIS, January 2007

Kim-Bossard, M., 'Challenging Homogeneity in Contemporary Korea: Immigrant Women, Immigrant Laborers, and Multicultural Families', *Education about Asia* 23, no. 2 (Fall 2018), pp. 38–41

Kim, J., 'China and Regional Security Dynamics on the Korean Peninsula', in C.M. Lee and K. Botto (eds), *Korea Net Assessment: Politicized Security and Unchanging Strategic Realities* (Washington, DC: Carnegie Endowment for International Peace, 2020), pp. 55–65

King Abdullah University of Science and Technology, 'KAUST', https://www.kaust.edu.sa/en (accessed 28 July 2021)

King Faisal Center for Research and Islamic Studies, 'Vision 2030 and Reform in Saudi Arabia: Facts and Figures, April 2015–April 2021', May 2021

Kingsbury, M.A., 'Beyond Attitudes: Russian Xenophobia as a Political Legitimation Tool', *E-International Relations*, 30 April 2017

Kingsley, P., 'Egypt "Suffering Worst Economic Crisis since 1930s"', *The Guardian*, 16 May 2013

Kirby, P., 'Why has Russia Invaded and What does Putin Want?', BBC News, 9 March 2022

Kirişci, K., Turkey's Foreign Policy in Turbulent Times, Chaillot Paper no. 92 (Paris: EUISS, 2006)

Kirka, D., 'UK Trade with EU Plunges after Brexit, Hurting Economy', AP News, 12 March 2021

Kissane, C., and A. Varga, 'Russia's Drilling in the Arctic Is a Threat to the World – and to Itself', *World Politics Review*, 9 July 2020

Kissinger, H., *Diplomacy* (New York: Simon & Schuster, 1994)

Kitchen, K., and B. Drexel, 'Quantum Computing: A National Security Primer', American Enterprise Institute, April 2021

Klare, M.T., 'Global Warming Battlefields: How Climate Change Threatens Security', *Current History* 106 (November 2007), pp. 355–61

Klubnikin, K., and D. Causey, 'Environmental Security: Metaphor for the Millennium', *Seton Hall Journal of Diplomacy and International Relations* 3, no. 2 (2002), pp. 104–33

Kneuer, M., 'Autocratic Regimes and Foreign Policy', *Oxford Research Encyclopedias*, 26 September 2017, https://doi.org/10.1093/acrefore/9780190228637.013.392

know.space, *Size and Health of the UK Space Industry 2020. Summary Report for the UK Space Agency* (May 2021)

Kobara, J., 'Japan to Scrap 1% GDP Cap on Defence Spending: Minister Kishi', *Nikkei Asia*, 20 May 2021

Kocs, S.A., 'Explaining the Strategic Behaviour of States: International Law and System Structure', *International Studies Quarterly* 38, no. 4 (1994), pp. 535–56

Kogan, E., 'A Ticking Bomb? Chinese Immigration to Russia's Far East', *European Security and Defence*, 14 May 2019

Kojala, L., 'Baltic Security: The Same Challenges Remain, Even during a Pandemic', Foreign Policy Research Institute, 28 May 2020

Konish, L., 'Bipartisan Plan to Fix Social Security Draws Criticism', CNBC, 20 April 2021

Koop, A., 'Mapped: The 25 Poorest Countries in the World', *Visual Capitalist*, 22 April 2021

Kopp, D., 'Opinion: Deadly Effects of Rwandan Genocide Still Felt Today', DW, 6 April 2014

Korabik, K.M., 'Russia's Natural Resources and Their Economic Effects', Penn State College of Earth and Mineral Sciences, 1 December 1997, via the Internet Archive Wayback Machine, https://web.archive.org/web/20190720062114/https://www.ems.psu.edu/~williams/russia.htm

Korea Energy Economics Institute, *Energy Info Korea* (Ulsan: Korea Energy Economics Institute, 2018)

Korea.net, 'Becoming a Society That Respects Cultural Diversity', https://www.korea.net/AboutKorea/Society/Transformation-Multicultural-Society (accessed 30 June 2021)

Kostiner, J., 'Saudi Arabia and the Arab-Israeli Peace Process: The Fluctuation of Regional Coordination', *British Journal of Middle Eastern Studies* 36, no. 3 (2009), pp. 417–29

Krause-Pilatus, A., and S. Schüller, 'Evidence and Persistence of Education Inequality in an Early Tracking System: The German Case', IZA Discussion Paper no. 8545 (October 2014)

Krepon, M., and J. Thompson (eds), *Anti-Satellite Weapons, Deterrence and Sino-American Space Relations* (Washington, DC: Stimson Center, 2013)

Krikorian, S., 'France's Efficiency in the Nuclear Fuel Cycle: What Can "Oui" Learn?', International Atomic Energy Agency, 4 September 2019

Kristensen, H.M., and M. Korda, 'United Kingdom Nuclear Weapons, 2021', *Bulletin of Atomic Scientists* 7, no. 3 (2021), pp. 153–58

Kristensen, H.M., and R.S. Norris, 'Israeli Nuclear Weapons, 2014', *Bulletin of the Atomic Scientists* 70, no. 6 (2014), pp. 97–115

Kristof, L.K.D., 'Political Laws in International Relations', *Western Political Quarterly*, no. 11 (1958), pp. 598–606

Kristof, L.K.D., 'The Origins and Evolution of Geopolitics', *Journal of Conflict Resolution* 4, no. 1 (1960), pp. 15–51

Kroenig, M., *The Return of Great Power Rivalry: Democracy versus Autocracy from the Ancient World to the US and China* (Oxford: Oxford University Press, 2020)

Kruger, G., *Strategic Subversion: From Terrorists to Superpowers, How State and Non-State Actors Undermine One Another* (Bloomington, IN: Authorhouse, 2021)

KSA Ministry of Education, 'R&D in the Kingdom', https://rdo.moe.gov.sa/en/AbouttheProgram/Pages/RandDintheKingdom.aspx (accessed 30 June 2020)

KSA Vision 2030, 'Vision 2030: A Sustainable Saudi Vision', https://www.vision2030.gov.sa (accessed 30 June 2021)

Kubicek, P., 'Energy Politics and Geopolitical Competition in the Caspian Basin', *Journal of Eurasian Studies* 4(2) (2013), pp. 171–180

Kucera, J., 'Why Did Kazakhstan Give Up Its Nukes?', eurasianet, 15 May 2013

Kuhn, A., 'As Workforce Ages, South Korea Increasingly Depends on Migrant Labor', NPR, 2 June 2021

Kulkarni, S.S., and A. Pimpalkhare, 'India's Import Diversification Strategy for Natural Gas: An Analysis of Geopolitical Implications', Observer Research Foundation, Issue Brief no. 330, 6 December 2019

Kumar, N., and R. Rani, 'Regional Disparities in Social Development; Evidence from States and Union Territories of India', *South Asian Survey* 26, no. 1 (2019), pp. 1–27

Kumar, Y., *Geopolitics in the Era of Globalisation: Mapping an Alternative Global Future* (New York: Routledge, 2021)

Kurji, Z., 'Analysis of the Health Care System of Pakistan: Lessons Learnt and Way Forward', *Journal of Ayub Medical College Abbottabad* 28, no. 3 (2016), pp. 601–4

Kusuma, W., A.C. Kurnia and R.A. Agustian, 'South China Sea: Conflict, Challenge and Solution', *Lampung Journal of International Law* 3, no. 1 (2021), pp. 51–62

Kutcherov, V., M. Morgunova, V. Bessel and A. Lopatin, 'Russian Natural Gas Exports: An Analysis of Challenges and Opportunities', *Energy Strategy Reviews*, 30 (2020), pp. 1–10

Kuus, M., and K. Dodds, *The Routledge Research Companion to Critical Geopolitics* (London: Routledge, 2016)

Kuzio, T., 'Russia is Quietly Occupying Ukraine's Information Space', Atlantic Council, 27 June 2020

Lain, S., 'Russia Piles Up the Pressure on Ukraine', RUSI, Commentary, 6 April 2021, https://rusi.org/commentary/russia-piles-pressure-ukraine

Lam, J., 'Kazakhstan: Central Asia's Global Financial Hub', HKTDC Research, 31 July 2019

Lambert, F., 'How Mexico's Social Spending Reduced Poverty and Income Inequality', IMF Diálogo a Fondo, https://blog-dialogoafondo.imf.org/?page_id=11901 (accessed 18 June 2021)

Lambert, F., and H. Park, 'Income Inequality and Government Transfers in Mexico', IMF Working Paper, WP/19/148, 11 July 2019

Lancet, The, 'Russia's Alcohol Policy: A Continuing Success Story', 394, no. 10205 (5 October 2019), P1205

Lane, C., 'Top Universities in Australia 2021', QS Top Universities, 26 May 2021

Lantis, J.S., 'Strategic Culture: From Clausewitz to Constructivism', in J.L. Johnson, K.M. Kartchner and J.A. Larsen (eds), *Strategic Culture and Weapons of Mass Destruction: Culturally Based Insights into Comparative National Security Policymaking* (New York: Palgrave Macmillan, 2003), pp. 33–52

Lantis, J.S., 'Strategic Culture: From Clausewitz to Constructivism', *Strategic Insights* 4, no. 10 (October 2005), n.p.

Larsen, B., *Arab Republic of Egypt: Cost of Environmental Degradation: Air and Water Pollution* (Washington, DC: World Bank, 2019)

Latif, A., 'Afghan Refugees in Pakistan Pin Hopes on US Pullout', Anadolu Agency, 21 April 2021

Latif, A., 'Pakistan Sitting on a Ticking AIDS Bomb', *Pakistan Tribune*, 6 October 2006, https://web.archive.org/web/20080111121613/http:/www. paktribune.com/news/index.shtml?156327

Lau, S., 'Lithuania Pulls out of China's "17 + 1" Bloc in Eastern Europe', Politico, 21 May 2021

Lauren, P.G., G.A. Craig and A.L. George, *Force and Statecraft: Diplomatic Challenges of Our Time*, 4th edn (New York and Oxford: Oxford University Press, 2007)

Lee, C.M., 'South Korea Is Caught between China and the United States', Carnegie Endowment for International Peace, 21 October 2021

Lee, J., A. Asiryan and M. Butler, 'Integration of the Central Asian Republics: The ASEAN Example', *E-International Relations*, 17 September 2020

Lee, J.-H., and J. Woo, 'Green New Deal Policy of South Korea: Policy Innovation for a Sustainability Transition', *Sustainability* 12, no. 23 (2020), pp. 1–17

Lee, M.M., *Crippling Leviathan: How Foreign Subversion Weakens the State* (Ithaca, NY: Cornell University Press, 2020)

Lee, N., '135 Million Americans Are Breathing Unhealthy Air, American Lung Association Says', CNBC, 22 April 2021

Lehmann, K.E., 'Can Brazil Lead? The Breakdown of Brazilian Foreign Policy and What It Means for the Region', *Rising Powers Quarterly* 2, no. 2 (2017), pp. 125–47

Lemma, B., 'CRISPR Dreams: The Potential for Gene Editing', *Harvard International Review* 40, no. 1 (2019), pp. 6–7

Leng, R., 'Influence Techniques among Nations', in P.E. Tetlock, J.L. Husbands, R. Jervis, P.C. Stern and C. Tilly (eds), *Behaviour, Society, and International Conflict: Volume III* (Oxford: Oxford University Press, 1993), pp. 126–89

Lepeska, D., 'Turkey Can Play a Constructive Role in Libya. But Will It?', *N OPINION*, https://www.thenationalnews.com/opinion/comment/turkey -can-play-a-constructive-role-in-libya-but-will-it-1.1232326 (accessed 30 June 2021)

Lerner, A., 'What's It Like to Be a State? An Argument for State Consciousness', *International Theory* 13, no. 2 (2021), pp. 260–86

Levick, E., 'The Drawbacks of Arctic Shipping', Global Risk Insights, 8 February 2018

Levite, A.E., and B. Tertrais, 'What Might the Middle East Look by 2025?', *CERI Strategy Papers*, 20 May 2008

Levitt, M., 'Hezbollah's Regional Activities in Support of Iran's Proxy Networks', Middle East Institute, 26 July 2021

Levy, A., 'Google Is Even More Influential than You Think', CNBC, 12 May 2015

Levy, I., 'How Iran Fuels Hamas Terrorism', Washington Institute for Near East Policy, *Policy Watch 3494*, 1 June 2021

Levy, J.S., *War in the Modern Great Power System 1495–1975* (Lexington: University of Kentucky, 2014 [1983])

Levy, K., S.M. Smith and E.J. Carlton, 'Climate Change Impacts on Waterborne Diseases: Moving toward Designing Interventions', *Current Environmental Health Reports* 5, no. 2 (2018), pp. 272–82

Lewis, A., 'Libya's Divisions', Reuters, 14 September 2018

Lewis, P., 'Create a Global Code of Conduct for Outer Space', Chatham House, 12 June 2019, https://www.chathamhouse.org/2019/06/create-global-code-conduct-outer-space

Lewis, S., 'Joe Biden Breaks Obama's Record for Most Votes Ever Cast for a US Presidential Candidate', CBS, 7 December 2020

Li, J., H. Zhao, L. Zheng and W. An, 'Advances in Synthetic Biology and Biosafety Governance', *Frontiers in Bioengineering and Biotechnology* 9 (2021), pp. 1–14

Li, K., 'China and India Trade Competition and Complementary Analysis of the "Belt and Road" Background', *Modern Economy* 9 no. 7 (2018), pp. 1213–27

Li, Y., 'A Zero-Sum Game? Repression and Protest in China', *Government and Opposition* 54, no. 2 (April 2019), pp. 309–35

Lietuvos Bankas Eurosistema, 'Tiesioginės užsienio investicijos Lietuvoje pagal šalį', 9 January 2018, https://web.archive.org/web/20180109194528/https:/www.lb.lt/lt/tiesiogines-uzsienio-investicijos-lietuvoje-pagal-sali-1

Lietuvos mokslo taryba (Lithuanian Science Council), 'Lietuvos ekonomikos ilgalaikio konkurencingumo iššūkiai' (Challenges to the Long-Term Competitiveness of the Lithuanian Economy) 2015, https://www.lmt.lt/data/public/uploads/2016/09/ekonomikos-moksliniu-tyrimu-programos-rekomendacijos.pdf, p. 18

Light Conversion, 'Light Conversion – About Us', 5 February 2018, http://lightcon.com/about-us.html

Lim, T., 'The Road to Multiculturalism in South Korea', *Georgetown Journal of International Affairs*, 10 October 2017

Liou, S., 'Chinese Immigration to Russia and Its Non-traditional Security Impact', *East Asia* 34 (2017), pp. 271–86

Local, The, 'How Switzerland Wants to Reduce Healthcare Costs', 26 August 2020

Looney, D., D. Wessel and K. Yilla, 'Who Owes All That Student Debt? And Who'd Benefit If We Were Forgiven?', Brookings Institution, 28 January 2020

Lopes da Silva, D., N. Tian and A. Marksteiner, *Trends in World Military Expenditure, 2020* (Stockholm: SIPRI, 2021)

Lorenzon, G., 'Corruption and the Rule of Law: How Brazil Strengthened Its Legal System', CATO Institute, Policy Analysis no. 827, 20 November 2017

Loveluck, L., 'Education in Egypt: Key Challenges' Chatham House, Background Paper, March 2012

Lovotti, C., E. Tafuro Ambrosetti, C. Hartwell and A. Chmielewska (eds), *Russia in the Middle East and North Africa: Continuity and Change* (Abingdon: Routledge, 2020)

Lowe, K., 'Five Times Immigration Changed the UK', BBC News, 20 January 2020

Lun, Y.H., K.H. Lai and T.C.E. Cheng, *Shipping and Logistics Management* (London: Springer, 2010)

Lust, E., (ed.), *The Middle East* (Washington, DC: CQ Press, 2019)

Ma, G., F. Peng, W. Yang, G. Yan, S. Gao, X. Zhou, J. Qi *et al.*, 'The Valuation of China's Environmental Degradation from 2004 to 2017', *Environmental Science and Ecotechnology* 1 (2020), pp. 1–10

Ma, T., S. Sun, G. Fu, J.W. Hall, Y. Ni, L. He, J. Yi *et al.*, 'Pollution Exacerbates China's Water Scarcity and Its Regional Inequality', *Nature Communications* 11, no. 650 (2020), pp. 1–9

Mabon, S., 'Israel-Palestine Conflict: Why Gulf Leaders Are Staying Quiet – For Now', *The Conversation*, 17 May 2021

Macdonald, F., 'This Map Shows All the Claims on the Arctic Seafloor', Science Alert, 18 August 20185, https://www.sciencealert.com/this-map -shows-all-country-s-claims-on-the-arctic-seafloor

Macdonald, G.J., 'Vaccine Makers Could Benefit from Synthetic Biology', *Genetic Engineering & Biotechnology News*, 29 June 2021

Maschmeyer, L., 'The Subversive Trilemma: Why Cyber Operations Fall Short of Expectations', *International Security* 46, no. 2 (Fall 2021)

Macias, A., 'List of Countries with Nuclear Weapons', CNBC, 16 March 2018

Macias, A., 'Trump Approves Plan to Withdraw 9,500 U.S. Forces from Germany', CNBC, 30 June 2020

Macias, A., 'US Sanctions Turkey over Purchase of Russian S-400 Missile System', CNBC, 14 December 2020

Macias, A., 'US Withdrawal from Afghanistan Is More than 90% Complete, Pentagon Says', CNBC, 6 July 2021

Macrotrends, 'Brazil Literacy Rate 1980–2021', https://www.macrotrends.net /countries/BRA/brazil/literacy-rate (accessed 30 June 2021)

Macrotrends, 'Egypt's Infant Mortality Rate 1950–2021', https://www .macrotrends.net/countries/EGY/egypt/infant-mortality-rate (accessed 30 June 2021)

Madramootoo, C., (ed.), *Emerging Technologies for Promoting Food Security: Overcoming the World Food Crisis* (Cambridge: Woodhead Publishing, 2015)

Magalhães, J. Calvet de, *The Pure Concept of Diplomacy*, trans. by B. Futscher Pereira (New York: Greenwood Press, 1988)

Magome, M., 'South Africa's President Fights Own Party over Corruption', AP News, 19 February 2021

Maizland, L., 'China's Fight against Climate Change and Environmental Degradation', Council on Foreign Relations, Backgrounder, 19 May 2021

Maizland, L., 'China's Repression of Uyghurs in Xinjiang', Council on Foreign Relations, Backgrounder, 1 March 2021

Maizland, L., 'India's Muslims: An Increasingly Marginalized Population', Council on Foreign Relations, Backgrounder, 20 August 2020

Maizland, L., and B. Xu, 'The US-Japan Security Alliance', Council on Foreign Relations, Backgrounder, 22 August 2019

Malan, M., 'How Rape Survivors' Long-term Risk of HIV Infection Can Lead to Heavier Sentences for Rapists', *News 24*, 1 December 2020

Malecka, M., 'Knowledge, Behaviour, and Policy: Questioning the Epistemic Presuppositions of Applying Behavioural Science in Public Policymaking', *Synthese*, 5 February 2021

Maloney, S., 'Iranian Protesters Strike at the Heart of the Regime's Revolutionary Legitimacy', Brookings Institution, 19 November 2019

Mandle, J., *Global Justice* (Cambridge: Polity Press, 2006)

Mandour, M., 'Sisi's Debt Crisis', Carnegie Endowment for International Peace, 20 November 2018

Mangold, P., *Superpower Intervention in the Middle East* (Abingdon: Routledge Revivals, 2013)

Mani, D., and S. Trines, 'Education in South Korea', WENR, 16 October 2018

Manky, D., 'The Hard Truth and Good News about the Fight against Cybercrime', *Forbes*, 17 May 2021, https://www.forbes.com/sites/fortinet /2021/05/17/the-hard-truth-and-good-news-about-the-fight-against -cybercrime/?sh=6437115519b5

Manne, R., 'Treatment of Asylum Seekers in Australia', La Trobe University, 5 March 2018

Mansour, A., 'Education and Development in Islamic World', 6 March 2020

Marbot, O., 'Egypt-Ethiopia: "Dam of Discord" Continues to Pressure Relations', *Africa Report*, 6 May 2021

Marcus, J., 'Why Saudi Arabia and Iran are Bitter Rivals', BBC News, 16 September 2019

Margulis, S., *Causes of Deforestation of the Brazilian Amazon*, World Bank Working Paper no. 22 (Washington, DC: World Bank, 2004)

Marin, P., S. Tal, J. Yeres and K. Ringskog, *Water Management in Israel: Key Innovations and Lessons Learned for Water Scarce Countries*, Water Global Practice Technical Paper (Washington, DC: World Bank, 2017), pp. 17–32

Markwica, R., *Emotional Choices: How the Logic of Affect Shapes Coercive Diplomacy* (Oxford: Oxford University Press, 2018)

Marlowe, J., 'Israel's Mizrahi Activists Are Fighting the Racist Nation-State Law', *The Nation*, 27 May 2021

Maron, J., 'What Led to the Genocide against the Tutsi in Rwanda?', Canadian Museum for Human Rights, https://humanrights.ca/story/what -led-to-the-genocide-against-the-tutsi-in-rwanda (accessed 27 July 2021)

Martens, C. de, *Le guide diplomatique* (Leipzig: F.A. Brockhaus, 1866)

Marteu, E., 'Saudi Arabia and the Israel-Palestine Conflict: Between a Rock and a Hard Place', *The Conversation*, 24 June 2018

Martin, M., and T. Owen, *Routledge Handbook of Human Security* (New York: Routledge, 2014)

Mathews, N., 'Pakistan Invests in Infrastructure, but Many Obstacles Stand in the Way of Construction', *Engineering News Record*, 13 April 2021

Matlary, J., 'Much Ado about Little: The EU and Human Security', *International Affairs* 84, no. 1 (2008), pp. 131–43

Matters, J., 'Biden and Putin's First Meeting Won't Reset US Relations with Russia', *The Conversation*, 15 June 2021

Matto, M., 'India's Water Crisis: The Clock Is Ticking', Down to Earth, 21 June 2019

Mau, V., 'Russia's Human Capital Challenge', OECD, 2013, https://www.oecd .org/russia/russias-human-capital-challenge.htm

Mavrellis, C., *Transnational Crime and the Developing World* (Washington, DC: Global Financial Integrity, 2017), pp. 3–21

Mbaku, J.M., 'The Controversy over the Grand Ethiopian Renaissance Dam', Brookings Institution, 5 August 2020

McCarthy, N., 'The Countries Leading the World in Scientific Research', World Economic Forum, 13 January 2020

McDougall, W.A., 'Why Geography Matters … but Is So Little Learned', *Orbis*, Foreign Policy Research Institute, 1 April 2003

McIntosh, K., E. Moss, R. Nunn and J. Shambaugh, 'Examining the Black-White Wealth Gap', Brookings Institution, 27 February 2020

Meacham, C., 'Why Does US-Brazil Defense Cooperation Matter?', Center for Strategic and International Studies, 1 December 2015

Medina, L., and F. Schneider, 'Shadow Economies around the World: What Did We Learn over the Last 20 Years?', IMF Working Paper no. 18/17, January 2018

Medvedev, D., M. Piatkowski and S. Yusuf, 'Will China Become a Global Innovation Champion? Keeping the Global Innovation System Open Will Be Key', World Bank Blogs, 14 May 2020

Megoran, N., 'Revisiting the "Pivot": The Influence of Halford Mackinder on Analysis of Uzbekistan's International Relations', *Geographical Journal* 70, December 2004

Mehta, K., 'Locating Xinjiang in China's Eurasian Ambitions', Observer Research Foundation, Occasional Paper, 25 September 2018

Meiser, J.W., 'Introducing Liberalism in International Relations Theory', *E-International Relations*, 18 February 2018

Melcangi, A., 'Egypt Recalibrated Its Strategy in Libya Because of Turkey', Atlantic Council, 1 June 2021

Mello, D., 'Brazil Still Seen among Most Corrupt Countries', Agência Brasil, 24 January 2021

Mercer, J., 'Feeling Like a State: Social Emotion and Identity', *International Theory* 6, no. 3 (2014), pp. 515–35

Merkezi, H., 'Turkey Ranks First in Violations in between 1959–2011', English Bianet, 15 May 2012

Mete, B., A. Gunduz, S. Bolukcu, H.K. Karaosmanoglu, D. Yildiz, M.M. Koç, O.A. Aydın *et al.*, 'HIV Care in Istanbul, Turkey: How Far Is It from the

UNAIDS 90-90-90 Targets?', *International Journal of STD and AIDS* 30, no. 13 (2019), pp. 1298–1303

Meyers, T., 'Responding to Turkey's Devastating Earthquake', *Direct Relief*, 7 December 2021

Mfeka, B., 'Brain Drain Is Another Threat to Economic Reforms and Recovery', IOL News, 14 October 2020

Mfundza Miller, S., and M. Muller, 'South Africa's Energy Crisis Has Triggered Lots of Ideas: Why Most Are Wrong', *The Conversation*, 22 January 2020

Michel, N., 'Colonialism: "France Has to Acknowledge the Contradictions in Its History", Ayrault', *Africa Report*, 6 July 2020

Middle East Monitor, 'Ex-adviser to UAE Crown Prince Compares Iran's "Occupation" of Gulf Islands to Israel Occupation', 5 January 2021

Miller, A.D., 'How Israel and the Arab World Are Making Peace without a Peace Deal', Carnegie Endowment for International Peace, 27 May 2020

Miller, J., 'Hugo Grotius', *The Stanford Encyclopedia of Philosophy* (Spring 2021 edition)

Mills, R., and F. Alhashemi, *Resource Regionalism in the Middle East and North Africa: Rich Lands, Neglected People* (Washington, DC: The Brookings Institution, 2018), https://www.brookings.edu/research/resource-regionalism-in-the-middle-east-and-north-africa-rich-lands-neglected-people/

Milne, R., 'Sweden's Government on Brink ahead of No-Confidence Vote', *Financial Times*, 17 June 2021

Min-Seok, K., 'The State of the North Korean Military', C.M. Lee and K. Botto (eds), *Korea Net Assessment: Politicized Security and Unchanging Strategic Realities* (Washington, DC: Carnegie Endowment for International Peace, 2020

Minakov, M., 'Ukraine's Political Agenda for the First Half of 2021', Focus Ukraine, 22 January 2021

Ministère de l'Écologie, de l'Énergie, du Développement durable et de la Mer (France), *Repères : Chiffres clés du transport: Édition 2010* (Key Transportation Figures: 2010 Edition) (La Défense: 2010), via the Internet Archive Wayback Machine, https://web.archive.org/web/20100601124351/http:/www.developpement-durable.gouv.fr/IMG/pdf/Chiffres_transport-pdf.pdf

Ministère de l'Europe et des Affaires Étrangères (France), 'Development Assistance', https://www.diplomatie.gouv.fr/en/french-foreign-policy/development-assistance (accessed 21 July 2021)

Ministère de l'Europe et des Affaires Étrangères (France), 'France and Cyber Security', https://www.diplomatie.gouv.fr/en/french-foreign-policy/security-disarmament-and-non-proliferation/fight-against-organized-criminality/cyber-security (accessed 21 Juy 2021)

Ministère de l'Europe et des Affaires Étrangères (France), 'France Relance Recovery Plan: Building the France of 2030', France Diplomacy, https://www.diplomatie.gouv.fr/en/french-foreign-policy

/economic-diplomacy-foreign-trade/promoting-france-s-attractiveness
/france-relance-recovery-plan-building-the-france-of-2030 (accessed 21
July 2021)

Ministry of Education and Science of Ukraine, 'Science in Ukraine',
https://mon.gov.ua/eng/science/nauka/nauka-v-ukrayini (accessed 22
June 2021)

Ministry of Foreign Affairs of Japan, 'Japan-US Security Treaty', https://www
.mofa.go.jp/region/n-america/us/q&a/ref/1.html (accessed 30 June 2021)

Ministry of Foreign Affairs of Japan, 'Japan's Foreign Policy to Promote
National and Worldwide Interests', 2017, https://www.mofa.go.jp/policy
/other/bluebook/2017/html/chapter3/c030105.html

Ministry of Foreign Affairs of Japan, 'Japanese Territory Q&A', https://www
.mofa.go.jp/territory/page1we_000007.html (accessed 30 June 2021)

Ministry of Foreign Affairs of the People's Republic of China, 'China's
Policies on Asia-Pacific Security Cooperation', January 2017

Ministry of Foreign Affairs (Turkey), 'Turkey's Policy on Water Issues', https://
www.mfa.gov.tr/turkey_s-policy-on-water-issues.en.mfa (accessed 23 July 2021)

Ministry of National Defence, Republic of Lithuania, 'Lithuanian
Armed Forces Continue Contributing to International Operations', 23
January 2021, https://kam.lt/en/news_1098/current_issues/lithuanian
_armed_forces_continue_contributing_to_international_operations.html

Ministry of National Defence, Republic of Lithuania, 'NATO', Accessed 30
June 2021. https://kam.lt/en/international_cooperation_1089/nato_1282.
html (accessed 30 June 2021)

Minority Rights Group, 'Kurds', https://minorityrights.org/minorities
/kurds-2 (accessed 30 June 2021)

Minshull, R., *Regional Geography: Theory and Practice* (New York: Routledge,
2017)

Mishra, M. K., 'Sustainable Development: Linking Economy and
Environment in the Era of Globalization', Working Paper, ZBW – Leibniz
Information Centre for Economics, Kiel, Hamburg (2020)

Mitrova, T., 'Russia's Energy Strategy', Atlantic Council Eurasia Center,
July 2019, pp. 1–2

Mkrtchyan, N.V., 'Migration in Rural Areas of Russia: Territorial Differences',
Population and Economics 3, no. 1 (2019), pp. 39–51

Mlambo, V.H., and T. Cotties Adetiba, 'Brain Drain and South Africa's
Socioeconomic Development: The Waves and Its Effects', *Journal of Public
Affairs* 19, no. 4 (2019), p. e1942

Mncayi, N.P., 'South African Graduates May Be Mostly Employed, but Skills
and Jobs Often Don't Match', *The Conversation*, 13 April 2021

Mohapatra, S., 'Pre-Budget Ground Reality: The Indian Middle Class under
Modi 1.0 and 2.0', *Economic Times*, 23 January 2021

Monaghan, A., 'Pharmaceutical Industry Drives British Research and
Innovation', *The Guardian*, 22 April 2014

Monteiro, N.P., and K.G. Ruby, 'IR and the False Promise of Philosophical Foundations,' *International Theory* 1, no. 1 (2009), pp. 15–48

Monye, J., and O. Abang, 'Taxing the Informal Sector – Nigeria's Missing Goldmine', Bloomberg Tax, 15 October 2020

Moon, S., 'Decrease in the Growth of Domestic Demand in Korea', Korea Institute for International Economic Policy, December 2015

Moon, S., 'Power in Global Governance: An Expanded Typology from Global Health', *Globalization and Health* 15, 74 (2019), pp. 3–4

Moore, S., 'Nanotechnology in the United Kingdom Market Report', AZO Nano, 10 January 2020

Moravcsik, A., 'Europe Is Still a Superpower', *Foreign Policy*, 13 April 2017

More, M., 'On Becoming Posthuman', *Free Inquiry* 14, no. 4 (1994), pp. 38–41

Morris, C., 'Turkey Elections: How Powerful Will the Next Turkish President Be?', BBC News, 22 June 2018

Morris, H., 'For Irregular Workers, Korea's Labor Market Embeds Unfairness', *Asia Times*, 21 February 2018, https://asiatimes.com/2018/02 /irregular-workers-koreas-labor-market-embeds-unfairness

Moscow Times, 'Council of Europe Urges Russia to Release Navalny Immediately', 21 June 2021

Muggah, R., 'Lessons from Organised Crime Task Forces: Brazil and Beyond', Global Initiative, 16 October 2017

Mukashev, A., 'How Is the Fight against Corruption in Kazakhstan Taking Place', Central Asian Bureau for Analytical Reporting, 28 May 2020

Munshi, N., 'Nigeria Infrastructure Splurge to Boost Economy', *Financial Times*, 17 February 2021

Murphy, J., 'Is the Arctic Set to Become a Main Shipping Route?', BBC News, 1 November 2018

Murray, C., 'Mexico Human Trafficking Cases Rise by a Third but Many States Found Lagging', Reuters, 22 January 2020

Musingafi, M.C.C., and T. Tom, 'Fresh Water Sources Pollution: A Human Related Threat to Fresh Water Security in South Africa', *Journal of Public Policy and Governance* 1, no. 2 (2014), pp. 72–81

Naff, T., *Water in the Middle East: Conflict or Cooperation?* (New York: Routledge, 2020)

Nagel, T., 'The Problem of Global Justice', *Philosophy and Public Affairs* 33, no. 2 (2005), pp. 113–47

Narasimhan, T., 'ISRO on Cloud Nine as India Joins "Cryo Club"', *Business Standard*, 7 January 2014

NASSCOM, 'The IT-BPM Industry in India 2017: Strategic Review' https:// nasscom.in/knowledge-center/publications/it-bpm-industry-india-2017 -strategic-reviewNathan, M., 'India's Water Crisis: The Seen and Unseen', DownToEarth, 19 March 2021, https://www.downtoearth.org.in/blog /water/india-s-water-crisis-the-seen-and-unseen-76049

National Academies of Sciences, Engineering and Medicine, *The Growth of World Population: Analysis of the Problems and Recommendations for Research and Training* (Washington DC: The National Academic Press, 1963)

National Archives, 'Extract from the Official Account of the Bomber Command by Arthur Harris, 1945', http://www.nationalarchives.gov.uk /education/heroesvillains/g1/cs3/g1cs3s1.htm (accessed 12 January 2021).

NATO Energy Security, 'Centres of Excellence', https://enseccoe.org/en /about/6 (accessed 30 June 2021)

NATO Slovenija, 'Neutral European Countries: Austria, Sweden, Finland, Ireland', http://nato.gov.si/eng/topic/national-security/neutral-status /neutral-countries (accesed 21 June 2021)

Naumann, K., J. Shalikashvili, The Lord Inge, J. Lanxade and H. van den Breemen, with B. Bilski and D. Murray, *Towards a Grand Strategy for an Uncertain World: Renewing Transatlantic Partnership* (Lunteren, Netherlands: Noaber Foundation, 2007)

Naval Technology, 'Royal Canadian Navy Receives Delivery of Second AOPS Patrol Ship', 16 July 2021

Navarro, V., *Neoliberalism, Globalization, and Inequalities: Consequences for Health and Quality of Life* (London: Routledge, 2020)

Nawaz, M., and G. Naeem, Coastal Hazard Early Warning Systems in Pakistan: Gap Analysis (Oxford: Oxfam GB, 2016)

NDTV, 'Election Results 2014: Narendra Modi Wins India. BJP and Allies Cross 300 Seats', 17 May 2014

Nederman, C., 'Niccolò Machiavelli', *The Stanford Encyclopedia of Philosophy* (Summer 2019)

Neom News, 'Neom Saudi Arabia', http://neomsaudicity.net (accessed 30 June 2021)

Neom, 'Neom: An Accelerator of Human Progress', https://www.neom.com /en-us (accessed 28 July 2021)

Neufeld, M., A. Bobrova, K. Davletov, M. Štelemėkas, R. Stoppel, C. Ferreira-Borges, J. Breda, J. Rehm, 'Alcohol Control Policies in Former Soviet Union Countries: A Narrative Review of Three Decades of Policy Changes and Their Apparent Effects', *Drug and Alcohol Review* 40, no. 3 (2020), pp. 350–67

New Defence Order Strategy, 'Russian-Kazakh Military Cooperation Agreement', https://dfnc.ru/en/vtc/russian-kazakh-military-cooperation -agreement (accessed 30 June 2021)

Newman, D., 'Borders and Conflict Resolution', in T.M. Wilson and H. Donnan (eds), *A Companion to Border Studies* (Hoboken, NJ: John Wiley & Sons, 2012), pp. 249–66

News18, '20% Sailor Shortage in Navy, 15% Officer Posts Vacant in Army, Nirmala Sitharaman Tells Parliament', 27 December 2017

News International, 'Pakistan's Pivotal Role in Regions' Peace, Security: Foreign Minister', 17 October 2019, https://www.thenews.com.pk/latest /542436-pakistan-playing-pivotal-role-in-region-s-peace-security-fm

Newsletter for the European Union, 'Internal Migration in China', 25 February 2019

Newsville Times, 'Drought in the Western United States Sets a 122-Year Record', 23 July 2021

Newton, C., 'A History of the US Blocking UN Resolutions against Israel', Al Jazeera, 19 May 2021

Ni, V., 'China Announces Three-Child Limit in Major Policy Shift', *The Guardian*, 31 May 2021

Nicolas, F., 'The Economic Pillar of Korea's New Southern Policy: Building on Existing Assets', *Asie.Visions*, no. 120, Ifri, February 2021

Nieblas-Bedolla, E., 'Legalisation of Undocumented Immigrants in the USA', *The Lancet* 397, no. 10268 (2021), pp. 25–26

Nikkei Asia, 'China Passes US as Top Japanese Export Buyer, Topping 20%', 22 January 2021

No Borders Law Group, 'Australia Needs 250,000 New Migrants a Year: Study', https://www.noborders-group.com/news/australia-needs-more-migrants (accessed 20 July 2021)

Noorbala, A.A., A. Saljoughian, S.A. Bagheri Yazdi, E. Faghihzadeh, M.H. Farahzadi *et al.*, 'Evaluation of Drug and Alcohol Abuse in People Aged 15 Years and Older in Iran', *Iranian Journal of Public Health* 49, no. 10 (2020), pp. 1940–46

Nouvel, P., 'De la biologie synthétique à l'homme synthétique' (From Synthetic Biology to Synthetic Man), *Comptes rendus biologies* 338, nos 8–9 (2015), pp. 559–65

Nuclear Engineering International, 'France to Decide on New Nuclear Build after 2022', 14 January 2020

Nuclear Threat Initiative, 'Pakistan', https://www.nti.org/countries/pakistan/ (accessed 29 November 2021)

Nunn, R., J. Parsons and J. Shambaugh, 'A Dozen Facts about the Economics of the US Health-Care System', Brookings Institution, 10 March 2020

Nurjanov, A., 'EU, Kazakhstan Intend to Deepen Energy Ties', *Caspian News*, 30 March 2021

Nurtazin, S., S. Pueppke, T. Ospan, A. Mukhitdinov and T. Elebessov, 'Quality of Drinking Water in the Balkhash District of Kazakhstan's Almaty Region', *Water* 12, no. 2 (2020), pp. 1–14

Nye, J.S., Jr, 'Hard, Soft and Smart Power', in A.F. Cooper, J. Heine and R. Thakur (eds), *The Oxford Handbook of Modern Diplomacy* (Oxford: Oxford University Press, 2013)

Nye, J.S., Jr, *Power in the Global Information Age: From Realism to Globalization* (New York: Routledge, 2004)

Nye, J.S., Jr, *Soft Power: The Means to Success in World Politics* (New York: Public Affairs, 2004)

Nye, J.S., Jr, 'The Future of American Power: Dominance and Decline in Perspective,' *Foreign Affairs* 89(6), 2010

Obaji, S., 'Nigeria Is Not a Failed State, but It Has Not Delivered Democracy for Its People', *The Conversation*, 19 November 2020

O'Brien, J., 'How Quantum Computing Could Be One of the Most Innovative Climate Change Solutions', World Economic Forum, 17 December 2019

O'Donnell, J., 'St. Augustine', *Encyclopaedia Britannica*, 9 November 2021

Observatory of Economic Complexity, 'Israel: Exports', OEC World, https://oec.world/en/profile/country/isr (accessed 30 June 2021)

Observatory of Economic Complexity, 'South Korea', https://oec.world/en/profile/country/kor (accessed 18 November 2021)

Odgaard, O., and J. Delman, 'China's Energy Security and Its Challenges towards 2035', *Energy Policy* 71 (August 2014), pp. 107–17

O'Donnell J., 'St. Augustine', *Encylopaedia Britannica*, 9 November 2021.

OECD Better Life Initiative, 'How's Life in Sweden?', 2020, https://www.oecd.org/sweden/Better-Life-Initiative-country-note-Sweden.pdf

OECD, Directorate for Science Technology and Innovation, 'R&D Tax incentives: Brazil, 2019', December 2019, https://www.oecd.org/sti/rd-tax-stats-brazil.pdf, p. 2

OECD, 'Education at a Glance 2019: Japan', https://www.oecd.org/education/education-at-a-glance/EAG2019_CN_JPN.pdf

OECD, 'Education at a Glance 2019: Mexico', https://www.oecd.org/education/education-at-a-glance/EAG2019_CN_MEX.pdf

OECD, 'Education at a Glance 2016: Russian Federation', https://read.oecd-ilibrary.org/education/education-at-a-glance-2016/russian-federation_eag-2016-76-en#page1

OECD, 'Education at a Glance 2019: United Kingdom', https://www.oecd.org/education/education-at-a-glance/EAG2019_CN_GBR.pdf

OECD, 'Education GPS: Lithuania', 2020, https://gpseducation.oecd.org/CountryProfile?primaryCountry=LTU&treshold=10&topic=EO

OECD, 'Education Policy Outlook: Germany', June 2020, https://www.oecd.org/education/policy-outlook/country-profile-Germany-2020.pdf

OECD, 'Education Policy Outlook: Turkey', June 2020, https://www.oecd.org/turkey/country-profile-Turkey-2020.pdf

OECD, 'Employment by Education Level', https://data.oecd.org/emp/employment-by-education-level.htm (accessed 30 June 2021)

OECD, 'Employment Rate (Indicator)', 2021, https://doi: 10.1787/1de68a9b-en 2021 (accessed 13 September 2021)

OECD/European Observatory on Health Systems and Policies, *Lithuania: Country Health Profile 2019: State of Health in the EU* (Paris: OECD Publishing and European Observatory on Health Systems and Policies, Brussels, 2019)

OECD, 'Fertility Rates', https://data.oecd.org/pop/fertility-rates.htm (accessed 30 June 2021)

OECD, 'Foreign Population', https://data.oecd.org/migration/foreign-population.htm#indicator-chart (accessed 9 March 2020)

OECD Green Growth Studies, *Addressing Industrial Air Pollution in Kazakhstan* (Paris: OECD Publishing, 2019)

OECD, 'Israel', https://gpseducation.oecd.org/CountryProfile?primaryCountry=ISR&treshold=10&topic=EO (accessed 30 June 2021)

OECD, 'Korea Should Adapt Its Migration Programmes to Ensure Continued Success in the Face of Expected Challenges', 28 January 2019

OECD, *Lessons from PISA for Korea* (Paris: OECD Publishing, 2014)

OECD, 'Lithuania Economic Snapshot: Economic Forecast Summary (May 2021)', https://www.oecd.org/economy/lithuania-economic-snapshot (accessed 22 July 2021)

OECD, 'Lithuania – Overview of the Education System (EAG 2020)', https://gpseducation.oecd.org/CountryProfile?primaryCountry=LTU&treshold=10&topic=EO (accessed 22 July 2021)

OECD, *OECD Economic Surveys: Lithuania 2018* (Paris: OECD Publishing, 2018)

OECD, *OECD Economic Surveys: Switzerland 2019* (Paris: OECD Publishing, 2019)

OECD, 'OECD Job Strategy: Israel', https://www.oecd.org/israel/jobs-strategy-ISRAEL-EN.pdf (accessed 30 June 2021)

OECD, *OECD Reviews of School Resources: Kazakhstan 2015* (Paris: OECD Publishing, 2015)

OECD, 'Reducing the Gap between Skill Supply and Demand in Korea', https://www.oecd-ilibrary.org/sites/dfe47455-en/index.html?itemId=/content/component/dfe47455-en (accessed 30 June 2021)

OECD, *Reforming Kazakhstan: Progress, Challenges and Opportunities* (Paris: OECD Publishing, 2017)

OECD, *Reviews of National Policies for Education: Education in Saudi Arabia* (Paris: OECD Publishing, 2020)

OECD, *Reviews of National Policies for Education: Education Policy in Japan: Building Bridges towards 2030* (Paris: OECD Publishing, 2018)

OECD, *OECD Reviews of Public Health: Korea: A Healthier Tomorrow* (Paris: OECD Publishing, 2020)

OECD, *SME and Entrepreneurship Policy in Brazil 2020*, OECD Studies on SMEs and Entrepreneurship (Paris: OECD Publishing, 2020)

OECD, 'Social Spending', https://data.oecd.org/socialexp/social-spending.htm (accessed 30 June 2021)

OECD, 'Swedish Economic Snapshot - Swedish Economic Forecast Summary (December 2021)', https://www.oecd.org/economy/sweden-economic-snapshot/ (accessed 13 January 2022)

OECD, 'Switzerland: Trade and Investment Statistical Note', 2017

OECD, *Working Together for Local Integration of Migrants and Refugees in Paris* (Paris: OECD Publishing, 2018)

Office of the United States Trade Representative, 'United States-Mexico-Canada Agreement', https://ustr.gov/trade-agreements

/free-trade-agreements/united-states-mexico-canada-agreement (accessed 1 October 2018)

Official Information Source of the Prime Minister of the Republic of Kazakhstan, 'Review of Kazakhstan's Healthcare System: Results of 2020 and Plans for 2021', 1 March 2021, https://www.primeminister.kz/en/news /reviews/review-of-kazakhstans-healthcare-system-Results-of-2020-and -plans-for-20215968

Okonjo-Iweala, N., 'Africa Can Play a Leading Role in the Fight against Climate Change', Brookings Institution, 8 January 2020

Oliveira, C.S., A. Roca and X. Goula, *Assessing and Managing Earthquake Risk: Geo-scientific and Engineering Knowledge for Earthquake Risk Mitigation: Developments, Tools, Techniques* (Dordrecht: Springer, 2006)

Oloruntoba, R., 'Cyber Attacks Can Shut Down Critical Infrastructure. It's Time to Make Cyber Security Compulsory', *The Conversation*, 27 May 2021

Olsen, R., 'UK Says China Breached Hong Kong Handover Treaty for Third Time', *Forbes*, 14 March 2021

O'Neill, J., 'Household Income Inequality, UK: Financial Year Ending 2020', Office for National Statistics, 21 January 2021, https://www.ons .gov.uk/peoplepopulationandcommunity/personalandhouseholdfinances /incomeandwealth/bulletins/householdincomeinequalityfinancial /financialyearending2020

Onursal, R., 'Why the Kurdish Conflict in Turkey Is So Intractable', *The Conversation*, 18 October 2019

OPEC, 'Saudi Arabia', https://www.opec.org/opec_web/en/about_us/169.htm (accessed 30 June 2021)

Open Access Government, 'How Can Japan Remain a World Competitor in Science and Technology', 23 September 2020

Orend, B., 'Justice after War', *Ethics & International Affairs* 16, no. 1 (2002), pp. 43–56

Organization for Security and Economic Co-operation in Europe, *Best-Practice Guide for a Positive Business and Investment Climate* (Vienna: OSCE, 2006)

Organization for Security and Economic Co-operation in Europe, 'Parliamentary Elections, 18 August 2007', https://www.osce.org/odihr /elections/57937 (accessed 30 June 2021)

Organization for Security and Economic Co-operation in Europe, 'Presidential Election, 4 December 2005', https://www.osce.org/odihr /elections/kazakhstan/eoms/presidential_2005

Organisation of Islamic Cooperation, 'History', https://www.oic-oci.org /page/?p_id=52&p_ref=26&lan=en (accessed 24 June 2021)

Organisation of Islamic Cooperation, 'Member States', https://www.oic-oci .org/states/?lan=en (accessed 30 June 2021)

Ostroukh, A., and A. Marrow, 'World Bank Tells Russia: Simplify Laws to Draw Foreign Investment', Reuters, 25 March 2021

Ottaway, M., and S. Mair, 'States at Risk and Failed States: Putting Security First', Carnegie Endowment for International Peace and German Institute for International and Security Affairs, Policy Outlook, September 2004

Oxfam International, 'Brazil: Extreme Inequality in Numbers' https://www .oxfam.org/en/brazil-extreme-inequality-numbers (accessed 20 July 2021)

Oxfam International, Rigged Rules and Double Standards: Trade, Globalisation, and the Fight against Poverty (Oxford: Oxfam, 2002)

Oxford Analytica, 'Mexico's Brain Drain to Continue Unabated', *Expert Briefings*, 2018

Oxford Business Group, 'Educational Reforms to Improve Teaching Quality in Saudi Arabia', in *The Report: Saudi Arabia 2020* (OBG, 2020)

Oxford Business Group, 'More Private Sector Participation to Stimulate Growth in Saudi Arabia Industry', in *The Report: Saudi Arabia 2018* (OBG, 2018)

Oxford Dictionary of Phrase and Fable, 'Artificial Intelligence', https://www .oxfordreference.com/view/10.1093/oi/authority.20110803095426960 (accessed 26 July 2021)

Ozturk, I., *Energy Dependency and Security: The Role of Efficiency and Renewable Energy Sources*, Working Paper no. E-37113-PAK-1, (London: International Growth Centre, 2014)

Pakistan Alliance for Girls Education, 'Education Budget of Pakistan', https:// page.org.pk/education-budget-of-pakistan (accessed 22 Juy 2021)

Palveleva, L., and R. Coalson, 'Echoes of War and Collapse: Russia's Demographic Decline as Small 1990s Generation Comes of Age', Radio Free Europe/Radio Liberty, 12 January 2020

Pamlin, D., and S. Armstrong, *Global Challenges: 12 Risks that Threaten Human Civilisation: The Case for a New Category of Risks* (Stockholm: Global Challenges Foundation, 2015)

Panda, A., 'Climate Change, Displacement, and Managed Retreat in Coastal India', Migration Policy Institute, 22 May 2020

Park, C.H., *The Three Enduring Legacies of the Pacific War in East Asia* (Washington, DC: Wilson Center, 2020

Parker, J.D., 'The Spillover Effects of the Syrian Civil War', in H. Moodrick-Even Khen, N.T. Boms and S. Ashraph (eds), *The Syrian War: Between Justice and Political Reality* (Cambridge: Cambridge University Press, 2020), pp. 198–216

Parrado, E., N. Woods and M. Kuritzky, 'What are Frontier Risks and How Can We Prepare for Them?', World Economic Forum, 2 June 2021

Parshotam, A., 'Sliding towards Disaster: Migration in European African Relations', SAIIA, 18 October 2018

Pascual, C., 'The Geopolitics of Energy: From Security to Survival', Brookings Institution, January 2008

Patel, N.V., 'Why Japan is Emerging as NASA's Most Important Space Partner', *MIT Technology Review*, 22 July 2020

Patrick, S.M., 'John Kerry and the Blurring of the Foreign and the Domestic', Council on Foreign Relations, 22 February 2013

Patz, J.A., P.R. Epstein, T.A. Burke and J.M. Balbus, 'Global Climate Change and Emerging Infectious Diseases', *JAMA: Journal of the American Medical Association* 275, no. 3 (1996), pp. 217–23

Pauwels, A., 'Preventing Terrorism in the South', EUISS, Brief no. 6, 8 March 2017, pp. 1–4

Pavid, K., 'Aspirin, Morphine and Chemotherapy: The Essential Medicines Powered by Plants', Natural History Museum, 19 February 2021, https://www.nhm.ac.uk/discover/essential-medicines-powered-by-plants.html

Peabody, B., 'Brexit Is Probably the United Kingdom's Death Knell', *Foreign Policy*, 3 February 2021

Pearson, E., 'Seven Years of Suffering for Australia's Asylum Seekers, Refugees', Human Rights Watch, 16 July 2020

Pedrozo, R.P., 'International Law and Japan's Territorial Disputes', *Review of Island Studies*, 6 February 2018

Pereira, R.H., C.K.V. Braga, L.M. Servo, B. Serra, P. Amaral, N. Gouveia and A. Paez, 'Geographic Access to COVID-19 Healthcare in Brazil Using a Balanced Float Catchment Area Approach', *Social Science and Medicine* 273 (March 2021), pp. 1–12

Permanent Mission of Switzerland to the United Nations Office, 'Facts and Figures about International Geneva', https://www.eda.admin.ch/missions/mission-onu-geneve/en/home/geneve-international/faits-et-chiffres.html (accessed 30 June 2021)

Perrin, D., 'Nobel Prize for CRISPR Honors Two Great Scientists – And Leaves out Many Others', *The Conversation*, 8 October 2020

Persson, I., and J. Savulescu, 'The Moral Importance of Reflective Empathy', *Neuroethics* 11, no. 2 (2018), pp. 183–93

Peter, L., 'Is Russia Going to War with Ukraine and Other Questions', BBC News, 13 April 2021

Peters, A., and A. Hindocha, 'US Global Cybercrime Cooperation: A Brief Explainer', *Third Way*, 26 June 2020

Peterson, E.R., *Addressing Our Global Water Future*, Center for Strategic and International Studies with Sandia National Laboratories (Washington, DC: CSIS, 2005)

Peterson Institute for International Economics, 'Case Studies in Sanctions and Terrorism', 2007, https://www.piie.com/commentary/speeches-papers/case-78-8-and-92-12

Peterson, S., 'Russia, Iran Harden against West', *Christian Science Monitor*, 18 October 2007, http://www.csmonitor.com/2007/1018/p06s02-woeu.html

Petro Online, 'Why Does Russia Want to Nationalise Its Oil and Gas Industry?', 9 July 2016, https://www.petro-online.com/news/fuel-for-thought/13/breaking-news/why-does-russia-want-to-nationalise-its-oil-and-gas-industry/39472

Pettit, P., 'The Globalized Republican Ideal', *Global Justice and Non-Domination* 9, no. 1 (2016), pp. 47–68

Pew Research Center, 'Religion and American Foreign Policy: Prophetic, Perilous, Inevitable', 5 February 2003

Pew Research Center, 'The Future of World Religions: Population Growth Projections, 2010–2050', 2 April 2015

Phelps, E.A., K.M. Lempert and P. Sokol-Hessner, 'Emotion and Decision Making: Multiple Modulatory Neural Circuits', *Annual Review of Neuroscience* 37 (2014), pp. 263–87

Phillips, D.L., 'The Truth about Turkey's Role in Syria', Columbia University Institute for the Study of Human Rights, 1 March 2021, http://www.human rightscolumbia.org/news/truth-about-turkey%E2%80%99s-role-syria

Pillai Rajagopalan, R., 'The Outer Space Treaty: Overcoming Space Security Governance Challenges', Council on Foreign Relations, 23 February 2021

Pimm, S.L., G.J. Russell, J.L. Gittleman and T.M. Brooks, 'The Future of Biodiversity', *Science* 269, no. 5222 (1995), pp. 347–50

Pind Foundation, *Niger Delta Annual Conflict Report: January to December 2020*, https://pindfoundation.org/niger-delta-annual-conflict -report-january-december-2020

Pinson, G., and C. Morel Journel (eds), *Debating the Neoliberal City* (London: Routledge, 2017)

Pitman, T., and H. Forsyth, 'Should We Follow the German Way of Free Higher Education?', *The Conversation*, 17 March 2014

Plaza, C.V., V. de A. Guimarães, G. Ribeiro and L. Bahiense, 'Economic and Environmental Location of Logistics Integration Centers: The Brazilian Soybean Transportation Case', *TOP: An Official Journal of the Spanish Society of Statistics and Operations Research* 28, no. 3 (2020), pp. 749–71

Podesta, J., and P. Ogden, 'The Security Implications of Climate Change', *Washington Quarterly* 31, no. 1 (2007–8), pp. 115–38

Polaniy, J., 'How Many Minutes to Midnight? A High-Level Panel Convenes to Check the State of the "Doomsday Clock' in R. Braun, R. Hinde, D. Krieger, H. Kroto and S. Milne (eds), *Joseph Rotblat: Visionary for Peace* (London: Wiley, 2007)

Pollmann, M., and N. Yashiro, 'Resolved: Japan Has Not Done Enough to Bolster Immigration', Centre for Strategic and International Studies, *Debating Japan* 3, no. 6 (2020), n.p.

Polyzos, S., and D. Tsiotas, 'The Contribution of Transport Infrastructures to the Economic and Regional Development', *Theoretical and Empirical Researches in Urban Development* 15, no. 1 (2020), pp. 5–23

Population Reference Bureau, 'Israel's Demography Has a Unique History', 9 January 2014

Port Technology International Team, 'Is the Arctic Route the Future of Shipping?', Port Technology, 5 November 2018

Poverty USA, 'The Population of Poverty USA', https://www.povertyusa.org
/facts (accessed 30 June 2021)

Power Technology, 'Managing Nuclear Waste in France: The Long and Short
Game', 2 May 2018

Power Technology, 'Power Plays: The Role of Energy in Modern Geopolitics',
26 April 2018

Poznansky, M.J., *Saved by Science: The Hope and Promise of Synthetic Biology*
(Toronto: ECW Press, 2020)

Primin, O., 'Clean Water of Russia: Problems and Solutions', *IOP
Conference Series: Materials Science and Engineering* 365, no. 2
(2018), pp. 1–7

Pryke, J., 'The Risks of China's Ambitions in the South Pacific', Brookings
Institution, 20 July 2020

Prytz, A., 'COVID-Recovery Budget Needs to Invest in Public Education,
Says Union', *The Age*, 30 August 2020

Pugh, J., L. Pycroft, A. Sandberg, T. Aziz and J. Savulescu, 'Brainjacking in
Deep Brain Stimulation and Autonomy', *Ethics and Information Technology*
20 (2018), pp. 219–38

Pulse, 'S. Korea to Raise Retirement Age Revision as Official Agenda Next
Year', 15 April 2021

Puranen, B., and O. Widenfalk, 'The Rentier State: Does Rentierism Hinder
Democracy', in M. Moaddel (ed.), *Values and Perceptions of the Islamic
and Middle Eastern Publics* (New York: Palgrave Macmillan, 2007),
pp. 160–78

Puri-Mirza, A., 'Banking Industry in Saudi Arabia – Statistics and Facts',
Statista, 17 December 2020

Puri-Mirza, A., 'Share of Female Graduates Saudi Arabia 2010–2019', Statista,
16 March 2021

Prusa, A., and B. Vasconcelos Cimatti, 'Too Hot: The Threat to Amazon
Biodiversity', Argentina Project, Wilson Center, 21 May 2021

Pycroft, L., 'Brainjacking – A New Cyber-Security Threat', *The Conversation*,
23 August 2016

Pycroft, L., S.G. Boccard, S.L. Owen, J.F. Stein, J.J. Fitzgerald, A.L. Green
and T.Z. Aziz, 'Brainjacking: Implant Security Issues in Invasive
Neuromodulation', *World Neurosurgery* 92 (2016), pp. 454–62

Qazizai, F., and D. Hadid, 'The Taliban Are Getting Stronger in Afghanistan
as US and NATO Forces Exit', NPR, 5 June 2021

Qin, V.M., B. McPake, M.Z. Raban, T.E. Cowling, R. Alshamsan, K.S. Chia,
P.C. Smith, R. Atun and J.T. Lee, 'Rural and Urban Differences in Health
System Performance among Older Chinese Adults: Cross-Sectional
Analysis of a National Sample', *BMC Health Services Research* 20, no. 1
(2020), pp. 1–14

Quillin, B., 'Changing Global Demographics: The Certain Future', *BBVA*, 14
October 2019

Quinn, C., 'Tehran and Washington Signal Slow Going for Nuclear Deal', *Foreign Policy*, 30 July 2021, https://foreignpolicy.com/2021/07/30/iran-nuclear-deal-raisi-sanctions

Radio Free Europe, 'Russia, Kazakhstan Replace Decades-Old Military Cooperation Agreement', 16 October 2020

Rafferty, J.P., '9 of the Biggest Oil Spills in History', Encyclopaedia Britannica, https://www.britannica.com/list/9-of-the-biggest-oil-spills-in-history

Raiser, M., 'Brazil Can Improve Education by Copying Its Own Successes', Brookings Institution, 6 March 2018

Rajabi, S., 'Unemployment in Iran a Problem with Political and Social Dimensions', *Iran Focus*, 17 May 2021

Rakhmat, M.Z., 'The Quiet Growth in Indonesia-Israel Relations', *The Diplomat*, 11 March 2015

Ramani, S., 'Russia's Strategic Transformation in Libya: A Winning Gambit?" RUSI, Commentary, 28 April 2021

Ramsey, P., 'Force and Political Responsibility', in E.W. Lefever (ed.), *Ethics and World Politics: Four Perspectives* (Baltimore: Johns Hopkins University Press, 1972), pp. 43–73

Randall, A., 'Climate Change Driving Migration into China's Vulnerable Cities', Climate and Migration Coalition (Accessed 30 July 2021)

Randall, C., 'CAM Study Reveals: German Carmakers Are Most Innovative', Electrive, 10 December 2019

RANE Worldview, powered by Stratfor, 'The Strategic Importance of the Caspian Sea', 19 May 2014

Rapoza, K., 'Kazakhstan Opens Astana International Financial Center in Hopes to Become Eurasian Financial Hub', *Forbes*, 26 June 2018

Rapoza, K., '"Strategic Competition": US Looks to Kazakhstan to Expand Ties', *Forbes*, 25 April 2021

Rasheed, M.F., 'The Concept of Power in International Relations', *Pakistan Horizon* 48, no. 1 (1995), pp. 95–99

Rasmussen, R.C., 'An Emerging Strategic Geometry – Thawing Chokepoints and Littorals in the Arctic', Center for International Maritime Security, 3 June 2020

Rathmell, A., and A. Mellors, 'Building Effective Institutions', *SDGs: The People's Agenda*, 1 March 2016

Rawls, J., *A Theory of Justice*, rev. edn (Oxford: Oxford University Press, 1999)

Razin, A., 'Israel's Immigration Story: Winners and Losers', National Bureau of Economic Research, Working Paper no. 24283, February 2018, pp. 10–12

Regan, H., '21 of the World's 30 Cities with the Worst Air Pollution Are in India', CNN, 25 February 2020

Regional Comprehensive Economic Partnership, 'RCEP: A New Trade Agreement That Will Shape Global Economics and Politics', https://rcepsec.org/2020/11/26/rcep-a-new-trade-agreement-that-will-shape-global-economics-and-politics (accessed 25 June 2021)

Reid, D., 'New York Stretches Lead over London as the World's Top Financial Center, Survey Shows', CNBC, 19 September 2019

Reif, K., and S. Bugos, 'UK to Increase Cap on Nuclear Warhead Stockpile', Arms Control Association, April 2021

Reiff, N., '10 Biggest Oil Companies', *Investopedia*, 10 September 2020

Rejali, S., and Y. Heiniger, 'The Role of Digital Technologies in Humanitarian Law, Policy and Action: Charting a Path Forward', *International Review of the Red Cross* 913 (March 2021)

Remy, M., 'CO_2: La France moins pollueuse grâce au nucléaire' (CO_2: France Pollutes Less Thanks to Nuclear Energy), *L'Usine Nouvelle*, 18 June 2010

Republic of Lithuania, 'Programme of the Eighteenth Government of the Republic of Lithuania', Resolution no. XIV-72, 11 December 2020

Republic of South Africa, 'How Unequal is South Africa?', 4 February 2020, http://www.statssa.gov.za/?p=12930

Republic of South Africa, 'South Africa's Updated Draft Nationally Determined Contribution (NDC) Launched', 30 March 2021, https://www.environment.gov.za/mediarelease/creecy_indc2021draftlaunch _climatechangecop26

Repucci, S., and A. Slipowitz, 'Freedom in the World 2021: Democracy under Siege, Freedom House, 2021

Reuters, 'Dozens Detained in Rare Kazakhstan Independence Day Protests', 16 December 2019

Reuters, 'Germany Sets Tougher CO_2 Emission Reduction Targets after Top Court Ruling', 5 May 2021

Reuters, 'Germany's Scholz Rejects Further Hike of Retirement Age to 68', 8 June 2021

Reuters, 'Mexico Loses 12 Million Jobs, Workers in Informal Sector Grow', 30 June 2020

Reuters, 'Remittances to Mexican Families Rise to Record High for February', 5 April 2021

Reuters, 'Russia Begins TurkStream Gas Flows to Greece, North Macedonia, 5 January 2020

Reuters, 'Saudi Arabia Doubles Private Sector Jobs in 30-Month Period', 19 January 2014

Reuters, 'South Africa Plans Special Court to Help Unblock Land Redistribution', 1 March 2021

Reuters, 'UPDATE 2 – Nigeria's Government Expects Economy to Contract by 3.4% in 2020', 5 May 2020

Reveron, D.S., N.K. Gvosdev and J.A. Cloud (eds) *The Oxford Handbook of US National Security* (Oxford: Oxford University Press, 2018)

Rhodes, C., G. Hutton and M. Ward, 'Research and Development Spending', House of Commons Library, Research Briefing, 16 March 2021

Riedel, B.O. *Avoiding Armageddon: America, India, and Pakistan to the Brink and Back* (Washington, DC: Brookings Institution Press, 2013)

Riley, L.W., A.I. Ko, A. Unger and M.G. Reis, 'Slum Health: Diseases of Neglected Populations', *BMC International Health and Human Rights* 7, no. 1 (2007), pp. 1–6

Riono, P., and S.J. Challacombe, 'HIV in Indonesia and in Neighbouring Countries and Its Social Impact', *Oral Diseases* 26, no. S1 (30 August 2020), pp. 28–33

Riordan, S., *The New Diplomacy* (Cambridge: Polity Press, 2003)

Ritchie, H., and M. Roser, 'Indonesia: CO_2 Country Profile', Our World in Data, https://ourworldindata.org/co2/country/Indonesia (accessed 30 June 2021)

Ritchie, H., and M. Roser, 'South Africa: CO_2 Country Profile', Our World in Data, https://ourworldindata.org/co2/country/south-africa (accessed 30 June 2021)

Ritter, K., 'Pollutants and Heavy Metals Taint Moscow's Water Supply', Circle of Blue, 12 April 2018

Robin, R.T., *The Making of the Cold War Enemy: Culture and Politics in the Military-Intellectual Complex* (Princeton, NJ: Princeton University Press, 2003)

Robinson, K., 'The Arab Spring at Ten Years: What's the Legacy of the Uprisings?', Council on Foreign Relations, 3 December 2020

Robinson, K., 'What Is the Iran Nuclear Deal?', Council on Foreign Relations, Backgrounder, 18 August 2021

Robinson, K., 'What Is US Policy on the Israeli-Palestinian Conflict?', Council on Foreign Relations, Backgrounder, 27 May 2021

Robinson, K., 'Yemen's Tragedy: War, Stalemate, and Suffering', Council on Foreign Relations, Backgrounder, 5 February 2021

Roden, L., 'The Four Big Security Challenges Facing Sweden Today', *The Local*, 16 March 2017

Rodionova, Z., 'World's Largest Corporations Make More Money than Most Countries on Earth Combined', *The Independent*, 13 September 2016

Roell, M.-S., and M.D. Zurbriggen, 'The Impact of Synthetic Biology for Future Agriculture and Nutrition', *Current Opinion in Biotechnology* 61 (2020), pp. 102–9

Romy, K., 'Banking Secrecy Remains a Business Model for Swiss Banks', Swissinfo.ch, 5 February 2021

Rosenau, W., 'Subversion Old and New', *War on the Rocks*, 24 April 2014

Rosenau, W., *Subversion and Insurgency*, RAND Counterinsurgency Study, Paper 2 (Santa Monica, CA: RAND Corporation, 2007)

Rosenbaum, A., 'Is Israel's Scarcity of Water a Blessing in Disguise?', *Jerusalem Post*, 7 January 2021

Ross, D., *Statecraft: And How to Restore America's Standing in the World* (New York: Farrar, Straus and Giroux, 2007)

Rosser, A., 'Beyond Access: Making Indonesia's Education System Work', Lowy Institute for International Policy, 21 February 2018

Rousseau, R., 'Kazakhstan's Strategic and Military Relations with Russia', *Diplomatic Courier*, 20 July 2011

Rowlingson, K., *Does Income Inequality Cause Health and Social Problems?* (York: Joseph Rowntree Foundation, 2011), p. 5

Roy, J.S., 'Leadership in a Multipolar World: Can the United States Influence Cooperation between China and Russia?', *National Bureau of Asian Research*, 8 April 2018

Ruggie, J.G., 'What Makes the World Hang Together? Neo-utilitarianism and the Social Constructivist Challenge', *International Organization* 52, no. 4 (Autumn 1998)

Rumer, E., R. Sokolsky and P. Stronsky, 'Russia in the Arctic – A Critical Examination', Carnegie Endowment for International Peace, Paper, 29 March 2021

Ruparelia, S., 'India's Farmers Are Right to Protest against Agricultural Reforms', *The Conversation*, 24 January 2021

Russell, M., 'The Russian Economy: Will Russia Ever Catch Up?', European Parliamentary Research Service Publications Office, 11 March 2015

Ryall, J., 'Japan's "Appalling" Gender Equality Record Puts Spotlight on Sexism', DW, 5 April 2021

Ryall, J., 'Japan's Territorial Disputes: China, South Korea, Russia and More', *SCMP*, 26 February 2021

Sabaghi, D., 'The Middle East Looks to Innovate Its Way out of a Water Crisis', *World Politics Review*, 14 April 2021

Saballa, J., 'Australian Military to Establish New $7 Billion Space Division', *The Defence Post*, 20 May 2021

Sachs, J., 'The New Geopolitics', *Scientific American*, 22 May 2006

Safranski, M., 'Why Some Are Calling Thomas P.M. Barnett Our Age's George F. Kennan', History News Network, http://hnn.us/articles/9212 .html

Saied, M., 'Spotlight on Egypt to Help Mediate with Hamas', *Al-Monitor*, 18 May 2021

Saiymova, M., S. Smagulova, R. Yesbergen, G. Demeuova, B. Bolatova, B. Taskarina and A. Ibrasheva, 'The Knowledge-Based Economy and Innovation Policy in Kazakhstan: Looking at Key Practical Problems', *Academy of Strategic Management Journal* 17, no. 6 (2018), n.p.

Salata, A., 'Race, Class and Income Inequality in Brazil: A Social Trajectory Analysis', *SciELO Brasil* 63, no. 3 (2020), pp. 1–40

Sanandaji, N., 'So Long, Swedish Welfare State?', Foreign Policy, 5 September 2018

Sanchez, W.A., 'The Future of US-Kazakhstan Relations', *Georgetown Journal of International Affairs*, 28 May 2010

Sanghi, A., and S. Yusuf, 'Russia's Uphill Struggle with Innovation', World Bank, 17 September 2018

Santander, 'France: Foreign Investment', https://santandertrade.com/en/portal /establish-overseas/france/foreign-investment (accessed 30 July 2021)

Santander, 'South Africa: Foreign Investment', https://santandertrade.com
  /en/portal/establish-overseas/south-africa/foreign-investment (accessed 22
  July 2021)
Santander, 'South Korea Foreign Trade in Figures', https://santandertrade
  .com/en/portal/analyse-markets/south-korea/foreign-trade-in-figures
  (accessed 30 June 2021)
Santos, R.E., R.M. Pinto-Coelho, M.A. Drumond, R. Fonseca and
  F.B. Zanchi, 'Damming Amazon Rivers: Environmental Impacts of
  Hydroelectric Dams on Brazil's Madeira River According to Local Fishers'
  Perception', *Ambio* (A Journal of the Human Environment) 49, no. 10
  (2020), pp. 1612–28
Sartbayev, B., 'Kazakhstan Aims to Become a Destination for Global
  Investment', *Foreign Policy*, https://foreignpolicy.com/sponsored
  /kazakhstan-aims-to-become-a-destination-for-global-investment
  (accessed 22 July 2021)
Sassi, F., 'What the "Power of Siberia" Tells Us about China-Russia Relations',
  The Diplomat, 7 December 2019
Satei, S., 'The Legal Status of the Northwest Passage: Canada's Jurisdiction
  or International Law in Light of Recent Developments in Arctic Shipping
  Regulation?', in L.P. Hildebrand, L.W. Brigham and T.M. Johansson
  (eds), *Sustainable Shipping in a Changing Arctic* (Cham: Springer, 2018),
  pp. 241–52
Satoh, S., and E. Boyer, 'HIV in South Africa', *The Lancet* 394, no. 10197 (10
  August 2019), p. 467
Saunders, R.A., and V. Strukov (eds), *Popular Geopolitics: Plotting an Evolving
  Interdiscipline* (Abingdon: Routledge, 2018)
Schaeffer, K., 'A Look at the Americans Who Believe There Is Some Truth
  to the Conspiracy Theory That COVID-19 Was Planned', Pew Research
  Center, 24 July 2020, https://www.pewresearch.org/fact-tank/2020/07/24/a
  -look-at-the-americans-who-believe-there-is-some-truth-to-the-conspiracy
  -theory-that-covid-19-was-planned
Schell, J., *The Fate of the Earth* (New York: Alfred A. Knopf, 1982)
Schewe, E., 'Settlements and the Israel-Palestine Conflict: Background
  Reading', *JSTOR Daily*, 19 May 2019, https://daily.jstor.org/israeli-settlement
  -palestine-background-readings/
Schuette, L., 'Should the EU Make Foreign Policy Decisions by Majority
  Voting?', Centre for European Reform, 15 May 2019
Schwab, K., (ed.), *The Global Competitiveness Report 2015–2016* (Geneva:
  World Economic Forum, 2015)
Schwab, K., (ed.), *The Global Competitiveness Report 2018* (Geneva: World
  Economic Forum, 2018)
Schwartz, Y., 'Can Israel and Jordan Cooperate to Save the Dying Dead Sea?',
  National Geographic, 6 December 2018
Science and Technology Australia, 'Australia Can't Afford to
  Lose R&D Investment in Recovery', 27 March 2020, https://

scienceandtechnologyaustralia.org.au/australia-cant-afford-to-lose-rd
-investment-in-recovery

Scientific American, Without a Treaty to Share the Arctic, Greedy Countries
Will Destroy It', 1 December 2017

Scoblic, J.P., 'Review: *Diplomacy*, by Henry Kissinger', *Brown Journal of World
Affairs* 1, no. 2 (1994), pp. 399–404

Scott, B., 'Five Eyes Blurring the Lines between Intelligence and Policy', *The
Interpreter* (Lowy Institute), 27 July 2020

Scott, D., 'Two Sisters. Two Different Journeys through Australia's Health
Care System', *Vox*, 15 January 2020

Scroll, 'India Latest Health Scorecard: More Heart Disease, a Surge in
Diabetes and a Rising Suicide Rate', 16 September 2018, https://scroll.in
/pulse/894452/india-latest-health-scorecard-more-heart-disease-a-surge
-in-diabetes-and-a-rising-suicide-rate

Scroxton, A., 'UK Plans "Full Spectrum" Approach to National Cyber
Security', *Computer Weekly*, 15 March 2021

Sempa, F.M., 'Halford Mackinder's Last View of the Round World', *The
Diplomat*, 23 March 2015

Sen, A.K., 'A Rising China Has Pacific Islands in Its Sights: US Lawmakers
Seek Ways to Deepen Engagement with a Critical Region', United States
Institute for Peace, 23 July 2020

Senvic, K., R.W. Hood Jr and T.J. Coleman III, 'Secularism in Turkey', 2017,
pp. 2–9, https://www.researchgate.net/publication/322962600_Secularism
_in_Turkey

Shackman, A., and T. Wager, 'The Emotional Brain: Fundamental Questions
and Strategies for Future Research', *Neuroscience Letters*, no. 693
(March 2019), pp. 68–74

Shahid, J., 'Pakistan's Deforestation Rate Second Highest in Asia: WWF',
DAWN, 15 August 2020

Shaikh, B., 'Private Sector in Health Care Delivery: A Reality and Challenge
in Pakistan', *Journal of Ayub Medical College Abbottabad* 27, no. 2 (2015),
pp. 496–98

Shapiro, D., and N. Yefimova-Trilling, 'Russian Population Decline in
Spotlight Again', *Russia Matters*, 13 September 2019

Sharifzoda, K., 'Why Is Kazakhstan a Growing Destination for Central Asian
Migrant Workers?' *The Diplomat*, 13 June 2019

Sharma, A., '10 Facts about Sanitation in Pakistan', The Borgen Project, 21
March 2020

Sharma, M., 'Environmental Degradation Draining Pakistan's Economy',
Down to Earth, 16 July 2014

Sharp, J.M., 'US Foreign Aid to Israel', US Congressional Research Service,
updated 16 November 2020

Sharudenko, A., '10 Facts about Healthcare in the Russian Federation', The
Borgen Project, 18 June 2020

Shead, S., 'China's Spending on R&D Hits a Record $378 Billion', CNBC, 1 March 2021

Sheehan, M., *The International Politics of Space* (New York: Routledge, 2007)

Sheen, D., 'Black Lives Do Not Matter in Israel', Al Jazeera, 29 March 2018

Shelton, T., 'Taliban Taking Back Territory as Australian and US Forces Prepare to Leave Afghanistan by September', ABC News, 18 June 2021

Sheludkov, A., J. Kamp and D. Müller, 'Decreasing Labor Intensity in Agriculture and the Accessibility of Major Cities Shape the Rural Population Decline in Postsocialist Russia', *Eurasian Geography and Economics* 62, no. 4 (2021), pp. 481–506

Sheridan, M.B., 'Violent Criminal Groups are Claiming More Territory', *Washington Post*, 29 October 2020

Sheykhi, M.T., 'Population Surge Threatens Water Supply in Iran', Water World, 1 April 2003

Shin, M., 'Conflict between South Korea and Japan Surges Again with Court's "Comfort Women" Decision', *The Diplomat*, 26 January 2021

Shinoda, H., 'The Politics of Legitimacy in International Relations: A Critical Examination of NATO's Intervention in Kosovo', *Alternatives* 25, no. 4 (2000), 515–36

Shorrocks, A., J. Davies and R. Lluberas, *Global Wealth Report*, 10th edn (Zürich: Credit Suisse, 2019)

Sikkink, K., 'Transnational Politics, International Relations Theory, and Human Rights', *Political Science and Politics* 31, no. 3 (1998), pp. 517–23

Simsek, A., 'Support for Muslim Brotherhood Isolates Turkey', DW, 21 August 2013

Singer, P.W., 'AIDS and International Security', *Survival* 44, no. 1 (2002), pp. 145–58

Singh, M., 'The Curious Case of Pakistan's Democracy', Global Risks Insights, 20 September 2018

Singh Verma, A., 'A Case for the United States' Ratification of UNCLOS', *Diplomatist*, 2 May 2020

Siripala, T., 'US and Japan Name China as Threat to International Order', *The Diplomat*, 17 March 2021

Siripurapu, A., and M. Speier, 'Is Rising Student Debt Harming the US Economy?', Council on Foreign Relations, 13 April 2021

SIPRI Military Expenditure Database (1949–), updated annually, https://www.sipri.org/databases/milex

Skinner, K., and R.A. Berman, 'Biden's Surrender to Merkel on Nord Stream 2', *Foreign Policy*, 26 July 2021

Slater, J., 'India Is No Longer Home to the Largest Number of Poor People in the World. Nigeria Is', *Washington Post*, 14 July 2021

Sleet, P., 'Water Resources in Pakistan: Scarce, Polluted and Poorly Governed', Future Directions International, 31 January 2019

Sloan, G., *Geopolitics, Geography and Strategic History* (London: Routledge, 2018)

Smith, B., 'South Korea: Environmental Issues, Policies and Clean Technology', AZO Clean Tech, 9 July 2015

Smith, B., 'United Kingdom: Environmental Issues, Policies and Clean Technology', AZO Clean Tech, 9 June 2015

Snow, D.M., *National Security for a New Era: Globalization and Geopolitics*, 2nd edn (New York: Pearson Longman, 2007)

Snyder, S., 'Water in Crisis: India', The Water Project, https://thewaterproject .org/water-crisis/water-in-crisis-india (accessed 14 July 2021)

Snyder, S.A., 'The US-South Korea Summit: A Relationship Restored?', Council on Foreign Relations, 25 May 2021

Snyder, S.A., G. Lee, Y.H. Kim and J. Kim, *Domestic Constraints on South Korea's Foreign Policy* (New York: Council on Foreign Relations, 2018)

Solingen, E., 'The New Multilateralism and Nonproliferation: Bringing in Domestic Politics', *Global Governance* 1, no. 2 (1995), pp. 205–27

Solis, M., 'Japan's Democratic Renewal and the Survival of the Liberal Order', Brookings Institution, 22 January 2021

Solomon, A.B., 'Inside Iran: Iran's Demographic Problem', *Jerusalem Post*, 25 January 2014, https://www.jpost.com/features/front-lines/inside-iran-irans -demographic-problem-339246

Solomon, S., 'From 1950s Rationing to Modern High-Tech Boom: Israel's Economic Success Story', *Times of Israel*, 18 April 2018

Soloshcheva, M.A., 'The Uyghur Terrorism: Phenomenon and Genesis', *Iran & the Caucasus* 21, no. 4 (2017), pp. 415–30

Sørensen, G., *The Transformation of the State: Beyond the Myth of Retreat* (London: Palgrave, 2004)

Sotamayor, K., 'The One-Child Policy Legacy on Women and Relationships in China', Independent Lens, 5 February 2020

South Korean Ministry of Foreign Affairs, 'Panmunjom Declaration for Peace, Prosperity and Unification of the Korean Peninsula', 11 September 2018, http://www.mofa.go.kr/eng/brd/m_5478/view.do?seq=319130&srchFr =&srchTo=&srchWord=&srchTp=&multi_itm_seq=0&itm_seq_1=0&itm _seq_2=0&company_cd=&company_nm=&page=1&titleNm=

Souza Dias, M.O. de, R.M. Filho, P.E. Mantelatto, O. Cavalett, C.E.V. Rossell, A. Bonomi and M.R.L.V. Leal, 'Sugarcane Processing for Ethanol and Sugar in Brazil', *Environmental Development* 15 (2015), pp. 35–51

Space.com, 'China's Space Program', https://www.space.com/topics/china -space-program (accessed 30 June 2021)

S&P Global, 'India's Infrastructure Push Needs New Model, Strong State Support to Succeed', 12 April 2021, https://www.spglobal.com /marketintelligence/en/news-insights/latest-news-headlines/india-s -infrastructure-push-needs-new-model-strong-state-support-to-succeed -63343927

Spoonley, P., 'Far-Right Extremists Still Threaten New Zealand, a Year on from the Christchurch Attacks', *The Conversation*, 10 March 2020

Spring, A., and C. Earl, 'Australia's Biodiversity at Breaking Point – a Picture Essay', *The Guardian*, 15 May 2019

Springfield, C., 'Accounting for Israel's Economic Boom', *International Banker*, 6 June 2018

Stanicek, B., 'Hagia Sophia: Turkey's Secularism under Threat', European Parliamentary Research Service, PE 652.026, July 2020, pp. 1–2

Starr, S.F., 'Is This Central Asia's ASEAN Moment?', *The Diplomat*, 5 December 2019

State Council of the People's Republic of China, '2020: China's GDP Expands by 2.3% to Top 101.6 Trillion Yuan', 19 January 2021, http://english.www.gov.cn/news/videos/202101/19/content_WS60064cecc6d0f725769441ba.html

State Secretariat for Economic Affairs (Switzerland), 'Swiss International Cooperation', 5 March 2021, https://www.seco-cooperation.admin.ch/secocoop/en/home/strategy/focus/international-cooperation.html

State Security Department of the Republic of Lithuania and Defence Intelligence Security Service under the Ministry of National Defence, *National Threat Assessment 2021* (Vilnius: State Security Department of Lithuania, 2021)

Statista, 'African Countries with the Highest Gross Domestic Product (GDP) in 2020', https://www.statista.com/statistics/1120999/gdp-of-african-countries-by-country (accessed 30 June 2021)

Statista, 'Brazil: National Debt from 2016 to 2026 in Relation to Gross Domestic Product', 19 October 2021. https://www.statista.com/statistics/271041/national-debt-of-brazil-in-relation-to-gross-domestic-product-gdp

Statista, 'Countries with the Highest Military Spending Worldwide in 2020 (in Billion US Dollars)', https://www.statista.com/statistics/262742/countries-with-the-highest-military-spending/ (accessed 4 August 2021)

Statista, 'Crimes and Violence in Brazil: Statistics and Facts', 14 September 2021, https://www.statista.com/topics/7017/crime-and-violence-in-brazil

Statista, 'Defense Spending UK 2021', https://www.statista.com/statistics/298490/defense-spending-united-kingdom-uk (accessed 30 June 2021)

Statista, 'Distribution of Oil and Non-Oil Revenue in Saudi Arabia in 2020', https://www.statista.com/statistics/1154249/saudi-arabia-oil-and-non-oil-revenue-share (accessed 30 June 2021)

Statista, 'Egypt – Inflation Rate from 1986 to 2026 (Compared to the Previous Year)', https://www.statista.com/statistics/377354/inflation-rate-in-egypt (accessed 20 July 2021)

Statista, 'Female Labor Participation Rate in South Korea from 2003 to 2020', https://www.statista.com/statistics/641654/south-korea-female-labor-force-participation-rate (accessed 23 July 2021)

Statista, 'Healthcare in Russia: Statistics and Facts', 22 April 2021, https://
www.statista.com/topics/4824/health-care-in-russia

Statista, 'Indonesia: Unemployment Rate from 1999 to 2020', https://www
.statista.com/statistics/320129/unemployment-rate-in-indonesia (accessed
21 July 2021)

Statista, 'Internal Migration in Russia from 2009 to 2019', https://www
.statista.com/statistics/1009980/internal-migration-russia-by-federal
-district (accessed 30 June 2021)

Statista, 'Iran: Unemployment Rate from 1999 to 2020', https://www.statista
.com/statistics/294305/iran-unemployment-rate (accessed 21 July 2021)

Statista, 'Israel: Total Population from 2016 to 2026', Accessed 30 June 2021.
https://www.statista.com/statistics/526560/total-population-of-israel
(accessed 30 June 2021)

Statista, 'Japan: Degree of Urbanization from 2010 to 2020', https://www
.statista.com/statistics/270086/urbanization-in-japan (accessed 30
June 2021)

Statista, 'Japan: Distribution of GDP across Economic Sectors from 2008
to 2018', https://www.statista.com/statistics/270093/distribution-of-gross
-domestic-product-gdp-across-economic-sectors-in-japan (accessed 30
June 2021)

Statista, 'Japan GDP in Current Prices from 1986 to 2006', https://www
.statista.com/statistics/263578/gross-domestic-product-gdp-of-japan
(accessed 30 June 2021)

Statista, 'Japan: National Debt from 2016 to 2026 in Relation to GDP', https://
www.statista.com/statistics/267226/japans-national-debt-in-relation-to
-gross-domestic-product-gdp (accessed 30 June 2021)

Statista, 'Kazakhstan: GDP in Current Prices from 1996 to 2026', https://
www.statista.com/statistics/436143/gross-domestic-product-gdp-in
-kazakhstan (accessed 30 June 2021)

Statista, 'Kazakhstan: Ratio of Military Spending to Gross Domestic Product
(GDP) from 2009 to 2019', https://www.statista.com/statistics/810452
/ratio-of-military-expenditure-to-gross-domestic-product-gdp-kazakhstan
(accessed 30 June 2021)

Statista, 'Kazakhstan: Unemployment Rate from 1999 to 2020', https://www
.statista.com/statistics/436179/unemployment-rate-in-kazakhstan (accessed
30 June 2021)

Statista, 'Leading Lobbying Industries in the United States in 2020, by
Total Lobbying Spending', https://www.statista.com/statistics/257364/top
-lobbying-industries-in-the-us (accessed 24 July 2021)

Statista, 'Number of Deaths Attributable to Air Pollution in Japan between
2010 and 2019', https://www.statista.com/statistics/935022/number-deaths
-air-pollution-japan (accessed 30 June 2021)

Statista, 'Number of Prisoners on Death Row in the United States in 2019,
by Race', https://www.statista.com/statistics/629895/number-of-death-row
-inmates-by-race-us (accessed 30 June 2021)

Statista, 'Pakistan: Ration of Military Spending to Gross Domestic Product (GDP) from 2009 to 2019', https://www.statista.com/statistics/810540 /ratio-of-military-expenditure-to-gross-domestic-product-gdp-pakistan (accessed 22 July 2021)

Statista, 'Percentage of Population Deemed Functionally Literate in Brazil from 2007 to 2018' https://www.statista.com/statistics/1130373/brazil -functional-literacy (Accessed 30 June 2021)

Statista, 'Percentage of the US Population Who Have Completed Four Years of College or More from 1940 to 2020, by Gender', https://www.statista .com/statistics/184272/educational-attainment-of-college-diploma-or -higher-by-gender (accessed 24 July 2021)

Statista, 'Population Density in South Korea from 2000 to 2020', 15 June 2021, https://www.statista.com/statistics/756232/south-korea-population-density

Statista, 'Population of Japan from 1995 to 2019 with a Forecast until 2025, by Age Group', https://www.statista.com/statistics/612575/japan-population -age-group (accessed 22 July 2021)

Statista, 'Population of Registered Foreigners in South Korea from 2010 to 2019', 5 March 2021, https://www.statista.com/statistics/1068529/south -korea-registered-foreigners-number

Statista, 'Population Projection for Russia 2021–2036, by Scenario', https:// www.statista.com/statistics/1009186/russia-population-projection-by -scenario (accessed 30 June 2021)

Statista, 'Poverty Headcount Ratio in Kazakhstan from 2007 to 2017', https:// www.statista.com/statistics/818364/poverty-headcount-ratio-in-kazakhstan (accessed 30 June 2021)

Statista, 'Poverty Rate in Japan from 1991 to 2018', https://www.statista.com /statistics/1172622/japan-poverty-rate (accessed 30 June 2021)

Statista, 'Poverty Rate in the United States from 1990 to 2019', https://www .statista.com/statistics/200463/us-poverty-rate-since-1990 (accessed 30 June 2021)

Statista, 'Private Education Rate of Students in South Korea in 2020, by Type of Tutoring', https://www.statista.com/statistics/1043943/south -korea-private-education-participation-rate-by-tutoring-type (accessed 23 July 2021)

Statista, 'Proportion of Children Living in Poverty in OECD Countries in 2018', https://www.statista.com/statistics/264424/child-poverty-in-oecd -countries (accessed 22 July 2021)

Statista, 'Russia: GDP Spent on R&D', https://www.statista.com/statistics /461754/share-of-gdp-expenditure-on-research-and-development-russia (accessed 20 June 2021)

Statista, 'Russia: Unemployment Rate from 1999 to 2020', Accessed 30 June 2021. https://www.statista.com/statistics/263712/unemployment-in -russia (accessed 30 June 2021)

Statista, 'Share of Elderly People Suffering from Diagnosed Chronic Diseases in South Korea in 2017, by Number of Diseases', https://www.statista.

com/statistics/944213/south-korea-seniors-with-chronic-conditions-by
-number-of-diseases (accessed 30 June 2021)

Statista, 'South Africa: Unemployment Rate from Q1 2019 to Q1 2020, by Population Group', https://www.statista.com/statistics/1129481 /unemployment-rate-by-population-group-in-south-africa (accessed 30 June 2021)

Statista, 'South Korea's National Health Expenditure as a Percent of GDP from 2000 to 2019', https://www.statista.com/statistics/647320/health -spending-south-korea (accessed 23 July 2021)

Statista, 'South Korea: Urbanization from 2010 to 2020', 6 July 2021, https:// www.statista.com/statistics/455905/urbanization-in-south-korea

Statista, 'The 20 Countries with the Largest Gross Domestic Product (GDP) in 2020', 16 June 2021, https://www.statista.com/statistics/268173/countries -with-the-largest-gross-domestic-product-gdp

Statista, 'Total Expenditure on Health as a Percentage of Gross Domestic Product (GDP) in France from 1980 to 2019', https://www.statista.com /statistics/429197/healthcare-expenditure-as-a-share-of-gdp-in-france/ (accessed 30 July 2021)

Statista, 'Total Health Expenditure as Share of GDP in Turkey from 2000 to 2019', https://www.statista.com/statistics/893497/health-expenditure-as -share-of-gdp-in-turkey (accessed 30 June 2021)

Statista, 'Total Population of France from 1982 to 2021, in Millions', https:// www.statista.com/statistics/459939/population-france/ (accessed 30 July 2021)

Statista, 'Total Population of Turkey 2016 to 2026', https://www.statista.com /statistics/263753/total-population-of-turkey (accessed 30 June 2021)

Statista, 'United States National Debt from 2016 to 2026', https://www.statista .com/statistics/262893/national-debt-in-the-united-states (accessed 30 June 2021)

Statistics Indonesia, 'Mengulik Data Suku di Indonesia' (Analysis of Tribal Data in Indonesia), https://www.bps.go.id/news/2015/11/18/127/mengulik -data-suku-di-indonesia.html (accessed 29 July 2021)

Stavljanin, D., and P. Baumgartner, 'Persian Might: How Strong Is Iran's Military?', Radio Free Europe, 9 January 2020

Steffen, L., 'Saudi Arabia Plans to Cut Emissions by 60% by Planting 50 Billion Trees', *Intelligent Living*, 6 May 2021

Steger, M.B., and R.K. Roy, *Neoliberalism: A Very Short Introduction* (Oxford: Oxford University Press, 2021)

Steinfeld, D., 'The US-Canada Northwest Passage Dispute', *Brown Political Review*, 8 April 2020

Stern, J., 'Germany Will Never Back Down on Its Russian Pipeline', *Foreign Policy*, 25 February 2021

Stock, J., M. Daniel and T. Goldstein, 'Partnerships Are Our Best Weapon in the Fight against Cybercrime. Here's Why', World Economic Forum, 21 January 2020, https://www.weforum.org/agenda/2020/01

/partnerships-are-our-best-weapon-in-the-fight-against-cybercrime-heres -why

Stokes, B., 'Hostile Neighbors: China vs. Japan', Pew Research Center, 13 September 2016

Stokes, M., 'Migrants Are Doing the Jobs South Koreans Sneer At', *Foreign Policy*, 28 January 2021

Stolberg, A.G., *How Nation-States Craft National Security Strategy Documents* (Carlisle, PA: Strategic Studies Institute, US Army War College, 2013)

Stone, J., 'German Elections: Far-Right Wins MPs for First Time in Half a Century', *The Independent*, 24 September 2017

Streusand, D.E., 'Geopolitics versus Globalization', in S.W.J. Tancredi (ed.), *Globalization and Maritime Power* (Washington, DC: National Defence University Press, 2002), pp. 41–56

Strukov, D., G. Indiveri, J. Grollier and S. Fusi, 'Building Brain-Inspired Computing', *Nature Communications* 10 (2019), pp. 1–6

Study Group on Europe's Security Capabilities, 'A Human Security Doctrine for Europe: The Barcelona Report', presented to the EU High Representative for Common Foreign and Security Policy, Javier Solana, Barcelona, 15 September 2004

Stuenkel, O., 'Latin America Is Too Polarised to Help Stabilize Bolivia', *Foreign Policy*, 13 November 2019

Suarez, K., R. Romo and J. Berlinger, 'Mexico's President Loses Grip on Power in Mid-Term Elections Marred by Violence', CNN World, 7 June 2021

Subramanyam, G., 'In India, Dalits Still Feel Bottom of the Caste Ladder', NBC News, 13 September 2020

Sudmeier-Rieux, K., H. Masudire, A. Rizvi and S. Rietbergen, *Ecosystems, Livelihoods and Disasters: An Integrated Approach to Disaster Risk Management*, Ecosystem Management Series no. 4 (Gland: IUCN, 2006)

Suleman, M., 'What's Going on at the Iran-Pakistan Border?', *The Diplomat*, 23 April 2021

Summers, T., 'How the Russian Government Used Disinformation and Cyber Warfare in 2016 Elections – An Ethical Hacker Explains', *The Conversation*, 27 July 2018

Sun, Y., 'Defining the Chinese Threat in the Arctic', The Arctic Institute, 7 April 2020

Sundaram, K., Chaudhary, A. 'China Back as India's Top Trade Partner even as Relations Sour', *Economic Times*, 23 February 2021

Suneja, K., 'Record Growth in April Exports, Trade Deficit Swells to $15.24 Billion', *Economic Times*, 3 May 2021

Sur, P., 'Under India's Caste System, Dalits Are Considered Untouchable. The Coronavirus Is Intensifying That Slur', CNN, 16 April 2020

Sussman, B., 'The List: Best and Worst Countries for Cybersecurity', Secure World Expo, 13 November 2019

Sustainable Governance Indicators, 'Environmental Policies', https://www
.sgi-network.org/2018/South_Korea/Environmental_Policies (accessed 23
July 2021)

Sutarsa, I.N., A.W. Prastyani and R. Al Adawiyah, 'Raising National Health
Insurance Premiums Doesn't Solve Indonesia's Health-Care Problems: This
Is What Needs to Be Done', *The Conversation*, 11 June 2020

Suttmeier, R.P., 'How China Is Trying to Invent the Future as a Science
Superpower', *Scientific American*, 9 July 2021

Suwanu Europe, 'Water Scarcity Increases in Turkey', 19 January 2021

Swissinfo, 'Major Drug Trafficking Network Busted in Zurich', 3
December 2020

Tadjbakhsh, S., and A. Chenoy, *Human Security: Concepts and Implications*
(New York: Routledge, 2007)

Takenaka, K., Y. Takemoto and Y. Obayashi, 'Japan Vows Deeper Emission
Cuts as Biden Holds Climate Summit', Reuters, 22 April 2021

Taşpınar, Ö., 'Turkey: The New Model?', Brookings Institution, 25 April 2012

Taylor, C., 'Renewables Could Displace Fossil Fuels to Power the World by
2050, Report Claims', *CNBC*, 23 April 2021

Taylor, R., 'What Can Australia Do about China? Ask Our Neighbours',
Business News, 8 December 2020

TB Facts, 'How Many People Have TB in India', https://tbfacts.org/tb
-statistics-india (accessed 30 June 2021)

Tedeneke, A., 'Brazil's Small and Medium-Sized Entreprises Join Fourth
Industrial Revolution', 7 November 2019

Telles, E., 'Racial Discrimination and Miscegenation: The Experience in Brazil,'
UN Chronicle, https://www.un.org/en/chronicle/article/racial-discrimination
-and-miscegenation-experience-brazil (Accessed 30 June 2021)

Terzic, B., *Energy Independence and Security: A Reality Check*, Deloitte Center
for Energy Solutions (Westlake, TX: Deloitte University Press, 2013)

Tesón, F., *Humanitarian Intervention: An Inquiry into Law and Morality*, 3rd
ed (New York: Brill, 2005)

Thatcher, M., *Statecraft: Strategies for a Changing World* (New York: Harper
Perennial, 2003)

Thomas, D., 'Is South African Transformation Dead?', *African Business*, 1
September 2020

Thomas, M., 'Poverty in Kazakhstan Is Like a Small Business', The Borgen
Project, 6 August 2020

Thompson, A. "How Governments Use Big Data to Violate Human Rights."
The Conversation, 13 January 2019. https://theconversation.com/how
-governments-use-big-data-to-violate-human-rights-109537

Thucydides, *History of the Peloponnesian War*, trans. by Rex Warner
(Harmondsworth: Penguin Classics, 1972)

Thurston, C.W., 'Brazil Emerges as Regional R&D Center', *Coatings World*, 13
March 2020

Tian, N., A. Fleurant, A. Kuimova, P.D. Wezeman and S.T. Wezeman, *Trends in World Military Expenditure, 2018* (Stockholm: SIPRI, 2019)

Tian, N., A. Kuimova, D. Lopes da Silva, P.D. Wezeman and S.T. Wezeman, *Trends in World Military Expenditure, 2019* (Stockholm: SIPRI, 2020)

Tilley, J., 'Hard Evidence: Do We Become More Conservative with Age?', *The Conversation*, 4 October 2015

Timperley, J., 'The Carbon Brief Profile: Brazil', 7 March 2018

Timperley, J., 'The Carbon Brief Profile: Japan', 25 June 2018

Tingting, D., 'In China, the Water You Drink Is as Dangerous as the Air You Breathe', *The Guardian*, 2 June 2017

Tjønneland, E.N., 'Crisis at South Africa's Universities – What Are the Implications for Future Cooperation with Norway?', *CMI Brief* 16, no. 3 (2017)

Tol, G., 'Viewpoint: Why Turkey Is Flexing Its Muscles Abroad', BBC News, 16 October 2020

Tol, G., and Y. Işık, 'Turkey-NATO Ties Are Problematic, but There Is One Bright Spot', Middle East Institute, 16 February 2021

Tolhurst, K., 'It's 12 Months since the Last Bushfire Season Began, but Don't Expect the Same This Year', *The Conversation*, 10 June 2020

Tomlin, R., 'Four Ways to Reduce Healthcare Costs', *Medical Economics*, 11 February 2020

Toon, O.B., C.G. Bardeen, A. Robock, L. Xia, H. Kristensen, M. McKinzie, R.J. Peterson, C.S. Harrison, N.S. Lovenduski and R.P. Turco, 'Rapidly Expanding Nuclear Arsenals in Pakistan and India Portend Regional and Global Catastrophe', *Science Advances* 5, no. 10 (2 October 2019)

Torul, O., and O. Oztunali, 'On Income and Wealth Inequality in Turkey', *Central Bank Review* 18, no. 3 (2018), pp. 95–106

Tosun, M., 'Turkey Deals Heavy Blow to Drug Trafficking in 2020', Anadolu Agency, 3 January 2021

Trading Economics, 'Japan: Employment in Agriculture', https://tradingeconomics.com/japan/employment-in-agriculture-percent-of-total-employment-wb-data.html (accessed 30 June 2021)

Trading Economics, 'South Africa Unemployment Rate', https://tradingeconomics.com/south-africa/unemployment-rate (accessed 30 June 2021)

Trading Economics, 'Turkey – Research and Development Expenditure', July 2021, https://tradingeconomics.com/turkey/research-and-development-expenditure-percent-of-gdp-wb-data.html

Tran, H., 'Do Deficits Matter? Japan Shows They Do', Atlantic Council, 6 July 2020

Tran, M., 'Mali: A Guide to the Conflict', *The Guardian*, 16 January 2013

Transparency International, 'Corruption Perceptions Index 2020, https://www.transparency.org/en/cpi/2020/index/ (accessed 16 November 2021)

Transparency International, 'Mexico', https://www.transparency.org/en/countries/mexico (accessed 30 June 2021)

Trenin, D., 'UK Security Review: Implications for Russia', Carnegie Moscow Center, 2 April 2021

Tress, L., 'High Tech Workforce Growing but Lacks Skilled Employees, Report Says', *Times of Israel*, 27 February 2020

Trofimov, Y., 'The European Union Is Punching Below Its Weight in World Affairs', *Wall Street Journal*, 17 December 2019, https://www.wsj.com/articles/the-european-union-is-punching-below-its-weight-in-world-affairs-11576578603

True, J., 'Soft Power or Smart Power? Flipping Australia's White Paper', Australian Institute of International Affairs, 27 November 2017

Tsavvko Garcia, R., 'Diversity in Brazil Is Still Just an Illusion', Al Jazeera, 22 October 2020

Tsubogo, M., 'The Role of Civil Society and Participatory Governance in Japanese Democracy', *Japanese Political Science Review* 2 (2014), pp. 39–61

Tsugane, S., 'Why Has Japan Become the World's Most Long-Lived Country: Insights from a Food and Nutrition Perspective', *European Journal of Clinical Nutrition* 75 (2021), pp. 921–28

Tsuji, T., 'Japan Targets Vietnam for First ASEAN Oil-Sharing Deal', *Financial Times*, 26 April 2021

Tuathail, G.Ó., 'Problematizing Geopolitics: Survey, Statesmanship and Strategy', *Transactions of the Institute of British Geographers* 19, no. 3 (1994), pp. 259–72

Tuathail, G.Ó., *Critical Geopolitics: The Politics of Writing Global Space* (Minneapolis: University of Minnesota Press, 1996)

Tugushev, A., 'The Porto Franco Regime in Canadian and Russian Sea Ports as an Instrument of Socio-Economic Development in the Arctic', The Arctic Institute, 9 June 2020

Turner, C., 'America's Schools Are "Profoundly Unequal," Says US Civil Rights Commission', NPR, 11 January 2018

Tyers, R., and Y. Zhou, 'An All-Out Trade War with China Would Cost Australia 6% of GDP', *The Conversation*, 30 November 2020

Tyrovolas, S., C. El Bcheraoui, S.A. Alghnam, K.F. Alhabib, M.A.H. Almadi, R.M. AlRaddadi, N. Bedi *et al.*, 'The Burden of Disease in Saudi Arabia 1990–2017: Results from the Global Burden of Disease Study 2017', *The Lancet* 4, no. 5, May 2020

Ueckerdt, F., R. Dargaville, H.-C. Gils, D. McConnell, M. Meinshausen, Y. Scholz, F. Schreyer and C. Wang, *Australia's Power Advantage: Energy Transition and Hydrogen Export Scenarios: Insights from the Australian-German Energy Transition Hub* (Melbourne and Potsdam: Energy Transition Hub, September 2019)

UK Department for Business, Energy and Industrial Strategy, 'Crude Oil and Petroleum: Production, Imports and Exports 1890 to 2020', 29 July 2021, https://www.gov.uk/government/statistical-data-sets/crude-oil-and-petroleum-production-imports-and-exports

UK Department for Business, Energy and Industrial Strategy, 'UK Research and Development Roadmap, updated 21 January 2021, https://www.gov .uk/government/publications/uk-research-and-development-roadmap/uk -research-and-development-roadmap

UK Department of International Trade, 'UK Innovation', https://www.great .gov.uk/international/content/about-uk/why-choose-uk/uk-innovation (accessed 30 June 2021)

UK Government, 'UK Agrees Historic Trade Deal with Australia', 15 June 2021

UK MI5, 'FAQ about MI5', Accessed 30 June 2021. https://www.mi5.gov.uk /faq/what-are-the-biggest-current-threats-to-national-security (accessed 30 June 2021)

UNCTAD, Investment Policy Hub, 'Turkey Introduced a New R&D Support Package', 1 March 2016

UNCTAD, *Review of Maritime Transport 2020* (New York: UNCTAD, 2020)

UN Department of Economic and Social Affairs, 'International Migration Report 2015', https://www.un.org/en/development/desa/population /migration/publications/migrationreport/docs/MigrationReport2015.pdf

UN Department of Economic and Social Affairs, 'The 17 Goals', https://sdgs .un.org/goals (Accessed 30 June 2021)

UN Division for Ocean Affairs and the Law of the Sea, 'Commission on the Limits of the Continental Shelf (CLCS): Outer Limits of the Continental Shelf beyond 200 Nautical Miles from the Baselines: Submissions to the Commission: Submission by the Kingdom of Norway', 20 August 2009, https://www.un.org/Depts/los/clcs_new/submissions_files/submission_nor .htm

UNDP, *Human Development Report 1998* (New York: Oxford University Press, 1998)

UNDP Nigeria, 'Sustainable Development Goals', https://www.ng.undp.org /content/nigeria/en/home/sustainable-development-goals.html (accessed 20 June 2021)

UNDP, *The Next Frontier: Human Development and the Anthropocene: UNDP Human Development Report 2020* (New York: UNDP, 2020)

UN Environmental Indicators, 'Greenhouse Gas Emissions', July 2010, via the Internet Archive Wayback Machine, https://web.archive.org /web/20100310190132/http:/unstats.un.org/unsd/environment/air_co2 _emissions.htm

UN Environment Programme (UNEP), '*Global Environment Outlook – GEO-6: Summary for Policymakers* (Cambridge: Cambridge University Press, 2019)

UN Environment Programme, 'Great East Japan Earthquake and Tsunami', https://www.unep.org/explore-topics/disasters-conflicts/where-we-work /japan/great-east-japan-earthquake-and-tsunami (accessed 30 June 2021)

UN General Assembly, 'Committee on Contributions', https://www.un.org /en/ga/contributions/honourroll.shtml (accessed 30 June 2021)

UN Inter-agency Group for Child Mortality Estimation, 'Mortality Rate, Infant: India', https://data.worldbank.org/indicator/SP.DYN.IMRT .IN?locations=IN (accessed 30 June 2021)

UN Office for Disarmament Affairs (UNODA), 'Arms Trade'

UN Office for Outer Space Affairs, Treaty on Principles Governing the Activities of States in the Exploration and Use of Outer Space, including the Moon and Other Celestial Bodies, Resolution 2222 (XXI), adopted 27 January 1967, entered into force 10 October 1967

UN Office for the Coordination of Humanitarian Affairs, 'Regional Outlook for the Horn of Africa and Great Lakes Region: January-March 2017', 24 February 2017

UN Office of the High Commissioner for Human Rights (OHCHR):

'Advancing Indigenous Peoples' Rights in Mexico', https://www.ohchr.org/en /NewsEvents/Pages/IndigenousPeoplesRightsInMexico.aspx (accessed 18 June 2021)

'China: UN Experts Deeply Concerned by Alleged Detention, Forced Labour of Uyghurs', 29 March 2021

'Committee on the Elimination of Racial Discrimination Examines Australia's Report', 28 November 2017, https://www.ohchr.org/en /NewsEvents/Pages/DisplayNews.aspx?NewsID=22460&LangID=E

Convention on the Elimination of All Forms of Discrimination against Women, ratified 18 December 1979, entered into force 3 September 1981, 1249 UNTS 13Convention on the Law of the Sea, ratified 10 December 1982, came into force 16 November 1994, 1833 UNTS 397

Convention on the Rights of the Child, ratified 20 November 1989, entered into force 2 September 1990, 1577 UNTS 3Declaration on the Rights of Disabled Persons, 9 December 1975 Declaration on the Rights of Disabled Persons, A/RES/3447 (XXX), 9 December 1975

International Covenant on Economic, Social and Cultural Rights, adopted 16 December 1966, came into force 23 March 1976, 999 UNTS 171. 'Monitoring Asylum in Australia', https://www.unhcr.org/asylum-in -australia.html (accessed 20 July 2021)

'Pakistan', https://www.unhcr.org/pakistan.html (accessed 30 June 2021)

'Refugees and Asylum Seekers in Turkey', https://www.unhcr.org/tr/en /refugees-and-asylum-seekers-in-turkey (accessed 30 June 2021)

'Refugees in Iran', https://www.unhcr.org/ir/refugees-in-iran (accessed 30 June 2021)

UN Office on Drugs and Crime, 'Indonesia: Terrorism Prevention', https:// www.unodc.org/indonesia/en/issues/terrorism-prevention.html (accessed 21 July 2021)

UN Office on Drugs and Crime, 'Mexico, Central America and the Caribbean', https://www.unodc.org/unodc/en/drug-trafficking/mexico -central-america-and-the-caribbean.html (accessed 18 June 2021)

UN Trust Fund for Human Security, 'What Is Human Security?, https://www .un.org/humansecurity/what-is-human-security (accessed 10 May 2021)

UN Women, 'Facts and Figures: Economic Empowerment', https://www
     .unwomen.org/en/what-we-do/economic-empowerment/facts-and-figures
     (accessed 30 June 2021)
UNAIDS, 'Brazil', https://www.unaids.org/en/20191011_country_focus
     _Brazil (accessed 30 June 2021)
UNAIDS, 'Kazakhstan', https://www.unaids.org/en/regionscountries
     /countries/kazakhstan (accessed 30 June 2021)
UNAIDS, 'Pakistan', https://www.unaids.org/en/regionscountries/countries
     /pakistan (accessed 30 June 2021)
UNAIDS, 'South Africa', https://www.unaids.org/en/regionscountries
     /countries/southafrica (accessed 22 July 2021)
UNESCO Institute of Statistics, 'How Much Does Your Country Invest
     in R&D?', http://uis.unesco.org/apps/visualisations/research-and
     -development-spending (accessed 18 June 2021)
UNESCO Institute of Statistics, 'Indonesia', http://uis.unesco.org/en/country
     /id (accessed 10 August 2021)
UNESCO Institute of Statistics, 'Iran (Islamic Republic of)', http://uis.unesco
     .org/en/country/ir?theme=science-technology-and-innovation (accessed 21
     July 2021)
UNESCO Institute of Statistics, 'Israel', http://uis.unesco.org/en/country/il
     (accessed 30 June 2021)
UNESCO Institute of Statistics, 'Kazakhstan', http://uis.unesco.org/en
     /country/kz?theme=education-and-literacy (accessed 30 June 2021)
UNESCO Institute of Statistics, 'Literacy Rate, Adult Male: Egypt, Arab
     Republic', September 2021, https://data.worldbank.org/indicator/SE.ADT
     .LITR.MA.ZS?locations=EG
UNESCO Institute of Statistics, 'Lithuania', http://uis.unesco.org/country/LT
     (accessed 30 June 2021)
UNESCO Institute of Statistics, 'Lithuania: Education and Literacy', http://
     uis.unesco.org/country/LT (accessed 22 July 2021)
UNESCO Institute of Statistics, 'Nigeria', http://uis.unesco.org/en/country/ng
     (accessed 20 June 2021)
UNESCO, 'Non-Governmental Organizations, Centres of Expertise
     and Research Institutes', https://ich.unesco.org/en/ngo-centers-and
     -institutions-00329 (accessed 30 June 2021)
UNESCO Institute of Statistics, 'South Africa', Accessed 30 June 2021. http://
     uis.unesco.org/en/country/za (accessed 30 June 2021)
UNESCO Institute of Statistics, 'United Kingdom of Great Britain and
     Northern Ireland', http://uis.unesco.org/country/GB (accessed 30
     June 2021)
Ung-Kono, V., '10 Facts about Education in Switzerland', The Borgen Project,
     17 July 2016
Ungku, F., 'Indonesia's New Law to Take Years to Reverse Oil and Gas Output
     Slump', Reuters, 24 February 2020
UNICEF, 'HIV and AIDS', https://www.unicef.org/hiv (accessed 24 July 2021)

UNICEF Indonesia, 'Nutrition', https://www.unicef.org/indonesia/nutrition (accessed 21 July 2021)

UNICEF Indonesia, 'Water, Sanitation and Hygiene', https://www.unicef.org /indonesia/water-sanitation-and-hygiene (accessed 21 July 2021)

UNICEF Pakistan, 'Education', https://www.unicef.org/pakistan/education (accessed 30 June 2021)

UNICEF, 'Take Action to Eliminate Female Genital Mutilation by 2030', 6 February 2019

UNHCR, 'Somalia Refugee Crisis Explained', https://www.unrefugees.org /news/somalia-refugee-crisis-explained (accessed 24 June 2021)

UNHCR, 'Syria Refugee Crisis', https://www.unrefugees.org/emergencies /syria/ (accessed 30 June 2021)

United Nations, 'Loss of Autonomy in Indian-Administered Jammu and Kashmir Threatens Minorities' Rights – UN Independent Experts', 18 February 2021

United Nations, 'Resolving Israel-Palestinian Conflict "Key to Sustainable Peace" in the Middle East: Guterres', 4 February 2021, https://news.un.org /en/story/2020/02/1056722

United Nations, 'Status of Treaties, United Nations Framework Convention on Climate Change', in United Nations Treaty Collection, https://treaties .un.org (accessed 20 November 2019)

United Nations, 'The Sahel: Land of Opportunities', 29 June 2018, https:// www.un.org/africarenewal/sahel

United Nations, United Nations Charter, 1945

United Nations, United Nations Treaty Collection, https://treaties.un.org

United Nations, 'Unprecedented Impacts of Climate Change Disproportionately Burdening Developing Countries, Delegate Stresses, as Second Committee Concludes General Debate', 8 October 2019

United Nations, 'World Population Projected to Reach 9.8 Billion in 2050, and 11.2 Billion in 2100', 21 June 2017

UniversityRankings.ch, 'QS World University Rankings 2021', https://www .universityrankings.ch/results/QS/2021

UN News, 'WHO Chief Warns against COVID-19 "Vaccine Nationalism", Urges Support for Fair Access',18 August 2020

US Bureau of International Labor Affairs, '2019 Findings on the Worst Forms of Child Labor', https://www.dol.gov/sites/dolgov/files/ILAB/child_labor _reports/tda2019/Egypt.pdf

US Central Intelligence Agency, 'Crude Oil – Proved Reserves', *The World Factbook*, https://www.cia.gov/the-world-factbook/field/crude-oil-proved -reserves/country-comparison

US Central Intelligence Agency, 'Israel', *The World Factbook*, updated 5 November 2021, https://www.cia.gov/the-world-factbook/countries /israel

US Central Intelligence Agency, *The World Factbook*, https://www.cia.gov /the-world-factbook/countries

US Congress, *Energy and the Iranian Economy: Hearing before the Joint Economic Committee*, Senate Hearing 109–720, 25 July 2006 (Washington, DC: US Government Printing Office, 2007)

US Congressional Research Service, 'Changes in the Arctic: Background and Issues for Congress', updated 12 October 2021

US Congressional Research Service, 'Iran's Foreign and Defence Policies', 11 January 2021

US Congressional Research Service, 'South Korea: Background and US Relations', 26 May 2021

US Congressional Research Service, 'The Social Security Retirement Age', 8 January 2021

US Congressional Research Service, 'The United Kingdom: Background, Brexit, and Relations with the United States', 16 April 2021

US Department of Defense, 'Iran Military Power Report Statement', 19 November 2019, https://www.defense.gov/Newsroom/Releases/Release/Article/2021009/iran-military-power-report-statement

US Department of Health and Human Services:

Centers for Disease Control and Prevention, 'Global Health Pakistan', https://www.cdc.gov/globalhealth/countries/pakistan/default.htm (accessed 30 June 2021)

Centers for Disease Control and Prevention, 'HIV in the United States: The Stages of Care', November 2014

Centers for Disease Control and Prevention, 'Leading Causes of Death', https://www.cdc.gov/nchs/fastats/leading-causes-of-death.htm (accessed 30 June 2021)

Centers for Disease Control and Prevention, 'Why It Matters: The Pandemic Threat', *Updates from the Field*, no. 26 (Winter 2017), updated 2020 and 2021

US Department of State, Bureau of Counterterrorism, 'Country Reports on Terrorism 2019: Indonesia', https://www.state.gov/reports/country-reports-on-terrorism-2019/indonesia (accessed 21 July 2021)

US Department of State, Bureau of Near Eastern Affairs, 'Background Note: Egypt', March 2008

US Department of State, Bureau of Western Hemisphere Affairs, 'US Relations with Mexico: Bilateral Relations Fact Sheet', 16 September 2021, https://www.state.gov/u-s-relations-with-mexico

US Department of State, Office of International Religious Freedom, '2018 Report on International Religious Freedom: Nigeria', https://www.state.gov/reports/2018-report-on-international-religious-freedom/nigeria

US Department of State, Office of the Spokesperson, 'US-India Joint Statement on Launching the US-India Climate and Clean Energy 2030 Partnership', 22 April 2021

US Department of State, Office to Monitor and Combat Trafficking in Persons, '2020 Trafficking in Persons Report: Turkey', https://www.state.gov/reports/2020-trafficking-in-persons-report/turkey

US Department of State, Overseas Security Advisory Council, 'Brazil 2020 Crime and Safety Report: Rio de Janeiro', 13 May 2020

US Department of State, Overseas Security Advisory Council, 'Democratic Republic of the Congo 2019 Crime and Safety Report', 4 April 2019

US Department of State, Overseas Security Advisory Council, 'Switzerland 2020 Crime and Safety Report: Bern', 31 July 2020

US Department of State, '2020 Country Reports on Human Rights Practices: Indonesia', https://www.state.gov/reports/2020-country-reports-on -human-rights-practices/Indonesia

US Department of State, 'Kazakhstan Profile', https://2009-2017.state.gov /outofdate/bgn/kazakhstan/47484.htm (accessed 30 June 2021)

US Department of State, 'U.S. Relations with Germany', 21 June 2021, https:// www.state.gov/u-s-relations-with-germany

US Department of State, 'U.S. Relations with Saudi Arabia', 15 December 2020 https://www.state.gov/u-s-relations-with-saudi-arabia/

US Department of State, 'U.S. Relations with Turkey', 20 January 2021, https://www.state.gov/u-s-relations-with-turkey

US Embassy and Consulate in Kazakhstan, 'Kazakhstan Has the Highest Percent of Awareness among People Living with HIV in Central Asia', https://kz.usembassy.gov/hiv-awareness (accessed 30 June 2021)

US Embassy in Berlin, 'U.S.-German Economic Relations Factsheet', May 2006, via the Internet Archive Wayback Machine, https://web.archive .org/web/20110511123309/http:/germany.usembassy.gov/germany/img /assets/9336/econ_factsheet_may2006.pdf

US Energy Information Administration, 'Country Analysis Executive Summary: Mexico', 30 November 2020

US Energy Information Administration, 'Oil and Natural Gas Production Is Growing in Caspian Sea Region', 11 September 2013

US Energy Information Administration, 'Oil and Petroleum Products Explained: Where Our Oil Comes From', 8 April 2021

US Energy Information Administration, 'Russia – Analysis', 31 October 2017

US Energy Information Administration, 'The Bab el-Mandeb Strait Is a Strategic Route for Oil and Natural Gas Shipments', 27 August 2019

US Energy Information Administration, 'The Danish and Turkish Straits Are Critical to Europe's Crude Oil and Petroleum Trade', 18 August 2017

US Energy Information Administration, 'The Strait of Hormuz Is the World's Most Important Oil Transit Chokepoint', 20 June 2019

US Energy Information Administration, 'The Suez Canal and SUMED Pipeline are Critical Chokepoints for Oil and Natural Gas Trade', 23 July 2019

US Institute of Peace, 'The Current Situation in Iraq', Fact Sheet, 4 August 2020

US International Trade Administration, 'South Korea – Country Commercial Guide', updated 13 August 2021, https://www.trade.gov/knowledge -product/korea-air-pollution-control

US Office of the Directory of National Intelligence:

National Intelligence Council, 'Global Trends 2025: A Transformed World', November 2008, www.dni/nic/NIC_2025_project.html

National Intelligence Council, 'Nonstate Actors: Impact on International Relations and Implications for the United States', 23 August 2007, https://fas.org/irp/nic/nonstate_actors_2007.pdf

US White House, 'Fact Sheet: President Biden Sends Immigration Bill to Congress as Part of His Commitment to Modernise Our Immigration System', 20 January 2021

US White House, 'Fact Sheet: President Biden Sets 2030 Greenhouse Gas Pollution Reduction Target Aimed at Creating Good-Paying Union Jobs and Securing US Leadership on Clean Energy Technologies', 22 April 2021

US White House, 'Fact Sheet: The American Jobs Plan', 31 March 2021

USAID, 'Eliminating HIV', 1 December 2020, https://www.usaid.gov/kazakhstan/success-stories/dec-2020-eliminating-hiv

USAID, 'Global Health Nigeria', last updated 12 July 2021, https://www.usaid.gov/nigeria/global-health

USAID, 'New USAID Program to Strengthen Transboundary Water Cooperation in Central Asia', 30 September 2020

USIP China-North Korea Senior Study Group, *China's Role in North Korea Nuclear and Peace Negotiations* (Washington, DC: United States Institute of Peace, 2019)

Uz-Zaman, Q., 'Low Earnings and Agricultural Neglect Push Pakistan into Food Insecurity', Eco-Business, 14 December 2020

Vaishnav, M., 'The Decay of Indian Democracy: Why India No Longer Ranks among the Lands of the Free', *Foreign Affairs*, 18 March 2021

Vaisse, J., *Transformational Diplomacy*, Chaillot Paper no. 103 (Paris: EUISS, 2007)

Vanderhill, R., S.F. Joireman and R. Tulepbayeva, 'Between the Bear and the Dragon: Multivectorism in Kazakhstan as a Model Strategy for Secondary Powers', *International Affairs* 96, no. 4 (2020), pp. 975–93

Vanderveen, A.M., 'Healthcare in Kazakhstan: Problems and Solutions', The Borgen Project, 17 August 2020

Van de Vuurst, P., and L.E. Escobar, 'Perspective: Climate Change and the Relocation of Indonesia's Capital to Borneo', *Frontiers in Earth Science* 8 (2020), pp. 1–6

Vandome, C., and J. Hamill, 'South Africa: A First Shot at Corruption', Chatham House, 19 May 2021

Vaswani, K., 'The Sleepy Island Indonesia Is Guarding from China', BBC News, 20 October 2014

Vatanka, A., 'Russia, Iran, and Economic Integration on the Caspian', *Middle East Institute*, 17 August 2020

Venkatachalam, K.S., 'Destroy India's Caste System before It Destroys India', *The Diplomat*, 4 August 2016

Ventura, L., 'Poorest Countries in the World in 2021', *Global Finance*, 21 May 2021

Verma, A.K., 'India's True Hydropower Potential Remains Untapped', *The Hindu Business Line*, 14 May 2020

Versluis, J.-M., and J. de Lange, 'Rising Crime Rate, Low Prosecution Rates: How Law Enforcement in SA Has All but Collapsed', *City Press/News 24*, 21 October 2019

Vespa, J., L. Medina and D.M. Armstrong, 'Demographic Turning Points for the United States: Population Projections for 2020 to 2060', US Census Bureau, February 2020

Vieira Filho, J.E.R., and A. Fornazier, 'Agricultural Productivity: Closing the Gap between Brazil and the United States', *Cepal Review* 118 (2016), pp. 203–20

Vijayakumar, A., 'Japan's Rise as a Space Powe', *Japan Times*, 28 January 2020

Vincze, H., 'One Voice, but Whose Voice? Should France Cede Its UN Security Council Seat to the EU?', Foreign Policy Research Institute, 20 March 2019

Vinelli, A., and C.E. Weller, 'The Path to Higher, More Inclusive Economic Growth and Good Jobs', Center for American Progress, 27 April 2021

Vinelli, A., and C.E. Weller, 'Move Fast and Think Big: 7 Key Principles for the Economic Package America Needs Now', Center for American Progress, 4 February 2021

Vivanco, J.M., 'López Obrador Threatens Judicial Independence', Human Rights Watch, 26 April 2021

VOA News, 'In Fast-Aging China, Elder Care Costs Loom Large', 23 May 2021

VOA News, 'Egypt: A Third of Population Lives in Poverty', 30 July 2019

VOA News, 'Turkish Operation Increases Conflict among Kurds in Iraq', 21 June 2021

Vohra, A., 'Iran is Trying to Convert Syria to Shiism', *Foreign Policy*, 15 March 2021

Waal, T. de, 'What Next after the US Recognition of the Armenian Genocide?', Carnegie Europe, 30 April 2021

Wadhams, P., *A Farewell to Ice: A Report from the Arctic* (Oxford: Oxford University Press, 2017)

Wæhler, T. Austin, and E. Sveberg Dietrichs, 'The Vanishing Aral Sea: Health Consequences of an Environmental Disaster', *Tidsskriftet*, 3 October 2017

Wahba, A.L., 'Egypt Asks for UN Help in Long-Running Ethiopian Dam Dispute', Bloomberg, 12 June 2021

Walker, P., and N. Parveen, 'Racial Disparities in the UK: Key Findings of the Report – and What Its Critics Say', *The Guardian*, 31 March 2021

Walt, S.M., 'It's Time to End the "Special Relationship" with Israel', *Foreign Policy*, 27 May 2021, https://foreignpolicy.com/2021/05/27/its-time-to-end -the-special-relationship-with-israel

Waltz, K.N., *Theory of International Politics*, 1st edn (New York: McGraw-Hill, 1979)

Walzer, M., 'Just and Unjust Occupations', *Dissent*, Winter 2004

Walzer, M., *Just and Unjust Wars: A Moral Argument with Historical Illustrations*, 3rd edn (New York: Basic Books, 2000)

Walzer, M., *Thick and Thin: Moral Argument at Home and Abroad* (Notre Dame, IN: University of Notre Dame Press, 1994)

Wang, J., and B. Wang, 'Turkish Islamic Movement after Conservatives in Power', *Asian Journal of Middle Eastern and Islamic Studies* 12, no. 2 (2017), pp. 55–68

Ward, M., 'Economy in March 2021: Post-Brexit Trade Data and Consumer Confidence', House of Commons Library Insight, 26 March 2021

Ward, M., 'Statistics on UK-EU Trade', House of Commons Library Research Briefing, 10 November 2020

Waslekar, S., 'Water Is More than a Strategic Resource: We Need to Acknowledge That', World Economic Forum and Project Syndicate, 26 January 2017

Water Aid, 'Pakistan', https://www.wateraid.org/where-we-work/pakistan (accessed 22 July 2021)

WaterLex, 'Legal Country Mapping: Germany', 6 July 2018, http://humanright2water.org/wp-content/uploads/2020/07/WL-Country-Mapping-Germany.pdf

Watson, R.T., I.R. Noble, B. Bolin, N.H. Ravindranath, D.J. Verardo and D.J. Dokken, Land Use, Land-Use Change, and Forestry, Intergovernmental Panel on Climate Change Special Report (Cambridge: Cambridge University Press, 2000)

Weaver, C., 'Russia Cuts Gas Supplies to Belarus', *Financial Times*, 21 June 2020, https://www.ft.com/content/a94728f8-7d21-11df-8845-00144feabdc0

Weber, A.C., and C.L. Parthemore, 'Lessons from Kazakhstan', Belfer Center for Science and International Affairs, January 2017

Wegren, S.K., 'Rural Inequality in Post-Soviet Russia', *Problems of Post-Communism* 61, no. 1 (2014), pp. 52–64

Wei, L., 'China's Xi Ramps up Control of Private Sector: "We Have No Choice but to Follow the Party"', *Wall Street Journal*, 10 December 2020

Weinzierl, M., 'Space, the Final Economic Frontier', *Journal of Economic Perspectives* 32, no. 2 (2018), pp. 173–92

Weiss, M., 'How Israel Used Desalination to Address Its Water Shortage', *Irish Times*, 18 July 2019

Weitz, R., 'Continuity and Change in US Policies Towards the Caspian Region', MEI, 2 April 2020

WENR, 'Education in Brazil', 14 November 2019

Wesolowsky, T., 'Lithuania Says Lukashenka Is Flooding Baltic State's Border with Migrants', Radio Free Europe, 18 June 2021

Wettengel, J., 'Gas Pipeline Nord Stream 2 Links Germany to Russia, but Splits Europe', Clean Energy Wire Factsheet, 14 June 2021, https://www .cleanenergywire.org/factsheets/gas-pipeline-nord-stream-2-links-germany -russia-splits-europe

Whineray, D., '5 Reasons Why US-Europe Tensions Will Grow in the 2020s – and How to Stop It', Carnegie Endowment for International Peace, 16 January 2020

Whiting, K., 'An Expert Explains: What is RCEP, the World's Biggest Trade Deal?', World Economic Forum, 18 May 2021

WHO Europe, 'Budgetary Space for Health in Ukraine', Health Policy Paper Series no. 20/01, July 2020

Wickiser, J.K., K.J. O'Donovan, M. Washington, S. Hummel and F.J. Burpo, 'Engineered Pathogens and Unnatural Biological Weapons: The Future Threat of Synthetic Biology', *Combating Terrorism Center Sentinel* 13, no. 8 (2020), pp. 1–7

Widianto, S., 'Indonesian Military Says Troops Suspected of Killing 2 Papuan Civilians', Reuters, 14 July 2021

Wijaya, T., and S. Nursamsu, 'The Trouble with Indonesia's Infrastructure Obsession', *The Diplomat*, 9 January 2020

Wilcox, D.J., 'The Israeli-Palestinian Peace Process: Lessons from Oslo', *E-International Relations*, 14 September 2020

Wilson Center, 'Secularism and Islam in France', 16 June 2021

Wilson, G., 'Minimizing Global Catastrophic and Existential Risks from Emerging Technologies through International Law', *Virginia Environmental Law Journal* 31, no. 2 (2013), pp. 307–64

Winkler, H., 'Why South Africa's Electricity Blackouts Are Set to Continue for the Next Five Years', *The Conversation*, 30 March 2021

Winnekens, F., 'Global Aging 2016: German Reforms Start to Tackle to Cost of Aging', S&P Global, 12 January 2016

Winter, D.A., A. Muhanna-Matar, M. Haj Salem, M. Musbah and A. Tohamy, 'The Role of Sub-National Authorities from the Mediterranean Region in Addressing Radicalisation and Violent Extremism of Young People', European Committee of the Regions, 2017, https://cor.europa.eu/en/engage /studies/Documents/Radicalisation-Violent-Extremism-Young%20People.pdf

Wintour, P., 'Raisi's Election Victory Raises Difficulties as Iran Nuclear Deal Talks Resume', *The Guardian*, 20 June 2021

Wintour, P., 'Yemen Civil War: The Conflict Explained', *The Guardian*, 20 June 2019

Wintour, P., and J. Borger, 'Trump Attacks China over COVID "Plague" as Xi Urges Collaboration in Virus Fight', *The Guardian*, 22 September 2020

WIO News, 'Pakistan Will Achieve 5 Per Cent GDP Growth in Next Fiscal: Finance Minister', 24 May 2021, https://www.wionews.com/south-asia /pakistan-will-achieve-5-per-cent-gdp-growth-in-next-fiscal-finance -minister-387073

Wolfers, A., *Discord and Collaboration: Essays on International Politics* (Baltimore: Johns Hopkins University Press, 1962)

Wolverton, M., 'Contesting the High Ground', *Mechanical Engineering* 141, no. 7 (July 2019), pp. 54–59

World Atlas, 'How Many Islands Are There in Indonesia?', https://www.worldatlas.com/articles/how-many-islands-does-indonesia-have.html (accessed 9 August 2021)

World Atlas, 'The Ethnic Groups of Afghanistan', https://www.worldatlas.com/articles/ethnic-groups-of-afghanistan.html (accessed 24 June 2021)

World Bank, '45 Million Egyptians to Benefit from Improvements to the Public Health System', 27 June 2018

World Bank, 'Access to Energy Is at the Heart of Development', 18 April 2018

World Bank, 'China Product Exports and Imports to Middle East and North Africa 2019'

World Bank, 'Curbing Desertification in China', 4 July 2019

World Bank, 'Economics of Adaptation to Climate Change', 6 June 2011

World Bank, 'Egypt: Job Creation for Better Livelihoods', 22 February 2021

World Bank, 'Greater Productivity, Investment in People Can Put Russia Back on Path to Sustainable and Inclusive Growth', 12 January 2017

World Bank, 'Helping India Overcome Its Water Woes', 9 December 2019

World Bank, 'In Ukraine, Labor, Taxation, and Social Policies Must Be Upgraded to Address Rising Inequality, Says World Bank', 25 September 2018

World Bank, 'Islamic Republic of Iran', 30 March 2021, https://www.worldbank.org/en/country/iran/overview

World Bank, *Kazakhstan: The Challenge of Economic Diversification amidst Productivity Stagnation: Country Economic Update Fall 2018* (Washington, DC: World Bank, 2018)

World Bank, 'New World Bank Report Looks at Turkey's Rise to the Threshold of High-Income Status and the Challenges Remaining', 10 December 2014

World Bank, *Inequality and Economic Development in Brazil: World Bank Country Study* (Washington, DC: World Bank, 2004)

World Bank, 'Russia among Global Top Ten Improvers for Progress Made in Health and Education, Says World Bank Report', 16 September 2020

World Bank, 'Turkey: Transforming Health Care for All', 27 April 2018, https://www.worldbank.org/en/about/partners/brief/turkey-transforming-health-care-for-all

World Bank, 'Universal Health Coverage for Inclusive and Sustainable Development', https://www.worldbank.org/en/topic/health/publication/universal-health-coverage-for-inclusive-sustainable-development (accessed 30 June 2021)

World Bank, 'World Bank in India: India Overview', https://www.worldbank.org/en/country/india/overview#2 (accessed 21 July 2021)

World Bank, 'World Development Indicators: Population Dynamics', http://
wdi.worldbank.org/table/2.1 (accessed 30 June 2021)

World Bank Data (unless otherwise stated accessed between June and
August 2021)

World Data Lab, 'World Poverty Clock', https://worldpoverty.io (accessed 14
July 2021)

World Economic Forum, 'Global Arms Sales Captured in Four Charts', 18
December 2018

World Economic Forum, 'How the One-Party State May Shape Our Future', 2
August 2019

World Economic Forum, 'Wild Wide Web', https://reports.weforum.org
/global-risks-report-2020/wild-wide-web (accessed 30 June 2021)

World Food Programme, 'Somalia', https://www.wfp.org/countries/somalia
(accessed 30 June 2021)

World Food Programme, 'Yemen Emergency', https://www.wfp.org
/emergencies/yemen-emergency (accessed 30 June 2021)

World Health Organization, 'Ageing and Health', https://www.who.int/china
/health-topics/ageing (accessed 24 July 2021)

World Health Organization, 'Factsheet 99 on Rabies', 17 May 2021, https://
www.who.int/news-room/fact-sheets/detail/rabies

World Health Organization, 'Germany Country Health Profile 2019', http://
www.euro.who.int/__data/assets/pdf_file/0005/419459/C (accessed 9
March 2021)

World Health Organization, 'Mexico', 2018, https://www.who.int/nmh
/countries/mex_en.pdf (accessed 18 June 2021)

World Health Organization, 'World Health Organization Assesses the
World's Health Systems', 7 February 2000

World Inequality Database, 'Lithuania', https://wid.world/country/lithuania
(accessed 30 June 2021)

World Nuclear Association, 'Nuclear Power in Brazil', updated August 2021

World Nuclear Association, 'Nuclear Power in France', January 2021, http://
www.world-nuclear.org/information-library/country-profiles/countries-a-f
/france.aspx

World Nuclear Association, 'Uranium and Nuclear Power in Kazakhstan',
https://world-nuclear.org/information-library/country-profiles/countries
-g-n/kazakhstan.aspx (accessed 30 June 2021)

WorldOmeter, 'Egypt Population', https://www.worldometers.info/world
-population/egypt-population (accessed 19 July 2021)

WorldOMeter, 'Russia Oil', https://www.worldometers.info/oil/russia-oil
(accessed 24 June 2021)

World Politics Review 'What Comes Next in the Standoff between the US and
Iran?', 29 October 2021

World Population Review, 'Crime Rate by Country 2021', https://
worldpopulationreview.com/country-rankings/crime-rate-by-country
(accessed 30 June 2021)

World Population Review, 'Pakistan Population 2021', https://
worldpopulationreview.com/countries/pakistan-population (accessed 9
August 2021)

World's Top Exports, 'World's Top Export Countries', Accessed 21 June 2021.
https://www.worldstopexports.com/worlds-top-export-countries (accessed
21 June 2021)

World, The, 'Historic Election Marks Transition in Pakistan', PRX/WGBH, 14
May 2013

World Vision, 'Global Water Crisis: Facts, FAQs, and How to Help', 16
April 2021

World Wildlife Fund, 'Six Ways Loss of Arctic Ice Impacts Everyone', https://
www.worldwildlife.org/pages/six-ways-loss-of-arctic-ice-impacts-everyone
(accessed 30 July 2021)

World Wildlife Fund, 'Water Scarcity', https://www.worldwildlife.org/threats
/water-scarcity (accessed 30 July 2021)

Wright, Q., 'Design for a Research Project on International Conflicts and
the Factors Causing Their Aggravation or Amelioration', *Western Political
Quarterly* 10, no. 2 (1957), pp. 263–75

WTO, 'Regionalism: Friends or Rivals?', Understanding the WTO: Cross
-Cutting and New Issues, https://www.wto.org/english/thewto_e/whatis_e
/tif_e/bey1_e.htm (accessed 13 January 2022)

WWF, 'Seals', https://www.worldwildlife.org/species/seals (accessed 12
January 2021)

Wyne, A., 'The Need to Think More Clearly about "Great-Power
Competition"', RAND, 11 February 2019

Xu, Y., *China, Africa and Responsible International Engagement* (New York:
Routledge, 2017)

Yachyshen, D., 'Russia Now Has a Position in Libya. What Next?', Foreign
Policy Research Institute, 23 November 2020

Yacoubian, M., 'What is Russia's Endgame in Russia?', United States Institute
of Peace, 16 February 2021

Yahya, M. 'Nigeria Must Lead on Climate Change', UNDP, 4 October 2019

Yale University, '2018 EPI Results', 23 July 2019, epi.envirocenter.yale.edu

Yale University, '2020 Environmental Performance Index: Country Profile:
Indonesia', 9 June 2020, https://epi.yale.edu/sites/default/files/files/IDN
_EPI2020_CP.pdf

Yamaguchi, K., 'Japan's Gender Gap', *Finance and Development* 56, no. 1
(2019), pp. 25–28

Yang, C., 'Japan's Dream for UN Security Council Seat Crushed by Its
Historical Mirages', *Global Times*, 26 September 2020

Yasaveev, I., 'Not an Epidemic, but a Global Problem: The Authorities'
Construction of HIV/AIDS in Russia', *Medicine (Baltimore)* 99, no. 21
(2020), pp. 1–5

Yau, N., 'Tracing the Chinese Footprints in Kazakhstan's Oil and Gas
Industry', *The Diplomat*, 12 December 2020

Yergin, D., 'Ensuring Energy Security', *Foreign Affairs* 82, no. 2 (2006), pp. 69–82

Yeung, J., J. Griffiths and N. Gan, 'The US Is Sanctioning Chinese Officials over Alleged Abuse of Uyghurs in Xinjiang. Here's What You Need to kKnow', CNN, 25 March 2021

Yi, Y.J., 'History of Poverty in South Korea', The Borgen Project, 25 February 2020

Yilmaz, Z., and B.S. Turner, 'Turkey's Deepening Authoritarianism and the Fall of Electoral Democracy', *British Journal of Middle Eastern Studies* 46, no. 5 (2019), pp. 691–98

Yonzan, N., C. Lakner and D.G. Mahler, 'Is COVID-19 Increasing Global Inequality?', *Data Blog* (World Bank), 7 October 2021

Yoo, J., 'Marcus Tullius Cicero, De Officiis', Hoover Institution, 6 February 2019

Yu, R., Y. Chen, L. Li, J. Chen, Y. Guo, Z. Bian, J. Lv *et al.*, 'Factors Associated with Suicide Risk among Chinese Adults: A Prospective Cohort Study of 0.5 Million Individuals', *PLOS Medicine* 18, no. 3 (2021), p. e1003545

Zacharias, D.C., 'Brazilian Offshore Oil Exploration Areas: An Overview of Hydrocarbon Pollution', *Revista Ambiente & Agua* 15, no. 5 (2020), pp. 1–20

Zakaria, F., 'The Future of American Power: How America Can Survive the Rise of the Rest', *Foreign Affairs* 87, no. 3 (2008), pp. 18–43

Zaken, D., 'Push to Revamp Education Funding Falls Flat in Israel', Al-Monitor, 20 July 2020

Zehfuss, M., *Constructivism in International Relations: The Politics of Reality* (Cambridge: Cambridge University Press, 2002)

Zeitoun, M., and M. Dajani, 'Israel Is Hoarding the Jordan River – It's Time to Share', *The Conversation*, 19 December 2019

Zhang, Jian, China's Energy Security: Prospects, Challenges and Opportunities, CNAPS Visiting Fellow Working Paper (Washington, DC: Brookings Institution, 2011)

Zhang, Jie, 'The Gender Ratio of Chinese Suicide Rates: An Explanation in Confucianism', *Sex Roles: A Journal of Research* 70, nos 3–4 (2014), pp. 146–54

Zheng, S., 'China Targets Energy Security as Risks from US Rivalry Grow', *South China Morning Post*, 9 March 2021

Zhenqiang, P., 'The US-Europe-China Triangle in an Increasingly Multipolar World', Konrad Adenauer Stiftung, January 2006

Zhihai, X., 'Rethinking Japan's Energy Security 8 Years after Fukushima', *The Diplomat*, 21 March 2019

Zhupankhan, A., K. Tussupova and R. Berndtsson, 'Water in Kazakhstan, a Key in Central Asian Water Management', *Hydrological Sciences Journal* 63, no. 5 (2018), pp. 752–62

Ziesing, K., '2021 Defence Budget at a Glance', *Australian Defence Magazine*, 11 May 2021

Zivitski, L., 'China Wants to Dominate Space, and the US Must Take Countermeasures', *DefenseNews*, 23 June 2020

Zmigrod, L., and M. Tsakiris, 'Computational and Neurocognitive Approaches to the Political Brain: Key Insights and Future Avenues for Political Neuroscience', *Philosophical Transactions of the Royal Society B* 376, no. 1822

Zollner, B., 'Surviving Repression: How Egypt's Muslim Brotherhood Has Carried On', Carnegie Middle East Center, 11 March 2019

Zubascu, F., 'Funding Synergies to Nudge EU Countries Closer to 3% R&D Spending Target by 2030', *Science Business*, 1 March 2021, https://sciencebusiness.net/news/funding-synergies-nudge-eu-countries-closer-3-rd-spending-target-2030

Index

Also by Nayef R.F. Al-Rodhan:

Emotional Amoral Egoism

A Neurophilosophy of Human Nature and Motivations

What makes us who we are? Are we born good or evil? Do we have free will? What drives our behaviour and why? Can technology change what it means to be human? In this thoroughly revised second edition of *Emotional Amoral Egoism*, Professor Nayef Al-Rodhan demonstrates the impact of our innate predispositions on key issues, from conflict, inequality and transcultural understanding to Big Data, fake news and the social contract. However, it is the societies we live in and their governance structures that largely determine how we act on our innate predispositions. Consequently, Al-Rodhan proposes a new and sustainable good governance paradigm, which must reconcile the ever-present tension between the three attributes of human nature ('Emotional Amoral Egoism') and the nine critical needs of human dignity.

This book is a perfect resource for enlightened readers, academics and policy makers interested in how our innate instincts and tendencies shape the world we live in, and how the interplay between neurophilosophy and policy can be harnessed for pragmatic and sustainable peace, security and prosperity solutions for all, at all times and under all circumstances.

'This ambitious and wide-ranging book offers [a] forceful argument that . . . our political thinking needs to be inspired by the neuro-psychological consequences of our brain chemistry.' – **Professor Michael Frieden**, University of Oxford

Published 28 October 2021

Hardback ISBN: 978 0 7188 9572 3
Paperback ISBN: 978 0 7188 9573 0
PDF ISBN: 978 0 7188 4833 0
ePub ISBN: 978 0 7188 4834 7

Also by Nayef R.F. Al-Rodhan:

Sustainable History and Human Dignity

A Neurophilosophy of History and the Future of Civilisation

'I hope that the path laid out in this book attracts many followers.' – **President Jimmy Carter**

In *Sustainable History and Human Dignity*, Professor Nayef Al-Rodhan shows that it is the human quest for sustainable governance, balancing the ever-present tension between nine human dignity needs and three human nature attributes (emotionality, amorality & egoism), that has and will most profoundly shape the course of history. Beginning with an 'Ocean Model' of a single collective human civilisation, Al-Rodhan constructs a common human story comprised of multiple geo-cultural domains and sub-cultures with a history of mutual borrowing and synergies. If humanity as a whole is to flourish, all of these diverse geo-cultural domains must succeed. Only thus can lasting peace and prosperity be achieved for all, especially in the face of 'Civilisational Frontier Risks' and highly disruptive technologies in the twenty-first century.

'A pioneering work that puts neuroscience to the service of history, and uses history as a guide to the future. A profound and important book.'
– Professor Eugene Rogan,
University of Oxford

Published 25 December 2014

Hardback ISBN: 978 0 7188 9570 9
Paperback ISBN: 978 0 7188 9571 6
PDF ISBN: 978 0 7188 4831 6
ePub ISBN: 978 0 7188 4832 3